Capitalism and Material Life
1400-1800

Fernand Braudel was born in 1902 in the French province of Meuse, and educated at the Lycée Voltaire Paris and at the Sorbonne where he took a degree in history. Graduating in 1923, he went to teach history in Constantine, Algeria, and stayed there till 1932. He then returned to Paris and taught at the Lycée Condorce and the Lycée Henri IV from 1932 to 1935, before joinin the Faculty of Arts in Saõ Paulo, Brazil for three years. During the war he served on the Rhine frontier until he was captured in 1940, spending the rest of the war years as a prisoner in Germany. It was during this time that he wrote his great work, *The Mediterranean and the Mediterranean World at the time of Philip II*. He has been a member of the École Pratique des Hautes Études since 1938, for a time its President, and since 1949 he has been Professor of Modern History at the Collège de France. Professor Braudel holds honorary doctorates from universities all over the world. He is the author of several books, and is editor of the review, *Annales (Économies, Sociétés, Civilisations)* founded by Lucien Febvre and Marc Bloch.

Capitalism
and Material Life
1400-1800

Fernand Braudel

Professor of French History at the Collège de France, Paris

Translated by Miriam Kochan

FONTANA/COLLINS

First published in 1967 by Librairie Armand Colin
First English edition 1973 George Weidenfeld & Nicolson Ltd
Published in Fontana 1974

© 1967 Librairie Armand Colin
English translation © 1973 George Weidenfeld & Nicolson Ltd

ISBN 0 633502 0

Printed in Great Britain
William Collins Sons & Co Ltd Glasgow

To Paule Braudel

Contents

MAPS

DIAGRAMS

TABLES

Preface

Let us assume then that there is a material life, or better still a material civilisation, mingled with – although by nature distinct from – a more full-blooded, often dominant economic life. Routine predominates at the level of everyday life: corn is sown as it was always sown, maize planted, rice fields levelled, ships sail the Red Sea as they always sailed it. The distinction between this life – more passive than active, repeated for centuries on end – and an economic life that benefits from it but implies calculation and demands vigilance, is not immediately apparent.

However, the core of the problem is not the distinction between these layers of intermingled activity. We are concerned at all times to take into consideration an enormous mass of history barely conscious of itself. Nearly everything depended on its immense inertia, the repeated checks it suffered, its old sometimes antediluvian choices, its structures. If man usually remained within the limits of the possible, it was because his feet were sunk in this clay.

Let us also assume that man's whole life is restricted by an upper limit, always difficult to reach and still more difficult to cross. This boundary between possibility and impossibility is established for every period (even our own). It marks the line between what can, with effort, be attained and what remains denied to men, in the past because food supplies were insufficient, populations too large or too small, labour not sufficiently productive, the taming of nature scarcely begun. An examination of this limit will be the subject of this first book, starting at the bottom level with material life, the ground floor (as it were) of history. But this bottom level is never simple and never completely static. It has gentle slopes along which the whole mechanism slides. None the less an extension of the limit of possibility is not sufficient by itself to ensure immediate progress. Road communications only achieved a new state of perfection on the eve of the creation of the railways, in the 1830s, when the old overland transport systems – until then lagging behind even the technical possibilities – were made faster, more efficient and more democratic.

For these and other reasons the frontier zone between possibility and impossibility barely moved in any significant way, from the fifteenth to the eighteenth century. It was only successfully crossed in the last years of the eighteenth century, and then only at a few points. It was the following century that saw a violent breakthrough, revolution, total upheaval of the world. This lends our book a certain unity. We are going on a long journey, far removed from the opportunities and practices which are a normal part of present-day life. It will take us to another planet, another world of men. We could, of course, visit Voltaire at Ferney and (as fantasy is free) have a long chat with him without any great sense of surprise. The men of the eighteenth century were contemporaries on the level of ideas. Their minds and passions were the same as ours, or at least near enough to prevent total disorientation. But if we spent a few days with the master of Ferney, all the details of material life, even his personal hygiene, would shock us. Tremendous distances would open up between him and us: lighting in the evenings, heating, transport, food, illness and its cures. 'In Phillip II's time' notes a historian (of Voltaire's time, let it be added) 'it was not possible to travel from Manilla to Escorial in twenty-four hours'. This detail, selected from thousands of others, supplies the key. To make the requisite journey back down the centuries, it is essential to discard all the facts of our environment once and for all, in order to rediscover the rules which enclosed the world in stability for such a long period – an almost inexplicable stability in view of the fantastic changes that followed.

Introduction

A general history always requires an overall model, good or bad, against which events can be interpreted. 'No theory, no history,' said Werner Sombart. The model in the present case suggests itself: the lives of men certainly progressed, from the fifteenth to the eighteenth centuries, as long as the word 'progress' is not taken in its current sense of rapid and uninterrupted growth. The advance occurred very slowly over a long period and was broken by sharp recessions. The right road was reached, and thereafter never abandoned, only during the eighteenth century, and then only by a few privileged countries. Thus, before 1750 or even 1800 the march of progress could still be affected by unexpected events, even disasters. Despite economic crises it was maintained over long periods by the initiative of groups of men, not individuals (the exceptions prove the rule), and in countless varied and obscure ways. The quest for progress, with the discussions it involves and the circumstances that throw light on it, clearly lies along the major axis of this work. But we have not arrived at any simple conclusions or any dogmatic sociological analysis of progress for these past centuries. We have tried to find a model, an overall view; not a general theory. We do not claim to have done so.

What advice would a modern economist retrospectively give to those economies which broke down so often – genuinely under-developed countries before the term was known – and to their confused inhabitants grappling with their material fate? How would he analyse those situations, if they were presented to him today? If the problem were solved, this book would be remarkably clear and simple. But it is not solved. Moreover, not one but thousands of problems are involved, varying with time and place. There is probably a certain family likeness, but the difference between the Indians of the Saint Lawrence and the France of Louis xiv is as great as, if not greater than, that between the United States and a newly independent state in Black Africa today.

These contrasts certainly activated the coherent life of the world as a whole, in the same way as differences in voltage activate an electric current; but they were, in effect, external distinctions. They are only part of the story. Every economy, society and civilisation is a world unto itself, divided internally and shared unequally amongst its members. Each of these individual mechanisms must therefore be taken to pieces and put together again to bring out the resemblances, similarities, recurring features and hierarchies among their components. Such comparisons require a precise vocabulary, hardly the one used by the men of the time, but rather that of the present-day human sciences, rethought in the context of the past. At least a dozen essential words must be understood for the sake of clarity.

Material life, consisting of very old routines, inheritances and successes, is there at the root of everything. Agriculture for example – the way of life of most people throughout the world before the eighteenth century (and even beyond that critical threshold) – goes back thousands of years before the fifteenth century, when this book begins. This is true of corn, rice, maize, the domestication of animals and basic cookery; that is, of some of man's longest-lasting early practices. Elementary tools are as old as cultivated plants, and the same can almost be said of the still fairly simple tools that increased or facilitated physical effort: lever, lathe, pedal, crank and winch. It is equally true of windmills and watermills, which were twelfth-century revolutions in the Western world. The expression *material life* will therefore be deliberately used throughout the book to denote repeated actions, empirical processes, old methods and solutions handed down from time immemorial, like money or the separation of town from country. It is an elementary life but neither entirely passive nor, above all, completely static. It has moments of acceleration and occasionally of surprise: new plants become acclimatised, techniques improve and spread, changes occur in processes employed by blacksmiths, weavers and, still more, by miners and shipbuilders. These changes take place slowly but steadily. Money and towns play a continually increasing part and some innovations are of decisive importance.

The term *economic life* will generally be used to imply a higher and more privileged level of daily life, with a wider radius and involving constant care and calculation. It is born of trade, transport, differentiated market structures, and of contact between already industrialised countries and those still primitive or underdeveloped, between rich and poor, creditors and borrowers, monetary and pre-monetary economies. It is, in fact, already almost a system in itself.

This said, can the awkward word *capitalism* be of any use in denoting a third stage? This modern expression (it was coined at the latest about 1870) only became current in political, social and then scientific discussion at the beginning of the present century. Karl Marx did not use it. Since then it has been much used and perhaps abused. But is it possible to replace it or, for the sake of prudence, limit its anachronistic employment in reference to earlier centuries? If we use it so much it is because there is a need for it, or for a word serving the same purpose; because it points to certain forms of economic life in past centuries that are already modern, as though oriented to the future. The activities of Jacques Coeur, Charles VII's silversmith, reflect *some* form of capitalism. Capitalism, with its rules, attitudes, advantages and risks, has betokened modernity, flexibility and rationality from its earliest beginnings. It is in the vanguard of the economic life of the past.

However, nascent capitalism clearly does not cover the whole of economic life. There are at least three levels and three spheres: everyday material life, very widespread, concerned with basic necessities and short-range; economic life, calculated, articulated, emerging as a system of rules and almost natural necessities; and finally the more sophisticated capitalist mechanism, which encroaches on all forms of life, whether economic or material, however little they lend themselves to its manœuvres.

Can we say that between the fifteenth and eighteenth centuries capitalism widely extended its field of action; that the realm of economic life was considerably enlarged; but that about 1800 most men still lived at the humble level of material life outside these rational orders and their never disinterested operations?

In fact these three levels are simplifications, and their value is limited. We will try to sketch out a few others as we go along, always with the same purpose in mind: to catalogue, classify, pinpoint reciprocal interplay and distinguish certain recurring features. We will thus speak of *primitive* or *subsistence economies, semi-monetary economies, market economies*; and of *primitive cultures, developed cultures, civilisations*. These are the terms – the tools – employed by economists and ethnographers. Without straining the vocabulary it can be maintained that a capitalist civilisation was gradually gaining ground. For example trade on the Gulf of Guinea from the sixteenth century onwards was characteristic of trading relations between a still primitive culture (Black Africa) and a civilisation (Europe), where the more developed partner adopted the economic language of the more backward, in this instance barter and primitive currency.

What would a present-day economist do in these conditions if some unkind providence transported him to the land of Philip the Fair in 1302, to Venice in 1600, or even introduced him to Law, the magician, in 1716, and then asked him to take stock, draw up the requisite balance sheets, and draft a plan to accelerate the growth of the economy concerned? He would, of course, only be allowed the bare means available in 1302, 1600 or 1716 respectively, and not those at his disposal today. He would obviously have to revise his theories from start to finish. Assuming he accomplished this, he would first have learnt that he had only a very small number of means of limited scope at his disposal and that his possibilities of action were likewise restricted. There was, of course, money, because we have placed him in Europe – but intrepid hands manipulated money even before Philip the Fair. There was taxation – but here again the idea of tightening the fiscal screw was not a new one. He could probably embark on a series of minor improvements, if only in matters concerning roads, tolls or accountancy.

But what would that achieve? He would see too many changes result in too much immobility or quasi-immobility, however violent they may have been in the short term. He would never have a manageable economy in front of him, nor really hold a whole people in his net, bending them to the decisions of leaders or specialists. Practically everything would elude him because political obedience is one thing and economic obedience another. But, more than anything else, his efforts would come up against insurmountable obstacles: the hazards of harvest, the slowness or lack of transport, incomprehensible and contradictory demographic movements hostile attitudes, lack of reliable statistics, and the chronic deficiency of power resources.

Man was locked in an economic condition that reflected hi human condition. He was an unconscious prisoner of the frontier marking the inflexible boundaries between the possible and the impossible. Before the eighteenth century his sphere of action was tightly circumscribed, largely limited to what he could achieve by physical effort. Whatever he did, he could not step over a certain line – and this line was always drawn close to him. He did not even reach it most of the time. That was possible only for individuals, groups or civilisations peculiarly favoured by circumstances. Those who succeeded usually did so ruthlessly at the expense of others. For this advance, though always limited, required an infinite number of victims.

Two approaches are therefore possible in this book: one could look at the victors first of all and then give a rapid outline of the others, the masses and their history. This is the usual course, although that history is the history of the majority. But we can reverse the order, and put the masses themselves in the foreground, although they lie, as it were, outside the lively, garrulous chronicles of history. We have chosen the latter approach. The present volume is therefore devoted to material civilisation: the repeated movements, the silent and half-forgotten story of men and enduring realities, which were immensely important but made so little noise. The second volume will return to the victors and the structure of economic life, to the achievements and techniques of capitalism, to a modernity that was often surprising because it was in advance not only of events but sometimes, though rarely, of accepted possibilities.

However, the essential problem will remain the same in both volumes: how could it decay and break up, this order, this complex system of life, this *ancien régime* on a world-wide scale? and having attained the limits of the possible, how did it surmount its obstacles? How did it – how could it – break the barrier? And why, once this was achieved, was it only to the advantage of a privileged few?

Weight of Numbers

Men and things make up material life. The study of things, of everything man makes or uses – food, housing, clothing, luxury, tools, coinage or its substitutes, framework of village and town – is not the only way of analysing daily life. The number of people who share the wealth of the world is also significant. The outward feature that immediately differentiates the present world from mankind before 1800 is the recent astonishing increase in the numbers of people. World population doubled during the four centuries covered by this book; nowadays it doubles every thirty or forty years. This is obviously the result of material progress. But the number of people is itself as much cause as consequence of this progress.

In any case number is a first-class pointer. It provides an index of success and failure. In itself it outlines a differential geography of the globe with continents that are barely populated on the one hand and regions already overpopulated on the other, civilisations face to face with forms of life still primitive. It indicates the decisive relationships between the diverse human masses. Curiously enough, this differential geography is often what has changed least over the centuries.

What has changed entirely is the rhythm of the increase in life. At present it registers a continuous rise, more or less rapid according to society and economy but always continuous. Previously it rose and then fell like a series of tides. This alternate demographic ebb and flow characterised life in former times, which was a succession of downward and upward movements, the first almost but not completely cancelling out the second. These basic facts make almost everything else seem secondary. Clearly, our starting point must be man. Only afterwards can we talk about things; and then we must take care not to be diverted by their colourful variety.

1 Guessing the world population

The difficulty is that if world population even today is only known within a 10% margin of error, our information concerning earlier populations is still more incomplete. Yet everything, both in the short and long term, and at the level of local events as well as on the grand scale of world affairs, is bound up with the numbers and fluctuations of the mass of people.

Ebb and flow

Between the fifteenth and eighteenth centuries populations rose or fell; everything was in a state of change. When the number of people increased, production and trade also increased. Wasteland and woodland, swamp and hill came under cultivation; manufactures spread, villages and towns expanded, the number of men on the move multiplied; and there were many other positive reactions to the challenge set by the pressure of population-increase. Of course, wars and disputes, privateering and brigandage grew proportionately; armies or armed bands also flourished; societies created *nouveaux riches* or new privileged classes on an unusually large scale; states prospered – both an evil and a blessing; the frontier of possibility was more easily reached than in ordinary circumstances. These were the usual symptoms. But demographic growth is not an unmitigated blessing. It is sometimes beneficial and sometimes the reverse. When a population increases, its relationship to the space it occupies and the wealth at its disposal is altered. It crosses critical thresholds and at each one its entire structure is questioned afresh. The matter is never simple and unequivocal. A growing increase in the number of people often ends, and always ended in the past, by exceeding the capacity of the society concerned to feed them. This fact, commonplace before the eighteenth century and still true today in some backward countries, sets an insuperable limit to further improvement in conditions. For when they are extreme, demographic increases involve a deterioration in the standard of living; they enlarge the always horrifying total of the underfed, poor and uprooted. A balance between mouths to be fed and the difficulties of feeding them, between manpower and jobs, is re-established by epidemics and famines (the second preceding or accompanying the first). These extremely crude adjustments were the predominant feature of the centuries of the *ancien régime*. But the main point for the observer is that everything takes place within the framework of vast and more or less observable movements.

We can pinpoint a prolonged population rise in the West between 1100 and 1350, and another between 1450 and 1650. A third, after 1750, was not followed by a regression. Here we have three broad and comparable periods of biological expansion. The first two, which occurred in the middle of our period, were followed by recessions which were extremely sharp between 1350 and 1450 and decidedly severe between 1650 and 1750. Nowadays any growth in backward countries brings a fall in the standard of living but fortunately not a decline in numbers (at least not since 1945).

Every recession solves a certain number of problems, removes pressures and benefits the survivors. It is pretty drastic, but none the less a remedy. Inherited property became concentrated in a few hands immediately after the Black Death in the middle of the fourteenth century and the epidemics which followed and aggravated its effects. Only good land was cultivated (less work for greater yield). The standard of living and real earnings of the survivors rose. Thus in Languedoc between 1350 and 1450 the peasant and his patriarchal family were masters of an abandoned countryside. Trees and wild animals overran fields that once had flourished. But soon the population again increased and had to win back the land taken over by animals and wild plants, clear the stones from the fields and pull up trees and shrubs. Man's very progress became a burden and again brought about his poverty. From 1560 or 1580 onwards in France, Spain, Italy and probably the whole Western world, population again became too dense. The monotonous story begins afresh and the process goes into reverse. Man only prospered for short intervals and did not realise it until it was already too late.

But these long fluctuations can also be found outside Europe. At approximately the same times China and India probably advanced and regressed in the same rhythm as the West, as though all humanity were in the grip of a primordial cosmic destiny that would make the rest of man's history seem, in comparison, of secondary importance. Ernst Wagemann, an economist and demographer, held this view. The synchronism is evident in the eighteenth century and more than probable in the sixteenth. It can be assumed that it also applied to the thirteenth and stretched from the France of St Louis to the remote China of the Mongols. This idea would both shift and simplify the matter. 'The development of population,' wrote Wagemann, 'must be attributed to causes very different from those that led to economic, technical and medical progress.' This is a remark to bear in mind. Obscure, yet prophetic in its way, it will help towards a better grasp of an authentic history of the world.

In any case these fluctuations, which occurred more or less simultaneously from one end of the inhabited world to the other, make it easier to envisage the existence of numerical relationships between the different human masses which have remained relatively fixed over the centuries: one is equal to another, or double a third. When one is known, the other can be worked out; eventually, therefore, the total for the whole body of people can be assessed, though with all the errors inherent in such an estimate. It is tremendously important to work out this global figure. However inaccurate and inevitably inexact, it helps to determine the biological evolution of humanity considered as a single entity, a single *stock* as statisticians would say.

The lack of statistics

Nobody knows the total population of the world between the fifteenth and eighteenth centuries. Statisticians working from the conflicting, sparse and uncertain figures offered by historians cannot agree. It would seem at first glance as if nothing could be constructed on such doubtful foundations. It is none the less worth trying.

The figures are few and not very reliable at that. They apply only to Europe and, as a consequence of some admirable research, to China. In these two cases, we have censuses and estimates that are almost valid.

What about the rest of the world? There is nothing, or almost nothing, on India, careless of its history in general, and unconcerned with the statistics that might shed light on it. There is nothing in fact on non-Chinese Asia, outside Japan. There is of course nothing on Oceania, only skimmed by European travellers in the seventeenth and eighteenth centuries: Tasman reached New Zealand in May 1642 and Tasmania, the island to which he gave his name, in December of the same year; Cook reached Australia a century later, in 1769 and 1783; and Bougainville arrived at Tahiti, the New Cythera (which, by the way, he did not discover) in April 1768. In any case, is there really any need to discuss these thinly inhabited areas? Statisticians estimate two million for the whole of Oceania, whatever the period under consideration. Nor is there anything definite on Black Africa, south of the Sahara, except conflicting figures on the extent of the slave trade from the sixteenth century onwards – and it would be difficult to deduce all the rest from these, even if they were reliable. Lastly, there is nothing certain relating to America, apart from two contradictory calculations.

For Alfred Rosenblatt there is only one method: the deductive. He starts from present-day figures and calculates backwards. For the whole of the Americas just after the Conquest this approach produces a very low figure: between ten and eleven million people. And this would have dropped still further to eight million in the seventeenth century. It did not increase again until the beginning of the eighteenth century, and then only slowly. However American historians at the University of California (Cook, Simpson, Borah – 'The Berkeley School') made a series of calculations and extrapolations based on partial contemporary figures known for some regions of Mexico immediately after the European Conquest. The resulting totals are very inflated: eleven million in 1519, according to the estimate put forward in 1948. In 1960, the addition of new documents or reappraisal of the old brought that already huge figure to 25 million inhabitants for Mexico alone. After that the population is reckoned to have decreased rapidly: 1532, 16,800,000; 1548, 6,300,000; 1568, 2,650,000; 1580, 1,900,000; 1595, 1,375,000; 1605, 1,000,000. A slow revival began after 1650 and became clearly defined after 1700.

These fanciful figures might lure us into assuming a total of some 80 to 100 million people for the whole of America in about 1500. No one is prepared to accept this blindly, despite the evidence of archaeologists and of so many of the chroniclers of the Conquest, including Father Bartolomé de Las Casas. What is quite certain is that the European Conquest brought a colossal biological slump to America, perhaps not in the ratio of ten to one but certainly enormous and quite incommensurate with the Black Death and its concomitant catastrophes in Europe in the disastrous fourteenth century. This was partly due to the hardships of ruthless warfare and to the unparalleled burden of labour for the colonists. But the Indian population at the end of the fifteenth century suffered from a demographic weakness, particularly because of the absence of any substitute animal milk. Mothers had to nurse their children until they were three or four years old. This long period of breast-feeding severely reduced female fertility and made any demographic revival precarious. Furthermore the Amerindian population, already barely holding its own, was overtaken by a series of terrible bacterial attacks similar to those dramatically spread by white men in the Pacific in the eighteenth and, more especially, the nineteenth century.

Diseases imported from Europe spread more rapidly than European animals, plants and men. Smallpox appeared in a virulent form in the Caribbean as early as 1507. It reached Peru in 1519 and 1520, even before the conquerors had set foot there; it reached Brazil in 1560, Canada in 1635. This disease, against which Europe was partially immunised, cut deep into the native populations. The same was true of measles, malaria, yellow fever, dysentery, leprosy, plague (the first rats are said to have reached America in about 1544–6), venereal diseases (an important subject which will be dealt with later), tuberculosis, typhus, typhoid and elephantiasis. All these diseases, whether carried by Whites or Blacks, took on a new virulence. We must make a conscious effort to stop thinking of yellow fever as native to tropical America, Panama or Rio de Janeiro. It probably came from Africa. In Indonesia and Oceania, a remote and long-sheltered part of the world, malaria for example arrived late. It appeared in Batavia and destroyed it in 1732. It is true that uncertainty and controversy still surround the question of the true origin of diseases (for example typhus and tuberculosis) but there is no doubt about certain invasions by virulent bacteria: the Mexican population collapsed under colossal epidemics; of smallpox in 1521 and of an ill-defined 'plague' in 1546, which appeared for a second time in 1576 and 1577 (when it may have been typhus) and caused two million deaths.

The cautious calculations of Rosenblatt and the romantic inventiveness of the Berkeley historians can thus be reconciled. Both sets of figures may be true or probable, depending on whether they refer to the period before or after the Conquest. We will therefore disregard the opinions of Woytinski and Embree. The latter once asserted that 'there were never more than ten million people between Alaska and Cape Horn at any time before Columbus'. Today this is doubtful.

How to calculate

The example of America shows that simple (even over-simple) methods can be applied to certain relatively reliable figures to arrive at others. Historians, accustomed to accept only things proved by irrefutable documentation, quite justifiably find these uncertain methods disturbing. Statisticians share neither their misgivings nor their timidity. 'We may be criticised for not dealing in minutiae,' says a sociological statistician, Paul A. Ladame; 'we would reply that details are not important: the order of magnitude is the only interesting fact.' The order of magnitude will give us the probable upper and lower limits.

In this debate where both sides are right (or both wrong) we will take a look at the position from the calculators' point of view. Their method always assumes that there are ratios which if not fixed are at least very slow to change between the various populations of the globe. This was the opinion of Maurice Halbwachs. In other words the population of the world has an almost unvarying structure, so that the numerical relationships between the different human groups are, roughly speaking, always the same. The Berkeley School deduced a total for the whole of America from partial Mexican statistics. Similarly, Karl Lamprecht and later Karl Julius Beloch calculated figures valid for Germania from approximate statistics for the population of the Trèves region in about 800. The problem is always the same: starting from known figures and reckoning on a basis of probable proportions to calculate probable, more comprehensive figures that will determine an order of magnitude. The range thus deduced will obviously never be entirely valueless as long as its limitations are recognised. Real figures would be better, but they do not exist.

The balance of Europe and China

We have used a series of figures for the populations of Europe and China, calculated on the one hand and considerably adapted on the other. They are summarised in diagram 1.

The figures for Europe were produced by K. Julius Beloch (1854–1929), the great forerunner of historical demography. I have however added to them so that they cover Europe to the Urals, thus incorporating Eastern Europe. The figures proposed for the Balkan peninsula, Poland, Muscovy and the Scandinavian countries are very dubious and scarcely more probable than those that statisticians suggest for Oceania or Africa. I think however that the extension is essential: it gives Europe the same area for any period that may be considered and achieves a better balance between an enlarged Europe on one side and China on the other. This balance was

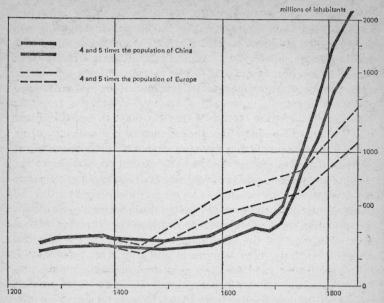

millions of inhabitants

4 and 5 times the population of China

4 and 5 times the population of Europe

Diagram 1 World population from the thirteenth to the nineteenth century

confirmed as soon as reasonable – though not absolutely reliable – statistics appeared in the nineteenth century.

The statistics for China are based on official censuses, but are not on that account, of course, unquestionably valid. They are concerned with tax and other levies, which means they are very likely to involve fraud and deception. A.P. Usher was right to think that the figures were, on the whole, too low; accordingly he increased them, with all the uncertainty an operation of this type involves. The latest historian to venture into this field of hypothetical calculations has done the same thing. The original figures reveal flagrant impossibilities, increases and decreases abnormally large even for the Chinese. They probably often measure the level of 'order and authority in the Empire as much as the level of population'. Thus the overall figure fell by seven million in 1647 as compared with the preceding year, at the time of the vast Won San-Kouei peasant revolt. The absentees were not dead; they were avoiding central authority. Had they come to heel, the statistics would have registered a sharp increase far exceeding even the maximum possible natural increase of the population.

8

In addition, the censuses were not always made on the same basis. Before 1735 they only comprised the *jen-ting*, tax-payers, men aged between sixteen and sixty. Their number therefore has to be multiplied, assuming that they represented 28% of the total population. After 1741 on the other hand the census counted the actual number of persons and gave the population as 143 million, while calculations based on the number of *jen-ting* had produced a figure of 97 million for 1734. The two totals *can* be correlated, since the sums involved allow plenty of scope for humorous invention, but the exercise will satisfy no one. However specialists do agree that these figures are, broadly speaking, valid; and the oldest statistics – relating to the China of the Mings (1368-1644) – are by no means the most questionable.

We can thus see the sort of material we shall have to work with. These figures, represented on a graph, only establish an approximate balance between Europe (extended to the Urals) and China (limited to the main territory of its provinces). Furthermore the balance today is also approximate: China, 700–750 million, Europe to the Urals, 600 million. But approximate as it is, this broad equality is probably one of the most important facts of world history in the last five or six centuries. It offers a starting point for our approximate calculations of world population.

World population

According to the first valid statistics, which became available in the nineteenth century (the first real census – for England – was in 1801), China and Europe each represented roughly a quarter of all mankind. Obviously the validity of applying this proportion to the past is not automatically guaranteed. Europe and China, both then and now, are the most highly populated regions of the world. Since their rates of increase were higher than elsewhere, it might perhaps be appropriate to use a ratio of one to five for the period before the eighteenth century rather than of one to four, for either continent, in relation to the rest of the world. The precaution is just another indication of our uncertainty.

We will therefore apply the coefficients of four or five to the two curves for China and Europe to obtain four probable curves of world population, corresponding respectively to four (or five) Europes, or four (or five) Chinas. We shall have a complex curve which marks out a wide zone of possibilities (and errors) between the lowest and the highest figures on this graph. The line giving the development of the population of the world from the fourteenth to the eighteenth century would lie between these limits.

These calculations show an overall rise in world population between 1300 and 1800 (obviously we do not record the violent but short-term regressions already mentioned). The rise would be expressed in the following manner. If we select the lowest estimate (250 million) for our starting point 1300–50 and the highest (1380 million in 1780) for our point of arrival, a rise of over 400 % would be registered. When we fix the starting point at its maximum, 350, and the finishing point as 836 (the lowest figure given by Wilcox and Carr Saunders), we would still have an increase of 138 %. Taken over a period of half a millennium, it would correspond to a regular average growth (the regularity is obviously purely theoretical) of the order of 1·73 per 1000, a movement that would have been barely perceptible over the years if it had been constant. None the less the population of the world probably doubled during this immense period of time. Neither economic crises, disasters nor massive mortality prevented the upward movement. This is indubitably the basic fact in world history from the fifteenth to the eighteenth century – and not solely at the level of material life: everything had to adapt to the general pressure.

Western historians will hardly find this surprising. They are aware of the numerous indirect signs (occupation of new territory, emigration, clearing of new land, agricultural improvements, urbanisation) that corroborate the statistical data. On the other hand the conclusions and explanations they have deduced from them remain debatable. They thought the phenomenon was limited to Europe, but it is a fact – and the most important and disturbing fact that we will record in this book – that man surmounted the manifold obstacles to his numerical advance *in all the lands he occupied*. If this population-growth is not solely European but world-wide, several theories and explanations will have to be revised.

Questionable figures

We have adopted the statisticians' method of using the best-known figures – in this case, those for Europe and China – to estimate world population. Statisticians will have nothing to say against such a procedure; however, they themselves have tackled the same problem in a different way. They split up the operation and calculated the population of each of the five 'parts' of the world in turn. It is useful to examine their conclusions and the reasons for certain divergences between different experts.

It will be remembered that they attributed two million inhabitants to Oceania during the whole period. This is of little consequence, since the tiny figure is immediately absorbed in our margin of error. But their figure of 100 million for Africa over the whole period is worth questioning. This constant level of the population of Africa seems to us improbable, and the estimate made on this basis has obvious repercussions on the estimate for the whole.

We have summarised the experts' estimates in a table. Note that all their calculations begin late – in 1650 – and that they are all on the high side, even the recent research by United Nations services. On the whole I think these estimates are too high, at least in so far as they concern Africa primarily, and Asia.

		1650	1750	1800	1850	1900	1950
Oceania		2	2	2	2	6	13*
Africa		100	100	100	100	120	199**
Asia		257* 330** 250***	437* 479** 406***	602** 522***	656* 749** 671***	857* 937** 859***	1 272*
America		8* 13** 13***	11* 12·4** 12·4***	24·6** 24·6***	59 59 59	144 144 144	338*
Europe (including Russian Europe)		103* 100** 100***	144* 140** 140***	187** 187***	274* 266** 266***	423* 401** 401***	594*
Totals	1	470	694		1 091	1 550	2 416
	2	545	733·4	915·6	1 176	1 608	
	3	465	660·4	835·6	1 098	1 530	

World population in millions from 1650 to 1950

Sources: * United Nations Bulletin, December 1951. ** Carr Saunders. *** Kuczynski.
Figures without an asterisk are common to the three sources.
Carr Saunders' figures for Africa are given to the nearest 100.

It is rash at the starting point in 1650 to attribute the same figure (100 million) both to Europe, which was then dynamic, and to Africa, which was then backward (with the possible exception of its Mediterranean coast). It is no more reasonable to give Asia in 1650 both the lowest figure in the tables (250 or 257 million) and the very high figure of 330 rather hastily accepted by Carr Saunders.

Africa certainly had a hardy population in the middle of the seventeenth century. It withstood the increasing drain caused from the middle of the sixteenth century by the slave trade to America, while the earlier drain towards Islamic countries did not cease until the twentieth century. It could only have done so by virtue of some sort of biological strength. Its resistance to European penetration provides a further proof of health. The Black continent, unlike Brazil, did not open up to the Portuguese in the sixteenth century without defending itself. Evidence shows a fairly compact peasant life, with beautiful peaceful villages spoiled by the nineteenth-century European advance.

The European might however have persisted in his attempts to seize lands in Black Africa if he had not been halted at the coasts by diseases. Intermittent or continuous fevers, 'dysentery, phthisis and dropsy', as well as numerous parasites, all took a very heavy toll of Europeans. They were as great an obstacle to advance as the bravery of the warlike tribes. Furthermore the rivers were broken by rapids and bars: who would sail up the wild waters of the Congo? Again, the American adventure and trade with the Far East were mobilising all available energy in Europe, whose interests in any case lay elsewhere. The Black continent supplied of its own accord gold dust, ivory and men, and cheaply too. Why ask more of it? As for the slave trade, it did not involve the vast numbers of men we all too readily assume. It was even limited in extent towards America, if only by the capacity of transport. By way of comparison total Irish immigration between 1769 and 1774 only amounted to 44,000, or fewer than 8,000 a year. Likewise a thousand Spaniards on an average left Seville for America annually in the sixteenth century. But, even if we assume that the slave trade involved the completely unthinkable figure of 50,000 a year (it would in fact only have reached this level – if at all – as the nineteenth century neared its end), such a total would only accord with an African population of 25 million at the most. In fact the population of 100 million attributed to Africa has no reliable basis. It merely reverts to the first very dubious overall estimate that Gregory King supplied in 1696 (95 million). Thereafter, everybody has been content to repeat his figure.

However, population estimates are available which make it possible to check these statistics. For example J.C. Russell estimates the population of North Africa in the sixteenth century at 3,500,000 (I personally had estimated it at two million, but without sound arguments). Fiscal data supplied by the work of Omer Lutfi Barkan allow us to suggest a maximum figure of between four and five million for Egypt in the sixteenth century. However this seems large to me in comparison with the 2,400,000 inhabitants for Egypt given much later by estimates for 1798. But today the populations of North Africa and Egypt are equal, each representing a tenth of African humanity. We are therefore left with a choice between 24, 35 and 50 million, depending on which of the three figures we adopt. The first refers to the end of the eighteenth century; the other two to the sixteenth. None of these approximations approaches the figure of 100 million. There is naturally no proof. In the first place our figures for the sixteenth century are very dubious. If we take them as indicators we also accept the fact that there was a demographic decline in the eighteenth century, which is still to be proved. It is true that in 1798 (when our data is reliable) Egypt had suffered a great deal since its sixteenth-century splendour. The *Voyage en Egypte et Syrie* which Volney made in 1782-3 did not depict Egypt as bursting with health. It is doubtful that it represented a tenth of the African population at that time. Thus we will remain uncommitted as far as fixing a figure is concerned, but we can fairly confidently reject the figure of 100 million.

The figures for Asia are also excessive, but it is not such a serious matter in this case. Carr Saunders thinks that Wilcox's figure of 70 million for the population of China in about 1650 – six years after the Manchus had taken Peking – is wrong. He boldly proceeds to double it (150 million). Everything relating to this period of change in Chinese history is open to question (for example, the *jen-ting* could simply be ordinary fiscal units). Wilcox, for his part, based his calculations on the *Toung Hwa Louh* (translated by Cheng Hen Chen). Even if we assume that his figure is too low, we still need to take into account the terrible havoc wrought by the Manchu invasion. A.P. Usher calculated a figure of 75 million for 1575 and 101 for 1661. The official figure for 1680 is 61; the figure given by one author is 98, by another 120. But these were for 1680, when the Manchu régime had finally been established. A traveller in about 1639 mentioned some 60 million inhabitants and he still counted 10 people per household, an unusually high coefficient even for China.

The extraordinary demographic increase in China did not begin until 1680, or more accurately until the reoccupation of Formosa in 1683. China was protected by wide continental expansion that later took her people to Siberia, Mongolia, Turkestan and Tibet. At that time China was engaged in extremely intensive colonisation within its own boundaries. All the low-lying lands and hills that could be irrigated were developed, followed by the mountainous areas where forest-clearing pioneers multiplied. New crops introduced by the Portuguese in the sixteenth century clearly spread more widely at this period – ground nuts for example, sweet potatoes and, above all, maize, before the arrival of ordinary potatoes from Europe (which did not become significant in China until the nineteenth century). This colonisation met no great obstacle until about 1740. After that the portion of land reserved to each individual gradually diminished as the population indubitably increased more rapidly than cultivable space.

These deep-seated changes help us to pinpoint a Chinese 'agricultural revolution' intensified by a powerful and overlapping demographic revolution. Probable figures are as follows: 1680, 120 million; 1700, 130; 1720, 144; 1740, 165; 1750, 186; 1761, 198; 1770, 246; 1790, 300; 1850, 430. When in 1793 George Staunton, secretary to the English ambassador, asked the Chinese what the population of the Empire was, they answered proudly, if not frankly: 353 million.

But to return to the population of Asia. It is usually estimated at two to three times that of China. Two rather than three, because India does not really seem to be equal to the Chinese mass. An estimate (30 million) of the population of the Deccan in 1522, based on dubious documents, would give a figure of 100 million inhabitants for the whole of India. This is higher than the contemporary official Chinese figure – but nobody is obliged to accept it.

Moreover, at the end of the century, India was attacked by the great epidemic of plague and famines which ravaged the northern countries after 1596. The whole Indian economy declined and regressed in the seventeenth century. An unpublished French estimate in 1797 put the population of India at 155 million, while China had officially claimed 275 million as from 1780. Kingsley Davis' statistical deductions do not back up this lower level for India. But we cannot accept his figures blindly.

In any case, if we assume that Asia was demographically equal to two or three times China, its figures for 1680 would be 240 or 360 million; 600 or 900 in 1790. We must repeat that we prefer the lower figures, especially for the period around the middle of the seventeenth century. The total for the population of the world in about 1680 would be obtained by adding up the following: Africa 35 or 50 million; Asia 240 or 360; Europe 100; America 10 and Oceania 2. This gives us the same order of magnitude as our first calculation, with the same margin of doubt.

The relationship between the centuries

Spatial calculations, continent by continent, need not exclude the more difficult calculations on the time axis, century by century. Paul Mombert provided the first model for this, relating to Europe in the period 1650–1850. He based his work on two hypotheses: first, that the most recent figures are the least uncertain; second, that when working backwards from the most recent to the most ancient levels plausible rates of increase between them must be assumed. This involved accepting the figure of 266 million for Europe in 1850 and deducing (on the basis of a rise that is quite obviously not as' steep as W. F. Wilcox assumes) the figure of 211 for 1800, 173 for 1750, and 136 and 100 for 1650 and 1600 respectively. The figure for the eighteenth century is thus very high in relation to current estimates; part of the gains usually conceded to the nineteenth century have been given to the eighteenth. (I obviously cite these figures with due reservation.)

We have therefore now arrived at the concept of *reasonable* annual rates of growth, roughly corroborated by some partial investigations: from 1600 to 1650, 6·2 per 1000; from 1650 to 1750, 2·4; from 1750 to 1800, 4; from 1800 to 1850, 4·6. We come back to K. Julius Beloch's figures for 1600 (nearly 100 million inhabitants for all Europe). But we have no valid index to follow the process further back from 1600 to 1300. This was an eventful period when we know a wide recession occurred between 1350 and 1450, followed by a sharp rise between 1450 and 1650.

We can probably, at our own risk, revert to Paul Mombert's ready solution. The least unreliable figure for 1600 is 100 million Europeans. This marked the peak of a long rise with three possible gradients: one of 6·2 per 1000, as indicated by the increase between 1600 and 1650; another of 2·4 per 1000 from 1650 to 1750; and the last of 4 per 1000 from 1750 to 1800. Logically we should at least refer to this last percentage if only to take into account the intensity, suggested though not established, of the rise between 1450 and 1600.

This would produce a figure of approximately 55 million inhabitants for Europe in 1450. Now, if we concur with all other historians in thinking that the Black Death and its consequences robbed the continent of at least a fifth of its manpower, the figure for 1300–50 would be 69 million. I do not consider this figure improbable. The early devastation and poverty of Eastern Europe and the astonishing number of villages that disappeared throughout Europe during the 1350–1450 crises all point to the possibility of this high level, in the region of Julius Beloch's reasonable estimate (66 million).

Some historians regard the sharp revival in an extended sixteenth century (1451–1650) as a compensation for earlier recessions. Our figures would represent a compensation and then a further addition. All this is obviously very debatable.

The old inadequate explanations

The question at issue mentioned at the beginning of the discussion remains: the *general* rise in world population. The old account must in any case be revised in the light of the demographic increase in China, which was as marked and as undeniable as in Europe. Historians who persist in the old way of explaining Western demographic movements by the fall in urban mortality, the advance in hygiene and medicine, the decline in smallpox, the numerous drinking-water supply systems, the decisive fall in infant mortality, plus a general fall in the mortality rate and a younger average age of marriage, should abandon it as inadequate and outmoded.

These factors are very important in their own right. But we must somehow or other find similar or equally significant explanations for China. I agree that different explanations are possible for the demographic increases in Europe in the seventeenth century and in the eighteenth, as one expert has suggested: explaining it in one instance by more children and in the other by more old people. Another expert has expressed the same theory: 'In the seventeenth century the bulge in the age column would have run from bottom to top; in the eighteenth century from top to bottom.' Admittedly the increase did assume several forms. But a fall in the average age of marriage or a leap in the birth rate does not apply to China, where marriages had always been 'early and fertile'. As for the hygienic condition of the towns, the huge city of Peking housed three million people in 1793, according to an English traveller, and was probably less extensive than London, which had nothing approaching this enormous figure. The congestion of families in the low-built houses is beyond imagining. Hygiene could make no progress here.

We have the same problem within Europe itself. How can we explain the rapid rise in the population of Russia (it doubled between 1722 and 1795: from 14 to 29 million) when doctors and surgeons were in short supply and there was no sanitation in the towns?

Outside Europe, how can we explain the eighteenth-century rise in both the Anglo-Saxon and the Hispano-Portuguese populations of America, where neither doctors nor hygiene were particularly in evidence – certainly not in Rio de Janeiro (capital of Brazil since 1763) which had regular visitations of yellow fever and where syphilis raged in an endemic state (as in all Hispanic America) and putrefied its victims 'down to the bone'? In short, therefore, every population could have grown in its own individual way. But why did all the increases occur at approximately the same time?

The space available to man would certainly have increased greatly everywhere – particularly with the general economic revival of the eighteenth century, although it would have started earlier than that. All the countries in the world colonised themselves at that time, settling their empty or half-empty land. Europe benefited from a surplus of living space and of food, thanks to overseas trade and also to the European East which, according to the Abbé de Mably, was emerging from 'barbarism'. Southern Russia made as much progress in this direction as for example Hungary, which was covered in forest and swamps, and where the aggressive frontier of the Turkish empire had for so long been maintained; from that time on, the frontier was pushed far back southwards. There is no need to emphasise the increase in space and colonisation in America. But it was also true in India, where colonisation began of the black lands of the *regur* in the Bombay region. It was even more the case in China, which was engaged in filling up so many spaces and deserts in or near its own lands. 'However paradoxical it may seem,' wrote René Grousset, 'if the history of China must be compared with that of any other great human collectivity, the history of Canada or the United States must be selected. In both cases what was involved, essentially and beyond political vicissitude, was the conquest of immense virgin country by a race of tillers who found only a small semi-nomad population there before them.' This expansion continued – or rather was resumed – with the eighteenth century.

However if this resumption of expansion was general and world-wide, the reason was an increase in the number of people. It was more consequence than cause. Space had, in fact, always been there for the taking, and within easy reach whenever men wanted or needed it. Even today, in our 'finite world' (as a term borrowed from mathematics describes it) and where an economist states that 'humanity no longer has a second Mississippi valley or a territory like Argentina at its disposal', we are not short of empty space. The equatorial forests, the steppes, even the arctic regions and the true deserts where modern techniques may hold many surprises in store are still there to be exploited.

Basically this is not the question. The real question is: why did these phenomena occur at the same time throughout the world when the space had always been available? The simultaneity is the problem. The international economy, effective but still so fragile, cannot assume sole responsibility for such a general and powerful movement. It too is as much consequence as cause.

Climatic rhythms

One can only imagine one single general answer to this almost complete coincidence: changes in climate. Today they are no longer dismissed by academics as a joke. Recent detailed research by historians and meteorologists shows uninterrupted fluctuations in temperature, pressure systems and rainfall. These variations affect trees, rivers, glaciers, the level of the seas, and the growth of rice and corn, olive trees and vines, men and animals.

Now the world between the fifteenth and eighteenth centuries consisted of one vast peasantry, where between 80% and 95% of people lived from the land and from nothing else. The rhythm, quality and deficiency of harvests ordered all material life. And these changes happened at the same time everywhere, which the specialists explain by the fascinating but provisional hypothesis of the variations in the speed of the jet stream, for example. Thus a general cooling-down process occurred in the northern hemisphere in the fourteenth century. The number of glaciers and ice-floes increased and winters became more severe. One historian suggests that the Vikings' route to America was cut off by dangerous ice at that time. Another thinks that some dreadful climatic drama finally interrupted European colonisation in Greenland, the evidence being the bodies of the last survivors found in the frozen earth. The Black

Death did not bear the sole responsibility for the passing of former wealth and wonders in Europe.

Similarly the 'little ice age' (to use Dr Shove's expression) during Louis xiv's reign was more of a tyrant than the Sun King. Everything moved to its rhythm: cereal-growing Europe and the rice fields and steppes of Asia; the olive groves of Provence and the Scandinavian countries where snow and ice, slow to disappear in normal circumstances, no longer left the corn sufficient time to ripen: this was the case in the terrible year of 1690. Natural disasters also multiplied in China in the middle of the seventeenth century – disastrous droughts, plagues of locusts – and a succession of peasant uprisings occurred in the interior provinces, as in France under Louis xiii. All this gives additional meaning to the fluctuations in material life, and possibly explains their simultaneity. The possibility of a certain physical and biological history common to all mankind would give the globe its first unity well before the great discoveries, the industrial revolution or the interpenetration of economies.

If, as I have thought for a long time, the climatic explanation is correct, we must take care not to over-simplify it. Climate is a very complex system and its effect on the lives of plants, animals and people only comes about via very devious routes that vary according to place, crop and season. In temperate western Europe, for example, there is 'a negative correlation between the quantity of rainfall from 10 June to 20 July and a positive correlation between the percentage (of sunny days) in the period from 20 March to 10 May and the number of grains of corn'. In the past too many examples of these direct effects of climate involved marginal lands or marginal crops, like corn in Sweden. 'If you want to attach serious consequences to a climatic deterioration,' according to one distinguished expert, 'the first essential is that it should have had a great influence ... on the countries which are the most highly populated and the largest cereal producers.' This is quite obvious. But we shall not prejudge the results of future research. We shall merely bear in mind the congenital frailty of man in relation to the colossal forces of nature. Historians studying *ancien régime* economy see it as becoming increasingly dependent on the sequence of good and bad harvests. One cannot avoid concluding that this background partly depended on the climate and its changes. We know how important an ordinary delay in the monsoon can be, even today.

It is amusing to think that the men of former times would not have been put out by this climatic explanation, implicating as it does the heavens. They found it all too tempting to explain the course of everything terrestrial, including individual or collective destinies and disease, by the stars. In 1551 Oronce Finé, a mathematician and dabbler in the occult, made the following diagnosis in the name of astrology: 'If the Sun, Venus and the Moon are in conjunction in the sign of Gemini (the Twins), writers will gain for that year and servants will rebel against their masters and lords. But there will be a great abundance of wheat on the land and roads will be unsafe for the abundance of thieves.'

2 A scale of reference

The consequences that emerge when these orders of magnitude have been roughly assessed implicitly govern the entire theme of this book. Thus the great problem at the elementary level of arithmetical fact is the ratios between the present and the time of the *ancien régime*: history is fundamentally the realisation of these vital differences deriving from number. But it is still difficult to discard and break away from our obsession with present-day perspectives unless we continually refer back to some scale of reference.

The present world population (known to within about 10%) is 3,300,000,000. Compared with the very approximate figures we gave, this is some four times the figure for 1800 or ten times the figure for 1300. These coefficients of one to ten or one to four, and their intermediate values, are not magic numbers that explain everything; all the more so as they apply to things that are never absolutely the same: mankind today is not really ten times as large as mankind in 1300 or 1350, even purely from the biological point of view, because the age pyramid is not identical; far from it. However, a comparison of the simple figures by themselves opens some wide perspectives.

Towns, armies and navies

Thus the towns and armies we, as historians, meet on our journeys back to pre-nineteenth-century times are small by our standards.

Cologne, at the intersection of two Rhine waterways – one up and the other down stream – and of important overland routes, was the largest town in Germany in the fifteenth century. Yet it numbered only 20,000 inhabitants at a time when the rural and urban population in Germany was in a ratio of about ten to one and when a degree of urban congestion was already clearly apparent. A group of 20,000 was a significant concentration of people, energy, talents, and mouths to feed – much more so, proportionately speaking, than a community of 100,000 to 200,000 people today. We only have to think of the importance of the robust culture of Cologne in the fifteenth century. Similarly we can justifiably say that Istanbul in the sixteenth century, with at least 400,000 inhabitants (and probably 700,000), was an urban monster, comparable in proportion to the largest agglomerations today. It needed every available flock of sheep from the Balkans to support it; rice, beans and corn from Egypt; corn and wood from the Black Sea; and oxen, camels and horses from Asia Minor. It also required every available man from the Empire to renew its population in addition to the slaves brought back from Russia after Tartar raids or from the Mediterranean coasts by Turkish fleets. All these slaves were offered for sale at the market of Besistan, in the heart of the enormous capital.

The armies of mercenaries who squabbled over Italy at the beginning of the sixteenth century also seem very small to us – between 10,000 and 20,000 men, ten to twenty pieces of cannon. These imperial soldiers with their remarkable leaders (Pescaire, the *Connétable* de Bourbon, de Lannoy, Philibert de Chalon) who routed the other armies of mercenaries commanded by Francis I, Bonnivet or Lautrec, numbered no more than 10,000 odd troops together with German lansquenets and Spanish arquebusiers, all of them picked men, but worn out as rapidly as the Napoleonic army between the striking of the camp at Boulogne and the Spanish war (1803–8). They took the stage from La Bicoque (1522) to Lautrec's defeat at Naples (1528), reaching their zenith at Pavia (1525). But these 10,000 mobile, furious and pitiless soldiers represented a far greater force than 50,000 or 100,000 men would do today. Had there been more of them in earlier times there would have been no means of moving or feeding them, except in a country with infinitely rich land. The victory of Pavia was the triumph of the arquebusiers and even more of empty stomachs. Francis I's army was too well fed and protected from enemy cannon, between the walls of the town of Pavia which it was besieging and the ducal park, a game reserve surrounded by walls, where the battle unexpectedly took place on 24 February 1525.

In the light of this, certain feats, however inconsiderable they may seem by today's standards, regain their significance. The Spanish administration's ability to move galleys, fleets and *tercios* across the lands and seas of Europe from its large supply points at Seville, Cadiz (later Lisbon), Malaga and Barcelona was really remarkable. Lepanto (7 October 1571), the scene of the confrontation between Islam and Christendom, was another striking achievement. The fleets of the two enemies between them carried a total of at least 100,000 men, either on the slender galleys or on the large round boats that accompanied them. A hundred thousand men! Imagine any fleet today carrying 500,000 or a million men. Fifty years later, in about 1630, Wallenstein's record achievement in gathering 100,000 soldiers under his command was an even greater feat, presupposing exceptional organisation of food supplies. Villars' army, victorious at Denain (1712), numbered 100,000 men, but this was the last-ditch effort of a country fighting for its life. The figure of 100,000 soldiers seems to have become normal in later years – at least in theory. Dupré d'Aulnay, Commissioner for War in 1744, explains that to provide for these numbers a massive delivery would have to leave the supply lines every four days carrying, at a rate of 120,000 rations a day (because some men received double rations), altogether 480,000 rations (800 per carriage). 'This would require only 600 carriages and 2,400 horses, harnessed in fours,' he concludes. Such organisation seems to have been commonplace; there were even iron travelling ovens to bake the bread ration. But a treatise on artillery at the beginning of the seventeenth century setting out the varied needs of any army equipped with cannon chooses the figure of 20,000 men.

The proposition these examples illustrate can be repeated in innumerable other cases: the loss to Spain caused by the expulsion of the Moors (1609–14) – a minimum of 300,000 according to quite reliable calculations; to France by the repeal of the Edict of Nantes; to Black Africa by the slave trade with the New World; again to Spain by the process of populating the New World with white men (departures in the sixteenth century at a possible average rate of 1000 annually; 100,000 in all). The relative smallness of all these figures represents a general problem: Europe, because of its political partition and the lack of flexibility in its economy, was not capable of dispensing with any more men. Without Africa it could not have developed the New World for thousands of reasons, notably the climate, but also because it could not divert too much manpower from its own labour force. Contemporaries probably exaggerate easily, but the effects of emigration must have been felt on Sevillian life for Andrea Navagero to have said in 1526: 'So many people have left for the Indies that the town (Seville) is scarcely populated and almost in the hands of women.'

K.J. Beloch followed a similar line of thought when he tried to make a fair assessment of seventeenth-century Europe divided between the three great powers who contested it: the Ottoman empire, the Spanish empire, and France under Louis XIII and Richelieu. He calculated that they each commanded a human mass of about 17 million in the Old World – and arrived at the conclusion that this was the level beyond which a country could aspire to the role of a great power.

A France prematurely overpopulated

As we go along many other comparisons will suggest equally important explanations. Suppose that the world population in about 1600 was an eighth of its present total and that the population of France (calculated on its present-day political boundaries) was 20 million, which is probable but not absolutely certain. England then numbered at most 5 million. If both countries had increased at the average world rate, England would number 40 million inhabitants today and France 160 million. This is a quick way of saying that France (or Italy, or even Germany in the sixteenth century) was probably already overpopulated; that France, in relation to its capacity at that period, was encumbered with too many people, too many beggars, useless mouths, undesirables. Brantôme was already saying that it was as 'full as an egg'. Emigration, in the absence of any deliberate official policy, was organised as best it could be – to Spain in the sixteenth and seventeenth centuries in some volume, and later to the American 'islands'. Otherwise it was the haphazard consequence of religious exile, during 'that long blood-letting of France that began in 1540 with the first systematic persecutions (of the Protestants) and only ended in 1752–3, with the last great emigration movement following the bloody repressions of Languedoc'.

Historical research has recently shown the extent (hitherto unknown) of French emigration to the Iberian countries. It is proved by statistical surveys as well as by continued emphasis in travellers' accounts. Cardinal de Retz expressed extreme surprise in 1654 at hearing everyone in Saragossa (where there was a very great number of French artisans) speaking his language. In the following year Antoine de Brunel wondered at the amazing number of *gavachos* (the pejorative nickname given to the French) in Madrid; 40,000 he thought, who 'disguised themselves as Spaniards or claim that they are Walloons or from Lorraine or Franche-Comté to conceal the fact that they are French and to avoid being beaten up as such'.

The French supplied the Spanish capital with artisans, odd-job men and retailers attracted by expectations of high salaries and profits. This was particularly true of masons and building workers. They also invaded the countryside: Spanish land would often have remained uncultivated without the peasant who came from France. These details indicate abundant, continuous and socially-mixed emigration, an obvious sign of French overpopulation. Jean Hérauld, lord of Gourville, states in his memoirs that there were 200,000 French in Spain (1669) – an enormous but by no means improbable figure.

Thus the deliberate birth control which appeared, or rather assumed prominence, with the eighteenth century took place in a country that had suffered the scourge of numbers for centuries. 'The husbands themselves,' wrote Sébastien Mercier (1771), 'taking care in their raptures to keep from adding a child to the household.' Should this not be seen as a reaction, explicable on many grounds, to the long past of obvious overpopulation?

Density of population and level of civilisation

Given its dry-land area of 150 million square kilometres, the present average density of the world, with its 3·3 thousand million human beings, is 22 inhabitants to one square kilometre. The same calculation for the period between 1300 and 1800 would give the figure of two inhabitants to a square kilometre at the lowest estimate and five or six at the highest. Suppose we then calculate the actual area covered nowadays by the most populated regions (190 inhabitants or more per square kilometre). This would give us the main area of present-day dense *civilisations*, that is to say (and this calculation has been worked out over and over again), 11 million square kilometres. On this narrow belt 70% of all human beings (over two thousand million) are concentrated. Man leaves the globe nine-tenths empty, often by force of circumstances, but also through neglect and because history, a succession of interminable efforts, has decided otherwise.

'Men did not spread evenly over the world,' writes Vidal de La Blache, 'they originally gathered in the manner of ants.'

Anthills – the term at first glance seems highly inappropriate to describe the heaviest densities of population in earlier times. By our standards the really dense population that goes to make up a civilisation was nowhere in existence between 1400 and 1800. In fact the world at that time was already divided by the same partition and the same asymmetry into small, heavily–populated areas and vast, empty, lightly peopled regions. Here again the figures must be seen in perspective.

We know, almost exactly, the location of the civilisations, developed cultures and primitive cultures throughout the whole world in about 1500, on the eve of the impact of the European Conquest of America. Contemporary documents, later accounts, and research by past and present ethnographers have yielded a valid map, because we know that the cultural boundaries vary little in the course of the centuries. Man lives from choice in the framework of his own experience, trapped in his former achievements for generations on end. When we say man we mean the group to which he belongs: individuals leave it and others are incorporated but the group remains attached to a given space and to familiar land. It takes root there.

The map of the world in about 1500 (p. 26) drawn by the ethnographer Gordon W. Hewes is self-explanatory. It distinguishes 76 civilisations and cultures, that is 76 areas of varied shape and size into which the 150 million square kilometres of dry land are divided. This map is very important and we will need to refer to it often. We will therefore examine it carefully from the outset. The 76 pieces of the jigsaw are classified, from area 1, Tasmania, to the 76th and last, Japan. There is no difficulty in reading the terms of classification, starting from the most elementary cultures: (1) 1 to 27 consist of primitive peoples, gatherers and fishermen; (2) 28 to 44, nomads and stockbreeders; (3) 45 to 63, peoples practising a still deficient form of agriculture, primarily peasants using hoes; they are oddly distributed in an almost continuous belt around the world; (4) finally, 64 to 76, civilisations; relatively dense populations possessing multiple assets and advantages: domestic animals, swing-ploughs, ploughs, carts, and above all towns. There is no need to emphasise that these last 13 pieces of the jigsaw are the developed countries, those parts of the world with the densest populations.

It must be added that the classification at the top levels is debatable on two scores. Do 61 and 62 – the Aztec or Mexican civilisation

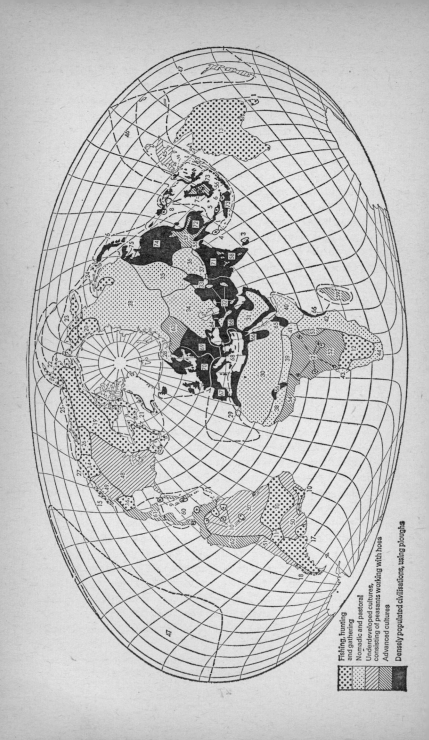

Fishing, hunting
and gathering

Nomadic and pastoral

Underdeveloped cultures,
consisting of peasants working with hoes

Advanced cultures

Densely populated civilisations, using ploughs

Map 1 Civilisations, 'cultures' and primitive peoples c. 1500 (after G. W. Hewes)

1. Tasmanians. 2. Congo Pygmies. 3. The Vedda (Ceylon). 4. Andamanese. 5. Sakai and Semang. 6. Kubu. 7. Punan (Borneo). 8. Negritos of the Philippines. 9. Ciboneys (Antilles). 10. Gé-Botocudos. 11. Gran Chaco Indians. 12. Bushmen. 13. Australians. 14. Great Basin. 15. Lower California. 16. Texas and north-eastern Mexico. 17. Patagonia. 18. Indians of the southern coast of Chile. 19. Athabascans and Algonkin (northern Canada). 20. Yukaghir. 21. Eastern and central Eskimos. 22. Western Eskimos. 23. Kamchadal, Koryak, Chukchi. 24. Ainu, Gilyak, Gol'dy. 25. North-west coast Indians (United States and Canada). 26. Columbia Plateau. 27. Central California. 28. Reindeer-herding peoples. 29. Canary Islands. 30. Sahara nomads. 31. Arabian nomads. 32. Pastoral mountain peoples in the Near East. 33. Pastoral peoples of the Pamir region and the Hindu Kush. 34. Kazakh-Kirghiz. 35. Mongols. 36. Pastoral Tibetans. 37. Settled Tibetans. 38. Western Sudanese. 39. Eastern Sudanese. 40. Somali and Galla of north-eastern Africa. 41. Nilotic tribes. 42. East-African stock-rearing peoples. 43. Western Bantu. 44. Hottentots. 45. Melanesian Papuans. 46. Micronesians. 47. Polynesians. 48. American Indians (Eastern United States). 49. American Indians (Western United States). 50. Brazilian Indians. 51. Chilean Indians. 52. Congolese peoples. 53. Lake-dwellers of East Africa. 54. Guinea coasts. 55. Tribes of the Assam and the Burmese highlands. 56. Tribes of the Indonesian highlands. 57. Highland peoples of Indo-China. 58. Mountain and forest tribes of central India. 59. Malagasy. 60. Caribbean peoples. 61. Mexicans, Maya. 62. Peru and the Andes. 63. Finns. 64. Caucasians. 65. Ethiopia. 66. Settled Muslims. 67. South-western Europe. 68. Eastern Mediterranean. 69. Eastern Europe. 70. North-western Europe. 71. India (this map does not differentiate between Muslims and Hindus). 72. Lowlands of South-east Asia. 73. Indonesian lowlands. 74. Chinese. 75. Koreans. 76. Japanese.

and the Inca or Peruvian civilisation – have full right to be placed at that level? The answer is yes as far as ability, brilliance, art and original turn of mind are concerned. It is equally so if we consider the ancient Mayas' wonderful science of calculation and the longevity of these civilisations: they survived the terrible impact of the European Conquest. On the other hand, the answer is no when we note that they used only hoes and digging sticks; that they had no large domestic animals (except llamas, alpacas and vicuñas); that they had no knowledge of the wheel, arch, cart or metallurgy in iron (known to the still modest cultures of Black Africa for centuries, even millennia). According to our criteria of material life, the answer is on the whole in the negative. We have the same misgivings and reservations about 63, the Finnish groups, which were then scarcely affected by the neighbouring civilisations.

The remaining 13 civilisations, seen on a world scale, form a long, thin ribbon round the whole of the Old World, a narrow belt of springs, tilled fields and dense populations, spaces that man held as securely as was then possible. Furthermore, as we have left the exceptional case of America on one side, we can say that the places where civilised man was to be found in 1500 were the places he had inhabited in 1400 and would inhabit in 1800, and even today. The list is simply drawn up: Japan, Korea, China, Indochina, the Indian Archipelago, India, Islam and the four varied facets of Europe (the Mediterranean Latin, the richest; the Greek, the most unfortunate, submerged by the Turkish conquest; the northern, the hardiest; and the Russo-Lapp, the roughest). Two odd cases need to be added to the list: 64, the robust Caucasian civilisations and 65, the ineradicable civilisation of the Abyssinian tillers.

Here we have a total of perhaps 10 million square kilometres (almost twenty times the territory of present-day France), a tiny area, a belt of high densities very clearly specified and recognisable, *mutatis mutandis*, in the present-day geography of the world (where, we repeat, 70% of all human beings live on 11 million square kilometres). If we accept this present-day percentage of the population living in civilisations in relation to the population as a whole and take our extremes of reference into account, the kilometric density of the developed zones between 1300 and 1800 would lie between 19 and 47·5. If we stop with K.J. Beloch at 1600, the average would lie between 23 and 24. This is an important threshold: if 17 million men was the minimum requirement for power in Europe at that time, the level at which overcrowding became apparent and provided the density necessary to the life and prosperity of a civilisation was some 20 people to the square kilometre. This figure, or rather this order of magnitude, must be remembered; it clarifies many situations which we could not understand *a priori*.

Continuing in 1600: Italy, which was well populated, had 44 inhabitants to the square kilometre; the Netherlands 40; France 34; Germany 28; the Iberian peninsula 17; Poland and Prussia 14; Sweden, Norway and Finland about 1·5 (but they were imprisoned in a prolonged and primitive middle age and remained on the margins of Europe, with only small areas of territory participating in its life). And China, with its seventeen provinces (the eighteenth, Kan-Sou, came under Chinese Turkestan at that time), had a density scarcely over 20 (1578).

Yet these levels, which seem so low to us, already pointed to obvious overpopulation. Wurtemburg, the most populous area of Germany (44 per square kilometre) at the beginning of the sixteenth century, was far and away the best place for the recruitment of lansquenets; France, with a level of 34, was a vast emigration zone; Spain had only 17. However the wealthy and already 'industrialised' countries of Italy and the Netherlands supported a heavier load of people and kept them in their own lands. For overpopulation is a matter of both the number of men and the resources at their disposal.

A.P. Usher distinguishes three levels of population in historical demography. He places the population of the pioneer zones (thinking back to the United States, he calls them 'frontier' people) at the bottom of the scale. This is a population at its very beginnings, in a space which has not, or hardly, been developed by man. The population in his second stage (China, India before the eighteenth century, Europe before the twelfth or thirteenth) ranges between 15 and 20 people to the square kilometre. Lastly, he has the 'dense' population of over 20. Jean Fourastié indicates the same figure as the traditional ratio in France: one man for two hectares of arable land, that is to say, still following the eighteenth-century norms (arable land being half the gross area), 25 inhabitants per square kilometre. William Petty says much the same thing: one man per acre.

These comments only take us to the threshold of the basic problems of a history of population. Among other things we still need to know the relationship between the urban and rural populations (this relationship is perhaps the basic indicator of growth in earlier history) and also the form the rural groups took, according to the norms of human geography. Near St Petersburg, at the end of the eighteenth century, the sordid farms of the Finnish peasants were scattered over the countryside fairly remote from each other; the houses of the German colonists were clustered together; and by comparison the Russian villages were large concentrations. Central Europe north of the Alps had fairly small villages, as in Bavaria. We had the opportunity in Bohemia of looking at several surveys of the former estates of the Rosenbergs and Schwarzenbergs, near the Austrian frontier, a country of artificial lakes filled with carp, pike and perch. The central archives at Warsaw also contain many cadastral maps. We were struck by the very small size of the many villages in central Europe in the seventeenth and eighteenth centuries; very often they consisted of only a dozen or so houses. How far removed they are from the village-towns of Italy or the large market-towns between the Rhine, the Meuse and the Paris basin. But surely the small size of the village in so many eastern and central European countries was one of the basic causes of the fate of the peasantry? It was all the more vulnerable vis-à-vis the nobility because of its lack of population.

Other points inferred from Gordon W. Hewes' map

At least three points emerge from the map:
(1) The permanence of the sites occupied by the 'cultures' (the first achievements) and the 'civilisations' (man's second achievement), for these sites have been reconstructed by a simple deductive method. Their boundaries have not changed. Their distribution therefore forms as marked a geographical feature as the Alps, the Gulf Stream or the course of the Rhine.
(2) The map also shows that man had already explored and exploited the whole world for centuries or millennia before the triumph of Europe. He was only stopped by major obstacles: vast expanses of sea, impenetrable mountains, dense forests (as in Amazonia, North America or Siberia) and immense deserts. Even so, closer inspection reveals that there was no expanse of sea able to escape man's spirit of adventure for very long and guard its secrets (the ancient Greeks knew about the monsoons in the Indian Ocean); no mountain mass that failed to reveal its access and passes; no forest man did not penetrate; no desert he did not cross. As for the 'habitable and navigable' parts of the world, there is not the slightest doubt: the smallest patch already had an owner before 1500 (and before 1400 or

1300 as well). Even the forbidding deserts of the Old World harboured their share of humanity, in the form of the great nomadic
peoples we shall mention later in this chapter. In short, the world
was 'discovered' a long time ago, well before the Great Discoverers.
Even the inventory of vegetable wealth had been drawn up so
precisely 'since the beginning of written history, that not one single
nutritious plant of general usefulness has been added to the list of
those previously known, so careful and complete was the exploration
to which the primitive peoples subjected the plant world'.

Europe therefore neither discovered America and Africa, nor
desecrated the mysterious continents. The nineteenth-century
explorers of central Africa, so greatly admired in the past, travelled
on the backs of the Black bearers. Their great mistake, Europe's
mistake at that juncture, 'was to think they were discovering a sort
of New World'. Similarly the discoverers of the South-American
continent, even the *bandeirantes paulistas* (who set off from the town
of São Paulo, founded in 1554), for all their wonderful epics, merely
rediscovered the old tracks and rivers, with canoes used by the
Indians, during the sixteenth, seventeenth and eighteenth centuries.
And they were generally guided by the *Mamelucos* (Portuguese and
Indian halfbreeds). The same adventure was repeated, to the profit
of the French, from the Great Lakes to the Mississippi in the seventeenth and eighteenth centuries, thanks to Canadian halfbreeds,
the *bois brûlés* as they were called. Europeans very often rediscovered
the world with the eyes, legs and brains of others.

Europe's own achievement was to discover the Atlantic and to
master its difficult stretches, currents and winds. This late success
gained it the doors and routes of the seven seas. Thenceforth the
maritime organisation of the world was at the service of white men.
Fleets, ships and still more ships ploughed the seas; seafaring
peoples, ports and shipbuilding yards — these were the glory of
Europe. Peter the Great made no mistake on his first voyage to the
West (1697): he went to work in Holland, in the shipbuilding yards
of Saardam, near Amsterdam.

(3) One final comment: the small areas of dense population were
not all of the same kind. The Indian Archipelago and Indochina
were really only seed-beds with a few populated regions, compared
with the solidly occupied zones (Western Europe, Japan, Korea,
China). India itself was not fully occupied by its mixed civilisations.
Islam was a series of coasts — of *sahels* — on the margins of empty
spaces, on the edges of deserts, rivers and seas, hugging the sides of

Black Africa, on the coast of the Slaves (Zanzibar) and the Niger loop, where it built and rebuilt its quarrelsome empires. Even Europe merged into emptiness towards the east, beyond the wild marches.

Wild men and animals

It is always very tempting to see only the civilisations. They are the main thing. Besides, they have expended a vast amount of skill on rediscovering their former selves, their tools, costumes, houses, practices, even their traditional songs. Their museums are there to be visited. Consequently we know a great deal about them and their distinctive artefacts: the windmill from China turns horizontally; the blades of the scissors of Istanbul are hollowed with wide interior concavities, their luxury spoons are made of wood from the pepper plant; Japanese and Chinese anvils are different from ours; not one nail was used to build the boats on the Red Sea and the Persian Gulf, and so on. And each has its own plants, domestic animals (or in any case its own way of treating them), its most common type of dwelling, its own foods. The mere smell of cooking can evoke a whole civilisation.

However not all the beauty of the world nor all the salt of the human earth was contained in the civilisations. The land outside them was permeated with primitive life which sometimes even crossed their territory or encircled their boundaries, and vast expanses rang hollow with emptiness. These were the places of wild men and animals, of the old peasant agricultures – the Golden Age, the paradise to which the civilised look back in their search for freedom from restriction.

The Far East yields the most numerous examples of this wild humanity: the islands of the Indian archipelago, the mountains of China, the north of the Japanese island of Yeso, Formosa or the heart of India. The European lands were free of these 'wild' tribes who burned up the high-ground forest and grew rice on the dry land they had cleared. Europe domesticated its mountain people very early on, tamed them by not treating them as if they were pariahs. In the Far East, by contrast, no such communication or co-operation occurred. The innumerable clashes that took place there were unmercifully brutal. The Chinese waged an unceasing war against their wild mountain population, stock-raisers living in stinking houses. It was the same in India. In 1565, in the peninsula of the

Deccan, the Hindu realm of Vidschayanagar was annihilated on the battlefield of Talikota by the Muslim cavalry and artillery of the sultans of the north. The conqueror did not occupy the enormous capital immediately. It was left defenceless and without carts or beast of burden, which had all departed with the army. The wild people from the surrounding brush and jungle then swooped down upon it – Brindscharis, Lambadis and Kurumbas – and pillaged it from end to end.

But these savages were already, as it were, confined and encircled by disapproving civilisations. The real savages lived elsewhere on appalling land, but in a state of complete freedom, beyond the boundaries of the populated countries. They were the *Randvölker*, the marginal people known to German geographers and historians as the *geschichtlos* people – people without history (but is this true?). Some time ago 12,000 Tchoutes lived on 800,000 square kilometres in the far north of Siberia; a thousand Samoyeds occupied 150,000 square kilometres of the frozen peninsula of Yamal. Because 'the poorest groups generally require the greatest space'; or, to put it another way, only an elementary life can be maintained by digging up roots and tubers and trapping wild animals in these vast and hostile spaces.

In any case, as soon as man declines in numbers wild animals multiply, even if the land seems poor or useless. They are to be found wherever man is not. One seventeenth-century traveller describes tigers prowling round Asian villages and towns, catching by surprise fishermen asleep in their boats in the Ganges delta. The ground around the mountain hamlets in the Far East is still cleared even today to keep the man-eaters at a distance. No one feels safe after nightfall, not even inside a house. One man went out of his hut in a small town near Canton, where the Jesuit father de Las Cortes and his fellow sufferers were imprisoned (1626), and was carried off by a tiger. A fourteenth-century Chinese painting represents an enormous tiger ocellated with pink, like some pet monster, amongst the flowering branches of fruit trees. This was all too true throughout the Far East.

Siam is a valley of the River Menam; its waters were alive with rows of houses on piles, bazaars, families crowded on to boats, two or three towns, including the capital. They were flanked by rice fields and then by great forests where the water penetrated vast expanses. The rare patches of forest that were permanently free from water harboured tigers and wild elephants (and, according to

Kämpfer, even chamois). There were other monsters; for example lions in Ethiopia, North Africa and Persia, near Bassorah and on the route from north-west India to Afghanistan. Crocodiles swarmed in the rivers of the Philippines, wild boar on the coastal plains of Sumatra, India and the Persian plateaux; wild horses were to be seen north of Peking. Wild dogs howled in the mountains of Trebizond and prevented Gemelli Careri from sleeping. Wild life in Guinea included small cows that were hunted incessantly. However, both hunter and hunted took flight at the sight of bands of elephants and hippopotamuses, 'sea-horses' that ravaged 'the fields of rice, millet, and other vegetables' in the same regions. 'One sometimes sees troupes of three or four hundred at a time.' 'Wild' animals and even 'small elephants' were encountered in the vast expanses of southern Africa, empty and barbarous well beyond the Cape of Good Hope, living side by side with men 'who lived more like beasts than men'. This is the moment to recall the North African elephants at the time of Carthage and Hannibal, across the centuries and at the other end of the continent; and the elephant hunts, again in the north but this time towards the Congolese interior, known from the end of the sixteenth century.

The whole of Europe, from the Urals to the Straits of Gibraltar, was the domain of wolves, and bears roamed in all its mountains. The omnipresence of wolves and the attention they aroused make wolf-hunting an index of the health of the countryside, and even of the towns, and of the character of the year gone by. A momentary inattention, an economic setback, a rough winter, and they multiplied. In 1420 packs entered Paris through a breach in the ramparts or unguarded gates. They were there again in September 1438, attacking people this time outside the town, between Montmartre and the Saint-Antoine gate. In 1640 wolves entered Besançon by crossing the Doubs near the mills of the town and 'ate children along the roads'. Francis I created grand masters of the wolf-hunts in about 1520. They organised round-ups needing the participation of lords and villagers. There was an example of this in 1765, again in the Gevaudan 'where the ravages of the wolves make one believe in the existence of an unnatural monster'. 'It appears,' wrote a Frenchman in 1779, 'that they are trying to annihilate the species in France, as they did in England six hundred years ago, but it is not easy to round them up in a country as vast and as open on all sides as ours, although it might be practicable in an island like Great Britain.' Even in the matter of wolves France did not escape its position as a geographical crossroads, welded to the countries of the continent and the distant forests of Germany and Poland.

The hazel-grouse, pheasants, white hares and white partridges in the Alps, or the red-legged partridges roused by the horses of Thomas Münzer (a Nuremburg doctor who with his friends travelled in the mountainous Valence hinterland in 1494) offer a more attractive picture. There was an abundance of game in the Rauhe Alb in Wurtemburg in the sixteenth century, but the peasants were forbidden to use large dogs on them; this right was reserved for the foresters. In addition to wild boar, stags, bucks, gazelles, lions, tigers, bears and hares, Persia was swarming with prodigious quantities of pigeons, wild geese, ducks, turtledoves, crows, herons and two types of partridge.

Naturally, the larger the space, the more freely animal life multiplied. Father Vertiss (1682) saw fantastic hunts when he travelled with the Emperor of China's enormous suite (100,000 horses) in Manchuria, and grumblingly and exhaustedly participated in them: a thousand stags and sixty tigers were killed in one day. Mauritius was still empty of people in 1639, but turtledoves and hares were so numerous and so unafraid that they were caught by hand. In Florida in 1690 'quantities of wild pigeons, parrots and other birds were so numerous that boats often came away full of birds' eggs'.

Of course everything was magnified in the New World: there was a superabundance of uninhabited regions (*despoblados*) interspersed with a few tiny towns at enormous distances from each other. The twelve large wooden carrioles drawn by thirty pairs of oxen that accompanied the bishop of Santiago de Chile, Lizarraga, in 1600, took about twenty days to travel from Cordoba to Mendoza, in what later became Argentina. Indigenous animals were few, with the exception of the ostrich, towards the south. Instead, the empty countryside had been filled with animals (horses and cattle) brought from Europe, and these had multiplied. Enormous herds of wild oxen had worn regular paths across the plain; they remained at liberty until the nineteenth century. The silhouettes of the herds of wild horses huddled together sometimes looked like vague hillocks against the horizon. In the pampas where not the tiniest piece of wood could be found, 'not even as large as a little finger', a *chapeton*, a newcomer to America, caught a glimpse of one such small hillock in the distance and cried out in delight: 'Let's go and cut some wood!'

We could stop on that anecdote, but there is an even better

example. This was Siberia, which was opened up to the Russians at the same time as America to Western Europeans. The vast and almost empty Kamchatka peninsula gradually came to life with the beginning of the eighteenth century. Hunters and merchants were attracted to it by fur-bearing animals. The skins were brought up to Irkutsk by merchants and from there reached either China, via the neighbouring fair of Kiakhta, or Moscow and thence the West. The fashion for sea-otter dates from that period. Previously it was only used for clothing by hunters and natives. The hunt suddenly assumed gigantic proportions with the sharp rise in prices. The trappers, the *promyschlennik*, either followed the animals in canoes and waited until they were forced to surface for breath or held off until the first ice-floes formed, when hunters and dogs could reach the otters (clumsy out of the water) easily. They then ran from one otter to another stunning them as they passed, finishing them off later. Sometimes fragments of ice-floe broke off, carrying hunters, dogs and otter corpses out to the open sea. Kamchatka was quickly cleared of its beautiful animals as a result of this hunting. The trappers had to look farther afield, as far as the American coast, even as far as the heights of San Francisco, where Russians and Spaniards clashed at the beginning of the nineteenth century – without making any great impact on the mainstream of history.

A sort of primitive animal life existed over vast expanses, even at the close of the eighteenth century. The tragic innovation into these paradises was man. The craze for furs explains why the sailing ship, *The Lion*, carrying the Ambassador, Macartney, to China, discovered five terribly dirty inhabitants (three French and two English) on the island of Amsterdam, in the Indian Ocean, around the fortieth degree of latitude south, on 1 February 1793. Boats from Boston which sold at Canton either beaver skins from America or seal skins from the island itself had set the five men ashore during an earlier trip. They had organised gigantic slaughter (25,000 animals during a summer season). Seals were not the only fauna on the islands. There were penguins, whales, sharks and dogfish, as well as innumerable other kinds of fish. 'Hooks and lines speedily procured enough fish to feed for a week the crew of *The Lion*.' Tench, perch, and particularly crayfish were found in profusion in fresh-water channels. 'The sailors . . . let down into the sea baskets, in which were baits of sharks' flesh. In a few minutes the baskets being drawn up, were found half-filled with crayfish.' The birds were a fresh source of wonder: albatrosses with yellow beaks, great black petrels, 'silver birds' and blue petrels. Blue petrels were night birds hunted by birds of prey and also by the seal-hunters who attracted them with lighted torches – so successfully that they 'kill multitudes of them. They constitute indeed the principal food of these people who think it very good. This blue petrel is about the size of a pigeon . . .'

3 The end of an old biological régime

What was shattered in both China and Europe with the eighteenth century was an old biological régime, a collection of restrictions, obstacles, structures, proportions and numerical relationships that had hitherto been the norm.

Preserving the balance

There is always a correlation between the patterns of births and deaths. Under the *ancien régime* the two coefficients were both at around the same figure: 40 per 1000. What life added, death took away. The parish registers of the small commune of La Chapelle-Fougcrets (today part of the suburb of Rennes) recorded 50 baptisms in 1609. Reckoning on the basis of 40 births per 1000 inhabitants and therefore multiplying the number of baptisms by 25, it is possible to suggest that the population of this large village was around 1250 – if the parish register figures are accepted. The English economist William Petty reconstructed the population on the basis of deaths in his *Political Arithmetic* (1690), multiplying the figure by 30 (which was actually an under-estimate of the death rate).

In the short term, credit and debit kept pace, so that when one side gained, the other reacted. In 1451 we are told that plague carried off 21,000 people; that in 1452 4000 marriages were celebrated. Even if these figures are exaggerated, as everything would seem to indicate, the compensation is obvious. In 1581 790 people – ten times more than in normal times – died at Salzewedel, a small place in the old Brandenburg Marches. Marriages fell from 30 to 10. But in the following year, despite the reduced population, 30 marriages were celebrated, followed by numerous compensatory births. Immediately after a plague that was said to have halved the population of Verona in 1637 (but the chroniclers exaggerated freely), the soldiers of the garrison – almost all French and numerous enough to

37

have escaped the plague – married the widows, and life regained its hold.

When the balance was not restored quickly enough the authorities intervened: Venice, normally so jealously closed, passed a liberal decree on 30 October 1348, just after the terrible Black Death, granting complete citizenship (*de intus et de extra*) to every individual who would come and settle there with his family and possessions within the period of a year. It must be added that the towns, as a general rule, only survived thanks to new blood from outside. But ordinarily people came of their own accord.

Increases and declines therefore alternated in the short term, regularly compensating each other. This is constantly demonstrated (up to the eighteenth century) by the serrated double curves of births and deaths for anywhere in the West – in Venice and Beauvais for example. Epidemics would, when necessary, soon finish off the younger children (who were always in danger) and everyone would be rendered vulnerable by the precarious means of support. The poor were always the first to be affected. Innumerable 'social massacres' occurred in these centuries. In 1483 at Crépy near Senlis, 'a third of that town is begging in the countryside and old people are dying in squalor every day'.

Life only gained over death in the eighteenth century and thereafter overtook it fairly regularly. But counter-attacks were still possible: in France in 1772-3, and during the crisis of 1779-83. These sharp alarms indicated the insecure character of an improvement which came late and was at the mercy of the always hazardous balance between food requirements and possibilities of production.

Famine

Famine recurred so insistently for centuries on end that it became incorporated into man's biological régime and built into his daily life. Dearth and penury were continual, and familiar even in Europe, despite its privileged position. A few overfed rich do not alter the rule. It could not have been otherwise. Cereal yields were poor; two consecutive bad harvests spelt disaster. These disasters were often absorbed in the Western world, possibly because of the climate. This was not the case in Muscovy, with its harsh, unreliable climate, nor in India which had to go far afield to procure foodstuffs it did not produce in sufficient quantity at home, nor in China where floods and drought seemed apocalyptic catastrophes.

Yet the 'miracle' crops – maize and potatoes – were only established late in Europe. Maize arrived in Portugal and Biscay in the sixteenth century but only reached Venice at the beginning of the seventeenth. It came to the plains of Gascony at the end of that century, and the distant Danubian provinces only in the nineteenth. Apart from its early success in Ireland and Germany, the potato is practically outside the chronological scope of this book. It hardly appeared before 1770 in Burgundy, where it was known as a truffle, *treuffe, pataque* or *cartoufle.* 'However, it had a local circulation on the eve of the Revolution.'

For these and other reasons famine only disappeared from the West at the close of the eighteenth century, or even later. When climatic severity intervened, whole populations could be 'faced with the inevitable' once again. A privileged country like France is said to have experienced 10 general famines during the tenth century: 26 in the eleventh; 2 in the twelfth; 4 in the fourteenth; 7 in the fifteenth; 13 in the sixteenth; 11 in the seventeenth and 16 in the eighteenth. We obviously give this eighteenth-century summary without guarantee as to its accuracy: the only risk it runs is of over-optimism, because it omits the hundreds and hundreds of local famines (in Maine, in 1739, 1752, 1770 and 1785 for example), which did not invariably coincide with country-wide shortages.

Cologne experienced 22 years of high prices (*Teuerungsjahre*), that is to say of famine, between 1437 and 1493. Later Germany had a large share of setbacks and suffering. There are still examples in the eighteenth century: famines in Silesia in 1730; in Saxony and southern Germany in 1771–2; in and beyond the boundaries of Bavaria in 1816–17. On 5 August 1817, the town of Ulm held thanksgiving ceremonies to celebrate the return to normal life with the new harvest. But this *Teuerungsjahre* made possible a sharpened awareness of the mechanism of such crises.

Another statistic from a report of 1767 indicates that in Tuscany the 316 preceding years included 111 years of famine compared with only 16 of good harvests. It is true that Tuscany was hilly, that it concentrated on vines and olive trees, and that, thanks to its merchants, it had been able to count on Sicilian grain (which it could not live without) since before the thirteenth century.

Furthermore it would be rash to conclude that the towns, habitual grumblers, were the sole victims of these acts of God. They had warehouses, reserves, corn exchanges, purchases from abroad – in fact a whole policy directed towards future contingencies,

Paradoxically the countryside sometimes experienced far greater suffering. The peasants lived in a state of dependence on merchants, towns and nobles, and had scarcely any reserves of their own. They had no solution in case of famine except to turn to the town (*il s'éborgeai[t] dans la ville*, according to a Dijon chorus in 1636) where they crowded together, begging in the streets and often dying in public squares, as in Venice and Amiens in the sixteenth century.

The towns soon had to protect themselves against these regular invasions, which were not purely by beggars from the surrounding areas but by positive armies of the poor, sometimes from very far afield. Beggars from distant provinces appeared in the fields and streets of the town of Troyes in 1573, starving, clothed in rags and covered with fleas and vermin. The rich citizens of the town soon began to fear 'sedition' by these miserable wretches and 'in order to make them leave, the rich men and the governors of the aforesaid town of Troye were assembled to find the expedient to remedy it. The resolution of this council was that they must be put outside the town ... To do this, an ample amount of bread was baked, to be distributed amongst the aforesaid poor who would be assembled at one of the gates of the town, without being told why, and after the distribution to each one of his bread and a piece of silver, they would be made to leave the town by the aforesaid gate which would be closed on the last one and it would be indicated to them over the town walls that they go to God and find their livelihood elsewhere, and that they should not return to the aforesaid Troye before the new grain from the next harvest. This was done. After the gift the dismayed poor were driven from the town of Troye ...'

The attitude of the bourgeois hardened considerably towards the end of the sixteenth century, and even more in the seventeenth. The problem was to place the poor in a position where they could do no harm. In Paris the sick and invalid had always been directed to the hospitals, and the fit, chained together in pairs, were employed at the hard, exacting and interminable task of cleaning the drains of the town. In England the Poor Laws, which were in fact laws *against* the poor, appeared at the end of Elizabeth's reign. Houses for the poor and undesirable gradually appeared throughout the West, condemning their occupants to forced labour in workhouses, *Zuchthaüser* or *Maisons de force* for example, that body of semi-prisons, united under the administration of the *Grand Hôpital de Paris*, founded in 1656. This 'great enclosure' of the poor, mad and delinquent, as well as sons of good family placed under supervision by their parents, was one psychological aspect of seventeenth-century society, relentless in its rationality. But it was perhaps an almost inevitable reaction to the poverty and increase in numbers of the poor in that hard century.

This was Europe. Things were far worse in Asia, China and India. Famines there seemed like the end of the world. In China everything depended on rice from the southern provinces; in India, on providential rice from Bengal, but vast distances had to be crossed and this contribution only covered a fraction of the requirements. Every crisis had wide repercussions. The famine of 1472, which hit the Deccan particularly harshly, caused large numbers who had escaped its consequences to emigrate to Gujarat and Malwa. In 1596 a violent famine extended over all north-west India.

The cataclysms were often irremediable, such as the terrible and almost general famine in India in 1630-1. A Dutch merchant left an appalling description of it: 'People wandered hither and thither,' he wrote, 'helpless, having abandoned their towns or villages. Their condition could be recognised immediately: sunken eyes, wan faces, lips flecked with foam, lower jaw projecting, bones protruding through skin, stomach hanging like an empty sack, some of them howling with hunger, begging alms.' The customary dramas ensued: wives and children abandoned, children sold by parents, who either abandoned them or sold themselves in order to survive, collective suicides. . . . Then came the stage when the starving split open the stomachs of the dead or dying to 'eat their entrails'. 'Hundreds and hundreds of thousands of people died,' the merchant continued, 'to the point when the country was entirely covered with corpses which stayed unburied, and such a stink arose that the air was filled with it and pestilential.'

Even when documents are not as detailed, one item is enough to convey the horror. In 1670 a Persian ambassador went to pay his respects to the Great Mogul, Aurenge-Zebe. He returned home accompanied by 'innumerable slaves' (who were to be taken away from him at the frontier) whom 'he had had for almost nothing because of famine'.

We return hardened, consoled or resigned to privileged Europe as if from some nightmare journey. Western Europe only encountered similar horrors during the first dark centuries of the middle ages or else on its eastern borders, which were backward in so many respects.

If one wants to measure 'the catastrophes of history by the proportion of victims claimed', wrote one historian, 'the 1696-7 famine in Finland must be regarded as the most terrible event in European history'. A quarter or a third of the Finnish population disappeared at that time. The East was the bad side of Europe. Famine raged there long after the eighteenth century, despite desperate recourse to 'famine foodstuffs' – wild herbs and fruit, formerly cultivated plants found amongst the weeds in fields, gardens, meadows, or the outskirts of forests.

However, this situation did sometimes recur in Western Europe, particularly in the seventeenth century, with the 'little ice age'. In the Blésois in 1662 a witness reported that 'such poverty had not been seen for five hundred years'. The poor were on a diet of 'cabbage runts, with bran soaked in cod water'. The protest the Electors of Burgundy sent to the king in the same year recorded that 'famine this year has put an end to over seventeen thousand families in your province and forced a third of the inhabitants, even in the good towns, to eat wild plants'. A chronicler adds that: 'Some people ate human flesh.' Ten years earlier, in 1652, the same chronicler had indicated that 'the people of Lorraine and other surrounding lands are reduced to such extremities that, like animals, they eat the grass in the meadows, and particularly those from the villages of Pouilly and Parnot in Bassigny ... and are black and as thin as skeletons'. In 1693 a Burgundian noted 'the price of grain was so high throughout the realm that people were dying of hunger'; in 1694 near Meulan (today Seine-et-Oise) corn was harvested before it was ripe, 'large numbers of people lived on grass like animals'; the terrible winter of 1709 threw innumerable vagrants on to all the roads of France.

All these gloomy examples should obviously not be placed one after another. All the same let us not be too optimistic. The accounts of food deficiencies and the illness they caused cannot be deceptive: scurvy (which came into its own with the great sea voyages); pellagra from the eighteenth century, which resulted from an exclusive diet of maize; beri beri in Asia. The persistence of gruel and sops in the popular diet, and the bread made with inferior flours and only cooked once a month or every two months are equally revealing. The bread was almost always hard and mouldy. It was cut with an axe in some regions. In the Tyrol brown bread made from ground corn and very long-lasting was baked two or three times a year. The *Dictionnaire de Trévoux* (1771) says quite bluntly: 'The peasants are usually so stupid because they only live on coarse foods.'

Epidemics

One bad harvest was just about bearable; if there were two, prices went mad and famine set in. Famine was never an isolated event. Sooner or later it opened the door to epidemics, which have their own individual cycles. Plague was the great, the terrible fear. 'A many-headed hydra', 'a strange chameleon', it assumed such varied forms that contemporaries unconsciously confused it with other diseases. Leader of the dance of Death, it was 'a fixture, an inherent part of men's lives'.

In fact it was only one disease among many others, intermingled in their frequent travels and contagions as a result of chaotic social mixing and the vast human repositories created thereby, where disease could lie dormant until its next explosion. A whole book could be written on dense civilisations, epidemics, endemics and on the cycles according to which these determined travellers disappear and come back. To mention only smallpox: in 1775, when inoculation was beginning to be discussed, a medical book considered it 'the most general of all diseases'; ninety-five in every hundred people were affected; one in seven died.

But a doctor today would at first glance scarcely know where he was among these diseases, obscured by their old names and the sometimes unusual descriptions of their symptoms. Furthermore there is no guarantee that they are always comparable to the diseases known today. Diseases change and have a history of their own, which depends on a possible modification of bacteria and viruses and of the human landscape on which they live. Pure chance led Gaston Roupnel in 1922, with the help of a parasitologist friend, to discover that the purple fever or purpura at Dijon and elsewhere in the seventeenth century was actually exanthematic typhus (transmitted by fleas). This was the same 'purple fever' which in about 1780 'mowed down the poor Parisians of the Faubourg Saint-Marcel by the hundreds ... the gravediggers' arms were falling off ...' But the question of the 'purple' remains to be solved.

What would the present-day doctor make of the plague in 1348 as described by Guy de Chauliac, whose *Grande Chirurgie* went into sixty-nine editions between 1478 and 1895? He gave two characteristic stages of the disease: first stage, quite long (two months), fever and spitting of blood; second stage, abscesses and pulmonary weakness. How would he diagnose the 1427 epidemic, inexplicably christened *dendo* in Paris and described as a hitherto unknown

43

malady? 'It begins in the back, as if one had a bad case of kidney stones, and is followed by the shivers; for eight to ten days one cannot drink, eat or sleep properly.' Then there was 'a cough which was so bad that when listening to a sermon people could not hear what the preacher was saying because of the great noise from the coughers'. This was undoubtedly some sort of special influenza virus, like the 'Spanish flu' after the First World War or the 'Asian flu' that invaded Europe around 1956–8. Estoile described another variety:

At the beginning of April (1595) the King (Henry IV) became very ill with a catarrh which distorted his whole face. Catarrhs like this were prevalent in Paris because it was very cold there for the time of year: they caused several strange and sudden deaths *with the plague* [the italics are ours] which spread in diverse places in the town; they were all scourges from God, which nonetheless produced as little visible improvement in conduct amongst the great as amongst the small.

The sweating sickness, the *suette anglaise*, in the reign of Henry VIII, which was not confined to England, was the same sort of thing: influenza with pulmonary complications. An Italian correspondent from Paris (31 January 1529) describes it after the event and recommends the patient to sweat through sheets and mattress without uncovering himself. He describes how a man from Ragusa wanted to change his shirt and died instantly.

And what was the disease that caused the epidemic in Madrid in August 1597 which, we are told, was 'non-contagious' and caused swelling of groin, armpit and throat? After the fever had broken out the sufferer was cured in five or six days and recovered slowly, or died immediately. It must be added that these were poor people, who lived in damp houses and slept on the ground.

There is another difficulty: different diseases break out simultaneously. 'They have scarcely anything in common except infection, such illnesses as diphtheria, *cholérine*, typhoid fever, *picotte*, smallpox, purple fever, the *bosse, dendo, tac* or *harion*, the *trousse galant* or *mal chaud*; or again whooping cough, scarlatina, grippe, influenza . . .' This list was drawn up for France, but it applies elsewhere with variations. The current diseases in England were intermittent fevers, sweating sickness, chlorosis or 'green sickness', jaundice, consumption, falling sickness or epilepsy, vertigo, rheumatism, gravel, stones.

The undernourished, unprotected population could offer little resistance to these massive attacks. I must admit that I was not entirely convinced by the Tuscan proverb I have often quoted: 'The best remedy against malaria is a well filled pot.' But during the famine in Russia, in 1921–3, an unimpeachable observer recorded that malaria broke out throughout the country and manifested the same symptoms as in tropical zones in the region of the Arctic circle. Undernourishment on all the evidence was an important factor in the spread of diseases.

There is another rule with no exceptions: epidemics jump from one human mass to another. Alonso Montecuccoli, sent to England by the Grand Duke of Tuscany, wrote (2 September 1603) that he would cross from Boulogne and not from Calais, where the English plague, following the trade route, had just arrived. This is but a small example in comparison with the powerful waves that began in China and India and brought the plague to the West, via the ever-active relay points of Constantinople and Egypt. Tuberculosis was also an old scourge of Europe: Francis II (tubercular meningitis), Charles IX (pulmonary tuberculosis) and Louis XIII (intestinal tuberculosis) all fell victim to it (1560, 1574, 1643). But a form of tuberculosis more virulent than the established variety arrived in the eighteenth century. In any case it was the leading disease of Romantic Europe and of the nineteenth century as a whole. Cholera also came from India, where it existed in an endemic state. It became general in the Peninsula in 1817 and then burst its bounds and swelled to a violent and terrible pandemic that soon reached Europe.

Another visitor, this time during the centuries actually covered by our study, was syphilis. Its origins are prehistoric, primitive skeletons having been found which bear its marks. There were known clinical cases before 1492. But syphilis sprang up again after the discovery of pre-Columbian America: a revenge, it was said, on the part of the conquered people. Perhaps the most probable of the four or five theories supported by doctors today is the one that considers the disease broke out – or rather broke out again – as a result of sexual relations between the two races (the influence of the *treponema pertenne* on the *treponema pallidum*). In any case, the terrifying character of syphilis was revealed in Barcelona from the time of the celebrations of Columbus' return (1493), and it then spread rapidly. It was an epidemic, rapid and mortal illness. Within the space of four or five years it toured Europe, moving from one country to another under misleading names: Neapolitan disease, *mal français*, the French disease, or *lo mal francioso*; France, by virtue of its geographical position, won this war of words. The surgeon-barbers of the Hôtel-Dieu as early as 1503 were claiming that they could cure the disease by cauterisation with red-hot irons. This virulent form of syphilis reached China in 1506–7. Afterwards, and with the help of mercury, it assumed its classical attenuated form in Europe, evolving slowly with its cures and specialist hospitals (the Spittle in London). Before that stage was reached it had probably attacked every level of society at the end of the sixteenth century, from beggars (male and female) to nobles and princes. Malherbe, known as the Père Luxure, 'boasted that he had sweated out the pox three times'. Gregorio Marañon, a famous historian and doctor, added a basis of hereditary syphilis to the customary diagnosis contemporary doctors made on Philip II. This can be retrospectively applied, without risk of error, to all princes of the past. Thomas Dekker (1572–1632), the dramatist, put into words what everyone in London was thinking when he said: 'As every throng is sure of a pick-pocket, as sure as a whoore is of the clyents all Michaelmas Tearme, and of the pox after the Tearme.'

The plague

The enormous dossier of evidence on the plague is constantly growing. The disease was at least two-fold: pulmonary plague, a new form of illness that came to light with the pandemic of 1348 in Europe; and the older bubonic plague (buboes form in the groin and become gangrenous). These were the marks of God, 'God's tokens' or more usually simply 'tokens': in French, *tacs*, like the metal or leather counters tradesmen put into circulation. 'It can happen that just one can prove fatal . . .' The Black Death (pulmonary) was due to a virus transmitted by fleas from the *Mus Rattus*. It used to be said that these rats invaded Europe and its granaries immediately after the Crusades, avenging the East as the *teponema pallidum* avenged America in the early days of its discovery in 1492.

This over-simple and moralistic explanation should probably be abandoned. The *Mus Rattus*, the black rat, was noticed in Europe from the eighth century, even in the Carolingian period; the same applies to the brown rat (*Mus Decumanus*) which was not itself a carrier of plague germs and according to popular lore eliminated the *Mus Rattus*, the species responsible for the epidemics. Finally, the Black Death did not, as used to be thought, arrive in central Europe in the thirteenth century, but in the eleventh at the latest. Moreover the brown rats settled in the cellars of houses, while the domestic rat chose to live in granaries, close to food supplies. Their invasions overlapped before the process of exclusion began.

All this does not mean that rats, and fleas from rats, did not play a part in spreading disease. On the contrary, a very intensive study (30,000 documents are involved) of the outbreaks of plague at Uelzen in Lower Saxony in 1560–1610 proves that they did. If the retreat of the disease in the eighteenth century is to be explained by external (exogenous, as economists would say) conditions, we can cite the substitution of stone for wooden houses after the great urban fires of the sixteenth, seventeenth and eighteenth centuries, increased personal and domestic cleanliness, and the removal of small domestic animals from dwellings – all conditions conducive to the breeding of fleas. But medical research in these fields is still continuing, even since Yerson discovered the specific bacillus of the plague in 1894, and discoveries that could modify present theories are still possible. For example, the bacillus itself is said to be preserved in the soil of certain areas of Iran and capable of infecting rodents. Were these danger zones therefore by-passed by the normal routes leading to Europe in the eighteenth century? We can at least tentatively suggest that India and China, so frequently accused by historians, were not entirely to blame.

Whatever the cause or causes, the scourge was subdued in the West in the eighteenth century. It made its last spectacular appearance in the famous plague of Marseilles in 1720. But it continued to be deadly in Eastern Europe: Moscow experienced a murderous plague in 1770. The Abbé de Mably wrote (in about 1775): 'The war, the plague or Pugachev have certainly carried off as many men as the partition of Poland.' Kherson in 1783 and Odessa in 1814 received further terrible visitations. The last large-scale attacks known in Europe were not in Russia but in the Balkans, in 1828–9 and 1841. This was the Black Death, and once again wooden houses played a part in its spread.

Bubonic plague, for its part, remained endemic in hot and humid areas: southern China, India and at the very gates of Europe in North Africa. The plague of Oran (described by Albert Camus in La Peste) was in 1942.

The above account is extremely incomplete. But the over-plentiful documentation defeats the historian's good intentions by its very quantity. Preliminary research work would be required to construct annual charts of the localisation of the disease. They would indicate its depth, extent and repeated violence: Besançon reported plague

40 times between 1439 and 1640; Dôle fell victim in 1565, 1586, 1629, 1632 and 1637; in the sixteenth century the whole of the Limousin was attacked 10 times, Orleans experienced it on 22 occasions; Seville, the heart of the world, was hit particularly hard in 1507-8, 1571, 1582, 1595-9, 1616, and 1648-9. Losses were heavy every time, even if they fell short of the chroniclers' exaggerated figures, and even if there were 'little' plagues and some false alarms.

Accurate calculations for Bavaria from 1621 to 1635 produce appalling averages: for every 100 deaths in a normal year Munich counted 155 in an abnormal year; Augsburg 195; Bayreuth 487; Landsburg 556 and Strauling 702. Children under a year old were primarily affected on each occasion, and women tended to be more susceptible than men.

Descriptions and examples must be compared – in the same way as all these figures have to be investigated and compared – because they often present the same drama, list the same more or less effective measures (quarantines, surveillance, inhalants, disinfection, blocked roads, close confinement, health certificates – *Gesundheitspässe* in Germany, *cartas de salud* in Spain), the same suspicions and the same social pattern.

At the first sign of the disease the rich whenever possible took hurried flight to their country houses; no one thought of anything but himself: 'This disease is making us more cruel to one another than we are to dogs,' noted Samuel Pepys in August 1665. And Montaigne told how he wandered in search of a roof when the epidemic reached his estate, 'serving six months miserably as a guide' to his 'distracted family, frightening their friends and themselves and causing horror wherever they tried to settle'. The poor remained alone, penned up in the contaminated town where the State fed them, isolated them, blockaded them and kept them under observation. Boccaccio's *Decameron* is a series of conversations and narratives in a villa near Florence at the time of the Black Death. Maître Nicolas Versoris, lawyer in the Paris Parlement, left his lodgings in August 1523. But three days after he reached his pupils' country house at the 'Grange Batelière', then outside Paris, his wife died of the disease – an exception that confirms the value of the customary precaution. The plague in Paris in that summer of 1523 once again struck at the poor. Versoris wrote in his *Livre de Raison*: 'death was principally directed towards the poor so that only a very few of the Paris porters and wage-earners who had lived there in

48

large numbers before the misfortune, were left. . . . As for the district of Petiz Champs, the whole countryside was cleared of poor people who previously lived there in large numbers.' One bourgeois from Toulouse placidly wrote in 1561: 'the aforesaid contagious disease only attacks poor people . . . let God in his mercy be satisfied with that. . . . The rich protect themselves against it.' J.-P. Sartre was right when he wrote in reference to the first pandemic in the fourteenth century (but his comment is valid for all its manifestations): 'The plague only exaggerates the relationship between the classes: it strikes at the poor and spares the rich.'

It also multiplied what we would call dereliction of duty: municipal magistrates, officers and prelates forgot their responsibilities; in France whole parlements emigrated (Grenoble 1467, 1589, 1596; Bordeaux 1471, 1585; Besançon 1519; Rennes 1563, 1564). Cardinal d'Armagnac quite naturally forsook his town of Avignon, when it was affected by the disease in 1580, for Bedarrides and then Sorgues; he only returned after ten months' absence when all danger had disappeared. 'He could say,' a bourgeois of Avignon noted in his journal, 'the opposite of the Gospel, *Ego sum pastor et non cognovi oves meas.*' But it is pointless to heap abuse on Montaigne, mayor of Bordeaux, who did not resume his post at the time of the 1585 epidemic, or on François Dragonet of Fogasses, rich Avignon citizen of Italian origin, whose leases provided for a time when he would be obliged to leave the town (which he did in 1588, during a fresh plague) and lodge with his farmers: 'In case of contagion (God forbid), they will give me a room at the house . . . and I will be able to put my horses in the stable on my way there and back, and they will give me a bed for myself.' When plague broke out in London in 1664 the Court left the town for Oxford and the richest members of the population hastened to follow suit with their hurriedly assembled families, servants and baggage. There was no litigation in the capital; 'the lawyers were all in the country'; ten thousand houses were abandoned, some with deal planks nailed over doors and windows; doomed houses were marked with a cross in red chalk. We will never know how much Daniel Defoe's retrospective (1720) account of the 1664 plague of London is consistent with the customary pattern, repeated thousands of times with the same actions (the dead thrown 'for the most part on to a cart like common dung'), the same precautions, despair and discrimination.

No disease today, however great its ravages, gives rise to comparable acts of folly or collective dramas.

A reliable observer who escaped the plague at Florence in 1637 describes the barricaded houses and forbidden street only opened to allow in food supplies; the occasional priest might pass by, but more frequently it would be a patrol, or the coach of a privileged individual granted rare permission to break the seal on the interior of the town for a moment. Florence was dead: no business activities and no religious services – except for the odd mass which the officiant celebrated at the corner of the street and in which the people participated from behind closed windows.

Father Maurice de Tolon, writing about the plague of Genoa in the same year in *Le Capucin charitable*, enumerated the precautions to be taken: do not talk to any suspect person from the town when the wind is blowing from him towards you; burn aromatics for disinfection; wash or better still burn clothes and linen belonging to suspected cases; above all pray; and help the guards. The extremely wealthy town of Genoa, the background to these comments, was subjected to clandestine looting because its rich palaces were abandoned. Meanwhile the dead piled up in the streets; the only way to rid the town of carcasses was to load them on to boats which were put out to sea and burned. As a sixteenth-century specialist, I must admit that the scenes presented by the plague-stricken towns in the following century, and their fatal losses, have long surprised me and continue to do so. The situation clearly deteriorated from one century to the next. Plague was in Amsterdam throughout every year from 1622 to 1628 (the toll: 35,000 dead). It was in Paris in 1612, 1619, 1631, 1638, 1662, 1668 (the last). It should be noted that after 1612 in Paris 'the sick were forcibly removed from their homes and transferred to the Hôpital Saint-Louis and to the maison de Santé in the faubourg Saint-Marcel'. Plague was in London five times between 1593 and 1664–5, claiming, it is said, a total of 156,463 victims.

Everything improved in the eighteenth century. Yet the plague of 1720 in Toulon and Marseilles was extremely virulent. According to one historian, a good half of the population of Marseilles succumbed. The streets were full of 'putrid bodies, gnawed by dogs'.

The cycle of diseases

Diseases appeared and alternately established themselves and retreated. Some disappeared. This happened in the case of leprosy, which may well have been conquered in Europe in the fourteenth or fifteenth centuries by Draconian isolation measures. (Today, strangely enough, lepers at large never spread infection.) It also happened with the plague, which disappeared in the eighteenth century when the West had arrived at its privileged position; with cholera in the nineteenth century; and with tuberculosis and syphilis, which are now in retreat before the miracle of antibiotics. One cannot however make any definite claims for the future, because syphilis is said to be reappearing today with some virulence.

Some historians will not hesitate to think, and I agree with them, that every disease has its own autonomous life, independent of the endless correlations we suggest. The correlations with economic crises, trade exchanges and the abnormal interchange during times of war would at most be only minor accidents in a history linked with other factors: rodents, parasites, bacilli, viruses, or some form of merchandise, whether in store or circulation. Their histories would still be cyclical, however, with a beginning, recurrences, surprise outbreaks, and sometimes an end.

In fact these virulent attacks and retreats might have originated from the fact that humanity had lived behind barriers for so long, dispersed, as it were, on different planets, so that the exchange of contagious germs between one group and another led to catastrophic surprise attacks, depending on the extent to which each had its own habits, resistance or weakness in relation to the pathogenic agent concerned. The unity of the world led to a dramatic telescoping. American syphilis reached China (1506–7) more rapidly than American maize (1597). In the opposite direction, grippe wrought havoc amongst the Indians in America, where it had been unknown. In 1588 grippe attacked (but did not kill) the whole population of Venice and even emptied the Grand Council: this had never happened during a plague. The wave went on to reach Milan, France, Catalonia and then America. The word *grippe*, in the sense of a disease which grips or seizes, may only date from the spring of 1743. But it caught on. On 10 January 1768, Voltaire wrote: 'Grippe, on a world tour, passed our Siberia (Ferney near Geneva, where he lived), and laid hold a little of my old and sickly face.'

By that time diseases had become common to all mankind, just as the world had become a single entity in other ways.

Life expectation

Before the nineteenth century, man, wherever he lived, could only count on a short expectation of life, with a few extra years in the case of the rich: '... notwithstanding the baneful luxuries in which the European rich indulge, and the disorders of repletion, inactivity and vice to which they are subject,' according to one English traveller (1793), 'the mean duration of their lives exceeds about ten years that of their inferiors, whom excessive fatigue had contributed to wear out before their time; whom poverty had deprived of the means of proportional comfort and subsistence. ...'

This separate demography for the rich is lost in the scale of our averages. In the Beauvaisis in the middle of the seventeenth century 'over a third of the children died every twelve months; only 58% reached their fifteenth year'; people died on average at about the age of twenty. Thousands of details demonstrated the precariousness and brevity of life in those far-off times. 'No one will be surprised to see the young Dauphin, Charles (the future Charles V), govern France at the age of seventeen, in 1356, and disappear in 1380 at forty-two with the reputation of a wise old man.' Anne de Montmorency, the *Connétable* who died on horseback at the battle of Porte Saint-Denis at the age of seventy-four (1567) was an exception. Charles V was an old man when he abdicated at Ghent in 1555 at the age of fifty-five. His son, Philip II, who died at seventy-one (1598), had aroused the liveliest hopes and fears amongst his contemporaries at each danger signal during his twenty-year period of failing health. Finally none of the royal families escaped the terrifying rate of infant mortality of the period. A 'guide' to Paris in 1722 lists the names of princes and princesses laid to rest since 1662 in the Val-de-Grâce founded by Anne of Austria: they are mainly children a few days, months or years old.

The poor endured an even harsher fate. In 1754 an 'English' author could still note: 'Far from being well-to-do, the peasants in France do not even have the necessary subsistence; they are a breed of men who begin to decline before they are forty for lack of a return proportionate to their efforts: humanity suffers by comparing them with other men and above all with our English peasants. With the French labourers, their external appearance alone proves the deterioration of their bodies. ...'

As for Europeans who lived outside their continent, they did not always know 'how to subject themselves to the habits and diet of the countries to which they have newly come and (obstinately) pursue their own fancies and passions there ... with the result that they find their graves'. This comment was made in 1690. Another, written at the same time, concerned Bombay: 'Deaths in the course of a year are so frequent there that it has become proverbial: two harvests in Bombay make up the age of a man.' At both Goa, where 'the Portuguese are freely magnificent', and Batavia, another pleasure city for the European, the other side of an elegant and expensive existence was the frightful mortality rate. Rough colonial America was no more charitable. Remarking upon the death of George Washington's father, Augustine, at the age of forty-nine a historian wrote: 'But he died too soon. To succeed in Virginia, you had to survive your rivals, neighbours and wives ...'

The same applied to non-Europeans. At the end of the seventeenth century a traveller remarked: 'Despite the abstemiousness which prevails amongst the Siamese ... they do not appear to live any longer' than people in Europe. A Frenchman wrote of the Turks in 1766: 'They grow old as we do when they can escape the terrible scourge of the plague which continually devastates this Empire....' Osman Aga, a Turkish interpreter who learnt German during a long period of captivity in 1688–99 and described his life in Christendom in a lively and sometimes picaresque fashion, was married twice. Only two children of the three daughters and five sons born of his first marriage survived; his second marriage produced three children with two survivors.

1400–1800: A long-lasting biological *ancien régime*

Thus the facts of the biological *ancien régime* we are discussing are, roughly speaking, the balance between births and deaths, very high infant mortality, famine, chronic undernourishment and virulent epidemics. These oppressions hardly relaxed with the advances of the eighteenth century, and then certainly in different ways in different places. Only part of Europe, not even all Western Europe, began to break free.

The advance was slow. We historians run the risk of forcing the pace. Renewed outbreaks of mortality still marked the whole of the eighteenth century; in France we have already mentioned them. They are also evident in the decennial averages for Bremen (where deaths exceeded births from 1710 to 1729 and from 1740 to 1799); at Königsburg in Prussia where deaths, at an average rate of 32·8 per

1000 from 1782 to 1802, reached 46·5 in 1772, 45 in 1775 and 46 in 1776. Think of the repeated bereavements in the family of Johann Sebastian Bach. J.P. Süssmilch, the founder of social statistics, said in 1765: 'In Germany . . . peasant and poor die without ever having employed the slightest remedy. No one ever thinks of the doctor, partly because he is too far away, partly . . . because he is too expensive. . . .' The same story comes from Burgundy at the same period: 'The surgeons live in the town and never leave it without a fee.' At Cassy-les-Vitteaux, a visit from a doctor and medicaments cost forty-odd livres. 'The unfortunate inhabitants today would rather die than call in surgeons to help them.'

At this time women were terribly vulnerable because of repeated childbirth. However although boys were more numerous than girls at birth (it is still 102 as compared with 100 today), all the figures we possess since the sixteenth century show that there were more women than men in the towns and even in the country (with a few exceptions, including Venice for a short period and later St Petersburg). The villages of Castile, where investigations were made in 1575 and 1576, all had a surplus of widows.

In any summing-up of the major characteristics of this *ancien régime* the important thing to isolate is probably its capacity for short-term revival, which was as powerful if not as rapid as the sudden disasters that struck down the living. In the long term, compensatory movements set in imperceptibly but ultimately had the last word. The ebb never entirely removed what the preceding tide had brought in. This difficult and marvellous long-term rise was the triumph of the force of numbers, on which so much depended.

4 The many against the few

A final category of comments is necessary, or rather offers an irresistible temptation. The world is divided and organised according to the force of numbers which gives each living mass its individual significance and fixes its level of culture and efficiency, its biological (and economic) rhythm of growth, and its pathological destiny. We have briefly shown that China, India and Europe were enormous reservoirs of diseases, active or dormant and quick to spread.

But this is not the only information to be derived from numbers.

They also illuminate the relationships between the living masses themselves, and these relationships concern not only periods of peace – in exchange, barter, trade – but the history of war. A book devoted to material life can scarcely ignore war. It is a multiform activity, always present, even at the earliest historical level. And numbers pre-determine its most obvious features, lines of force, repetitions and typologies. In battle, as in everyday life, not everyone has the same opportunities. Groups can be almost unerringly classified according to their numbers into masters and subjects, proletarians and privileged, facing the possibilities, the normal opportunities of the time.

In this sphere as in others, numbers are certainly not the only factors at work. Technology weighs heavily in war, as well as in peace. But even if technology does not favour *all* dense populations equally, it is none the less always a product of numbers. These statements seem obvious to twentieth-century man. Numbers to him mean civilisation, power, the future. But could the same be said of earlier times? Numerous examples immediately suggest the contrary. However paradoxical it may seem – and it seemed paradoxical to Fustel de Coulanges examining the respective fates of Rome and Germania just before the barbarian invasions – the unsophisticated and less numerous side sometimes won or *seemed to win* – as Henri Pirenne has often shown and as Hans Delbrück demonstrated by calculating the ridiculously small number of barbarians who conquered Rome.

Against the barbarians

When civilisations are defeated or seem to be defeated, the conqueror is always a 'barbarian'. It is a figure of speech. A barbarian to a Greek was anyone who was not Greek, to a Chinaman anyone not Chinese. The great pretext for European colonisation in the past was bringing 'civilisation' to barbarians and primitive peoples. Of course, it was the civilised peoples who gave the barbarian his reputation, and at best he only half deserved it. We need not go to the other extreme and believe implicitly in the defence of Attila by the historian Rechid Saffet Atabinen, but what certainly does require revision is the myth of barbarian strength. Whenever the barbarian won, it was because he was already more than half civilised. He had spent a long time in an antechamber and knocked not once but ten times before gaining admission to the house. He was, if not completely civilised, at least deeply imbued with the adjacent civilisation.

This is what the classic case of the Teutons confronting the Roman Empire in the fifth century proves. But the process was also constantly repeated in the history of the Arabs, Turks, Mongols, Manchus and Tartars. The Turks and Turcomans were the transporters and caravaners *par excellence* on the routes from central Asia to the Caspian and Iran.

They visited adjacent civilisations and often became completely integrated into them. The Mongols of Ghengis Khan and Kublai, barely (if at all) emerged from their Shamanism, do not give the impression of unsophisticated barbarism. They soon fell captive to Chinese civilisation in the east and to visions of Islam in the west, being cut off and uprooted from their own destiny. The Manchus, who conquered Peking in 1644 and then the rest of China, were a mixed people. Mongol elements were numerous, but Chinese peasants had moved into Manchuria beyond the Great Wall of China very early on. Barbarians if you like, but imbued with Chinese influence beforehand, and driven to their conquest by the social and economic difficulties of the huge land of China by a sort of remote control.

Above all, the barbarian only triumphed in the short term. He was very rapidly absorbed by the conquered civilisation. The Germans 'barbarised' the Empire and then drowned in the land of wine; the Turks became the standard-bearers of Islam from the twelfth century; Mongols, then Manchus, were lost amongst the Chinese masses. The door of the conquered house closed behind the barbarian.

The disappearance of the great nomads before the seventeenth century

It must also be noted that the 'barbarians' who were a real danger to civilisation belonged almost entirely to one category of men: the nomads of the deserts and steppes in the heart of the Old World – and it was *only* the Old World that experienced this extraordinary breed of humanity. These arid and abandoned lands formed an endless explosive fuse from the Atlantic to the waters of the Pacific. It burst into flames at the slightest spark and burned along its entire length. For when a dispute arose among these horse- and camel-men, as harsh on each other as they were on other peoples, or a drought or a population increase drove them out from their pasturage, they invaded their neighbours' lands. As year followed year, the repercussions from these movements extended over thousands of miles.

They represented speed and surprise at a period when everything moved slowly. On the Polish frontier the alarm that any threat of Tartar cavalry regularly set off, even in the seventeenth century, almost immediately caused a mass levy. Fortresses had to be equipped and stores laid in, and if there was still time, guns supplied, horsemen mobilised and barricades set up. If, as on so many occasions, the raid succeeded -- across the mountains and the empty spaces of Transylvania for example -- it hit town and countryside like a scourge, beyond comparison even with what the Turks did. At least the Turks customarily withdrew their troops at the start of winter, after Saint George's Day. The Tartars remained on the spot, wintering with their families, eating the countryside down to the root.

Furthermore these raids (we can recapture the sense of terror they created from contemporary Western news-sheets) were nothing compared with the great nomad conquests in China and the Indies. Europe had the advantage of escaping them, despite various recorded episodes (Huns, Avars, Hungarians, Mongols). It was protected by the barrier of the Eastern peoples. Its peace was founded on their misfortunes.

The nomads' strength also lay in the carelessness and relative weakness of the men who held the approaches to the civilisations. Northern China was underpopulated before the eighteenth century -- an empty space for anyone to enter. In India the Muslims took the Punjab early on -- in the tenth century -- and thenceforth the gates to Iran and the Khyber Pass were no longer shut. The strength of the barriers in eastern and south-eastern Europe varied from century to century. The nomads' world rotated between these areas of negligence, weakness and sometimes ineffectual vigilance. A physical law drew them now westwards, now eastwards, according to whether their explosive life would ignite more easily in Europe, Islam, India or China. Eduard Fueter's classic work drew attention to a cyclonic zone, an enormous vacuum in 1494 over the fragmented Italy of princes and urban republics. All Europe was attracted towards this storm-creating area of low pressure. In the same way hurricanes persistently blew the peoples of the steppes eastwards or westwards, according to the lines of least resistance.

For example China under the Mings drove the Mongols out in 1368 and burned their great centre at Karakorum in the Gobi desert. But the long period of inertia that followed the victory caused a powerful nomad return eastwards. The space created behind the advance of their first waves tended to attract new ones and the movement had repercussions farther and farther westwards, at intervals of one, two, ten and twenty years. The Nogais crossed the Volga from west to east in about 1400, and then the current slowly began to turn. The peoples who had flowed towards the West and frail Europe for over two centuries now turned eastwards for the next two or three, attracted by the weakness of distant China. Our map summarises this change of direction. Its decisive episodes were the conquest of northern India by Baber (1526) and the capture of Peking by the Manchus in 1644. The hurricane had once again struck India and China.

In the west, however, Europe was breathing more easily. The Russian seizure of Kazan and Astrakhan in 1551 and 1556 was not achieved solely by gunpowder and arquebuses; reduced nomadic pressure in southern Russia also facilitated the Russian drive towards the black earth country of the Volga, Don and Dniester. In the course of this action old Muscovy lost a number of its peasants, who fled from the strict authority of their lords. The land they abandoned passed into the hands of new arrivals: peasants from the Baltic countries and Poland. The gaps this group left unoccupied were filled in their turn, and at the appropriate moment, by peasants from Brandenburg or Scotland. It was a sort of a relay race. This is the view that two distinguished historians, Alexandre and Eugène Kulischer, take of this silent history, this man-slide from Germany to China. Its currents run underground, as though concealed beneath the skin of history (map 2).

Later the conquest of China by the Manchus led to a new order in the 1680s. Northern China, protected and shielded by advance posts – Manchuria, where the conquerors had come from, then Mongolia, Turkestan and Tibet – was repopulated. The Russians, who had seized Siberia without opposition, met Chinese resistance along the valley of the Amur and were obliged to recognise the treaty of Nertchinsk (7 September 1689). The Chinese consequently went 'from the Great Wall up to the neighbourhood of the Caspian Sea'. Even before this success, the manifold world of pastoral peoples had turned back towards the west, crossing in the opposite direction the narrow gateway of Dzungaria, the classic route for migration between Mongolia and Turkestan. Only this time the vast masses in flight no longer found a door open to receive them. In the west they

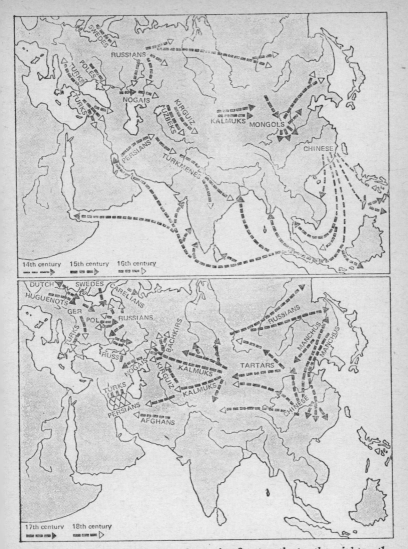

Map 2 Eurasian migrations from the fourteenth to the eighteenth century. The difference between the two maps is clear: on the first, overland migrations move from West to East, on the second from East to West. Note on the first map the Chinese maritime expansion, of such importance at the beginning of the fifteenth century, and the convergence of overland movements on India and China. On the second, the re-establishment of order by the Manchus in the seventeenth century (capture of Peking, 1644) leads to a huge Chinese expansion inland and the halt of the Russians. The nomads are pushed back towards the West and Russian Europe. (*After* A. & E. Kulischer.)

met resistance from a new Russia under Peter the Great and the forts, strongholds and towns of Siberia and the lower Volga. Russian literature in the following century is full of accounts of these repeated battles.

In the event, the great career of the nomads ended here. Gunpowder had triumphed over speed. Even before the end of the eighteenth century civilisation had won at Peking and Moscow, Delhi and Teheran (after the lively Afghan crisis). The nomads, condemned to stay at home, appeared in their true colours: a poor species of mankind put in its place and destined to remain there. In short, they represent an exceptional case of a long parasitical existence that came to an end once and for all. It is almost a marginal episode despite its very widespread repercussions.

The conquest of space

As a general rule, the civilisations played and won. They won their struggles against 'cultures' and primitive peoples. Even better, they also won their war against empty space. In this last case, everything had to be built up from scratch. And this was the Europeans' great good fortune in three-quarters of America. The Russians enjoyed the same advantage in Siberia, and the British in Australia and New Zealand. How lucky it would have been for the Whites in South Africa if the Boers and the British had not been called upon to face Black pressure.

In Brazil the primitive Indian slipped away when the Portuguese appeared. The Paulist *bandeiras* scattered over more or less empty land. In less than a century the adventurers from São Paulo had overrun, although not colonised, half the South-American continent, from the Rio de la Plata to the Amazon and Andes, in their pursuit of slaves, precious stones and gold. They met no resistance until the Jesuits formed their Indian reserves, which the *paulistas* shamelessly pillaged.

The same process was repeated by the French and British in North America and the Spaniards in the north Mexican deserts, faced with a few rough Chichimec Indians. They were still being systematically hunted down in the seventeenth century; every year, starting from November, they were run to earth 'like wild animals'. Things were more difficult in Argentina and particularly in Chile, because the Indian had at least acquired the horse from his conqueror; the Araucanians continued to be tough adversaries until the beginning of the twentieth century. The real issue was not conquest of men (they were annihilated) but of space. Thenceforth it was distance that had to be conquered. In the sixteenth century the means of this silent conquest were the slow carts from the Argentine pampas drawn by pairs of oxen, the caravans of mules from Iberian America or the covered wagons of the nineteenth-century westwards trek in the United States. The journey regularly ended at a colonisation front, a pioneer zone from which everything sprang up. The colonists' life started from rock bottom in this distant border country: their numbers were too few for social life to impose itself; everyone was his own master. This attractive anarchy lasted for some time before order was established. Meanwhile the frontier would have moved a little farther towards the interior and the same temporary anarchic scenes would be re-enacted. This is the moving frontier that Joseph Turner romantically interpreted (1922) as the real birth of America and of its strongest original characteristics.

The easy conquest of empty or almost empty space also lay open to the great Russian expansion in the sixteenth century, when salt merchants, fur-hunters and cossacks successfully took possession of Siberia. Sharp resistance broke out but soon collapsed. Towns sprang up — fortresses, road stations, bridges, staging-posts for carriages, horses and sledges (Tobolsk in 1587, Okhotsk in 1648, Irkutsk near Lake Baikal in 1652). For a certain doctor of Swiss origin with the Russian armies, Siberia even in 1815 was remembered only by exhausting days on horseback which could only end when a small stronghold or town offering the necessary accommodation had been reached. If a merchant travelling by sledge in winter missed his stopping point he ran the risk of being irretrievably buried beneath the snow with his retinue, animals and merchandise. A road and urban system slowly took shape. The Amur basin was reached in 1643, the immense Kamtchatka peninsula discovered in 1696. Russian explorers reached Alaska in the following century and colonists settled there in 1799. These were rapid but precarious acquisitions and all the more remarkable for that. When Bering moved to Okhotsk for his voyages of discovery in 1726 he found only a few Russian families in the citadel there. In 1719 John Bell travelled on a main road to Siberia and 'for six days saw neither houses nor inhabitants'.

The resistance of cultures

When the advance was no longer into empty space everything became more complicated. This is quite a different story. There is no possibility of confusing the *Ostsiedlung*, the famous 'Germanic colonisation' of eastern lands, and the saga of the American frontier, despite the efforts of comparative history. Colonists from Germania in the broad sense (often from Lorraine or the Netherlands) were able to settle east of the Elbe from the twelfth to the thirteenth century and even in the fourteenth by means of political or social arrangements and also by force. The newcomers built their villages in the midst of vast forest clearings, laid out their houses along the roads, probably introduced heavy ploughs with iron ploughshares, created towns and imposed German law on both these and the Slav towns – the Magdeburg law for the mainland and the Lübeck for the seas. This involved an immense migration. But the colonisation took place within an already established Slav people who had a more or less compact organisation and were destined to resist the newcomers, and when necessary to shut them out. Germania's misfortune was its late formation and the fact that it only began its march eastwards after the settlement of the Slav peoples, who were more firmly attached to their land and dependent on their towns (this is proved by excavations) than was formerly believed.

The same process recurs in connection with Russian expansion, not in Siberia, which was almost empty, but also in the sixteenth century towards the southern rivers, Volga, Don and Dniester. This expansion was also marked by unhampered peasant colonisation. The steppe between the Volga and the Black Sea was not densely settled but was overrun by nomad peoples – the Nogais and Tartars from the Crimea. These formidable horsemen were the vanguard of Islam and of the vast Turkish empire that supported them and occasionally threw them forward. It had even saved them from the Russians by supplying them with firearms, an asset the defenders of the khanates of Kazan and Astrakhan had lacked in the 1550s. They were therefore not adversaries to be scorned. Tartar raids took them to the near by lands of Transylvania, Hungary, Poland and Muscovy, which they cruelly devastated. In 1572 one of their raids captured Moscow. The Tartars sold innumerable Slav prisoners (Russians and Poles) as slaves on the Istanbul market. It is known that Peter the Great's attempt to open 'a window' on the Black Sea in 1696 failed; the failure was not made good until Catherine II's reign a hundred years later. Even then the Tartars were not eliminated; they remained in occupation until the Second World War.

Furthermore colonisation by Russian peasants would have been unthinkable without the strongholds and military borders and without the help of those outlaws the Cossacks. As horsemen, they could counter an adversary with extreme mobility; as boatmen, they went up and down the rivers, carrying their boats from one reach to another; some 800 of them came from the Tanais in about 1690 to throw their canoes into the Volga in pursuit of the 'Kalmyck Tartars'; as sailors, they pirated the Black Sea in boats crammed with sail, from the end of the sixteenth century. That side of modern Russia was therefore not built on a *tabula rasa* – any more than the Russian advance into the Caucasus or Turkestan in the nineteenth century (which once again brought it face to face with Islam) took place effortlessly or without surprise.

Other examples could support this account: the late and ephemeral colonisation of Black Africa by the European powers in the nineteenth century or the conquest of Mexico and Peru by the Spaniards. These immature civilisations, which were really cultures, collapsed in the face of a small number of men. Today these countries are once more Indian or African.

A culture is a civilisation that has not yet achieved maturity, its greatest potential, nor consolidated its growth. Meanwhile – and the waiting period can be protracted – adjacent civilisations exploit it in a thousand ways, which is natural if not particularly just. History is full of examples of this type of economic exploitation; the trade along the coasts of the Gulf of Guinea, a familiar feature from the sixteenth century, is typical. The Kaffirs of Mozambique on the shores of the Indian Ocean claimed that if the monkeys 'do not talk it is because they are afraid that they will be made to work'. But they themselves made the mistake of talking and buying cotton goods and selling gold dust. The strong always adopted the same very simple tactics: the Phoenicians and Greeks in their trading-posts and colonies; the Arab merchants on the Zanzibar coast from the eleventh century; the Venetians and Genoese at Caffa and Tana in the thirteenth century; and the Chinese in the Indian Archipelago, which had been their market for gold dust, spices, pepper, slaves, precious woods and swallows' nests even before the thirteenth century. During the period covered by this book a host of Chinese transporters, merchants, usurers, pedlars and middlemen exploited these 'colonial' markets. If China has remained so uninventive and so backward at the capitalist level, despite its intellectual power and its discoveries (paper money for example), it is to the extent that this exploitation was so easy and widespread. The Chinese had things too easy.

It is only a step from market to colony. The exploited have only to cheat, or to protest, and conquest immediately follows. But it has been proved that the cultures, the semi-civilisations (the term is even applicable to the Tartars in the Crimea) were no mean adversaries. They were pushed back but they reappeared; they were wrong enough to survive. They could not be permanently deprived of their future.

Civilisation against civilisation

When civilisations clash the consequences are dramatic. Today's world is still embroiled in them. One civilisation can get the better of another: this was the case with India following the British victory at Plassey (1757), which marked the beginning of a new era for Britain and the whole world. Not that Plassey, or rather Palassy, near present-day Calcutta, was an exceptional victory. The French could claim that Dupleix or Bussy were just as successful. But Plassey had immense consequences, which is how great events are recognised: they have a sequel. In the same way the absurd Opium War (1840–2) marked the beginning of a century of 'inequality' for China, colonised without really being so. As for Islam, it foundered completely in the nineteenth century, with the possible exception of Turkey. But China, India and Islam (or rather its various parts) recovered their independence with the series of decolonisation measures after 1945.

So stormy conquests looked at retrospectively, through the eyes of men today, seem like episodes, whatever their duration. They came into being more or less suddenly, then collapsed one fine day like stage sets.

All this destiny, much simplified and seen from such a height, is not entirely dominated by numbers. It is not simply a matter of strength or sheer weight. But it must be remembered that numbers played their part throughout the centuries. They account for some regular aspects of material life and some of its limitations. If wars are excluded a whole social, political and cultural (religious) area is immediately left out of count. But such exchanges in themselves have little meaning because they are often mutually unequal.

Europe cannot be understood without its slaves and its subject economies. China similarly cannot be understood if we ignore the savage cultures within the country that defied it and the distant conquered lands outside it that lived in its orbit. All this figures in the balance of material life.

We have used numbers to give a first glimpse of the different destinies of the world between the fifteenth and the eighteenth centuries. Men were divided into great masses as unevenly equipped to deal with their material life as the different groups within a given society. Thus the collective personalities who will be introduced in the pages that follow are presented on a world scale. They will appear even more in the second volume, which will be devoted to the pre-eminence of economic life and capitalism; categories that probably separate the world more sharply than material life into developed and backward regions, according to a classification with which the dramatic reality of the present world has made us familiar.

2

Daily Bread

Men's diet between the fifteenth and the eighteenth centuries essentially consisted of vegetable foods. This is obvious in relation to pre-Columbian America and Black Africa; it is glaringly so in the Asiatic rice-growing civilisations, not only in earlier times but today. The early settlement and then the spectacular increase in population in the Far East were only possible because of the small amount of meat eaten. The reasons for this are very simple. If the choices of an economy are determined solely by adding up calories, agriculture on a given area will always have the advantage over stock-raising; for better or worse, it feeds ten to twenty times as many people. Montesquieu made the point with reference to the rice-growing countries: 'Land which elsewhere is used to feed animals there directly serves as sustenance for men.'

But every population-increase beyond a certain level involves greater recourse to vegetable foods – everywhere, and not only from the fifteenth to the eighteenth centuries. The choice between cereals and meat depends on the number of people. This is one of the great tests of material life: 'Tell me what you eat, and I will tell you who you are.' The German proverb, which hinges on a play on words, says the same thing in its own way: *Der Mensch ist was er isst* (man is what he eats). His food bears witness to his social status and his civilisation or culture.

A journey from a culture to a civilisation, or from a low density of population to a relatively high one, involves significant changes in diet for a traveller. Jenkinson, the leading merchant of the Muscovy Company, arrived in Astrakhan in 1558 from distant Archangel. There he came upon the nomad Nogais camped in the neighbourhood, who had 'neither towns nor houses'. The Englishman heard nothing from his hosts but jokes and gibes about the Russians. How could they be men like other men when they spent their whole lives in one place 'breathing in their own stink', when they ate corn and drank more corn (beer or vodka being made from grain)? The

Nogais drank milk and ate meat, which was quite a different story. Jenkinson continued his journey across the deserts of Turkestan, risking death from thirst or hunger. When he reached the valley of the Amu Darya, he found fresh water, mare's milk and meat from wild horses, but no bread. The same differences and gibes between stock-raisers and agriculturalists are found in the very heart of the West, between the people in the lands of Bray and cereal-growers in the Beauvaisis, between the Castilians and the stock-raisers of Béarn whom the southerners jeered at but who gave back as good as they got.

Europe, which was wholly carnivorous, was the great exception to all this. For several centuries from the middle ages its tables had been loaded with meat and drink, worthy of Argentina in the nineteenth century. This was because the European countryside, beyond the Mediterranean shores, had long remained half empty with vast lands for pasturing animals. Later on its agriculture left ample facilities available for stock-raising. But Europe's advantage declined after the seventeenth century. The general rule of vegetable supremacy seemed to be re-asserting itself with the increase in population in Europe up to at least the middle of the nineteenth century. Then and only then scientific stock-raising and massive arrivals of meat from America, salted and then frozen, enabled it to break its fast.

Furthermore the European, true to his long-established tastes, regularly and promptly demanded they be catered for when he was overseas. Abroad, the lords and masters ate meat. They stuffed themselves with it unrestrainedly in the New World, recently invaded by herds from the Old. Their appetite for meat roused opprobium and astonishment in the Far East: 'You must be a very great lord in Sumatra,' said one seventeenth-century traveller, 'to have a boiled or roast chicken, which moreover has to last for the whole day. Therefore they say that two thousand Christians (meaning Westerners) on their island would soon exhaust the bullocks and poultry.'

These dietary choices and the decisions they imply were the result of very old processes. Maurizio goes so far as to write: 'A thousand years brings scarcely any changes in the history of diet.' In fact the broad outlines of man's dietary history are marked and controlled by two ancient revolutions. At the end of the Paleolithic Age the 'omnivores' moved on to hunting large animals. 'Great carnivorism' was born and the taste for it has never disappeared: 'this need for flesh, for blood, this "hunger for nitrogen" or, if you prefer, for animal protein.'

The second revolution, in the fifth millennium before the Christian era, was neolithic agriculture; it saw the arrival of cultivated cereals. Now fields were cultivated at the expense of hunting-ground and extensive stock-raising. As the centuries passed a larger and larger number of people were reduced to eating vegetable foods, raw or cooked, often insipid and always monotonous whether they were fermented or not: gruels, sops and bread. Thenceforth history shows two opposing species of humanity: the rare meat-eaters and the innumerable people who fed on bread, gruel, roots and cooked tubers. In China in the second millennium 'the administrators of the great provinces were termed . . . meat-eaters'. In ancient Greece it was said that 'the eaters of barley gruel have no desire to make war'. An Englishman centuries later (1776) stated: 'You find more courage among men who eat their fill of flesh than among those who make shift with lighter foods.'

Having said this, we will concentrate first on the food of the majority between the fifteenth and the eighteenth centuries and therefore on those foods supplied by agriculture, the oldest industry of all. Now in every case agriculture had from the start to count on one of the dominant plants, and then organise itself according to this ancient choice of priority on which everything or almost everything thenceforth depended. Three of them were brilliantly successful: corn, rice and maize. They continue to share world arable land between them today. The 'plants of civilisation', they have profoundly organised man's material and sometimes his spiritual life, to the point where they have become almost ineradicable factors. Their history and the determinism they exercise over the peasantry and the general life of man are the subject of the present chapter. Our journey from one to the other of these cereals will take us round the world.

1   Corn

Corn is primarily – but not only – found in the West. Well before the fifteenth century it grew on the plains of northern China side by side with millet and sorghum. It was 'planted in holes' there and not reaped but 'uprooted with its whole stem', with a hoe. It was exported by the Yun Leang Ho – 'the grain-bearing river' – up to

Peking. It was even found from time to time in Japan and southern China where, according to Father de Las Cortes (1626), the peasant sometimes succeeded in obtaining a corn harvest between two harvests of rice. This was simply an extra, because the Chinese 'did not know how to knead bread any more than they knew how to roast meat' and because, as a minor product, corn (in China) is always cheap. Sometimes they made a sort of bread from it, cooked in steam over a cauldron and mixed 'with finely chopped onions'. The result, according to one Western traveller, was 'a very heavy dough that lay like a stone on the stomach'. Biscuit was made at Canton in the sixteenth century, but it was for Macao and the Philippines. Corn also provided the Chinese with vermicelli, gruels and lard cakes, but not bread, which was considered 'insipid'.

An 'excellent' corn was also present in the dry plains of the Indus and in the upper Ganges, and immense caravans of oxen effected exchanges of rice and corn across all India. In Iran a rudimentary type of bread, a plain biscuit made without leaven, was generally on sale at a low price. It was often the result of enormous peasant labour. In the neighbourhood of Ispahan for example, 'the corn lands are heavy and need four or even six oxen to till them. And a child is placed on the yoke of the first pair to drive them on with a stick.' And of course corn grew all round the Mediterranean, even in the Sahara, and especially in Egypt. As the Nile floods in summer the crops there are invariably produced in winter, when the water has receded from the land. The climate at this time of year is scarcely favourable to tropical plants but it suits corn.

With Europe as its starting point, corn made numerous distant conquests. Russian colonisation carried it eastwards to Siberia, beyond Tomsk and Irkutsk; as early as the sixteenth century the Russian peasant established its success in the black earth country of the Ukraine (where Catherine II eventually completed her conquests in 1793). Corn had triumphed there well before that date, even somewhat inopportunely: 'At present,' states a report of 1771, 'piles of corn the size of houses, enough to feed all Europe, are again rotting in Podolia and Volhynia.' The same catastrophic superabundance happened in 1784. Corn was 'at such a low price in the Ukraine that many landowners have abandoned its cultivation', noted a French agent. 'However, stocks of this grain are already so plentiful that they not only feed a large part of Turkey but even supply exports for Spain and Portugal.' And for France as well, via Marseilles. Boats from Marseilles took on corn from the Black Sea either in the Aegean islands or in the Crimea, for example at Gozlev, the future Eupatoria, the crossing of the Turkish straits being effected by predictable administrative collusion.

The great period of 'Russian' corn came later. The arrival in Italy of boats loaded with Ukrainian corn in 1803 seemed like a disaster to the landowners. The same threat was denounced in the French Chamber of Deputies a little later in 1818.

Corn had crossed the Atlantic from Europe well before these events. In Iberian America it had to compete with excessively hot climates, destructive insects and rival crops (maize and manioc). Its success in America came slowly: in Chile; on the banks of the St Lawrence; in Mexico; and more slowly still in the English colonies in America, in the seventeenth and particularly the eighteenth centuries. At that time Boston sailing ships carried flour and corn to the sugar lands of the Caribbean, then to Europe and the Mediterranean. In the nineteenth century corn triumphed in Argentina, southern Africa, Australia, the Canadian prairies and the Middle West, everywhere asserting 'by its presence the expansion characteristic of European civilisation'.

Corn and secondary cereals

To return to Europe: at first examination, corn appears for what it is – a complicated phenomenon. It would be better to put it in the plural – *los panes*, as so many Spanish texts say. In the first place there were different qualities of corn; in France the best was often called 'the head of the corn'; sold side by side with it were medium-quality corn, 'small corn' or maslin, a mixture of corn and another cereal, often rye. Moreover wheat was never grown by itself. Despite its great age, even older cereals grew alongside it. Spelt, a corn with a 'dressed grain', was still present in fourteenth-century Italy and in the Palatinate in 1697. Millet covered vast expanses. When Venice was besieged by the Genoese in 1378, it was saved by its stocks of millet. In the sixteenth century the Venetian government deliberately kept stocks of this long-lasting cereal (it could sometimes be kept for twenty or so years) in the fortified towns of the Terra Firma. And millet rather than corn was sent to the *presidios* in Dalmatia or the islands of the Levant when they were short of food. Millet was still grown in Gascony, Italy and central Europe in the eighteenth century. But it produced a very coarse foodstuff to judge by the comments of a Jesuit at the end of the century. He admired the use

the Chinese made of their various millets and exclaimed: 'With all
our progress in the sciences of curiosity, vanity and uselessness, our
peasants in Gascony and the Bordelais *Landes* are as little advanced
as they were three centuries ago in methods of making their millet
into a less uncivilised and less unhealthy food.'

Wheat had other and more important associates; for example
barley, which was used to feed horses in the southern lands. 'No
barley harvest, no war', could have been said in the sixteenth
century and later of the long Hungarian frontier where battles
between Turks and Christians were inconceivable without cavalry.
Towards the north, hard corn gave way to soft corn, barley to oats
and more especially rye, which came late to the northern lands – no
earlier than the great invasions of the fifth century it seems. After
that it would have become established and spread there at the same
time as triennial rotation. Boats from the Baltic, very soon attracted
from farther and farther afield by hungry Europe, carried as much
rye as corn. First they came as far as the North Sea and the Channel,
then to the Iberian ports on the Atlantic and finally, on a massive
scale at the time of the great crisis of 1590, as far as the Mediterranean. All these cereals were used to make bread, even in the eighteenth century, when wheat was in short supply. 'Rye bread,' wrote
a doctor, Louis Lemery, in 1702, 'is not as nourishing as corn
and relaxes the stomach a little.' Barley bread, he added, 'is refreshing but less nourishing than corn and rye'; only the northern
peoples made bread from oats 'which suits them very well'. But
it is a fact that France in 1716 undoubtedly produced more rye
than corn.

Another expedient was rice, which had been imported from the
Indian Ocean since classical antiquity. Traders in the middle ages
rediscovered it in the commercial ports of the Levant, and in Spain
where the Arabs had established the crop very early on: rice from
Majorca was sold at fairs in Champagne in the fourteenth century.
From the fifteenth century onwards it was grown in Italy and sold
at a low price on the market at Ferrara. A person who laughed
easily was said to have eaten rice soup – a play on words: *Che aveva
mangiato la minestra di riso.*

Rice later spread into the lands of the peninsula, bringing into
being vast estates (up to 1,000 hectares) in Venetia, Lombardy,
Piedmont, even in Romagna, Tuscany, Naples and Sicily. When these
rice fields succeeded, their capitalist organisation turned the
peasant labour force into a proletariat. It had already become *il riso*

amaro, the bitter rice, harsh taskmaster to the men who produced it. Similarly rice played an important role in the Turkish Balkans. It also reached America; at the end of the seventeenth century Carolina became a great exporter via England.

In fact it was an emergency foodstuff in the West, barely tempting the rich, despite a certain use made of rice cooked in milk. Boats laden with rice from Alexandria in Egypt were 'an expedient to feed the poor' in France in 1694 and 1709. As early as the sixteenth century rice flour was mixed with other flours to make bread for the people during famines in Venice.

In France it was eaten in hospitals, military barracks and ships. Distributions to the people by Paris churches often included 'economical rice' mixed with mashed turnips, pumpkins and carrots, cooked in water. The saucepans were never washed so as not to waste the leftovers and deposit. According to the experts, cheap bread could be made from rice mixed with millet and distributed to the poor 'so that they could be satisfied from one meal to the next'. This was somewhat equivalent to China's provision for its poor 'who could not buy tea': hot water in which beans and vegetables had been cooked, plus cakes of 'crushed beans made into a paste'. The same beans, boiled as usual, 'providing a sauce to soak the food. . . .' Can these have been soya beans? In any case the product was inferior, intended to satisfy the hunger of the poor, like rice or millet in the West.

There is everywhere an unmistakable correlation between corn and supplementary cereals. It already appears in the curves that can be drawn for English prices after the thirteenth century. Relative to one another these prices were constant during a fall but not during a rise, as rye, the food of the poor, rose sharply during periods of scarcity to even higher points than wheat at times. Oats, on the other hand, lagged behind.

'The price of corn always increases much more than that of oats,' taught Dupré de Saint-Maur (1746) because of 'our custom of living on wheaten bread (the rich at least – my correction) while horses are put to graze in the countryside as soon as the price of oats rises'. Corn and oats is much the same as saying people and horses. The normal ratio was three to two, according to Dupré de Saint-Maur (he called it a 'natural' ratio like the old economists who wanted all prices to be in a natural relationship, of one to twelve in the case of gold and silver). 'In a given period, whenever a *setier* (approximately eight pints) of oats . . . was selling at around a third less than a *setier* of corn, things were in their natural relationship.' A breakdown in this ratio was a sign of famine, and the greater the discrepancy the more serious the famine. 'In 1351 a *setier* of oats was worth a quarter of a *setier* of corn, in 1709 a fifth, in 1740 a third. Thus prices were higher in 1709 than in 1351, and in 1351 than in 1740. . . .'

This argument is probably sound within the limits of the facts immediately available to the author. To say that it is an accurate guide to the period from 1400 to 1800 is another matter. For example, between 1596 and 1635 and probably during the greater part of the sixteenth century, oats were worth roughly half what corn was worth in France. The 'natural' ratio of three to two only appeared in 1635. It would be too simple to follow Dupré de Saint-Maur and conclude that there was a rise in prices brewing in the sixteenth century and to blame this on the troubles of the period, arguing that things returned to normal in about 1635 with the return of relative internal peace. It could just as well be argued that France under Richelieu entered what the textbooks call the Thirty Years War in 1635; therefore the price of oats – without which there could be no horses, cavalry or artillery trains – rose sharply.

All the bread crops added together never created abundance; Western man had to adapt himself to chronic scarcities. He compensated for them in the first place by the regular consumption of vegetables or flour substitutes made from chestnuts and buckwheat which was grown in Normandy and Brittany from the sixteenth century onwards, being sown after the corn harvest and ripening before winter. Buckwheat, incidentally, is not a gramineae but a polygonaceae. No matter – to man it was 'black corn'. Chestnuts yielded flour, and biscuit known as 'tree bread' in the Cévennes and Corsica. In Aquitaine (where they were called *ballote*) and elsewhere, they often filled the role taken over by potatoes in the nineteenth century. People relied on chestnuts to a larger degree in the southern lands than is usually thought. Charles v's major-domo, living with his master at Jarandilla near Yuste in the Castilian Estremadura (1556), noted: 'It is the chestnuts that are good here, not the corn, and the corn is horribly expensive.'

On the other hand consumption of 'bread made from acorns and roots' in Dauphiné during the winter of 1672–3 was highly unusual and a symptom of terrible famine. Lemery incredulously reported in 1702 that 'there are still places where these acorns are used for the same purpose'.

Dried vegetables, lentils, beans, black, white and greyish-brown peas and chick-peas – these real supplementary cereals were also a cheap source of protein. The Venetian documents called them *menudi* or *minuti* (minor foods). When a village in Terra Firma lost its *menudi* following a summer tornado, as frequently happened, the misfortune was immediately reported to the Venetian authorities and induced their intervention. The thousands of documents that place these minor foodstuffs on an equal footing with corn itself prove that they were considered 'cereals'. For instance a boat from Venice or Ragusa could be commissioned to load either corn or beans at Alexandria in Egypt. A Captain-General of Grenada looking for chick-peas and beans for the fleet wrote that they were difficult to come by in sufficient quantity and that their 'price was the same as corn' (2 December 1539). A Spanish letter from a *presidio* in Africa in about 1536 mentioned that the soldiers there preferred *garbanzos* (chick-peas) to corn or biscuit. A bad harvest for corn and wine, noted a Venetian memorialist in 1629, but pretty good for vegetables, *ma di minuti honestamente*. One made up for the other. Excavations in villages in Bohemia dating from the early middle ages reveal that the ancient diet was based on peas much more than corn. The *Preiscourant* for Bremen in 1758 gave the prices of cereals and vegetables one after another (*Getreide* and *Hülsenfrüchte*).

Corn and crop rotation

Corn cannot be cultivated on the same land for two years running without serious harmful effects. It has to be rotated. Hence the amazement of Westerners in China at the sight of rice growing continually 'on the same ground', wrote Father de Las Cortes (1626), 'which they never leave fallow any year, as in our Spain'. In Europe, and wherever it was cultivated, corn was sown in a different field from one year to the next. The space it required had to be two or three times the surface area it occupied, according to whether it could return to the same 'break' one year in two or three. It was therefore caught up in a two- or three-year rotation.

It is true that systems or régimes based on no fixed frequency were also practised in Europe – on poor soil or where cultivation was carried on in an old-fashioned way. The ground was cultivated and then abandoned and left to lie fallow for years on end. These temporary crops were always the despair of agronomists in the past; in 1777 one of them referred to the land around 'Mayenne . . . black and difficult to cultivate; it is even more so around Laval where . . .

the best ploughmen with six oxen and four horses can till only fifteen or sixteen *arpents* (one *arpent* equals approximately an acre) a year. This is why land is left fallow for eight, ten or twelve years in succession.' On the other hand, more scientific rotation extending over longer periods than the biennial or triennial systems appeared fairly early on in regions that were heavily populated and therefore forced to depart from custom. In Flanders, certainly as early as the fourteenth century, they strove to alternate cereals and fodder. Later, *koppelstelsel* in Holland was the succession of five years of crops following five previous years of pasturage, and so on. Some areas of Germany in the sixteenth century practised similar rotations over periods four or five years apart. It was reaction on the part of the German nobility in the seventeenth century that re-established or consolidated triennial rotation in association with sheep-rearing. In northern Italy fairly early progress was apparent: in the Vercellese, rotation followed a four-year pattern in about 1700, a five-year pattern around 1800.

Very roughly, Europe was divided between two systems. In the south, corn and other bread grains took half of the cultivated land in turn, the other half lying fallow, in *barbechos* as they say in Spain. In the north the land was divided into three fields: winter cereals, spring cereals sown in spring, and fallow. In Lorraine in recent times, around the village which formed the central point, the three fields (corn, oats and fallow) still divided the land like the sectors of a roughly drawn circle extending to the near-by forest. In successive years, corn replaced fallow, oats replaced corn and fallow replaced oats. This was the cycle of triennial rotation; in the third year the situation was the same as at the beginning. There were therefore two systems: in one, land under corn lay fallow for a longer period; in the other it always covered a larger area, proportionately, as long as it was entirely sown to corn – which was in fact never the case. The grain in the south was richer in gluten; in the north the yield was higher, but the quality of the soil and the climate also played a part.

Such an outline is only very roughly true: there was cultivation 'in thirds' (fallow for two years) in the south, in the same way as biennial rotation persisted in certain places in the north (for example in northern Alsace, from Strasbourg to Wissemburg). Triennial rotation had developed later than biennial rotation, which continued to exist over quite large areas.

Naturally mixtures were the general rule on the boundaries of the two great European systems. A survey of Limagnes in the sixteenth century notes the tangle of biennial and triennial rotations depending on soil, labour force and level of peasant population. There was even a small region of three-yearly rotation in the extreme south of the 'biennial' zone, around Seville, in about 1755, which seems similar to northern rotation.

But let us set these variations to one side. As a rule there was always a dead period, a rest from cultivation of grain, whether rotation revolved on a two- or three-yearly basis. This dead period enabled the soil lying fallow to regain its richness in nourishing salts, especially when it was manured and then tilled. Repeated tilling was supposed to aerate the soil, prevent weeds and prepare the ground for abundant harvests. Jethro Tull (1674–1741), one of the apostles of the English agricultural revolution, recommended repeated tilling as strongly as manuring and rotation of crops. Documents even mention seven tillings, including those preceding sowing. Three tillings (in spring, autumn and winter) were already the rule in England and Normandy in the fourteenth century. In Artois (1328), the land reserved for corn 'was well worked with four furrows (tillings), one in winter and three in summer'. In Bohemia on the Czernin domains in 1648, three or four tillings, depending on whether the land was intended for rye or corn, were the general rule. Here are the words of a Savoy landowner (1771): 'In certain places we wear ourselves out with incessant tilling and we till four or five times in order to have a single harvest of wheat – which is often of very average quality.'

In any case crop rotation permanently kept one field fallow, which meant, very often, an area of pasturage. In addition, after harvesting in July or August the stubble fields of wheat, barley, rye or oats were opened for the pasturage of sheep. In short, the wheatlands, unlike the rice fields, were not isolated worlds, closed in on themselves. They were thrown open to stock-raising – to their own stock and to stock from adjacent regions, particularly from mountainous areas, all the more so as cultivated land only formed a part of the village territory. Beyond the gardens, ploughed fields and vineyards were forests, wasteland, mown meadows and grass verges that until quite recently in Little Poland fed the cows and goats and the flocks of geese of the poor. These were the flocks the humanist Thomas Platter encountered in Silesia when as a vagabond child he followed students who were vagabonds themselves, serving both as their servant and their scapegoat. In the same way transhumance in

Castile from the heights of Segovia, Soria or Cuenca to the desolate plains and plateaux of La Mancha would never have been possible if there had not been access to the vast stony pasturage, the wasteland beyond the close-set fields surrounding the villages or, after July, the blank sheet of stubble in the very heart of the cultivated land.

Manuring, harnessing and the labour force

Cultivation of corn ultimately favoured the infiltration of necessary livestock. It was necessary because corn required careful manuring. This treatment was never given to oats or to any 'spring wheat', with the result that the yield from oats, which were sown more closely than corn, was normally half that of wheat – the reverse of present results. Manuring necessarily depended on livestock, and the fact that there were more animals in the north was one of the reasons for the superiority of northern lands. However even in those privileged regions the fairly general absence of artificial meadows before the eighteenth century and even later limited stock-raising and therefore the yield from the land.

The landowner closely supervised manure intended for corn. A lease granted by the Carthusian monks in Picardy in 1325 provided for arbitration by men of experience and integrity in case of dispute in this matter. In Bohemia a register of manurers, a *Dungerregister*, was kept on the vast (probably too vast) domains. Even around St Petersburg 'they manure with dung mixed with straw: they till the soil twice for all cereals, three times for *Winterroggen*' (winter rye – the source is a German observer). In Basse-Provence in the seventeenth and eighteenth centuries calculations were continually made and remade of the loads of manure required, of what had been spread, and also of what the *mège*, the farmer, had not supplied. One lease even provided that manure should be checked by authorised persons before being spread and that its production should be supervised.

There were substitute manures – manure crops, ashes and dead leaves kept in peasants' courtyards or village streets – but the principal source of manure remained livestock – never human beings, as in the towns and countryside of the Far East (in the West urban refuse was only used around certain towns, such as Valencia in Spain or some Flemish cities).

In short, corn and stock-raising were complementary, particularly when the use of harnessed animals spread. It would have been impossible for a man who could dig two hectares a year at the most (he comes far below horses and oxen in the league of strength) to prepare the vast cultivated land unaided. Harnessed animals were necessary – horses in northern lands, oxen and mules (an increasing number of mules) in the south.

Thus, to quote Ferdinand Lot, there evolved in Europe 'a complicated system of relations and customs so well cemented together that there were no possible fissures', with obvious regional variations. Plants, animals and people each had their place in it. In fact the whole system was inconceivable without the peasants, the harnessed animals and the livestock in the countryside under grain – or without the herds coming from outside according to the rhythm of the seasons, and the seasonal labour force for harvesting and threshing (for harvesting and threshing were done by hand).

It is hard to know what to admire most in this system: the break in agricultural work to the advantage of stock-raising and the use of animals – a combination clearly originally adopted in the Western and Mediterranean countryside – or the opening-up of low-lying fertile territory to a labour force from poor land, very frequently rough highland regions. Innumerable examples (the southern Jura and Dombes, the Massif Central and Languedoc) demonstrate that the partnership was a basic rule of life. It would perhaps be better to talk of a double system. To interfere with it thoughtlessly always was dangerous.

There are thousands of examples of the invasion of animals and men. An immense crowd of harvesters arrived every summer in the Tuscan Maremma, where fever was so prevalent, in search of high wages (up to five *paoli* a day in 1796). Malaria regularly claimed innumerable victims there. The sick were then left to fend for themselves in huts near the animals, with a little straw, some foul water, coarse bread and an onion or a head of garlic. 'Many die without medicine and without a priest.'

Low yields, compensations and disasters

Corn's unpardonable fault was its low yield: it did not provide for its people adequately. We have already pointed this out at length. All recent studies establish the fact with an overwhelming abundance of detail and figures. Yields from the fifteenth to the eighteenth centuries are disappointing wherever surveys have been made. The harvest from one grain sown was often five, and sometimes much less.

As the grain required for the next sowing had to be deducted, four grains were therefore produced for consumption from every one sown. What does this yield represent in quintals and hectares? Before embarking on these simple calculations we must warn the reader to be wary of their simplicity. Probability in these matters is not enough and, furthermore, everything varied with the fertility of the land, the methods of cultivation and changes in climate from year to year. *Productivity*, the relationship between what is produced and the total effort expended to produce it (labour is not the only factor involved), is a difficult value to calculate, and certainly a variable.

Having said this, we will assume that, as today, between one and two hectolitres of corn were sown per hectare (without taking into account the fact that the grains were smaller and that therefore the number in a hectolitre used to be larger) and start from an average of 1·5 hectolitres of seed. At 5 from 1, 7·5 hectolitres, or about 6 quintals would be obtained. It is a very low figure. But Olivier de Serres confirms it: 'The farmer generally has something to be happy about when his land yields him an average of five or six from one. . . .' Quesnay (1757) says the same about 'small-scale farming', which was still very much the predominant system in France in his own period: 'Each *arpent* giving on an average four from one . . . the seed deducted and not including the tithe. . . .' In the eighteenth century in Burgundy, according to a modern historian, 'the normal yield from an average soil, seed deducted, was generally five or six quintals to the hectare'. Such figures are very probable. France had perhaps 25 million inhabitants around 1775. It more or less managed to live from its corn, what it exported equalling what it imported over the years. If we accept the figure of four hectolitres per inhabitant per year for the consumption of bread grain, the country needed to produce 100 million hectolitres or 80 million quintals. In fact production had in addition to supply grain for sowing and for feeding animals and had therefore to be far above this figure. According to a high estimate by J.C. Toutain, it was in the order of 100 million quintals. If we accept a figure of 15 million hectares for the area sown, we come back to a production figure of six quintals. We therefore remain within the limits of our first estimate, in the neighbourhood of five to six quintals (the figure is on the low side but scarcely open to doubt).

But although the answer seems reasonable it far from indicates the whole complexity of the problem. Chance samples of reliable book-keeping present us with figures far above or far below our approximate average of five or six quintals to the hectare.

Heinrich Wächter's impressive calculations for the *Vorwerk-Domänen* – large estates owned by the Teutonic Order and then by the Duke of Prussia (1550 to 1695) – which deal with almost 3000 totals, give average yields as follows (quintals per hectare): wheat 8·7 (but only a minute crop was involved); rye 7·6 (in view of the latitude, rye tended to become the most important grain); barley 7; and oats only 3·7. Higher figures, although they are still low, were given by a survey in Brunswick (for the seventeenth and eighteenth centuries this time): wheat 8·7; rye 8·2; barley 7·5; and oats 5. One might think that these were record figures for a later period. But an Artois landowner at the beginning of the fourteenth century, Thierry d'Hirecon, who was concerned with the good administration of his estates, obtained the following yields from one grain sown on one of his properties at Roquestor (for 7 known years between 1319 and 1327): 7·5; 9·7; 11·6; 8; 8·7; 7; 8·1. Similarly, Quesnay indicated that the large-scale farming he advocated produced yields of 16 quintals per hectare, a record amount to notch up to the credit of modern capitalist agriculture. But we will return to this later.

As opposed to these unusually high figures there is abundant information of another kind. The recent study by Leonid Zytkowski which establishes a general average for Poland indicates the low level of yields from the sixteenth to the eighteenth century: bad harvests (less than 2 grains from 1 sown) accounted for 13·5% of the total; 'normal' harvests (from 2 to 4 from one) 63%; and good harvests (over 4·0) only 23·5%. The same poor results were obtained from Hungarian harvests from the sixteenth to the eighteenth century. Hungary of course only became a great corn-producing country in the nineteenth century. Neither did the old farmland in the West always show a higher yield. In Languedoc, from the sixteenth to the eighteenth century, the sower's 'hand was heavy', often two and even three hectolitres of seed to the hectare. Oats, barley, rye or corn were grown too closely together and choked each other, as Alexander von Humboldt was still able to observe across the whole of Europe. These massive sowings only produced wretched yields in Languedoc: 2·2 from 1 in the sixteenth century (1584–5); four from one (that is ten hectolitres or eight quintals per hectare) in the seventeenth. The improvement 'for the classic cereals' was only established after 1725 (six from one).

Increased cultivation and higher yields

These low averages did not prevent a slow and continuous advance, as wide investigations undertaken by B.H. Slicher van Bath (1963) prove. What he accomplished was to group together all the known figures for cereal yields, which were almost meaningless in isolation. Compared, they point to a long-term advance. This slow-motion race gives us the opportunity to distinguish groups of runners who moved at the same pace. They were led by (1) England, Ireland and the Netherlands; (2) France, Spain and Italy; (3) Germany, the Swiss Cantons, Denmark, Norway and Sweden; (4) Bohemia in the wide sense, Poland, the Baltic countries and Russia.

If a single yield is calculated for the four principal cereals (corn, rye, barley and oats) – so many grains harvested from one sown – it is possible to distinguish four phases, A, B, C, D, according to group and yield obtained:

CEREAL YIELDS IN EUROPE (1200–1820)

A *Before 1200–1249*	*Yield of 3 to 3·7 from 1*
1. England 1200–1249	3·7
2. France before 1200	3
B *1250–1820*	*Yield of 4·1 to 4·7*
1. England 1250–1499	4·7
2. France 1300–1499	4·3
3. Germany, Scandinavian countries 1500–1699	4·2
4. Eastern Europe 1550–1820	4·1
C *1500–1820*	*Yield of 6·3 to 7*
1. England, Netherlands 1500–1700	7
2. France, Spain, Italy 1500–1820	6·3
3. Germany, Scandinavian countries 1700–1820	6·4
D *1750–1820*	*Yield above 10*
1. England, Ireland, Netherlands 1750–1820	10·6

Source: B.H. Slicher van Bath.

So there were a series of slow and modest advances from A to B, from B to C and C to D. They do not exclude relapses of fairly long duration, for example from 1300 to 1350, from 1400 to 1500, and from 1600 to 1700 (the dates are approximate). Neither do they exclude sometimes quite marked variations from one year to another. But the main thing to remember is the long-term advance of 60% to 65%. It will also be noted that progress in the last phase, 1750–1820, was made in the most densely populated countries, England, Ireland and the Netherlands. A correlation obviously exists between the rise in yields and the rise in population. One last point: the initial advances were relatively the strongest, as calculations would show; the advance from A to B was proportionally greater than from B to C. The transition from three from one to four from one represented a decisive step, the establishment (roughly speaking) of the first towns in Europe, or the revival of those that had not gone under during the high middle ages. For towns obviously depended on a surplus of cereal production.

DECLINES IN CEREALS (1250–1750)

		Yields from 1 grain sown	Decreases %
England	1250–99	4·7	16
	1300–49	4·1	
	1350–99	5·2	14
	1400–49	4·6	
	1550–99	7·3	13
Netherlands	1600–49	6·5	
Germany	1500–99	4·4	18
Scandinavia	1700–49	3·8	
Eastern Europe	1550–99	4·5	17
	1650–99	3·9	

Source: B. H. Slicher van Bath.

Not surprisingly the area sown was often extended, particularly during each population-increase. Sixteenth-century Italy was racked by intensive land-improvement schemes in which Genoese, Florentine and Venetian capitalists invested enormous sums. The slow toil of winning back land from water – from rivers, lagoons and swamps – from forests and heathland, tortured Europe incessantly and condemned it to superhuman effort. All too often these exertions were accomplished to the detriment of peasant life. The peasants were as much the slaves of corn as of the nobility.

'Agriculture,' a present-day historian rightly says, 'is the greatest industry of the Renaissance and modern times.' But as an industry it was always in difficulty. Even in the large food-producing regions of the north, the newly cultivated lands were only makeshift economic ventures that proved inefficient in the long run. To extend the cultivation of corn was to meet with decreasing yields (we have already mentioned this for Poland; a graph by Heinrich Wächter shows the same thing in precise terms for Prussia; the same process was equally evident in Sicily). This was a general rule and the cultivation of corn at two from one proved pointless.

Local and international trade in corn

As the countryside lived off its harvests and the cities off the surplus, it was sensible for a town to obtain its provisions from within striking distance – 'from its own possessions', according to advice given by a resolution at Bologna as early as 1305. This provisioning from within a radius of between twenty and thirty kilometres avoided the difficulties of transport as well as the always hazardous recourse to foreign suppliers. It functioned all the better because towns almost everywhere controlled the adjacent countryside. In France until Turgot and 'the Flour War', even until the Revolution, the peasant was obliged to sell his corn at the market of the nearby town. During the troubles accompanying the summer famine of 1789 the rioters knew where to lay their hands on those grain merchants reputed to be hoarders: everybody knew them. This was probably true all over Europe. For instance, there was no place in eighteenth-century Germany without measures against 'usurers', grain hoarders, *Getreidewucher*.

This life based on local exchanges did not go on without hitches. Every bad harvest obliged the towns to appeal to more fortunate areas. Corn and rye from the north probably reached the Mediterranean as early as the fourteenth century. Even earlier than this Italy was receiving Byzantine and later Turkish corn. Sicily had always been a great supplier – equivalent to Canada, Argentina or the Ukraine in a later period.

These suppliers on which the large towns depended had to be easily accessible – on the sea or the banks of navigable rivers, since water transport was preferable for heavy goods. Picardy and the Vermandois exported to Flanders by the Escaut and to Paris by the Oise in years of good harvests up to the end of the fifteenth century. Champagne and Barrois supplied Paris in the sixteenth century, the corn leaving Vitry-le-François to make the sometimes perilous journey down the Marne. At the same period barrels of corn left Burgundy by the Saône and Rhône, with Arles as a corn station for these upstream consignments. When Marseilles feared famine it turned to its good friends the Consuls of Arles. Later, particularly in the eighteenth century, it became a great port itself for 'corn from the sea'. Then it was to Marseilles that the whole of Provence appealed in difficult times.

From the sixteenth century onwards northern corn played a growing part in international trade in cereals – often to the disadvantage of the exporting country itself.

The large quantity of grain that Poland exports every year [a dictionary of commerce explains (1797)] would give the impression that this country is one of the most fertile in Europe. But those who know it and its inhabitants will judge otherwise, because even if there are fertile and well-cultivated regions there, elsewhere there are more fertile regions which are even better cultivated and which still do not export grain. The truth is that the nobles are the only landowners there and the peasants are slaves, and the former, in order to maintain themselves, appropriate the toil and products of the latter, who form at least seven eighths of the population and are reduced to eating bread made from barley and oats. Whereas the other peoples of Europe consume the major part of their best grain, the Poles retain only a small portion of their wheat or rye so that one might say they only harvest it for foreign lands. Thrifty nobles and bourgeois eat rye bread themselves, wheaten bread being only for the tables of the great lords. It is no exaggeration to say that a single town in other European states consumes more wheat than the whole realm of Poland.

These underpopulated or underdeveloped countries able to supply Europe with the grain it lacked were almost always on the margins – to the north, or east (the Turkish empire), or even to the south (Barbaresque lands, Sardinia, Sicily). The process was subject to frequent revision. One granary closed and another opened. In the seventeenth century it was Sweden (Livonia, Estonia, Scania); after 1689, England, under the impetus of export subsidies which encouraged enclosure; in the eighteenth century, the English colonies in America.

The attraction in each case was ready cash. The rich always paid cash down in the corn trade. The poor succumbed to the temptation and, of course, those who made the biggest profits were the middlemen, like the merchants who speculated on corn in the blade in the kingdom of Naples and probably elsewhere. Venice in 1277 was already paying for corn from Apulia in gold bullion. Similarly the tiny Breton boats that usually carried the corn needed by Seville and particularly Lisbon, in the sixteenth and seventeenth centuries, carried away its counterpart either in silver or in 'red gold' from Portugal, a practice forbidden in any other trade. Exports of corn from Amsterdam to France and Spain in the seventeenth century were also paid for 'in cash'. An Englishman said in 1689, 'our abundant corn [has maintained] our balance of trade'.

None the less the quantities involved in this essential commerce were never as large as might at first be thought. There were about 60 million people in the Mediterranean area in the sixteenth century. At a rate of three hectolitres per head, total consumption would have been 180 million hectolitres each year, or 145 million quintals. A rough calculation indicates that maritime trade involved one or two million quintals or barely 1% of total consumption. If we start with a consumption figure of four hectolitres per inhabitant, the percentage would be even lower.

Did the situation change after the sixteenth century? In 1635 a witness stated that Danzig at the height of its power exported 'over 700,000 barrels' of corn, each holding a demi-last (a last is equal to ten quintals). Exports would thus have totalled 3·5 million quintals. Double this figure to obtain the total for all the north and we arrive at 7 million quintals to the credit of the corn trade. Add the million that Europe could procure from the Mediterranean and we have 8 or 9 million to meet a total consumption of 300 million hectolitres or 240 million quintals (100 million inhabitants at a rate of three hectolitres). We are still at a modest level – 3%.

This long-distance trade holds endless fascination. It is extraordinary to think that the Bardi of Florence, in the service of Pope Benedict XII, succeeded in sending corn from Apulia to Armenia in 1336; that Florentine merchants managed to handle between five and ten thousand tons of Sicilian corn every year in the fourteenth century; that the Grand-Dukes of Tuscany, Venice and Genoa moved tens of thousands of tons of grain from the Baltic and the Black Sea, through the agency of international merchants and letters of exchange on Nuremburg and Antwerp, to make up for shortages during the calamitous 1590s in the Mediterranean; that wealthy but still backward Moldavia sent 350,000 hectolitres on an annual average to Istanbul in the sixteenth century; and that a boat from Boston arrived at Istanbul loaded with American flour and grain at the end of the eighteenth century.

We may also wonder at the docks and warehouses set up at

departure points (in the Sicilian *caricatori*, in Danzig, Antwerp – important from 1544 – Lübeck and Amsterdam) and at arrival points like Genoa or Venice (forty-four warehouses in Venice in 1602). We can admire the facilities available for this trade: the tickets, the grain *cedules* for the Sicilian *caricatori* for example.

However, taking everything into account, this trade remained marginal, spasmodic and more closely supervised than anything subjected to the attentions of the Inquisition. Large-scale systems of purchase, warehousing and distribution – essential for regular long-distance trade in heavy and perishable merchandise – did not appear until the eighteenth century, if then. Even in the sixteenth century neither Venice, Genoa nor Florence had big independent merchants specialising even to a small extent in trade in grain (except possibly the Florentine Bardi Corsi). They engaged in it during times of great crisis when the opportunity offered. It is true that the great Portuguese firms, including the Ximenes, who financed the vast movement of northern corn to the Mediterranean during the massive crisis of 1590 earned a return of between 300% and 400%; but they were not necessarily typical. Generally, big merchants found little profit in this risky and restrictive trade. In fact no concentration appeared in the corn trade until the eighteenth century. 'Trade in corn,' someone at Marseilles remarked during the famine of 1773, 'has been restricted to a small number of merchants who have imposed their own law.' From that time the international market slowly broke away from the immediate natural conditions (harvests determining prices) that generally governed short-distance supply.

We know of various large transactions in corn, for instance important purchases by Gustavus Adolphus in Russia; purchases by Louis xiv on the Amsterdam market just before his invasion of Holland in 1672; and Frederick ii's urgent order to buy 150,000 to 200,000 bushels of rye immediately in Poland, Mecklenburg, Silesia, Danzig and other foreign places (which led to difficulties with Russia) issued on 27 October 1740, the day after he learned of the death of Emperor Charles vi. In these large transactions much depended on the military policy of the states. And the example of Frederick ii shows that in cases of emergency it was necessary to approach all the grain-producers at the same time because of the lack of substantial stocks. Furthermore, obstacles to free trade were endlessly multiplied, so that movement became even more difficult. The case of France during the last years of the *ancien régime* demonstrates this. In its efforts to do the right thing the royal administration brushed aside too-free private initiative and created a monopoly of trade in corn to its own advantage, or rather the advantage of its agents and the merchants in its service, all at its own expense and to its own greatest prejudice. The old system was incapable of providing for the supply of the enlarged towns and gave rise to monstrous. abuses and repeated extortion, from which the legend of the Famine Pact was born. In this case we can say that there was truly no smoke without fire.

All this was very serious. Corn was France's whole life, as it was of all the West. We know about the 'Flour War' which followed Turgot's untimely measures in support of the free movement of grain. 'When they have pillaged the markets and the bakers' shops,' said a contemporary, 'they can pillage our houses and slit our throats.' He added: 'They are beginning to ransack the farms, why not ransack the castles?'

Corn and calories

A man today requires 3500 to 4000 calories a day if he belongs to a rich country and a privileged class. These levels were not unknown before the eighteenth century. But they were less frequently the norm than today. None the less as we need a reference point for our calculations we will use this figure of 3500 calories. Earl J. Hamilton arrives at the same high level in his calculations of the nutritive value of the meals intended for the crews of the Spanish fleet in the Indies in about 1560. This was certainly a record, if we accept (despite Courteline's authority and wisdom) the accuracy of the official figures.

We know of even higher levels at the tables of princes or privileged classes (for example at Pavia at the Collegio Borromeo at the beginning of the seventeenth century); but such isolated cases should not deceive us. As soon as we begin to calculate the averages (for the great urban masses, for example) the level often falls to around 2000 calories. This was the case in Paris just before the Revolution. Of course the few figures we possess never hold the exact answer to the problems that concern us, especially as there is dispute over the reliability of calories as the test of a healthy diet (which demands a balance between carbohydrates, fats and protein). For example, should wine and alcohol be included in the calory intake? It has become established practice never to attribute more than 10% of the calory intake to drink. What is drunk over and above that percentage

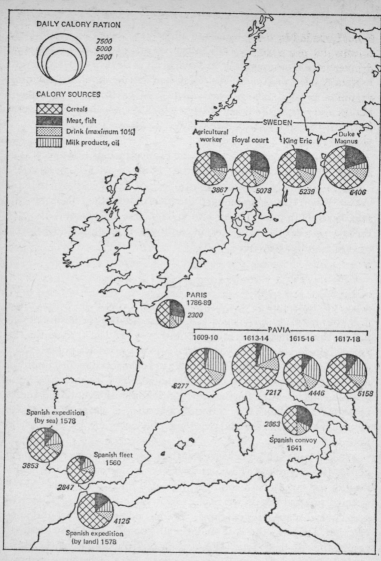

DAILY CALORY RATION

7500
5000
2500

CALORY SOURCES

Cereals
Meat, fish
Drink (maximum 10%)
Milk products, oil

SWEDEN

Agricultural worker — 3867
Royal court — 5078
King Eric — 5239
Duke Magnus — 6406

PARIS 1786-89 — 2300

PAVIA

1609-10 — 6277
1613-14 — 7217
1615-16 — 4446
1617-18 — 5158

Spanish expedition (by sea) 1578 — 3853

Spanish fleet 1560 — 2847

Spanish convoy 1641 — 2863

Spanish expedition (by land) 1578 — 4125

Diagram 2   Some diets of the past, reckoned in calories. The map is based on a few relatively privileged menus. It would be necessary to find thousands of examples, from different periods and every social level, to establish a valid map for Europe. (*From* F. Spooner, *Régimes alimentaires d'autrefois*) is not included in the calculations – which does not mean that the surplus did not count as far as the health and expenditure of the drinker were concerned.

None the less general rules do become apparent (diagram 2). For example, the distribution of the various types of foodstuffs reveals the diversity or, much more often, the monotony of diet. Monotony is obvious every time the share of carbohydrates (cereals in nearly every case) is far in excess of 60% of intake expressed in calories. The share of meat, fish and dairy products is then fairly limited and monotony sets in. Eating consists of a lifetime of consuming bread, more bread, and still more bread and gruels.

On these criteria, it would appear that northern Europe was characterised by a larger consumption of meat, and southern Europe by a larger share of carbohydrates, except obviously in the case of military convoys when meals were improved by barrels of salted meat and tunny fish.

Not surprisingly the tables of the rich were more varied than those of the poor, the difference being marked by quality rather than quantity. Cereals only represented 52% of calories on the Spinolas' luxurious table at Genoa around 1614–15. At the same date they formed 81% of the consumption of the poor at the Hospital for Incurables (one kilogram of corn is equivalent to 3000 calories and one kilogram of bread to 2500). If other dietary categories are compared, the Spinolas consumed twice as much meat and fish and three times as much dairy produce and fats as the inmates of the hospital. Similarly we can be sure that if the boarders at the Collegio Borromeo (1609–18) were overfed (their almost incredibly large intake of food amounted to between 5500 and 7000 calories daily) they were not overfed in a particularly varied way. Cereals represented up to 73% of the total. Their food was not, could not be, particularly interesting.

Sooner or later a more varied diet became common in towns everywhere where assessment is possible, at the very least more varied than in the countryside. Cereals only accounted for 50% of the total, or about a pound of bread a day in Paris, where daily consumption in 1780 was about 2000 calories. Moreover this corresponds to figures (both earlier and later) for average Parisian bread consumption: 540 grams in 1637; 556 in 1728–30; 462 in 1770; 587 in 1788; 463 in 1810 and 500 in 1820. We certainly cannot vouch for these quantities – any more than we can vouch for the figure of 120 kilograms per person, which seems (though the calculation is

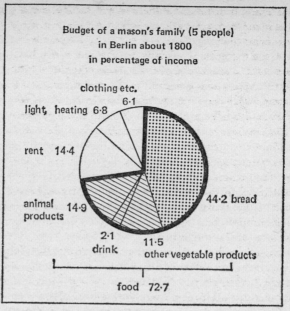

Budget of a mason's family (5 people)
in Berlin about 1800
in percentage of income

clothing etc.
6·1

light, heating 6·8

rent 14·4

animal products 14·9

2·1 drink

11·5 other vegetable products

44·2 bread

food 72·7

Diagram 3   Budget of a mason's family in Berlin about 1800. Compare it with the calculations of the average expenditure on food of the Parisian in 1788 and 1854 (p. 91). Bread here represents considerably more than half the family's food budget, an enormous proportion in view of the relative price of cereals. (*After* W. Abel.)

doubtful) to have been the annual consumption in Venice at the beginning of the seventeenth century. However other indications suggest the existence of an exacting and well-paid working class in Venice, and also the extravagant habits of old-established citizens of substance.

In general there is no doubt whatsoever that bread was consumed on a substantial scale in the country, much more so than in the town, and amongst the lowest levels of the working classes. According to Le Grand d'Aussy in 1782, a working man or a peasant in France ate two or three pounds of bread a day, 'but people who have anything else to eat do not consume this quantity'. However one can see construction workers in southern Italy even today dining on enormous loaves accompanied, almost as a flavouring, by a few tomatoes and onions significantly called the *companatico*: something to go with the bread.

The triumph of bread arose of course because corn — as well as alcohol made from grain (the addition by a Polish historian incidentally confirms the propensity of peasants in his country to drink and not only eat their grain) — was the least expensive foodstuff in relation to its calorific content. In about 1780 it cost eleven times less than meat, sixty-five times less than fresh sea fish, nine times less than fresh-water fish, three times less than butter and oil. Corn, the primary source of energy, came only third in expenditure after meat and wine in budgets calculated for the average Parisian in 1788 and 1854 (only 17% of total expenditure in both cases) (diagram 3).

Corn, which we have necessarily so maligned, is thus reinstated. It was the manna of the poor, and its price was the most sensitive general index of the food market. 'This,' wrote Sébastian Mercier in 1770, 'is the third consecutive winter when bread has been dear. During the past year half the peasants needed public charity and this winter will be the last straw, because those who until now have lived by selling their effects now have nothing left to sell.' For the poor, if corn gave out, everything gave out. This side of the matter must not be forgotten: the slavery in which corn held producers, middlemen, transporters and consumers. There were constant mobilisations and alarms. 'The corn which feeds man has also been his executioner,' said, or rather repeated, Sébastian Mercier.

The price of corn and the standard of living

To correlate the two is hardly an exaggeration. In Europe corn represented approximately half man's daily existence. Its price varied incessantly, at the mercy of stocks, transport, bad weather preceding and therefore governing harvests, at the mercy of the harvests themselves, and finally according to the time of year. Our retrospective graphs of corn prices look like the oscillations of a seismograph. The lives of the poor were all the more affected by these variations, because they were rarely able to escape seasonal increases in price by laying in large stocks at the right time. Can we take the variations in corn prices as a sort of barometer of the standard of living of the masses in the short and long term?

We have the choice of few, invariably imperfect, methods of working this out. We can compare the price of corn with wages, but many wages were paid in kind or partly in kind, partly in money. We can calculate wages in terms of corn or rye. We can fix the average price of one typical 'shopping basket' (Phels Brown's method). Finally we can adopt as our unit the hourly wage of the most underprivileged workers, usually hodmen or plasterers' labourers. This last method, employed by Jean Fourastié and his pupils, notably René Grandamy, has its advantages. What do these 'real' prices ultimately show? They certainly indicate that a quintal of corn remained below 100 hours' work until about 1543, and then continued above that critical line up to about 1883. This, roughly speaking, is what French conditions (and conditions outside France, in the West, which were similar) suggest. A worker has approximately 3000 hours of work at his disposal every year; his family (of four) consumes approximately twelve quintals a year. It is always serious when the 100-hours-for-one-quintal line is crossed; to cross the 200 is a danger signal; 300 is famine. In René Grandamy's opinion the 100 line was always crossed either by a rocketing rise, as in the middle of the sixteenth century, or by a sharp drop, as in 1883. Once the line was crossed in either direction the movement always proceeded rapidly. Thus real prices fluctuated in the unfavourable direction during the centuries covered by this book. The only favourable period would have followed the Black Death, which makes necessary a systematic revision of previous opinions.

The conclusion therefore points to a low level of town wages and to the poverty of the people in the country where wages in kind fluctuated to almost the same rhythm. The rule for the poor was therefore fairly plain: they were obliged to fall back on secondary cereals, 'on less expensive products which still provided a sufficient number of calories, to abandon foods rich in protein in order to consume foodstuffs based on starch'. In Burgundy, on the eve of the French revolution, 'the peasant, apart from the small farmer, eats little wheat. This luxury cereal is reserved for sale, for small children and for a few rare celebrations. It supplies the purse rather than the table ... Secondary cereals make up the main part of the peasant's food: *conceau* or maslin, rye in fairly rich homes, barley and oats in the poorest, maize in Bresse and in the Saône valley, rye and buckwheat in Morvan.' Average consumption in Piedmont in about 1750 was as follows (in hectolitres): corn 0·94; rye 0·91; other grains 0·41; chestnuts 0·45.

Bread of the rich, bread and gruel of the poor

There are different grades of bread just as there are various types of corn. In Poitiers in December 1362, 'when the price of a *setier* of wheat reached twenty-four sous, there were four types of bread: *choyne* bread without salt, salted *choyne* bread, *safleur* bread and *reboulet* bread'. *Choyne* bread (probably 'the canon's bread'; the French for canon is *chanoine* and *choyne* would be a contracted form) with or without salt, was superior-quality white bread made from boulted flour. *Safleur* bread (the name is still used) contained the full flour, not subjected to boulting. *Reboulet* was probably made from flour 90% boulted, and contained that fine bran 'which is still called *riboulet* in the Poitou dialect'. These four qualities corresponded to calm periods of moderate corn prices. Only three categories were authorised when prices were low, or rather reasonable, but seven widely different qualities could be manufactured when they rose; which meant in effect a whole range of inferior bread. Nothing is more typical of the extent to which social inequality was the general rule (we have taken Poitiers from amongst thousands of other examples). Bread was sometimes bread in name alone. Often there was none at all.

Europe remained faithful to an old tradition and continued to feed on coarse soups and gruels until the eighteenth century. These were older than Europe itself. The *puls* of the Etruscans and ancient Romans were basically millet. *Alica*, another gruel, had a starch or bread basis; there was also the Phoenician *alica*, a luxury dish containing cheese, honey and eggs. Before it was made with maize *polenta* was a gruel of barley grains, toasted and then ground and often mixed with millet. Oats were used in Artois in the fourteenth century (probably earlier and certainly later) 'to prepare curds, a gruel very common among the rural population'. A gruel made of millet was current in Sologne, Champagne and Gascony in the fourteenth century and until the eighteenth. In Brittany there was also a thick gruel called *grou* made from buckwheat and water or milk. Doctors in France at the beginning of the eighteenth century recommended gruel on condition that it was 'made with rich oats'.

These old practices have not entirely disappeared today. Scots and English porridge is a gruel made from oats; *kasha* in Poland and Russia is made from ground and toasted rye, cooked like rice. A British grenadier in the Peninsular campaign in 1809 cooking a makeshift dinner was unwittingly linked to an old tradition: 'We prepared this wheat,' he tells, 'by boiling it like rice or, if it were more convenient, we crushed the grain between two flat stones and then boiled it so that we had a sort of thick dough.' A young Turkish *sipahi*, Osman Aga, captured by the Germans at the time of the taking of

Limova near Temesvar in 1688, was even more resourceful, much to his guards' surprise. The regular bread, the *Profond-Brot*, being exhausted, the quartermaster distributed rations of flour to the soldiers (they had been without supplies for two days). Osman Aga was the only person who knew how to knead it with a little water and cook it under the hot ashes of the fire, having been, he said, in similar circumstances before. This was much like the bread – in any case the unleavened bread – kneaded and cooked under ashes that is often eaten in Turkey and Persia.

White bread was therefore a rarity and a luxury. 'In all French, Spanish and English homes,' wrote Dupré de Saint-Maur, 'there are not more than two million men eating wheaten bread.' If the statement is accurate it would mean that three or four million people out of the 100 million consumers in Europe ate white bread. Even at the beginning of the eighteenth century 'half the rural population feeds on non-bread-making cereals and rye', and a lot of bran was left in the mixture of grains that went to make the bread for the poor. Wheaten bread and white bread, *choyne* bread, remained a luxury for a long time. It existed early on, but for the exclusive use of the rich. In 1581 young Venetians on the road to Compostela in Spain broke into an isolated house near the Duero to appease their hunger. There they found 'neither real bread, nor wine, nothing but five eggs and a large loaf made of rye and other mixtures which we could scarcely bear to look at, and of which some of us were able to eat one or two mouthfuls'.

Of even higher quality than white bread, soft bread became popular in Paris fairly early on. It was made from the finest flour, with the addition of barm (in place of 'true' yeast). When milk was added to the mixture it became the 'Queen's bread' that Maria de Medici adored. In 1669 the Faculty of Medicine vainly condemned the use of barm, but it continued to be used for 'rolls'. Women carried bushels full of it 'balanced on their heads in the manner of milkmaids' to the bakers' shops each morning. Soft bread of course remained a luxury. As a Parisian said (1788): 'with its firm golden crust it seems to rebuke the Limousin cob ... it looks like a noble amongst rustics'. These luxuries, however, were only available in times of abundance. In times of dearth, as in Paris in September 1740, two decrees of the Parlement promptly forbade 'the making of any types of bread except second quality'. Soft bread and rolls were prohibited; so was the use of powder widely used on wigs at that period.

The real revolution in white bread only occurred between 1750 and 1850. At that period wheat took the place of other cereals (as in England) and bread was increasingly made from flours that had had most of the bran removed. At the same time the view gained ground that only bread, a fermented foodstuff, suited the health of the consumer. Diderot considered all gruel indigestible 'not having yet been fermented'. In France, where the revolution in white bread began early, a National School of Bakery was founded in 1780. Shortly afterwards Napoleon's soldiers introduced this 'precious commodity, white bread' all over Europe. None the less, taking the continent as a whole, the revolution was amazingly slow and not completed before 1850. But its influence on what kind of crops were grown was felt well before its final success, because of the traditional demand of the rich and the new demand of the poor. 'Wheat was predominant (near Paris) in the plain of France, the rich Multien and the Vexin, from the beginning of the seventeenth century, but not until the end of the century in the Valois, Brie and Beauvaisis. North-western France remained loyal to rye.'

We should bear in mind this French advance in the matter of white bread. Where is good bread eaten if not in Paris? asked Sébastian Mercier: 'I like good bread, I know it and I can tell it at a glance.'

Buying or baking bread at home

The price of bread did not vary; its weight did. Roughly speaking, variable weight was the general rule throughout the Western world. The average weight of bread sold in the bakers' shops in Saint Mark's Square or on the Rialto in Venice varied in an inverse ratio to the price of corn. Regulations published at Cracow in 1561, 1589 and 1592 indicate the same practices: unvarying prices and variable weights. They fixed what must have been the equivalents in bread, of variable quality and weight, of one *grosz* (a coin) – six pounds of rye bread or two pounds of wheaten bread in 1592.

There were exceptions to this, including Paris. The regulation of July 1372 distinguished three types of bread: *Chailli* bread, blistered or *bourgeois* bread and *brode* bread (a brown bread). Their respective weights for the same price were one, two and four ounces. At this period, therefore, the usual system of constant prices and variable weights was in force. But after 1439 the respective weights of the three types of bread were fixed once and for all at half a pound, one pound and two pounds. 'Thenceforth, it was the price of bread that changed with the price of corn.' This was probably because of the authorisation to sell 'cooked bread' by weight granted at a very early date to bakers working outside the capital – at Gonesse, Pontoise, Argenteuil, Charenton, Corbeil, etc. Bread in Paris, as in London, was bought at one of the ten to fifteen markets in the town much more than at bakers' shops.

Bakers throughout Europe were then important people, more important even than the millers, because they bought corn direct and therefore played the part of merchants. But their production was intended only for a part of the consuming public. Domestic ovens, even in towns, must be taken into account in the production and public sale of household bread. In Cologne in the fifteenth century, in Castile in the sixteenth and even today, peasants from the neighbouring countryside arrived in the towns at daybreak to sell bread. In Venice it was the ambassadors' privilege to be supplied with country bread from the outskirts. It was reputed to be superior to the produce of the Venetian bakers. Similarly, numerous wealthy houses in Venice, Genoa and elsewhere had their own granaries and ovens. One muses over the idea of a town market where corn was sold in small measures (still preserved in the Augsburg museum). How was the corn then ground?

Genoa was the scene of great excitement in August 1673 when the question of forbidding domestic baking was raised.

The people are grumbling [the French consul explained]. It seems that [the nobles of the town] want to force everyone to buy bread at the markets and it is said that there are gentlemen [i.e. local businessmen] who offer one hundred and eighty thousand *écus* a year to have this privilege of making bread because ... the custom is that everyone makes his own bread at home, and with this law passed no one will be able to do so, which will be a very great expense because bread is sold at the markets ... at a price of forty lires a *mina* and is only worth about eighteen, besides which the aforesaid bread sold is good on the day it is made and is bitter and cannot be eaten on the next. This affair is causing a great stir and yesterday morning a notice was found stuck up on Saint-Sire Square where the ancient nobility assembles, which spoke strongly against the government and threatened that its tyranny would be evaded.

These practices were further complicated because although corn could be kept in a relatively good state of preservation at that period (it was still often kept in the ear and threshed several times a year in the barns), flour could hardly be preserved at all. Grinding was therefore necessary almost every day of the year, in the mills. Mills at that time were situated at the approaches to every village and town, sometimes even in the middle of them, on any stretch of water that happened to be handy. Every time these mills broke down – for example in Paris when the Seine froze or overflowed – there were immediate difficulties in supplies. It is not surprising that windmills were installed on the fortifications of Paris and that some people continued to favour and use the handmill.

2 Rice

Rice is as much a tyrant as corn, if not a greater one.

Many readers of a recent history of China by a distinguished historian may have been amused at the author's constant comparisons: one emperor was the Hugues Capet of China, another the Louis XI, or the Louis XIV, or the Chinese Napoleon. To understand the world of the Far East the Westerner has to refer to his own circumstances. So we will refer to corn when talking of rice. Both plants are gramineae and both natives of dry countries. Rice was later adapted to a semi-aquatic cultivation, which ensured its high yields and popularity. But one characteristic still reveals its origin: like corn, its roots require a rich supply of oxygen, which stagnant water cannot give. Consequently, however static the water in a rice field may appear, it is always in motion at some time so that oxygenation is possible. Hydraulic technology had therefore alternately to suspend and create motion.

Rice dominates life in the Far East and in the world, both more and less than corn. More, because it does not, like corn, feed its millions at a rate of 50% to 70%, but of 80%, 90% or even more. Unhusked, it keeps better than corn. On the other hand, over the world as a whole, corn is more important. Today it occupies over 200 million hectares, rice 125. But rice yields almost twice as much as corn per hectare, an average of 20·5 quintals against 12. On the whole, the two products balance out at around 250 million tons (against 225 of maize). But the figure for rice is questionable. It applies to unrefined rice, which loses 20% to 25% of its weight when unhusked. The figure then falls to 200 million tons, far below corn or even maize, where the husk is retained. Another disadvantage is that rice holds the record for the man-handling it requires.

It must be added that, despite spreading in Europe, Africa and

America, rice is still largely limited to the Far East, to the tune of 95% of present production; and that it is most frequently consumed locally, so that there is no trade in rice comparable to trade in corn. The only important trade before the eighteenth century was from southern to northern China, by the Imperial Canal and to the profit of the Court at Peking; or again from Tonkin, present-day Cochin China, and Siam, in this case in the direction of India, which always suffered from a shortage of food. There was only one exporting area in India: Bengal.

Rice cultivated dry and in paddy fields

Rice and corn, like so many other cultivated plants, are natives of the dry valleys of central Asia. But corn became popular much earlier than rice, possibly in about 5000 BC as compared with 2000 BC. Corn therefore had a lead of tens of centuries. For a long time rice made a poor showing amongst dry-land plants. The first Chinese civilisation did not know of it and was founded instead on three gramineae grown on the vast denuded lands of northern China. They are still standard crops today: sorghum, with stems four to five metres high, corn and millet. This, according to an English traveller (1793), was 'the Barbadoes millet distinguished by the Chinese under the name of *Kow leang* or lofty corn. It is cheaper than rice in all the northern provinces where it was probably the first grain cultivated, as it appears in Ancient Chinese books that measures of capacity were originally ascertained by the numbers of this grain which they contained. Thus one hundred grains would fill a *choo*. . . .' A European traveller in northern China (1774) was delighted to dine on a dish of 'millet cooked with sugar'. Gruels made from wheat and millet are still very common there today.

Compared with this early progress, tropical, wooded and swampy southern China long remained a region of secondary importance. Like the Pacific islanders today, its inhabitants lived on yams – liana tubers used to make a nourishing flour – or taro (colocasia), a plant similar to beetroot. Its leaves are still a characteristic of the small earthbanks in China today, proof that taro was once important there. The American plants – sweet potato, manioc, potato and maize – did not cross the sea to join yam and colocasia until after the European discovery of the New World. They met resistance from the rice-growing civilisation, well established by then. Manioc only became established in the region of Travancore in the Deccan, and the sweet potato in China in the eighteenth century, in Ceylon and on the distant Sandwich Islands of the Pacific Ocean.

Aquatic rice is said to have become established in India first and then to have reached southern China overland or by sea, possibly in about 2150 or 2000 BC. It settled in slowly, in the standard form in which we now know it, and as it spread the hourglass of Chinese life turned: the new south took over the dominance of the old north – especially as the north had the misfortune to open on the deserts and routes of central Asia and would later suffer invasions and devastation. From China, cultivation of rice then reached the islands, the Philippines and Japan, the last step before the first century of the Christian era. So began its gradual displacement of millet.

Even today paddy fields cover very small areas in the Far East (probably 95% of the total land devoted to rice, but still only 70 million hectares). Outside this zone rice managed to spread over enormous spaces somehow or other as a dry-land plant. This poor-quality rice is the staple foodstuff of certain underdeveloped peoples. Imagine a burnt and cleared corner of a forest in Sumatra, Ceylon or the highlands of Annam. The grain is sown broadcast on the cleared earth without any preparatory work (the tree stumps are left where they are and the ground is not tilled; the ashes serve as fertiliser). It ripens in five and a half months. A few crops – tubers, aubergines, various vegetables – can then be tried in its wake. This system completely exhausts the poor soil. The following year another section of the forest has to be cleared. With decennial rotation, this type of cultivation theoretically demands one square kilometre for fifty inhabitants, in fact for about twenty-five, as a good half of the mountainous ground is unusable. If the rotation necessary to restore the forest is not ten but twenty-five years (as is most frequently the case), the density will be ten to the square kilometre.

The 'fallow forest' invariably yields a fine soil easily worked by primitive tools. The system works well, provided, obviously, that the population does not increase excessively and that the destroyed forest grows again after each successive burning. This system of cultivation has various local names: *ladang* in Malaysia and Indonesia, *ray* or *rai* in the Vietnam mountains, *djoung* in India, and *tavy* in Madagascar where rice was introduced by Arab sailors around the tenth century. They are all simple forms of life, supplemented by 'the farinaceous marrow of the sago palms', or the produce of the bread-fruit tree. They are a far cry from the methodical production of the paddy fields but very far also from the exhausting labour they demand.

The miracle of the paddy fields

So much has been written about the paddy fields that we can give a fairly complete account of them. Drawings in a Chinese work of 1210, the *Keng Tche Tou*, already show the chequered pattern of the paddies, irrigation pumps worked by pedals, the planting and harvesting of the rice, and 'the same plough as today, yoked to a single buffalo'. The picture is the same whatever the date, even today. Nothing seems to have changed.

What is striking at first glance is the extraordinarily intensive utilisation of the land: 'All the plains are cultivated,' wrote the Jesuit Father du Halde (1735). 'One sees neither hedges, ditches nor almost any trees, so afraid are they of losing an inch of land.' That other admirable Jesuit, Father de Las Cortes, had said the same thing a century before: 'there was not an inch of land ... not the smallest corner that was not cultivated'. The paddies are divided by flimsy earthbanks into sections some fifty metres along each side. Water flows in and out of them. Fortunately the water is muddy and therefore restores the fertility of the soil and does not suit the malaria-carrying anopheles mosquito. The clear water in hills and mountains, on the other hand, favours mosquitoes; so the *ladangs* and *ray* are regions of endemic malaria and therefore of limited demographic growth. In the fifteenth century Angkor Wat was a thriving capital, with rice fields irrigated by muddy water. Siamese attacks were not solely responsible for its destruction; they only upset the balance of its life and work. The water of the canals cleared and malaria triumphed, and, with it, the invading forest. Similar dramas seem to have occurred in seventeenth-century Bengal. If the rice field was too small and flooded by adjacent clear water, the destructive onslaught of malaria was unleashed. Malaria was omnipresent in the depression between the Himalayas and the Siwalik hills, where there are so many clear springs.

Water is certainly the great problem. It can submerge the plants: in Cambodia the unparalleled adaptability of floating rice, capable of growing roots nine to ten metres long, had to be used to combat the enormous variations in water level. Bringing in and then draining off water is another difficulty. Sometimes it is brought along bamboo conduits from high-ground springs; sometimes drawn from wells, as in the Ganges plain and often in China; or, as in Ceylon, from large reservoirs — but the tanks that collect the water are almost always at a low level, sometimes sunk deeply into the ground. In some places it was therefore necessary to irrigate a paddy field on higher ground, hence the rudimentary norias and pedal pumps that can still be seen today. To replace them by steam pumps or electric pumps would be to forfeit cheap human labour. Father de Las Cortes saw them functioning: 'They sometimes draw water,' he noted, 'with a handy little machine, a sort of noria that does not require horses. It is the easiest thing in the world [according to him] for a single Chinaman to make this device rotate with his feet.' Sluices also were needed to make the water flow from one paddy to the next. Of course, the system chosen depends on local conditions. When no type of irrigation is possible, the earthbanks of the rice fields serve to retain rainwater, which is enough to support a very large area of cultivation in the plains of the monsoon lands of Asia.

All in all an enormous concentration of work, human capital and careful adaptation was involved. Even then nothing would have held together if the broad lines of this irrigation system had not been firmly integrated and supervised from above. This implies a stable society, state authority and incessant large-scale works. According to one specialist, the Imperial Canal of the Blue River at Peking was also a vast irrigation system. The increase in the number of rice fields implied an increase in state control. It also implied the concentration of villages, as much because of the collective requirements of irrigation as because of the dangerousness of the Chinese countryside.

The rice fields therefore brought high populations and strict social discipline to the regions where they prospered. If southern China was dominant in about 1100, it was because of rice. As early as 1390 the population of the south was three times that of the north: 45 million to 15, according to the official figures. And the real achievement of the rice fields was not their continuous use of the same cultivable area, nor their water technology designed to safeguard the yield, but the two or sometimes three harvests they produced every year.

Let us compare the present-day calendar in Lower Tonkin. The agricultural year there begins with sowing in February; in June, five months later, the harvest is gathered in – the largest one, 'the fifth-month harvest'. Speed is required to ensure the tenth-month harvest, five months later. The rice fields are emptied of water in

June to allow the rice to ripen. When the harvest has been hurriedly transported to the granaries, the rice fields have to be retilled, levelled, fertilised and flooded. There is ńo question of sowing the seed broadcast; germination would take too long. The young rice plants are reared in a nursery, where they grow extremely closely together on richly fertilised soil, then thinned out ten to twelve centimetres apart. The nursery, abundantly manured with human excrement or urban refuse, plays a crucial part, saving time and making the young plants stronger.

The sequence of these hurried labours is fixed by a strict agricultural timetable everywhere. In Cambodia the first tilling after the rains, which leave pools of water, 'wakes up the rice field'. The ground is tilled once from the circumference inwards and then from the centre outwards. The peasant walks beside his buffalo so as not to leave hollows behind him that would fill with water. He draws one or many diagonal channels across the furrows to drain off excessive water; he also has to pull up the weeds and leave them to rot, drive away the crabs that infest insufficiently deep water and take the precaution of pulling out the seedlings with his right hand and beating them against his left foot 'to knock the earth from the roots, which are further cleansed by being rinsed in water. . . .'

Proverbs and familiar figures of speech bear witness to these tasks. In Cambodia, when the water is brought into the fields of seedlings, they call it the 'drowning of partridges and turtledoves'; when the first panicles appear they say that 'the plant is pregnant'; the rice field then takes on a golden hue the 'colour of a parrot's wing'. A few weeks later, at harvest-time, when the grain 'where the milk has formed becomes heavy', comes the game (or almost a game) of stacking the sheaves in 'mattresses', 'lintels', 'flying pelicans', 'dogs' tails' or 'elephants' feet'. Threshing completed, the grain is winnowed to remove 'the promise of the paddy' (the strict meaning of *paddy* is 'rice in the husk').

There are therefore two harvests, both of rice, or farther north one of rice and the other of corn, rye or millet. Sometimes three harvests are possible, two of rice and one in between of corn, barley, buckwheat or vegetables (turnips, carrots, beans, Nankin cabbages). The rice field is thus a factory. In Lavoisier's time one hectare of land under corn in France produced an average of five quintals; one hectare of rice field often bears thirty quintals of rice in the husk. Unhusked, this means twenty-one quintals of edible rice at 3500 calories per kilogram, or the colossal total of 7,350,000 calories per hectare, as compared with 1,500,000 for corn and only 340,000 animal calories if that hectare were devoted to stock-raising and produced 150 kilograms of meat. These figures demonstrate the enormous advantage of the rice field and of vegetable foodstuffs. The Far Eastern civilisations' preference for vegetarianism certainly does not spring from idealism.

Rice lightly boiled in water is daily food, like bread in the West. One cannot help thinking of the Italian *pane e companatico* when noting the meagre accompaniment to the rice ration of a well-fed peasant in the Tonkin delta in modern times: 'five grams of pork, ten grams of *nuoc mam* (fish sauce), twenty grams of salt and a quantity of green leaves with no calorific value' to 1000 grams of white rice (representing 3500 calories out of a total of 3565). In 1735, Father du Halde mentions that a Chinaman who had spent the day working incessantly 'often in water up to his knees, in the evening . . . would think himself lucky to find rice, cooked herbs, with a little tea. It must be noted that rice in China is always cooked in water and is to the Chinese what bread is to the European, never giving rise to distaste.' The ration, according to Father de Las Cortes, was: 'a small bowl of rice and water without salt, which is the usual bread in these regions' — or rather four or five of these bowls 'which they raise to their lips with their left hand, holding two sticks in their right, hastily conveying it to their stomachs, as if they were throwing it into a bag, blowing on it first of all'. There was no point in mentioning bread or biscuit to these Chinese. When they had corn they ate it in cakes kneaded with lard.

These Chinese 'rolls' delighted Gemelli Careri and his fellow travellers in 1774. They improved them with 'a little butter' and thus made up for the fasts the mandarins had imposed on them. Perhaps we can venture the idea of a dietary choice by a civilisation, a dominant taste, even a passion, of which the European has not the slightest understanding, Gemelli Careri no more than any other. The choice is the result of a conscious preference, a feeling for what is best. To stop cultivating rice would be to lose caste. 'The men in the monsoon lands of Asia,' said a geographer, 'prefer rice to tubers and gruel cereals' or bread. Japanese peasants today cultivate barley, corn, oats and millet, but only between rice harvests or when only dry cultivation is possible. They never eat these cereals — 'which they think dreary' — except from necessity. This explains why rice at present extends as far towards the Asiatic north as possible, up to 49° north, in regions where we would expect other crops.

The entire Far East lived on a diet of rice and its by-products, even the European settlers in Goa. Wine made from rice 'was as intoxicating as the best Spanish wine'. 'A wine,' according to another source, 'tending towards the colour of amber and with a taste of Spanish wine, which they use as an everyday drink.' A very strong spirit can also be made from rice, 'forbidden in France, together with spirit made from grain and molasses'.

Diet therefore consisted of a great deal of rice and little meat or no meat at all. Its overwhelming importance in these circumstances can be imagined; variations in its price in China affected everything, including the daily pay of the soldiers, which rose and fell with it on a kind of sliding scale. It was even more marked in Japan, where rice was actual currency before the crucial reforms and changes of the seventeenth century.

Rice owes its fame to the second harvest. When does it date from?

A sinologist recently fixed it at about the seventeenth or eighteenth century, with all the usual reservations, which enabled him to explain the large population-increase in the latter part of the seventeenth and in the eighteenth century. But this decisive revolution must surely have happened earlier. Father de Las Cortes saw the double harvest in the Canton area with his own eyes in 1626 and it was not new then. He noted that from the same land 'they obtain three consecutive harvests in one year, two of rice and one of corn at forty and fifty from one seed sown, because of the moderate heat, atmospheric conditions and most excellent soil, much better and more fertile than any soil in Spain or Mexico'. We may doubt the forty or fifty from one, but the impression of abundance remains.

As for the date, the choice of early rice (called Champa – from the centre and south of Annam) made quicker ripening of the grain possible in about the eleventh century. The innovation gradually reached the hot provinces, one by one. By the thirteenth century the present system had been established. Another explanation must therefore be found for the rise in population of the eighteenth century.

The importance of rice

The success of and preference for rice raises a number of issues. So does corn, the dominant plant in Europe, but there is one difference: historical information on Asia is all too often lacking.

The rice fields occupy a very small part of China, not only of

Chinese territory but of available cultivable space. Hills, not to mention mountains, and even plains, are not generally subject to the meticulous chequered lay-out or terraces of rice paddies. It is true that outside China (for example in Java and in the Philippines) some hills are furrowed by level strips of rice cultivation, and even the lower slopes of mountains or the very mountains themselves. In China too, as in Japan, rice extends into land bordering on other crops. But the scale is insignificant, at the most a few supplementary margins. Karl Wittfogel has calculated that Chinese land in the rice-growing region is divided into dry zones, gardens and rice paddies in the following ratios: dry zones 1000, paddies 300, and gardens 100. These gardens are narrow, minute patches of land, usually with a well; every Chinaman complements his food supplies there. The low proportion of cultivated land results in a concentration of population and crops in very small areas. Roughly speaking, cultivated land in southern China today represents 7% to 10% of the total, while in northern China, which escapes the exclusive tyranny of rice, figures of 30% and 40% (even 68% in Chan Tong) are the general rule.

The land outside this rice-growing zone, for example from Ning Po to Peking, is an area of 'deserted and terrible mountains', a broken-up landscape planted only with pines and a few rare complementary crops.

The Far East disdained and rejected what Europe found in its mountains – developed assets of manpower and animal herds and a flourishing way of life. What lost opportunities! But how could the Chinese utilise their mountains when they had no understanding of forestry or stock-raising, when they consumed no milk or cheese and very little meat, and when they never tried to integrate the mountain populations? To paraphrase Pierre Gourou, imagine the Jura or Savoy without flocks, ruthlessly cleared of trees and with the active population concentrated in the plains and by the shores of lakes and rivers. The cultivation of rice and the habits it has implanted in the Chinese are partly responsible for this.

The explanation is also to be sought in a long and still obscure history. 'Contrary to what Chinese tradition itself teaches, irrigation was a relatively late development in China. All evidence indicates that the technique was established between the fifth and the first centuries BC, contemporary with the first developments in Chinese iron metallurgy...' China therefore came late to hydraulics and the intensive production of cereals, and did not create its typical historical countryside before the Han period. This is 'one of the great facts, if not the essential fact in the history of man in the Far East'. At the earliest, this countryside was created during the century of Pericles, to return to Western chronology. It was not fully established before the success of early southern rice, which brings us to between the eleventh and the twelfth centuries, the period of our Crusades. In fact it is only recently (given the terribly slow tempo of civilisations) that classical China in a material sense appeared, emerging from a long agricultural revolution that destroyed and renewed its institutions.

There is nothing comparable to this in Europe, where the agrarian civilisation of the Mediterranean lands – corn, olive trees, vines and stock-raising – was established well before the Homeric legends and where pastoral life flowed down from one stage of the mountains to the next, down to the level of the plains. Telemachus remembered living among dirty acorn-eating mountain-dwellers in the Peloponnese.

The southern Chinaman, concerned only with himself, did not fail in the conquest of the mountains; he did not attempt it. Having driven off almost all the domestic animals and closed his door on the wretched mountain-dwellers with their dry rice, he prospered, but he had to become a jack-of-all-trades: draw the plough when the need arose; haul in the boats, or lift them up to move them from one reach to another; transport timber, and foot it along the roads with news and letters. The buffalo on the rice fields, fed on short rations, did hardly any work. Horses, mules and camels were only to be found in the north (but the north was not rice-growing China). Rice-growing China in the last resort represents the triumph of a peasantry closed in upon itself. The cultivation of rice was not in the first instance orientated towards the outside world, towards new lands, but towards the towns, which were in existence early on. It was refuse and human excreta from the towns and muck from their streets that fertilised the rice fields. This resulted in continual exchanges between peasants who came to the towns to acquire the precious fertiliser in return for 'wood, herbs or linseed oil'. It also resulted in the intolerable smells over towns and village fields. The symbiosis between countryside and town was stronger than in the West, which is saying a great deal. Rice as such was not the cause of all this, but its success was. It imprisoned towns and countryside in its restrictions.

Japan at the time of the Tokugawa, and India

But very clearly the urban economy was not an inactive prisoner. Recent studies have shown that peasant life in Japan, however heavily handicapped by a genuinely feudal régime, adapted itself to the demands of the market economy whose influence becomes clear with the beginning of the seventeenth century. Slow progress was made in the production of rice, following improvements in seeds, irrigation and water drainage systems, peasants' hand tools, and especially because of the use of richer and more plentiful manures than human or animal excrement: dried sardines and colza, soya and cotton cake, for example. These manures often represented 30% to 40% of working expenses.

Research reveals increases (obviously uneven but probably general). In the Tokyo region: 100 in 1736–41; 102 in 1802; but near Osaka, the greatest trading centre in Japan: 100 in 1727–35; 156 in 1800–6. Not surprisingly, for in Osaka and in all western Japan the increasing commercialisation of agricultural products resulted in the establishment of a large-scale trade in rice, with merchant monopolists. It also brought a sharp rise in complementary crops: cotton, colza, hemp, tobacco, vegetables, mulberries, sugar cane, sesame and corn. Cotton and colza were the most important, colza in association with the rice crop, cotton with corn. These crops increased gross income from agriculture but required double or triple the amount of fertiliser used in the rice paddies and twice as much manpower. In the fields outside the rice paddies, barley, buckwheat and turnips were combined in a three-crop system. While rice was still subject to a very heavy rent in kind (50% to 60% of the harvest was paid over to the landowners) these new crops led to the payment of rents in money. They linked the rural world to a new economy and account for the appearance of peasants who if not rich were at least comfortably off, though the properties still remained tiny (from two to three hectares). This demonstrates, if demonstration is necessary, that rice is also a complex entity with many different facets – different according to time and place – and that Western historians are only beginning to see them.

We are only just beginning because the historical information at our disposal is decidedly meagre. We know nothing or almost nothing about India and its old agricultural problems. Rice encircles peninsular India, borders the lower Indus and covers the wide delta and lower valley of the Ganges. But it leaves a huge area to corn and even more to millet, which can be grown on less fertile land. On the other hand, there are no tubers, or very few, to restore the balance of a constantly difficult food situation, except in Travancore where manioc is widespread. In contrast to China, animals – oxen and buffalo – play a considerable part as draught animals and beasts of burden, but their excreta is dried and used as fuel, not as manure. For religious reasons human excreta is not utilised, again in contrast to the Chinese example, and above all the vast herds of cattle are not used for food, except for milk and melted butter (only produced in small quantities owing to the poor condition of the livestock which are generally not kept under cover and hardly fed at all).

In fact, rice and other grains provide for the life of the vast 'sub-continent' very unsatisfactorily. The famines we have already mentioned are eloquent testimony to this. Rice was obviously not wholly to blame; the responsibility was shared. It was not even the sole begetter of yesterday's and today's overpopulation in India and elsewhere. It only makes overpopulation possible. To quote a fine geographer of Asia, Pierre Gourou: 'Men can be more numerous on a given territory if they eat little.' And malnutrition remains the general rule in the Far East today as it did in the past.

3 Maize

Maize is a fascinating subject to complete our study of the dominant plants. We have decided after reflection not to include manioc, which only serves as a basis for primitive and generally small-scale cultures in America. Maize, on the other hand, sustained the brilliance of the Inca and Aztec civilisations or semi-civilisations, both of which were its authentic creations. It then rose to remarkable popularity on a world scale.

Origins

Everything is straightforward in this case, even the question of origins. As a result of some doubtful texts and interpretations, eighteenth-century scholars thought that maize had come both from the Far East (yet again) and America, where Europeans discovered it at the time of Columbus' first voyage. The first proposition is unquestionably wrong. Maize only reached Asia and Africa (where certain remains, even certain Yoruba sculptures, might still be misleading) from America. Archaeology must have and has had the last word in this matter. Although ears of maize are not preserved in ancient layers, its pollen can be fossilised. Fossilised pollen has been found around Mexico City, where deep excavations have been carried out. The town in the past was on the edge of a lagoon which was drained so that the ground subsided and considerable settlement occurred. Numerous excavations of the old swampy soil of the town have revealed grains of maize pollen at a depth of fifty to sixty metres – that is to say from thousands of years ago. The pollen is either of the same type as the maize cultivated today or from at least two species of wild maize.

The problem has just been elucidated by recent excavations in the valley of Tehuacan, 200 kilometres south of Mexico City. The dryness of this region, which becomes an immense desert every winter, has preserved grains of ancient maize, chewed-up leaves and the stalks of ears. Plants, men and man-made objects have been found around points where underground water rose to the surface. Cave dwellings have supplied the excavators with considerable material and in one stroke yielded up the whole retrospective history of maize.

In the older layers you can see all the modern types of maize disappear one by one. . . . Only a primitive maize is present in the very oldest, from seven or eight thousand years ago, and everything indicates that it was not yet cultivated. This wild maize was a small plant. . . . The ripe ear only measured two to three centimetres, with only fifty or so grains, situated at the axil of feeble bracts. The ear has a very fragile axis and the leaves surrounding it do not form a lasting sheath, so that the seeds must have been easily disseminated.

Wild maize was thus able to ensure its survival. In cultivated maize, on the other hand, the grains are imprisoned by leaves that do not open when the grain is ripe. Man has to lend a hand.

Of course the mystery is not entirely solved. Why did this wild maize disappear? The herds, notably the goats, brought in by the Europeans may have been responsible. In what country did it originate? That it was America is accepted, but research still has to fix the exact birthplace in the New World of this plant so marvellously transformed by man. Paraguay, Peru and Guatemala have been suggested; Mexico has just shown a more ancient claim. But archaeology too may have some surprises in store. And just as if the matter were destined to be left with no definitive solution, experts still talk or at least dream of a further centre of the original diffusion of maize, in upper Asia, cradle of almost all world cereals, or in Burma.

Maize and American civilisations

In any case maize had long been part of the American landscape when the Aztec and Inca civilisations established themselves in the fifteenth century. Sometimes it was combined with manioc, as in eastern South America; sometimes it was grown alone, either as a dry crop or on the irrigated terraces of Peru and the shores of the Mexican lakes. As far as dry cultivation is concerned, the system is much the same as the cultivation of rice in *ladang* or *ray*. It is enough to have seen the great brushwood fires on the Mexican plateau, the Anahuac, to imagine the rotations in the cultivation of maize on a dry countryside, a new section of forest or brush being cleared every year. The system is called *milpa*. Gemelli Careri noticed it in the mountains near Cuernavaca a little way from Mexico in 1697: 'There was only grass,' he noted, 'so dry that the peasants burned it to fertilise the land.'

Intensive cultivation of maize is found on the shores of the Mexican lakes, and even more spectacularly on terraces in Peru. When the Incas came down by the Andes valleys from the heights of Lake Titicaca they had to find land for their increasing population. The mountain was cut out in steps, linked by stairways and irrigated by a series of canals. Iconographic documents are very evocative of this culture: they show peasants with digging sticks and their women laying down the seeds; then the grain, rapidly ripened, had to be defended against birds and animals. At harvest-time the ear was pulled out with the stalk, which was rich in sugar and a valuable foodstuff. It is instructive to compare such naïve drawings by Poma de Ayala with some photographs taken in upper Peru in 1959. They show the same peasant vigorously driving in an enormous digging stick and hoisting up large lumps of earth while the woman lays down the grain. In the seventeenth century in Florida, Correal saw the natives manipulating heavy poles in March and July and burying the seeds.

Maize is a miraculous plant; it grows quickly and its grain is edible even before it is ripe. The harvest from one grain sown was between 70 and 80 in the dry zone of colonial Mexico; in the Michoacan, a yield of 150 from one was considered low. Almost incredible record yields are mentioned of 800 from one on very good land near Queretaro. It was even possible to obtain two harvests in Mexico in hot or temperate country; one of *riego* (with irrigation), the other of *temporal* (as a result of rainfall). Thus, in the colonial period, we can imagine yields of between five and six quintals a hectare, similar to those on small properties today. But maize has always been a crop that demands little effort. The archaeologist Fernando Márquez Miranda recently gave an excellent account of the advantages enjoyed by peasants cultivating maize: it required them to work only fifty days in the year, one day in seven or eight, according to season. They were, therefore, free. Too free. Maize on the irrigated terraces of the Andes or on the lakesides of the Mexican plateaux brought about theocratic totalitarian systems and all the leisure at the disposal of the countryside was used for immense Egyptian-type public works. (It is arguable whether the cause was indeed maize, or irrigation, or the denseness of the societies, oppressive from mere weight of number.) Without maize, the giant Mayan or Aztec pyramids, the cyclopean walls of Cuzco or the wonders of Machu Pichu would have been impossible. They were achieved because maize virtually produces itself.

The problem is really this: on one hand we have a series of striking achievements, on the other, human misery. As usual we must ask: who is to blame? Man of course. But maize as well.

All this suffering, and for what? The maize cake, that poor daily bread, 'those cakes cooked on a slow fire on earth plates' or the grains popped over a fire. Neither is an adequate food. What is lacking is meat; meat is persistently absent. The maize-growing peasant in Indian regions today is still too often in a wretched condition, particularly in the Andes. His food consists of maize, more maize and dried potatoes (our potatoes are known to have originated in Peru). Cooking is done in the open air on a hearth built of stones. The one room in the low hut is shared by animals and people alike. Their unchanging clothes are woven from llama wool on rudimentary looms. Their only resort is to chew cocoa leaves, which numb the pangs of hunger, thirst, cold and fatigue, and to drink beer made from sprouted (or chewed) maize, *chicha*, which the Spaniards discovered in the West Indies and propagated, at least in name, throughout Indian America. Even more popular is *sora*, the strong Peruvian beer. Both were dangerous drinks vainly forbidden by sensible authorities. They enabled these sad, weak populations to escape from themselves in Goyaesque scenes of drunkenness.

There is a serious difficulty: maize is not always within easy reach. It stops half-way up the slopes of the Andes, because of the cold. Elsewhere it occupies limited areas. The grain must therefore be moved around, whatever the cost. The dramatic migration of the Yura Indians south of the Potosi, even today, takes them down from their inhuman heights – at an altitude of 4000 metres – towards the maize regions. Providential saltworks, which they work like stone quarries, provide them with currency of exchange. Every year, in March, men, women and children, all on foot, embark on a journey of at least three months there and back in search of maize; bags of salt stand like ramparts near their camps. This is a small and insignificant example of one of the ways in which maize or maize flour have been moved around since the very distant past.

In the nineteenth century Alexander von Humboldt in New Spain and Auguste de Saint-Hilaire in Brazil noted the transport of maize by mules, with its stopping places, ranches, stations and fixed routes. Everything depended on it, even the mines. There is no saying who profited most – the miners in search of silver, the gold-washers, or the food merchants. Any stoppage in the traffic and the consequences immediately affected the mainstream of history.

We can believe Rodrigo Vivero, Captain-General of Panama at the beginning of the seventeenth century: silver from the Potosi mines arrived at the port of Panama from Arica, via Callao. The valuable cargo then crossed the isthmus and reached Porto Belo on the Caribbean Sea, first by caravans of mules and then by boat on the river Chagres. Muleteers and boatmen had to be fed, otherwise there would be no transport. But Panama lived solely on imported maize, either from Nicaragua or Caldera (Chile). In 1626, during a barren year, the situation was only saved by the dispatch of a boat from Peru loaded with 2000 to 3000 *fanegas* of maize (100 to 150 tons) which enabled the silver to travel over the heights of the isthmus.

Maize outside America

Maize broke out of its American confinement in the sixteenth century, thanks to the Portuguese and Spaniards. But the process of acclimatisation was slow. The Portuguese took it to Black Africa and Morocco, and also to Asia, Burma and China where, as we have already said, it is thought to have arrived in 1597. We can follow its trail in the Old World, especially in Europe. One of its earliest successes was in the Basque country, another in Morocco. Curiously enough, its presence in Gascony remained unobtrusive for a long time, until the eighteenth century. It was at Udine in Venetia a century earlier, in about 1600, and thenceforth quoted regularly on the markets. A century later it was in Hungary and Rumania *Millasse* in the south of France, Italian *polenta* and Rumanian *mamaliga* therefore hardly come within the chronological scope of this book, like potatoes, haricot beans (possibly) and tomatoes (debatable) – those other gifts from the New World. The foreigner was given a multitude of different names on its travels. In Lorraine it is called 'Rhodes corn'; in the Pyrenees, more understandably, 'Spanish corn'; in Tuscany, 'Sicilian corn'; in Provence, 'Barbary' or 'Guinea' corn; in Egypt, 'Syrian doura'; in Italy, very often *grano turco*; in Germany and Holland, 'Turkish corn'; in Russia it has the same name but with the Turkish word for corn, *koukourou*; in Turkey on the other hand it is 'Rooms corn'; in Franche-Comté, 'turky', and so on. In every case it was the poor who bought it, an opportunity, as in the south of France, to save wheat for selling and for supplying the rich. In Burgundy in the eighteenth century '*les gaudes*, maize flour cooked in an oven, are the peasants' food and are exported to Dijon'.

Rice and potatoes also started off in this modest way in Europe. Attempts were first made to produce flour and bread from potatoes, but the results were unsuccessful and for a long time they were the food of the poor and wretched, *agonfle-bougres* ('belly filler for the poor'). So true is it that dietary customs and taboos touch the very roots of civilisations; they rarely change overnight. The poor are the first to bear the brunt of the experiment.

In the 'Kongo', maize was called *Masa ma Mputa*, 'the ear from Portugal'. In fact it was imported from America by the Portuguese at the beginning of the sixteenth century. But a traveller in 1596 tells us that it was rated below the other grains and was used to feed pigs, not humans. Times have certainly changed since then: for example in Benin, in the Yoruba country, maize has slowly become the most important crop and has been incorporated in the cycle of legends – unquestionable proof of its success. Proof, in addition, that eating is a complex element of material life.

4 The rest of the world

It is clear that maize was not a dominant plant on the same scale as corn or rice before the eighteenth century. The proof is that, taking the world as a whole, the space it occupied barely touched the lands of tillage, swing ploughs, ploughs and harnessed animals, and that it largely involved primitive peasants who worked with their hands, using either digging sticks or hoes.

In fact these peasants were a category apart, like a separate species of humanity. To consider their fate is to turn our attention away from the dominant plants (except maize) – that is, away from the civilisations that have been favoured by history and so arrogate to themselves the front of the stage. We could have written a whole book on corn without any difficulty; but the result would have been misleading. The fate of things grown is predominantly a matter of the fate of their cultures. If we deny the title of dominant plant to manioc, as we have unhesitatingly done, it is because it was adopted by the primitive cultures of the poorest pre-Columbian societies and afterwards rejected in favour of corn or maize or even rice; because it remained the food of the Black slaves in the West Indian sugar plantations; the Whites only ate it (cassava) when they were forced to by blockades of the islands. Cassava was a high-grade flour; manioc (cassava is produced from the root of manioc, cut, washed, dried and grated) according to one historian is actually 'the crop chosen to prevent food-shortages in savannah lands'. But plants, like people, only succeed with the connivance of circumstances. It was the mainstream of history that passed manioc by.

Cultivation with the hoe

What is striking even today is the vast extent of the land where work is done mainly with either a digging stick (a sort of primitive hoe) or a hoe. These lands form a belt round the whole world (map 3) comprising Oceania, pre-Columbian America, Black Africa and a large part of south and south-east Asia (where they border and sometimes cross the territory of the tillers). In the south-east particularly (Indochina in the broad sense) there is a mixture of the two types of agriculture.

We can say: (1) That this feature of the globe is extremely old and applies over the whole chronological range of this book; (2) that the people involved are remarkably homogeneous, with inevitable local variations; but (3) that as the centuries go by they naturally find themselves less and less protected from outside influences.

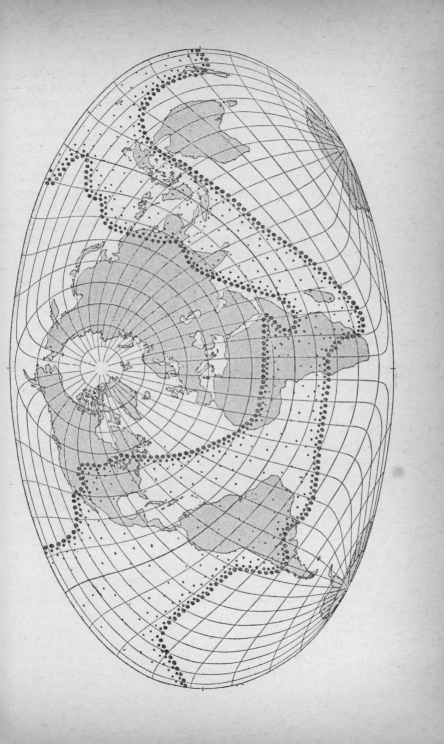

(1) *A feature of ancient times*

If prehistorians and ethnologists – who are still arguing the point amongst themselves – are to be believed, cultivation with the hoe was the result of a very ancient agricultural revolution, even earlier than the revolution that gave birth to agriculture with harnessed animals in about the fourth millennium BC. It may go back to the fifth millennium and be lost in the darkness of prehistory. Like the other revolution, it is said to have originated in peninsular India or more probably ancient Mesopotamia – in any case, from experience that had been passed on from earliest times and had continued as the result of the endless repetition of a lesson learned.

From our point of view it is unimportant whether the distinction between agriculture with or without the plough is valid, because what is involved in either case is the determinism of tools. An original book by Ester Boserup (1966) explains that in systems of the *ladung* type, described above (p. 99), if space is restricted any increase in mouths to be fed results in a shorter fallow period for the reconstitution of the forest. And the change of tempo in its turn will make the transition from one tool to another necessary. The tool, according to this theory, is the result and no longer the cause. The digging stick is adequate – and sometimes not even needed – for sowing broadcast and planting seeds or cuttings amidst ashes and charred wood (remember that the tree stumps are left in the ground). But if the forest does not grow again, because of the rapid return of cultivation, grass moves in. Burning it is not enough because fire does not destroy the roots. The hoe is then essential for weeding. We see this happening in Black Africa where cultivation takes place both on patches of burnt forest and patches of burnt savannah. Finally, when the tempo of harvest is increasingly accelerated, making necessary constant preparation of the land, the swing plough or ordinary plough move in on the vast expanses laid bare and cleared of all shrub formation.

This amounts to saying that our peasants with their hoes are backward communities, that because demographic pressure is still light they have not been forced into the skills and oppressive toil reserved to the drivers of harnessed animals. Father Jean François of Rome (1648) gives us an accurate picture of the agricultural activity of the Congo peasants during the rainy season: 'Their manner of cultivating the land,' he wrote, 'demands little work because of the great fertility of the soil [we obviously do not accept this reason]; they do not plough or dig, but scratch the earth a little with a hoe to cover the seed. In return for this slight effort, they reap abundant harvests, provided that rainfall is not deficient.' We can conclude that the labour of the peasant with a hoe was more productive (considering time and effort spent) than that of the tillers in Europe or the rice-growers in Asia. Neither soil nor climate were responsible for the privileged position this primitive work enjoyed, but rather the immense extent of fallow made available because of the low level of population.

(2) *A homogeneous human type*

The breed of men with hoes was characterised – and this is the most striking fact about them – by a fairly marked homogeneity of goods, plants, animals, tools and customs. We can say that the house of the peasant with a hoe, wheresoever it may be, is almost invariably rectangular and has only one storey. He is able to make coarse pottery, uses a rudimentary hand loom for weaving, prepares and consumes fermented drinks (but not alcohol), and raises small domestic animals – goats, sheep, pigs, dogs, chickens and sometimes bees (but not cattle). He lives off the vegetable world round about him: bananas, bread-fruit trees, oil palms, calabashes, taros and yams.

Naturally variations occur between the large zones of cultivation with the hoe. For example we find cattle, buffalo and oxen in the African steppes and savannahs, probably as the result of an old diffusion via the Abyssinian tillers. The banana tree, which has always been cultivated (the fact that it cannot reproduce by seeds but only by cuttings proves the antiquity of its cultivation) and is characteristic of zones under the hoe, is absent in marginal regions. This is true of the Sudanese lands north of the Niger and of New Zealand where the (to them) severe climate surprised the Polynesians (Maoris) when their wonderful venture led on to its stormy coasts canoes with outriggers between the ninth and the fourteenth centuries AD.

But the main exception concerns pre-Columbian America. The peasants with hoes responsible for the retarded and weak civilisations of the Andes and the Mexican plateaux were descended from populations of Polynesian origin who crossed the Pacific and reached America in several waves (possibly in the sixth or seventh centuries BC). They would be the real redskins; the yellow race could only claim the natives of southern South America or northern North America as its own. In any case, red or yellow, these newcomers did not find readily available the plants and facilities to which they were accustomed. They had to utilise local resources — manioc, sweet potatoes, potatoes and maize; particularly maize, which made possible the enormous extension of the hoe towards the temperate zones, in the north and south of the continent, well beyond the tropical or hot lands of the narrow manioc region.

(3) Recent mixtures

With the social mixing set in motion by the maritime integration of the world modifications became increasingly numerous and new combinations of crops appeared. I have already mentioned the arrival in the Congo of manioc and maize, two of the benefits resulting from Portuguese navigation and trade. The newcomers grew only moderately well among the established plants: maize and manioc side by side with various kinds of millet, white or red. Millet was mixed with water to give a sort of *polenta* which when dried would keep for two or three days. 'It serves as bread and is in no way harmful to the health.' Similarly vegetables, also imported by the Portuguese – cabbages, gourds, lettuces, parsley, chicory, garlic – did not usually prosper by the side of the natives' peas, red haricots and beans. But they did not disappear.

The African food-producing trees formed the most distinctive setting: kolas, banana trees, and particularly palm trees. There were many different varieties of palm, providing oil, wine, vinegar, textile fibres and leaves. 'The products of the palm are to be found everywhere: in fences and roofs of houses, in traps for game and in the fisherman's eel-pot, in the public treasury (pieces of material served as money in the Congo), in clothing, cosmetics, therapeutics and foodstuffs.'

In short, these populations and societies dependent on rudimentary but long-established agriculture should not be underestimated. Think of Polynesian expansion, for example; they occupied an enormous maritime triangle, from Hawaii to Easter Island and New Zealand in the thirteenth century: no mean achievement. But civilised man has driven them far into the background. He has obliterated, devalued their achievement.

Primitive peoples

There were, however, far more primitive peoples, living in those areas totally without agriculture corresponding to the first categories

of W. Gordon Hewes' map (map 1). We get to know of them in the
wake of the European travellers, with the increase of curiosity in the
eighteenth century. Food gatherers, hunters, fishermen – they attract
our attention from the four corners of the world.

One example will be enough. In Kamtchatka the engraver and
traveller J.B. Le Prince saw and depicted the native fishermen of the
coasts in about 1735: 'The Kamtchadales,' explains the commentary
to one of his engravings, 'prepare fish for drying and melt the fat in
wooden vessels by means of stones heated over the fire.' Note the
antiquated method. In the engraving the stones are gripped by what
seem to be huge wooden spoons with very long handles. Fish are
hanging up in their hundreds.

We could cite many similar examples in the vast northern hemisphere with its wide, unbroken expanses. In the southern hemisphere
we would only have to follow Tasman or Cook on the coasts of
Tasmania or Australia. But the situation is the same everywhere,
whether it concerns Eskimos in the Great North, Negritos in the
Philippines, or pygmies in the African forests: primitive populations
who have somehow to take what they need to survive from the wild
flora and fauna surrounding them.

Eating other people's bread

Wherever observation is possible in the varied world we have tried
to evoke, we see an order of precedence among foodstuffs, a kind of
hierarchy. Stability is the general rule within any system, especially
at the level of everyday life: rice pilaf in Persia with a little – very
little – bread; rice 'cooked dry' or 'half-cooked' in China which 'that
nation uses for bread and meat' with a little pork fat sometimes,
with which everything 'in China is prepared ... [as] they use
neither butter nor oil there, because there is no olive oil, but only
oil from rape and a few other seeds to burn in lamps, and for
cooking for the poor ...'; corn in Europe; maize in America and so
on.

The difficulty of real innovation in this network of traditional
customs and needs can be imagined. If there was a revolution, as in
Europe, it was made up of slow and time-consuming changes.

There was no active conflict except where two opposing foodstuffs
met – which means every time an individual found himself away
from home, from his own customs and daily diet, and confronted by
others. Europeans provide the best examples; their experience,

repeated so many times, reveals the dietary frontiers and the difficulties of crossing them. In the countries opened up to their curiosity or their exploitation they never abandoned their customs: wine, alcohol, meat, ham that came from Europe and sold like gold in the Indies, even when worm-eaten. They had to have their bread at any price. In China Gemelli Careri procured corn and had it made into biscuits and cakes 'when biscuit was lacking, because rice cooked dry, as it is served in this country, and with no seasoning whatsoever, does not suit my stomach'. In the Panama isthmus, where corn would not grow, flour came from Europe. Bread was therefore a luxury. 'It is scarcely to be found except amongst Europeans settled in the towns and rich Creoles, and they only use it when taking chocolate or eating caramel sweets.' At all other meals they served maize cakes, a sort of *polenta*, and even cassava 'flavoured with honey'.

When that indefatigable traveller Gemelli Careri arrived at Acapulco from the Philippines in February 1697, he naturally did not find wheaten bread. This happy surprise was reserved for a later occasion, on the road to Mexico City in the Massatlan *trapiche*, where 'we found … good bread, which is no small thing in these mountains where all the inhabitants eat only maize cakes'. This is an occasion to recall the considerable cultivation of corn on irrigated or non-irrigated land (*riego* or *secano*) in New Spain, intended for export to the towns. On Tuesday, 12 March 1697, Careri witnessed a popular commotion in Mexico City: 'A sort of uprising occurred today; the populace went to ask for bread under the Viceroy's windows.' Measures were immediately taken to prevent the people from burning the Palace, 'as had been done at the time of the Earl of Galoe in 1692'. Was this 'populace' composed of Whites, as we think likely? Let us assume that it was, so that we can bring the chapter to a somewhat hasty conclusion: white bread, white man. In America it would go without saying. If on the other hand, half-castes, Indians and Black slaves from the town were involved, then it is most probable that what they were demanding under the always ambiguous name of 'bread' was only maize.

3

Superfluity and Sufficiency:
Food and Drink

The main foods of the majority of men – corn, rice and maize – is a
relatively simple subject. As soon as we begin to consider less
ordinary foodstuffs (including meat) and the very varied needs of
clothing and housing, we move into a far more complex sphere
where superfluity and bare necessity are constantly to be found side
by side. The problem would perhaps be clearer if we began by comparing the condition of the majority – the food, houses and clothes of
the general run of men – with that of the minority, the privileged,
those whose way of life we may call luxurious. Distinguishing
between the ordinary and the exceptional will involve us in a difficult
and flexible procedure, because classifications are inevitably imperfect and luxury cannot be identified once and for all with the
necessary precision. It is an elusive, complex and contradictory
entity.

For example, sugar was a luxury before the sixteenth century;
pepper was still a luxury in the closing years of the seventeenth;
alcohol and the first 'aperitifs' at the time of Catherine de Medici;
swansdown beds or the Russian boyars' silver cups before Peter the
Great. The first flat plates, very probably made of silver, which
Francis I ordered from a silversmith in Antwerp in 1538, were also a
luxury. The first deep plates, known as 'Italian', were mentioned in
the inventory of Cardinal Mazarin's possessions in 1653. Other
sixteenth- and seventeenth-century luxuries were forks and glass
window panes, both of which originated in Venice. But the manufacture of glass panes – the glass was no longer made with potassium
after the fifteenth century but with soda, which gave a more trans-
parent material, easy to smooth – spread to England in the following
century thanks to coal-firing. So, using a little imagination, we may
assume that the Venetian fork and English glass met at Lyons. It is
also surprising to think that the chair is still a luxury, a rarity in

Islam and India even today. Handkerchiefs were another luxury. Erasmus in his *Civility* explains: 'To wipe the nose on the cap or sleeve belongs to rustics; to wipe the nose on the arm or elbow to pastrycooks; and to wipe the nose with the hand, if by chance at the same instant you hold it to your gown, is not much more civil. But to receive the excreta of the nose with a handkerchief turning slightly away from noble people is an honest thing.' Oranges likewise were still a luxury in England in the Stuart period: they appeared around Christmas and were preciously guarded until April or May. And we have said nothing yet on the inexhaustible subject of dress.

Luxury therefore has many facets, according to the period, country or civilisation in question. In contrast, the social drama, without beginning or end, with luxury as its prize and its theme, scarcely changes at all, a choice spectacle for sociologist, psychoanalyst, economist and historian. The privileged and the onlookers – the masses who watch them – must of course agree to a certain amount of connivance. Luxury does not only represent rarity and vanity, but also social success, fascination, the dream that one day becomes reality for the poor, and in so doing immediately loses its old glamour. Not long ago a medical historian wrote: 'When a food that has been rare and long desired finally arrives within reach of the masses, consumption rises sharply, as if a long-repressed appetite had exploded. Once popularised the food quickly loses its attraction . . .' The appetite becomes sated. The rich are thus doomed to prepare the future life of the poor. It is, after all, their justification: they try out the pleasures that the masses will sooner or later grasp.

Such games are full of futility, pretentiousness and caprice. 'We find extravagant praise of turtle soup amongst English eighteenth-century authors: it is delicious, a sovereign remedy for consumption and weakness, it arouses the appetite. No state dinner [like the Lord Mayor's banquet in the City of London] was without turtle soup.' Also in London we hear of 'roast mutton stuffed with oysters'. Economically extravagant, Spain paid cash for the wigs the wicked northern lands made for it. 'But what can we do about it?' asked Ustariz in 1717. At the same time the Spaniards were buying the loyalty of a few sheikhs in North Africa with black tobacco from Brazil. And if we believe Laffemas, adviser to Henry IV, the French, who always behaved like savages, 'receive baubles and strange merchandise in exchange for their treasures'.

Similarly Indochina and the Indian Archipelago provided gold dust, spices, precious woods – sandalwood and rosewood – slaves and rice in exchange for Chinese trifles: combs, lacquer boxes, and coins made of copper mixed with lead. But it is comforting to find that China, in its turn, committed similar acts of folly for swallows' nests from Tonkin, Cochin China and Java, or 'paws of bears and various other wild animals which arrive salted from Siam, Cambodia, or Tartary'. Finally, to return to Europe: 'What a wretched luxury porcelains are!' exclaimed Sébastian Mercier in 1771. 'One tap of a cat's paw can do more damage than the devastation of twenty arpents of land.' Nevertheless the price of Chinese porcelains was falling at that time and soon they no longer served as anything but common ballast for boats returning to Europe. The moral is not surprising: every luxury dates and goes out of fashion. But luxury is reborn from its own ashes and from its very defeats. It is really the reflection of a difference in social levels that nothing can change and that every movement recreates. An eternal 'class struggle'.

It applies not only to classes but also to civilisations. Civilisations were incessantly cyeing each other, acting out the same drama as the rich played in relation to the poor. But this time it was reciprocal, and therefore created currents and led to accelerated exchanges, from near and far. In short, as Marcel Mauss wrote, 'it is not in production that society found its impetus; luxury is the great stimulus' – an idea recently forcefully supported by Werner Sombart. According to Gaston Bachelard 'the attainment of the superfluous causes greater spiritual excitement than the attainment of necessities. Man is a creature of desire and not a creature of need.' Jacques Rueff, the economist, goes so far as to repeat that 'production is the daughter of desire'. Probably no one will deny the existence of this impetus or these needs. What the various sciences of man and history will find more difficult to accept is that an ineradicable and primordial mechanism is involved, even in present-day societies and in the face of rampant mass luxury. Or else we shall have to further extend the meaning of the word luxury, never so simple to define as these brilliant formulations would lead us to believe. Luxury for Werner Sombart was the zealous creator of early modern capitalism and its beginning coincided with the period of the princely courts in the West, of which the pontifical court at Avignon was the prototype. In fact there is no society without different levels. And with the slightest social variation comes luxury, in the past as today. It would be possible to discourse at length on what was luxury in ancient Rome.

On the other hand, there is no doubt that before the nineteenth century and its innovations, luxury was more like the action of an engine often running in neutral than an element of growth, proof that the facilities of material life and of the economy could only produce limited and superficial phenomena, though all the more brilliant for that. Hence we shall suggest that a certain type of luxury was, could only be, a fact (or a disease) of the *ancien régime*, and that it characterised societies and economies inexorably limited in their growth, in which men were imprisoned until the Industrial Revolution and its consequences. If we wished to sermonise (but where would that take us?) and to retain the economists' language we would say: before the nineteenth century (and often after it) luxury was the unjust, unhealthy, brilliant and anti-economic utilisation of any surplus produced in a given society. And to the supporters of luxury, I quote the words of an American biologist, Theodosius Dobzhansky: 'I for one, do not lament the passing of social organisations which used the many as a manured soil in which to grow a few graceful flowers of refined culture.'

1 Luxury and the foods of the masses

The two sides are clearly visible at first glance: luxury and poverty, superabundance and penury. Luxury is the more conspicuous spectacle, the better documented and also the more attractive to the armchair observer today. The other side proves depressing, however unwilling one may be to accept a Michelet-type romanticism, all too natural in the circumstances.

A belated luxury

We can risk the generalisation that there was no real luxury or sophistication of eating habits in Europe before the fifteenth or sixteenth centuries. It is very possible in this respect that the West lagged behind the other Old World civilisations.

In any case, it is approximately at the beginning of the period covered by this book that cooking became, in Italy, a skilful and expensive art with precepts and decorum of its own. The Senate at Venice was very early on protesting at the expensive feasts the young nobles held; in 1460 it forbade banquets costing half a ducat a head. The *banchetti*, of course, continued. Marin Sanudo's *Diarii* have preserved some of the menus and prices from these princely meals, on gala days of the Carnival. As if fortuitously they ritually contained the dishes forbidden by the Venetian government: partridges, pheasants, peacocks, and so on. Slightly later, when Ortensio Lando in his *Commentario delle più notabili e mostruose cose d'Italia* (printed and reprinted in Venice from 1550 to 1559) attempted to list foods available to charm gourmet palates in the towns of Italy, he had almost too great a choice: sausages and saveloys from Bologna, *zampone* (a sort of stuffed pig's leg) from Modena, round pies from Ferrara, *cotognata* (quince jam) from Reggio, cheese and *gnocchi* with garlic from Piacenza, marzipan from Sienna, *caci marzolini* (March cheeses) from Florence, *luganica sottile* (fine sausage) and *tomarelle* (mince) from Monza, *fagiani* (pheasant) and chestnuts from Chiavenna, fish and oysters from Venice, even *eccellentissimo* bread (a luxury in itself) from Padua, not forgetting the wines whose reputation later grew.

Thus emerged the elaborate cooking known to every mature civilisation; the Chinese in the fifth century, the Muslim in the eleventh and twelfth centuries, the West with the Italian achievement. And then the French. From the sixteenth century onwards France came more and more to be the homeland of fine fare, where precious recipes were created and others collected from the four corners of Europe and the world; the place where the presentation and the ceremonial of those profane festivals of gourmandising and *bon ton* were perfected.

If this were so, was it not the result of the abundance and variety of French resources, which were able to surprise even a Venetian? Girolamo Lippomano, ambassador in Paris in 1557, went into ecstasies over the omnipresent opulence: 'There are innkeepers who will feed you at their houses at all prices: for one *tester*, for two, for one écu, for four, for ten, for even twenty per person, if you so wish. But for twenty-five écus, you will be given manna in soup or roast phoenix: in fact everything that is most precious on earth.' However, great French cooking was perhaps only established later, with the Regency and the active good taste of the Regent; or even later still, in 1746, when 'Menon's *Cuisinière bourgeoise* finally appeared, a valuable book which rightly or wrongly has certainly run through more editions than Pascal's *Provinciales*'. Even a Parisian maintained in 1782 that 'people have only known how to eat delicately for the last half century'. However that may be, in 1788 a gourmet was able to list the following culinary resources of France: turkey with truffles from Périgord, *pâtés-de-foie-gras* from Toulouse, partridge *terrines* from

Nérac, *pâté* of fresh tunny fish from Toulon, larks from Pézenas, cooked brawn from Troyes, woodcock from the Dombes, capons from the Pays de Caux, hams from Bayonne, cooked tongue from Vierzon and even sauerkraut from Strasbourg.

But no one ever has the last word in these things. A Frenchman unhesitatingly declared in 1827: 'The art of cooking has made more progress in the last thirty years than in any century before.' It is true that he had before him the magnificent sight of a few large 'restaurants' in Paris (where the 'innkeepers' had not long since become 'restaurateurs'). In fact fashion governs cooking like clothing. The famous sauces fall into disrepute one fine day and thenceforth elicit nothing but condescending smiles. 'The new cooking,' wrote the author of the *Dictionnaire Sentencieux* (1768), who seems to have had a dry sense of humour, 'is all juice and jelly.' '*Soup* . . .' says the dictionary, 'which everyone ate in former times is rejected today as too bourgeois and too old a dish, on the pretext that stock relaxes the fibres of the stomach.' The same went for 'pot herbs', the vegetables which the 'refinement of the century has almost banished as a vulgar food! . . . Cabbages are no less healthy, nor less excellent', but all the peasants ate them throughout their lives.'

Other small changes gradually occurred. Turkeys came from America in the sixteenth century. A Dutch painter, Joachim Buedkalaer (1530–73) was probably among the first to include one in a still life, today in the Rijksmuseum, Amsterdam. We are told that turkeys multiplied in France with the restoration of internal peace in the reign of Henry IV. 'It was turkeys,' a Frenchman wrote in 1779, 'which in some way caused the geese to disappear from our tables, on which they formerly held the place of honour.' Do the fat geese of Rabelais' period belong to a past age of European gluttony?

We might also follow fashion in food through the revealing history of certain words which are still in use but which have changed in meaning several times: *entrées*, *entremets*, *ragoûts*, etc. Similarly with 'good' and 'bad' ways of roasting meat – but that story would be endless.

These matters of luxury and fashion only touched a certain part of Europe. There, food and the art of eating gradually freed themselves from tradition, beliefs and ancient ritual. Formerly eating and drinking were not merely necessities or, occasionally, social luxuries, but definite community activities, means of intercourse between man and society, men and the material world, and man and the supernatural universe. A historian says: 'The tomb and the altar were the first tables laden with food and drink.' The gods and the dead claimed their share. Even the most highly developed West continued to bear the marks of these ancient rites, especially at the popular level and in the countryside. This was even more striking towards Eastern Europe, where the clock of history is slow, even in the Balkans influenced for such a long time by Byzantine civilisation. Gifts from the rich, open tables maintained by nobles, fasts multiplied by the Church, and public feasting and carousing cut across an almost invariably hard life. When the Guild of Tanners of Salonika nominated new masters it habitually invited (up to the nineteenth century) the whole town to share its rejoicing and feasts in the nearby countryside. And in revolutionary Paris, an immense civic meal 'between the Feast of the Supreme Being and the memorable ninth of Thermidor', required over 20,000 tables to be laid out in the street, in front of houses and in the public squares. The whole town took part.

Carnivorous Europe

There was, as we have said, no sophisticated cooking in Europe before the fifteenth century. The reader must not let himself be dazzled by feasts like those given by the ostentatious court of the Valois of the house of Burgundy: fountains of wine, set-pieces, and children disguised as angels descending from the sky on cables. Ostentatious quantity prevailed over quality. At best, this was a luxury of greed. Its striking feature was the riot of meat – a long-lasting feature of the tables of the rich.

Meat, in all its forms, boiled or roasted, mixed with vegetables and even with fish, was served 'in a pyramid' on immense dishes called *mets* in France. 'Thus all the roasts placed on top of one another formed a single *mets*, and the very varied sauces for them were offered separately. They did not even think twice about piling up the whole meal on a single vessel and this dreadful hotch-potch was also called a *mets*.' We have French cookery books dated 1361 and 1391 mentioning *assiettes* (plates) in the same sense: a meal of six *assiettes* or *mets* comprised what we would call six courses. All of them were lavish and to our eyes often unexpected. A single *mets* out of four offered – our source is the *Ménagier de Paris* (1393) – consisted of the following: *pâtés* of beef, rissoles, lamprey, two broths with meat, white fish sauce, plus an *arboulastre*, a sauce made with butter, cream, sugar and fruit juice. The book gives the recipe for each of these items but we

would not advise a cook today to take them literally. All experiments
have turned out badly.

Consumption of meat on this scale does not seem to have been a
luxury reserved exclusively to the very rich in the fifteenth and
sixteenth centuries. Even in 1580 Montaigne noted dish-stands in
inns in Upper Germany equipped with several compartments to
enable the servants to offer at least two dishes of meat at the same
time and replenish them easily up to the seven dishes Montaigne
observed on certain days. Meat abounded in butchers' shops and
eating houses: beef, mutton, pork, poultry, pigeon, goat and lamb.
As for game, a treatise on cooking, possibly dating from 1306, gave a
fairly long list available in France; wild boar was so common in
Sicily in the fifteenth century that it cost less than butcher's meat;
Rabelais' list of feathered game is interminable: herons, egrets, wild
swans, bitterns, cranes, partridges, francolins, quails, wood pigeons,
turtledoves, pheasants, blackbirds, larks, flamingoes, water fowl,
divers, etc. Except for large items (boar, stag, roe deer) the long
price list for the Orleans market (from 1391 to 1560) indicates
regular and abundant supplies of game: hare, rabbit, heron, partridge, woodcock, lark, plover, teal. The description of the Venice
markets in the sixteenth century is equally rich. Is it not after all only
natural in a West which was only semi-populated?

We should not accept too readily the complaints, often in literary
form, about the food of the poor peasants, robbed by the rich of
'wine, wheat, oats, oxen, sheep and calves, leaving them only rye
bread'. There is proof to the contrary.

In Germany an ordinance by the Dukes of Saxony in 1482 ran
'let it be understood by all that the craftsmen must receive a total of
four courses at their midday and evening meals; on a meat day: one
of soup, two of meat, one of vegetables; for a Friday or a meat-less
day: one of soup, one of fresh or salted fish and two of vegetables. If
the fast has to be extended, five courses: one of soup, two sorts of fish
and two vegetables. And in addition, bread, morning and night.'
And again with the addition of *kofent*, a light beer. It might be
argued that this menu was for craftsmen, who were citizens. But in
Oberhergheim in Alsace in 1429 if a peasant doing statute labour
did not want to eat with the others in the *Maier's* (the steward's)
farm, the *Maier* had to send 'two pieces of beef, two pieces of roast
meat, a measure of wine and two pfennig-worth of bread' to the
man's house. There is more evidence on the same subject. A foreign
observer in Paris in 1557 said that 'pork is the habitual food of poor

people, those who are really poor. But every craftsman and every merchant, however wretched he may be, likes eating venison and partridge at Shrovetide just as much as the rich.' Of course these rich and prejudiced observers begrudged the poor the slightest luxury they indulged, and, as if it were all part of the same thing: 'there is no labourer nowadays,' wrote Thoinot Arbeau (1588), 'who does not want oboes and sackbuts (a type of trumpet with four branches) at his wedding.'

Tables laden with meat presuppose regular supplies from the countryside or from nearby mountains (the Swiss Cantons); Germany and northern Italy were supplied even more plentifully from the eastern regions of Poland, Hungary and the Balkan countries, which still sent half-wild cattle westwards on foot in the sixteenth century. No one turned a hair at the sight of 'extraordinary herds of 16,000 and even 20,000 oxen' at a time pouring into the largest cattle fair in Germany at Buttstedt near Weimar. In Venice herds from the East arrived overland or via shipping points in Dalmatia; they were rested before slaughter on the Lido island, which was also used for testing artillery pieces and as quarantine for suspect boats. Offal, particularly tripe, was one of the everyday foods of the poor in the town of Saint-Marc. In 1498 Marseilles butchers bought sheep from as far afield as Saint-Flour, in the Auvergne. Butchers as well as animals were imported from these distant regions. In the eighteenth century the butchers of Venice were often mountain-dwellers from Grisons, quick to cheat on the selling price of offal; in the Balkans, Albanian and later Epirot butchers and tripe merchants have continued to emigrate to far-off lands up to the present day.

From 1350 to 1550 Europe probably experienced a favourable period as far as individual life was concerned. Following the catastrophes of the Black Death living conditions for workers were inevitably good as manpower had become scarce. Real salaries have never been as high as they were then. In 1388, canons in Normandy complained that they could not find anyone to cultivate their land 'who did not demand more than what six servants made at the beginning of the century'. The paradox must be emphasised since it is often thought that hardship increases the farther back towards the middle ages one goes. In fact the opposite is true, as far as the standard of living of the common people – the majority – is concerned. Before 1520–40, peasants and craftsmen in Languedoc (still little populated) ate white bread. The fact cannot be misleading. The deterioration becomes more pronounced as we move away from the 'autumn' of the middle ages; it lasted right up to the middle of the nineteenth century. In some regions of Eastern Europe, certainly in the Balkans, the downward movement continued for another century, to the middle of the twentieth.

Meat consumption after 1550

Things began to change in the West after the middle of the sixteenth century. Heinrich Müller wrote in 1550 that in Swabia 'in the past they ate differently at the peasant's house. Then, there was meat and food in profusion every day; tables at village fairs and feasts sank under their load. Today, everything has truly changed. For some years, in fact, what a calamitous time, what high prices! And the food of the most comfortably-off peasants is almost worse than that of day-labourers and valets previously.' Historians have been wrong in not taking account of this repeated evidence or in persistently interpreting it as man's morbid need to praise the past. 'How far away is the time, oh comrades,' explained an old Breton peasant (1548), 'when it was difficult for an ordinary feast day to pass by without someone from the village inviting all the rest to dinner, to eat his chicken, his gosling, his ham, his first lamb and his pig's heart.' 'In my father's time,' a Norman gentleman wrote in 1560, 'we ate meat every day, dishes were abundant, we gulped down wine as if it were water.' Before the Religious Wars, another witness noted, the 'village people (in France) were so rich and endowed with all possessions, their houses so well furnished, so well stocked with poultry and animals that they were noblemen'. Things had truly changed. Thenceforth cereals were at a premium. Their prices rose to such unduly high levels that there was no money for buying extras. Meat consumption diminished in the long term until about 1850, as we have said.

It was a strange regression. It is true that there were breathing spaces and exceptions. In Germany, for example, just after the Thirty Years War, livestock quickly built up its strength again in a land often empty of people; or in the important agricultural regions of Auge and Bessin (Normandy) when constantly rising meat prices and constantly falling corn prices between 1770 and 1780 led to the substitution of stock-raising for the cultivation of grain, at least until the great fodder crisis of 1785. This quite naturally resulted in unemployment, and a considerable mass of the small peasantry, then in the grip of a demographic growth with far-reaching consequences, was reduced to begging and vagabondage. But the respites did not last for long and the exceptions do not invalidate the rule. The craze, the obsession with tilling and corn, continued. The number of butchers in the small town of Montpezat in the Bas-Quercy steadily decreased: eighteen in 1550, ten in 1556; six in 1641; two in 1660; one in 1763. Even if its inhabitants also decreased during that period they did not decline in a ratio of eighteen to one.

Figures for Paris indicate an average annual consumption of between 50 and 60 kilograms of meat from 1751 to 1850. But Paris is Paris and these eighteenth-century figures are questionable. A calculation by Lavoisier at the beginning of the Revolution put average consumption in France at 46 pounds (each of 488 grams) or some 20 kilograms, and the figure still seems on the high side. Annual consumption in Hamburg (but the town is on the threshold of Denmark, a source of livestock supplies) in the eighteenth century was 60 kilograms of meat *per capita* – although it is true that this only included 20 kilograms of fresh meat.

With the modern period the advantage enjoyed by carnivorous Europe diminished. The real remedies did not appear before the middle of the nineteenth century as a result of the widespread creation of artificial meadows, the development of scientific stock-raising, and the exploitation of distant stock-raising areas in the New World. Europe remained hungry for a long time. The territory of Melun, covering 18,800 hectares in the Brie, consisted of 14,400 hectares of arable land in 1717 and an almost negligible 814 of meadow. And 'the farmers only keep what is absolutely indispensable for their agricultural needs', selling fodder at a good price in Paris (for the numerous horses in the capital). It is true that corn on the tilled land yielded twelve to seventeen quintals per hectare in a good harvest. This competition was an irresistible temptation.

.There were, as we have said, degrees of regression. It was more pronounced in the Mediterranean countries than in the northern regions, with their rich pasturage. Poles, Germans, Hungarians and English seem to have been less rationed than others. In England there was even a real revolution in meat in the eighteenth century within the agricultural revolution. A Spanish ambassador is said to have remarked about the great London market of Leadenhall (1778): 'More meat is sold in a month than is eaten in the whole of Spain during a year.' However, even in a country like Holland where 'official' rations were high (if not strictly apportioned), diet remained unbalanced before the improvements of the end of the eighteenth century: beans (perhaps not originating from America as was believed some time ago), a little salted meat, bread (made from barley or rye), fish, a small quantity of bacon, occasionally game. But game was normally for peasants or nobles. The town poor had barely heard of it; for them there were 'turnips, fried onions, dry if not mouldy bread' or sticky rye bread and 'small beer' (the 'double' was for the rich or for drunkards). The Dutch middle classes also lived frugally. The *hutsepot*, the national dish, did of course contain meat, either beef or mutton, but it was finely minced and always used sparingly. The evening meal was often only gruel made from left-over bread soaked in milk. Amongst doctors, 'the discussion opened at just the right time to find out if a meat diet was good or harmful'. 'As far as I am concerned,' Louis Lemery wrote (1702), 'without entering into all these arguments which seem to me pretty useless, I believe one can say that the use of animal flesh can be advisable, provided it is in moderation. ...'

Concomitant with the decrease in the meat ration, consumption of smoked and salted meat clearly increased. Werner Sombart spoke, not without justification, of a revolution in salting at the end of the fifteenth century to feed ships' companies at sea. But in the Mediterranean the role of salted fish and still more of the traditional biscuit as the basic menu for sailors on board ship remained unchanged, as it always has. The almost exclusive realm of salted beef (*vaca salada*) began at Cadiz, with the immense Atlantic, where it was supplied by the Spanish administration from the sixteenth century onwards. Salted beef came primarily from the north, particularly Ireland, which was also an exporter of salted butter. But the administration was not the only interested party. As meat proved a luxury, salted foods became the ordinary diet of the poor (which soon included the Black slaves in America). 'Salt beef was the standard winter dish' in England, in the absence of fresh food after the summer season. In Burgundy in the eighteenth century 'pork provides the greatest part of the meat consumed in the peasant's household. Few inventories do not mention a few portions of bacon in the salting tub. Fresh meat is a luxury reserved to convalescents, and moreover so expensive that one cannot always satisfy this requirement.' In Italy and Germany, sausage pedlars (*Wursthändler*) were part of the landscape of the towns. From Naples to Hamburg, from France to the vicinity of St Petersburg, salted beef and, still more, salted pork furnished the poor of Europe with their meagre meat ration.

There were probably exceptions here as well. In 1658 Mademoiselle de Montpensier tells us that peasants of the Dombes 'are well-dressed . . . [that they have not] paid taxes'. She adds: 'They eat meat four times a day.' The claim would need confirmation but is possible, as man's dietary condition varied from one region to another. There were peasants and peasants. And the Dombes remained a wild, unhealthy country in the seventeenth century. Now animals, domestic or not, are most plentiful precisely in countries still relatively untenanted by man. Thus it is probable that we twentieth-century men would have found the ordinary meal in Riga at the time of Peter the Great, or at Brusa in Anatolia 'where everything is good, bread, meat, fish and fruit' more satisfying than its equivalent in Berlin, Vienna or even Paris. We should recall one historian's remark that 'man is no poorer in many deprived countries than in wealthy countries', as the standard of living is a matter of the number of people and the total resources at their disposal.

Europe's privileged position

Europe remained in a privileged position, though less so. It is enough to compare it with other civilisations. 'In Japan,' said a Spaniard (1609), 'they only eat meat from game which they kill by hunting.' In India the population luckily had a horror of meat foods. The soldiers of the Great Mogul Aurenge-Zebe were very undemanding, according to a French doctor: 'Provided they have their *kicheris* or a mixture of rice and other vegetables over which they pour browned butter . . . they are content.' This mixture was actually made of 'cooked rice, beans and lentils mashed up together'.

In China meat was extremely rare. A small amount of fish, which even a Chinaman of rank ate without cleaning, sometimes supplemented the daily meal of rice cooked in water. Father de Las Cortes describes how one day during his forced stay in 1626 he 'put the small fish heads [he found in his bowl of rice] on one side and got ready to give them to the dog; the master of the house forestalled me and lifted them out of my bowl on the ends of his sticks in order to eat them himself'. There was no meat and almost no slaughtered animals. The domestic pig (fed on scraps from the table and sometimes a little rice), poultry, game, even dogs offered for sale in special butchers' shops or on doorsteps 'skinned or half cooked', or carried in crates like suckling pigs or young goats in Spain: all these animals did not add up to a very significant total and could not have satisfied the appetite of a determinedly carnivorous population.

Even the rich mandarins 'nibble a few mouthfuls of pork or chicken or whatever meat is placed on their tables as if to whet their appetites. For however rich and great they are, the meat they eat is infinitesimal in quantity and,' concluded Father de Las Cortes, 'if they did eat it as we Europeans do, all the types of meat they possess would not in any way suffice to assure them of such a diet: the fertility of their China would not stand up to it.' A Neapolitan who crossed China from Canton to Peking and back in 1696 was infuriated by the vegetable foods, in his opinion badly cooked, and whenever he could, bought chickens or eggs, pheasants, hares, ham, or partridges from his lodgings or markets. On his return from Peking he even noted 'there would have been the wherewithal to provide good fare at the inns; but the fact that the Chinese do not want to spend more than the normal price means that the host only serves up bad pork and spoiled chicken, stinking meat'. In about 1735 a European observer concluded: 'The Chinese eat very little butcher's meat.' He added: 'They therefore need less land to feed animals.' A correspondence between Jesuits sums up the situation (1779): 'Proportionately speaking, there are at least ten oxen in France for every one in China.'

The evidence of Chinese literature testifies to the same thing. In Ming times a proud father-in-law confides: 'The other day my son-in-law came bringing me two pounds of dried meat here on this dish.' A butcher is full of admiration for a high personage 'who had more money than the Emperor himself' and whose house harboured scores of relatives and servants. Irrefutable proof of his wealth: he 'buys 4000 to 5000 pounds of meat during the year!' The complete menu for one feast consisted of 'swallows' nests, chicken, duck, cuttlefish, and bitter cucumbers from Kwang Tung . . .' And there was no end to the dietary requirements of one young and capricious widow: eight *yen* of medicaments daily, duck one day, fish the next, fresh vegetables and soup made of bamboo shoots on another occasion, or again oranges, biscuits, water-lilies, fruit, salted crawfish and, naturally, wine. . . . The only accumulation of meat in China was in front of the Emperor's palace at Peking, and here again it only consisted of masses of game, sent from Tartary and preserved by the cold winter weather in 'rows as long as the range of one or two musket shots' (1688).

The same moderation and frugality existed in Turkey where dried beef, *pasterme*, was not only food for soldiers in the field. Apart from the enormous consumption of mutton in the Seraglio, the average in

Istanbul from the sixteenth to the eighteenth century was about one sheep or a third of a sheep per person per year. And Istanbul was well off. In Egypt, which seems at first glance the granary of plenty, 'the way the Turks live,' said a traveller in 1693, 'is one continual penance. The meals, even of the richest, are composed of bad bread, garlic, onion and sour cheese; when they add boiled mutton it is a great feast for them. They never eat chicken or other fowl, although they are cheap in that country.'

If the Europeans' privilege was in the process of diminishing on their own continent, it was making a fresh start for some of them elsewhere with the abundance of a new middle ages. This was the case both in the European East – in Hungary for example – and in colonial America, in Mexico, Brazil (in the São Francisco valley which was invaded by wild herds and where a thriving civilisation based on meat was established to the advantage of Whites and halfbreeds), more still southwards, around Montevideo and Buenos Aires, where horsemen would kill a wild animal for just one meal. Such massacres did not cancel out the improbably rapid increase in free livestock in Argentina, but they did in the north of Chile. All that survived around Coquimbo at the end of the sixteenth century were dogs who had returned to the wild state.

Meat dried in the sun (the *carne do sol* of Brazil) was readily available to coastal towns and the Black slaves on the plantations. *Charque*, boned and dried meat produced in the *saladeros* of Argentina (once again intended for slaves and the European poor), was to all practical purposes invented at the beginning of the nineteenth century. A delicate traveller was doomed to eat nothing but 'slices of cows and buffalos dried in the sun ...' on the galleon from Manila to Acapulco, at the end of the seven or eight months of the interminable journey (1696). They 'are so hard that one cannot chew them without beating them thoroughly with a piece of wood, from which they do not greatly differ, nor digest them without a strong purgative'. The worms swarming in this awful food were a further source of disgust. But carnivorous necessity obviously knew few laws. Thus despite a certain repugnance the filibusters of the West Indies, like the Africans, killed and ate monkeys (preferably young ones); unfortunates and poor Jews in Rome bought buffalo meat, sold in special butchers' shops and viewed with horror by the majority. Oxen were not killed and eaten in Aix-en-Provence until around 1690 because meat of that sort had long been reputed to be unhealthy.

The extravagances of the table

After the fifteenth and sixteenth centuries only a few privileged people in Europe ate luxuriously. They consumed huge quantities of rare dishes. What was left went to their servants, and what was left after that was sold to food-dealers, even if it had gone rotten. Typical of such extravagance was the transport of a turtle to Paris from London; 'this is a dish (1782) which costs a thousand écus; seven or eight gluttons can gorge themselves on it'. By comparison wild boar grilled over a fire seems commonplace. 'Yes,' the same witness tells us, 'I saw it on the gridiron with my own eyes; St Lawrence's boar was not bigger. It was surrounded with live coals, larded with *foie gras*, flamed with fine fats, flooded with the fullest-flavoured wines, and served in one piece with its head . . .' The guests then barely sampled the various quarters of the animal. These were the whims of princes. For the king and the wealthy houses, the caterers filled their baskets with the best of the meat, game and fish on the market. Smaller fry were sold low-quality cuts and at higher prices than the rich paid. What is worse, this merchandise was generally adulterated. 'The butchers of Paris on the eve of the Revolution were supplying the large houses with the best of the beef; they sold the people the worst and even then added bones, which were ironically called *réjouissances* (a *double-entendre* which meant either rejoicings or make-weights).' The very worst pieces, which the poor ate, were sold outside butchers' shops.

Hazel grouse and ortolans were other rare dishes. Some sixteen thousand *livres*' worth of these birds were consumed at the Princess of Conti's wedding (1680). The ortolan, a bird of the vineyard, abounded in Cyprus (from where it was exported to Venice preserved in vinegar in the sixteenth century); it was also found in Italy, Provence and Languedoc. There were also green oysters, and new oysters from Dieppe or Cancale which arrived in October, and strawberries and pineapples grown in greenhouses in the Paris region. The rich also indulged in elaborate – often over-elaborate – sauces, which mingled all conceivable ingredients: pepper, spices, almonds, amber, musk, rose water . . . And let us not forget the costly cooks from Languedoc, the best in Paris, who sold their services at enormous prices. If the poor wanted to participate in these feasts they had to get in with the servants or go to the *regrat* at Versailles where left-overs from the royal table were sold. A quarter of the town fed on them without any compunction. 'Someone enters, sword at side, and buys a turbot and a head of salmon, a rare and delicate morsel.' He might have done better to have gone to an eating house in the Rue de la Huchette in the Latin Quarter, or to the Quai de la Vallée (the quay for poultry and game), and treated himself to a capon *au gros sel* fished out of 'the ever-ready pot' hanging from a wide pot-hanger, where it would be boiling with a mass of other capons. He could eat it piping hot at home, 'or four steps away, washing it down with a Burgundy wine'.

Laying the table

Table luxury also included crockery, silver, tablecloths, napkins, lighted candles and the whole setting of the dining-room. It was customary in Paris in the sixteenth century to rent a beautiful house, or better still gain admittance to one through the paid collusion of the caretaker. The caterer would then deliver the dishes for the temporary host to entertain his friends. Sometimes he settled in until the real owner dislodged him. 'In my time,' said an ambassador (1557), 'Mgr Salviati, the Papal Nuncio, was forced to move house three times in two months.'

There were sumptuous inns as well as sumptuous houses. At Châlons (sur-Marne), 'we lodged at *La Couronne*,' Montaigne noted (1580), 'which is a beautiful hostelry and serves one on silver plates'. It must have posed quite a problem to lay a table for 'a company of thirty persons of high estate whom you want to entertain lavishly'. The answer is given in a cookery book with an unexpected title, *Les Loisirs des campagnes* (The Leisures of the Countryside) by Nicolas de Bonnefons, published in about 1650. The answer: lay fourteen places on one side, fourteen on the other and, as the table is rectangular, one person at the 'top end' plus 'one or two at the bottom'. The guests will be 'the space of a chair apart'. 'The tablecloth (must) reach to the ground on all sides. There will be several salt pots and table mats in the centre for the extra dishes.' The meal will have eight courses, the eighth and last, by way of example, being composed of 'dry or liquid' jams, crystallised sweets, musk pastilles, sugared almonds from Verdun, musky and amber-scented sugar . . .' The maître d'hôtel, sword at side, will order the plates to be changed 'at least at every course and the napkins at every two'. But this careful description, which even specifies the way the dishes will be 'rotated' on the table at each course, omits to say how the table should be laid for each guest. At this period he would certainly be given a plate, spoon and knife, less certainly an individual fork, and glass and bottle were certainly not placed in front of him. The rules of propriety remain uncertain; the author recommends a deep plate for soup as an elegance, so that the guests could serve themselves with all they wanted at one time 'without having to take spoonful after spoonful from the dish, because of the dislike some might have for others'.

A table laid in the modern way and our present table manners are the result of many details that custom has imposed slowly, one by one, and in ways that vary according to region. Spoon and knife are fairly old customs. However the use of a spoon did not become widespread until the sixteenth century, and the same is true of the custom of providing knives – before that the guests brought along their own – and putting an individual glass in front of each person. Courtesy formerly dictated that he emptied the glass and passed it on to his neighbour, who did the same. Or else, when requested, the manservant brought the required drink, wine or water, from the pantry or the dresser near the guest table. When Montaigne crossed southern Germany in 1580 he noted that 'everyone has his goblet or silver cup at his place; the man serving takes care to refill this goblet immediately it is empty, without moving it from its place, pouring wine therein from a distance away out of a tin or wooden vessel with a long spout'. This elegant solution economised on the effort demanded of the staff, but it required every guest to have a personal goblet in front of him. In Germany in Montaigne's time every guest also had his own plate, either tin or wooden; sometimes a wooden bowl underneath and a tin plate on top. We have proof that wooden plates continued to be used in some places in the German countryside, and probably elsewhere, until the nineteenth century.

But for a long time before these more or less tardy refinements guests were satisfied with a wooden board or 'trencher', a slice of bread on which the meat was placed. The large dish then sufficed for everything and everybody: everyone selected the morsel they wanted and picked it up with their fingers. Montaigne noted that the Swiss 'use as many wooden spoons with silver handles as there are people [note that each guest had his own spoon] and a Swiss is never without a knife, with which he takes everything; and he scarcely ever puts his hand in the dish'. Wooden spoons with metal handles (not necessarily silver) are preserved in museums, together with various types of knife. But these were old implements.

This is not the case with forks. The very large fork with two prongs, used to serve meat to the guests and to manipulate it on the stove or in the kitchen, is probably old, but not the individual fork, despite some exceptions.

The individual fork dates from about the sixteenth century and spread from Venice, from Italy in general and probably Spain. In any case its diffusion was slow. Montaigne did not use it. He accuses himself of eating too fast, so fast that 'I sometimes bite my fingers in my haste'. Félix Platter mentions it in Basle, early on, in about 1590, and was surprised not to see it in use when he was a student at Montpellier. An English traveller in 1608 discovered it in Italy, found it amusing and then adopted it, incurring the mockery of his friends who christened him *forciferus*, fork-carrier. Could the use of ruffs have obliged wealthy guests to use forks? It is unlikely. For example in England no forks appeared in inventories before 1660. Their use only became general in about 1750. Anne of Austria can therefore be pardoned for her life-long habit of plunging her fingers into the dishes of meat. The Viennese court did the same until 1651. This accounts for the numerous napkins presented to the guests, although the custom only spread to private life in Montaigne's time as he himself tells us. It also explains the custom of hand-washing with ewer and bowl, repeated several times during a meal.

The slow adoption of good manners

Taken as a whole these changes, representing a new code of behaviour, were adopted gradually. Even the luxury of a room used solely for meals only became current in France with the sixteenth century, and then only among the rich. Before then the nobleman ate in his vast kitchen.

The whole ceremonial of the meal meant large numbers of servants in the kitchen and around the guests, and not only at Versailles where the *Grand* and *Petit Commun* were mobilised for the meal or 'the King's meat', as it was called. All this new luxury only reached the whole of France or England with the eighteenth century. 'If people who died sixty years ago came back,' wrote Duclos in about 1765, 'they would not recognise Paris as far as its tables, costumes and customs are concerned.' The same was probably true of all Europe, in the grip of an omnipresent luxury, and also of its colonies where it had always tried to establish its own customs. Hence Western travellers thought even less of the customs and habits of the wide world and looked down on them more than ever.

Gemelli Careri was surprised when his host, a Persian, almost a nobleman, received him at his table (1694) and used 'his right hand instead of a spoon to pick up rice so as to put it on the plate (of his guests)'. Or read what Father Labat (1728) has to say about the Arabs in Senegal: 'They do not know what it is to eat off tables . . .' No one found favour with these fastidious arbiters except the refined Chinese, seated at their tables with their glazed bowls, and carrying the knives and sticks they used for eating in a case in the belts of their gowns.

However, an Austrian ordinance of 1624 for the landgraviate of Alsace still laid down for the use of young officers the rules to be observed when invited to an archduke's table: to present themselves in clean uniform, not to arrive half drunk, not to drink after every mouthful, to wipe moustache and mouth clean before drinking, not to lick the fingers, not to spit in the plate, not to wipe the nose on the tablecloth, not to gulp drink like animals . . . Such instructions make the reader wonder at the state of manners in Richelieu's Europe.

At the table of Christ

Nothing is more instructive on these journeys into the past than the pictures painted before these late refinements. Pictures representing the meals of the past are innumerable – particularly Christ's last meal, the Last Supper, depicted thousands of times ever since there have been painters in the West; or Christ's meal with Simon, the wedding at Cana, the table of the pilgrims of Emmaus. If we ignore the figures for the moment and only look at the tables, the embroidered tablecloths, the seats (stools, chairs, benches), and above all the plates, dishes and knives, we can see that no fork was included before 1600 and almost no spoons either. Instead of plates there are slices of bread, round or oval pieces of wood or slightly hollow tin discs – they are the spots of blue which appear on the majority of south German tables. The trencher of stale bread, often placed on a wooden or metal slab, was intended 'to soak up the juice from the carved joint'. This bread plate was then distributed to the poor. There is always at least one knife – sometimes extra large when it is the only one available and has to serve for all the guests – and often small individual knives. Of course, the wine, bread and lamb are in evidence at the mystic gathering. And of course the Last Supper is not a lavish or luxurious meal; the event transcends earthly sustenance. None the less, Christ and his apostles eat like Ulm or Augsburg bourgeois; for the scene is almost the same whether it represents the marriage at Cana, Herod's feast, or the meals served to some master of Basle, surrounded by family and attentive servants, or the Nuremburg practitioner painted with his friends at his house-warming in 1593. As far as we know, Jacopo Bassano (1599) painted one of the first forks to figure in a Last Supper.

Everyday foods: salt

It is time to pass on to the everyday. Salt calls us to order very effectively because this ultra-common commodity was the subject of a universal and necessary trade. It was indispensable to people and animals and for preserving meat and fish – and all the more important as governments had an interest in it. It was a great source of wealth to states and merchants, in Europe and China alike. We will return to that point. Being a necessity, the trade overcame all obstacles and exploited all facilities. As a heavy material it utilised riverways (going up the Rhône for instance) and shipping in the Atlantic. Not a single rock salt mine remained unexploited. Protest-ant fishermen of the north had to fetch their salt from Brouage, Setubal or San Lucar de Barrameda because the salt-pans on the Mediterranean and Atlantic were all in sunny lands, Catholic countries. The trade was always carried on, despite wars, and to the great profit of vast consortia of merchants. Slabs of salt from the Sahara reached Black Africa by caravans of camels, despite the desert, and were exchanged for gold dust, ivory from elephants' tusks or black slaves. Nothing is more indicative of the irrepressible demands of this trade.

The small Swiss canton of Valais demonstrates the same thing in terms of economy and distances to be covered. Resources and population in these lands flanking the upper Rhône valley were in perfect balance, except for iron and salt – particularly salt, which the inhabitants needed for stock-raising, cheeses and salting. Salt had to cover great distances to reach these Alpine cantons: it came from Peccais (Languedoc) 870 kilometres away, via Lyons; from Barletta, 1300 kilometres away, via Venice; and, also via Venice, from Trapani, 2300 kilometres away.

Essential, irreplaceable, salt was a sacred food ('salted food is synonymous with holy food both in ancient Hebrew and the current Malagasy language'). In the Europe of insipid farinaceous gruels consumption of salt was large (twenty grams daily per person, double the present figure). One doctor historian even thinks that the peasant uprisings against the *gabelle*, the salt tax, in western France in the sixteenth century, can be explained by a hunger for salt which the tax thwarted. Furthermore an odd detail here and there informs us – or fortuitously reminds us – of numerous uses of salt which are not immediately obvious: for example, for making botargo in Provence or for domestic preserving which spread in the eighteenth century: asparagus, fresh peas, mushrooms, morels, artichoke hearts and so on.

Everyday foods: milk products, fats, eggs

Nor does luxury come into the realm of cheeses, eggs, milk and butter. Cheeses arrived in Paris from Champagne and Brie ('the Angelot cheeses') and were often bought from *regrattiers*, those all-purpose retail merchants in touch with convents and the neighbouring countryside. Cheese from Montreuil and Vincennes was sold there 'freshly curdled and drained, in little baskets woven from wicker or rushes', *jonchées*. In the Mediterranean, Sardinian cheeses, *formaggio cacio* or *salso*, were exported everywhere – to Naples, Rome, Leghorn, Marseilles and Barcelona. They left Cagliari in boat-loads and sold even more cheaply than the cheeses from Holland, which were invading the markets of Europe and the whole world by the eighteenth century. As early as 1572 thousands of Dutch cheeses were unlawfully reaching Spanish America. Cheeses from Dalmatia and enormous wheels of cheese from Candia were sold in Venice. Cheese consumed in Marseilles in 1543 included some from the Auvergne, where it was so plentiful that it formed the principal basis of diet in the sixteenth century. In the previous century 'cheese from the Grande-Chartreuse in Dauphiné ... was considered excellent and was used to make *fondues* and cheese on toast'. Large quantities of Swiss gruyère were consumed before the eighteenth century: 'It comes from a place situated in the canton of Fribourg and is imitated in the mountains and valleys of Franche-Comté so well that you cannot tell one from the other.'

Cheese, a source of cheap protein, was one of the great foods of the people in Europe, greatly missed by any European forced to live far away and unable to get it. French peasants made fortunes in about 1698 by carrying cheeses to the armies fighting in Italy and Germany. Nevertheless, particularly in France, cheese had not yet won its great reputation. Cookery books gave it only a small place, describing neither its qualities nor its individual names. Goats' cheese was scorned and considered inferior to cows' or ewes'. As late as 1702 a doctor recognised only three great cheeses: 'Roquefort, Parmesan and those from Sassenage in Dauphiné ... served at the most refined tables.' Roquefort at that time recorded a sale of over 6000 quintals every year. Sassenage was a mixture of cows', goats' and ewes' milk, boiled together. Parmesan (like the 'marsolin' of Florence which later went out of fashion) had been an acquisition of the Italian wars, after the return of Charles VIII.

Mention must be made of the great place these humble but vital foodstuffs — milk, butter, cheese — occupied throughout Islam as far as the Indies. A traveller noted in 1694 that the Persians spent little; they 'are satisfied with a little cheese and sour milk in which they soak the local bread, which is as thin as a wafer, tasteless and very brown; in the morning they add rice to this (or pilau) sometimes only cooked with water'. But pilau, often a stew with rice, distinguished the tables of the comfortably-off. In Turkey milk products were almost the sole food of the poor: sour milk (yoghourt) accompanied 'in the summer months by cucumbers or melons ... an onion, a leek ... or stewed dried fruit'. Along with yoghourt, mention must also be made of *kaymak*, a slightly boiled cream, and the cheeses preserved in leather bottles (*tulum*), in wheels (*tekerlek*), or in balls, like the famous *cascaval* which the Wallachian mountain-dwellers exported to Istanbul and even to Italy. This was a cheese made of ewes' milk subjected to repeated boiling, like *cacio cavallo* in Sardinia and Italy.

But the vast and persistent exception of China in the East must not be forgotten. China remained deliberately ignorant of milk, cheese and butter. Cows, goats and sheep were raised purely for meat. So what was the 'butter' Gemelli Careri thought he was eating? Japan shared China's repugnance on this score. Even in villages where oxen and cows are used to work the land the Japanese peasant still does not eat dairy products and thinks them 'un-wholesome'; he draws the small quantities of oil he requires from soya.

Milk was consumed in such large quantities in the towns of the West that problems of supply appeared very early on. In London consumption increased every winter, when all the wealthy families moved to the capital; it decreased in summer for the opposite reason. But, winter or summer, it was the subject of gigantic fraud. Milk was watered on a wide scale by dairy farmers and retailers.

There was 'a large landowner in Surrey [1801] who has a pump [in his dairy farm] which is known as the black cow, because it is painted in that colour, and he makes sure that it supplies more milk than all the cows put together'. Let us pass on to the daily scene in Valladolid a century earlier, when over four hundred asses thronged the streets bringing milk from the neighbouring countryside and supplying the town with curd cheeses, butter and cream. A Portuguese traveller praised the quality and cheapness of these products. Everything was plentiful in Valladolid, a capital which Philip III was soon to abandon for Madrid. Over seven thousand birds were sold daily on the poultry market; the mutton there was the best in the world, the bread excellent, the wine perfect. But its supply of milk products was particularly unusual for Spain.

Butter remained limited to Northern Europe, except for the immense zones of rancid butter from northern Africa to Alexandria in Egypt and beyond. The remainder of the continent used pork fat, lard and olive oil. France epitomises this geographical division of culinary resources. A veritable river of butter flowed through the lands of the Loire, in Paris and beyond. 'Practically no sauce is made without it in France,' said Louis Lemery (1702). 'The Dutch and the northern peoples use it even more than we do and it is claimed that it contributes to the freshness of their complexion.' Actually the use of butter did not really spread until the eighteenth century, even in Holland. It characterised the cooking of the rich. It distressed Mediterranean people when they were obliged to live in or cross these strange countries; they thought that butter increased the number of lepers. The wealthy cardinal of Aragon was careful to take his own cook when he travelled to the Netherlands in 1516, and carried a sufficient quantity of olive oil in his luggage.

Eighteenth-century Paris, so well set in its comforts, had an ample supply of butter at its disposal – fresh, salted (from Ireland and Brittany), and even clarified in the Lorraine manner. A good part of its fresh butter arrived from Gournay, a small town near Dieppe where merchants received the butter unrefined and then kneaded it again in order to eliminate the whey it still contained. 'They then make it into large blocks, of between forty and sixty pounds, and send it to Paris.' As snobbery is always with us, according to the *Dictionnaire Sentencieux* (1778) 'there are only two types of butter which the fashionable world dares mention: butter from Vanvre [*sic*] and butter from the Frévalais', in the vicinity of Paris.

Eggs were widely eaten. Doctors repeated the old precepts of the

Salerno School – let them be eaten fresh and not overcooked: *Si sumas ovum, molle sit atque novum.* And there were numerous recipes for keeping eggs fresh. Their market price is a valuable indicator: eggs were a cheap commodity and their price accurately followed the fluctuations of the economic situation. A statistician can reconstruct the movement of the cost of living in the sixteenth century from a few eggs sold in Florence. Their price alone is a valid measure of the standard of living or the value of money in any given town in any given country. At one time in seventeenth-century Egypt 'one had the choice of thirty eggs, two pigeons or one fowl for a sou'; on the road from Magnesia to Brusa (1694) 'provisions are not dear: seven eggs can be bought for one *para* (one sou), a fowl for ten, a good winter melon for two, and as much bread as you can eat in a day for the same price'. In February 1697 the same traveller, this time near Acapulco in New Spain, noted: 'The innkeeper made me pay a piece of eight (thirty-two sous) for a fowl, and eggs were one sou each.' Eggs were thus superabundant everywhere. Montaigne's surprise in the German inns was therefore understandable: they never served eggs there, he wrote, 'except hard, cut into quarters in salads'. There were greater surprises to come. Montesquieu, leaving Naples and returning to Rome (1729), was astonished 'that in this ancient Latium the traveller finds neither a chicken nor a young pigeon, nor often an egg'.

But in Europe these were exceptions and not the rule that applied to the vegetarian Far East, where China, Japan and India never made use of this rich and commonplace item of diet. Eggs were very rare there and formed scarcely any part of the food of the people. The famous Chinese ducks' eggs, preserved in pickling brine for thirty days, were a delicacy of the rich.

Everyday seafoods

The sea was enormously important. It could have been even more so. Vast regions were barely aware of its foods, however accessible they were.

This was more or less the case in the New World, despite the huge shoals in the fishing grounds of the Caribbean where boats often made miraculous hauls on the way to Vera Cruz; despite the great wealth of the coasts and banks of Newfoundland, which supplied food almost exclusively to Europe (although barrels of cod reached the eighteenth-century English colonies and the American plantations in the southern states); despite the salmon that swam up the cold rivers of Canada and Alaska; despite the resources of the Bay of Bahia where an influx of cold waters from the south made whale-hunting possible and accounts for the presence of Basque harpooners as early as the seventeenth century. In Asia only Japan and southern China from the mouth of the Yang-tse-Kiang to the island of Hainan went in for fishing. Elsewhere it would seem that only a few boats, as in Malaysia or around Ceylon, were so engaged – if we except some oddities like the pearl fishermen in the Persian Gulf, near Bandar Abass (1694) who 'preferred their sardines (dried in the sun) to the pearls the merchants bought, as more reliable and easier to fish'.

In China where fresh-water fishing and fish-breeding yielded large profits (sturgeon were caught in the lakes of the Yang-tse-Kiang and in the Pei Ho), fish was often preserved in the form of a sauce obtained by spontaneous fermentation, as in Tonkin. But even today consumption there is insignificant (0·6 kilograms per person per year). The sea does not manage to penetrate the continental mass. Only Japan was widely fish-eating. It has kept this characteristic and today is on a par with carnivorous Europe (forty kilograms per person per year and the leading fishing fleet in the world after Peru). The abundance comes from the richness of its internal sea, and still more from the proximity of the Yeso and Sakhaline fisheries, at the meeting point of enormous masses of cold waters from Oya Shivo and warm waters from Kouro-chivo – just as Newfoundland is at the confluence of the Gulf Stream and the Labrador current in the north Atlantic. The meeting of plankton from hot and cold waters helps the rapid breeding of fish.

Europe is not so well provided for but it has many sources of supply at short and long range. Fish was all the more important here as religious rulings multiplied the number of fast days: 166 days, including Lent, observed extremely strictly until the reign of Louis XIV. Meat, eggs and poultry could not be sold during those forty days except to invalids and with a double certificate from doctor and priest. To facilitate control the 'Lent butcher' was the only person authorised to sell prohibited foods at that time in Paris, and only inside the area of the Hôtel Dieu. This led to a huge demand for fresh, smoked and salted fish.

However, fish was not always plentiful around the coasts of Europe. The much-vaunted Mediterranean had only limited resources – tunny from the Bosporus, caviar from the Russian rivers (choice food for Christian fasts as far afield as Abyssinia), dried squids and octopus, always a providential food for the Greek archipelago. Tunny was also trapped in the madragues of North Africa, Sicily, Andalusia and the Portuguese Algarve. Lagos was a great shipping point for whole boat-loads of barrels of tunny bound for the Mediterranean and the north. And there were limited resources, such as tunny, sardines and anchovies, on the coast of Provence.

By comparison, the resources of those narrow northerly inland seas – the Channel, North Sea and Baltic – and even more those of the Atlantic, were superabundant. The Atlantic coasts of Europe were the scene of lively fishing expeditions in the middle ages (salmon, mackerel, cod). The Baltic and North Sea have been centres of large herring fisheries since the eleventh century; they were the making of the Hanse and then of fishermen from Holland and Zealand. A Dutchman, William Benkelszoor, is said to have discovered in about 1375 the rapid method of gutting herrings and salting them on the boat where the fishermen could barrel them immediately. But some authors think that barrelling was only perfected in about 1447. Curiously enough, the herring left the Baltic in 1473. Thenceforth boats from Holland and Zealand fished on the barely covered sands of the Dogger Bank and in the open sea off the English and Scottish coasts, as far as the Orkneys. Other fleets gathered at these rich grounds. In the sixteenth century, at the height of the conflicts between Valois and Hapsburgs, herring truces were duly concluded to ensure Europe's continued supplies.

Herrings were exported to western and southern Europe by sea, along rivers, by carriage and by pack animals. Bloaters and red and white herrings arrived in Venice: white herrings were salted, the red were smoked, and bloaters had been bloated, that is slightly smoked and slightly salted. The *chasse-marées*, carriers of fresh sea fish, could often be seen hurrying towards large towns like Paris – poor fellows urging on wretched horses weighed down with fish and oysters. Their cry: 'Herrings fresh last night' can be heard in *Les cris de Paris* by the musician Janequin. In London, eating a barrel of oysters with wife and friends was a minor luxury and one the young and economical Samuel Pepys could treat himself to.

But sea fishing was hardly sufficient to satisfy Europe's hunger. Recourse to fresh-water fish becomes more and more essential as we move farther away from sea coasts, towards the central and eastern continental lands.

No river, no stream, not even the Seine at Paris, was without its authorised fishermen. The distant Volga was a colossal reserve. The Loire was famous for salmon and carp; the Rhine for perch. A Portuguese traveller to Valladolid in the first years of the seventeenth century found supplies of sea fish rather deficient and not always of high quality, in view of the time they took to reach the city. There were sole, *escabèches* of sardines and oysters, and sometimes coalfish, all the year round; and excellent dorado came from Santander during Lent. But our traveller was startled by the unbelievable number of magnificent trout coming from Burgos and Medina de Rioseco and sold daily on the markets, sometimes so many that half the town could be fed on them. Artificial ponds and the fish-breeding on the large estates in the south of Bohemia have already been mentioned. The general consumption of carp was a distinctive feature of Germany. During the period of high prices in 1817 observers mentioned the price of carp amongst other prices as a measure of the rise.

Cod fishing

Thus it was a true revolution when, as early as the end of the fifteenth century, the large-scale exploitation of cod began on the Newfoundland banks. It provoked a scuffle between Basques, French, Dutch and English, the strongest driving out the less protected. The Spanish Basques were eliminated and access to the fishing grounds remained in the hands of the powers with the strongest navies: England and France.

The great problem was how to preserve and transport the fish. The cod was either prepared and salted on board the Newfoundland boat, or dried on land. Salted cod was the 'green cod' 'which has just been salted and is still all wet'. Boats specialising in green cod were of light tonnage with ten or twelve fishermen on board, plus sailors who cut, cleaned and salted the fish in the hold – often full to the beams of the bridge. Their practice was to drift with the tide once they had 'embanked' (arrived on the Newfoundland banks). On the other hand, quite large sailing ships were used to bring back dried or dressed cod. They dropped anchor when they arrived off the coast of Newfoundland and the fishing expedition was continued in boats. The fish was dried on land by complicated processes.

Every sailing ship, whatever sort of cod it carried, had to be 'victualled' before it set out — to take on board salt, naval stores, flour, wine, alcohol, lines and fish-hooks. Fishermen from Norway and Denmark still went to San Lucar de Barrameda near Seville at the beginning of the seventeenth century to obtain a type of salt of unequalled quality for preserving fish. Naturally the merchants advanced it to them; the borrowers had to pay it back in fish when they returned from America.

This was the custom at La Rochelle during its period of prosperity in the sixteenth and seventeenth centuries. Numerous sailing ships, often of a hundred tons because quite large holds were required ('Cod is bulky rather than heavy'), put into port there every spring. They had twenty to twenty-five men on board, which shows the importance of manpower in this thankless job. The 'bourgeois victualler' advanced the owner flour, tools, drink and salt, according to the terms of a 'charter-party', legalised by a notary. Near La Rochelle, the little port of Olonne alone equipped up to a hundred sailing ships and sent several thousand men to the other side of the Atlantic every year. As the town numbered 3000 inhabitants the owners had to engage sailors from as far afield as Spain. In any case once the boats had left, the money the bourgeois had advanced 'on bottomry' floated at the whims of the fish and the sea. No repayment would be made until the return, after June. Furthermore a valuable bonus awaited the first boats to put in. The race was usually won by a native of Olonne. The victorious skipper was assailed in his inn by the bourgeois amidst arguments, brawls and solicitations. It was a singularly profitable victory. Everyone would be waiting for the new fish. Our man of Olonne then sold the 'little hundred' cod (110 to the 100 according to custom) at up to 60 livres, while the 'thousand' a few days later sold for no more than 30 livres.

The fishing here was inexhaustible. Cod on the immense, scarcely-covered undersea mountain of the great Newfoundland bank were as numerous 'without exaggeration ... as the grains of sand covering the bank'. 'It is God who gives us cod in Newfoundland,' wrote a native of Marseilles in 1739. A century earlier a French traveller had already explained: 'One can truly say that the best trade in Europe is to go and fish cod because it costs nothing [he meant by this no cash outlay, which is both true and false] to have the aforesaid cod, except the effort of fishing and selling; you make good Spanish coin out of it and a million men live on it in France.' The last figure is obviously inflated. But 500 boats and possibly 10,000 fishermen are not excessive estimates for France alone in the eighteenth century, and there were also their families and the middlemen. At the end of this century cod represented 60% of the tonnage of the French fishing fleet, 45% of its crews and 45% of its income. The figure of 1500 vessels and 25,000 to 30,000 sailors might perhaps be obtained for all Europe in the eighteenth century, with the addition of American fishermen from Boston, and including boats fishing off the coasts of Iceland, the Orkneys, Norway, Lapland and in the open sea off Heligoland. If we calculate at a rate of 100 tons of fish per boat we arrive at 150,000 tons of foodstuff at the lowest estimate. It is true that many boats did not carry 100 tons and that those, like the Olonne fleet, which left in December and succeeded in making two journeys and having two seasons were rare. The risk was of bad weather forcing them to 'disembank' hurriedly at some time. By way of comparison, the Dutch fishing fleet in 1750 (standing at 86,000 tons) numbered 1000 boats and brought back 175,000 tons of fish from two fishing seasons, primarily herrings, sardines, mackerel, and cod preserved in barrels (300 cod-fishing boats at the most in 1699).

The correspondence of a Honfleur merchant (a contemporary of Colbert) acquaints us with the requisite distinctions in quality: 'gaff' cod, which was exceptionally large, and 'merchant', ling and codling, small green cod, which were however still better than the rejects – the enormous mass of 'spoilt' goods, either salted too much or too little, or damaged by the stackers' heels. As green cod was sold in pieces and not by weight (like dried cod), sorters able to distinguish between merchandise at a single glance and to gauge quantities had to be employed. One of the problems facing these cod merchants was to prevent the arrival on the Honfleur market of herrings from Holland (subjected to stiff duties) and even more, herrings caught at banned periods, particularly after Christmas, by a few wretched fishermen from Normandy. The fish at that time of year was not good quality, and as it was caught in quantity, sold at low prices: 'As soon as this herring appears, it is difficult to sell a cod's tail.' Whence arose the royal prohibition which the honest cod fishermen approved.

Every port specialised in a type of fish, depending on the preferences of the zone it supplied. Dieppe, Le Havre and Honfleur supplied Paris, which ate green cod; Nantes supplied the varied tastes of the Loire region; Marseilles absorbed half the French catch of dried cod on an average but re-exported part of it to Italy. Numerous vessels from Saint Malo also sailed directly to Italian ports, notably Genoa, from the seventeenth century.

Much is known about the way Paris was supplied with green (or, as it is still called, white) cod. The first fishing fleets (leaving in January, returning in July), and then the second (leaving in March, returning in November and December), led to two lots of supplies, the first small, the second more abundant but exhausted by about April. There followed a shortage which lasted for three months – April, May, June – and affected the whole of France. And 'moreover this is a season when vegetables are still scarce, eggs dear and little fresh-water fish is eaten'. Hence the sudden value and high price of the green cod which the English fished off their own coasts and which was redistributed to Paris through the port of Dieppe, a mere intermediary on this occasion.

Nearly all the fleets suspended their fishing operations during the great maritime quarrels for world domination: wars of succession in Spain and Austria, the Seven Years War, the War of American Independence. Only the strongest powers continued to enjoy their cod.

A gradual increase in the catch is perceptible, though not calculable; and there was certainly a rise in average tonnage, although barely any change in the duration of the round trip (a month to six weeks). The miracle of Newfoundland was the continual reconstitution and superabundance of supplies. The banks of cod fed on plankton and were also particularly fond of whiting, driving them out of Newfoundland waters and towards the coasts of Europe where fishermen caught them. It would even seem that cod was numerous on the coasts of Europe in the middle ages. Later it would have moved westwards.

Europe jumped at this proffered food; it was a godsend, especially for the poor. Cod was 'a foodstuff abandoned to the working classes' said one sixteenth-century author. The same applied to the flesh and fat of whales, which were very much coarser (except for the relatively esteemed tongue) but still eaten by the poor during Lent until the time when the fat was converted into oil and widely used for lighting, soap and various manufactured products. Whale meat then disappeared from the market. It was no longer eaten except 'by Kaffirs near the Cape of Good Hope, a semi-savage people', said a treatise of 1619, which none the less mentioned the use in Italy of fat from salted whales, known as 'Lenten lard'. In any case, industrial requirements were sufficient to maintain an increasingly active whale hunt: for example the Dutch sent 6995 ships to the Spitzburg area between 1675 and 1721 and harpooned 32,908 whales, depopulating the adjacent seas. Boats from Hamburg looking for whale oil regularly traversed the seas of Greenland.

The decline in the vogue for pepper after 1650

Pepper occupies a peculiar position in the history of food. An ordinary seasoning we are far from considering indispensable today, it was for many centuries associated with spice, the primary object of trade with the Levant. Everything depended on it, even the dreams of the fifteenth-century explorers. 'As dear as pepper' was a common saying.

Europe had had a very old passion for pepper and spices – cinnamon, cloves, nutmeg and ginger. We must not be too quick to call it a mania. Islam, China and India shared the taste, and every society has its crazes for particular foods that become almost indispensable. They express the need to break the monotony of diet. A Hindu writer said: 'When the palate revolts against the insipidness of rice boiled with no other ingredients, we dream of fat, salt and spices.'

It is a fact that the poorest and most monotonous diets in underdeveloped countries today are those which most readily resort to spices. By spices we mean all types of seasoning in use in our period (including pimento, which came from America under many names) and not merely the glorious spices of the Levant. There were spices on the tables of the poor in Europe in the middle ages: 'thyme, marjoram, bay leaves, savory, aniseed, coriander and particularly garlic, which Arnaud de Villeneuve, a famous thirteenth-century doctor, called the peasants' theriac'. The only luxury product amongst these local spices was saffron.

The Roman world from the time of Plautus and the older Cato was passionately fond of *silphium*, a mysterious plant from Libya which disappeared in the first century of the Empire. When Caesar emptied the public treasury in 49 he found over 490 kilograms of *silphium*. Later came the fashion for a Persian spice, *asa foetida*: 'its alliaceous and fetid smell earned it the name of *stercus diaboli*, devil's dung'. It is still used in Persian cooking today. Pepper and spices came late to Rome, 'not before Varro and Horace, and Pliny was surprised by the favour pepper found'. In his time its use was widespread and prices were relatively modest. According to Pliny fine spices were even cheaper than pepper, which was not the case in later years. Pepper ultimately had its own specialised storehouses in

Rome, *horrea piperataria*, and when Alaric seized the town in 410 he took five thousand pounds of pepper with it.

The West inherited spices and pepper from Rome. It is probable that both were later in short supply, in Charlemagne's time, when the Mediterranean was all but closed to Christianity. But compensation followed rapidly. In the twelfth century the craze for spices was in full swing. The West sacrificed its precious metals for them and engaged in the difficult Levant trade which meant travelling half-way round the world. The passion was so great that along with black and white pepper (both genuine peppers, the colour depending on whether or not the dark coating was left on) Westerners bought 'long pepper', also from India, and a substitute product like the bogus pepper or *malaguetta* which came from the Guinea coast from the fifteenth century onwards.

Cookery books show that the mania for spices affected everything: meat, fish, jam, soup, luxury drinks. Who would dare cook game without using 'hot pepper', as Douet d'Arcy counselled as early as the beginning of the fourteenth century? The advice of *Le Ménagier de Paris* (1393) was to 'put in the spices as late as possible'. Its recipe for black pudding ran as follows: 'take ginger, clove and a little pepper and crush together'. In this booklet *oille*, 'a dish brought back from Spain' and consisting of a mixture of various meats, duck, partridge, pigeon, quail and chicken (to all appearances the popular *olla podrida* of today), also becomes a mixture of spices, 'aromatic drugs', eastern or otherwise, nutmeg, pepper, thyme, ginger and basil. Spices were also consumed in the form of preserved fruits and elaborate powders to treat any disease medicine might diagnose. They were all reputed 'to drive off wind' and 'favour the seed'.

In fact there was nothing in common between this spice-orgy and the late and moderate consumption known to the Roman world. It is true that the Romans ate little meat (even in Cicero's time it was the object of sumptuary laws). The medieval West, on the other hand, was carnivorous. We might assume that the badly preserved and not always tender meat cried out for the seasoning of strong peppers and spicy sauces, which disguised its poor quality. Present-day doctors are aware of the existence of very curious psychological processes with regard to smells. It would seem that there is a sort of mutual exclusion between the taste for seasonings 'with a bitter smell, like garlic and onion . . . and the taste for more delicate seasonings with sweet and aromatic smells, reminiscent of the scent of flowers'. The first category was dominant in the middle ages.

Things were probably not as simple. In any case consumption of spice increased in the sixteenth century (until then, it had been a great luxury) with the sharp rise in deliveries following Vasco da Gama's voyage. The increase was particularly marked in the north, where purchases of spices far exceeded those in the Mediterranean regions. The spice-market shifted from Venice and its *Fondaco dei Todeschi* to Antwerp (with a short sojourn at Lisbon) and then to Amsterdam, so the trade was not governed by simple considerations of commerce and navigation. Luther, who exaggerated, claimed that there were more spices than corn in Germany. The large consumers were in the north and east. Pepper and spices seem to have been in greater demand in places where they had on the whole arrived later. Was this luxury in the north and east a new luxury? When Abbé Mably reached Cracow he was served with wine from Hungary and 'a very plentiful meal which might have been very good if the Russians and the Confederates had destroyed all those aromatic herbs used in such quantities here, like the cinnamon and nutmeg that poison travellers in Germany'. It would seem therefore that in eastern Europe the taste for strong seasoning and spices was still medieval in style at that date, while the ancient culinary customs were to some extent disappearing in the West. But this is conjecture and not fact.

A historian tells us (1896) that in the West 'when spices could appear on every table and were no longer a proof of luxury and wealth, perhaps people stopped valuing them so highly and their use was more and more restricted'. A cookery book of 1651 (François de La Varenne) and Boileau's satire (1665) ridiculing the misuse of spices point to the same conclusion.

As soon as the Dutch reached the Indian Ocean and the Indian archipelago they did their utmost to restore and then maintain for their own profit the monopoly in pepper and spices against the Portuguese (whose trade however was never eliminated) and soon against English competition and later French and Danish. They also tried to control supplies to China, Japan, Bengal and Persia, and were able to compensate for a slack period in Europe by a sharp rise in their trade with Asia. The quantities of pepper reaching Europe via Amsterdam (and outside its market) probably increased, at least until the middle of the seventeenth century, and then were maintained at a high level. Annual arrivals in about 1600 before the Dutch success were possibly in the order of 20,000 present-day quintals, hence an annual quota of 20 grams per inhabitant for 100 million Europeans. Consumption may well have been in the order of 50,000 quintals in about 1680, more than double the figure at the time of the Portuguese monopoly. The sales of the *Oost Indische Companie* from 1715 to 1732 suggest that a limit was reached. What is certain is that pepper ceased being the dominant spice-trade commodity it was in the days of Priuli and Sanudo and the undisputed supremacy of Venice. Pepper still held first place in the trade of the Company in Amsterdam in 1648–50 (33% of the total). It fell to fourth in 1778–80 (11%) after textiles (silk and cotton, 32·66%), spices (24·43%) and tea and coffee (22·92%). Was this a typical case of the ending of a luxury consumption and the beginning of a general one? Or the decline of excessive use?

For this decline the popularity of new luxuries – coffee, chocolate, alcohol and tobacco – can legitimately be blamed; perhaps also the spread of new vegetables which gradually began to vary Western diet (asparagus, spinach, lettuce, artichokes, peas, green beans, cauliflower, tomatoes, pimentoes, melons). These vegetables were mostly the product of European, and especially Italian, gardens. (Charles VIII brought the melon back from Italy.) They were sometimes native to Armenia, like the cantaloup, rarely definitely to America, apart from the potato.

One last but rather unconvincing explanation remains. A general decrease in meat consumption took place after 1600 or even earlier, which meant a break with former diet. Concurrently the rich adopted a simpler style of cooking, in France at least. German and Polish cooking may have been behindhand and have also had better supplies of meat and therefore a greater need for pepper and spices. But this explanation is only conjectural and those we gave before may suffice until fuller information is available.

There is proof of a certain saturation of the European market; a German economist (1722) and an 'English' witness (1761) both reported that the Dutch had 'sometimes to burn large quantities of pepper and nutmeg . . . or throw them into the sea to maintain the price'. Furthermore, Europeans had no control over the fields of pepper trees outside Java, and Pierre Poivre's efforts in the îles de France et de Bourbon where he was governor (1767) only seem to have been of passing interest; the same was true of similar attempts in French Guiana.

As nothing is ever simple, the seventeenth century which saw the break with spices in France fell madly in love with perfume. It invaded stews, pastries, liqueurs and sauces: amber, iris, rose water, orange-flower water, marjoram, musk, and so on. 'Scented waters' were even spooned over eggs!

Sugar conquers the world

Sugar cane is native to the Bengal coast, between the Ganges delta and Assam. The wild plant later reached gardens where for a long time it was cultivated for its sugar water and then sugar, regarded as a cure at that period: it appears in doctors' prescriptions in Sassanid Persia. Similarly, medicinal sugar vied with honey in general prescriptions in Byzantium. It appears in the pharmacopaea of the Salerno School in the tenth century. Before that date it had begun to be used as a foodstuff in India and in China where the cane was imported in about the eighth century AD. It quickly adapted itself to the hilly area of Kwang Tung, in the neighbourhood of Canton – predictably enough, because Canton was already the largest port in ancient China and had a wooded hinterland (sugar production required a great deal of fuel). For many centuries Kwang Tung provided the main part of Chinese production, and in the seventeenth century the *Oost Indische Companie* had no difficulty in organising exports from there to Europe.

Cane was in Egypt in the tenth century and sugar was already being produced by an advanced process. The Crusaders met it in Syria. After the fall of Acre, with Syria lost (1291), sugar passed into the hands of the Christians and rapidly established itself in Cyprus. The beautiful Catherine Cornaro, wife of the last of the Lusignans and last queen of the island (the Venetians seized it in 1479) was descended from the Cornaros, Venetian patricians and in their day 'sugar kings'.

Even before its success in Cyprus sugar brought by Arabs had prospered in Sicily and then in Valencia. It was in Moroccan Sousse at the end of the fifteenth century, touched Madeira, then the Azores, the Canaries, the island of São Thomé and Prince's Island in the Gulf of Guinea. Very shortly afterwards it reached Brazil where its prosperity was consolidated in the second half of the sixteenth century. From Brazil, as a result of the Dutch expulsion from Recife in 1654 and the Holy Office's persecutions of Portuguese *marranos*, cane and sugar mills reached Martinique, Guadeloupe, Dutch Curaçao, Jamaica and Santo Domingo. The great period for these new areas began in about 1680.

Thenceforth production showed an uninterrupted increase. Mas

Latrie, the historian of Cyprus, estimated that the island produced 2000 Venetian quintals, that is about 100 tons at the end of the fifteenth century. But Santo Domingo alone produced 70,000 at its peak in the eighteenth century. In 1800 England consumed 150,000 tons of sugar annually, almost fifteen times more than in 1700, and Lord Sheffield was right when he noted in 1783: 'The consumption of sugar can increase considerably. It is scarcely known in half of Europe.' Consumption in Paris just before the Revolution was 5 kilograms per person per year (on the doubtful reckoning of a population of 600,000); in 1846 (and this figure is more reliable) consumption was only 3·62 kilograms. An estimate for the whole of France in 1788 gives a theoretical average consumption of one kilogram. We can be certain that sugar was still a luxury item despite public favour and the relative fall in its price. The sugar loaf hung over tables in many peasant households in France. Directions for use: hold your glass up to it briefly so that the sugar can melt into it.

The low level of production was also the result of the late establishment of sugar beet. It was known however as early as 1575 and the German chemist Markgraff had isolated sugar from it in solid form in 1747. Its career only began with the Continental Blockade and required almost another century to reach its full extent.

Sugar cane cultivation was limited to hot climates, which was why it did not cross to the north of the Yang-tse-Kiang in China. It also had special marketing and industrial requirements. Sugar demanded a large labour force (in America the Black slaves) and expensive installations – the *yngenios* in Cuba, New Spain and Peru, equivalent to the *engenhos de assucar* in Brazil, the *engins* or sugar mills in the French islands, and the English 'engines'. The cane had to be crushed by rollers arranged in various ways and worked by animals, waterpower, wind or elbow grease, as in China where moreover rollers were not always used. The sap of the plants required treatment, preparation, precautions and long heating in copper vats. When crystallised in clay moulds it produced raw sugar or *muscovado*; when filtered in white clay, clayed sugar or moist sugar. It was then possible to obtain ten different products, plus alcohol. Raw sugar was very often refined in Europe, at Antwerp, Venice, Amsterdam, London, Paris, Bordeaux, Nantes and Dresden. The operation was almost as profitable as the production of the raw material. This gave rise to conflicts between refiners and sugar growers, the colonists of the islands who dreamed of manufacturing everything on the spot, or as they said 'setting themselves up in white' (in white sugar).

Cultivation and production therefore required capital and chains of intermediaries. Where intermediaries did not exist, sales rarely went beyond the local market; this remained the case in Peru, New Spain and Cuba until the nineteenth century. If the sugar islands and the coast of Brazil prospered, it was because they were situated within easy reach of Europe, given the speed and capacity of contemporary ships.

There was an additional obstacle: 'To feed a colony in America,' Abbé Raynal explains, 'it is necessary to cultivate a province in Europe.' For the sugar-growing colonies could not feed themselves, as the cane left little space for food crops. This is the characteristic of sugar as a monoculture in north-east Brazil, the West Indies, and Moroccan Sousse (where archaeology is bringing to light vast installations from the past). In 1783 England sent 16,576 tons of salted meat, beef and pork, 5188 flitches of bacon and 2559 tons of preserved tripe to its own West Indies (Jamaica particularly). Food for the slaves in Brazil was secured by importing tons of cod from Newfoundland, *carne do sol* from the interior (*sertão*), and soon by *charque* (dried meat) shipped from Rio Grande do Sul. The saving of the West Indies was salted beef and flour from the English colonies in America: in exchange the colonies obtained sugar and rum – rum which very shortly afterwards they were able to produce for themselves.

To sum up: we must not be too quick to talk about a sugar revolution. Sugar was established very early but progressed extremely slowly. It was still not widespread on the threshold of the nineteenth century. We cannot conclude that sugar graced every table in the world. Scarcely is that statement uttered, however, than we think of the agitations provoked by lack of sugar in revolutionary Paris at the time of *le maximum*.

2   Drinks, stimulants and drugs

Even a short history of drinks must discuss the old and the new, the popular and the refined, together with the various changes that occurred with the passage of time. Drinks are not only foodstuffs: they have always served as drugs, a means of escape. Sometimes, as with certain Indian tribes, drunkenness is even a means of communication with the supernatural. Be that as it may, the rise of alcoholism was continuous in Europe during the centuries that concern us. And then exotic stimulants were coming in: tea, coffee and, not least, tobacco in all its forms, an unclassifiable 'dope', neither food nor drink.

Water

Paradoxically we must begin with water. It was not always readily available and, despite specific advice from doctors who claimed that one sort of water was preferable to another for a particular disease, people had to be content with what was on hand: rain, river, fountain, cistern, well, barrel or a copper receptacle in which it was wise to keep some in reserve in every provident household. Sea water was distilled by alembic in the Spanish *presidios* in North Africa in the sixteenth century; otherwise water would have been brought from Spain or Italy. We hear of the desperate plight of some travellers across the Congo in 1648 who, starving, tired to death and sleeping on the bare ground, had to 'drink water [which] resembled horse's urine'.

Another great problem was the lack of fresh water on board ship. There was no way of keeping it drinkable, despite so many recipes and jealously guarded secrets. Finally whole towns – and very wealthy ones at that – were poorly supplied with water. This applied to Venice where the wells in the public squares or the courtyards of palaces were not (as is often thought) dug right down to the underground fresh-water level, below the bed of the lagoon. They were cisterns half-filled with fine sand through which rain water was filtered and decanted and then oozed into the well running down through the centre. When no rain fell for weeks on end, the cisterns ran dry; this happened when Stendhal was staying in the city. If there was a storm they were tainted with salt water. Even in normal weather they were inadequate for the enormous population of the town. Fresh water had to be brought from outside, not by aqueduct but by boats filled in the Brenta and sent to Venice daily. These *acquaroli* of the river even formed an autonomous guild at Venice. The same unpleasant situation prevailed in all the towns of Holland, reduced to using cisterns, wells and dubious canal waters.

There were a few aqueducts in use: the deservedly famous ones at Istanbul, and the one at Segovia, the *puente* (repaired in 1481), which dated from Roman times and astounded visitors. Portugal had aqueducts at Coimbra, Tomar, Villa do Conde and Elvas all functioning in the seventeenth century. The new Spring Water aqueduct built in Lisbon in the eighteenth century took water to the outlying square of the Rato. Everyone quarrelled over water from this fountain, where carriers went to fill red kegs with iron handles which they carried on the backs of their necks. Appropriately, Martin v's first concern when he reoccupied the Vatican after the Great Schism was to restore one of the demolished aqueducts of Rome. Two new aqueducts had to be built to supply the large town at the end of the sixteenth century: the *Aqua Felice* and the *Aqua Paola*. In Paris the Belleville aqueduct was repaired in 1457; in conjunction with the one at Pré-Saint-Gervais it supplied the town until the seventeenth century. The Arcueil aqueduct, reconstructed by Maria de Medici, brought water from Rungis to the Luxembourg Palace. Large hydraulic wheels raised river water to supply towns everywhere (Toledo 1526; Augsburg 1548) and drove powerful lift-and-force pumps for this purpose. The Samaritaine pump, built between 1603 and 1608, yielded 700 cubic metres of water every day, drawn from the Seine and redistributed to the Louvre and the Tuileries; in 1670 the pumps of the Notre Dame bridge drew 2000 cubic metres from the same source. Water from aqueducts and pumps was distributed about the towns through terra cotta pipes (as in Roman times) or wooden pipes (hollowed tree trunks fixed together, as in northern Italy from the fourteenth century and at Breslau from 1471). The use of lead piping, recorded in England from 1236, remained limited.

In sixteenth-century Paris the left bank of the Seine had nothing but wells; the right bank had a few fountains in addition, dry for half the year. The Seine remained the best provider. Its water, sold by carriers, was supposed to possess all the virtues: first, to bear boats best, as it was muddy and therefore heavy (a Portuguese envoy noted this in 1641); then, to be excellent for the health – which we may be allowed to doubt. 'A number of dyers pour their dye three times a week into the branch of the river which washes the Pelletier quay and between the two bridges,' said an eye witness (1771). 'The arch which forms the Gêvres quai is a seat of pestilence. All that part of the town drinks infected water.' It is true that this was soon remedied. And after all Seine water was better than water from the wells on the Left Bank, which were never protected from terrible infiltrations and with which the bakers made their bread.

This river water was a natural purgative and of course 'unpleasant for foreigners' but they could always add a few drops of vinegar or buy filtered and 'improved' water – or better still, a product called the King's water, or the best and most expensive, the so-called Bristol water. These refinements were unknown before about 1760. 'One drank water [from the Seine] without really bothering about it.'

Twenty thousand carriers earned a living (though a poor one) supplying Paris with water, taking some thirty 'loads' (two buckets at a time) to the highest levels at two sous a load. It was therefore the beginning of a revolution when the Perrier brothers installed two steam pumps at Chaillot in 1782, 'very curious machines' which raised water 110 feet from the low level of the Seine 'by ordinary steam from boiling water'. This was in imitation of London, which had had nine such pumps for a long time. The Saint-Honoré district, the wealthiest and therefore the most able to pay for such progress, was the first to be served. But people were worried: what about the fate of the twenty thousand water carriers if the number of machines increased? And furthermore the venture shortly turned into a financial scandal (1788). But all the same, with the eighteenth century the problem of supplying drinkable water was clearly posed and the solutions seen and sometimes achieved.

Despite everything, progress was slow. In every town in the world the water carrier was indispensable. One Portuguese traveller in Valladolid in Philip III's time praised the excellent water sold in delightful demi-johns and ceramic jugs of all shapes and colours. In China the water carrier used two pails, as in Paris, balancing them at each end of his pole. But a drawing of Peking in 1800 also shows a large barrel on wheels, with a bung at the back. An engraving of about the same period explains 'the way in which women carry water in Egypt' in two jars, reminiscent of ancient amphorae: a large one on the head supported by the left hand, a small one held flat on the right hand by a graceful movement of the bent arm. Many fountains were built in Istanbul as a result of the religious requirement to wash frequently every day under running water. The water drunk there was probably purer than anywhere else; which may be why Turks today still pride themselves on being able to recognise the taste of the water from the different springs – just as Frenchmen boast that they can tell the wine from different vineyards.

Another amenity in Istanbul was the snow water sold in streets everywhere in summer for a small sum. It was also available in Valladolid where a Portuguese, Bartolome Pinheiro da Veiga, at the beginning of the seventeenth century was amazed that it was possible to treat oneself to 'cold water and iced fruit' during the hot months, and at a reasonable price. In Peking the ice was broken up into large blocks every winter and stored in specially prepared 'ice wells'. But snow water was mostly a great luxury, reserved for the wealthy. This was the case in France, which only developed a taste for it at the time of Henri III, and around the Mediterranean where boats loaded with snow sometimes made quite long voyages. The Knights of Malta were supplied by Naples; one of their requests, in 1743, stated that they would die if they did not have 'this sovereign remedy' to break their fevers.

Wine

The whole of Europe drank wine; only a part of Europe produced it. Although the vine (if not wine) had its successes in Asia, Africa and more still in the New World – zealously remodelled in the obsessive image of the Old – only Europe really mattered.

Wine-producing Europe consisted of all its Mediterranean countries and an area to the north added to it by the perseverance of the vine-growers. As Jean Bodin says: 'The vine cannot grow beyond the forty-ninth parallel because of the cold.' A line drawn from the mouth of the Loire on the Atlantic coast up to the Crimea and beyond as far as Georgia and Trans-Caucasia sets the northern boundary of the commercial cultivation of the vine – one of the great hinges in the economic life of Europe and its eastern extensions. In the Crimea area wine-growing Europe is very narrow, just a fringe along the seashore. None the less it is a very old implantation and in ancient times they used to bury the foot of the vine before the beginning of winter to protect it from the cold winds of the Ukraine.

Outside Europe wine followed in the wake of Europeans. Great feats were accomplished in acclimatising the vine in Mexico, Peru, Chile (reached in 1541) and in Argentina, after the second foundation of Buenos Aires in 1580. In Peru vineyards rapidly prospered in the hot and fever-ridden valleys because of their proximity to Lima, an exceptionally wealthy town. They prospered still more in Chile where the soil and climate were propitious; vines were already growing amongst the *cuadras*, the blocks of the first houses of the growing town of Santiago. In 1578 Drake seized a boat loaded with Chilean wine in the open sea off Valparaiso. The same wine, carried on the backs of mules or llamas, reached the high point of Potosi. But vines were not planted in California until the end of the seventeenth and in the eighteenth centuries, during the last north-ward thrust of the Spanish empire.

However, its most brilliant successes were in mid-Atlantic, between the Old and the New World, in the islands (both new Europes and pre-Americas), and notably Madeira, where the production of red wine was increasingly substituted for sugar. Then came the Azores, a half-way point where ships could take on board good wines with a high alcohol content. When politics intervened (Lord Methuen's treaty with Portugal was in 1704), it was more convenient to carry them than French wines from La Rochelle or Bordeaux. Finally the Canaries, notable Tenerife, exported white wine on a large scale to Anglo-Saxon and Iberian America, and even to England.

In southern and eastern Europe wine came up against the un-yielding obstacle of Islam. It is true that the vine maintained itself throughout the land controlled by Islam, and wine proved an indefatigable clandestine traveller. Innkeepers near the Arsenal in Istanbul sold it daily to Greek sailors, while Selim, son of Suleiman the Magnificent, was only too fond of Cyprus liqueur wine. In Persia (where the Capuchin friars had vine arbours and wines — which were not used solely for mass), wines from Chirz and Ispahan had a reputation and customers. They travelled as far as the Indies in enormous glass demi-johns protected by wicker, actually manufac-tured in Ispahan. What a pity that the Great Moguls who succeeded the Sultans of Delhi after 1526 were not content with these strong Persian wines instead of taking to rice spirit, arak!

However the subject of wine is best summed up in the context of Europe, and we must go back to that long line from the Loire to the Crimea, the northern limit of the vine. On one side of it there were the peasant producers and consumers, accustomed to local wine, to its treachery and its benefits alike; on the other, large customers — not always experienced drinkers, but with specific requirements and generally a partiality for wines with a high alcoholic strength. Englishmen very early on established the great reputation of Malm-sey, liqueur wines from Candia and the Greek islands. Later they launched port, malaga, madeira, sherry and marsala, all famous wines with a high alcohol content. The Dutch created the popularity of all types of spirits from the seventeenth century onwards. Thus northerners had their own special palates and tastes. The southern people looked jeeringly upon these drinkers who, in their opinion, did not know how to drink and emptied their glasses in one gulp.

Jean d'Auton, chronicler of Louis XII, saw German soldiers suddenly start drinking (*trinken*) like this when they pillaged the castle of Forli. And there they were again staving in the barrels and rapidly becoming dead drunk during the terrible sacking of Rome in 1527. Sixteenth- and seventeenth-century German engravings of peasant festivities almost invariably show one of the guests turning round on his bench to throw up his excess of drink. When Félix Platter from Basle stayed in Montpellier in 1556 he admitted that 'all the boozers' in the town were German and were to be found snoring under barrels, the chosen victims of countless tricks.

This large northern consumption gave rise to large-scale trade with the south: by sea, from Seville and Andalusia to England and Flanders; or along the Dordogne and the Garonne to Bordeaux and the Gironde; from La Rochelle or the Loire estuary; along the Yonne, from Burgundy to Paris, and then beyond as far as Rouen; along the Rhine; across the Alps (large German carriages, which the Italians called *carretoni*, arrived immediately after every wine harvest to look for new wines from the Tyrol, Brescia, Vicenza, Friuli and Istria); from Moravia and Hungary to Poland; a little later by Baltic routes, from Portugal, Spain and France, right up to St Petersburg and the violent but undiscriminating Russian thirst. Of course the whole population of northern Europe did not drink wine. Only the rich did as a rule; then there were a few bourgeois, the odd prebendal monk in Flanders in the thirteenth century; or the Polish nobleman in the sixteenth who thought he would lose caste if he were satisfied with the same home-brewed beer as his peasants.

The wine that travelled about in this way and was awaited and greeted with joy everywhere was new wine. For wine did not keep from one year to the next; it turned sour. And clarifying, bottling, and the regular use of corks may have been unknown until the seventeenth century. But in the following century everything was in order, and collecting old empty bottles for wine merchants was one of the lucrative activities of London thieves. On the other hand, for a very long time wine was transported in wooden barrels (jointed and ringed staves), no longer in the amphorae of Roman times (in spite of persistent survivals here and there). The wine did not always keep well in these barrels, which had been invented in Roman Gaul. The Duke of Mondejar advised Charles V on December 2, 1539 that large quantities of wines should not be bought for the navy. If they 'are to turn into vinegar, it is better that they remain with their owners than with your Majesty'. As late as the eighteenth century a dictionary of commerce was surprised that the Romans had considered 'the age of wines as their claim to excellence, while in France wines are thought to be stale (even those from Dijon, Nuits and Orleans, the most suitable of all for keeping) when they reach the fifth or sixth leaf' [year].

The vintage wines did not establish themselves before the eighteenth century. The best-known possibly owed their reputation less to their merits than to the convenience of the routes in their vicinity and particularly to their proximity to a large town or waterways (this was just as true of the small vineyard of Frontignan on the coast of Languedoc as of the large vineyards in Andalusia, Portugal, Bordeaux and La Rochelle). Paris alone absorbed the 100,000 or so barrels (1698) produced by the vines of Orleans; wines from the Kingdom of Naples – *greco, latiño, mangiaguerra, lacryma christi* – were near the enormous clientele of Naples and even Rome. Champagne, which began to be produced during the first half of the eighteenth .century, took time to displace the old local red, grey and white wines. But the job was done by the middle of the eighteenth century when all the great vintages of today had established their eminence. 'Taste,' wrote Sébastien Mercier in 1788, 'the wines of the Romanée, Saint-Vivant, Cîteaux and Graves, both red and white ... and insist on Tokay if you meet it. In my opinion, it is the greatest wine in the world and only the masters of the world should drink it.' Savary's *Dictionnaire de Commerce* lists all the wines in France in 1762 and places 'those of Champagne and Burgundy' at the top. It also mentions: 'Chablis, Pomar, Chambertin, Beaune, le Clos de Vougeau, Volleney, la Romanée, Nuits, Mursault. . . .' Obviously with the increasing differentiation of vintages, wine was developing more and more into a luxury product. This was the time when according to the *Dictionnaire sentencieux* (1768) the new expression *sabler le vin de champagne* (meaning to toss off a drink) was coming into fashion amongst the smarter set.

But here, we are interested more in the ever-increasing number of ordinary drinkers than in these refinements and their history, which could easily lead us too far out of our way. Drunkenness increased everywhere in the sixteenth century. Consumption in Valladolid reached 100 litres per person per year in the middle of the century; in Venice the seignory was obliged to take new and severe action against public drunkenness in 1598; in France Laffemas was quite positive on that point at the beginning of the seventeenth century. This widespread urban drunkenness never required high-quality wine; coarse types of vines with high yields were becoming general in commercial vineyards. In the eighteenth century the movement reached the countryside itself (the taverns there were the ruin of the peasants) and became more pronounced in the towns. Mass consumption became general with the establishment of the *guingettes* at the gates of Paris, outside the boundaries of the town, where the *aides*, the tax of 'four sous admittance for one bottle which intrinsically is only worth three . . .' was not chargeable.

> Commoners, artisans, grisettes,
> All leave Paris and run to the guingettes.
> Two pints for the price of a single booze
> On two boat's benches, without cloth or serviettes,
> You'll drink so much in these Bacchic stews
> That out of your eyes the wine will ooze.

This prospectus for the poor, below a contemporary engraving, was not without some truth. Hence the popularity of the suburban taverns: the famous Courtille, near the Belleville 'gate', founded by Ramponeau whose name, according to a contemporary, 'is a million times better known to the multitude than Voltaire's and Buffon's'; or 'the famous beggars' saloon' at Vaugirard where men and women danced barefoot in a tumult of dust and noise. 'When Vaugirard is full the people [on a Sunday] stream back to the Petit Gentilly, the Porcherons and the Courtille: the next day you see empty barrels by the dozen in front of wine merchants' stalls. The people drink enough for the whole week.' In Madrid too, 'good wine can be drunk cheaply outside the town, because you do not pay the taxes there which amount to more than the price of the wine'.

Consumption in Paris on the eve of the Revolution was in the order of 100 litres per person per year, which is not scandalous in itself. In fact wine, principally low-quality wine, had become a cheap foodstuff. Its price even fell relatively every time corn became too expensive. One historian has suggested that wine could have been a compensation (like other forms of alcohol) – that is to say, cheap calories every time bread was short. Or is the explanation more simply that purses emptied by the high prices during famine periods left fewer customers for wine and therefore its price inevitably dropped? In any case we should not measure the standard of living by those conspicuous debaucheries. And we should remember that wine, calories or not, was often a means of escape; what the Castilian peasant still calls a *quita-penas*, drowner of sorrows. This is the red wine that Velasquez's two comrades are drinking (Museum of Budapest) or the golden yellow wine that looks even more precious in the long fluted glasses and the magnificent rounded glaucous goblets of Dutch paintings; here, wine, tobacco, women of easy virtue and the music of violinists (which became fashionable in the seventeenth century) are combined for the drinker's delight.

Beer

With beer we will still stay in Europe – if we leave out the American maize beer which we have mentioned in passing, and the millet beer which for the Black peoples of Africa filled the ritual role of 'bread and wine with Westerners', and also if we do not inquire too much into the distant origins of this very old beverage. For in fact beer was known in both ancient Babylon and Egypt. The Roman Empire, which did not like it much, generally met it far away from the Mediterranean, at Numantia, for example, which Scipio besieged in 133 BC, in Gaul, and on the tables of the poor almost everywhere. The Emperor Julian the Apostate (361–3) drank it once and immediately scorned it. There were barrels of beer at Trèves in the fourth century. It was also known in China long before the Christian era. Centuries later, beer became the drink of the poor and the barbarian in the West. It was available right across Charlemagne's vast empire and in his own palaces where master brewers were instructed to make good beer, *cervisam bonam ... facere debeant.*

It can be made by brewing wheat or oats, barley or millet, or sprouted barley (malt). One type of grain is never treated by itself: brewers today add hops and rice to barley. Malt, which gradually came to predominate, is crushed, brought to the boil, mixed with yeast, and then left to ferment. Beer, as a present-day English historian repeats, is 'a soup' with multiple ingredients. Old recipes added poppy seeds, mushrooms, aromatics, honey, sugar, bay leaves, butter and breadcrumbs. Beer made with hops (which pass on their bitter taste and act as a preservative) is said to have originated in the monasteries of Roman Gaul. It is recorded in Germany between the ninth and twelfth centuries. It reached England late, in the fifteenth. As the chorus has it, with some slight exaggeration (but hops were forbidden until 1556):

Hops, Reformation, bays and beer
Came into England all in one year.

Beer became established outside the vine-growing region and was really at home in the vast zone comprising the northern lands, from England to the Netherlands, Germany, Bohemia, Poland and Muscovy. It was produced in the towns and on noblemen's estates in central Europe where 'the brewers are generally liable to cheat their masters'. The peasants on the Polish estates consumed up to three litres of beer a day. Naturally the beer region had no precise western or southern boundaries. It even fairly rapidly extended southwards, particularly in the seventeenth century with the Dutch advance. A brewery was even established in Bordeaux at that time, not far from the Château-Trompette, in the suburb of Chartreux. Even Seville is thought to have had a brewery in 1542. In the West there was a wide and indistinct frontier zone where the establishment of a brewery caused a great stir. It included Lorraine, for example, where vineyards were mediocre and yields uncertain, and could stretch as far as Paris. Le Grand d'Aussy (*La vie privée des Français*, 1782) thought that as beer was the drink of the poor every difficult period saw an extension of its consumption; conversely, good times, economically speaking, turned beer drinkers into wine drinkers. He appended a few examples drawn from the past, adding: 'Have we ourselves not seen the disasters of the Seven Years War (1756–63) produce similar effects? Towns which had only known wine before that time began to drink beer, and I myself know certain places in Champagne where four breweries were set up in the same town in a single year.'

Beer went through a long period of difficulty in Paris from 1740 to 1780 (though it was an economically good period in the long term). The number of brewers fell from 75 to 23 and production from 75,000 hogsheads (one hogshead equals 286 litres) to 26,000. The poor brewers then had to worry about the apple crop every year and try to make up their losses from beer by their earnings from cider. Their situation had not improved by the time of the Revolution. Wine remained the great winner: its consumption in Paris from 1781 to 1786 rose to an annual round figure of 730,000 hectolitres, as compared with 54,000 of beer (or a ratio of 1 to 13). But Le Grand d'Aussy's theory was confirmed during the period of obvious economic difficulty from 1821 to 1830, when wine consumption in Paris was at an average of 917,000 hectolitres as compared with 140,000 of beer; the ratio then was of 1 to 6·5.

Beer was not solely the mark of poverty. It was not solely the English small beer brewed at home to wash down the daily ration of cold meat and oat cake. From the sixteenth century the Netherlands had a luxury beer for the rich, imported from Leipzig, as well as a popular type. In Germany, Bohemia and Poland, a large growth in urban brewing pushed the light beer made by lord and peasant, often without hops, into second place. There is an immense literature on this subject. Beer, as well as the shops where it was consumed, was the object of legislation. The towns supervised its production; for example, brewing was only allowed between Michaelmas and Palm Sunday in Nuremburg. Books appeared praising the virtues of different and increasing varieties of beer. One by Heinrich Knaust in 1575 listed the names and nicknames of famous beers and described their medicinal qualities for drinkers. But in Muscovy, where everything was behind the times, the consumer still obtained his 'barley-beer' from the 'public canteen' in 1655, at the same time as he bought his spirits, salted fish, caviar and black sheepskins imported from Astrakhan and Persia – all these purchases destined to fill the coffers of a commercial and monopolist state.

Cider

A few words about cider. It originated in Biscay where the cider apple trees came from; they appeared in Cotentin, the Caen region and the Pays d'Auge towards the eleventh or twelfth century. Cider was mentioned in these regions in the following century. It should be noted that the vine was also present there, although to the north of its commercial boundary. The newcomer did not interfere with wine; it competed with beer and met with some success, since beer was made from grain and drinking it sometimes meant going without bread.

Then apple trees and cider extended their territory. They arrived in eastern Normandy (lower Seine and Pays de Caux) at the end of the fifteenth and the beginning of the sixteenth centuries. A representative sent by the province to the States General could still say in 1484 that the great difference between lower and upper Normandy (eastern Normandy) was that one had apple trees and the other did not. Furthermore beer and more particularly wine (such as the wine from the vineyards in the sheltered bends of the Seine) were holding their own in upper Normandy. Cider only made headway in about 1550, and, of course, amongst people of small account. Its success was more evident in Lower Maine since it became the drink of the rich there from the fifteenth century onwards (at least in the south-west of the province), beer remaining the drink of the poor. At

Laval, however, the rich resisted until the seventeenth century. For a long time before they succumbed they preferred bad wine to cider, which they left to masons, servants and chambermaids. Perhaps this minor change can be attributed to the regression in the seventeenth century. Naturally Normandy was too near to Paris for cider's success not to affect the capital. But a Parisian consumed an average of 121·76 litres of wine between 1781 and 1786; 8·96 of beer and 2·73 of cider. Cider came well and truly last and in Germany, for example, met competition from cider made from wild apples, a very second-rate drink.

The belated popularity of alcohol in Europe

The great innovation, the revolution in Europe was the appearance of brandy and spirits made from grain – in a word: alcohol. The sixteenth century created it; the seventeenth consolidated it; the eighteenth popularised it.

Brandy was obtained by distilling, 'burning' wine. The operation required an apparatus, the still or alembic (*al*, the Arab definite article, and *ambicos* from the Greek, a vase with a long neck for distilling liquid). But we do not know if the Greeks and later the Romans used such an apparatus, *a fortiori* whether or not they passed them on to the West, through the intermediary of Islam once again. One single fact is beyond doubt: there were stills in the West from the twelfth century and therefore the possibility of distilling all sorts of alcoholic drink.

The distillation of wine was practised solely by apothecaries. Brandy, resulting from the first distillation, and spirit of wine, resulting from the second (theoretically 'free from all humidity') were medicines. Alcohol was possibly discovered in about 1100, in southern Italy 'where the Salerno school of medicine was the most important centre of chemical research' of the period. The first distillation had been attributed (probably wrongly) to Raymond Lulle, who died in 1315, or to a curious itinerant doctor, Arnaud de Villeneuve, who taught at Montpellier and Paris and died in 1313 on a journey from Sicily to Provence. He wrote a work entitled *La conservation de la jeunesse*. According to him, brandy, *aqua vitae*, accomplished the miracle of preserving youth, dissipated superfluous body fluids, revived the heart, cured colic, dropsy, paralysis, quartan ague, calmed toothache and gave protection against plague. But his miracle cure brought Charles the Bad, of execrable memory, to a

terrible end (1387); doctors had enveloped him in a brandy-soaked
sheet sewn up with large stitches for greater efficiency so that it
fitted tightly round the patient. A servant held a candle up close to
try to break one of the threads, and sheet and invalid went up in
flames.

Brandy remained a medicine for a long time, particularly against
plague, gout and loss of voice. It was also used fairly early on to
produce liqueurs like the Italian *rossolo*, made from raisins and an
aromatic plant of the drosera species. However the liqueurs made in
Germany with decoctions of spices were still pharmaceutical products in the fifteenth century. The change only became apparent in
the last years of that century and the first years of the next. Brandy
must have had other patrons besides the sick at Nuremburg in 1496,
because the town was obliged to forbid the free sale of alcohol on
feast days. A Nuremburg doctor in about 1493 even wrote: 'In view
of the fact that everyone at present has got into the habit of drinking
aqua vitae it is necessary to remember the quantity that one can
permit oneself to drink and learn to drink it according to one's
capacities, if one wishes to behave like a gentleman.' There is therefore no doubt that by then *geprant Wein*, 'burnt' wine, *vinum ardens* or,
as other texts call it, *vinum sublimatum*, had been born.

Brandy only broke away from doctors and apothecaries very
slowly. Louis XII did not grant the guild of vinegar-makers the
privilege of distilling it until 1514. In 1537 Francis I divided the
privilege between vinegar-makers and victuallers – giving rise to
quarrels indicating that the game was already worth the candle. At
Colmar the movement took place earlier. From 1506 the town controlled wine distillers and brandy merchants, and their product
thenceforth figured in its fiscal and customs returns. Brandy rapidly
took on the appearance of a national industry. At first it was entrusted
to the wet coopers, a powerful trade association in a land of prosperous vineyards. But, as was to be expected, the wet coopers did excellent business and the merchants attempted to seize it after 1511. It
was fifty years before they succeeded. The quarrel continued because
the wet coopers again obtained the right to distil in 1650, though on
condition that they handed over their production to the merchants,
among whom we find many of the Colmar patriciate. The trade
already had a high standing.

Unfortunately we do not have enough evidence to enable us to
sketch out the geography and chronology of the first brandy industry.
Some indications relating to the Bordeaux region suggest that an

early distillery was operating at Gaillac in the sixteenth century and that brandy was sent to Antwerp as early as 1521; but we cannot be sure. *Acquavite* only made its appearance in Venice – at least in customs tariffs – in 1596. There is hardly any question of it before the seventeenth century in Barcelona. Beyond these indications it would indeed seem that as far as brandy is concerned the northern countries – Germany, the Netherlands and France north of the Loire – were in advance of the Mediterranean lands. The role of promoters, if not of inventors, was really played by Dutch merchants and sailors, who made the distilling of wines general on the Atlantic coasts of Europe in the seventeenth century. Engaged in the largest wine-trade of the period, they had got to grips with the many problems posed by transport, preservation and sweetening. The addition of spirits gave even the most feeble wines new body. As they were more valuable than the same volume of wine, transport costs were correspondingly less. And contemporary taste was beginning to favour brandy.

Helped by demand, distillation of wines spread far inland, the question of transport being less important for spirits than for wine. Thus distillation was established in the vineyards of the Loire, Poitou, Bordeaux, Périgord and Béarn (Jurançon wine is a mixture of wine and brandy). Thus evolved the international reputations of Cognac and Armagnac in the seventeenth century. Everything helped in this success: the type of vine (such as *Enrageant* or *Folle Blanche* in Charente), supplies of wood available, proximity to navigable waterways. After 1728 some 27,000 casks of brandy from Cognac were sent through the port of Tonnay-Charente. Even poor wine from the Meuse region in Lorraine was distilled in about 1690 (and perhaps earlier) in the same way as grape marc (to make white brandy), and all these products travelled along the river to reach the Netherlands. Brandy gradually came to be made wherever the raw material was available. Inevitably it poured out of the vine-growing lands of the south: Andalusia near Jerez, Catalonia, Languedoc.

Production rose rapidly. Sète exported 12,640 hectolitres in 1699 – the product of the distillation of 63,200 hectolitres of wine; 62,096 from 310,480 hectolitres of wine in 1753; the record figure of 68,806 from 344,030 in 1755 just before the Seven Years War, which was disastrous for exports. At the same time the price fell: 25 francs per *verge* (equal to 7·6 litres) in 1595; 12 in 1698; 7 in 1701; 5 in 1725. A slow increase after 1731 brought prices back to 15 in 1758.

Of course prices depended on the various qualities – above the lowest limit fixed by the 'Dutch test': a sample was removed during the distillation process and a phial half filled with the specimen. A thumb was placed over the phial and it was turned upside down and shaken. If the air entering the liquid formed bubbles of a certain shape the brandy had the alcoholic content necessary to make it of marketable quality. Below the specified limit it had to be thrown out or subjected to fresh distillation. Average quality was called three-six and contained 79 to 80 degrees of alcohol; three-eight, at the top of the scale, was pure wine spirit with 92 to 93 degrees.

Production remained difficult and on the scale of a craft-type organisation. Stills were only inadequately and empirically modified until Weigert's (1773) and Magellano's (1780), which made continuous cooling by a double current possible. The crucial changes that made it possible to distil wine in one operation came even later. They were the work of a little-known inventor, born in 1778, Edouard Ardant. They lowered manufacturing costs and contributed to the enormous spread of alcohol in the nineteenth century.

Consumption increased by leaps and bounds. It soon became the custom to give alcohol to soldiers before battle. According to a doctor in 1702, this did not produce 'a bad effect'. The soldier became a habitual drinker and the production of brandy, when the need arose, a war-time industry. An English military doctor even stated (1763) that wine and alcoholic beverages tended to suppress 'putrid diseases' and were thus indispensable for the good health of the troops. Similarly the porters at the *Halles*, both men and women, became accustomed to drinking brandy diluted with water, but flavoured with long pepper, a good means of contending with the tax on wine entering Paris. The clientele of smoking-rooms – popular taverns where 'idle' working-class smokers took their pleasure – did the same.

Alcohol was also in demand for 'apéritifs' (known at that time as *ratafias*) which we would call liqueurs. 'Inflammable spirits,' wrote Doctor Louis Lemery in his *Traité des Aliments*, 'have a slightly pungent and often empyreumatic taste ... To remove the disagreeable taste, several compositions have been invented, which have been given the name of ratafia and which are nothing more than brandy or spirit of wine flavoured with a mixture of different ingredients.' Eighteenth-century Paris drank 'Sète waters', aniseed, frangipane and claret waters (made like 'claret' wine, that is strengthened by spices soaked in them), ratafias with a fruit base, Barbados waters, with a sugar and rum base, celery water, fennel water, *mille fleurs* water, lily water, 'divine' waters, coffee waters, and so on. The great centre for the production of these 'waters' was Montpellier, near the brandy supplies of Languedoc. Paris was obviously the big customer. Montpellier merchants set up a vast warehouse in the Rue de la Huchette where taverners obtained supplies wholesale. What had been a luxury in the sixteenth century had become an everyday amenity.

Brandy was not the only drink to spread through Europe and the world. A product of West Indian sugar cane, rum had become popular in England, Holland and the English colonies in America more than in the rest of Europe. It was an honourable adversary. In Europe brandy made from wine met brandy made from cider (which produced the incomparable calvados in the seventeenth century), from pears, plums and cherries (kirsch, which came from Alsace, Lorraine and Franche-Comté, was used as a medicine in Paris in about 1760). Maraschino from Zara, famous in about 1740, was the jealously guarded monopoly of Venice. Marc-brandy and alcohols made from grain were lesser but still formidable opponents. The distillation of grape marc began in about 1690 in Lorraine. In contrast to brandy, which needed a low heat, it required a high temperature and therefore large quantities of wood. The plentiful forests in Lorraine played their part. But this type of distillation gradually spread, for instance in Burgundy (the marc produced there was soon the best known of all) and also in all the vineyards of Italy each of which had its *grappa*.

The great competitors (rather like beer versus wine) were alcohols made from grain: *Kornbrand*, vodka, whisky, Hollands and gin, which became established north of the commercial boundaries of the vine without our knowing exactly when they began to spread. Their great advantage was their modest price.

The lands along the northern boundaries of the vine-countries naturally presented a mixture of tastes: England, which was open to brandy from the continent and rum from America (punch began to enjoy success there), drank its own whisky and gin. Holland was exactly at the meeting point of all the wine brandies and all the grain-based alcohols in the world, to say nothing of rum from Curaçao and Guiana. All these alcoholic drinks were quoted on the Amsterdam Stock Exchange: rum at the head, followed by brandy, and then, far behind these noble leaders, grain alcohols. Germany between the Rhine and the Elbe also had a two-fold consumption: in 1783 Hamburg received 4000 casks of brandy from France (500

litres per cask, making 20,000 hectolitres). The region where alcohol
made from grain was consumed almost exclusively only really began
beyond the Elbe and around the Baltic. In 1783 Danzig received no
more than a hundred or so casks of brandy which were reshipped,
after being scented with cummin, to Stockholm, another town
devoted to grain-based alcohols.

Alcohol succeeded all too well in Europe, which discovered in it
one of its everyday stimulants, a cheap source of calories and
certainly an easily accessible luxury, with vicious consequences. And
the watchful state soon found that it too could profit.

Alcoholism outside Europe

Every civilisation found its own answer or answers to the problem
of drinks, particularly alcoholic drinks. Any fermentation of a
vegetable product produces alcohol. The Indians in Canada found
their solace in maple juice; the Mexicans, before and after Cortes,
in *pulque* made from agaves which 'intoxicates like wine'; the poorest
Indians in the West Indies or South America, in maize or manioc.
Even the simple Tupinambas, whom Jean de Léry met in the bay of
Rio de Janeiro in 1556, on feast days drank a beverage made from
manioc chewed up and then left to ferment. Elsewhere there was
palm wine, a fermented sap. Northern Europe had its own saps of
birch trees and its beers made from cereals; it was responsible for the
success of mead (fermented honey water) until the fifteenth century.
Very early on, the Far East had wine made from rice, preferably
glutinous rice.

Did the still give Europe the advantage over all these peoples –
the possibility of making any super-alcoholic beverage it chose?
Rum, whisky, *kornbrand*, vodka, calvados, marc, brandy, and gin all
had to go through the cooled tube of the still. To answer this
question we would need to investigate the origins of alcohol made
from rice (arak) and find out if it existed before or after the Western
revolution of the sixteenth century. If Father Ricci, who reached
China in 1583 and died there in 1610, was not mistaken, the Chinese
did not know how to extract the essential juices from plants at that
time: it might follow that they did not know how to distil them, and
that therefore they may not have known the still. But that is a rather
hasty conclusion.

In fact the travellers do not supply the answer. They do establish
the presence of arak (*arrequi*) among privateers in Algiers at the

beginning of the seventeenth century. A traveller at Gujarat, in 1638, Mandeslo, claimed that *terry* from coconut palms 'is no less delicious than wine'. He adds: 'From rice, sugar and dates they make arac, which is a type of brandy much stronger and more agreeable than that made in Europe.' But no one tells us how this particular brandy was made and particularly when it began to be distilled.

Many uncertainties still remain. There is no doubt, however, about the alcohol content of arak and saké, that 'amber-coloured' rice wine. Kämpfer, an experienced doctor, described the 'sacki' he drank in Japan (1690) as a sort of beer, made particularly in the village of Temusii in the vicinity of Osaka. It was drunk warm – to drink it cold would be dangerous for the health – and was 'as strong as Spanish wine', a handsome compliment to a beer. On the other hand the *lau* he tasted in Siam was a sort of liqueur wine, a *Branntwein*, which travellers mentioned along with 'araka'. By contrast, Chinese wine was a 'real beer' made from rough millet or rice, according to a Jesuit correspondent in 1781. Fruit was often added to it 'either fresh or preserved or dried in the sun. ... To distinguish the different sorts of wine, they are called by the names of what has been added.' Thus there were 'quince wines, cherry, grape'. Slightly later, in China, in 1793, George Staunton drank 'a yellow vinous liquor [rice wine] and also distilled spirit'. The spirit seemed to be better made than the wine, which was generally cloudy, had a flat taste and turned sour fairly quickly. The spirit was clear and rarely had a bitter taste. It was made with millet in the northern provinces, with rice in the southern. 'The strength of some of it,' served up to the English (those who like Staunton accompanied the English ambassador Macartney), 'was, upon trial, ascertained to be above the common proof for ardent spirits.' The Jesuit fathers made the same comment: the only brandy the Chinese drank regularly 'has been passed through the still again and is so strong that it burns almost like alcohol'. We must add that it was drunk hot. The Chinese, according to Staunton, called spirits 'hot wine, *show-choo*'. The name is familiar, but we are at the end of the eighteenth century. Historians today generally think that alcohol and the means of making it were brought to the Far East from the West by Muslims in the fifteenth century.

Scarcely have we restated this cautious account than the need arises for renewed questioning of the specialists' hypotheses. For example, Sassanid Persia almost certainly possessed the stills needed to distil perfume. Al Kindi, in the ninth century, not only mentioned the distillation of perfumes but also described the apparatus used for the purpose. He spoke of camphor, which is known to be obtained from the distillation of camphor wood. Now camphor was a very early product in China. There is nothing to stop us thinking that alcohol was even invented in China in about the ninth century and took its place in the long list of Chinese inventions which were to travel to neighbouring lands. 'In the thirteenth century,' a present-day historian writes, 'the Mongols enthusiastically indulged in all sorts of Chinese brandy.' Ghengis Khan in his *Book of Dicta* even begged his people to give up alcohol ('the *Syrma* and the *Darassun*'). The Chinese could have passed on to the Mongols 'gunpowder which enabled them to blow up castles and towns throughout Persia, and rice spirit and millet spirit (*Shao-Hung* and *Shao-Chiu*), alcohols made from grain that might have led to their degeneration in less than a century'. *Araq* or *araqi* also means 'spirit' or 'soul' in Persia and the Islamic countries. In Kashmir a certain sultan, Iskander II (1465–7), died from drinking too much 'brandy'. It was said that 'he kept all the brown sugar to himself for its distillation'. The evidence is all the more important as the techniques of the Chinese and of the Tamerlane period in Persia were passed on via Kashmir: paper, gunpowder and soap. All these comments, taken from an unpublished paper by my colleague Aly Mazaherei, suggest an answer different from the usual explanation. Chinese precocity would surprise no one. At the level of general history it would make necessary a return to the old version – that the alembic and the distillation of plants came from Asia via the Muslims at the time of the Crusades.

It is impossible to cut this discussion short. The Jesuit fathers' accounts (1780) seem to establish the existence of alcoholic drink obtained from successive boilings without a still. A letter states that 'according to the last editor of the *Peu-tsao kang mou*, the invention of alcohol made from grain is not old in China and only goes back to the Yuen dynasty, that is to say towards the end of the thirteenth century'. We are neither farther forward nor reassured.

On the other hand, it is undeniable that brandy, rum and *agua ardiente* (alcohol made from cane) were Europe's poisoned gifts to the civilisations of America. All probability suggests that this was also the case with *mezcal*, produced by distilling the heart of the agave and much more alcoholic than the *pulque* made from the same plant. The Indian peoples suffered tremendously from the alcoholism in which they were encouraged to indulge. It would really seem as if the civilisation of the Mexican plateau, losing its ancient framework and taboos, abandoned itself to a temptation which wrought havoc with it after 1600. State revenue from *pulque* in New Spain was equal to half the revenue from the silver mines! It was deliberate policy on the part of the new masters. In 1786 the Viceroy of Mexico, Bernardo de Galvez, expressed his satisfaction at its results and, noting the Indian's taste for drink, recommended that it be spread amongst the still innocent Apaches in the north of Mexico. Apart from the profits to be expected, there was no better way of creating 'a new need which forces them to recognise very clearly their obligatory dependence with regard to ourselves'. The English and French had already done the same in north America, the French propagating brandy, despite all royal prohibitions, the English rum.

Chocolate, tea, coffee

At nearly the same time as the discovery of alcohol, Europe, at the centre of the innovations of the world, discovered three new drinks, stimulants and tonics: coffee, tea, and chocolate. All three came from abroad: coffee was Arab (originally Ethiopian); tea, Chinese; chocolate, Mexican.

Chocolate

Chocolate came to Spain from Mexico, from New Spain, in about 1520 in the form of loaves and tablets. Not surprisingly it was in the Spanish Netherlands slightly earlier (1606) than in France. The anecdote about Maria Theresa (her marriage to Louis XIV took place in 1659) drinking chocolate on the sly, a Spanish habit she was never able to lose, may well be true. The person who really introduced it into France a few years earlier was said to have been Cardinal Richelieu (brother of the minister, he was archbishop of Lyons and died in 1653). It is possible, though chocolate at that time was regarded as a medicine quite as much as a foodstuff: 'I have heard one of his servants say,' reported a witness later, 'that he [the cardinal] took it to moderate the vapours of his spleen and that he got this secret from some Spanish nuns who brought it to France.' Chocolate reached England from France in about 1657.

These first appearances were discreet and fleeting. Madame de Sévigné's letters mention that chocolate was either all the rage at court or out of favour, according to the day or the gossip. She herself worried about the dangers of the new beverage, having like others got into the habit of mixing it with milk. In fact chocolate did not become established until the French Regency. The Regent made it popular. At that time 'to go to the chocolate' meant to attend the prince's levée, to be in his good books. Nevertheless its popularity should not be exaggerated. We are told that in Paris in 1768 'the great take it sometimes, the old often, the people never'. The only area where it triumphed was Spain: every foreigner made fun of the thick chocolates, perfumed with cinnamon, which were the delight of the inhabitants of Madrid. A Jewish merchant, Aaron Colace, whose correspondence has been preserved, had good reason to settle in Bayonne in about 1727. From this town he was able to watch the Peninsular market while maintaining business connections with Amsterdam and its market in colonial goods (notably cocoa from Caracas, which often made this unexpected detour).

In December 1693 Gemelli Careri offered chocolate to a Turkish Aga at Smyrna, and had cause to regret it. The Aga 'was either intoxicated by it [which is unlikely] or smoke from the tobacco produced that effect, for he flared up at me violently, saying that I had made him drink a liquor to upset him and take away his powers of judgment'.

Tea

Tea came with the Portuguese, Dutch and English from China where its use had spread ten or twelve centuries earlier. The transfer to Europe was long and difficult: leaves, teapots, and porcelain cups had to be imported, together with a taste for this exotic drink, which Europeans had first known in the Indies where tea was very widely used. The first cargoes of tea arrived at Amsterdam in 1609, on the initiative of the *Oost Indische Companie*.

The tea plant was a bush from which the Chinese peasant plucked leaves. The first small and tender leaves – the smaller the better – produced imperial tea. Tea leaves were dried either by heat from a fire (green tea) or in the heat of the sun (the tea then fermented and blackened to form black tea). Both types were rolled by hand and sent out in 'large chests lined with lead into which they were crushed like grapes'.

The new drink was not mentioned in France until 1635 or 1636 in Chancellor Séguier's circle, but it had by no means yet acquired the freedom of the city. This was brought home to a medical student when he defended his thesis on tea in 1648: the thesis was rejected and the copy apparently burned.

The English East India Company began to import tea in 1646.

Samuel Pepys drank it for the first time at home on 28 June 1667. In fact European tea consumption did not become considerable until 1720–30 when direct trade between Europe and China began. Until then the major part of this trade had been carried on via Batavia, founded by the Dutch in 1617. Chinese junks bringing their usual cargoes to Batavia also carried a small quantity of rough tea which was the only variety that would keep and survive the long journey. The Dutch for a time succeeded in paying for this tea from Fou Kien with bales of sage instead of silver. Sage was also used in Europe to prepare a drink, one with highly praised medicinal qualities. But the Chinese were not won over; tea fared better in Europe.

Some forty years later the English overtook the Dutch. Exports from Canton in 1766 were as follows: 6 million pounds (weight) on English boats, 4·5 on Dutch, 2·4 on Swedish, 2·1 on French; making a total of 15 million pounds, about 7000 tons. Veritable tea fleets gradually grew up. Increasing quantities of dried leaves were unloaded at all ports with 'Indies quays': Lisbon, Lorient, London, Ostend, Amsterdam, Gothenburg, sometimes Genoa and Leghorn. The figures rose enormously: 28,000 'pics' (one picul equals about 60 kilograms) left Canton annually between 1730 and 1740; 115,000 from 1760 to 1770; 172,000 from 1780 to 1785. George Staunton, taking 1693 as the starting point, could infer that 'an increase of 1 in 400' had occurred a century later. In his day it was estimated that every inhabitant of England and America drank his pound of tea a year. And yet only a tiny part of Western Europe – Holland and England – had taken to the new drink on a large scale. France consumed a tenth of its own cargoes at the most. Germany preferred coffee. Spain hardly tried it.

Is it true to say that the new drink replaced gin in England? (The English government had taken the tax off gin production to combat the invasion of imports from the continent.) Was it a remedy for the undeniable drunkenness of London society in the reign of George II? Or did the sudden taxation of gin on the one hand and the general rise in grain prices on the other favour the newcomer – reputed in addition to be an excellent remedy for colds, scurvy and fevers? Such might have been the end of Hogarth's 'gin alley'. In any case tea won the day and the State subjected it to vigilant taxation (as in the American colonies which later used it as a pretext for revolt). In fact an unprecedented contraband trade brought in six or seven million pounds from the continent every year, via the North Sea, the Channel and the Irish Sea. All the ports and Indies companies as well as high finance in Amsterdam and elsewhere participated in the smuggling. Everyone was in on it, including the English consumer.

This picture covers only north-west Europe and one important customer is missing – Russia. Tea may perhaps have been known there in 1567, though it hardly came into general use before the treaty of Nertchinsk (1689) and more particularly before the establishment of the Kiatka fair, south of Irkutsk, very much later in 1763. A document in the archives at Leningrad dating from the end of the century and written in French states that:

[The goods] that the Chinese bring ... are a few silk fabrics, a few varnished objects, not many porcelains, large quantities of material from Canton which we call *nankins* and the Russians call *chitri*, and very considerable quantities of green tea. It is infinitely superior to the tea Europe receives across the immense seas, and thus the Russians are forced to pay as much as twenty francs a pound for it although they rarely resell it for more than fifteen or sixteen. To compensate for the loss, they never fail to raise the price of their furs, almost the sole commodity they supply to the Chinese, but the trick turns much less to their advantage than to the profit of the Russian government, which levies a tax of twenty-five per cent on everything bought and sold.

Nevertheless Russia imported less than 500 tons of tea at the end of the eighteenth century. It was a far cry from the 7000 tons consumed by the West.

To conclude this chapter on tea in the West, note that it took Europe a very long time to find out how to lay hands on the plant. The first tea shrubs in Java were only planted in 1827 and in Ceylon from 1877, immediately after the island's coffee shrubs had practically been destroyed.

The popularity of tea in Europe – even limited to Russia, the Netherlands and England – was an immense innovation. But the event is insignificant when measured on a world scale. Even today the essential business of tea is carried on in China, the largest consumer and producer. Tea there plays the same kind of role as the vine on the shores of the Mediterranean. Both vine and tea have their geographical zones where their very ancient cultivation has been gradually changed and perfected. Minute and repeated attentions are necessary to satisfy the requirements of generations of knowledgeable consumers. According to Pierre Gourou, the Chinese 'have sharpened their taste to the point of being able to distinguish between teas from the various localities, and to establish a subtle hierarchy. . . . All this is strangely reminiscent of viticulture at the other extremity of the Old World, also the result of thousands of years of progress accomplished by a civilisation of sedentary peasants.'

Every plant of civilisation creates a state of strict bondage. The soil of the tea plantations has to be prepared, the seeds sown, the tea plants pruned so that they remain shrubs instead of growing into trees 'which they are in the wild state'; the leaves carefully plucked then treated on the same day, dried either naturally or by heating, rolled and then dried again. In Japan the drying/rolling operation can be repeated six or seven times. Certain qualities can then sell for huge prices – the quality of the product depending on its type, on the soil, even more on the season when it is picked (the young spring leaves are more scented than the others), and finally on the treatment that differentiates green teas from black. The best green teas are used for the powdered tea the Japanese dissolve in boiling water (instead of simple infusion) according to an old Chinese method (forgotten in China itself) reserved for the famous tea ceremony, the *Cha-no-yu*. According to an eighteenth-century memoir, this was such a complicated ceremony that to learn the art of it properly 'you need a teacher, just as in Europe you need one to learn to dance, to bow, to fence etc.'.

For tea certainly had its ritual – like wine, like any self-respecting plant of civilisation. Even in poor households in China and Japan boiling water was always in readiness to make tea at all hours of the day. No guest would ever be received without being offered a cup of tea. In well-off Chinese homes, a source informs us in 1762:

There are very suitable implements for that purpose, such as a decorated table [the traditional low table], with a small stove beside it, boxes with drawers, bowls, cups, saucers, spoons for jam, crystallised sugar in pieces shaped like nuts, to hold in the mouth whilst drinking the tea, for this has least effect on its good taste, and uses up less sugar. All this is accompanied by various preserves, both dry and liquid, the Chinese having a much better understanding of how to make them dainty and attractive than European confectioners.

It must however be added that according to a nineteenth-century traveller in northern China where tea did not grow well, 'the members of the lower classes only know it as a luxury and sip hot water with as much pleasure as the well-to-do take their infusion of green tea – they are content to give it the name of tea'. Was it the social custom of tea that spread this strange *ersatz* of hot water? Or was everything generally drunk hot in China, as in Japan – tea, saké, alcohol made from rice or millet, and even water? 'If the Spaniards, who have a passion for drinking everything iced at all seasons, did as the Chinese do,' remarks a very sensible book (1762), 'they would not see so many diseases prevalent in their midst, nor so much dryness in their temperament.'

Tea, the universal drink in China and Japan, was adopted far less generally by the rest of the Far East. It was made into compact briquettes for long journeys and very early on carried from the Yang-tse-Kiang to Tibet by caravans of yaks, following what was probably the worst route in the world. Caravans of camels took the briquettes to Russia until the railway line was laid, and briquettes of tea are still in general consumption in certain regions of the USSR today.

Tea was also a success in Islam. Very sweet mint tea became a national drink in Morocco, but it only appeared there in the eighteenth century, introduced by the English, and did not become widespread until the following century. We do not know much about its travels in the rest of Islam. But it is a remarkable fact that all tea's successes occurred in countries where the vine was unknown: northern Europe, Russia, Islam. Should we infer that the plants of civilisation are mutually exclusive? 'Of the civilised countries that consume tea,' wrote a geographer, 'the Latin countries are the least important.' But the converse is also true for wine. In any case European wine and alcohol did not conquer the Far East.

Coffee

There is a danger that the history of coffee may lead us astray. The anecdotal, the picturesque and the unreliable play an enormous part in it.

The coffee shrub was once thought to be a native of Persia but more probably came from Ethiopia. In any case coffee shrub and coffee scarcely appeared before 1470. Coffee was being drunk in Aden at that date. It had reached Mecca by 1511 since in that year its consumption was forbidden there; the prohibition was repeated in 1524. It is recorded in Cairo in 1510 and Istanbul in 1517; thenceforth it was forbidden and re-authorised at regular intervals. Meanwhile it spread widely within the Turkish Empire, to Damascus, Aleppo (1532) and Algiers, and eastwards beyond the Empire to Persia and as far as Muslim India. Before the century ended coffee was at home in nearly all the Muslim world.

That is where coffee, and occasionally the coffee shrub, was discovered by Western travellers such as Prospero Alpini, an Italian doctor who reached Egypt in 1592, and the swaggering Pietro della Valle, who was in Constantinople in 1615:

The Turks [wrote della Valle] also have another beverage, black in colour, which is very refreshing in summer and very warming in winter, without however changing its nature and always remaining the same drink, which is swallowed hot. ... They drink it in long draughts, not during the meal but afterwards, as a sort of delicacy and to converse in comfort in the company of friends. One hardly sees a gathering where it is not drunk. A large fire is kept going for this purpose and little porcelain bowls are kept by it ready-filled with the mixture; when it is hot enough there are men entrusted with the office who do nothing else but carry these little bowls to all the company, as hot as possible, also giving each person a few melon seeds to chew to pass the time. And with the seeds and this beverage, which they call *kafoue*, they amuse themselves while conversing ... sometimes for a period of seven or eight hours.

Coffee arrived in Venice in about 1615, slightly later in Marseilles, in Lyons in about 1644. A traveller, Father de La Roque, brought the first grains to Paris in about 1644, together with coffee cups and the coffee pot. Coffee may possibly have reached London in 1650, Vienna in 1651, Sweden in 1674. All these dates are approximate.

In fact it was in Paris that it received the welcome which decided its success. In 1669 a Turkish ambassador, Suleiman Mustapha Raca, who entertained a great deal and had a knowledge of the world, offered his visitors coffee. 'The embassy failed but coffee succeeded.' A *Traité du Caphé* appeared in Lyons in 1670, without an author's name, perhaps written by Jacob Spon. Like tea, the new beverage was heralded as a marvellous remedy:

It dries up all scrofula, drives away wind, strengthens the liver, relieves dropsies by its purifying quality; sovereign equally for scabies and impurity of the blood, it revives the heart and its vital beat, relieves those who have stomach ache and have lost their appetite; it is equally good for those who have a cold in the head, streaming or heavy. ... The vapour which rises from it [helps] watering eyes and noises in the ears, sovereign remedy also for short breath, colds which attack the lungs, pains in the kidneys, worms; extraordinary relief after over-eating or over-drinking. Nothing better for those who eat a lot of fruit. ...

However, other doctors and public opinion claimed that coffee prevented men from having children.

As a result of this publicity and despite these accusations, coffee made ground in Paris. Pedlars appeared on the scene during the last years of the seventeenth century, Armenians dressed as Turks and wearing turbans, who carried trays in front of them with coffee pot, lighted stove and cups. Hatarioun, an Armenian known by the name of Pascal, opened the first stall to sell coffee in about 1670, in one of the booths of the Saint-Germain fair (held for centuries near the abbey on which it depended, on the site of the present Rue du Four and Rue Saint Sulpice). Business was not good for Pascal and he moved to the Right Bank of the Seine to the quai de l'Ecole du Louvre where at one time his customers consisted of a few Levantines and Knights of Malta. He then moved on to England. Despite his failure, other cafés opened. One of these was the Malibar café, with premises first in the Rue de Buci and then in Rue Férou, owned by another Armenian. The most famous was established in the modern style by an old waiter of Pascal's, an Italian, Procope, who was born in Sicily in 1650 and later called himself François Couteau or Descouteaux. He set up at the Saint-Germain fair, then in the Rue de Tournon, and finally in 1686 in the Rue des Fossés-Saint-Germain. This last café, the *Procope* – it is still there today – was near the elegant and busy centre of the town, at that time (before it moved to the Palais Royal in the eighteenth century) the Buci crossroads, or more properly the Pont Neuf. He had another piece of luck when the Comédie Française started up opposite his newly-opened café. The Sicilian's ability to set the right tone ensured his success. He knocked down the partitions between two adjoining houses, hung tapestries and mirrors on the walls, chandeliers from the ceilings, and sold preserved fruit and drinks as well as coffee. His stall was the rendezvous of the idle, of gossips, conversationalists, wits (Charles Duflos, future secretary of the Académie Française was one of the pillars of the establishment) and beautiful women. The theatre was near at hand and *Procope* also sold refreshments in a booth there.

The modern café could not remain the prerogative of one district or one street. In addition the movement of the town gradually militated against the Left Bank to the advantage of the Right, which was livelier, as a summary map of Parisian cafés in the eighteenth century demonstrates – a total of six to seven hundred. The reputation of the Café de la Régence, founded in 1681 in the Palais-Royal square, grew up at that time (later its fame became even greater and it moved to its present position in the Rue Saint-Honoré). The vogue the cafés enjoyed gradually lowered the social status of the taverns. The fashion was the same in Germany, Italy and Portugal. Brazilian coffee was cheap in Lisbon, and so was sugar, which was poured so copiously into it that, to quote one Englishman, the spoon stood up in the cup.

This fashionable drink was not fated to remain limited to the fashionable world. While all other prices were rising, superabundant production in the islands maintained the cost of a cup of coffee almost unchanged. In 1782 Le Grand d'Aussy explained that:

Consumption has tripled in France; there is no bourgeois household where you are not offered coffee, no shopkeeper, no cook, no chambermaid who does not breakfast on coffee with milk in the morning. In public markets and in certain streets and alleys in the capital, women have set themselves up selling what they call *café au lait* to the populace, that is to say poor milk coloured with coffee grounds which they buy from the kitchens of big houses. This beverage is in a tin urn equipped with a tap to serve it and a stove to keep it hot. There is usually a wooden bench near the merchant's stall or shop. Suddenly, to your surprise, you see a woman from Les Halles or a porter arrive and ask for coffee. It is served in large pottery cups. These elegant people take it standing up, basket on back, unless as a sensuous refinement they want to place their burden on the bench and sit down. From my windows overlooking the beautiful quai where I live [the quai du Louvre in the neighbourhood of the Pont Neuf] I often see this spectacle in one of the wooden booths that have been built from the Pont Neuf to the Louvre. And sometimes I have seen scenes which make me regret that I am not Teniers or Callot.

To correct this picture painted by an awful Parisian bourgeois, it must be said that perhaps the most picturesque or rather the most moving sight was the women pedlars standing at street corners when the workmen went to work at daybreak. They carried the tin urns on their backs and served *café au lait* 'in earthenware pots for two sous. Sugar was not much in evidence.' It was, however, enormously popular; the workmen 'have found more economy, more sustenance, more flavour in this foodstuff than in any other. As a result, they drink it in prodigious quantities, saying that it generally sustains them until the evening. Thus they eat only two meals, a large breakfast, and beef salad in the evening'; which meant slices of cold beef with parsley, oil and vinegar.

If there was such an increase in consumption – and not only in Paris and France – from the middle of the eighteenth century, it was because Europe had organised production itself. So long as the world market had depended solely on coffee shrubs around Mocha, in Arabia, European imports had perforce been limited. But coffee shrubs were planted in Java from 1712; on Bourbon island (Réunion) from 1716; on the island of Cayenne in 1722 (it had therefore crossed the Atlantic); in Martinique in 1723–30; in Jamaica in 1730; in Santo Domingo in 1731. These dates do not apply to production because the coffee shrubs had to grow and spread. Father Charlevoix writes in 1731: 'We are delighted to see coffee enriching our island [Santo Domingo]. The tree which produces it is already becoming as fine ... as if it were native to the country, but it needs time to get accustomed to the soil.' The last to come on to the market, coffee from Santo Domingo remained the least mentioned and the most plentiful of all: some 40 million pounds were produced in 1789, when European consumption fifty years before was perhaps 4 million pounds. Mocha always headed the list as far as price and quality were concerned, followed by coffee from Java and Bourbon island ('a small, bluish bean, like that of Java') when its quality was good, then by the products of Martinique, Guadeloupe and finally Santo Domingo.

Careful checks, however, warn us against exaggerating the figures for consumption. From about 1785–9 France imported 36,000 tons of coffee (half of it from Santo Domingo). Of this, 10,000 to 12,000 were re-exported and Paris only kept about a thousand tons for its own use. Some provincial towns still did not welcome the new beverage. The Limoges bourgeois only drank coffee 'as a medicine'. Only certain social categories – the postmasters in the north, for example – followed the fashion.

It was therefore necessary to go in search of new markets. The Dutch Indies Company was well aware of this; it supplied coffee to Persia and Muslim India, both of them loyal to Mocha, but the Company would have liked to dispose of its surplus from Java there too. If the 150 million Muslims are added to the 150 million Europeans, there was a possible market of 300 million – perhaps a third of all human beings – actual or potential coffee drinkers in the eighteenth century. Coffee had become a 'national commodity' like tea, a means of making money. An active capitalist sector had a financial interest in its production, distribution and success. It had a significant impact on Parisian social and cultural life. The café (the shop where the new drink was sold) became the rendezvous for men of fashion and the leisured, as well as a shelter for the poor. 'There are men,' wrote Sébastien Mercier (1782), 'who arrive at the café at ten in the morning and do not leave until eleven at night [the compulsory closing time, supervised by the police]; they dine on a cup of coffee with milk, and sup on Bavarian cream' [a mixture of syrup, sugar, milk and sometimes tea].

An anecdote illustrates the slow infiltration of coffee amongst the people. When Cartouche was about to be put to death (29 November 1721), his 'judge' who was drinking white coffee offered him a cup. 'He replied that this was not his drink and that he would prefer a glass of wine with a little bread.'

The stimulants: the glories of tobacco

Diatribes against the new drinks were numerous. Some wrote that England would be ruined by its possessions in the Indies, meaning 'the stupid luxury of tea'. Sébastien Mercier on his moralising walk across Paris in the year 2440 was conducted by a 'sage' who reprovingly told him:

> We have banished three poisons of which you used to make perpetual use — tobacco, coffee and tea. You used to put an evil powder in your noses that took away from you Frenchmen what little memory you had. You burned your stomachs with destructive liquors that hastened digestive action. Your common nervous diseases were due to that effeminate washing which removed the nourishing essence of animal life. . . .

In reality every civilisation needs dietary luxuries and stimulants. In the twelfth and thirteenth centuries the craze was for spices and pepper; in the sixteenth century for alcohol; then it was tea and coffee, not to mention tobacco. The nineteenth and twentieth centuries were destined to have new luxuries of their own, their good and evil drugs. In any case we like the Venetian text dating from the beginning of the seventeenth century which sensibly and not unhumorously specified that the tax on *acque gelate*, coffee and other *bevande* applied to all similar things *inventate o da inventarsi*, invented or yet to be invented. Michelet's view that coffee as early as the French Regency was the 'drink of the Revolution' was certainly exaggerated. But wiser historians also misrepresent the reality when they talk about the Great Century and the eighteenth century without mentioning the shortage of meat, the excesses of alcohol and the coming of coffee.

It may be an error of perspective on our part, but it seems to us that with the increase — or at least the continuation — of very serious dietary difficulties, humanity had need of compensation, according to a constant rule of its life.

Tobacco was one of these compensations. How should it be classified? Louis Lemery, 'Doctor Regent in the Faculty of Medicine of Paris, of the Royal Academy of Sciences', did not hesitate to include it in his *Traité des Aliments* (1702). The plant, he specified, 'is taken either by the nose, or in smoke or by chewing'. He also spoke of cocoa leaves, similar to myrtle leaves, which 'appease hunger and pain, and give energy'. He did not mention quinquina, although he alluded to opium, consumed amongst the Turks even more than in the West, a drug which it was 'dangerous to use'. What did escape him was the immense opium venture from India to the Indian archipelago (on one of the major lines of Islamic expansion) and already as far as China. The great turning point came after 1765, just after the conquest of Bengal, when a monopoly of poppy fields was established to the advantage of the East India Company; they had formerly been a source of income for the Great Mogul. Louis Lemery did not of course possess any of these facts in the early years of the century. Nor did he know about Indian hemp. Stupefacients, foods or medicines, these were great factors destined to transform and disturb men's daily lives.

We shall confine ourselves to tobacco. Between the sixteenth and seventeenth centuries it conquered the whole world, and enjoyed even greater popularity than tea or coffee, which was no mean achievement.

Tobacco originated in the New World. When Columbus arrived in Cuba on 2 November 1492 he saw the natives smoking rolled tobacco leaves. The plant and its name (either Caribbean or Brazilian) moved to Europe where it was for a fairly long time an object of curiosity in botanical gardens or known because of supposedly medicinal qualities. Jean Nicot, French ambassador at Lisbon (1560), sent Catherine of Medici tobacco powder to use against migraine, according to Portuguese practice. Jean Thevet, who also brought the plant to France, asserted that the natives of Brazil used it to eliminate superfluous fluids from the brain. Naturally at one point in Paris a certain Jacques Gahory (died 1576) attributed to it the virtues of a universal panacea.

The plant was cultivated in Spain in 1558 and spread rapidly to France, England (about 1565), Italy, the Balkans, and Russia. It was in the Philippines in 1575, having arrived with the 'Manila galleon'. In 1588 it was in Virginia, where production began to soar after 1612; in Macao after 1600, in Java in 1601, in India and Ceylon in about 1605–10. Its diffusion was all the more remarkable as there was no producer market – that is to say no civilisation – behind tobacco comparable to that for pepper at its distant beginnings (India), tea (China), coffee (Islam), even chocolate, which had the advantage of a high-quality culture in New Spain. Tobacco came from 'savage' areas in America; the production of the plant had therefore to be ensured before its blessings could be enjoyed. But it had one unique advantage: its great flexibility in adapting itself to the most varied climates and soils.

The outlines of the history of commercialised tobacco do not appear before the first years of the seventeenth century in Lisbon, Seville and above all Amsterdam, although snuff had begun to be popular in Lisbon at least from 1558. The first two of the three ways of using tobacco (snuff, smoking, chewing) were the most important. 'Powdered tobacco' rapidly acquired several forms, depending on the ingredients added: musk, amber, bergamot, orange blossom. There was a 'Spanish type' tobacco, and tobacco with 'perfume of Malta' or 'perfume of Rome', 'illustrious ladies taking as much as great lords'. Meanwhile 'smoking tobacco' was taken by pipes, later in cigars (the rolled leaves 'the length of a candle' that the natives of Spanish America smoked were not immediately imitated in Europe); later still, in cigarettes. Cigarettes appeared in Spain during the Napoleonic wars: it became the custom at that time to roll tobacco in a small piece of paper, a *papelito*. The *papelito* then reached France where it earned the approval of French youth. In between times the paper became thinner and the cigarette came into general use in the Romantic period.

We get our information about the early use of tobacco from violent government prohibitions (governments later came to realise the attractive possibilities of financial return and the Tobacco Monopoly was established in France in 1674). These prohibitions encircled the world: England 1604, Japan 1607–9, the Ottoman Empire 1611, the Mogul Empire 1617, Sweden and Denmark 1632, Russia 1634, Naples 1637, Sicily 1640, China 1642, the Papal States 1642, the Electorate of Cologne 1649, Wurtemburg 1651. Of course they were ignored, particularly in China where they continued in force until 1776. The use of tobacco was already universal in the Tche-li in 1640. In the Fou Kien (1664) 'everyone has a long pipe in his mouth, lights up, inhales and blows out the smoke'. Vast regions were planted with tobacco and China exported it to Siberia and Russia. By the end of the eighteenth century everyone in China smoked – men and women, mandarins and poor, 'down to toddlers two feet high'. So did the street urchins of Lisbon at the same period.

All types of tobacco and all the ways they could be used were known and accepted in China, including, from the seventeenth century, the consumption of tobacco mixed with opium, which came from the Indian archipelago and Formosa through the medium of the *Oost Indische Companie*. 'The best commodity to take to the East Indies,' says a report of 1727, 'is powdered tobacco, either from Seville or Brazil.' In any case the temporary decline in the popularity of tobacco in Europe in the eighteenth century, about which we have very little information, had no parallel in China or India. It goes without saying that this disfavour was only temporary – and we can even doubt whether it occurred at all when we see the Burgundy peasants and the rich of St Petersburg all giving themselves up to the pleasures of smoking at that time.

In Africa the vogue grew. The success of large tails of black tobacco from Bahia whose inferior quality was disguised by an admixture of molasses continued until the nineteenth century to stimulate a lively trade between Brazil and the gulf of Benin, where an active clandestine Black slave trade lasted until about 1850.

4

Superfluity and Sufficiency: Houses, Clothes and Fashion

In the last chapter we tried to draw the line between superfluity and sufficiency in an area ranging from meat to tobacco. To complete the picture and give us a further opportunity of studying the differences between poor and rich it remains to describe houses and clothes. After all, where is luxury more conspicuous than in the home, furniture and dress? At the same time we shall be able to make comparisons between civilisations, for none of them adopted the same styles.

1 Houses throughout the world

We cannot hope to look at all the kinds of houses built between the fifteenth and eighteenth centuries. We can do little more than pick out a few obvious general characteristics.

In almost all cases, fortunately, we will be dealing with unchanging fixtures, or at least with slow evolutions. Many preserved or restored houses refer us back not only to the eighteenth century but to the sixteenth and fifteenth, even earlier, as we can see in the Golden Road of the Hradschin in Prague, or in the marvellous village of Santillana, near Santander. An observer remarked in 1842 that Beauvais retained more of its ancient dwellings at that time than any other town; he described 'some forty wooden houses going back to the sixteenth and seventeenth centuries'.

Furthermore a house is built or rebuilt according to traditional patterns. Here more than anywhere else the strength of precedent makes itself felt. The masons called in to rebuild the houses of the rich at Valladolid after the terrible fire of 1564 were the unconscious representatives of the old Muslim crafts, and their beautiful new houses bore distinct marks of the past. The influence of customs and traditions is always present, for they constitute ancient legacies that can never be discarded. Typical of these is the way Islamic houses are closed in on themselves. The traveller was right when he said that all well-off homes in Persia in 1694 'are of the same architecture. There is always a room about thirty feet square in the middle of the building, at its centre a hollow full of water in the form of a small pond and surrounded by carpeting.' The standard pattern is even more true in the case of country-dwellers throughout the world. To have seen a very poor peasant's house being built from its frail wooden frame in the region of Vitoria north of Rio de Janeiro in 1937 is to possess an ageless document, valid for centuries before the present day. The same applies to the nomad's simple tent: it has come down through the centuries without change, often woven on the same primitive loom as in the past.

In short, a 'house', wherever it may be, was an enduring thing, and it bears perpetual witness to the slowness of civilisations, of cultures bent on preserving, maintaining and repeating.

Rich building materials: stone and brick

Repetition was all the more natural as building material varied little and imposed certain limitations on every region. This does not mean, necessarily, that civilisations lived absolutely according to the restrictions imposed by stone, brick, wood or earth. But these materials often did constitute long-lasting limitations. 'It is lack of stone,' a traveller noted, 'that obliges them [the Persians] to build walls and houses of earth.' In fact they were built of sun-dried bricks. 'Rich people decorate the outside walls with a mixture of whitewash, Muscovy green and gum which makes them look silvery.' None the less they were still unfired bricks, and geography explains why, though it does not explain everything. Human beings also had a say in the matter.

Stone was a luxury which had to be paid for; otherwise it was necessary to accept compromises, like mixing brick with stone, as Roman and Byzantine masons had already done and as Turkish and Chinese masons still regularly did; or using wood and stone; or reserving stone solely for the houses of princes and gods. Stone triumphed completely in Inca Cuzco, but only observatories, temples and stadiums enjoyed this privilege in the Maya kingdoms. Side by side with these monuments we must imagine the everyday huts made of branches and *pisé*, like those still to be seen around the ruins of Chichen Itza or Palenque in Yucatan today. In the same way the striking stone architecture of the rectangular towns in the Indian Deccan stretches northwards as far as the soft earth of the Indus-Ganges plain. This is the result of an old tradition. Yet Indian villages never had stone houses. The houses near Portuguese Goa in 1639 'are all made of straw, and small, having no opening other than a low and narrow door. Their furniture only consists of a few rush mats on which they lie down to sleep or to take their meals ... and they live almost entirely on rice and have earthenware pots to cook it. They smear their houses with cow dung because they believe it drives away fleas.'

This picture is still true today. Nothing has changed; the house remains drastically small, without hearth or window; the alley-like village street is crowded with animals which have no stables.

In the West and in the Mediterranean stone civilisation took centuries to evolve. Quarries had to be worked and stone selected that was easy to work and hardened in contact with the air. It meant a human investment for centuries on end.

There are innumerable sandstone, sand, rough limestone and gypsum quarries around Paris. The town cleared its own site in advance. Paris was built on enormous excavations, 'towards Chaillot, Passy and the old road from Orléans', under 'the whole suburb of Saint-Jacques, the Rue de la Harpe and the Rue de Tournon'. Rough limestone was widely quarried until the First World War, sawn up in yards in the suburbs and transported across Paris by heavy horse-drawn drays. Nevertheless we should not be misled: Paris was not always a stone town. Enormous work had to be done, starting in the fifteenth century, requiring hosts of carpenters from Normandy, roofers, makers of edge tools and masons from the Limousin (who were accustomed to hard work), tapestry-makers specialising in fine work, and innumerable plasterers. In Sébastien Mercier's day the road these plasterers took to return to their lodgings every evening was marked by the trail of their white footprints. And a great many houses of that period only had a stone foundation while the upper floors were still of wood. In the Petit-Pont fire on 27 April 1727 the wooden houses blazed fiercely like a 'great lime-kiln [into which] one saw whole beams fall'. The rare stone houses formed protective barriers stopping the advance of the fire. 'The Petit Châtelet, which is very well built,' noted a witness, 'saved the Rue de la Huchette and the Rue Galande area.'

Paris was thus for a long time a wooden town, like so many others – like Troyes, which went up in flames in the vast fire of 1547; like

Dijon, which still had wooden houses with thatched roofs in the seventeenth century. It was only then that stone began to be widely used, together with tiles, and in particular glazed tiles, which were beginning to make their appearance then. Houses in Lorraine towns and villages were covered with wooden shingles. Round tiles, regarded by a persistent but erroneous tradition as a Roman survival, were slowly adopted. In the seventeenth century it was necessary to forbid the use of straw and even irregular shingles to cover houses in certain villages of Wetterau near the Main. Indeed the advent of stone and tile was in some places achieved by coercion, and even by means of subsidies, while the straw roof remained a sign of the past and of poverty. In the Saône plain 'the tile roof, that symbol of prosperity, is rare' even in the eighteenth century. In a sketch of a small village in the Nuremburg region showing both tile and straw roofs we can certainly tell which ones belong to poor peasants and which to comfortably-off farmers.

Brick gradually replaced wood in buildings from England to Poland, but it did not predominate immediately. In Germany its success began precociously, though slowly, in the twelfth century.

London began to adopt brick from the Elizabethan period, at the same time as Paris became a stone city. The transformation was completed after the fire of 1666 – which 'consumed three-quarters of the town, over twelve thousand houses' – in the ensuing massive and inevitably unmethodical reconstruction. Similarly, all new buildings in Amsterdam were of brick in the seventeenth century. The brick was browned by protective coatings of tar, with frontons or cornices standing out as patches of white stone.

Poor building materials: wood, earth, fabric

Over large expanses in between these areas of expensive building, wood or wood in combination with clay and *pisé* continued to be used where geography and tradition were favourable: in Picardy, Champagne, the Scandinavian and Muscovite countries, the Rhineland regions and wherever a certain backwardness encouraged its retention. The painters of the Cologne school regularly depicted mud and half-timbered houses in the fifteenth century. In Moscow prefabricated wooden houses could be erected in a few hours or moved wherever the purchaser desired.

Because of earth tremors a wood and *pisé* house with a bamboo frame was adopted throughout the Far East. 'Ordinary houses' in

China, explained Father Ricci, 'are built of wood, and although the imperial palaces have brick walls their roofs are wooden and supported by wooden columns'. Bamboo was an excellent material, 'cylindrical and as hard as iron'. 'When it is mature a man has difficulty in bending it with both hands, and although hollow and as it were formed of joined pieces its nodes and junctures give it so much strength that it is commonly used to make the supports for small houses.' But these were inferior and often wretched houses, particularly in the villages. A French traveller who crossed China from Canton to Peking during the winter of 1774–5 says the same thing over and over again: at their best – near the Yang-tse-Kiang – peasant houses were built of bricks and covered with tiles; usually they were made of earth, with thatched roofs, and their leanto's were covered by 'pine leaves'. 'Low, rounded or almost flat', they were often astonishingly filthy.

According to an English traveller (1793):

The walls of the village houses [north of Peking] consisted mostly of indurated mud; or of masses of earth baked imperfectly in the sun, or moulded between planks ... or of wicker-work, defended by a coating of clay. The roofs were covered generally with straw, rarely with green turf. The apartments are divided by lattice-work hung with broad paper containing either the figures of deities or columns of moral sentences. A court or vacant space around the house, is enclosed with wattles or the stems of the *kow leang* [sorghum].

The style of the present-day house is reminiscent of these ancient descriptions. In its simplest form it is one narrow rectangle, at the most two or three rectangles, arranged around a courtyard closed by a wall. The doors and windows (when they exist) draw their light from this courtyard. Generally speaking the materials used are brick and tile in the south (a sign of wealth or tradition), *pisé* and thatch (sorghum or wheat-straw) in the north. Japanese houses are built more or less on the same principles, with the same thatched roof, but always on piles. As in very old Chinese houses (though the custom lapsed a long time ago) a large part of the external walls consists of sliding paper panels. They are always open in daytime and 'at night when the lamp is lit, they give the house the appearance of a lantern'.

Wood and earth were so important in China that every building (up to the present day) was called a 'great enterprise of earth and wood'. If the building was at all important or if it was princely or imperial, supplies of wood were the first consideration (particularly in denuded northern China) with 'its extravagant cost' in both men and money. The requisite wood was not always to be found near coastal zones or along usable waterways. A sixteenth-century official recalled a popular saying in Se-tchouan: 'For every thousand people who go into the mountains in search of wood, five hundred come back.' According to the same witness, at every proclamation demanding wood for imperial buildings the peasants in the Houpe and the Se-tchouan 'wept until they choked'.

The frailest dwelling is still the nomad tent. Its substance (felt, woven goat- or camel-hair) and also its shape and proportions vary. But, as we have said, this frail object persisted through the centuries. Was it only a makeshift solution? It only needed some new circumstance or opportunity for the nomad to settle down and change his style of dwelling. This probably occurred to some extent at the end of the Roman Empire; it happened more certainly during the Turkish conquests and the forced settlements which accompanied them in the Balkans; it could be observed in colonial Algeria in recent years and still may be seen in all the Islamic countries today.

Peasant houses in Europe

The two broad categories of houses throughout the world are obvious: rural and urban. The former, clearly the most numerous, were shelters rather than houses, intended to meet the rudimentary needs of men and domestic animals. We can scarcely add anything to the rapid resumé given in the preceding paragraphs about such vast regions as China and India. Here as elsewhere Europe is the only continent privileged in respect of our historical knowledge of it, though our knowledge is very limited.

The peasant house in Europe does not figure in literary documents. The classic description by Noël du Fail is only a rapid sketch of a Breton house of the middle of the sixteenth century. The same is true of a description – though an unusually detailed one – of a Finnish farm near St Petersburg (1790). It mentions the group of wooden huts, most of them in a state of collapse, that made up the farm: the house, a simple smoky room, two small stables, a Russian bath (a *sauna*), a stove to dry wheat or rye. The furniture consisted of a table, a bench, a cast-iron pot, a cauldron, a basin, a pail, some barrels, tubs, wooden or earthenware plates, an axe, a spade, a knife for slicing cabbages.

Drawings and paintings usually add a little more to our knowledge of the appearance of whole villages or the interiors of large houses where men and beasts lived together. We learn even more by studying the regulations governing village buildings.

In fact a village house was only built or repaired with the authorisation of the community or the seigniorial authority – which controlled access to the stone or clay quarries and to the forests where the wood to build houses grew. Six large trees had to be cut down for one house in Alsace in the fifteenth century and the same for a barn. These regulations also contain information on the way in which rushes, reeds or straw were woven at the top of a roof; on the stones that were added to shingles (wooden tiles) in the mountains so that the wind should not blow them down; on the relatively small fire risk represented by a thatched roof which had been exposed to the elements for a long time; on the excellent fertiliser provided by old straw roofs that had been replaced; on the food that such roofs could provide for cattle in times of distress (as in Savoy in the eighteenth century); on methods of mixing wood and clay or of arranging planks for the main room; on the custom of indicating inns by signs, either the hoop of a cask or a crown, as in Germany. Many details did not change until the nineteenth century, and even later – for example the village square; the wall which often sur-·rounded the cluster of houses; the church, which often served as a fortress; the water supplies (rivers, fountains, wells); and the arrangement of the peasant house into quarters for humans and animals and the barn for harvests. At Varzy (Nièvre), a small town in Burgundy, the houses of the rich are peasant in style and the inventories describing them in the seventeenth century scarcely mention more than one large habitable room, which was kitchen, bedroom and living-room all in one.

Excavations undertaken in the past twenty years on sites of deserted villages in the USSR, Poland, Hungary, Germany, Denmark, Holland, England and, recently, in France, are gradually making good a previously chronic lack of information. Ancient village houses discovered in the earth of the Hungarian *puzta* and elsewhere reveal shapes and details (for example the brick furnace) which were destined to endure. The first French excavations (1964 and 1965) were centred on three abandoned villages: Montaigut (Aveyron), Saint-Jean-le-Froid (Tarn) and Dracy (Côte-d'Or). The first was fairly large, the third rich in various objects, the second sufficiently cleared to be seen with 'its rampart, ditch, approach road, paved streets equipped with gutters, and one of its residential districts, its cemetery, two and probably three churches all built on the same site and of more striking dimensions than the last chapel, which is still visible'.

The lesson of these excavations is the relative mobility of villages and hamlets; they grew up, expanded, contracted, and also shifted their sites. Sometimes these 'desertions' were total and final – the *Wüstungen* mentioned by German historians and geographers. More often the centre of gravity within a given cultivated area shifted, and furniture, people, animals, stones, everything was moved out of the abandoned village to a site a few kilometres away. Even the form of the village could change in the course of these vicissitudes. The large compact village in Lorraine would seem to date from the seventeenth century. The *bocage vendéen* (the wooded district north-west of Poitou) in the Gâtine area of the Vendée dates from the same period, with the establishment of large farms, isolated from each other, which reshaped the landscape.

Many villages or houses have come down, although undoubtedly altered, to our own time. There are museum villages as well as museum towns where it is possible to go back towards a distant past, the great problem being to date the various stages with any precision. But extensive researches – the results have been published for Italy and the French results are still awaiting publication (a total of 1634 unpublished monographs) – give the outlines of a possible reconstruction. In places where life has not followed too precipitous a course, as in Sardinia, peasant dwellings can often be found intact, variously adapted to their functions of housing people and animals according to the different regions of the island.

Any traveller or tourist can see for himself the interiors of mountain houses preserved in the Innsbruck museum, or dwellings still standing in Savoy and so far unspoiled by holidaymakers, with their wooden chimney, known as the *borne*, where ham and sausages are smoked. Similarly, large seventeenth-century peasant houses can be seen in Lombardy, and there is a magnificent fifteenth-century *masia* in Catalonia with Roman vaults, arches and beautiful stone. In both cases the houses in question certainly belonged to that rare being, the comfortably-off peasant.

Urban houses and dwellings

It is even easier to visit the urban rich – in Europe of course, because apart from princely palaces practically nothing of the old houses outside Europe has been preserved – the fault of their poor materials. And good eye-witness accounts are lacking. We will therefore stick to Europe.

The Cluny Museum (hostel of the abbots of Cluny) opposite the Sorbonne in Paris was completed in 1498 (in less than thirteen years) by Jacques d'Amboise, brother of the cardinal who was Louis XII's minister for a long time. It gave temporary shelter to Louis XII's very young widow, Mary of England, in 1515. The house of the Guise family between 1553 and 1697 in the Marais district now holds the *Archives Nationales*, while in 1643-9 Mazarin lived in what is now the *Bibliothèque Nationale*. Jacques-Samuel, Comte de Coubert, son of Samuel Bernard (the richest merchant in Europe in Louis XIV's time) lived at 46, Rue du Bac a few metres away from the Boulevard Saint-Germain, in a house built between 1741 and 1744. Nine years later in 1753 its owner went bankrupt. If we go to a wonderfully preserved town like Cracow we can still visit the home of Prince Czartoryski, or Wierzynek; a very rich fourteenth-century merchant, in his house in the Market Square (the Rynek) where it is still possible to dine today. In Prague we would run the risk of losing our way on a visit to Wallenstein's immense and arrogant house on the edge of the Moldau. In Toledo the museum of the Dukes of Lerma is undoubtedly more authentic than El Greco's house.

At a more modest level we can trace the plans of sixteenth-century Parisian flats from the files of the *Archives Notariales*. Such dwellings were not, however, for everyone. When their numbers increased – inordinately as it seemed to seventeenth- and eighteenth-century Parisians – the poor continued to be housed even more abominably than they are today, which is saying a great deal.

Furnished rooms in Paris, generally kept by wine merchants or wigmakers, were dirty, infested with fleas and bugs, and served as a home for prostitutes, delinquents, foreigners and penniless youths recently arrived from the country. The police searched them remorselessly. People who were scarcely better off lived in the new *entresols* (built on the cheap by the architects, 'like cellars') or on the top floors of houses. Normally the social condition of the lodger deteriorated the higher he climbed. Poverty was the rule on the sixth or seventh floors, in attics and garrets. Certain individuals managed to emerge from it; Greuze, Fragonard and Vernet lived like that and 'did not blush for it', but what became of the others? In 1782, in the 'fauxbourg Saint-Marcel', the worst district of all, 'a whole family [often] occupies one single room ... where the wretched beds have no curtains, where cooking utensils lie side by side with chamber pots'. When rent quarter came round there were many hasty and shameful removals. The Christmas quarter, in the winter cold, was particularly severe. 'A porter puts absolutely all a poor chap's household possessions on his crochet: bed, mattress, chairs, table, cupboard, cooking utensils; he brings all his property down from a fifth floor [in one place] and takes it up to a sixth [in another] . . . So true is it that there is as much money in a single house in the Faux-bourg Saint-Honoré [in about 1782] as in the whole of the Saint-Marcel district . . .' And the district was periodically exposed to flooding from the Bièvre, 'the river of the Gobelins'. It was the same story in the little houses of small towns, like Beauvais, made of poor half-timbering, 'two up, two down and one family per room'.

Indeed the story was the same everywhere. In Dutch towns, even in Amsterdam, the poor were lodged in low houses or in the lower rooms of houses. These poor dwellings – which were the rule before the general prosperity of the seventeenth century – consisted of two rooms: 'the front room and the back room'. When wealth increased and houses became 'bourgeois', they generally only housed one family but they still had their narrow frontages. So they were extended in every possible way: upwards and downwards, in basements and upper storeys, in 'hanging rooms', in recesses and annexes. The rooms were linked by steps or narrow staircases like ladders. The room and bed where Saskia lay suffering was in an alcove behind the drawing-room in Rembrandt's house.

Luxury in the eighteenth century meant primarily the separation of the living habitats of the rich. The poor felt its consequences, but that is another question. On the one hand there was the home, the place for eating, sleeping, bringing up children. Here, the woman had nothing to do but exercise her role as mistress of the house, which (given the abundance of manpower) was crowded with a chattering domestic staff working or pretending to work, disloyal, but also frightened: one word, one suspicion, one theft meant prison or even the gibbet. On the other hand there was the house where the man worked, the shop where he sold, or the office where he spent the best part of his days. Until then there had been no such division: the master had his shop or his workshop in his own home, and housed his workmen and apprentices there. This gave merchants' and artisans' houses in Paris their characteristic form – narrow (in view of the price of land) and high: the shop was on the lower floors; the master's dwelling above, above that the workmen's rooms. Similarly, in 1619, every baker in London had his children, his servants and his apprentices under his own roof. The group constituted the 'family', with the master baker at its head. Even the king's secretaries in Louis XIV's reign sometimes had their ministerial offices in their own homes.

The change came in the eighteenth century. And we must assume that it came because of the very nature of large towns, because we find the same thing in Canton (as well as in Paris and London): in the eighteenth century Chinese merchants in communication with Europeans had their shops in one place, their houses in another.

It is unfortunate for a fair appreciation of the world that we know so little of the evolution of life outside Europe. The plans and pictures we give of the houses of Islam, China and India may seem – indeed are – of no particular age. Even the towns – the reader should refer to what we have to say about Peking (pp. 424–30) – do not yield up their real image, especially as the travellers who give us our information did not have Montaigne's meticulous curiosity: they chased after the great spectacles their potential readers expected, not the houses of Cairo, but the Pyramids; not the streets, shops or houses of notables in Peking or Delhi, but the forbidden imperial city with its yellow walls and the palace of the Great Mogul.

The urbanised countryside

It is obvious, however, that on a world scale the division between town and country houses is too categorical. The two species link up at the level of wealth, because – apart from a few changes like those which entirely transformed English villages in the sixteenth and seventeenth centuries – changes in the countryside were a reflection, a consequence of the wealth of the town. The town that had accumulated too much money invested it in the nearby countryside. It would have done so even if the rich had not been attracted by land, which carried a title to nobility, by the profitable or at least reliable income from rural jurisdiction, and by the comforts of seigniorial residences.

This return to the land was a prominent feature in the West. In the seventeenth century, when the economic situation changed, it became a craze. Noble and bourgeois property gradually spread out round the towns. Only outlying regions sheltered from these raging appetites remained peasant and old-fashioned. For the town proprietor supervised his possessions, rents and rights; he drew corn, wine and poultry from his lands; occasionally he stayed there and often had part of the buildings reconstructed for his own use, joining up plots of land and making enclosures.

The many seigniorial farms, landowners' dwellings and country houses around Paris can be accounted for in this way. So can the shooting boxes in the Provençal countryside; or the Florentine residences which in the sixteenth century created a second and equally rich Florence outside the main town; or the Venetian residences in the Brenta valley that drained the old city of its resources. In the eighteenth century urban palaces were scorned in favour of villas. The profit motive obviously played a part in all this, whether in the neighbourhood of Lisbon, Ragusa, Dijon, Marseilles, Bordeaux, Ulm, Nuremburg, Cologne, Hamburg, The Hague or London. Expensive residences were built throughout the English countryside in the eighteenth century. A 1779 miscellany gives descriptions with reproductions of eighty-four of these 'castles', notably the Duke of Oxford's seat at Houghton in Norfolk, begun by Walpole in 1722 and completed in 1735, with its immense rooms, marbles and galleries. One of the most beautiful journeys still to be made today is a search for eighteenth-century neo-classical villas in the outskirts of Naples, as far as Torre del Greco; from Barra to S. Giorgio, from Cremano to Portici in the vicinity of the Royal Palace; from Resina to Torre Annunziata. All these villas are luxurious, marvellous summer residences between the slopes of Vesuvius and the sea.

The urban colonisation of the countryside, so obvious in the West, also occurred in other places; witness the residences built by the rich of Istanbul on both banks of the Bosporus, or the raïs of Algiers on the Sahel hills, where the gardens are 'the most beautiful in the world'. If the phenomenon is not as obvious in the Far East it is because of the unsafe nature of the countryside, and more still the inadequacy of our documentation. A book by Bernardino de Escalante (1577) speaks (on the basis of what he had read and heard from other travellers) of the 'pleasure houses' of wealthy Chinese, 'with their gardens, groves of trees, aviaries, ponds'. A whole series of known Chinese texts, dating from at least the eleventh century, celebrate the charms and pleasures of these houses, in the midst of running water, always near an artificial pond with the 'purple and scarlet' blossoms of water lilies. To build up a library in such a place, to watch the swans or 'storks waging war against the fishes', or to stalk rabbits and pierce them with arrows 'at the entrance to their holes' were among the greatest pleasures life had to offer.

2 Interiors

Houses viewed from the outside are one thing, from within, another. Interiors are, however, an equally difficult subject to study, with all the same problems of classification and description in a frame of reference that must cover the whole world. Here again we can sketch the broad outlines of the picture by looking at what remains, what is slow to change. In the case of the universal poor, and of those impoverished civilisations that were static and closed in upon themselves, interiors barely changed at all. Only the West is distinguished by uninterrupted change. Such is the ruler's privilege.

The poor without furniture

The destitution of the poor goes without saying. If it is established for Europe, the richest civilisation and the one most ready to change, it will apply *a fortiori* to the rest. The poor in the towns and country-side of the West lived in a state of almost complete deprivation. Their furniture consisted of next to nothing, at least before the eighteenth century when a rudimentary luxury began to spread (chairs, woollen mattresses, feather beds) together with decorative peasant furniture, painted or painstakingly carved in certain regions. But this was an exception. Inventories made after death, completely reliable documents, testify almost invariably to the general destitution. Apart from a very small number of well-to-do peasants, the furniture of the day labourer and the small-scale agricultural worker in Burgundy even in the eighteenth century was identical: 'the pot-hanger, the pot in the hearth, the frying pans, the *quasses* (dripping pans), the *meix* (for kneading bread) ... the chest, the bedstead with four pillars, the feather pillow and *guédon* (eider-down), the bolster, sometimes a tapestry (cover) for the bed, the drugget trousers, the shirt, the gaiters, a few tools (shovels, pick-axe) ...' But before the eighteenth century the same inventories mention a few old clothes, a stool, a table, a bench, the planks of a bed, sacks filled with straw. Official reports for Burgundy between the sixteenth and the eighteenth centuries are full of 'references to people [sleeping] on straw ... with no bed or furniture' who were only separated 'from the pigs by a screen'. And we can see it for ourselves. A picture by Adrien Brouwer (1605–38) shows four peasants singing in chorus in a poorly furnished room: a few stools a bench and a barrel doing service as a table, on which is a dishcloth, crust of bread and jug. This was not by chance. Old barrels cut in half served all purposes in the village taverns, so dear to seventeenth-century Dutch painters. They were even cut away to form armchairs with backs. A canvas by J. Steen shows a young peasant being given a writing lesson by his mother, who stands near him; his desk is a plank laid over a barrel. And he did not even belong to the most wretched class, since the people around him knew how to read and write! A few words in an old thirteenth-century text provide another eloquent testimony: in Gascony, although 'rich in white bread and excellent red wine', the peasants 'seated round the fire, are accustomed to eat without a table and to drink out of the same goblet'.

All this is quite natural: poverty was everywhere. A typical French ordinance of 1669 orders the demolition of 'houses built on poles by vagabonds and useless members of society', on the edges of forests. These huts are reminiscent of those built by a few Englishmen when they escaped the plague of London in 1664 and took refuge in the woods. The situation in the towns was just as depressing: in Paris, in the suburbs of Saint-Marcel and even Saint-Antoine, only a few joiners were comfortably off; in Le Mans and Beauvais the weavers lived in penury. An inquiry of 1560 in Pescara, on the Adriatic, mentions 400 or 500 people out of a population of 2000 who had come down from the adjacent mountains or the Balkans and were already living a shanty-town existence in holes in the earth. And though it was small the town had its fortress, garrison, fairs, port, salt works and was, after all, situated in Italy in the second half of the sixteenth century when it was linked with the Atlantic and the wealth of Spain. In the very rich town of Genoa the homeless poor sold themselves as galley slaves every winter. In Venice poor wretches lived with their families on miserable boats, near the quays (the *fondamenta*) or under the bridges of the canals. They were the counterpart of the Chinese artisans who lived on board junks or sampans on the rivers of the towns with their families and domestic animals, endlessly travelling upstream or down in search of work.

Poor civilisations and unchanging interiors

The traditional civilisations remained faithful to their accustomed décor. A Chinese interior of the fifteenth century could just as well belong to the eighteenth, apart from certain variations – porcelains, paintings and bronzes. The traditional Japanese house was the same in the sixteenth or the seventeenth century as it is today, except for the coloured prints that came in during the eighteenth century. The same applies to the Indies. And the Muslim interior of the past can be glimpsed in the most recent examples.

The non-European civilisations, except for the Chinese, were poor in furniture. There were practically no chairs in India and no tables: in Tamil the word for table – *mecei* – derives from the Portuguese (*mesa*). There were no chairs in Black Africa where Benin artists were content to imitate European chairs. Neither were there chairs or for that matter high tables in Islam or the countries under its influence. The low table where guests sat round on cushions was still the general rule in Muslim Yugoslavia, at Mostar for example, a few years ago. In 1699 Dutch merchants were advised to take very strong paper to Muscovy; having few tables the Russians wrote mostly on their knees and so had to have a tough type of paper.

Of course the West was not superior in every respect to the rest of the world, which adopted ingenious solutions to the problems of housing and furniture that were often less expensive than the European. It had various points of superiority to its credit: Islam had its public baths (though inherited from Rome); Japan had the elegance and cleanliness of its most ordinary interiors and the ingenuity of its storage space.

In spring 1699 Osman Aga passed through Buda (recaptured by the Christians in 1686) on his difficult journey home to freedom (he had been taken prisoner, or rather reduced to slavery by the Germans at the capture of Lipova ten years earlier). There, he was thoroughly happy to be able to make his way to 'the magnificent baths of the town'. They were of course the Turkish baths on the bank of the Danube below the fortified town and had admitted everyone, without charge, since the time of the Ottoman domination.

Rodrigo Vivero considered that the Japanese houses he saw in 1609 did not look as beautiful from the street as houses in Spain, but their interiors were more beautiful. One can well imagine how such an impression might have been possible: everything in the most modest Japanese house was put away first thing in the morning as if removed from inquisitive eyes – the cushions from the bed, for example. Straw mats were placed everywhere, the partitions of the rooms let in the light and everything was in order.

And yet, there were also considerable disadvantages. There was no heating. For the most part the sun had to look after that, as in Mediterranean Europe. But it sometimes did not look after it very successfully. There was not even a fireplace in the whole of Turkish Islam (with the exception of the monumental fireplace in the Seraglio in Istanbul). A brazier was the only solution when supplies of charcoal for it were available. Muslim houses in present-day Yugoslavia are still without fireplaces. They did exist in Persia and in all the rooms of the rich, but in a narrow form 'because to avoid smoke and save wood, which is very expensive, the Persians burn it standing on end'. Neither were there fireplaces in India or the Indian archipelago (where they would not often have been necessary). Nor in Japan, though the cold there was acute: the baths the Japanese took in piping hot water, in the basins heated by wood fires which every house possessed, were as much a way of warming as cleansing themselves.

On the other hand, in northern China, which is as cold as Siberia in winter, the whole peasant family slept on a brick stove – furnace or oven – heated by smoke from a coal fire lit in the adjacent hearth. This stove was shaped like a low divan and also served as a seat in daytime. In rich households the flagstones of the floor themselves were heated by a hearth in the basement.

Frequently, therefore, there was no heating and almost no furniture. A few chests made of precious cedar-wood were known in Islam and used to store clothing and materials, the valuables of the household. Low tables were occasionally used there, and sometimes large copper trays balanced on wooden frames. In Turkish houses recesses in the walls of rooms served as cupboards. As for the rest, there were the wonderful brightly coloured woollen carpets, sometimes piled up on top of each other, for which Christendom has always had a passion. This was the furniture of a race of nomads.

Istanbul museums contain many treasures – precious fabrics, often embroidered with stylised tulips; spiral glasses (known as nightingales' eyes); magnificent spoons made of rock crystal, ivory or pepper wood and encrusted with copper, silver, mother of pearl or coral; porcelains from Cyprus and China; magnificent jewellery; and two or three extraordinary thrones completely encrusted with rubies,

emeralds, turquoises and pearls. The detailed summary of the
treasures seized from a Kurdish prince by the Turkish army in
July 1655 and put up for auction also gives the same impression:
ivory, ebony and cedar-wood boxes; chests encrusted with pearls
from Ceylon; flagons of rose water; perfume-pans; books printed in
the West; Korans embellished with precious stones; works by
famous calligraphers; innumerable carpets; hundreds of tiger skins;
silver candlesticks; porcelains from China; multicoloured cups,
bowls and plates from Iznik (Nicaea) ...

The two facets of Chinese furniture

No violent change occurred in China during the centuries which
concern us, but one characteristic distinguished it from all other
non-European countries – its abundant and refined furniture,
precious woods often imported from very far afield, lacquers, cupboards, cabinets with ingeniously contrived shelving, high and low
tables, chairs, benches and stools, beds, generally with curtains,
rather like those in the West in earlier days. Its most marked
originality (because it implied a whole way of life) was certainly the
use of a table, with chair, stool or bench. It should be noted, however, that this had not come down from primitive China. At the
time when Japan borrowed and meticulously copied all the artefacts
of the Tang civilisation of China (618–907), neither chair nor high
table was to be found there. In fact present-day Japanese furniture
exactly corresponds to ancient Chinese furniture: low tables,
elbow-rests for arms to make the squatting position more comfortable, mats (the Japanese *tatami*) on platforms of varying heights, low
storage furniture (cabinets and chests set beside each other),
cushions. Everything is adapted to life at floor level.

The chair probably arrived in China in the second or third
century AD, but took a very long time to become a general item of
furniture (the first known representation of it is in 535–40: a sculp-
tured stele in Kansas City Museum in the United States). It was
probably European in origin whatever detours it may have made to
arrive in China (via Persia, India or northern China). Moreover its
original Chinese name, still current today, means 'barbarian bed'.
It was probably first used as a seat of honour, either for lay or
religious purposes. And even recently in China chairs were reserved
for guests of honour and old people, while stools were used much
more frequently, as in Europe in the middle ages.

But the important thing is the seated position that chair and stool imply, and therefore a way of life unlike that of ancient China and the other Asiatic countries, indeed unlike all non-European countries. If the chair travelled via Persia or India, it met with no popular success on its way through those countries. However, high tables with various benches and seats can be seen in rustic inns and urban shops alike on a journey along a country road and through a Chinese town depicted on a thirteenth-century Chinese scroll.

For China this acquisition corresponded to a new art of living, which was all the more original in that it did not exclude the old way of life. As a result China possessed two forms of furniture, low furniture and high furniture. In the large living-room, so characteristic of all northern China, chair, stool and bench on the lower level were accompanied by a high table and a high cupboard (often with drawers; but the Chinese never knew of chiffoniers or chests-of-drawers consisting entirely of drawers, except belatedly and in isolated cases, in imitation of nineteenth-century Europe). Furniture of the old or Japanese variety was arranged on the higher level, on a brick platform the height of a bench, above the other part of the room. This was the *kang*, heated by interior piping, covered with mats or felt, cushions and brightly coloured carpet, with a very low table and equally low cupboards and chests. Here they slept in winter, protected from the cold, and here too they received their visitors, seated on the floor and drinking tea; here, the women sewed or wove their carpets. The Chinaman took off his shoes before going up on the *kang*, and wore only boots made of blue cloth with white padded soles (which self-respect demanded be always worn impeccably clean). Heating was not necessary in southern China but the two types of furniture were also to be found there. The scenes Father de Las Cortes sketched in the Canton region at the beginning of the seventeenth century show the Chinese seated on their chairs around a square table eating a meal. And the sedan chair he depicted was conceived on the same principle as the European sedan chair, however different its flimsy wood may have made it.

The rapid summary we have just given poses and does not solve the problems of what was, after all, a very striking change. To see it merely as the story of the chair and the numerous consequences of its introduction is one of those simplistic explanations that abound in past histories of technology. The reality was always much more complex (we will return to its broader implications in the following chapter). In fact a great surge of life took place in China (roughly speaking, before the thirteenth century) and also a sort of division between seated life and squatting life at ground level, the latter domestic, the former official: the sovereign's throne, the mandarin's seat, benches and chairs in schools. The subject would require research and analysis beyond our present scope; nevertheless it is worth while noting these two types of behaviour – almost two different biologies – in the everyday life of the world: the seated position and the squatting position. The latter is omnipresent except in the West, and the two only came together in China. To find the origins of this behaviour in Europe would take us back to antiquity and the very roots of Western civilisation.

However, we can summarise with a few examples. Appropriately the traveller in the Japanese ox-drawn cart squatted. A Persian miniature shows a prince sitting cross-legged on a wide throne. Until very recently the Cairo cabman who sat with a bundle of straw in front of his seat coiled up his legs even though he could have stretched them out. Ultimately, a biological difference is involved: resting on the heels in a kneeling position in the Japanese manner, or sitting cross-legged as they do in Islam and Turkey, or squatting as the Hindus so often do, is impossible or at the best difficult for a European. And the Japanese regard our way of sitting as so surprising that they call it 'hanging up the legs'. Gemelli Careri found no seat in the Turkish or rather Bulgarian coach in which he was travelling from Gallipoli to Adrianople in the winter of 1693. 'As I was not at all accustomed,' he wrote, 'to being seated on the ground, legs crossed Turkish fashion, I was very uncomfortable in this carriage, which had no seats and was made in such a way that there is no European who would not have been likewise inconvenienced.' The same traveller two years later was in a palanquin in the Indies and 'obliged to keep stretched out as in a bed'. An obligation which we would consider less of a hardship!

Black Africa

There were no compact towns of the Western or Chinese type on the fringes of the Gulf of Guinea, where European trade had established itself and penetrated inland. The peasantry was certainly deprived, from the very first villages described in travellers' accounts.

They lived in mud huts made with poles and reeds, 'round like dove-cotes', seldom whitewashed, without furniture (except mud vases and baskets), without windows, carefully filled with smoke every night to drive out gnats, the *maringouins*, which stung painfully. 'Not everyone is accustomed as they are,' wrote Father Labat (1728), 'to be smoked like hams and to be smitten with a smell of smoke which makes people sick when they first start to associate with the Negroes.' Historians and sociologists in Brazil maintain that runaway slaves living in the *sertão* (rough, open country) in independent republics, and even the town Blacks in their urban hovels (*mucambos*), lived a healthier life in the nineteenth century than their masters on the plantations or in the towns.

There were a few whitewashed huts alongside the ordinary huts in Africa, and this was already an advance, however slight, on the common lot. The 'Portuguese-style' houses (so called because they derived from the ancient conquerors, whose language the 'princes' still spoke) marked an even greater progress, though there were very few of them. These houses had 'open vestibules', and even 'small, very clean wooden stools' (so that visitors could sit down), tables, and certainly palm wine for special guests. It was in houses like these that the beautiful mulattas lived who held the hearts of the chiefs of the land or rich English merchants, which amounted to the same thing. The courtesan who ruled over the 'king' of Barre was clad in 'a little satin corset in the Portuguese style' and wore 'as a skirt, one of those beautiful loin cloths from the island of Saint Yague, one of the Cape Verde islands ... these are loin cloths of some consequence, as only distinguished people wear them; they are very beautiful and very fine'. This interesting sidelight proves that the usual opposing modes were also to be found in the vast expanse of Africa – destitution and luxury.

The West and its many different types of furniture

Compared with China and the rest of the world, the characteristic of the West in matters of furniture and interior arrangement was undoubtedly its taste for change, a relative rapidity of development which China never knew. In the West everything was constantly changing. Not of course from one day to the next; but nothing escaped a complex evolution. Each new step in a museum takes you to a new room, a changed scene. The scene of course changed quite differently in the different regions of Europe; only the major transformations were common to all, over and above considerable time-lags, imitations, and the more or less conscious assimilations of other styles.

The common life of Europe thus consisted of a medley of obstinately different colours: the north was not the same as the·south, the European West was not the New World, nor old Europe the new, expanding eastwards as far as wild Siberia. Furniture bears witness to these contrasts, affirming the identity of the small countries and the different social groups into which the Western world was divided. Finally, the furniture or rather the whole décor of houses bore witness to a broad economic and cultural movement carrying Europe towards what it itself christened the Enlightenment, progress.

Floors, walls, ceilings, doors and windows

Everything in the familiar setting of our present-day lives can be seen to be a heritage, an ancient acquisition: the desk I write on, the linen cupboard, the paper glued on the walls, the seats, the wooden floor, the plaster ceiling, the arrangement of the rooms, the fireplace, staircase, the ornaments, engravings and pictures. I can mentally reconstruct the ancient evolution from a simple present-day interior and as it were run the film backwards to take the reader back towards ancient luxuries which were, however ancient, slow to emerge. This will at least fix the landmarks, outline the main points of a history of furniture.

A room for human habitation has always had four walls, a ceiling, a floor, one or more windows and one or more doors.

For a long time floors at ground level were made of mud, then paved or tiled. Ancient miniatures often show magnificent tiling – an inexpensive luxury. Inlaid tiles were in use in the fourteenth century. 'Leaded' tiles (covered with an enamel with a graphite base) appeared in the sixteenth. By the seventeenth, ceramic tiling was everywhere, even in modest homes. Nevertheless there was no mosaic, at least in France, before the end of the seventeenth century. As for parquet in the modern sense, it appeared in the fourteenth century but only became really fashionable in the seventeenth, with many variations (bonded parquets, inlaid, in Hungarian points). The need for wood increased. Voltaire could write: 'Once oaks used to rot in the forests; today they are made into parquet floors.'

Ceilings for a long time were made of beams, of rough joists, only planed in wealthy homes, and generally concealed by fabrics. Originally, when there was an upper storey, the ceiling of the room below was the floor of the room above. The wooden ceiling with compartments came from Italy in the sixteenth century and was fashionable for a long time. Ceilings only began to be whitewashed in the eighteenth century.

The most curious ancient custom, which continued until the sixteenth century (and even later), was to cover the floors of the ground-floor rooms and the bedrooms with straw in winter and herbs and flowers in summer. 'The Rue du Fouarre, cradle of our Faculties of Letters and Sciences, owes its name to the straw with which the floors of the lecture rooms used to be covered.' The same custom prevailed in royal residences. Care was taken at a banquet given by the town of Paris for Catherine of Medici in June 1549 to scatter the room with fine aromatic herbs'. A picture (1581–2) of the ball on the duc de Joyeuse's wedding night shows the floor strewn with flowers. All the same, these flowers, herbs and rushes had to be changed. This was not always the case in England, at least according to Erasmus, so that dirt and refuse tended to collect there. Despite such disadvantages a doctor still recommends the use of scattered green herbs in 1613, 'in a handsome room, well-matted or hung with tapestries all round and paved below with rosemary, pennyroyal, oregano, marjoram, lavender, sage and other similar herbs'. The straw and herbs, with rushes or swordgrass arranged decoratively along the walls, disappeared before the woven straw mats which had always been known and were made in varied colours, with arabesques. They were soon replaced in turn by rugs. Thick and brightly coloured, they covered the ground, tables (right down to the floor), chests, and even the tops of cupboards. Later, in the eighteenth century, fitted carpet made its appearance everywhere.

Flowers, branches and rushes on the walls of rooms (painted with oils or size) gave way to tapestries which could 'be made from all sorts of material, such as velvet, damask, brocade, brocatelle, Bruges satin, caddis'. But Savary (1762) recommends that the description 'tapestry' should perhaps be limited to "Bergamot tapestries, gilded leathers (the *guadameciles* of Spain, known for centuries), tapestries made from wool shearings in Paris and Rouen, and other tapestries of quite new invention where the figures and landscapes of high-warp tapestry are well copied in various colours'. The fashion for these high-warp tapestries with figures goes back to the fifteenth century and is ascribed to the craftsmen of Flanders. The Gobelins workshops later brought them to technical perfection. But their high production costs were against them; in addition furniture, which became more widespread in the eighteenth century, limited their use: a chest of drawers or sideboard placed in front of them and there you were, as Sébastien Mercier explained, with your beautiful figures cut in two.

Wallpaper (it was known as *domino*) made decisive progress, helped by its cheapness. It was printed by *dominotiers*, by the same process used to make playing-cards.

This type of paper tapestry ... had for a long time only been used by country folk and the common people in Paris to decorate and to hang here and there in their huts, shops and rooms; at the end of the seventeenth century, however, it had been brought to such a degree of perfection and attractiveness that in addition to the large consignments sent to foreign countries and the principal towns of the realm there is no house in Paris, however magnificent, which has not got somewhere, either closet or some still more secret place, hung with it and quite pleasantly decorated (1762).

Besides, wallpaper was invariably found at the level of the attics, sometimes very simple with black and white stripes. For there was wallpaper and wallpaper: not all was like the expensive specimen (1770) in the Munich National Museum, which is in the Chinese style.

Occasionally walls were also covered with wood panelling. From the fourteenth century English joiners had produced panels in Danish oak to cover walls and combat the cold. Examples range from the neat and simple panels found in the small study of one of the Fugger's houses (sixteenth century) in Germany, to the large, lavishly carved, painted and gilded panels of eighteenth-century French salons, whose décor served as a model for all Europe, Russia included.

Until the seventeenth century doors were narrow, opened inwards and only let one person at a time pass through. Large double doors came later. Windows were usually simple solid wood shutters, as we can see from peasant dwellings in the eighteenth century. When the leaded glass window, the privilege of the church, spread to houses, the irregular glass set in lead was too heavy and also too valuable for the leaf to be movable. The problem was solved in various ways: in Germany a single opening leaf in a window with fixed glass was used. The Dutch solution combined fixed glazed panels with movable wooden panels. In France the glazed frames were often fixed; Montaigne noted that 'what makes the glass [in Germany] shine so brightly is that they have no fixed windows in our fashion', so that they can 'polish them very often'. Some open-

able windows also had panes made of parchment, cloth treated with
turpentine, oiled paper, and sheets of gypsum. White glass really
only appeared with the sixteenth century; it then spread slowly.
When Charles v reached Estramadura (1555) he was concerned
about buying glass before he came to the end of his journey. Montaigne, on the road to Germany (1580), noted that from Epinal
onwards: 'There is no village house, however small, which is not
glazed.' But two travellers from the Netherlands who reached Spain
in 1633 mention that glass disappeared from windows of houses
after they had crossed the Loire at Saumur. In 1779 glass brought
daylight to the rooms of the humblest Parisian workers, but our
informant adds that Lyons and certain other provinces had retained
the use of oiled paper, particularly for silk workers, because the light
it gave was 'softer'. This slowness we see in France was more marked
elsewhere. In Serbia panes of glass were not commonly to be seen in
windows until the nineteenth century. Another feature slow to
disappear was the use of several wooden crosspieces, necessary
because of the small size of the panes and the weight of the frame. It
was not until the eighteenth century that large windows became the
general rule, at least in the houses of the rich.

Painters, as we would expect, offer plenty of varied evidence of
this belated modernisation. There was never at any given moment a
typical Dutch-style window common to the whole of Europe, with
fixed panes (upper part) and opening solid wood (lower part).
There is such a window in an Annunciation by Schongauer.
Another from the same period only comprises one narrow panel of
opening glass; yet another has an external wooden shutter closing
over the fixed window. The wooden leaf would be either double or
single. Sometimes there were curtains inside, sometimes none. All in
all, there were many solutions to the problem of ventilating and
lighting houses, and also of mitigating the effects of cold and stopping
daylight disturbing the sleeper. Everything depended on climate and
custom. Montaigne was not pleased that in Germany he had no
'defence against the evening dew or the wind except ordinary glass,
which was not in any way covered with wood' (therefore without
external or internal shutters), and moreover the beds in German inns
had no curtains!

Chimneys

There were no chimneys before about the twelfth century. But
within a short space of time chimneys – hearths linked in one way or

another to the air outside – could be seen from Venice (where the high external chimneys were frequently depicted by its painters) right up to the North Sea and from the borders of Muscovy to the Atlantic.

The name chimney was for a long time given to hearths like those in rural houses at the beginning of the twentieth century: a wide vertical shaft leaving space, if need be, for two chimney-sweeps at a time. The draught was such that, near to the fire, one ran the risk of being 'toasted on one side while freezing on the other'.

At first the hearth had a brick base; later, in the seventeenth century, a metal plate. Andirons supported the logs. A vertical cast-iron plate called the back-plate and often decorated (some were very beautiful) stood on the hearth. In the chimney itself the pot-hanger, which enabled a pot – or more often a cauldron in which water was kept permanently hot – to be hung over the fire, was attached to a ring and equipped with notches allowing adjustments of height. Cooking was done on the hearth in front of the fire near the flames, or glowing embers were used to cover the lid of an iron pan. Frying pans with long handles made it possible to use the hottest part of the fire in comfort.

In rich households the fireplace naturally became the main decorative element of a room. Mantels were decorated with bas-reliefs, hoods with frescoes, and bases were moulded to terminate in consoles or capitals with human heads. The hood of a Bruges chimney dating from the end of the fifteenth century was decorated with an Annunciation from the school of Gérard David. As fire-places grew larger it became possible to fix stone benches on either side of the hearth, sometimes in front of walls decorated with *azulejos*, as in the house in Toledo said to have been El Greco's. It was here that people would sit when the fire had burnt down to embers and chat 'under the mantel of the chimney'.

Such a system may possibly have been acceptable for cooking, but it was a deplorable means of heating. The area round the fire offered the only refuge in a cold house when winter set in. The two fireplaces at the extremities of the Hall of Mirrors at Versailles did not succeed in heating its enormous expanse. It was advisable to wear furs for added protection. But even they were hardly sufficient. On 3 February 1695 the Palatine wrote: 'At the king's table the wine and water froze in the glasses.' The detail (there are many more that could be cited) is enough to evoke the discomfort of a seventeenth-century house. Cold weather, at that period, could be a public disaster, freezing rivers, halting mills, bringing packs of dangerous wolves out into the countryside, multiplying epidemics. When these hardships increased, as in Paris in 1709, 'the people died of cold like flies' (2 March). In the absence of heating since January (again according to the Palatine) 'all entertainments have ceased as well as law suits'.

Everything changed in about 1720: 'Since the Regent, we can claim that we manage to keep warm during the winter.' It was achieved as a result of an advance in 'caminology' for which chimney-sweeps and stove-setters were responsible. The hearth of the chimney was made narrower and deepened, the mantel lowered, the chimney shaft curved, as the straight chimney had had a persistent tendency to smoke. (One wonders how the great Raphael was able to cope with his appointed task of preventing the Duc d'Este's chimneys from smoking.) With a better draught it was possible to heat reasonably-sized rooms – not the apartments in Mansard's palaces, but certainly those in the town houses built by Gabriel. Chimneys with several hearths (at least two, said to be in the style of Popelinière) even made it possible to heat the servants' quarters. A revolution in heating thus belatedly took place.

But we must not suppose that there was any saving in fuel (as a book called *L'épargne-bois* had foreseen a century earlier in 1619). Having become more efficient, hearths increased astonishingly in number. Before winter set in, every town was filled with the activity of transporting and sawing up wood for heating. In Paris from the middle of October on the very eve of the Revolution:

There is a new problem in all districts of the town. The roads are cluttered up with thousands of carts laden with wood, which, as it is thrown down, sawn up and transported, puts all passers-by in danger of being crushed, bowled over or having their legs broken. The men unload roughly and hurriedly, throwing the logs off the top of the cart. The cobbles resound. The men are deaf and blind and only want to unload their wood promptly, to the danger of passing heads. Then comes the sawyer, plies his saw rapidly and throws the wood around him, without taking heed of anybody.

The same performance was repeated in every town. In Rome the wood merchant offered to deliver his merchandise to the door by donkey-cart. Although Nuremburg was situated amidst vast and accessible forests, an order of 24 October 1702 bade the peasants within its jurisdiction deliver half their stocks of wood to its market.

Furnaces and stoves

Montaigne rather hastily asserted that there were 'no chimneys' in Germany. Specifically, there were no fireplaces in the bedrooms or living-rooms of inns. There was always one in the kitchen. But Germans 'do not like anyone going into their kitchens'. The traveller could only warm himself in the vast living-room where meals were taken and where the earthenware stove, the *Kachelhofen*, stood. The chimney did not fit 'our style of life': 'They build hearths in the middle or in the corner of a kitchen and the chimney shaft runs along almost its whole width; it is a large opening, seven or eight feet square and ending right at the top of the building; this gives them the space to accommodate in one place their large sail, which in our houses would take up so much space in our shafts as to prevent the passage of the smoke.' This 'sail' was like the vanes of a windmill; they moved as the smoke and hot air rose and caused the spit to turn.

Stoves were also found well beyond Germany – in Hungary, Poland, Russia and soon in Siberia. They were ordinary ovens made of stone, brick and sometimes clay. In Germany from the fourteenth century the furnace was built in a lighter material – potters' clay (*Töpferthon*). The earthenware tiles covering it were often decorated. A bench stood in front for sitting or sleeping upon. Erasmus explained (1527): 'In the stove [that is in the room it heated] you take off your boots, you put on your shoes, you change your shirt, if you wish; you hang up your clothes, damp from the rain, near the fire and you draw near to dry yourself.' 'At least,' as Montaigne said, 'you burn neither your boots nor your face and you are free of the smoke of France.'

The large cast-iron stove appeared on the scene towards the end of the eighteenth century. In Russia often and in Siberia up to the eighteenth century the furnace had a single door opening on the outside of the house; the furnace heated the house and half-filled it with smoke. In the front part of the oven cooking was done 'with the embers remaining after the wood has been burned'.

Stoves made of glazed earthenware only appeared in France in about 1520, five years after Marignan. Their success began in the seventeenth century and was consolidated in the next. Fireplaces were still rare in Paris in 1571. It was often necessary to use a brazier for warmth. The poor of Paris continued to use braziers in the eighteenth century. They burned coal in them, which gave rise to frequent cases of poisoning. Fireplaces finally played a larger role in France than stoves, which continued to be used more in the cold eastern and northern countries. Sébastien Mercier noted in 1788: 'What a difference between a stove and a fireplace! The sight of a stove extinguishes my imagination.'

Furniture makers and the vanities of buyers

Interiors and furniture never changed very quickly, however pronounced the taste for change amongst the rich. Fashion evolved, but in slow motion. There were several reasons. The expense involved in renovation and refurnishing was enormous; more important, production possibilities remained limited. The mechanical saw worked by water did not exist until 1235; no material except oak was in general use until the sixteenth century, when the fashion for walnut and exotic woods began in Antwerp. More important still, everything depended on the crafts, which developed slowly. Joiners became independent from carpenters between the fifteenth and the sixteenth centuries; then cabinet-makers, long called 'marquetry and veneering joiners', appeared from the ranks of the joiners themselves, in the seventeenth century.

Carpenters had produced furniture and houses for centuries on end. The result was the large scale, the solidity and a certain unashamed roughness of 'Gothic' furniture – heavy cupboards hung from walls, enormous narrow tables, benches more often than stools or chairs, chests with powerful locks made from large, ill-squared planks 'fitted together with a flat joint and held by nailed iron bands'. Such things were baggage quite as much as furniture. Planks were smoothed with an axe: the plane, an old tool known in Egypt, Greece and Rome, only resumed its role in northern Europe in the thirteenth century. Planks were joined with iron nails. Mortise and tenon and dovetail joints slowly reappeared later, then wooden nails, pegs (a late technique), and iron screws, always known but never fully utilised until the eighteenth century.

All their tools – axes, hatchets, chisels, mallets, hammers, crossbow-lathes (for large pieces; to turn the foot of a table for example), handle- or pedal-lathes (for fine pieces) – had always been known and were in fact a heritage from far back, before the Roman world. The ancient tools and processes had been preserved in Italy, where there exists the only furniture we have dating from before 1400. There again, Italy had a lead and an advantage: it produced and propagated furniture, models for furniture and means of constructing furniture. Proof enough in the sixteenth-century Italian chests in the National Museum in Munich. With their complicated carving, stands, polished wood and sophisticated shapes, they are very different from chests of the same period in the rest of Europe. The drawers that belatedly appeared north of the Alps also arrived from the south via the Rhine valley. 'They only reached England in the fifteenth century.'

It was the general practice until the sixteenth century and on into the seventeenth to paint furniture, ceilings and walls. We have to imagine the ancient furniture with its carvings painted gold, silver, red and green, in palace, house and church alike. It was proof of a desperate hunger for light and bright colours in poorly lit, dark interiors. Furniture was sometimes covered with a fine cloth and plaster before it was painted so that the colour should not bring out any of the faults in the wood. Objects began to be plainly waxed and varnished at the end of the sixteenth century.

Particular items of furniture

How can we follow the complicated biography of each of these pieces of furniture? They appeared, changed, but scarcely ever disappeared, constantly sustaining the tyrannies of architectural style and the arrangement of interiors.

The habit of placing the bench in front of the fireplace probably gave rise to the narrow rectangular table; the guests sat on only one side of it, 'with their backs to the fire and their stomachs to the table'. According to the legend of King Arthur, the round table overcame the problem of precedence. But round tables could only become popular when there were chairs to go with them, and chairs were late acquiring their form and production on any large scale. The earliest were monumental singletons reserved for the master of the household; other people made do with benches and stools. Chairs for them only came much later.

Society – we might as well say vanity – was the arbiter in this matter of furniture. For example the dresser started life in the kitchen as an ordinary table on which were placed the dishes and loads of crockery required to serve a meal. In seigniorial houses a second dresser made its way into the drawing-room: on it were displayed the gold, silver and vermeil services, the bowls, *aiguières* and goblets.

Etiquette prescribed the number of shelves it should have according to the status of the master of the house – two for a baron, the number increasing with rank. A picture of Herod's feast shows a dresser with eight rows, marking the supreme royal dignity. The dresser finally moved out to the street itself on Corpus Christi day 'in front of the tapestries with which the houses were hung'. An English traveller, Thomas Coryate, was amazed to see so many dressers with silverware in 1608 in the streets of Paris.

We should, by way of example, be able to sketch out the history of cupboards from the heavy ancient cupboards strengthened with iron bands to the seventeenth-century models already becoming 'bourgeois' (according to a historian who had no great love for the 'frontons, entablatures, columns and pilasters' of the Louis XIII style). The massive sides of the old models were replaced by panels embedded – or joined by groove and tongue – in a framework. Cupboards could then reach considerable proportions, sometimes so vast that it was desirable to cut them in half. This created a new piece of furniture, the low cupboard, which never caught on. Cupboards thus became a piece of ostentation, occasionally richly carved and embellished. They lost this role in the eighteenth century, at least in luxurious houses and, relegated to the function of wardrobes, no longer appeared in reception rooms. But for centuries on end they remained the pride of peasant and working-class homes.

Importance and then insignificance; in any event, fashion was the winner, as we see with the cabinet, a piece of furniture with drawers or compartments to hold toilet articles, writing equipment, packs of cards and jewellery. There are examples of it in the Gothic style. Its popularity began in the sixteenth century. Renaissance cabinets decorated with *pietra dura* and German-type cabinets both enjoyed a vogue in France. Some of the cabinets produced under Louis XIV were very large. In the eighteenth century the popularity of the *secrétaire* was launched on the wave of its success.

But it is more useful to follow for a moment the fortunes of the chest-of-drawers, which soon gained the ascendancy. It was really the chest-of-drawers that dethroned the cupboard. It evolved in France at the very beginning of the eighteenth century. The idea behind the chest-of-drawers was probably that of several small chests placed on top of each other, and the first cupboards were probably chests stood on end. But idea and achievement took some time to materialise.

Launched by a new fashion into a century of refined elegance, the chest-of-drawers was immediately an item of luxury furniture. Its shape – rectilinear or curved, straight or bulging, bulky or slim – the marquetry, precious woods, bronzes and lacquers, closely followed the dictates of changing fashion, including the fashion for *chinoiserie* showing all the differences between the Louis XIV, Louis XV and Louis XVI styles with which we are familiar. A basic piece of furniture, reserved for the rich, it only came into general use in the nineteenth century.

But are the several histories of these items of furniture really the history of furnishing?

The general setting

However characteristic it may be, one piece of furniture does not reveal a whole picture; and the whole picture is all that matters. Museums, with their isolated objects, generally only teach the basic features of a complex history. The essential is not contained within these pieces of furniture themselves but is in their arrangement, whether free or formal, in an atmosphere, an art of living both in the room containing them and outside it, in the house of which the room is a part. How then did people live, eat and sleep in these separate and, of course, luxurious worlds?

The first precise evidence concerns late Gothic, and comes to us through Dutch and German pictures in particular, where furniture and objects are painted as lovingly as people, like a series of still lives. The Birth of Saint John by Jan van Eyck or an Annunciation by van der Weyden give a concrete idea of the atmosphere of the fifteenth-century living-room. A door open on to the succession of other rooms is enough to conjure up the kitchen or the bustle of the servants. It is true that the subject helps – Virgin Annunciations and births, whether by Carpaccio, the older Holbein or Schongauer, with their beds, chests, a beautiful open window, a bench in front of the fireplace, the wooden tub in which the new-born child is bathed, the bowl of soup carried to the woman after her confinement, are as evocative of the domestic framework as the subject of the Last Supper is of mealtime ritual.

Despite the very few pieces of furniture and their robust rusticity these late Gothic homes have, at least in northern countries, the warm intimacy of very cosy rooms, enclosed in folds of luxurious fabrics in bright and iridescent colours. Their only real luxuries are the curtains and covers for the beds, hangings on the walls and silky cushions. Fifteenth-century tapestries with their pure colours and luminous backgrounds strewn with flowers and animals also bear witness to this taste, this need for colour. It was as though the houses of the period were a response to the external world and like 'the cloister, the fortified castle, the walled town, the walled garden' acted as a protection against the dimly apprehended difficulties of material life.

However, from the period when Renaissance Italy, economically so far advanced, was engaged in producing new displays for princely and ostentatious courts, a completely different framework began to appear. It was solemn and more formal; its architecture and furniture (which repeated the same motifs and the same monumental lines in frontons, cornices, medallions and sculptures) aimed at a kind of social magnificence, at the grandiose. Fifteenth-century Italian interiors, with their colonnades, immense carved and canopied beds and monumental staircases, already give a strange foretaste of the Great Century and of that court life which was to be a sort of parade, a theatrical spectacle. Luxury there quite obviously became a means of government.

Let us jump two hundred years. In the seventeenth century the decoration of the house sacrificed everything to fashion, to social significance – in France, England and even the Catholic Netherlands. There were of course exceptions including Germany and Holland, where greater simplicity was the rule. Reception-rooms became immense, with very high ceilings, more open to the exterior, deliberately solemn, with a superabundance of ornaments, sculptures, decorative furniture (buffets, heavily carved sideboards), which supported equally decorative pieces of silverware. Plates, dishes and pictures hung on the walls, and the walls themselves were painted with complex motifs (as in the Rubens room with its decoration of grotesque figures). Tapestries, always in high favour, had changed their style and were also moving towards a certain grandiloquence and costly, subtle complication.

None the less this large reception-room – Versailles might pass for a symbol of it – was a *living* room. This same room with its theatrical décor where guests are shown gathered for a lavish meal also contained the heavily curtained bed, generally placed next to the fireplace. Seventeenth-century luxury was not aware of thousands of amenities – heating for a start. It was also unaware of privacy: when Louis xiv wanted to visit Madame de Montespan he had to cross Mademoiselle de La Vallière's apartment.

Privacy was an eighteenth-century innovation. Not that Europe abandoned fashionable display at that time; it made even greater sacrifices for the sake of social appearances. But the individual was soon to have his revenge. Housing and furniture changed because individuals wanted them to and because the large town favoured their inclination. In the rapidly growing towns – London, Paris, St Petersburg – everything became more and more expensive, luxury unrestrained. Space was in short supply and architects had to utilise to the maximum limited spaces bought at sky-high prices. The modern town house, the modern apartment, conceived for a less grandiose but also a more agreeable life, then became indispensable. An advertisement from the reign of Louis xv offers a rented apartment in Paris 'with ten rooms, divided into an ante-chamber, dining room, reception room, second reception room arranged for winter [therefore with heating], a small library, a small social room and bedrooms with wardrobes'. Such an advertisement would have been unthinkable in Louis xiv's time, when the rich lived in suites of rooms, everything was sacrificed to appearances and every room suited to every purpose. As a result of this dismantling of the home everyone thenceforth lived to some extent as he pleased.

The pantry was distinct from the kitchen, the dining-room from the drawing-room; the bedroom was established as a realm apart. Lewis Mumford thinks that from being a summer activity love then became an all-the-year-round pastime! We do not need to believe him (dates of births in the records even prove the contrary) but it is true that there came about an 'internal allocation of apartments' which had not existed in Rome, or in Tuscany under the Medicis, or in France under Louis xiv. 'Small houses with more sections [rooms],' wrote someone during the Regency, 'are more convenient; one has a lot of things in little space.' 'Our small apartments,' wrote Sébastien Mercier, 'are fashioned and arranged like round and polished seashells, and one lives with light and pleasure in spaces hitherto lost and really quite dark.' 'Moreover', added a sage, 'the ancient manner [immense houses] would be too dear; nowadays people are not rich enough.'

On the whole a distinction had been made between three types of space: that required for good manners or society; that for ostentation and magnificence; that for comfort.

Decorative furniture multiplied in the houses of the rich, but it was more delicate than before. Ornaments, vases, precious woods, mirrors, hangings, knick-knacks, pictures – these were the first to lead an invasion of interiors which was to continue and broaden in scope. The evacuated village along the Maginot line where we spent some months in 1939–40 offered the solitary visitor poor rooms cluttered with useless objects. Did the pernicious fashion start, as Lewis Mumford humorously suggested, because it was necessary to employ such a numerous domestic staff that there was no longer enough to keep them decently occupied? Therefore let them polish, dust and shine! But, if the ritual persisted, it was also because the mania corresponded to other needs. What might a psychoanalyst have to say about this accumulation of real and false wealth?

Luxury and comfort

Such luxury seems all the more false to us because it was not always accompanied by what we would call comfort. Heating was still poor, ventilation derisory, cooking done in a rustic manner, sometimes on a portable charcoal stove. Apartments did not always include English-style water-closets, although Sir John Harington had invented them in 1596. When they did exist the house still had to be cleared of pestilential odours in various ways. The problems posed by the defective emptying of cesspools in Paris even worried the Academy of Sciences in 1788. And chamber pots, as always, continued to be emptied out of windows; the streets were sewers. For a long time Parisians 'relieved themselves under a row of yews' in the Tuileries; driven from there by the Swiss guards, they betook themselves to the banks of the Seine, which 'is equally revolting to eye and nose'. This picture is from Louis XVI's reign.

A bathroom was a very rare luxury in these seventeenth- and eighteenth-century houses. Fleas, lice and bugs conquered London as well as Paris, rich interiors as well as poor. As for lighting, candles and oil lamps continued to be used in houses until the blue flame of gas lighting appeared in about 1808. But even the thousands of ingenious methods of early lighting from torch to lantern, sconce, flat candlestick or chandelier, as we see them in old pictures, were late in coming. A study has established that in Toulouse they only really became widespread in about 1527. Until then lighting had been almost non-existent. And they paid dearly for this 'victory over the night', which was such an object of pride and even ostentation. It required wax, tallow, olive oil (or rather a by-product of it known as 'hell oil') and increasingly in the eighteenth century, whale oil – which made for the success of fishermen from Holland

and Hamburg, then later in the nineteenth century from those United States ports which Melville was to describe.

So if we moderns were to enter into an interior of the past, we would very soon feel uncomfortable. However beautiful it might be – and it was often wonderfully so – what for them exceeded sufficiency would not be enough for us.

3   Costume and fashion

The history of costume is less anecdotal than would appear. It touches on every issue – raw materials, production processes, manufacturing costs, cultural stability, fashion and social hierarchy. Subject to incessant change, costume everywhere is a persistent reminder of social position. The sumptuary laws, therefore, expressed the wisdom of governments, but even more the anger of the upper classes when they saw the *nouveaux riches* imitate them. Neither Henry IV nor his nobility could consent to the wives and daughters of the Parisian bourgeoisie dressing in silk. But nothing has ever been effective against the passion to move up in the world or the desire to wear those clothes which, in the West, symbolised the slightest social promotion. Nor did governments ever prevent the ostentatious luxury of the great lords, or the extraordinary shows put on by those who had just become mothers in Venice, or the displays in Naples when burials took place.

It was the same in the poorest environments. At Rumegies, a village in Flanders, near Valenciennes, in 1696, a priest's journal tells us that the rich peasants sacrificed everything to luxury of dress 'the young men with hats trimmed with gold or silver, and all the rest; the girls with coiffures a foot high and their other clothes in proportion ...'. There they were, with 'unheard-of insolence frequenting taverns every Sunday'. But a little later the same priest wrote, 'Except for Sundays when they are in church or at the tavern, they [rich and poor] are so dirty that the girls are a cure for the men's concupiscence and the men for the girls'.' This puts the situation in the right light, against the backcloth of everyday life. In June 1680 Madame de Sévigné, half admiring, half indignant, actually received a 'beautiful little farmer's wife from Bodégat (Brittany) with her gown of Holland cloth cut away to show watered silk, and her slashed sleeves ...'. who owed her 8000 francs. But she was an exception, as were the peasants wearing ruffs at the parish feast in a German village in 1680. Usually all went barefoot, or almost so, and one glance even at a town market was enough to differentiate between middle and lower classes.

If society stood still . . .

If society remained more or less stable everything stayed put. And this was most frequently the case, right up to the highest rung of the established hierarchies. The mandarin's costume in China was the same from the outskirts of Peking, the new capital (1421), to the pioneer provinces of Se-tchouan and Yunnan and had been so from well before the fifteenth century. And the silk costume with golden embroidery drawn by Father de Las Cortes in 1626 was the same shown in so many eighteenth-century engravings, with the same 'many-coloured silk boots'. At home, mandarins dressed in simple cotton clothes. Their brilliant costumes were donned in the course of their duties and served as a social mask, an authentification of their official personality. The mask scarcely changed in the course of centuries, but then Chinese society itself scarcely moved at all. Even the upheaval of the Tartar conquest in 1644 hardly interfered with a centuries'-old stability. The new masters forced their subjects to wear their hair close-cropped (except for one lock) and altered the large robe of former times. But that was all and it did not constitute a great deal. 'In China,' noted a traveller in 1793, 'the form of clothing is rarely changed by fashion or whim. The dress which suits the status of the man and the season of the year when he wears it is always made in the same way. Even the women have scarcely any new fashions, other than in the arrangement of the flowers and other ornaments which they put on their heads.' Japan was also conservative, possibly despite itself after Hideyoshi's harsh reaction. For centuries it remained faithful to the *kimono*, an indoor garment hardly any different from the present-day kimono, and to the '*jinbaori*, a leather garment painted on the back' which was regulation wear for walking in the streets.

As a general rule no changes took place in these societies except as a result of political upheavals which affected the whole social order. When India was more or less conquered by the Muslims the costume of the Mogul conquerors (the *pyjama* and the *chapkar*) became the rule, at least for the rich. 'All the portraits of the Rajput princes [we know they were not Muslim] show them in court dress, with one exception, an incontestable proof that in general the high nobility has accepted the customs and manners of the Mogul sovereigns.' The same conclusions apply to the Turkish empire. Wherever the strength and influence of the Osmanli sultans made itself felt the upper classes adopted their costume – in far-off Algeria and in Christian Poland, where Turkish fashion only belatedly gave way (and then imperfectly) to French fashion in the eighteenth century. All these imitations, once adopted, scarcely changed over the centuries. Mouradj d'Osson confirms the impression in the *Tableau général de l'Empire ottoman*, which appeared in 1741. 'Fashions which tyrannise European women hardly disturb the fair sex in the east; hair styles, cut of clothing and type of fabric there are almost always the same.' Was this, as our author thought, because there were no fashion merchants in Levantine towns? In Algiers anyway, which had been Turkish since 1516 and remained so until 1830, female fashion changed little in three centuries. The detailed description supplied by a prisoner, Father Haedo, in about 1580, 'could be used, with very little correction, as a caption to engravings of 1830'.

If all the world were poor . . .

The question would not even arise. Everything would stay fixed. No wealth, no freedom of movement, no possible change. This was the fate of the poor everywhere. Their costumes, however beautiful or coarse, remained the same. The beautiful was represented by the feast-day costume, often handed down from parent to child. It remained more or less the same for centuries on end, despite the infinite variety of national and provincial popular costumes. Coarse homespun was the everyday working garb made from the least expensive local resources and varied still less.

The Indian women in New Spain in Cortes' day in their long and sometimes embroidered cotton tunics, later in woollen thread, were no different from those of the eighteenth century. Male costume on the other hand changed – but only to the extent to which conquerors and missionaries demanded clothing decently concealing the nudity of the past. The natives in Peru today are clad in the same fashion as in the eighteenth century: a square of homespun llama wool with an opening in the centre for the head – the *poncho*. The same applies, and has always done, to India: 'The Hindu,' wrote K.H. Panikkar, 'continues to wear a *dhoti*,' today as in the past. In China 'the villagers and lower classes have always worn cotton clothing in every sort of colour'; in fact this was a long shirt, gathered in at the waist. In

1609, and probably for centuries before, Japanese peasants were wearing kimonos lined with cotton. In his *Voyage d'Egypte* (1783) Volney expressed surprise at the Egyptian costume: 'That mass of material, rolled in folds round a shaven head; that long garment which falls from neck to heels, concealing the body rather than clothing it. . . .' This is an even older garment than the one worn by the rich Mamelukes and dating from the twelfth century. As for the costume which Father Labat describes the poor Muslims in Black Africa as wearing, it could hardly change when it was so meagre. 'They have no shirts; they envelop their bodies above their pants with a bit of material fixed at the belt; most of them go bare-headed and barefoot.'

The poor in Europe were more covered, but made no greater concession to caprice. Jean-Baptiste Say wrote in 1828: 'I confess that the unchanging fashions of the Turks and the other Eastern peoples do not attract me. It seems that their fashions tend to preserve their stupid despotism. Our villagers are to some extent Turkish in respect of fashions and one sees old pictures of the wars of Louis XIV where male and female peasants are represented in clothes barely differing from those we see today.' We can demonstrate the validity of the comment for an earlier period by a comparison of three items at the Munich Pinakothek: a picture by Pieter Aertsen (1508–75) and two canvases by Jan Breughel (1568–1625), all three depicting crowds at a market. A single glance is enough in every case to distinguish the humble vendors and fishermen from the groups of bourgeois customers and passers-by. Their costumes immediately give them away. A second fact to emerge is more curious. During the half-century or so separating the two painters, bourgeois costume changed considerably: Aertsen's Spanish-style high collars edged with simple fluting have been replaced by the true ruffs which both men and women are wearing in the Breughels, while the popular female costume (turned-down open collar, bodice, apron over a gathered skirt) has remained exactly the same. There is a difference in hair style, but that was probably regional. A widow living in a village in the upper Jura in 1631 received under the terms of her husband's will 'one pair of shoes and a chemise every two years and a dress of coarse cloth every three'.

Although peasant costume remained similar in appearance, certain important details did change. Thus, underwear came into general use, inside and outside France, towards the thirteenth century. It was customary in eighteenth-century Sardinia to wear the same shirt for a period of a year as a sign of mourning, which at least shows that the peasant knew about shirts and that not to change them was a sacrifice. On the other hand we see from many pictures that in the past – even in the fourteenth century – rich and poor slept naked in their beds.

Furthermore a certain eighteenth-century demographer remarks that 'scabies, tinea and all the skin diseases and others originating from lack of cleanliness were so common in the past only because of lack of linen'. In fact medical and surgical books prove that these diseases had not entirely disappeared in the eighteenth century, but they were on the retreat. The same eighteenth-century observer still mentions the widespread use of rough woollen clothing by peasants in his own day.

A French peasant [he writes] is badly dressed and the rags which cover his nudity are poor protection against the harshness of the seasons: however it appears that his state, in respect of clothing, is less deplorable than in the past. Dress for the poor is not an object of luxury but a necessary defence against the cold: coarse linen, the clothing of many peasants, does not protect them adequately . . . but for some years . . . a very much larger number of peasants have been wearing woollen clothes. The proof of this is simple, because it is certain that for some time a larger quantity of rough woollen cloth has been produced in the realm; and as it is not exported, it must necessarily be used to clothe a larger number of Frenchmen.

These were belated and limited improvements. The change in the French peasant's dress followed that of the English peasant. We should not however jump to the conclusion that the change was general. Just before the Revolution, still, peasants in the Chalonnais and the Bresse were only 'clad in coarse cloth dyed black' with the aid of oak bark, and 'this custom was so widespread that the woods all suffered thereby'. Moreover 'in Burgundy, clothing was not [at that time] a significant item in the [peasant] budget'. This was probably the case all over Europe as far as Russia, and especially in Germany where the peasant was still dressed in linen at the beginning of the nineteenth century. The shepherds depicted as characters in a manger scene in the Tyrol in 1750 have linen blouses falling to their knees, their legs and feet being bare or merely shod with a sole held on by a leather strap wound round the leg. In Tuscany, supposed to be a rich land, the countryman, even in the eighteenth century, was dressed exclusively in homespun fabrics, hempen cloth and cloth made of equal parts of hemp and wool (*mezzelane*).

Europe and the craze for fashion

We can now approach the Europe of the rich and of changing fashions without risk of losing ourselves in its caprices. First of all we know that fashionable whims only affected a very small number of people, but that they made a great deal of noise and show, because the rest, even the most wretched, looked on and encouraged them in their extravagance.

We also know that the craze for change year after year took some time to become really established. It is true a Venetian ambassador at the Court of Henry IV was already saying: 'A man ... is not respected if he does not have twenty-five to thirty suits of different types which he changes every day.' But fashion is not only a matter of abundance, quantity, profusion. It also consists in making a quick change at the right moment. It is a question of season, day and hour. In fact the sovereign authority of fashion was barely enforced in its full rigour before 1700. At that time the word gained a new lease of life and spread everywhere with a new meaning: keeping up with the times. Everything then assumed the appearance of fashion in its present sense. Before then things had not moved so fast.

If we go far back into the past we find unruffled times and ancient institutions like those we have described in India, China and Islam. The general rule was changelessness. Until towards the beginning of the twelfth century costumes in Europe remained entirely as they had been in Roman times: long tunics falling straight to the feet for women and to the knees for men.

There was no change until the boost in the economy after about 1300, when the West had seized control of the routes of the inland sea and appropriated their wealth. Proof, if any is required, that costume is linked to the possibilities of the material situation. In any case, costume changed: it began to be moulded, fitted to the body. Oderic Vital deplored these sartorial follies, in his opinion completely useless: 'The old costume has been almost completely swept aside,' he says, 'by new inventions.' He may possibly have been referring to the first of the changes in dress adopted by the rich, at the very beginning of European ascendancy. Others of course were to follow.

The fashions involved became established rather slowly. At the very beginning of the period covered by this book, in about 1400–50, princely costume was more or less the same at the four corners of Christendom: the same great coats, the same fine hats, the same shoes with long pointed toes. It is the same kind of universality (with its many variations) we find in Romanesque art and Gothic art, which emerged in all its intricate brilliance in the fifteenth century. But this graceful and slightly crazy costume, like the court of Charles VI, was not to survive through the centuries to come; it was but one link in a long chain of changes.

Thus in the sixteenth century the upper classes adopted the black cloth costume inspired by Spaniards. It was a sign of the political preponderance of the Catholic King's 'world-wide' empire. It succeeded the Renaissance Italian costume whose large, low-cut, square necks, wide sleeves and hairnets had set the fashion for a large part of feminine Europe. In the seventeenth century on the other hand brightly coloured French costumes gradually took over, even in the Spanish territories. The Spanish resisted at first but then yielded to the point where an Indian chief in distant Peru donned the new fashion, as may be seen in the portrait done of him by a seventeenth-century painter. The very heart of Spain, Madrid itself, had also been conquered, and Philip IV's illegitimate son, the second Don Juan of Austria, assured its success there. Not without difficulty. The court for a long time obstructed the *vestido de color*; a foreigner was only received there properly 'dressed in black'. An envoy from the Prince de Condé (then an ally of the Spaniards) could only obtain an audience after he had changed into the compulsory dark clothing. But Catalonia was won over to the new fashion in 1630, ten years before it revolted against Madrid. The Stadtholder's court in Holland also yielded to the craze at the same date, although recalcitrants were not rare; such was the Burgomaster Bicker, whom van der Helst depicted still wearing the high round collar. Could this diffusion be interpreted as an indication of the extent of the decadence of Spain and soon even of Holland?

Successive dominating influences suggest the same explanation we advanced for the expansion of Mogul costume in India or Osmanli costume in the Turkish empire. Europe was a single family, despite or because of its quarrels. The law was laid down by the strongest and the most admired, and not inevitably, as the French believed, by the most loved or the most refined. It is obvious that the political preponderances which affected the whole body of Europe – with the result that the direction of its progress or its very centre of gravity might suddenly change from one day to the next – did not affect the whole realm of fashion immediately. There were time-lags, aberrations, gaps, delays. French fashion was predominant in the seventeenth century but really only established its sovereignty in the eighteenth. Paris set the fashion for the four corners of Enlightened Europe with its mannequin dolls. They appeared very early on and thenceforth reigned undisputed. In Venice, long regarded as the capital of fashion and good taste in the fifteenth and sixteenth centuries, one of the oldest shops was called and still is called The Doll of France (*La Piavola de Franza*).

It is very obvious that the reduction of everything to one dominant fashion never took place without resistance on the part of some people. There was, as we have said, the immense inertia of the poor, situated as they were on the periphery of things, There was also – and this stands out above the general conformity – local resistance, regional partitioning. The despair of costume historians certainly springs from such schisms and aberrations. The Valois court of the house of Burgundy was too near Germany and too original to follow the fashion of the French court. The farthingale might have been in general use there in the sixteenth century or, to take a better example, furs might have enjoyed a long vogue, but everyone wore them in their own way. Ruffs could vary from discreet ruching to the enormous lace ruff Isabelle Brandt wore in the portrait in which Rubens depicts her by his side; or that worn by Cornelis de Vos' wife in the picture in the Brussels Museum showing her with the painter and her two small daughters. The Italian women noticed, and were shocked by, the profusion and wealth of the French women's jewellery at Maria de Medici's wedding, regarding such luxury as typical of *nouveaux riches*: the French were unversed in the art of choosing a jewel well and showing it off to advantage.

There is an account left by three young noble Venetian travellers. Handsome, happy to be alive, sensitive, intelligent and pleased with themselves, they found themselves in Saragossa one evening in May 1581, *doppo disnar*. A procession passed with the Holy Sacrament, followed by a crowd of men and women. 'The women were very ugly,' says the narrator mischievously, 'their faces painted in every colour, so that the effect was most strange, and they were wearing very high shoes or rathér *zocoli*, in the Venetian fashion, and mantillas in the fashion of all Spain.' Curiosity draws the travellers towards the spectacle. But whoever looks at other people must expect to be observed, noticed and pointed out in turn. Men and women passing in front of them begin to shriek with laughter and shout at them. 'All this simply,' writes our Francesco Contarini, 'because we were wearing *nimphe* (lace collarettes) broader than Spanish custom decreed. Some said: "All Holland has come to our town" (i.e. all Holland cloth, or some other play of words on *olanda*, the fabric used to make sheets and linen); others remarked: "What enormous lettuces!" From this we derived great amusement.'

Is fashion frivolous?

Fashion seems to enjoy freedom to act and to pursue its whims. In fact, its path is largely ordained in advance and its range of choice limited.

Its mechanism depends on the rules governing cultural transfers. And all diffusion of this type is by nature slow, involving a whole series of processes and constraints. The dramatist Thomas Dekker (1572–1632) amused himself by reflecting on the sartorial borrowings his compatriots had made from other nations –. "his Codpeece is in Denmarke, the collar, his Duble and the belly in France, the wing and narrow sleeve in Italy: the short waste hangs over a Dutch Botchers stall in Utrich: his huge Sloppes speakes Spanish: Polonia give him the Bootes." The pedigrees were not necessarily exact, but the diversity of the ingredients probably was, and it was not in one season that a recipe acceptable to all was to be produced.

Everything moved faster in the eighteenth century and therefore became more lively, but for all that, frivolity did not become the general rule in this boundless kingdom so enthusiastically described by witnesses and participants. Listen to Sébastien Mercier (without necessarily believing all he says), a good observer and talented diarist but certainly not a very great intellect: 'I fear,' he wrote in 1771, 'the approach of winter because of the harshness of the weather. . . . It is then that the noisy and insipid gatherings where all the useless passions exercise their ridiculous authority, are born. The taste for frivolity dictates the judgements of fashion. All the men are turned into effeminate slaves, all subordinated to the whims of the women. . . .' Here, let loose, is 'that flood of fashions, fantasies, amusements, not one of which will last'. 'If it took my fancy,' he wrote again, 'to give a treatise on the art of curling, into what state of astonishment would I throw my readers by proving that there are three or four hundred ways of cutting a gentleman's hair.' The tone is typical of Mercier, decidedly moralistic though always anxious to entertain. So it is tempting to take him more seriously when he appraises the development of feminine fashion in his period. Of women and the outmoded farthingale he wrote:

The hoops enclosing them, their multitude of beauty spots, some of which resembled veritable plasters – all that has disappeared, except for the immoderate height of their *coiffures*; ridicule has not been able to correct this last custom, but the defect is tempered by the taste and grace which direct the construction of the elegant edifice. Women, taking everything into account, are better dressed today than they have ever been; their attire combines lightness, decency, freshness and charm. These gowns made of light fabric [prints] are renewed more frequently than the gowns that glittered with gold and silver; they follow as it were the colours of the flowers of the different seasons. . . .

Here is testimony indeed. Fashion eliminates one style and imposes another – a double role representing a double difficulty. The innovation in question was printed calicos, relatively inexpensive cotton fabrics. But even they did not reach Europe overnight. And the history of textiles shows that quite clearly in the field of fashion everything depends on everything else.

Is fashion in fact such a trifling thing? Or, as we think, do these signs constitute evidence in depth concerning the energies, possibilities, demands and *joie de vivre* of a given society, economy and civilisation? When Rodrigo Vivero was returning from Manila (where he was temporarily Captain-General) in 1609 on board a large ship (two thousand tons) taking him back to Acapulco in New Spain, he was shipwrecked off the coast of Japan. The castaway almost immediately became an honoured guest of the islands (who were curious about the foreigner) and then a sort of ambassador extraordinary. He tried, but to no avail, to close the islands to Dutch trade and also, equally vainly, considered attracting miners from New Spain, so that the silver and copper mines of the archipelago might be better exploited. This rather appealing character was also a good and intelligent observer. One day he was chatting idly with the Shogun's secretary at Yedo. The secretary criticised the Spaniards for their pride, their reserve. He then proceeded to discuss their way of dressing, 'the variety of their costumes, a realm in which they are so inconstant that they are dressed in a different way every two years'. These changes could only be ascribed to their levity and the levity of the governments which permitted such abuse. As for him, he would show 'by the evidence of traditions and of old papers that his nation had not changed its costume for over a thousand years'.

The conversation is revealing. Costume is a language. It is no more misleading than the graphs drawn by demographers and price historians. In fact the future belonged to societies which were trifling enough, but also rich and inventive enough to bother about changing colours, material and style of costume, and also the division of the social classes and the map of the world. Everything is connected.

I have always thought that fashion resulted to a large extent from the desire of the privileged to distinguish themselves, whatever the cost, from the masses who followed them; to set up a barrier. 'Nothing makes noble persons despise the gilded costume so much [according to a Sicilian who passed through Paris in 1714] as to see it on the bodies of the lowest men in the world.' New 'gilded costumes' or new distinctive signs, whatsoever they might be, had therefore to be invented with the inevitable complaint each time: 'Everything is truly changed and the new bourgeois fashions for both men and women are identical to those adopted by people of quality' (1779). Pressure from followers and imitators obviously made for a lively race. And if this was the case, it was because prosperity granted privileges to a certain number of *nouveaux riches* and pushed them to the fore. A social ascent took place which was the declaration of a certain level of material well-being, and we come back to our former observation. Material progress occurred: without it nothing would have changed so quickly.

However the material explanation obviously does not solve the whole problem. Fashion is also a search for a new language to discredit the old, a way in which each generation can repudiate its immediate predecessor and distinguish itself from it (at least in the case of a society where there is conflict between generations). 'The tailors,' ran a text in 1714 'have more trouble inventing than sewing.' But the problem in Europe was precisely that of inventing, of pushing out obsolete languages. The stable values – Church, Monarchy – made all the greater effort to preserve the same appearance; nuns wore the costume of women in the middle ages; Benedictines, Dominicans and Franciscans remained faithful to their ancient style of dress. The ceremonial costume of the English monarchy went at least as far back as the Wars of the Roses. It was a deliberate reaction against the general current. Sébastien Mercier was not mistaken when he wrote (1782): 'When I see vergers I say to myself: everyone was dressed like that in Charles VI's reign.'

The geography of textiles

Before we conclude, the complicated history of costumes should take us on to a history of textiles and fabrics, to a geography of production and exchange, to the slow work of the weavers and the regular crises resulting from the scarcity of raw materials. Europe lacked wool, cotton and silk; China, cotton; India and Islam, light wool; Black Africa bought foreign fabrics on the shores of the Atlantic or the Indian Ocean in exchange for gold or slaves. That was how poor peoples paid for their luxury purchases.

Production zones were, of course, to some extent fixed. For example, an area where wool was produced took shape and remained fairly static from the fifteenth to the eighteenth centuries, if we do not take into account the experiment peculiar to America and its vicuña (very fine) and llama wool (coarse). The static zone covered the Mediterranean, Europe, Iran, northern India and cold northern China.

So China had its sheep. 'They shear them,' wrote Father Ricci, 'but they are far less skilful at utilising the wool than the Europeans, and though they greatly appreciate imported cloth they do not know how to weave wool to make clothing.' They only made a few serges 'very fine and very valuable ... generally worn by old men and people of standing during the winter'. This was because the Chinese had too great a choice. They had silk and cotton, as well as two or three vegetable fibres that were easy to work. And when winter came, mandarins and nobles in the north covered themselves with sables, while the poor were clad in 'sheepskins'.

Like the most humble cultural assets, textiles incessantly moved about, took root in new regions. Wool found the land of its choice in Australia in the nineteenth century. It is likely that silk first reached the European world in the Trajan period (52–117). Cotton left India and ran riot in China in the twelfth century; it reached the Mediterranean even earlier, in about the tenth century, via the Arab world.

Silk made the most striking of these journeys. Jealously guarded, it took centuries to reach the Mediterranean from China. At the outset the Chinese disapproved, as did the Sassanid Persians living between China and Byzantium and keeping vigilant watch in both directions. Justinian (527–65) was not only the builder of Saint Sophia, not only the author of the code which bore his name; he was the emperor of silk, having succeeded, after various vicissitudes, in introducing into Byzantium silk worms, white mulberries, the unwinding of cocoons and the weaving of the precious thread. Byzantium thereby earned a fortune which it jealously guarded for centuries.

However in the fifteenth century, when this book begins, silk had been in Sicily and Andalusia for almost four hundred years. It spread in the sixteenth century – together with the mulberry – to Tuscany, Venetia, Lombardy, lower Piedmont and along the Rhône valley, reaching Savoy in the eighteenth century. Had it not been for this silent advance of trees and silk-worm rearing, the silk industry inside and outside Italy would not have experienced the remarkable success it enjoyed from the sixteenth century onwards.

The cotton plant and cotton made equally spectacular journeys. Europe was familiar with the valuable fabric quite early on, particularly after the thirteenth century, when wool became scarce following the decrease in sheep-raising. An ersatz cloth, fustian, made with a warp of flax and a woof of cotton, spread at that time. It had a great vogue in Italy and an even greater one north of the Alps where *Barchent* began to achieve its great popularity in Ulm and Augsburg – the zone beyond the Alps which Venice dominated and inspired from afar. This great town was in fact the importing port for cotton – in the form of yarn or in balls of raw cotton (called cotton wool). Large ships left Venice twice a year in the fifteenth century to bring it back from Syria. It was, of course, also worked locally – in and around Aleppo for example – and exported to Europe. This coarse blue cotton cloth, similar to the material used for kitchen aprons nowadays, served as clothing for the people in southern France in the seventeenth century. Later, in the eighteenth, cotton goods from India arrived on European markets. These were the fine printed fabrics, the 'calicos' which delighted the feminine clientele until the time when the industrial revolution enabled the English to do as well as the skilful Indian weavers, and then to ruin them.

Flax and hemp stayed more or less in their original environment, moving slightly eastwards towards Poland, the Baltic countries and Russia, but barely leaving Europe. (However hemp did grow in China.) These textiles were not popular outside the Western countries (including America). Nevertheless they were extremely useful: sheets, table linen, underwear, sacks, overalls, peasant trousers, sailcloth and rope were all made from one or other or both of these textiles. Elsewhere, in Asia and even in America, cotton was inevitably substituted for them even for sails – although Chinese and Japanese junks preferred bamboo slats whose virtues continue to be praised by nautical experts.

We could fill pages if we now embarked on the history of cloth production and then on the characteristics of the innumerable and varied fabrics. We would also need a dictionary of the terms used, as many of the expressions that have come down to us did not always designate the same product and sometimes designated products which we cannot identify reliably.

However we shall put off returning to the large subject of the textile industries until the second volume of this work.

Fashion in the broad sense

Fashion does not only govern clothing. The *Dictionnaire sentencieux* defines the word thus: 'Ways of dressing, writing and behaving, which the French twist round and round in a thousand different ways to make themselves out more gracious, more charming and often more ridiculous.' Fashion in this sense affects everything and is the way in which each civilisation is orientated. It covers ideas as much as costume, the current phrase as much as the coquettish gesture, the manner of receiving at table, the care taken in sealing a letter. It is the way one speaks: for example it was said in 1768 that 'the bourgeois have servants, people of quality have lackeys, priests have valets'. It is a way of eating: the times of meals in Europe varied according to place and social class but also according to fashion. Dinner in the eighteenth century was what we would call lunch. 'Artisans dine at nine o'clock [in the morning], provincials at twelve, Parisians at two, business people at half-past two, nobles at three.' As for 'supper' [our dinner], it 'is taken at seven in small towns, at eight in large, at nine in Paris and at ten at court. Nobles and financiers sup regularly, the legal profession never, adventurers when they get the chance'. This gave rise to the semi-proverbial expression: 'The Robe [the legal profession] dines and Finance sups.'

Fashion is also the way of walking and of greeting one's acquaintances. Must the hat be raised or not? The custom of baring the head before kings in France is said to have come from the Neapolitan nobles, whose respect astonished Charles VIII and served as a lesson.

It is also the care given to body, face and hair. If we pause a moment at these three items, it is because they are simpler to follow than the others. It will be noticed that fashion in respect of them also records very slow oscillations like the trends economists discern beneath the sharp and slightly incoherent movements of day-to-day prices. These rather slow backward and forward movements were also one of the facets, one of the realities of luxury and European fashion between the fifteenth and the eighteenth centuries.

Bodily cleanliness left much to be desired at all periods and for everyone. The privileged mention the repulsive dirtiness of the poor very early on. An Englishman (1776) was astonished at the 'unbelievable uncleanliness' of the poor in France, Spain and Italy: it 'makes them less healthy and more disfigured than they are in England'. Let us add that the peasant practically everywhere hid behind his poverty, displayed it and used it to protect himself from nobleman or tax collector. But was the European privileged class itself so clean?

The custom for men 'to wear pants which are changed every day and which maintain cleanliness' instead of simple lined breeches was hardly established until the second half of the eighteenth century. And, as we have already mentioned, there were no baths, except in the large towns. The West even experienced a significant regression from the point of view of body baths and bodily cleanliness from the fifteenth to the seventeenth centuries. Naked public bathing was general for both sexes in the middle ages. The public baths disappeared, we are told, as a result of sixteenth-century contagions and of the terrible syphilis: at Frankfurt-am-Main they decreased to nine in 1530 from thirty-nine in 1387. Was this the result of fear of disease or because of a new modesty? We cannot make a clear division. In any case the whole idea of bathing began gradually to disappear in the West at the same time as the public bath. In the middle ages people bathed at home in wooden tubs ringed like barrels. However public baths were retained in Finland and Russia, even in villages, with a sort of medieval innocence. They reappeared in the West in the seventeenth century, but public baths at that time meant much the same as brothels for rich clients. The success of the Vigier baths (a hundred baths fed by water from the Seine) should not be exaggerated: 'Use of the bath was regarded rather as a means of curing certain diseases than as a means of cleanliness.' The comment came from a Parisian in 1827! The same Parisian, interested in past customs, was all too happy to point to the Directory period, when 'women bathers ... determined to throw aside the veils of modesty, appeared daily at the Vigier baths stripped even of Venus' girdle'.

The low level of soap production is hardly surprising in these conditions, although it had originated as far back as Roman Gaul. Scarcity of soap was a problem and was possibly one of the reasons for high infant mortality, according to Lewis Mumford. The hard soaps with soda from the Mediterranean were used for washing and included cakes of toilet soap, which had to be 'marbled and scented in order to enjoy the right to pass over the cheeks of all our dandies'. Liquid soap made with potash (in the north) was intended for washing sheets and other fabrics. A poor tally on the whole – yet Europe was the continent *par excellence* for soap. It was not to be found in China and only in very small quantities elsewhere. No underwear was worn in China and there were still victims for its leper hospitals in 1793.

We have to wait for the eighteenth century, and the discoveries it added to ancient heritages, for feminine beauty treatment. The coquette easily took five or six hours to dress, in the hands of her servants and even more under the care of her hairdresser, chatting with her priest or her 'lover'. Hair was the great problem. It was built up so high that the eyes of the beauties seemed to start out from the middle of their bodies. Make-up was an easier task, especially as foundations were spread on generously. Only the bright rouge of the cosmetics, obligatory at Versailles, offered a choice: 'Show me what rouge you wear and I will tell you who you are.' Perfumes were manifold, essences of violet or rose, iris or lily-of-the-valley, and Spain had imposed a taste for strong perfumes with a musk and amber base a long time previously. 'Every French woman,' noted an Englishman (1779), 'believes herself at her toilette the genius of taste and elegance in all her apparel, and she imagines that there are no ornaments that could be invented to embellish a human face which do not belong to her by exclusive right.' The *Dictionnaire sentencieux* confirms that this sophistication was already in an advanced state in the following definition: 'Dressing is the combination of all the powders, all the essences, all the foundations necessary to change a person's nature and make even ugliness and age young and beautiful. It is then that defects of the figure are made good, eyebrows put in shape, teeth replaced, faces made up, indeed when face and skin are changed.'

But the most frivolous subject was still hairstyle, even for men. Were they to wear their hair long or short? Were beard and moustache acceptable? It is surprising to see how much individual whims were held within bounds in such an individual matter.

At the beginning of the wars with Italy Charles VIII and Louis XII wore their hair long and were clean-shaven. The new fashion of beard and moustache, but with short hair, came from Italy. It was launched, we are told, by Pope Julius II (which is open to doubt) and later imitated by Francis I (1521) and Charles V (1524). The dates are tentative. What is certain is that the fashion reached the whole of Europe. 'When François Olivier, who later became Chancellor, presented himself at the Parlement in 1536 to be received as Maître des Requêtes his beard frightened the assembled Chambers and caused a protest on their part. Olivier was only received on condition that he abandoned his beard.' But the Church opposed even more vociferously than the Parlement the custom of 'fostering facial hair'. Royal jussive letters were still necessary in 1559 to impose a bearded bishop or archbishop on recalcitrant chapters, who had tradition and ancient fashion on their side.

Of course the chapters did not win. But the victors themselves tired of their success. In fact such fashions scarcely last a century at the most. Hair lengthened again and beards and moustaches shrank with the beginning of Louis XIII's reign. And, once again, so much the worse for the laggards. The object of the conflict had changed, not its meaning. Very soon wearers of long beards became 'more or less foreigners in their own country. Seeing them it was tempting to believe that they came from a far-off land.' Sully's experience is an indication of the change. When he came to the court at the invitation of Louis XIII, who wanted to consult him on an important matter, the young courtesans could not restrain their laughter on seeing the hero with a long beard, a suit no longer in current fashion, a grave demeanour and manners suited to the old court. Beards became less and less common until the point when 'Louis XIV has entirely abolished short beards. Only the Carthusian brothers have not abandoned them' (1773). For the Church, as always and in accordance with its nature, was reluctant to change: once it had accepted changes it inevitably retained them beyond their season. It protested again against fashion in about 1629, at the beginning of the vogue for 'artificial hair', which shortly led to wigs and then to powdered wigs. Could a priest officiate in a wig that hid his tonsure? This was the subject of bitter controversy. The progress of wigs continued unaffected and at the beginning of the eighteenth century Constantinople even exported 'fashioned goat's hair for wigs' to Europe.

The essential point in these chapters of trifles is the duration of successive fashions over a period of about a century. Disappearing at the time of Louis XIV, beards only came into fashion again with Romanticism and then disappeared after the First World War, in about 1920. Will they last another century? We shall neither exaggerate nor minimise the importance of all this. England, with fewer than 10 million inhabitants in about 1800, counted 150,000 wig-wearers, if the fiscal authorities are to be believed. On the other side we quote a text of 1779, which was probably accurate at least for France: 'The peasants and the common people ... have always managed somehow to shave their beards and have always worn their hair quite short and uncared for.' Without taking the declaration literally we can wager that the chances are that, once again, immobility was on one side, the side of the majority, and movement on the other, that of luxury.

What conclusions?

All these realities of material life – food, drink, housing, clothes and fashion – cannot be so infallibly correlated that we only have to point out the relationship once and for all. The distinction between luxury and poverty is only a first classification, recurring again and again and yet not precise enough in itself. Actually all these circumstances are not solely the result of restrictive needs: man feeds himself, lives and dresses, because he cannot do otherwise. But he could feed, live and dress differently. The sudden changes in fashion demonstrate this in a 'diachronic' manner, and the contrasts over the world's surface do the same at every juncture of history but in a synchronistic manner. We are not only in the realm of things but really of 'things and words', interpreting the last term in a wider sense than is usual. Our concern is with terminologies, with languages, with all that man brings to them and insinuates into them as in the course of his everyday life he makes himself their unconscious prisoner.

The important thing, if one is to follow the trend of pioneering works such as those by Mario Praz and Michel Foucault, is to see these commodities and these languages in their context – undoubtedly in an economic context, in the broad sense of the word; probably in a social context too. If luxury is not a good way of supporting or promoting an economy, it is a means of holding, of fascinating a society. Civilisations – strange collections of commodities, symbols, illusions, phantasms and intellectual models – work in this way. An order becomes established that operates down to the very depths of material life. It is inevitably self-complicating, being influenced by the propensities, the unconscious pressures, and all that is implicit in economies, societies and civilisations.

5

The Spread of Technology: Sources of Power and Metallurgy

Everything is technology: not only man's 'violent exertions' but also his patient and monotonous efforts to make a mark upon the external world; not only the brisk changes we are a little too quick to label revolutions (gunpowder, navigation on the high seas, printing press, wind- and water-mills, the first machinery) but also the slow improvements in processes and tools. Technology is also all those innumerable actions which certainly have no innovating significance but which are the fruit of accumulated knowledge: the sailor fixing his ropes, the miner digging his gallery, the peasant behind his plough, the smith at his anvil. 'I call technology,' said Marcel Mauss, 'a traditional effective action'; in short, the work of man upon himself and the training he has undertaken and perpetuated since the beginning of time.

Technology ultimately covers as wide a field as history and has, of necessity, history's slowness and ambiguities. Technology is explained by history and, in its turn, explains history, though the correlation in neither case is entirely satisfactory. This domain, co-extensive with the whole of history, does not involve one action but a multiplicity of actions and reactions and a series of interlinking cogs. It is not a linear process. Lefebvre des Noëttes, whose work is nevertheless to be admired, yielded to a simplistic materialism. It was not the shoulder harness that gradually put an end to the slavery of man after the ninth century by replacing the chest harness and increasing the traction power of horses (Marc Bloch has questioned this over-simplification). Nor was it the centreline rudder, originating from the northern seas, that from the twelfth century paved the way and then ensured the prodigious adventure of the maritime discoveries. Similarly we can accept as an amusing whim L. H. White's theory about spectacles, namely that when they came into general use in the fifteenth century they assisted the intellectual advance of the Renaissance by increasing the numbers of readers. As a matter of fact there were many other considerations involved. What about the printing press, the increasing use of interior lighting in houses? Imagine the hours of reading and writing gained. But above all, the motives behind this new passion for reading and knowing must be investigated. Was there not a desperate search for ancient manuscripts in Petrarch's time, well before the rise of spectacles?

In short we have always to reckon with a more general history, or if you like society in the broadest sense; technology is never the only factor in the discussion. We mean by society a slow, muted and complicated history; a memory that obstinately repeats known solutions, that avoids the difficulty and the danger of thinking up something else. Every invention that presented itself had to wait for years or even centuries before being introduced into real life. First comes the *inventio*, then, very much later, the application (*usurpatio*), society 'having attained the required degree of receptivity'. The scythe is an example of the process. The *Schnitter Tod*, death armed with a scythe, became an obsessive image following the epidemics that decimated the West in the fourteenth century. But the scythe was used exclusively to cut grass in meadows at that time. It was rarely the harvester's implement. The ears of corn were cut at varying heights, with a sickle. The straw was left standing for the flocks. In spite of the enormous urban growth, in spite of Europe's being reduced to a corn-growing country (the *Vergetreidung* of German historians), the use of the scythe to harvest corn did not become general before the beginning of the nineteenth century. Only then did the need for greater speed and a certain permissible degree of grain-wastage ensure the scythe's widespread predominance.

Of course hundreds of other examples show the same process. The steam engine, for example, was invented a long time before it launched the industrial revolution – or should we say before being launched by it? The history of inventions, taken by itself, is therefore only a deception. A splendid sentence by Henri Pirenne neatly sums up the question: 'America [when the Vikings reached it] was lost as soon as it was discovered, because Europe did not yet need it.'

What does this mean if not that technology is sometimes the possibility which men are not capable of attaining and fully utilising, primarily for economic and social reasons, and also for psychological reasons; and at other times the ceiling which materially and technically blocks their efforts? In the latter case, when one fine day the ceiling gives way, the technical breach becomes the point of departure for a rapid acceleration. Nevertheless the movement that overcomes the obstacle is never a simple *internal* development of technology or science, or certainly not before the eighteenth century.

The key problem: sources of power

Between the fifteenth and eighteenth centuries man had at his disposal his own strength and that of his domestic animals; also that of the wind, running water, wood, charcoal and coal – varied but still moderate sources of power. Progress would have consisted in speculating on coal (we know this in the light of future events) and particularly in using it systematically, in the form of coke, in iron metallurgy. Coal was in fact used in Europe from the eleventh and twelfth centuries, and in China, according to writings of the time, from the fourth millennium before the Christian era. But men took a very long time to realise that coal was anything more than a supplementary fuel. The discovery of coke itself did not immediately result in its use.

The human engine

Man and his muscles represent a poor engine. His power measured in horse-power (seventy-five kg to a height of one metre in one second) is derisory: between three and four hundredths of one horsepower against twenty-seven to fifty-seven hundredths for a cart horse. In 1739 Forest de Belidor maintained that seven men were required to do the haulage work of one horse. Other measurements in 1800 suggested that one man could 'till from 0·3 to 0·4 hectares, turn 0·4 hectares of meadow, harvest 0·2 hectares with a sickle, thresh about 100 litres of corn' per day; a more optimistic historian put it at two quintals. But even at that level the yield was low.

Nevertheless, according to a historian 'man in terms of potential work is one of the highest values for the lowest weight'. Furthermore, under Louis XIII, a man's daily wage was half a horse's (eight and sixteen sols). The tariff rightly over-estimated human labour because such an insignificant engine always had great flexibility and knew how to increase its brute strength. Man had tools at his disposal, some of them since the most distant past: hammers, axes, saws, tongs and spades; he also possessed rudimentary engines which he worked with his own strength: trepans, capstans, pulleys, cranes, jacks, levers, pedals, cranks and lathes. G. Haudricourt has suggested the appropriate term 'human engines' for the last three, which had come to the West from either India or China. The most complex human engine of them all was really the loom, which reduced everything to simple actions: the alternate movement of the feet worked the pedals, raising half the threads of the warp and then the other, while the hands threw the shuttle carrying the thread of the woof.

Man in himself therefore contains many possibilities; he combines skill and flexibility. A porter in Paris (according to an account dating from 1782) lifted on his back 'loads that would kill a horse'. P.G. Poinsot, in *L'Ami des cultivateurs* (1806), gives advice which is flabbergasting in view of its late date:

It would be desirable if all the land could be tilled with a spade. The labour would be much more profitable than with the plough and this implement is preferred in several cantons of France where great practice in handling it shortens the operation considerably, since one single man can turn over 487 square metres of earth at a depth of 65 centimetres in a fortnight, and such tilling is enough by itself, while tilling by plough must be repeated four times before heavy soil can be sown; furthermore the earth is never so well turned over nor crumbled up as with a spade. . . . It is clearly bad economy to till with a plough if a man has not a sizeable domain to cultivate, and this is the principal reason why almost all the small farmers are ruined. . . . Furthermore it has been proved that harvests from lands thus cultivated are triple those of the others. The spade used to cultivate the land must be at least double the length and strength of that used for gardens, which does not stand up to the efforts required to lift up compact earth and break it up sufficiently.

Neither was this purely theoretical. Day labourers in the countryside often cultivated their plots with pick-axes, if not with spades. This, as they said at Moutiers-en-Bresse in the eighteenth century, was farming by hand. It would be interesting to calculate what would have been the result if this Chinese-type tillage had been the rule instead of the exception. Would Western towns have been able to subsist in such conditions? Could they even have been created? And what would have happened to the livestock?

The lone man working with bare hands is a recurring figure in China in modern times. A traveller notes (1793): not only is human labour there 'the least costly, but it is not spared at all as long as it is sure of being put to good use' – a condition we need not believe.

Chinese man dug with a pick-axe, drew the plough in the place of the buffalo, distributed water, worked 'chain pumps', hulled grain, carried travellers, lifted enormous burdens, transported weights balanced on a long wooden lever resting on his shoulders, turned the millstone at paper mills and hauled boats despite the fact that 'in many other countries horses are used for this'. The highest lock on the Grand Canal from the Yang-tse-Kiang to Peking – called 'Tien Fi Cha', which means the Queen and the Mistress of the Sky – was not worked by opening and closing the gates, but by the action of capstans and ropes pulled by four to five hundred men, 'or an even larger number according to the weight and size of the boat'. Was Father de Magaillans right (1678) to hold up as an example the Chinese custom of accomplishing 'all sorts of mechanical work with many fewer instruments than we use'? Gemelli Careri, some years later (1697), also marvelled at the speed of the chair-carriers who went trotting along as fast as the 'little Tartary horses'. A Jesuit father at Peking in 1657 produced a fire-engine capable of throwing 'water to a height of a hundred palms' by manpower and wind. Yet even in India the noria and the sugar mill were turned by teams of animals. Another extreme example could be found in Japan in the nineteenth century: there is a picture by Hokusai that shows the almost incredible sight of sugar cane being milled solely by manpower.

The Jesuit fathers were still explaining matters in 1777:

The question of the utility of machines and working animals is not so easy to decide, at least for a country where the land is barely sufficient to feed its inhabitants. What use would machines and working animals be there? – to turn part of the inhabitants into philosophists [sic], that is to say into men doing absolutely nothing for society and making it bear the burden of their needs, their well-being, and what is even worse their comical and ridiculous ideas. When our country folk [the argument is expounded by Chinese Jesuits] find themselves either supernumerary or unemployed in a few cantons, they decide to go away and work in great Tartary, in the newly conquered countries where our agriculture is making progress. . . .

Which seems perfectly sensible. It is moreover true that at that time Chinese agriculture was being extensively developed. However it is also true that agricultural progress was incapable of keeping pace with let alone overtaking demographic progress.

When Aurenge-Zebe made his journey to Kashmir the camels had to be unloaded at the first slopes of the Himalayas; they were relieved by 15,000 to 20,000 porters, some forced to serve, others 'attracted by the bait of ten écus for a hundred pounds' weight'. At the house of correction in Bicêtre (1788), water used to be drawn from the wells by twelve horses, 'but tough and powerful prisoners have since been employed at this work, a wise and most advantageous economy'. And this is the moralist Sébastien Mercier talking! Similarly Black slaves could be seen on even later occasions replacing horses in the towns of Brazil, pulling heavily laden carts.

The precondition for progress was probably a reasonable balance between human labour and other sources of power. The advantage was illusory when man competed with machines inordinately, as in the ancient world and China where mechanisation was ultimately blocked by cheap labour. There were slaves in Greece and Rome, and too many highly efficient coolies in China. In fact there is never any progress without an enhancement of human life. When man has a certain cost price as a source of power, then it is necessary to think about aiding him or, better still, replacing him.

Animal power

Man was relieved by domestic animals early on, though the luxury was very unfairly distributed over the world. The history of these 'engines' will be clearer if we distinguish between Old and New Worlds from the beginning.

America

In America it all seems very straightforward. Llamas, 'the sheep of the Andes', were the only important heritage from the Amerindians. They were fairly poor carriers but unique in being able to adapt to the rarefied air of the high Cordillera. All the other animals (except for vicuñas and turkeys) came from Europe: oxen, sheep, goats, horses, dogs and poultry. The most important for economic life were the mules, which gradually became indispensable as carriers – except in North America, and certain areas of colonial Brazil, and even more in the Argentine pampas where wooden carts with high wheels, drawn by teams of oxen, remained the general rule until the twentieth century.

Everywhere else there were caravans of mules with their noisy bells. In New Spain in 1808 Alexander von Humboldt noted their importance for the transport of merchandise and maize flour, indispensable to life in every town, above all in rich Mexico. The same applied in Brazil, where Auguste de Saint-Hilaire was an observant witness some twelve years later. This traffic, with its compulsory stops and fixed routes, required mule 'stations' – as at Porto da Estrella, at the foot of the Serra do Mar near Rio de Janeiro. The owners of the convoys, the Brazilian *tropeiros*, financed cotton production and later coffee. They were the pioneers of an early capitalism.

In the vast kingdom of Peru in 1776 five hundred thousand mules were employed for trading along the coast or through the Andes and for drawing coaches in Lima. The kingdom imported about 50,000 of them a year from the Argentine pampas in the south. There they grew up in a wild state, watched over at a distance, and were then driven northwards by *peones* on horseback in enormous herds of several thousand animals as far as Tucuman and Salta, where their ferocious training began. They finally arrived in either Peru or Brazil, and would often end up at the enormous fair of Sorocaba, in São Paulo province. This production and trade reminded Marcel Bataillon of the automobile industry today and 'its internal market in a continent open to motorisation'.

The commerce gave primitive Argentina the chance to share in the silver of Peru and the gold of Brazil. Add the five hundred thousand mules in Peru to possibly the same number in Brazil and those in New Spain and elsewhere – Caracas, Santa Fé de Bogota, central America – and we have anything up to two million beasts, of burden or of saddle (rarely for hauling). Say one animal to every five or ten inhabitants; that represents an enormous 'mechanisation' effort in the service of precious metals, sugar or maize. There was nothing comparable anywhere else in the world, with the probable exception of Europe. Spain only counted 250,000 mules for 10 million inhabitants (or almost the whole population of Iberian America) in 1799. The disproportion would still be large if more accurate research modified the statistics for America.

Other European domestic animals also proliferated in the New World, particularly oxen and horses. Yoked oxen drew the heavy cart of the pampas and the *carro de boi*, with solid wheels and creaking wooden axle, typical of colonial Brazil. They also formed wild herds. This was the case in the Rio São Francisco Valley in Brazil, where a 'leather civilisation' recalls the similar scenes in the Argentine pampas and the Rio Grande do Sul, with their indulgence in grilled meat, eaten almost raw.

Despite their superabundance, here as everywhere else in the world horses represented a sort of violent and virile aristocracy, that of the masters and the *peones* leading the herds of animals. The most astounding horsemen in the world, the *gauchos*, were already riding the pampas at the end of the eighteenth century. A horse was worth almost nothing. Even an ox did not have a market price; it belonged to whoever caught it with a *lasso* or *bola*. A mule however sold for up to nine pesos in Salta. As a Black slave in Buenos Aires was often worth 200 pesos, the New World had it seems enhanced the status of man – and placed the whole animal kingdom in his power.

The Old World: camels and dromedaries

Nothing was more logical – or so it seems *a posteriori* at least – than the spread of camels and dromedaries to all the empty parts of the Old World, that interminable chain of hot and cold desert lands running uninterruptedly from the Atlantic Sahara to the Gobi desert. The hot deserts were the realm of dromedaries, animals susceptible to the cold and also unadapted to mountainous country. The cold deserts and mountains were the realm of camels, the division between them being on either side of Anatolia and Iran. As a traveller put it (1694): 'Providence has made two types of camel, one for hot countries, the other for cold.'

But this wise division was the result of a long process. Dromedaries only arrived in the Sahara at about the beginning of the Christian era and did not gather there in strength until the Arab conquests of the seventh and eighth centuries, and then the arrival of the 'great nomads' during the eleventh and twelfth centuries. Camels colonised the West between the eleventh and the sixteenth centuries, with the help of the Turkish advances into Asia Minor and the Balkans. Of course camels and dromedaries spread out from their respective regions. Dromedaries crossed Iran and went as far as India where they sold at high prices, like horses. They penetrated south of the Sahara to the borders of the Black world where canoes and carriers took over from them. At one time they even pushed as far northwards as Merovingian Gaul, while in the east they did not become fully established in the Balkan countries until the nineteenth century. In 1529 they brought supplies to the Turkish army under the walls of Vienna. Northern China, at the other end of the Old World, was likewise invaded by the camel drive. A traveller near Peking (1775) noticed a camel 'carrying sheep' on its back alongside the sedan chairs.

Although donkeys had been used in the Mediterranean area for a very long time Islam had a near-monopoly of this powerful animal for local transport, tilling, norias and for long-distance caravan connections with the Sahara, the Near East, and central Asia – a network of communications to be attributed to a resourceful ancient capitalism.

Dromedaries and camels carried fairly heavy loads – 700 pounds for less powerful animals, quite often 800 (around Erzerum for example), and 1000 to 1500 between Tabriz and Istanbul, according to a document of 1708. The pounds concerned were obviously the so-called light pounds (under 500 grams), the average load being roughly four to five of our quintals. A caravan of 6000 camels could carry 2400 to 3000 tons, or the load of 4 to 6 reasonable-sized sailing ships of that period. For Islam, long-time master of all internal communications in the Old World, the camel was the crucial element in her commercial supremacy.

The Old World: oxen and buffaloes

Oxen (as well as buffaloes and zebus) spread right across the whole Old World to the Siberian forest in the north, where reindeer (wild or domestic) predominated; in the south the tsetse fly of the African tropical forest barred their passage.

In India they were sometimes not put to work at all; some however were harnessed to ploughs, pulled gilded carriages, turned mills or were ridden by soldiers and nobles; or enormous convoys of up to ten thousand animals under the command of caravaneers of the curious Mouris caste would be used to transport corn and rice. In case of attack men and women defended themselves with volleys of arrows. When two caravans crossed on the narrow north Indian roads flanked by trees and walls, one line would wait for the other to pass by to avoid confusion. Other travellers might be blocked for two or three days, unable to move forward or backwards because of the animals. These Indian oxen were ill-fed and never stabled. Buffaloes in China, which were much rarer, were not fed if they did not work and had to make shift for themselves. They were rather wild and easily frightened by travellers.

A common sight, particularly in Europe even today (for example in Spanish Galicia), is a pair of yoked oxen drawing a wooden carriage with solid wheels. Oxen could also be harnessed like horses: this method was used by the Japanese and Chinese (the chest harness) and sometimes Europeans in the north (the shoulder harness). Oxen have immense possibilities as draught animals. Alonso de Herrera, a Spanish agriculturalist whose book appeared in 1513, advocated harnessing oxen and was not in favour of mules: mules were faster but oxen tilled more deeply and economically. François Quesnay took up the old discussion in 1758. In his time capitalist agriculture using horses was driving out traditional agriculture which primarily employed oxen. Tests today prove that horses have equal pulling power to oxen. But all things considered (the horse is quicker and its working day longer, but it eats more and depreciates in value much more in old age than the ox destined for the butcher's shop), the ox costs 30% more than its rival for an equal amount of work. A unit used to measure land in Poland in the seventeenth century corresponded to the surface that could be worked by 'one horse or a pair of oxen'.

The Old World: horses

Horses have been around for a long time. They were present in France in the Neolithic Age, as is proved by the vast ossuary discovered at Solutré near Mâcon which covers more than a hectare. They were in Egypt in the eighteenth century BC and crossed the Sahara in the Roman period. Did they perhaps originate in the regions surrounding the port of Dzungaria, in the very heart of Asia? In any case they became well distributed over Europe. Wild horses, or rather horses that had returned to a wild state, lived in the forests and thickets of north-west Germany, the Swiss mountains, Alsace and the Vosges in the sixteenth and seventeenth centuries AD. A cartographer, Daniel Spekle, mentions these wild horses in 1576 'in the forests of the Vosges, reproducing themselves, feeding themselves in all seasons. In winter, they shelter beneath rocks. . . . Extremely wild, they are very sure-footed on the narrow, slippery rock's.

They were, therefore, old Europeans. This centuries'-old contact helped to bring about the gradual improvement in harnessing (shoulder harnesses in the West in the ninth century, later saddles, stirrups, bits, reins, harness, tandem teams, shoes). In the Roman period horses were badly harnessed (the chest harness throttled them) and they could only draw a relatively light load: in terms of work they were not worth more than four slaves. In the twelfth century their performance suddenly improved, like an engine increased to four or five times its power, as a result of shoulder harnesses. Until then they had been animals of war; thenceforth they played a very large part in harrowing, tilling and transport. This important transformation was one of a series of changes which included demographic expansion, the spread of the heavy plough, the propagation of triennial rotation in the northern region, and increased yields – all factors in the rise of northern Europe.

However horses remained very unevenly distributed. There were relatively few in China: 'We have scarcely seen them,' said Father de Las Cortes (1626), 'in the Kingdom of Chanchinfu, and those we have seen are very small animals with short legs; they do not shoe them and do not use spurs. The saddles and bits are not as ours. [They were still wooden saddles and ordinary ropes instead of reins in the eighteenth century.] We have seen a few more in the Kingdoms of Fuchinsu and Canton, but never in large numbers. I have been told that there are many horses in the mountains who have returned to wild life, and that it is the practice to capture them and break them in.' As for mules, they were few in number and conspicuously 'small', according to another traveller, although they were sold at a higher price than horses 'because they are easier to feed and they work more'. If a traveller wanted to travel on horseback in China he would have been well advised to choose a good horse to start off with, since he would not have been able to change it; relay-points were reserved solely for the emperor's use. The sensible choice remained the sedan chair – light, quick and comfortable, with eight men taking turns to carry it. In the interior of China, or towards the north, only limited trust was placed in the small horses from Se-tchouan, Mongolia or Manchuria, bought at fairs at Ka Yuan, Kwang Min, or, after 1467, near Fu-Shun. Father de Las Cortes probably only saw southern China; horses were obviously more numerous in the north. But even if we accept Father de Magaillans' figures (1678), there were only between two and three million horses in the whole empire, which is five or six times fewer than in eighteenth-century Europe, the emperor alone maintaining half a million of them for his soldiers, his court and the relay-stations.

Horses were even rarer in India and Black Africa. Moroccan horses were indeed objects of great luxury, bartered for gold dust, ivory and slaves in the Sudan: twelve slaves for one horse at the beginning of the sixteenth century, and still as many as five later on. Fleets loaded with horses bought in Persia sailed for the Indies from Ormuz. A horse at Goa sold for as much as 500 *pardoes* or 1000 of the Great Mogul's rupees, whereas a young slave at the same period was worth between 20 and 25 *pardoes*.

How did these expensive horses live with neither barley nor hay?

For food [wrote Tavernier in 1664] the horses are given a species of large pea that is crushed between two small millstones and then left to soak because its hardness makes its digestion very lengthy. These peas are given to the horses morning and evening; they are made to swallow two pounds of rough black sugar, crushed with the same amount of flour, and a pound of butter in small balls which are pushed down their throats; after which their mouths are carefully washed out because they have an aversion to this food. In the daytime they are only given certain herbs from the fields which are pulled up by the root and which are also carefully washed so that no earth or sand remains.

In Japan, where carriages were normally harnessed to oxen (from Korea), horses were primarily nobles' mounts.

In Muslim countries horses were the aristocracy of the animal world. They constituted the striking power of Islam almost from its very beginning, even more so after its first great successes. And they were plentiful: a traveller (1694) saw caravans of 1000 horses in Persia. From a military point of view, the Ottoman Empire in 1585 consisted of 40,000 horses in Asia and 100,000 in Europe; according to an ambassador, hostile Persia had 80,000. In fact Asia won the race to produce war-horses – witness the vast numbers of them assembled at Scutari and then shipped to Istanbul.

Théophile Gautier in the nineteenth century in Istanbul marvelled at the sight of so many thoroughbreds from Nedj, Hedjaz and Kurdistan. He also described 'a type of Turkish cab', the *arabas* stationed opposite the landing stage in Scutari. It was a 'gilded and painted carriage', covered 'with a cloth fitted over a frame' and harnessed to 'black buffaloes or silver-grey oxen'. In fact in the nineteenth century horses were still reserved for soldiers, the rich, and nobles. In Istanbul horses might certainly turn the mills; and small horses, their feet shod in solid iron soles, provide transport in the Western Balkans. But they were menials. The traveller was not talking about these horses when he mentions that they were worth forty to fifty ducats at Mazagan in Morocco, while a Black slave of eighteen years fetched sixteen ducats and a child seven. Horses did not finally replace oxen and camels for tilling in Asia Minor until after the First World War, in about 1920.

To its cost, Europe was slow to develop its own resources when faced with this world of horsemen. After the battle of Poitiers (732) it had to increase its numbers of horses and horsemen to protect itself and survive: the large charger the armed horseman rode in battle, the palfrey which carried him in times of peace, and his valet's common cob. What was involved was a war effort on the part of both Islam and Christendom, with tensions and occasional respites. The Swiss victory over Charles the Bold's cavalry marked a return in the West to infantry, pikemen and later to arquebusiers. The Spanish *tercio* in the sixteenth century was the most effective development of the foot-soldier. Similarly the janissary inaugurated the reign of the unmounted soldier on the Turkish side. However, the Turkish Spahi cavalry (for a long time incomparably superior to Western cavalry) retained its importance at his side.

Good horses sold for high prices in Europe. When Cosimo de Medici was reinstalled at Florence in 1531 and created a guard of two thousand horsemen the ostentatious magnificence ruined him. In 1580 the Spanish cavalry briskly achieved an easy conquest of Portugal, but immediately afterwards the Duke of Alba was complaining of a lack of horses and carriages. The same shortage occurred in the following century, for example during the war of Catalonia (1640–59), and throughout Louis xiv's reign, when the French depended on the 20,000 or 30,000 horses they could rely on buying abroad during an average year.

Beautiful horses were bred in Naples and Andalusia: the large Neapolitan breed and the Spanish jennets. But it was impossible to buy one at any price without the gracious consent of the King of Naples or the King of Spain. Of course smuggling was rife on both sides; the *passador de cavalls* on the Catalonian frontier was even prepared to risk the thunderbolts of the Inquisition, which had been entrusted with this unwonted supervision. In any case it took a very rich man, like the Marquis of Mantua, to have his own agents engaged in prospecting markets in Castile and as far as Turkey and North Africa in order to buy beautiful horses, pedigree dogs and falcons. The Grand Duke of Tuscany, whose galleys (the Order of Saint-Etienne, founded in 1562) pirated the Mediterranean, often helped out Barbary privateers in return for gifts of beautiful horses. When relations with North Africa became easier in the seventeenth century Barbary horses were shipped to Marseilles and sold at the Beaucaire fairs. Shortly afterwards attempts were made to breed thoroughbreds from imported Arab horses in England in Henry viii's reign, then in France in Louis xiv's and in Germany, where stud farms increased in the eighteenth century. Buffon explained that 'it is from them [the Arab horses] that, either directly or indirectly, the most beautiful horses in the world are bred'. Breeds therefore gradually improved in the West; and livestock also increased. At the beginning of the eighteenth century the Austrian cavalry which made possible Prince Eugène's successes against the Turks was built up partly as a result of this progress.

But the important thing from our point of view is not war horses so much as cart- and plough-horses, both of which were frequently sturdy animals from northern, central or eastern Europe. It is worth noting this proletarian conquest, important not only for tillage but also for trade, army transports and artillery trains.

In September 1494 Charles VIII's army surprised the Italian population when its pieces of field artillery passed quickly by, drawn not by oxen but large horses 'clipped in the French style without tail or ears'. A manual of Louis XIII's day listed everything needed to mobilise a troop of 20,000 men equipped with artillery. It included amongst other things an enormous number of horses for the transport of cooking utensils, luggage and crockery belonging to the various officers, the field blacksmith's tools, the carpenter's, the surgeon's chests, but above all for the transport of pieces of artillery and their ammunition. The largest required at least twenty-five horses to carry the piece itself, plus at least a dozen for powder and shot.

Such were the duties of the large horses from the north which were increasingly exported southwards. Milan bought them from German merchants from the beginning of the sixteenth century; France from the Jewish dealers of Metz; they were in great demand in Languedoc. Clearly-defined breeding areas developed in France – Brittany, Normandy (Guibray fair), the Limousin and the Jura.

We do not know whether the price of horses showed a relative fall in the eighteenth century. Whatever the case, Europe was equipped and even overburdened with horses. In England horse thieves and receivers formed a social category of their own at the beginning of the nineteenth century. In France, just before the Revolution, Lavoisier calculated that there were 3 million oxen and 1,781,000 horses, including 1,500,000 engaged in agriculture (900,000 in regions where only horses were used, 600,000 where work was also done by oxen). And France at that time had 25 million inhabitants. If proportions were constant, Europe would have had 14 million horses and 24 million oxen at its disposal – an important contribution to the continent's power.

Mules were also used in Europe, in Spanish agriculture, in Languedoc and elsewhere. Quiqueran de Beaujeu mentions mules in Provence 'whose price is often higher than that of horses'. A historian has deduced the tempo of economic life in Provence in the seventeenth century from the number of mules and muleteers and their movements. Since carriages could only cross the Alps at certain points, like the Brenner pass, the other paths were left exclusively to mule transport. These animals were even described as 'large carriages' at Susa and all the other mule stations in the Alps. French Poitou should be noted among the important regions where asses and mules were reared.

Horses and urban transport

Every town depended on its horses for its daily provisioning, its internal communications and its hired carriages. Convoys arrived incessantly in eighteenth-century Paris, which probably used proportionately as many horses as it does motor cars today. These convoys were called 'carriages of horses', and consisted of files of ten to twelve animals, each attached to the tail of the one in front, with a blanket on the back and a sort of stretcher at each side. They were assembled in the district of Saint-Victor or on the Saint-Geneviève mountain, and there was a horse market in the rue Saint-Honoré for a long time.

Except for Sundays when boats took sightseers to Sèvres or Saint-Cloud (not always safely), the Seine was scarcely used for public transport, which moreover was almost non-existent. The vehicle for someone in a hurry was a hired carriage.

At the end of the century two thousand seedy cabs plied for trade in the town; they were drawn by broken-down horses and driven by foul-mouthed coachmen who had to pay out twenty sous a day for 'the right to drive on the highway'. Congestion was notorious and we have many descriptions of it. 'When the cabs are empty,' said a Parisian, 'they are fairly docile; around midday they are more difficult, in the evening they are unmanageable.' And they were unobtainable at rush hours, for example at dinner time (for such it was) around two o'clock in the afternoon. 'You open the door of the cab, someone else does the same on the other side; he gets in, you get in. It is then necessary to go to the commissioner of police for him to decide who shall have it.' At such times a gilded carriage might be seen blocked by a cab crawling slowly along in front of it, at a slow and measured pace, 'all broken down, covered with burnt leather and with planks in place of glass'.

The real responsibility for such congestion probably lay with Old Paris, that network of narrow streets often lined with sordid houses into which the population was crowded – particularly as Louis XIV had opposed the development of the town by an ordinance of 1672. This Paris had not changed since Louis XI's day. To overcome the difficulties, said a historian, 'would seem to require nothing short of a cataclysm to make a clean sweep of the old city, as the 1666 fire did in London and the earthquake in 1755 in Lisbon'.

Carriages had more room for manœuvre on the road from Paris to Versailles and back; they were drawn by horses that were nothing but skin and bone, but urged recklessly on 'all dripping with sweat'; these cabs were known as the *enragés*. 'Versailles is the land of horses.' They showed 'the same differences as exist amongst the inhabitants of the town: some are fat, well fed, well trained ... others ... with drooping neck and withers, only drawing carriages of court valets or provincials. ...'

The scene would have been the same in St Petersburg and London, where we have only to follow day by day Samuel Pepys' drives and excursions in hired coaches in Charles II's reign. Later he treated himself to the luxury of a private carriage.

It is difficult to imagine what these problems of transport meant, for goods as much as people. Every town was full of stables. The shoeing smith was a person of substance, his establishment being rather like the present-day garage. Nor should the provision of oats, barley, hay and straw be forgotten. In Paris 'anyone who does not like the smell of new-mown hay,' wrote Sébastien Mercier in 1788, 'does not know the pleasantest of perfumes; anyone who likes this smell should go in the direction of the Porte d'Enfer [it is still there today, south of the Place Denfert-Rochereau] twice a week. There he will find long lines of carts overloaded with hay: they ... are awaiting purchasers ... suppliers to houses which keep horses and carriages are there, examining the quality of the produce; all of a sudden they pull out a fistful of hay, feel it, smell it, and chew it; they are cup-bearers for the horses of Madame la Marquise.' But the Seine remained the great supply route. The fire that broke out on 28 April 1718, setting light to the arches of the Petit Pont and burning the houses on it and neighbouring dwellings, started on a boat loaded with hay. In London hay was bought at a market just outside Whitechapel bar, where in 1664 for example, a year of high prices, it sold at £4 a cartload. At the Perlachplatz market in Augsburg in the sixteenth century, October saw peasants offering piles of hay side by side with supplies of wood and game, and in Nuremburg pedlars with wheelbarrows sold the straw needed for the stables of the town.

Wind engines and water engines

The West experienced its first mechanical revolution in the twelfth and thirteenth centuries. Not so much a revolution, perhaps, as a whole series of slow changes brought about by the increased numbers of wind- and watermills. The power from these 'primary engines' was probably not very great – from two to five horse-power from a water-wheel, sometimes five and at the most seven from the sails of a windmill. But they represented a considerable increase of power in an economy where power supplies were poor. At that time (just as in the period of the industrial revolution in the nineteenth century) prices in Europe were rising, as were wages over the long term (Wilhelm Abel).

Water-wheels

Watermills were older and had a much greater importance than windmills. They did not depend on the irregularities of the wind, but on water which is on the whole less capricious. They were more widespread because they had been in existence for a long time, and also on account of the large number of streams and rivers, dams, diversions and aqueducts which could turn a wheel fitted with blades or paddles. Nor should power from the tides be forgotten; it was utilised, both in Islam and the West, even in places where the tides were slight. In 1533 a French traveller to the lagoon at Venice was full of admiration for the only watermill he could have seen on the island of Murano, moved 'by water from the sea on a wheel when the sea swells and subsides'.

The first watermill was horizontal, a sort of rudimentary turbine: it is sometimes called the Greek mill (because it appeared in ancient Greece) or the Scandinavian mill (because it was used in Scandinavia for a long time). It might just as well be called the Chinese or Corsican, or Brazilian, or Japanese, or of the Faroe Islands or central Asia, because water-wheels turned horizontally there until variously the eighteenth or twentieth centuries, developing a small amount of power able to move millstones slowly. It is no surprise to find these primitive wheels in Bohemia in the fifteenth century or in Rumania in about 1850. This type of mill, with vanes, even functioned up to about 1920 near Berchtesgaden.

It was a stroke of genius to move the wheel to the vertical position, which Roman engineers did in the first century BC. The energy was transmitted by gear wheels to a horizontal plane for the purpose of turning the millstone – which furthermore turned five times faster than the propelling wheel, thanks to the use of gears. These first engines were not always rudimentary. Archaeologists have discovered admirable Roman installations in Barbegal near Arles: an aqueduct over ten kilometres long in which the water was forced along by a series of eighteen wheels.

Nevertheless the late appearance of this Roman equipment was limited to a few points in the Empire and was used solely to grind corn. Now the thirteenth-century revolution that increased the number of water-wheels also extended their use to other purposes. The Cistercians built them in association with their iron-works in France, England and Denmark. Centuries went by until the day when no village in Europe, from the Atlantic to Muscovy, was without a miller and a wheel turning with the current, except where a piping system brought water from higher up.

The uses of the water-wheel had become manifold; it worked pounding devices for crushing minerals, heavy tilt hammers used in iron-forging, enormous beaters used by cloth fullers, bellows at iron-works; also pumps, millstones to grind knives, tanning mills and paper mills, which were the last to appear. We should also mention the mechanical saws that appeared in the thirteenth century – as shown in a sketch made about 1235 by that strange 'engineer' Villard de Honnecourt.

But mechanical saws were still no everyday sight. When Barthélemy Joly crossed the Jura and arrived at Geneva in 1603 he noticed mills in the Neyrolles valley at the outlet of the lake of Silan handling 'pine and fir wood which is thrown from the top of the precipitous mountains to the bottom, with a pleasing device by which several movements from bottom to top and in the opposite direction [these were made by the saw] proceed from a single wheel turned by water, the wood moving forward of its own accord ... and another tree following in its place with as much method as if it were done by men's hands'. It is obvious that this was indeed an unusual sight, worthy of inclusion in a travelogue.

With the extraordinary development of mining in the fifteenth century the finest mills worked for the mines, powering winches with a reversible action to raise buckets of ore, machines to ventilate galleries or to pump water by norias, bucket chains or even by lift-and-force pumps, and various controls that could set in motion mechanisms which were already complicated and which were to remain unchanged until and after the eighteenth century. These fine mechanisms are shown in the very beautiful plates in *De re metallica* by Georg Agricola (Basle 1556) which summed up earlier work and brought it up to date. And this at a time when some winches were still worked by hand or by teams of horses.

Curiously enough, there was an excessive supply of water machinery quite early on. The Rouen region possessed too many mills in relation to the needs of its economy from the thirteenth century. The noble built and repaired his watermills and put them to use or abandoned them and rented out the surrounding meadows, as economic circumstances dictated. A concentration to the advantage of the largest of them took place in the eighteenth century. But paddle-wheels made almost no progress, despite one or two ancient drawings by Leonardo da Vinci, and turbines scarcely appeared on the scene before the end of our period.

Fully utilised or not, river power was absolutely necessary. The 'industrial' towns (and what town at that time was not?) adapted themselves to the courses of rivers, moving near them, controlling the running water and taking on a Venetian appearance, at least along three or four distinctive streets. Troyes was a typical case; Bar-le-Duc always had a Tanners Street, on an offshoot of the river; Châlons, the cloth centre, did the same with the Marne (where there was a bridge called the Cinq Moulins – the Five Mills); Rheims with the Vesle; Colmar with the Ill; Paris with the Seine and the Bièvre. The royal manufactory of Gobelins was established on this last river in 1667. The same thing happened in Toulouse with the Garonne, where a fleet of 'floating mills', that is boats with wheels turned by the current, existed very early on and long remained in use. The Pegnitz made it possible for the many wheels of Nuremburg to turn inside the city walls and in the nearby countryside (180 were still operating in 1900). One Kämpfer, a travelling doctor from Westphalia who in 1690 wanted to give some idea of the flow of the river on an insignificant island in the Gulf of Siam where he was relaxing, remarked: 'Abundant enough to turn three mills.'

According to statistics, Poland (which had become Austrian) had 5243 watermills (and only twelve windmills) for two thousand square leagues and two million inhabitants at the end of the eighteenth century. This is an enormous figure at first glance, but the Domesday Book in 1086 actually recorded 5624 mills south of the Severn and Trent. It is enough to observe the innumerable small wheels visible in so many pictures, drawings and town plans, to understand how general they had become. If the proportion of watermills to population for Poland was the same elsewhere, there would have been 60,000 in France and not far off 500,000 to 600,000 in Europe on the eve of the industrial revolution.

Windmills

Windmills appeared very much later than water-wheels. They were previously thought to have originated in China; more probably they came from the high lands of Iran or from Tibet.

Mills turned in Iran from the seventh century AD, moved by vertical sails fitted to a wheel turning horizontally. The momentum from the wheel was transmitted to a central axis and set in motion a millstone to grind grain. Nothing was simpler: there was no need to adjust the direction of the wheel since it was always situated in the path of the wind. It had another advantage: no gear-wheel was required to transmit the energy to the millstone. The problem in the case of a grain mill always was to power a horizontal millstone, the *mola versatilis*, which crushed the grain on a stationary millstone placed beneath it. The Muslims were said to have spread these mills to China and the Mediterranean. Tarragona, at the northern limit of Muslim Spain, possessed windmills in the tenth century. But we do not know how they turned.

The great event in the West – as opposed to China where mills turned horizontally for centuries – was the transformation of the windmill into a wheel fitted vertically, as had happened to water-mills. Engineers say that the modification was a stroke of genius and that power was greatly increased. It was this new style of mill, a creation in itself, that spread in Christendom.

The statutes of Arles recorded its presence in the twelfth century. It was in England and Flanders at the same period. The whole of France welcomed it in the thirteenth century. It was in Poland and already in Muscovy in the fourteenth, conveyed thither by Germany. One small point: the Crusaders did not, as has been said, find wind-mills in Syria; they took them there. Time-lags were numerous, but in general northern Europe was more advanced than southern. For example the windmill arrived late in certain regions of Spain, notably La Mancha, so much so that according to one historian Don Quixote's alarm was very natural: those great monsters were new to him. The same did not apply in Italy; in 1319, in Dante's *Inferno*, Satan stretches out his enormous arms *come un molin che il vento gira*.

In the West the windmill caught current practice off its guard and so was often established by default. As opposed to watermills, which were almost always "communal" though they belonged to a nobleman, windmills only belonged to their owners; they could humorously be described as 'capitalistic'. In the Neubourg (Normandy) region in the seventeenth century, 'the construction of windmills even gave rise to a whole network of odd paths; as flour did not keep easily, it was necessary for grain to be carried to the mill frequently – on foot or by ass – and naturally it was taken there by the shortest route; all these paths (*chemins herbus* or *chemins verts*), some of which [have] become carriage ways', were thus superimposed haphazardly on the patchwork pattern of the fields.

Windmills were more expensive to maintain than other mills and costlier for the same amount of work, notably flour-milling. But they had other uses. The major role of the *Wipmolen* in the Netherlands in the fifteenth century (and still more after 1600) was to drive the bucket chains that drained water from the soil and poured it into canals. It therefore became one of the instruments used in the patient reclamation of the Low Countries' soil; they were located behind the dykes built up against the sea and along the lakes formed on the sites of over-exploited peatbogs. Another reason why Holland was the homeland of windmills was its situation in the centre of a great area of permanent westerly winds from the Atlantic to the Baltic.

Originally the whole mill pivoted on itself to align its sails in the direction of the wind, like the Brittany mills, called by the distinctive name of *chandeliers*. The whole mill was mounted on a central mast and a directing bar or 'tail-pole' enabled the body to pivot. It was best if the sails were situated as high as possible above ground level to catch the strongest wind, so the machinery of gear-wheels and millstones was placed at the top of the building (hence the need for sack-hoists). One small detail is worthy of note: the axis of the sails was never strictly horizontal, the tilt being regulated by trial and error. We can understand these simple machines from plans (like that of Ramelli, 1588) and mills still in existence – how they transmitted momentum, their braking systems, the possibility of substituting two lateral pairs of millstones for the single central pair, and so on.

It is scarcely more complicated to explain the working of a *Wipmolen*, which took its driving power from the top of the mill and retransmitted it to the base and the bucket chain that acted as a pump. The momentum was transmitted by a shaft through a hollow central mast. This gave rise to certain difficulties when *Wipmolen* were, as the opportunity offered, converted for the purpose of milling grain, but they were not insurmountable.

Quite soon, certainly in the sixteenth century, thanks to Dutch engineers, tower mills became widespread: their sails were adjusted at the top of the building, the only movable part. The difficulty with these mills, sometimes called 'smock mills' (because from a distance they looked like a peasant clad in his smock), was to facilitate the movement of the 'cap' on the fixed part of the mill by the use of wooden runners or various types of rollers. Inside, the problems to be solved remained the same: to adjust, control and stop the movement of the sails, to organise the slow descent from the mill-hopper of the grain, which crossed the body of the upper turning part of the millstone by the 'mouth'; the basic problem was to convert the momentum from the vertical plane of the sails to the horizontal plane of the millstones by gear-wheels.

More generally the great advance was the discovery that a single engine, a single wheel – whether wind- or watermill – could transmit its momentum to several implements: not to one millstone but to two or three; not to one saw but to a saw plus a tilt-hammer; not to one pile but to a whole series, as in a curious model (in the Tyrol) which 'pounded' corn instead of milling it (in this case the roughly crushed grain was used to make wholemeal bread which was more like biscuit than bread).

Sails: the European fleets

We are not concerned here with the whole question of boat sails, but with getting some idea of the power that sails put at the service of man. The sail was in fact one of the most powerful engines at his disposal. The example of Europe offers adequate proof. In about 1600 it had something in the order of 600,000 to 700,000 tons of merchant shipping; according to reliable statistics established in France probably in 1786, the European fleet had by then reached 3,372,029 tons. Its volume had therefore possibly quintupled in two centuries. At an average of three voyages a year this would represent a trade of ten million tons, equivalent to that of a large port today.

These figures do not enable us to calculate the power of the wind engines that shifted such a volume with the same reliability we would have in the case of a fleet of steam-driven cargo boats. It is true that around 1840, when sailing ships and steam ships existed side by side, it was estimated that steam did the work of about five sailing ships for equal tonnage. The European fleet was therefore equivalent to

600,000 to 700,000 tons of steam-driven cargo boats, and we can hazard a figure of between 150,000 and 233,000 horse-power, according to whether the power needed to propel a nautical ton in about 1840 is estimated at a third or a quarter of one horse-power. The figure would have to be considerably increased if we included war-time fleets.

Wood, a source of everyday power

Calculations of power today leave out work by animals and to some extent manual work by men; and often they ignore wood and its derivatives as well. But wood, the first material to be in general use, was an important source of power before the eighteenth century. Civilisations before the eighteenth century were civilisations of wood and charcoal, as those of the nineteenth were civilisations of coal.

Everything in the European scene points to it.

It is the technology of wood that inspires building, even in stone; it is from wood that means of overland and maritime transport, utensils and tools are manufactured. The carpenter's tools are made of wood, except for the cutting edge which is made as thin as possible; it is from wood that looms and spinning wheels, wine-presses and pumps are made; most ploughing implements are wooden; the swing plough is made entirely of wood, the plough most frequently has a wooden ploughshare fitted with a thin iron blade.

To our eyes nothing is more extraordinary than some of the complicated gear-wheels with their precision-fitting wooden pieces that can be seen for example in the Deutsches Museum, the museum of technology in Munich. Exhibits there even include several eighteenth-century clocks, made in the Black Forest, with works entirely of wood, as well as a rarer item, a round wooden watch.

The fact that wood was used everywhere carried enormous significance in the past. One of the reasons for Europe's power lay in its being so plentifully endowed with forests. In the face of it Islam was in the long run undermined by the poverty of its wood resources and their gradual exhaustion.

Probably all that ought to concern us here is the wood directly transformed into power for heating houses and for industries using heat, 'iron furnaces, glass works, tile works and charcoal workshops', and salt mines, which often used firing processes. But, apart from the fact that supplies of wood available for burning were limited by the other uses of wood, these other uses exerted too great an influence on the manufacture of all the implements producing energy for us to be able to omit them.

The numerous uses of wood

The forest enabled man to warm and house himself and make his furniture, tools, carriages and boats.

The type of wood he required varied. He used oak for houses; ten different types, ranging from fir to oak or walnut, were used for galleys; elm was used for gun carriages. The result was enormous devastation. No transport was too long or too costly for the needs of the arsenals: every forest was affected. Planks and timber loaded in the Baltic and Holland reached Lisbon and Seville in the sixteenth century; so did rather heavy but cheap ready-made boats which the Spaniards sent to America with no intention of bringing them back, leaving them to finish their career in the Caribbean or sometimes abandoning them to the ship-breakers as soon as they arrived. These were the lost boats, *los navios al través*.

Every fleet, in no matter what country, required for its construction the destruction of enormous expanses of forest. Ship-building in Colbert's time exploited the forestry resources of the entire kingdom; timber was transported by every navigable route, even small waterways like the Adour or the Charente. Fir from the Vosges was floated along the Meurthe and then transported up to Bar-le-Duc where the tree trunks were assembled into rafts on the Ornain. Next the Saulx, Marne and finally the Seine were used. France found itself excluded from the Baltic trade for the crucial supplies of masts for warships. The Baltic primarily supplied England via Riga and later St Petersburg. France did not think of exploiting the forests in the New World, particularly those of Canada (as the British did later).

The French navy was therefore obliged to use artificial masts made of pieces of jointed wood ringed with iron, but they lacked flexibility and broke if overloaded with sail. Compared with the English, French ships could never show an extra turn of speed. We can judge better by looking at the time when the situation was momentarily reversed during the English colonies' War of Independence in America: the English had to resort to the inferior type of mast, for the League of Neutrals closed the Baltic to them, and the advantage passed to their opponents.

This was not the only way in which forest reserves were wasted, nor even the most dangerous in the long run. The peasant, particularly in Europe, was continually pulling up trees to extend his tillage. Common land was the enemy of the forest. The forest of Orléans measured 140,000 arpents in Francis I's reign and only 70,000, it was said, a century later. The figures are not reliable, but certainly clearing of land from the end of the Hundred Years War (which favoured the invasion of field by forest) until Louis XIV's reign reduced wooded expanses to their lowest limits, which correspond more or less to those of today. Everything conspired against the forest; in 1519 a hurricane destroyed fifty to sixty thousand trees in the forest of Bleu, which linked the mountainous masses of Lyons with the woods of Gisors in the middle ages; tillage moved into the breach and the link was broken. Today the view of the land on an aeroplane journey from Warsaw to Cracow still shows the way in which the long fields thrust into the forest areas. If French forests were stabilised in the sixteenth and seventeenth centuries, was it the result of careful legislation (for example the great ordinance of 1573 and Colbert's measures); or was a balance naturally reached because the land that was still unexploited was too poor and not worth the effort?

Theorists, thinking primarily of the New World, have said that those who burned forests and set up cultivated zones in their place were duped. The destroyer exchanged an existing wealth for one to be created and not necessarily worth more. Such reasoning is obviously fallacious: forest wealth only existed when incorporated into the economy through intermediaries – shepherds tending their flocks (not only the pigs at acorn time), woodcutters, charcoal-burners, carters: a whole community whose profession it was to exploit, to utilise and to destroy. The forest was worth nothing unless it was used.

Immense forest areas still remained outside the clutches of civilisations before the nineteenth century: there were the Scandinavian forests; the Finnish forests; the almost uninterrupted forest between Moscow and Archangel, crossed by a narrow thread of roads; the Canadian forest; the Siberian forest linked by trappers to the markets of China and Europe; the tropical forests of the New World and the Indian archipelago, where precious woods were pursued instead of furs: campeachy wood in present-day Honduras, *pau brasil* ('brazil', which gave a red dye and was cut down on the coasts of north-east Brazil), teak from the Deccan, sandalwood and rosewood elsewhere.

Wood for burning

Wood also served for cooking, heating houses and for all the industries that used heat — altogether a large number of consumers for a wealth whose abundance was illusory. For even at that period a forest as a concentration of fuel could not be compared with even a very modest coal mine. Twenty to thirty years had to pass before it recovered its strength after being cut. At Wieliczka in Poland they had to give up using a heat-process on the saline water in the enormous mine after 1724 and be content with producing slabs of rock salt, because of the devastation of the surrounding forests.

Being a bulky material firewood had to be close at hand. It was ruinous to transport it more than thirty kilometres unless by waterway or sea. Tree trunks thrown into the Doubs could travel all the way to Marseilles in the seventeenth century. 'New' wood arrived in Paris in boatloads and 'floated' wood began to arrive from Morvan along the Cure and Yonne after 1549. Twelve years later it floated down the Marne and its tributaries from Lorraine and the Barrois. It took extraordinary skill to manœuvre these floats, up to 250 feet long, under the arches of the bridges. Charcoal reached Paris in the sixteenth century by way of Sens from the forest of Othe.

Immense rafts of wood came down the Polish rivers to the Baltic from the fourteenth century onwards. The same sight, on an even more grandiose scale, was to be seen in distant China. The rafts of wood from the Se-tchouan, the trunks tied together with a sort of 'wicker rope', were very long, according to Father du Halde (1735). 'The richer the merchant, the longer the rafts; some of them are half a league long.'

Wood was also transported over long distances by sea. For example there were the sailing ships that carried charcoal from Cape Corse to Genoa, and the ships from Istria and Quarnero that brought Venice its winter wood. The ships from Asia Minor that supplied Cyprus and Egypt sometimes towed tree trunks behind them. Even slender galleys were used to carry firewood to Egypt, drastically short of fuel.

However there were limits to this form of supply and most towns had to be content with what they could find close at hand. Platter, a citizen of Basle who finished his medical studies in 1595 at Montpellier, noted the absence of forests around the town.

The nearest is at the Saint-Paul glass works, a good three miles in the direction of Celleneuve. The firewood is brought from there in winter and sold by weight. One wonders where they would get it if the winter lasted a long time because they consume an enormous quantity of it in their fire-places, while shivering beside them. Stoves are unknown in this part of the land; the shortage of wood is so great that bakers fill their ovens with rosemary, kermes-oak and other bushes.

The shortage increased the farther south you went. Antonio de Guevara, the Spanish humanist, was right: fuel in Medina del Campo was more expensive than what was cooked in the pot. In Egypt the straw from the sugar cane was burned for want of any-thing better; in Corfu they burned the residue from squeezed olives, made into bricks and immediately put to dry.

This enormous provisioning meant a vast transport organisation, the maintenance of the waterways used for floating, as well as extensive commercial networks and the supervision of stocks – to which end governments increased the number of regulations and prohibitions. Nonetheless wood became rarer every day, even in richly endowed countries. The problem was to utilise it better. But it would appear that no attempt was made to economise in fuel in either glass- or iron-works. As soon as the radius from which a wood-burning factory drew its supplies became too large and costs in-creased, the most they did was try to shift it somewhere else. Or else they simply cut down on the amount of work it produced. A blast furnace 'built in Dolgyne in Wales in 1717' was not fired until four years later when 'enough charcoal had been accumulated for thirty-six and a half weeks' work'. It only operated for an average of fifteen weeks a year, because, as always, of lack of fuel. Furthermore it was the general rule in view of this constant shortage of supplies for 'blast furnaces only to function one year in every two or three, or even one year in five, seven or ten'. According to calculations by an expert, an average iron-works where the furnace was working two years on and two years off in the period before the eighteenth century absorbed the production of 2000 hectares of forest. The problems continually increased with the advance in the eighteenth century. 'In the Vosges trade in wood has become the trade of all the inhabitants: it is a case of who can fell more trees, and in a short time the forests will be completely destroyed.' It was from this crisis – latent in England from the sixteenth century – that in the course of time the coal revolution emerged.

And, of course, there was also the pressure of prices. In his *Oeconomies Royales* Sully went so far as to say 'that the price of all the commodities necessary for life would constantly increase and the increasing scarcity of firewood would be the cause'. The rise in price accelerated in 1715 and 'shot up with the last twenty years of the *ancien régime*'. In Burgundy 'timber can no longer be found' and 'the poor do without fires'.

It is very difficult to present the matter statistically, but we do have at least three rough estimates at our disposal. In 1942 when France was reduced to heating with wood the country is said to have used 18 million tons, about half of it in the form of firewood. In 1830 consumption amounted to 12 million tons for firewood alone. This consumption – enormous in a country much more sparsely populated than today – justifies *a posteriori* the very high estimates for consumption in Paris in the period before the Revolution: 10,000 loads of coal a year, 700,000 of charcoal (40 kilograms a load) and 700,000 cords of wood (800 kilograms a cord). If our conversions of measures are accurate, the wood alone would be equivalent to 560,000 tons, or a ton per inhabitant. The consumption of Europe should not be calculated on the basis of this very high figure, which reflects the wastefulness of Paris. But the figure for 1830 gives a lower limit: 12 million tons for France, or 120 million for Europe (10 times more).

It is on the basis of this figure of 120 million tons that we must try to conduct the hazardous calculation of the value in horse-power of wood as a source of power. Two tons of wood are equal to a ton of coal. If we assume that one horse-power hour represents the combustion of two kilograms of coal and that power was used at the rate of about three thousand hours per year, the power available will be in the order of ten million horse-power. These calculations, which I have shown to specialists, only give a very approximate order of magnitude and the reduction to horse-power is both outmoded and risky. But the size of the figure is not a complete aberration. We should remember that more weighty calculations than our own show that coal did not overtake wood in the economy of the United States until 1887!

Coal

Coal was not unknown to either China or Europe. In China it was used in Peking for domestic heating (for four thousand years according to Father de Magaillans), for cooking food in the houses of the mandarins and those in high positions, and also by 'blacksmiths, bakers, dyers and the like'. In Europe it was extracted in the eleventh and twelfth centuries – from the shallow basins in England for example, in the Liège basin, in the Saar, and in the small coal basins of the Lyonnais, Forez and Anjou – for lime kilns, domestic heating and for some processes in the iron-works (not all, at least not until anthracite or coke were available, coke coming in at the end of the eighteenth century). However, well before that date coal fulfilled the minor functions charcoal left it, in chaferies and splitting mills (where the iron was split up) and wire mills where the wire was drawn. And coal was transported over quite long distances.

The excise authorities in Marseilles in 1543 noted the arrival of 'brocz' of coal by the Rhône, probably from Alès. At the same period a peasant mine at La Machine, near Decize, yielded barrels (they called them 'fish' or 'loads') of coal, which were taken up to the small port of La Loge on the Loire. From there they were sent on by boat to Moulins, Orléans and Tours. Admittedly these were all small-scale enterprises. So too was the coal-firing employed at the Saulnot salt mines, near Montbéliard, as early as the sixteenth century. The Ruhr itself had to wait until the first years of the eighteenth century before coal assumed its importance. Similarly, it was only at that time that coal from Anzin was exported beyond Dunkirk to Brest and La Rochelle; then also that coal from the Boulonnais mines was utilised in Artois and Flanders for keeping the watchmen warm and for heating brick works and the forges of the shoeing smiths.

Within Europe there were only two achievements of any magnitude: in the Liège basin and in the Newcastle basin in England. Liège was already an 'arsenal', a metallurgical town, in the fifteenth century, and its coal was used to finish its products. Production tripled or quadrupled during the first half of the sixteenth century. Later its neutrality (Liège came under the authority of its bishop) helped it to prosper throughout the ensuing wars. The coal, which had already been extracted from deep galleries, was exported towards the North Sea and the Channel by the Meuse. Newcastle's success was on an even greater scale. It was an integral part of the coal revolution that modernised England after 1600, enabling fuel to be used in a series of industries with large outputs: the manufacture of salt by evaporating sea water; the production of sheets of glass, bricks, and tiles; sugar refining; the treatment of alum, previously imported from the Mediterranean and thenceforth developed on the Yorkshire coast; and there were also the bakers' ovens and the enormous amount of domestic heating that polluted London for centuries. Production in Newcastle continually increased stimulated by a rising consumption: 30,000 tons annually in 1563, 500,000 in 1658. Production around 1800 was probably in the neighbourhood of two million. The Tyne estuary was permanently filled with coal ships plying mainly between Newcastle and London. Their tonnage rose to 348,000 in 1786, at a rate of six round journeys a year. Part of this coal was exported; 'sea coal' travelled great distances, at least as far as Malta in the sixteenth century.

Very early on it was thought necessary to refine the coal before using it in iron production. It was done in primitive earth-covered furnaces of the same kind as those in which the combustion of wood had produced charcoal. The method of producing coke was known in England in 1627. The first combustion of coal in Derbyshire dates from 1642. Almost immediately the brewers in the region began to use coke instead of straw and ordinary coal for drying and heating the malt. 'This new fuel will give Derby beer the paleness and sweetness which will make its reputation,' ridding it of the unpleasant smell of ordinary coal. It duly became the leading beer in England.

But coke did not achieve immediate popularity in metallurgy. 'Coal can, with fire, be purged of the bitumen and sulphur it contains,' said an economist in 1754, 'so that by losing two-thirds of its weight and very little of its volume it remains a combustible substance but cleared of those parts that give off the unpleasant smoke for which it is criticised. . . .'

Nevertheless this 'coal cinder', as the same eighteenth-century economist called it, only achieved its first metallurgical success around 1780. We will have to return to this apparently incomprehensible delay. It is a good example of social inertia in the face of anything new.

The case of China is even more conclusive in this respect. We have indicated that coal played a part in domestic heating there, possibly millennia before Christ, and in iron metallurgy from the fifth century BC. In fact the firing of coal made the production and utilisation of cast iron possible very early on. This tremendous precocity did not lead to the systematic utilisation of coke during the extraordinary Chinese advance in the thirteenth century, although it was probably known then. Probably, not certainly. Otherwise, what an argument for our thesis: China, powerful as it was in the thirteenth century, would have had the means to make the crucial breakthrough of the industrial revolution, and failed to do so! The achievement was left to England at the end of the eighteenth century – and England itself had taken some time to utilise what was under its nose. Technology is only an instrument and man does not always know how to use it.

Conclusion

Let us return to Europe at the end of the eighteenth century to formulate two connected remarks: the first on the subject of power resources as a whole, the second on the machinery available.

(1) We can accurately classify available sources of power in descending order of importance: first, animal traction; 14 million horses, 24 million oxen, each animal representing a quarter horse-power – that is roughly 10 million horse-power; next, wood, possibly equivalent to 10 million horse-power; then water-wheels, between 1·5 million and 3 million horse-power; then manpower (50 million workers), representing 900,000 horse-power; finally, sails, at the most 233,000 horse-power, without counting the war fleet. This is obviously a far cry from the present-day power league. That was already self-evident. The interest of this incomplete calculation (in which, it should be pointed out, we have counted neither windmills, nor river fleets, nor charcoal, nor even coal) is simply to show that the first two positions were held by draught animals and firewood. To all intents and purposes, therefore, the economy was trapped in the old inflexible solutions, and it was this that hampered the development of mechanisation most of all, not any delay in the inventive urge. Many elaborate machines were working but still in slow motion. Mechanisation required large sources of power: they were not available until after the eighteenth century.

(2) But a preliminary stage was reached before the industrial revolution. The harnessing of horses, the flames from burning wood, rudimentary engines utilising wind and river currents, plus an increased number of men at work, all provoked a certain European growth from the fifteenth to the eighteenth century, a slow increase in strength, power and practical understanding. Increasingly active progress in the 1730s and 1740s was built upon this gradual advance. There was thus an often imperceptible or unrecognised industrial pre-revolution in an accumulation of discoveries and technical advances, some of them spectacular, others modest: various types of gear-wheels, jacks, articulated transmission belts, the 'ingenious system of reciprocating movement', the fly-wheel that regularised any momentum, rolling mills, more and more complicated machinery for the mines. And there were so many other innovations: looms for knitting and manufacturing ribbons, chemical processes. 'It was

during the second half of the eighteenth century that the first attempts were made to adapt lathes, borers and drilling machines [tools which had long been known] to industrial use.' It was the mechanisation of weaving and spinning processes at the same time that launched the English economy. Nevertheless what was lacking before these imagined or realised machines could be fully employed was a surplus of easily mobilised power.

Came steam and everything was, as if by magic, speeded up. But the magic can be explained: it had been prepared and made possible in advance. To paraphrase a historian (Pierre Léon), two connected movements were involved: evolution (a slow rise) and then revolution (an acceleration).

2 Iron: a poor relation

Men the world over in the fifteenth century, and *a fortiori* in the eighteenth, would certainly not have thought the description 'a poor relation' either serious or in accordance with the facts. What would Buffon, iron-master at Montbard, have had to say about it? Nevertheless from our point of view the observation is true.

Iron smelting did use by and large the same basic processes as it does today -- blast furnaces and power-hammers 'are the expression of the same basic principle' -- but the difference is one of scale. Whereas a blast furnace today 'can consume the equivalent of three train-loads of coke and iron ore in twenty-four hours', the most perfected of these furnaces in the eighteenth century only functioned intermittently; then, flanked by a forge with two fires, for example, it barely produced 100 to 150 tons of iron a year. Today production is calculated in thousands of tons; 200 years ago they talked about 'hundredweights', which were quintals of fifty present-day kilograms. That is the difference in scale. It divides two civilisations. As Morgan wrote in 1877: 'When iron succeeded in becoming the most important production material, it was the event of events in the evolution of humanity.' A book (1963) by a young Polish economist, Stefan Kurowski, goes as far as to maintain that all the vibrations of economic life can be grasped through the special case of the metallurgical industry: it summed everything up and ushered everything in.

But up to the beginning of the nineteenth century 'the event of events' had still not come to pass. In 1800 world production of the various forms of iron (cast iron, wrought iron, steel) had only risen at the very most to two million tons. Economic civilisation at that time was dominated by textiles (it was cotton after all that launched the English revolution) much more than by iron.

Metallurgy remained traditional, out of date and precarious. Of all the industries it was 'the one most linked to nature, its resources, its inner life', also to its hazards, to the fortunate abundance of ore, to the always insufficient forest (as we have seen) and to the variable power of the waterways. In the sixteenth century peasants in Sweden manufactured iron, but only during the rise of the spring waters; any fall in the rivers where the furnaces were built resulted in unemployment. Finally there were few or no really specialised workmen but too often simple peasants, as much in Alsace as in the Urals. Nor were there any entrepreneurs in the modern sense of the word. Many iron-masters in Europe were landowners above all and left their iron factories to stewards or farmers. A final hazard: demand was temporary, linked with wars that flared up and then died down.

The picture certainly did not appear in this light to contemporaries. They enthusiastically announced that iron was the most useful metal, and all of them had had an opportunity to see iron-works (at least a village forge or the forge of a shoeing smith), a blast furnace, a chafery, and a refinery. In fact local scattered production or supplying over short distances remained the general rule. Amiens in the seventeenth century bought iron from Thiérache, less than 100 kilometres from its markets, and redistributed it within a radius of 50 to 100 kilometres. For the preceding century we have the journal of a merchant in the small Austrian town of Judenburg in the Obersteiermark who brought together and shipped out iron, steel and metallurgical products from neighbouring iron-works and from the busy centre of Leoben. Details of purchases, sales, transports, prices and measures can be followed from day to day; there are bewildering lists of the innumerable grades, from raw and bar iron to various types of steel, wire (the heavy described as 'German', the thin as *Welsch*), not to mention needles, nails, chisels, stoves and 'white' iron utensils. And none of this went very far: even steel, a high-priced material, did not cross the Alps in the direction of Venice. Metallurgical products did not travel on a scale comparable to textiles, except for certain luxury items, like swords from Toledo, arms from Brescia or, to return to our Judenburg merchant, arbalests for hunting requested by Antwerp. The great trade in metallurgical products (from the Cantabrian region in the sixteenth century, from Sweden in the seventeenth, from Russia in the eighteenth) took advantage of sea and river routes and, as we will see, only involved modest quantities.

In short, before the nineteenth century in Europe (and naturally it was even truer outside Europe) the quantity of iron produced and used was not able to tip the balance of material civilisation. We are speaking of the period before the first smelting of steel (1740), before the discovery of puddling (1784); before the general use of coke for smelting, before the long sequence of famous names and processes: Bessemer, Siemens, Martin, Thomas. We are speaking of what was still another planet.

The beginnings of metallurgy

Iron smelting was discovered in the Old World and spread very early on, probably from the Caucasus, in the fifteenth century BC. All the Old World civilisations sooner or later learned this rudimentary skill, with varying degrees of efficiency. Only two spectacular advances occurred: the early advance in China, which appears doubly enigmatic (by its precocity on one hand, its stagnation after the thirteenth century on the other); and the later but crucial advance in Europe leading up to the industrial revolution.

China had an incontestable advantage. It was familiar with cast iron and coal firing perhaps as early as the fifth century BC, certainly as early as the first, and it probably knew about smelting ore with coke in the thirteenth century. Now Europe was not familiar with casting molten iron before the fourteenth century and smelting with coke, concerning which there had been conjectures in the seventeenth, only came into general use well after 1780.

This precocity poses a problem. The use of coal probably made very high temperatures possible; furthermore the ores used had a high phosphorus content and therefore melted at relatively low temperatures; finally, bellows with pistons worked by paddle-wheels produced a continuous blast and thus created high temperatures inside the furnaces. The Chinese processes had to solve the same problems as elsewhere: washing, breaking up and calcining the ore, hammering the red-hot iron on the anvil to rid it of impurities, refining it to obtain steel in certain rare cases. But Chinese casting gave a choice of two stages of smelting: to obtain iron after extensive decarbonisation, or steel if decarbonisation were incomplete (this decarbonisation was probably effected by passing a current of cold air across the molten iron). On the other hand the mixture of iron with molten iron gave the mass a higher degree of carbon than was the case with iron but lower than that of cast iron, and therefore produced steel.

Another Chinese prerogative was the soldering of mild steel to hard steel, which enabled the manufacture of remarkably high-quality sabres, so greatly appreciated that they spread to Japan, India and Islam. A recent article on Chinese sabres by Aly Mazaheri claims that the famous Durandal was only a replica of them, coming by way of Islam.

The extraordinary thing is the ensuing stagnation after the thirteenth century. No further progress was made. The skills of the Chinese smelters and ironsmiths were merely self-perpetuating. Smelting with coke, if it was known, did not develop. All this is difficult to pinpoint and explain. But the destiny of China as a whole poses the same problem, the same confusion; it has still not been properly accounted for.

Europe's late success took place in England after the 1780s. It concluded a long history too important for us to omit giving an account of its development, all the more so as its beginnings are fairly representative of the situation in the other Old World countries which could claim neither China's early nor Europe's final success.

The beginning of medieval metallurgy can be seen equally well in the Sieg or Saar Valleys or between the Seine and the Yonne. Iron ore was present almost everywhere; only almost pure (meteoric) iron was rare, exploited in Europe from the La Tène period. The ore was broken up, washed and if necessary calcined, then placed inside an oven in successive layers alternating with layers of charcoal. The form the oven took varied greatly: excavations on a hillside in the forest of Othe, between the Seine and Yonne, have brought to light rudimentary ovens without walls, 'wind ovens'. At the end of two or three days, after firing, a small mass of spongy iron and a good deal of dross was obtained. The iron then had to be worked by hand in the forges, reheated (subjected to several firings), then beaten on an anvil.

More complicated ovens, with walls but still not closed, appeared shortly. Natural ventilation (as in the case of an ordinary chimney) was no longer adequate. An example of this type revealed by excavations in Landenthal, in the Saar, is the oven that was in use between 1000 and 1100. It had baked clay walls moulded on wooden slats, a height of 1·5 metres, a maximum diameter of 0·65 (it was shaped conically), and two bellows. This example, with hardly any variations, was typical of a series of Corsican, Catalan and Norman ovens (the Norman for the treatment of *ossmurd*, the Swedish ore), all of them enclosed by walls but not shut at the top, worked by second-rate blowing machines and giving a low yield: ore with a 72% iron content would give a metallic mass in the order of 15%. Of course this applies to the metallurgy after the eleventh century practised by peasants in Europe (which lasted for such a long time) and by underdeveloped races in the Old World. In about 1720 Father Labat gave the following description of ironsmiths in Guinea:

There are never fewer than three working together. One of them blows the fire using a goatskin folded down the middle or two skins joined together with the places for the legs tightly bound, except for one, where there is a nozzle of iron or copper. They use all sorts of wood to heat their metal and never make charcoal. . . . The two others sit facing one another, the anvil on which they nonchalantly beat the metal between them.

Progress between the eleventh and fifteenth centuries in Styria and the Alps

The water-wheel resulted in decisive progress in Europe after the eleventh and twelfth centuries. The advance was very slow, but for better or for worse finally established in all the great producing regions. Iron-works moved from forests to riversides. Water power worked enormous bellows, pounding devices that broke up the ore and hammers that beat the iron after its various firings. This progress began with the installation of blast furnaces at the end of the fourteenth century. They appeared in Germany (or perhaps the Netherlands) and were soon in eastern France and the upper valley of the Marne, while manual iron-works continued in the forests of Poitou, the lower Maine and the whole of western France until the sixteenth century.

Styria was a good example of the new progress. The *Rennfeuer* (oven), entirely walled in, with hand bellows, appeared there in the thirteenth century. In the fourteenth century they had the *Stückofen* (bloomery furnace), higher than its predecessor and with a hydraulic blowing machine. At the end of the same century blast furnaces came in; they were similar to the *Stückofen* but even higher, with fore-hearths, and were grouped in the *Blähhaus* (the name appears in a document of 1389). The important thing was that smelting was achieved for the first time with the installation of enormous water-powered leather bellows and tunnels in the blast furnaces; which virtually means that cast iron was 'discovered' in the fourteenth century. Iron or steel could thenceforth be obtained as required from cast iron, their common starting point, by extensive decarbonisation (iron) or incomplete decarbonisation (steel). In Styria they set out to produce steel. But ancient metallurgy most frequently resulted in 'steeled iron' and not steel, until the innovations at the end of the eighteenth century.

Meanwhile the forge had moved away downstream from the blast furnace because in preserving its unity, the factory had become too large a fuel consumer and hampered in its supplies. A sketch of 1613 shows a *Blähhaus* in isolation, separated from the forge that functioned in association with it down-river. The forge is equipped with a large water-powered hammer – the 'German hammer' or tilt-hammer. An enormous oak beam forms its handle. Its head, an iron mass which could weigh between 500 and 600 pounds, was raised by a wheel with a stopping-block and then let fall back on the anvil. This enormous striking power had become necessary to work the raw metal, which was thenceforth produced in large quantities. However, as iron had to be reworked endlessly, small hammers with short, rapid blows were also used – they were called Italian hammers. Their prototype probably came from Brescia, the old iron capital, by way of workers from Friuli.

Another example illustrating the advance takes us to the Alps. It has the advantage of pointing out the considerable role of the Carthusians throughout the early rise of metallurgy. They were settled in the Alps, in Styria, Lombardy, Carinthia and Piedmont from the twelfth century and were 'intimately connected with the invention of (pre-)modern iron smelting'. They were said to have invented cast iron at Allevard in Dauphiné in the twelfth century, in any case clearly before Styria or elsewhere. This was the result of the early utilisation of a fierce form of ventilation by means of enormous water blasts that harnessed a complete alpine torrent. With the arrival of Tyrolean workers (from 1172) a method of refining cast iron by charcoal fire and the addition of scrap iron was said to have allowed them to produce steel, called natural steel. None of this chronology is very reliable.

In fact every centre had its individual stages, methods – particularly methods of refining – its secrets, customers, and its choices from amongst the various products. Techniques, however, have a tendency to become general whatever their origin, if only with the movement of craftsmen ready to move about. A tiny example of this occurred in about 1450 when two workers, 'natives of Liège', received a site on the Avalon near Senlis 'to make a waterfall to build a foundry or iron works'.

All blast furnaces were sooner or later in continuous operation. The oven was immediately reloaded with ore and charcoal after each casting. Interruptions for repairs or supplies took place at increasingly long intervals. And blast furnaces grew in size: they doubled their capacity between 1500 and 1700 to reach as much as 4·5 cubic metres and a daily yield of two tons of molten iron. The custom of retempering iron in molten iron to increase its carbon content also became general.

Semi-concentrations

Stimulated by wars, the demand for cuirasses, swords, pikes, arquebuses, cannons and iron bullets increased. Such urgent demands obviously did not last. Reconversion remained difficult, but iron or cast iron was used to make cooking utensils, cauldrons, saucepans, grates, andirons, chimney plates, ploughshares and all sorts of wrought-iron works of art. As these manifold demands used a considerable amount of material they led to concentrations or rather semi-concentrations, still rather uneven because problems of transport, fuel, the motive power available at any one point, supplies of victuals and the irregular pace of activity did not make highly intensive concentration possible.

At the end of the fifteenth century Brescia had perhaps 200 arms factories – *botteghe*, workshops with a master and three or four workers. A text mentions sixty thousand people working iron. The figure is exaggerated even though we have to take into account workers at the ovens (*forni*), at the forges (*fucine*) and water-wheels (*mole*), diggers and miners who extracted ore, and carters responsible for its transport, all of them scattered within a radius of twenty to thirty kilometres around the town, as far as distant Val Camonica.

The situation was the same in Lyons, which collected the products of a multitude of small metallurgical centres from over 100 kilometres around in the sixteenth century. In Saint-Etienne iron products in order of importance were: ironmongery, arquebuses, halberds, and, in lesser quantities, mountings for swords and daggers. In Saint-Chamond they manufactured ironmongery, arquebuses, buckles, rings, spurs, iron filings and implements required for throwing or for dying silk – copper basins, 'spindles for mills'. Secondary centres such as Saint-Paul-en-Jarez, Saint-Martin, Saint-Romain and Saint-Didier specialised in the manufacture of nails. Terre Noire manufactured domestic hardware; Saint-Symphorien *ulles* or iron pots'; Saint-André agricultural implements: spades, iron parts for swing ploughs. Slightly farther away Viverols produced 'bells for mules' (perhaps this was the place of origin of the bells the great Italian merchants of Lyons exported outside the kingdom). Bonnel-le-Château built up a reputation for the manufacture of 'clippers' (for shearing sheep).

Craftsmen, such as the nail-smiths, took their merchandise to the large towns themselves, making up the load their animal carried with a small quantity of coal. This proves that the industry used coal, that Lyons knew of its use for domestic heating (even in the lime-kilns in the Vaise district), and that the finished products of the metallurgical industry circulated better, or less poorly, than the raw material.

The same conditions – small-scale and relative dispersion of the production units, difficulty of transport – were the rule in the diversified hardware industry in and around Nuremburg, in seventeenth-century Swedish metallurgy, in the growth of industry in the Urals in the eighteenth century and in industrial methods in the Biscay or the Liège region. Concentration only took place where there were sea- or waterways: the Rhine, the Adriatic, the Meuse, the Bay of Biscay, the Ural river. The presence of the Atlantic at Biscay, together with rapid water courses, beech woods and rich mountain deposits, account for the early presence of an intensive metallurgical industry. 'Until the beginning of the eighteenth century Spain was still selling its iron to England and Spanish iron was used to equip the English ships that fought the Spanish fleets at sea.'

A few figures

We have already said that the world production figure of 2 million tons put forward for around 1800 appears excessive to us. In 1525 John Nef estimated production in Europe alone in the region of 100,000 tons. At the beginning of the sixteenth century Biscay and Guipuzcoa produced perhaps 15,000, Styria 8000 to 9000, Liège the same (but the estimate is for 1569), the whole of France 10,000, Germany 30,000, and England about 6000 (between 1536 and 1539). English production increased considerably in the sixteenth century and at the beginning of the seventeenth. In about 1640, on the eve of the civil wars, it may have risen to 75,000 tons. But production fell off and England did not touch the same figure again until about 1756.

The total production of Europe in around 1700, including Russia, was estimated at between 145,000 and 180,000 tons. A broad-based advance took place in the eighteenth century, clearly marked after 1780, especially in that part of Europe where the main progress had been achieved. If we follow it to its end in about 1830, the leap is prodigious: England produced 68,000 tons of iron in 1788, 125,400 in 1796, 250,000 in 1806, 678,000 in 1830. But by then the great threshold of the industrial revolution had been crossed. If we cross it backwards, the role played by iron instantly diminishes and it returns to the moderate level which seems to us to have been the general rule in former times.

Other metals

As historians we tend to place the production or trade of the masses in the foreground: not spices but sugar, or better still corn, not rare or precious metals but iron, the basis of everyday life, even in those centuries that were still not very eager to make use of it. The viewpoint is justified as far as rare metals of very modest use are concerned: antimony, tin, lead, zinc (which only came into use at the end of the eighteenth century); but the question is far from settled when precious metals – gold and silver – are involved. These metals gave rise to speculative enterprises with which proletarian iron was never concerned. A wealth of ingenuity was expended in the quest for silver – witness the beautiful diagrams in Agricola's book on mines, or the pits and galleries of Sainte-Marie-aux-Mines in the Vosges; it was for silver that the valuable deposits of mercury in Almaden in Spain were worked (the amalgam method made silver a metal of industrial production in the fifteenth century and particularly after the sixteenth century); for silver that mining progress (galleries, pumping out of water, ventilation) was accomplished.

It could even be maintained that copper played an equally great or perhaps more important role than iron at that time. Bronze pieces were the aristocrats of the artillery. Copper bottoms for boats became widespread in the eighteenth century. As early as the fifteenth the double smelting of copper by the lead process made it possible to separate the silver mixed in its ore. Copper was the third monetary metal, next to gold and silver. In addition it had the advantage of being relatively easy to smelt (one reverberatory furnace could yield thirty tons of copper daily). It was also favoured by early capitalism, which accounts for the steep rise of the copper mines at Mansfeld in Saxony in the sixteenth century, the boom in Swedish copper in the seventeenth, and the great speculation that Japanese copper (monopolised by the *Oost Indische Companie*) then represented. Jacques Coeur, and even more the Fuggers, were copper kings. It is copper that should be unhesitatingly backed on the Amsterdam stock market in the centuries to follow.

6

The Spread of Technology: Revolutions and Delays

As has been seen, the basic technological structure was a cumbersome one. Innovations infiltrated into it slowly and with difficulty. The great technological 'revolutions' between the fifteenth and eighteenth centuries were artillery, printing and ocean navigation. But to speak of revolution here is to use a figure of speech. Nothing took place at breakneck speed. And only ocean navigation ended by creating any upheaval or 'asymmetry' in the world. The usual result was for everything to become widespread: Arabic numerals, gun-powder, compasses, paper, silkworms, printing presses... No innovation remained at the service of one group, government or civilisation. Or if it did, it was because other groups did not really need it. The new techniques were established so slowly in their place of origin that neighbouring groups had time to learn about them. Artillery made its appearance in the West at Crécy, or to be more precise off Calais, in 1347. But it was not a major element in European warfare until Charles VIII's expedition to Italy in September 1494, after a century and a half of gestation, experiment and discussion.

Above all certain sectors remained stagnant: in the field of transport – though after Columbus the maritime integration of the globe was a reality – we still find the slow movements and impossibilities of an *ancien régime* disrupted but not yet done away with.

1 Three great technological innovations

The origins of gunpowder

'Western' nationalism impels historians of science and technology to deny or minimise Europe's borrowings from China. The discovery of gunpowder by the Chinese was not 'a legend' whatever Aldo Mieli – albeit a first-rate specialist in the history of science – may maintain. They were producing it with saltpetre, sulphur and crushed charcoal from the ninth century AD. The first firearms were also Chinese and are said to date from the eleventh century, though the first *dated* Chinese cannon is from the year 1356.

Was an independent discovery made in the West? The invention has been attributed to the great Bacon himself (1214–93) though there is no proof. Gunpowder certainly appeared in Flanders around 1314 or 1319: in Metz in 1324, in Florence in 1326, and in England in 1327. But it only assumed an important historical role when it was first used to fire projectiles. Perhaps this leads us to the battlefield of Crécy (1346) where the English *bombardiaux* did nothing but 'flabbergast' the French under Philip VI of Valois, according to Froissart; but we have no confirmation that Edward III used it at that time. He certainly used it the following year off Calais. But the new weapons only really came to the fore in the following century, at the time of the dramatic Hussite war, in the heart of Europe, the rebels having wagons with pieces of light artillery after 1427. Finally, artillery played a decisive role at the end of Charles VII's wars against the English – a good century after Calais – this time to the advantage of the French. Its new importance was linked to the discovery of gunpowder in grains, around 1420. This gave a sure and instantaneous combustion not obtained from the solid substance of the old mixtures, which did not allow air to penetrate completely.

Nonetheless we should not imagine that the presence of artillery was the rule. We have a rough idea that it played a part in Spain and North Africa from the fourteenth century. But when Ceuta, a vital town on the Moroccan coast, occupied by the Portuguese since 1415, was under a new attack from the Moors, a soldier of fortune who had gone thus far to fight the Infidels wrote: 'We shot stones at them with our machines with a fair amount of success ... The Moors, for their part, had their marksmen armed with slings and arrows ... They were shooting with a few catapults during the whole day.' Yet four years earlier, in 1453, the Turks had used a monstrous cannon under the walls of Constantinople. But even in Spain trebuchets were still in use at the time of the siege of Burgos, in 1475. In addition, it may be noted that saltpetre was known in Egypt by the name of 'Chinese snow' in about 1248; that cannons were certainly in use in Cairo from 1366 and in Alexandria in 1376; and that they were common in Egypt and Syria in 1389. This chronology – Calais 1347, China 1356, etc. – still does not give first place to either Europe or China as far as the invention of the cannon is concerned. L. White none the less maintains that if the first powder was Chinese, the first cannon, the 'gunpowder engine', was European.

Artillery becomes mobile

In the beginning pieces of artillery were short, light-weight weapons, stingily supplied with gunpowder (which was scarce and therefore expensive). We do not always know exactly what to make of their names. For example, the *ribaudequin* may have been a series of arquebus-like weapons assembled together in such a way as to suggest the machine-gun.

Pieces then became larger – from 136 to 272 kilograms on an average in the reign of Richard II (1376–1400), according to speci-mens preserved in the Tower of London. They were sometimes enormous bombards in the fifteenth century, like the German *Donnerbüchsen*, monstrous bronze tubes, bedded in wooden cradles, which posed almost insoluble problems when they had to be moved. The miracle cannon – *der Strauss*, the ostrich – lent to Emperor Maximilian by the town of Strasburg in 1499 to subdue the Swiss cantons moved so slowly that it only just escaped the enemy clutches in time. A more commonplace accident occurred in March 1500 when Lodovico Moro had 'six pieces of heavy artillery' brought for him to Milan from Germany: two of them broke on the journey.

Relatively mobile, large-bore artillery able to follow the move-ments of the troops had made its appearance before this period – the Bureau brothers' artillery for example, which was the instrument of Charles VII's victories at Formigny (1450) and Castillon (1453). Mobile artillery was drawn by teams of oxen in Italy: it was seen during the insignificant encounter of Molinacela in 1467. But cannon mounted on gun-carriages drawn by teams of powerful horses only made its appearance in Italy with Charles VIII in September 1494. It shot iron bullets (which quickly came into general use) instead of stone ones, and these missiles were no longer aimed solely at the houses in a besieged town but also at its walls. No fortified city, where the action had hitherto consisted of defending or surrendering the gates, resisted such point-blank bombardments. For the pieces were taken right up to the foot of the ramparts on the outer bank of the moats and immediately placed under the protection of *taudis* (hovels), according to Jean d'Auton, Louis XII's chronicler.

These weapons accounted for the chronic vulnerability of fortified towns for over thirty years: their ramparts were demolished like theatre sets. But counter-attack was gradually organised. Fragile stone ramparts were replaced by thick, scarcely raised ramparts built of earth, in which the shot lodged uselessly, and the defence artillery was set up on the highest platforms – the *cavaliers*. In about 1520 Mercurio Gattinara, Charles V's chancellor, claimed that twenty pieces of artillery were enough to protect Milan (and, behind the great city, the Emperor's domination of Italy) from the French. He was right. In 1525 the fortified town of Pavia immobilised Francis I's army which was taken by surprise from the rear by the Imperial forces on 24 February. Marseilles resisted Charles V in the same way in 1524 and 1536; similarly, Vienna resisted the Turks in 1529, Metz the Imperial forces in 1552. This is not to say that towns could not still be taken by surprise: Düren was in 1544, Calais in 1558, Amiens in 1596. However the fortress' revenge – the advent of skilled wars of siege and defence – was already foreshadowed, and only the strategy of Frederick II and of Napoleon was able to break out of it, but very much later because they were no longer concerned with taking towns but with destroying enemy manpower.

However, artillery gradually improved. It was rationalised, reduced to seven sizes of calibre by Charles V in 1544, to six by Henry II. The heaviest, earmarked for sieges or for defending towns, fired from 900 paces; the rest, called 'field' artillery, from only 400. Later development was slow: for example in France General de Vallière's system, dating from Louis XV, lasted until Gribeauval's reform (1776). The fine cannon then in use served through the Revolutionary Wars and those of the Empire.

Artillery on board ship

Cannon were installed on ships very early on, but there again in a very whimsical and strange fashion. In 1338 (therefore before Crécy) they were already on board the English ship *Mary of Tower*. But some forty years later, in 1377, twelve Castilian galleys destroyed with their cannon thirty-six English ships in the open sea off La Rochelle. The English ships were entirely without artillery and incapable of defending themselves. Yet, according to experts, it had become the general rule for English ships to be armed with artillery round about 1373. In Venice, there is nothing to prove that there was naval artillery on board the Seigniory's galleys during the inexpiable wars against Genoa (1378). But it was installed by 1440, and probably earlier. We can therefore probably assume that cannon were on board Turkish ships too. In any case in 1498 near Gallipoli a Turkish *schierazo* of over 700 *botte* (350 tons) fired stone shot, including one weighing 85 pounds, at the Venetians.

Of course this equipment was not installed overnight nor without difficulty. Long-barrelled cannon shooting straight and with direct fire were not at sea before about 1550; cannon-ports were still not a regular feature of round-hulled ships in the sixteenth century. In spite of the danger, unarmed ships were to be found side by side with armed vessels. I have mentioned the English misadventure off La Rochelle in 1377. But in 1520, at a time when French privateers on the Atlantic possessed artillery, Portuguese merchant ships had none. In 1520!

However, the increase in privateering in the sixteenth century soon forced all ships to carry pieces of artillery and expert gunners to use them. There was hardly any difference between war- and merchant-ships; at that time all were armed. This gave rise to strange quarrels of etiquette in the seventeenth century. For warships had the right to special salutes at the entrance to ports in Louis XIV's time, on condition (it is maintained) that they did not carry merchandise. And every one of them carried some.

Fairly firm rules soon governed naval armament, which was becoming general: so many men and so much artillery per ton capacity. In the sixteenth century, and still in the seventeenth, the scale was one piece for ten tons. Thus we can say that an English ship anchored at Bender Abassi on the scorching Persian coast in April 1638 was under-armed: it carried only 24 pieces for 300 tons. But the rule is very rough – there were various types of ships and various types of guns, and many other criteria of armament, even if only in terms of the number of crew. English ships in the Mediterranean and later on the interminable routes to the Indies from the end of the sixteenth century were normally over-armed, carrying more men and guns than others. Their half-decks were cleared of merchandise and therefore a more flexible defence was made possible. These were some of the reasons for their success.

There were others. The large ship had ruled the waves for a long time because it was safer, better defended and equipped with a larger number of guns of a higher calibre. But from the sixteenth century small ships achieved a staggering mercantile success because they could be loaded quickly and did not remain idle for long in port; they also enjoyed great success in war because they managed to be well-armed.

The Chevalier de Razilly explained this to Richelieu on 26 November 1626: 'What made large ships formidable formerly was that they carried large cannon and the average ships could only carry small ones, which were not capable of piercing the side of a large ship. But now this new invention is the quintessence of the sea, so much so that a vessel of 200 tons carries as heavy cannon as a vessel of eight hundred.' In case of an encounter the large one ran the risk of being the loser; the small one, faster and more manoeuvrable, could hit as it wished at its dead angles. The English and Dutch success on the seven seas was the triumph of small and middle-size tonnages.

Arquebuses, muskets, rifles

It is impossible to say exactly when the arquebus appeared. Probably towards the end of the fifteenth century; it was certainly in use during the first years of the sixteenth. The defenders at the siege of Brescia in 1512 'began to shoot their artillery and their arquebutes [sic] as thick as flies', according to the Loyal Serviteur. What got the better of the knights of yore was the arquebus, not the bombard or culverin. Artillery caused the downfall of fortified castles and, at one time, towns. But it was a bullet from an arquebus that brought down the noble Seigneur Bayard in 1524. 'God grant these wretched instruments had never been invented,' Monluc wrote later. He had raised, as he said, 700 to 800 men in Gascony in 1527 for M. de Lautrec and his expedition, which ended so unfortunately off Naples. 'This I did in a few days ... and they included four or five hundred arquebusiers; although there were but few in France at that time.'

Such comments and others like them give the impression that the armies in the service of France lagged behind the German, Italian and particularly the Spanish forces at the beginning of this change. At first the French word copied the German: *Hackenbüchse*; this produced *haquebute*. It then copied the Italian word: *archibugio*; which gave *arquebuse*. Perhaps the hesitancy is characteristic. There are many reasons for the French disaster at Pavia in 1525, but one was certainly the heavy bullet used by the Spanish arquebusiers. As a result the French increased the numbers of arquebusiers (one for every two pikemen). The Duke of Alba went further and divided his infantry in the Netherlands into two equal bodies: the same number of arquebusiers as pikemen. The ratio in Germany in 1576 was five pikemen to three arquebusiers.

In fact it was impossible to abandon the pike – still described as 'the queen of weapons' in the seventeenth century – because arquebuses took a long time to manipulate. They had to be rested on prongs, loaded and reloaded, and the fuse lit. Even when muskets replaced arquebuses Gustavus Adolphus still maintained one pikeman for every two musketeers. The invention in 1630 of the rifle, an improved musket adopted by the French army in 1703, was one of the factors that made the changeover possible. Also important in this context was the use of paper cartridges, known in the Great Elector's army in 1670 but not until 1690 in the French. A final factor was the adoption of bayonets, which did away with the fundamental double nature of the infantry. All infantry in Europe at the end of the seventeenth century had rifles and bayonets; but this development took two centuries to come about.

Production and budget

Artillery and firearms quite transformed inter-state warfare, economic life, and the capitalist organisation of arms production.

A certain concentration of the industry gradually took shape although it did not assume any decisive form, as the war industry remained many-sided. The same manufacturer did not produce gunpowder as well as arquebus barrels or side arms, or pieces of heavy artillery. Neither was power readily concentrated at any given point. It had to be sought out along river-courses and in forests.

Only rich states were capable of bearing the enormous costs of the new warfare. They eventually eliminated the great independent towns, which nevertheless managed to preserve their autonomy for a long time.

Montaigne could still admire the armoury when he passed through Augsburg in 1580. He would also have been able to admire the arsenal in Venice, an enormous factory with as many as three thousand workers at that period, summoned to work every morning by the great bell of Saint Mark. Of course every state had its own arsenals (Francis I founded eleven and the kingdom possessed thirteen by the end of his reign). They all had large arms depots. The main ones in England under Henry VIII were at the Tower of London, Westminster and Greenwich. The policy of the Catholic kings in Spain depended on the arsenals at Medina del Campo and Malaga.

But, until the industrial revolution, European arsenals most frequently consisted of a series of workyards, individual craft units rather than factories with a rationalisation of tasks. Artisans often even worked for the arsenal at some distance from it in their own homes. It was prudent to locate the mills where gunpowder was manufactured far away from the towns. Mills were normally found in mountainous regions or sparsely populated areas such as Calabria, near Cologne in the Eifel, and in the Pays de Berg. Twelve gunpowder mills had just been built in Malmédy in 1576 at the time of the uprising against the Spaniards. All mills – even those established in the eighteenth century along the Wupper, a tributary of the Rhine – produced their charcoal from alder, *Faulbaum*, in preference to any other wood. The charcoal had to be triturated with sulphur and saltpetre, then sifted to obtain either coarse or fine powder.

Venice, economical as usual, persisted in using the coarse powder which was less expensive than the fine. However, in 1588 the superintendent of its fortresses explained that it would have been better 'to use only the fine as do the English, French, Spaniards and Turks, who thus have only one single type of gunpowder for their arquebuses and cannon'. The Seigniory had six million pounds of this coarse powder in magazines at that time, or 300 shots for each of its fortresses' 400 pieces. Two million more pounds or an expenditure of 600,000 ducats would have been necessary to supply 400 shots. To sieve the powder to make it fine would have meant an additional expense of a quarter again, or 150,000 ducats. But as the necessary charge of fine powder was less by a third than that of the coarse, the result would still have been a gain.

The reader will excuse us for having dragged him into the bookkeeping of a past age. Its relevance is to show that Venice's security was 1800 ducats' worth of powder at the lowest estimate, or more than the equivalent of the annual receipts of the city itself. This shows the huge scale of war expenditure, even when there was no war. And the figures increased with the years: in 1588 the Invincible Armada carried northwards 2431 cannons, 7000 arquebuses, 1000 muskets, 123,790 bullets and shot (or 50 per piece), plus the necessary powder. But in 1683 France had 5619 cast-iron cannon on board its fleets and England 8396. We have come a long way from Gattinara's twenty pieces in 1520!

Metallurgical war industries sprang up: at Brescia on Venetian territory from the fifteenth century; around Graz in Styria very early on; around Cologne, Ratisbon, Nordlingen, Nuremburg and Suhl (the arsenal for Germany and the most important centre in Europe until its destruction by Tilly in 1634); also at Saint-Etienne where over 700 workers were employed in the 'powerful arsenal of the lame husband of Venus' in 1605. We must also mention the blast furnaces built in Sweden in the seventeenth century with capital from Holland or England. The Geer enterprises there were able to deliver in almost a single consignment the 400 pieces of artillery that enabled the United Provinces to block the advance of the Spaniards south of the Rhine delta in 1627.

The rapid progress of firearms stimulated the copper industries, particularly as cannon were manufactured from bronze, cast by the same process as church bells (the right combination – different from the one used for bells – eight parts of tin to ninety-two of copper, was already known in the fifteenth century). However, iron cannons (really cast-iron) appeared in the sixteenth century. Of the 2431 cannons of the Invincible Armada 934 were iron. This cheap cannon was to replace the expensive bronze pieces and to be manufactured on a large scale. There was a link between the development of artillery and the development of blast furnaces (like those set up by Colbert in Dauphiné).

But the cost of artillery did not end when it had been built and supplied with ammunition. It had also to be maintained and moved. The monthly bill for maintenance of the fifty pieces the Spaniards had in the Netherlands in 1554 (cannon, demi-cannon, culverins and serpentines) was over forty thousand ducats. To set such a mass in motion required a 'small train' of 473 horses for the mounted troops and a 'large train' of 1014 horses and 575 wagons (with 4 horses each), or 4777 horses in all, which meant almost 90 horses per piece. At the same period a galley cost about 500 ducats a month to maintain.

Artillery on a world scale

Technology itself was important on a world scale but so was the way it was utilised. The Turks – so skilled in earthworks, unequalled for digging pits during sieges, excellent gunners – had not succeeded in adopting the heavy cavalry pistols, manipulated with one hand, by 1550. Again, they 'do not reload their arquebuses as promptly as our men', according to a witness who saw them at the siege of Malta in 1565. Rodrigo Vivero, who admired the Japanese, noted that they did not know how to use their artillery, and that their saltpetre was excellent but their gunpowder second-rate. Father de Las Cortes said the same of the Chinese (1626): they did not shoot their arque- bus bullets with a sufficient charge of powder; and this powder, another witness later said, was bad, coarse and at the most good for firing salutes. Trade with Europeans introduced southern China to 'rifles seven palms long which took very small bullets, but they were more for pleasure than for use' (1695). Hence the importance of artillery schools in the West. They were frequently found in the towns (particularly those that felt themselves threatened), with their apprentice gunners who went off to the firing range every Sunday and came back led by a band. Despite the size of the demand, Europe was never short of gunners, arquebusiers or master smelters. Some of them wandered over the world, to Turkey, North Africa, Persia, the Indies, Siam, the Indian archipelago, and Muscovy. Until the death of Aurenge-Zebe (1707), the Great Mogul's gunners in India were European mercenaries. They were then replaced, and poorly at that, by Muslims.

As a result of these interchanges technology in the end served all sides. This was more or less true in Europe where victories cancelled each other out. If Rocroi in 1643 marked the triumph of French artillery (and we are not sure of it), it was at the best a tit-for-tat (in view of the arquebuses of Pavia). Certainly, artillery did not create any permanent imbalance of power in favour of one or another prince. It helped to raise the price of warfare and the efficiency of the state, and certainly entrepreneurs' profits. On a world scale it put Europeans in a privileged position – on the Far Eastern maritime frontiers and in America, where the cannon was of small importance but where the gunpowder of the arquebuses played a certain part.

Islam too had its share of victories and defeats. The taking of Grenada (1492) and the Spanish occupation of the North-African *presidios* (1497, 1505, 1509–10) were due to artillery; so was Ivan the Terrible's capture of Kazan (1551) and Astrakhan (1556) from Islam. But there were Turkish rejoinders: the capture of Constan- tinople (1453), Belgrade (1521), and the victory of Mohacs (1526). The Turkish war was supplied by Christian artillery (5000 pieces seized in Hungary from 1521 to 1541). It used its firing-power with terrifying effectiveness. At Mohacs Turkish artillery drawn up in the centre of the battlefield cut the Hungarian line in two. At Malta (1565) 60,000 bullets were shot at the defenders, at Famagusta (1571-2), 118,000. Moreover artillery gave the Turks a devastating advantage over the rest of the Islamic world (Syria 1516, Egypt 1517) and in their conflicts with Persia. In 1548 the large Persian town of Tabriz succumbed to an eight-day bombardment. We can also attribute to artillery the success of Baber's campaign when he destroyed India under the Sultans of Delhi with cannon and arque-buses on the battlefield of Panipat in 1526. Then there was that episode in 1636 when three Portuguese cannon taken on to the Wall of China put the Manchurian army to flight, assuring China under the Mings of almost ten extra years of life.

The balance sheet is not complete but we can nevertheless draw our conclusions. If we take into account both advances and retreats, artillery did not change the frontiers of the great cultural groups. Islam stayed where it was. The Far East was not fundamentally touched (Plassey was not until 1757). Above all, artillery gradually spread everywhere of its own accord, as far afield as Japanese pirate ships in 1554. In the eighteenth century no Malay pirate was without a cannon on board.

From paper to the printing press

Paper came from very far afield, again from China, passed on to the West via the Islamic countries. The first paper mills turned in Spain in the twelfth century. However, the European paper industry was not established in Italy until the beginning of the fourteenth century. In the fourteenth century, around Fabriano, a water-wheel operated 'beaters' — enormous wooden pounders or mallets — fitted with anvil-cutters and nails which tore the rags to shreds.

Water served both as motive power and ingredient. The production of paper required enormous quantities of clear water, so mills were sited on rapid rivers up-stream of towns that might pollute it. Venetian paper was produced around Lake Garda. The Vosges had paper factories very early on; so did Champagne, with a large centre at Troyes, and Dauphiné. Italian workers and capitalists played an important role in this expansion. Fortunately there was an abundance of old rags for raw material. Flax and hemp cultivation had increased in Europe from the thirteenth century. Linen cloth had replaced what woollen cloth there was. Old rope could also be used (as at Genoa). Nevertheless the new industry prospered so much that crises of supply arose. Law-suits broke out between paper-makers and itinerant rag-and-bone men – attracted by the large towns or the reputation of the rags in a specific region, Burgundy for example.

Paper had neither the strength nor the beauty of parchment. Its sole advantage was its price. A 200-page manuscript on parchment required the skins of 80 lambs, 'that is to say that the actual copying was the smallest expense of the operation'. But the flexibility and uniform surface of the new material automatically marked it out as the only solution to the problem of the printing press. As for the press itself, everything prepared the way for its success. The number of readers in the universities of the West and even outside them had increased considerably since the twelfth century. An enthusiastic clientele had created an increase in the number of copyists' work-shops and multiplied the numbers of correct copies; people were looking for rapid reproduction processes – for example by tracing illuminations, at least for the background. Veritable 'editions' of books appeared as a result of such methods. Two hundred and fifty copies of the *Voyage de Mandeville*, completed in 1356, have been preserved (73 in German and Dutch, 37 in French, 40 in English, 50 in Latin).

The discovery of movable type

It does not matter who invented movable type in the West towards the middle of the fifteenth century. It could have been Gutenburg (from Mainz) and his collaborators – which is probable – or Procope Waldfogel, from Prague, who settled in Avignon, or Coster from Haarlem, if he existed, or perhaps someone completely unknown. The problem is rather to know whether the discovery was a revival, an imitation, or a rediscovery.

For China had been familiar with the printing press since the ninth century. Japan printed Buddhist books in the eleventh. Pi Cheng 'invented movable type in ceramics ... held in a metal block' between 1040 and 1050. Under the rule of the Songs (960–1280), the use of movable type on wood spread as far as Turkestan. Metal letters were cast in Korea in 1390. Did a transfer take place? This is what Loys le Roy suggested, in 1576 – which means very late and unfortunately without proof. According to him the very old knowledge of the printing press in China 'has moved some people to believe that its invention was brought to Germany via Tartary and Muscovy and then communicated to the rest of the Christians'. We too connect the two experiences, the old and the new, but lack the intermediate link that would prove the relationship. However, enough travellers, and cultured travellers at that, made the journey to China and back for its invention in Europe to be a very doubtful theory.

In any case, copy or re-invention, the European printing press was established after a good deal of experiment and difficulty in about 1440–50. The movable type had to be produced from an alloy of precisely determined quantities of lead, tin and antimony (and antimony mines only seem to have been discovered in the sixteenth century) sufficiently resistant without being too hard. There were three essential operations: a very hard steel stamp bearing the character in a raised form had to be made; the character was then sunk into a copper (rarely lead) die; finally, the actual movable character was obtained by casting the alloy in the type mould. Then it was necessary to 'compose', lock up lines and spaces, ink them and press them on to the sheet of paper. The bar press made its appearance towards the middle of the sixteenth century and was barely altered until the eighteenth. The principal difficulty was that the letters wore out quickly. They had to be replaced by using the dies again and these in their turn wore out. In other words the whole process had to start all over again. It really needed the craftsmanship of a goldsmith. It is not surprising that the new invention emerged from their midst, and not, as has been maintained, from the manufacturers of wood-engravings – pages printed from blocks of carved and then inked wood. On the contrary, at one time these popular picture salesmen fought against the new invention. In 1462 Albrecht Pfister, a Bamburg printer, incorporated a wood engraving in a printed book for the first time. Competition thenceforth was impossible.

The printers' craft was slow to improve and was still virtually the same in the eighteenth century as when it began. 'Because the way printing was done up to 1787 (when François Ambroise Didot conceived the press which enabled a folio to be printed by one turn of the screw) was such that if Gutenburg had been resurrected and entered a printing shop at the beginning of Louis xvi's reign in France he would have immediately felt at home in it, save for a few minor details.'

The invention travelled around the world. Like the gunners

looking for hire, printing workers with makeshift equipment wandered at random, settled down when the opportunity offered and moved on again to accept the welcome of a new patron. Paris saw its first printed book in 1471, Lyons in 1473, Poitiers in 1479, Venice in 1470, Naples in 1471, Louvain in 1479 and Cracow in 1474. More than 110 European towns were known by their printing presses in 1480. Between 1480 and 1500 the process reached Spain, proliferated in Germany and Italy, and touched the Scandinavian countries. In 1500 236 towns in Europe had their own workshops.

One calculation puts the total of *incunabula* (books printed before 1500) at 20 million. Europe had perhaps 70 million inhabitants at that time. The movement gathered speed in the sixteenth century: 25,000 editions in Paris, 13,000 in Lyons, 45,000 in Germany, 10,000 in England, perhaps 8000 in the Netherlands. An average of 1000 copies printed should be reckoned for every edition, i.e. 140 to 200 million books from 140,000 to 200,000 editions. And Europe, up to and including its Muscovite borders, counted barely more than 100 million inhabitants by the end of the century.

Books and presses from Europe were exported to Africa, America, the Balkans (reached via Venice by itinerant printers from Montenegro), and Constantinople, where Western presses were taken by Jewish refugees. By way of Portuguese navigation, presses and movable type reached India and naturally Goa, the capital (1557); then Macao (1589) in the shadow of Canton. They had already reached Japan during its 'Christian' century: 1549-1638. If the invention had indeed originated in China, the process had gone full circle.

Printing and the mainstream of history

Valéry's comment on food could appropriately be applied to the printing press: 'Eating is a just pursuit: our food is shared equally between our vices and our virtues.' Printing presses and books from the fifteenth to the eighteenth century were shared equally between vice and virtue, the retrograde and the progressive thought of Europe.

Books were a luxury and since the beginning of their history were subject to the strict laws of profit, supply and demand. The printer's equipment was frequently renewed, the cost of labour high, paper represented over double the other costs, and returns from outlay were slow. All this made the printing house dependent upon moneylenders, who soon became masters of the networks of distribution. The publishing world had its Fuggers on a small scale as far back as the fifteenth century: Barthélemy Buyer (died 1483) in Lyons; Antoine Vérard, master of a Paris workshop devoted to calligraphy and the illumination of manuscripts, who then adopted the new processes and specialised in illustrated books for France and England; the Giunta family from Florence; Anton Koberger, perhaps the largest publisher of his time, who brought out at least 236 works in Nuremburg between 1473 and 1513; and Plantin, born in Touraine in 1514, who settled in Antwerp in 1549 with notable success.

Books, being merchandise, depended on routes, trade and fairs; fairs were held in Lyons and Frankfurt in the sixteenth century and in Leipzig in the seventeenth. Taken as a whole, traffic in books was a means of power at the disposal of the West. All thought draws life from contacts and exchanges. Books accelerated and enlarged the currents that the old hand-written books had created: hence there was a speeding-up process despite significant obstacles. Latin predominated at the time of the *incunabula* in the fifteenth century, and with it a religious and devout literature. Humanism had only the Latin and Greek editions of classical literature at the beginning of the sixteenth century to serve its aggressive cause. Slightly later the Reformation and then the Counter-Reformation made use of books to serve their cause.

We cannot say whom the printing press really served. It enlarged and invigorated everything. One consequence can perhaps be discerned. The great discovery that began the mathematical revolution of the seventeenth century was the discovery of (to adopt Oswald Spengler's phase) the number function, $y = f(x)$, in present-day terms. Now the idea of function depends on the concepts of the infinitesimal and of the limit, which were already in Archimedes' thought. But who knew about Archimedes in the sixteenth century? Some rare privileged individuals. On a couple of occasions Leonardo da Vinci looked for one of his manuscripts after someone had talked to him about it. Slow to turn towards scientific works, the printing press gradually took over this task and little by little reinstated Greek mathematics. As well as the works of Euclid and Apollonius of Perga (on conics), it put the triumphant thought of Archimedes within reach of all.

It may be that the relative lateness of these editions must bear the responsibility for the slow development of modern mathematics between the end of the sixteenth century and the beginning of the seventeenth. But without them success would have been delayed still further.

The Western achievement: ocean navigation

The conquest of the high seas gave Europe a world supremacy that lasted for centuries. This time technology – ocean navigation – did create 'asymmetry', an advantage on a world scale. In fact Europe's explosion on to all the seas of the world poses a great problem: how was it that ocean navigation was not shared by all the maritime civilisations of the world once the demonstration had been made? Theoretically they could all have entered the competition. But Europe remained alone in the race.

The navies of the Old World

It is all the more puzzling as the maritime civilisations had always known about each other and, taken together, covered the Old World in a continuous line from the European Atlantic to the Indian Ocean, the Indian archipelago and the marginal seas of the Pacific. Jean Poujade regarded the Mediterranean and the Indian Ocean as forming but one vast sea which he appropriately called 'the route to the Indies'. In fact 'the route to the Indies', the navigable axis of the Old World, runs (and always ran) from the Baltic and the Channel as far as the Pacific.

The Suez isthmus did not cut it in two. Moreover a branch of the Nile had joined the Red Sea over a period of several centuries (thus connecting it to the Mediterranean). This was Nechao's canal, as it was known, a 'Suez Canal' still functioning in St Louis' day but filled in soon afterwards. Venice and the Egyptians thought about opening it again at the beginning of the sixteenth century. Moreover, men, animals and dismantled ships crossed the isthmus. The fleet the Turks launched on the Red Sea in 1538, 1539 and 1588 was taken there in pieces on the backs of camels and put together again. Vasco da Gama's voyage (1498) did not destroy this old common life between Europe and the Indian Ocean. It made a new route for it.

Such contact did not necessarily imply any mixing. No one is more attached to his own way of doing things than the sailor, wherever he may be. The Chinese junks, despite so many advantages (sails, rudders, hulls with watertight compartments, compasses from the eleventh century, an enormous displacement from the fourteenth), reached Japan but did not venture beyond the Gulf of Tonkin in the south. Inferior Indonesian, Indian and Arab ships with triangular sails were to be found from Tourane to the distant shores of Africa. This was because – though it may be difficult to believe – the maritime frontiers of the civilisations were as rigid as their continental frontiers. Everybody kept to their own territory at sea as well as on land. Nevertheless neighbours visited each other: Chinese sails and junks were in the Gulf of Tonkin because Tonkin had been under Chinese domination. If the Suez isthmus was not a frontier – although it had the appearance and possibilities of one – it was because different civilisations occupied it regularly. Thus, when Islam established itself over a large part of the Mediterranean, it introduced the so-called 'Latin' or fore-and-aft sail, which was actually Indian and had originated in the Oman Sea. There Islam had found it. This piece of untypical history was necessary to establish the triangular sail in the Mediterranean. In our eyes it has become the very symbol of that sea.

Yet it was in fact borrowed, replacing the square sail used by all the Mediterranean peoples from the Phoenicians to the Greeks, Carthaginians and Romans. Moreover it met with opposition, particularly on the coasts of Languedoc, but this is only one small detail. There was still more opposition in Greek territory, as long as Byzantium held sway there through the strength of its squadrons and Greek fire-power. In any case, it is not surprising that triangular sails were in Portugal, for Portugal was strongly influenced by Islam.

On the other hand, in northern Europe where a vigorous maritime revival took place before the thirteenth century, square sails remained the general rule. Hulls were made especially strongly, with planks overlapping like the tiles of a roof (clinker-built). But the wonder to end all wonders was the axial rudder, operated from inside the ship and known as the centreline rudder.

All in all there were two different European navies – the Mediterranean and the northern – brought face to face and then intermingled by economic (not political) conquests. Genoan galleys, the large ships of the Mediterranean, appropriated the best of the northern trade after 1297 with the first commercial voyage direct to Bruges. The process was one of capture, domination and education. Lisbon's rise in the thirteenth century was as a port of call which gradually assimilated the lessons of an active, maritime, peripheral and capitalist economy. In these conditions the long ships of the

Mediterranean served as a pattern for the northern navies and suggested the precious Latin sails to them. Conversely, by a series of intermediaries, including the Basques, clinker construction and especially the centreline rudder of the northern ships, which improved their power to beat up to windward, were gradually introduced and accepted in Mediterranean yards. There were exchanges and intermixing, and these in themselves indicate that a new unit of civilisation was in the process of asserting itself: Europe.

The Portuguese caravel, dating from about 1430, was the issue of this marriage. It was a small clinker-built sailing ship with centreline rudder, three masts, two square sails and one Latin sail. The Latin sail running lengthways along the boat on a mast whose yard was higher and longer on one side than the other made it easy to slew the vessel round and steer it. The square sails ran across the width of the boat and were fitted to receive an astern wind. Once they had reached the Canaries, where trade winds blew uninterruptedly up to the Caribbean, caravels and other European ships could haul down their triangular sails and hoist square ones.

World water routes

The prize at stake was the opening-up of the water routes of the world. Around 1420 and still in 1430 all the seafaring men except for the extraordinary Polynesians were prisoners of narrow seas, 'Mediterraneans'. This was true even of the Indian Ocean, used in its northern zone between the barriers represented by the coasts of Africa, India, and the Malay peninsula.

There is no evidence that one rather than another of these peoples were winning the race. Phoenicians had sailed round Africa over 2000 years before Vasco da Gama. Irish sailors discovered the Faroes in about 690, centuries before Columbus, and Irish monks landed in Iceland in about 759; the Vikings rediscovered it in about 860. Eric the Red reached Greenland in 981 or 982 and Norsemen continued to be present there until the fifteenth or sixteenth centuries. A marvellous map dating from 1440 has just been discovered which is said to indicate the coast of the American continent beyond Greenland ('Vinland'). The Vivaldi brothers passed through the straits of Gibraltar with two galleys in 1291, en route to the Indies, and then got lost beyond Cape Juby. If they had succeeded in skirting Africa they would have set in motion the course of the major discoveries two centuries in advance.

This was all European. But from the eleventh century the Chinese seem, in retrospect, to have been unrivalled competitors. They had the advantage of the compass. Three centuries later, they had 'large junks with four bridges, divided into watertight compartments, rigged with four to six masts, able to carry twelve large sails and manned by a thousand men'. Under the rule of the Songs of the south (1127–1279) they ousted the small Arab craft from trade in the Sea of China. This represented a vigorous, clean sweep of their own front doorstep. In the fifteenth century Chinese squadrons made amazing voyages under the leadership of the great eunuch Tscheng Hwo, a Muslim and a native of Yunnan. His first expedition (1405–7) took him into the Indian archipelago with sixty-two large junks. The second (27,000 men, 48 ships, 1408–11) resulted in the conquest of Ceylon; the third (1413–17) in the conquest of Sumatra. The fourth (1417–19) and fifth (1421–2) were peaceful and led to exchanges of presents and ambassadors (the fourth to India, the fifth as far as Arabia and the Abyssinian coast). The sixth, a quick one, carried an imperial letter to the lord and master of Palembang in Sumatra. The seventh and last was perhaps the most spectacular. It left the port of Long Wan on 19 January 1431. For the rest of the year the fleet was anchored at the most southerly ports of Tche Kiang and Fu Kien. The voyage was continued in 1432 via Java, Palembang, the Malaccan peninsula, Ceylon, Calicut and finally Ormuz, the end of the voyage. Here, on 17 January 1433, the fleet landed a Chinese ambassador of Muslim origin, who might perhaps have reached Mecca. It returned to Nanking on 22 July 1433.

Then, as far as we know, everything stopped. It is true that China under the Mings had to face a renewed threat from the nomads of the north. The capital was transferred from Nanking to Peking (1421). This marked the end of an era. All the same, we can for a moment imagine what would have been the result of a possible spread of Chinese junks towards the Cape of Good Hope, or better still to the Cape Agulhas which served as a southern gateway between the Indian and Atlantic Oceans.

We can cite another example of wasted opportunity. Arab geographers (starting with Massoudi in the tenth century, who knew the Arab towns on the Zanzibar coast) had talked about the possibility of circumnavigating the African continent for centuries, contrary to Ptolemy's opinion. Their views coincided with the immutable opinion of the Christian Church which affirmed the unity of the liquid of the seas on the basis of the Bible. In any case

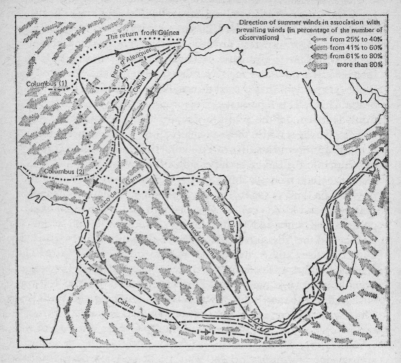

Map 4 The great discoveries – the routes across the Atlantic. This simplified map shows the summer positions of the northern and southern trade-winds, which change position according to season. The routes to and from the Indies followed certain fairly simple rules. Ships were driven south by the northern winds and used the southern trades to reach the coasts of Brazil. On the return journey the southern trades drove them northwards and they cut across the northern trades to the winds of the middle latitudes. The dotted line showing the return from Guinea (or the return *da Mina*, as the Portuguese said) shows that it was necessary to avoid the African coast on the return journey to Europe. Bartolomeo Dias, whose voyage preceded Vasco da Gama's, made the mistake of hugging the coast of Africa when sailing southwards. The difficulties of the early navigations, during which these rules gradually came to be recognised, were greater than has been imagined. To complete the picture we ought to mention the role of ocean currents, which both helped and hindered navigation.

information from Arab travellers and sailors had percolated as far as Christendom. Alexander von Humboldt thought that the strange voyage said to have been made by an Arab ship in about 1430 should be taken as fact. It was described in a caption on the map of the *geographus incomparabilis* of Venice by Fra Mauro (1457). The ship is said to have sailed for forty days and covered 2000 miles between sky and sea in 'the sea of Darkness', as the Arabs called the Atlantic Ocean. Its return took seventy days.

And yet the credit for solving the problem of the Atlantic, which was to solve all the others, was to fall to Europe.

The simple problem of the Atlantic

The Atlantic is three large wind and sea circuits shown on a map as three vast ellipses. Currents and winds take a boat in either direction with no effort on its part. Both the Vikings' circuit of the North Atlantic and Columbus' demonstrated it. Columbus' three ships were driven as far as the Canaries, then to the West Indies. The winds from the middle latitudes brought them back in the spring of 1493 via the Azores, after having taken them in the vicinity of Newfoundland. In the south a large circuit leads up to the coast of America, then carries on as far as the level of the Cape of Good Hope, at the southern tip of Africa. There was only one condition for successful navigation: look for the right wind and never let it go when you catch it. This was the usual practice on the high seas (map 4).

Nothing would have been simpler if ocean navigation had seemed a natural thing to sailors. But the early exploits of the Irish and Vikings had got lost in the mists of time. Before they could be revived Europe had to wake up to a more active material life, combine techniques from north and south, learn about compasses and navigational charts, and above all conquer its instinctive fear. Portuguese discoverers were in Madeira in 1422, in the Azores in 1427; they followed the line of the African coast. It was child's play to reach Cape Bojador, but the return journey, with a head wind and against the northern trade winds, proved difficult. It was equally easy to reach Guinea, with its slave market, gold dust and ersatz pepper. But here again the return journey involved cutting across the trade winds and getting back to the west winds, which meant sailing in the open sea for a month, as far as the Sargasso Sea. Similarly the return journey from Mina (São Jorge de Mina was founded in 1487) made it necessary to cut across contrary winds for days on end as far as the Azores.

In fact the greatest difficulty was to brave the venture and take the plunge. The courage required for such an unwonted feat has been forgotten – as probably our grandchildren will know nothing about the bravery of the astronauts today. 'It is quite well known,' wrote Jean Bodin, 'that the kings of Portugal . . . [have] sailed the high seas for a hundred years.' Now even in the seventeenth century seamen kept as close to the coast as possible. Tomé Cano, whose book appeared in Seville in 1611, says of the Italians: 'They are not sailors of the high seas.' To Mediterranean sailors, who went from one seaport tavern to the next, taking the plunge meant at the most going from Rhodes to Alexandria (four days in the open sea if all went well); or from Marseilles to Barcelona, following a chord of that dangerous arc of a circle – the Gulf of Lions; or going in a straight line from the Balearics to Italy, via Sardinia, and sometimes as far as Sicily. However, the best straight route in the maritime spaces linked to Europe during that *ancien régime* of ships and navigation was the journey from the Iberian peninsula to the mouth of the English Channel. It included the dramatic surprises of the stormy Bay of Biscay and the long swells of the Atlantic. When Ferdinand left his brother Charles v in 1522, the fleet carrying him from Laredo missed the Channel and found itself in Ireland. When Dantiscus (ambassador of the King of Poland) crossed from England to Spain in 1522, it was the most dramatic voyage of his life. Crossing the Bay of Biscay was certainly for centuries an apprenticeship to the savage high seas. Such apprenticeships and others were perhaps necessary conditions for the opening-up of the world.

But why only Europe? European observers and sailors were already wondering about this between the sixteenth and eighteenth centuries, when they had the very different navies of China or Japan before their eyes. Father Mendoza had an explanation in 1577: the Chinese were 'afraid of the sea, being people not accustomed to take risks'. The fact was that the Far Eastern sailors also went from one seaport tavern to the next. Rodrigo Vivero, travelling on the inland waterways of Japan between Osaka and Nagasaki – that is for twelve to fifteen days – declared 'that at sea, one sleeps almost every night on land'. The Chinese, Father du Halde stated (1693), were 'good coastal pilots but pretty bad pilots on the high seas'.

At the end of the eighteenth century George Staunton gave more thought to the matter as he had the opportunity of examining at leisure Chinese junks in the Gulf of Tche-li beyond the Yellow Sea. He observed the 'curious contrast and singular spectacle of the towering masts and complicated tackling of European ships, in the midst of the low, simple and clumsy, but strong and roomy junks of the Chinese. Each of the latter was of the burden of about 200 tons.' He noted the way the hold was divided up into compartments, the abnormal size of the two masts, 'each of which consisted of a single tree or piece of timber; each carrying a square sail generally made of split bamboo, and sometimes of matting composed of straw or reeds. The junks are nearly of the same flat form at both extremities. At one is a rudder, of a breadth almost equal to that of a London lighter. It is guided by ropes passing from it along each side of the vessel's quarter.'

The Jackall – the second English ship, which followed the ship of the line, *The Lion*, like a faithful servant – only carried 100 tons. In the Gulf of Tche-li it was outclassed by the junks with which it was competing. *The Jackall*, explained Staunton:

was built for navigating with the variable and frequently adverse winds of the European seas; and drawing on that account double the quantity of water, or, in other words, sinking to double the depth of junks, or Chinese vessels of equal burden. The inconvenience of falling much to leeward with a side wind, to which the flat-bottomed vessels of Europe are liable, is not very much felt in the Chinese seas, where vessels sail generally with the monsoon directly in their favour [he means with a following wind]. The sails, too, of Chinese junks are made to go round the masts with so much ease, and to form so acute an angle with the sides of the vessel, that they turn well to windward, notwithstanding the little hold they have of the water.

His conclusions:

The Chinese, indeed, enjoy a similar advantage (as the Greeks), as their seas resemble the Mediterranean by the narrowness of their limits, and the numerous islands with which every part of them is studded. It is to be observed, likewise, that the art of navigation, improved among Europeans, dates its origins nearly from the same period when their passions, or their wants, impelled them to undertake long voyages over the boundless ocean.

We are back where we started – no further forward after all that. Ocean navigation was the key to the seven seas of the world. But there is no proof that the Chinese and Japanese were incapable of seizing this key and using it, technically speaking.

In fact contemporaries and historians have been imprisoned in a search for a technical solution which they feel they must isolate at all costs. But perhaps the solution is not primarily technical. King John II ordered the Portuguese pilot who told him that it was possible to get back from the coast of Mina 'with any ship in good condition' to remain silent on threat of imprisonment.

There is a better example, a unique one as far as we know – the adventure of the Japanese junk that sailed from Japan to Acapulco in Mexico in 1610. A present from the Japanese, it brought back Rodrigo Vivero and his fellow castaways. It is true that the entire crew was European, but the experiment proved that technically speaking, junks were not incapable of braving the high seas. So much for the explanation on purely technical grounds.

Modern historians have even come up with the idea that the caravel did not owe its success so much to its sails and rudder as to its shallow draught which 'enabled it to explore coasts and estuaries', and even more to the fact that it was 'a ship of small dimensions, and so could be equipped relatively cheaply'! This is to belittle its role.

It is no easier to explain the ineffectiveness of Muslim boats. Their voyages straight across the Indian Ocean were probably easy, with the alternation of the monsoons, but they nonetheless implied considerable knowledge, the use of the astrolabe or Jacob's staff. And these were high-quality ships. The story of Vasco da Gama's Arab pilot who took the small Portuguese fleet to Melinda and guided it straight to Calicut is very revealing. How was it, in these circumstances, that the adventures of Sinbad the Sailor and his successors did not lead to Arab domination of the world? How was it that, to use an idea of Vidal de La Blache's, Arab navigation south of Zanzibar and Madagascar came to a halt at the violent current from Mozambique, which rushes southwards towards the approaches to the Atlantic? First we will reply by saying that these old Arab navigational achievements did lead Islam to dominate the Old World up to the fifteenth century, as we have had occasion to explain. Then why should they have looked for a route round the Cape when they had a Suez Canal (seventh to thirteenth centuries) at their disposal? And what would they want to find there? Islamic towns and merchants could already obtain gold, ivory and slaves on the coast of Zanzibar and across the Sahara in the Niger loop. There would have had to have been a 'need' for West Africa. Perhaps then the merit of the West, confined as it was on its narrow 'Cape of Asia', was to have needed the world, to have needed to venture outside its own front door. Nothing would have been possible, according to an expert in Chinese history, without the growth of the capitalist towns of the West at that time. They were the driving force. Without them technology would have been impotent.

This does not mean that it was money, capital, that was responsible for ocean navigation. On the contrary, China and Islam at that period were societies well endowed with what we today would call colonies. The West in comparison was still 'proletarian'. But the important thing was the long period of pressure after the thirteenth century that raised the level of its material life and transformed its whole psychology. What historians have called a lust for gold or a lust for the world or a lust for spices was in the technical sphere accompanied by a constant search for new utilitarian inventions and applications — utilitarian in the sense that they would be in the service of man, to ensure both the lightening and the greater efficiency of his labour. The accumulation of practical discoveries showing a conscious will to master the world and a growing interest in every source of power revealed Europe's true features and guaranteed its pre-eminence well before its success.

2 Transport

The victory over the ocean was an immense triumph and an immense innovation. It completed a global system of links. But it did so without altering that slowness and those defects in transport itself that remained permanent limitations on the economy of the *ancien régime*. Up to the eighteenth century sea journeys were interminable and overland transport almost paralysed. We are told that Europe established an enormous network of efficient roads from the thirteenth century. But we have only to look at the series of small paintings by Jan Breughel at the Pinakothek in Munich, for example, to realise that even in the seventeenth century and even in flat open country a road was not a clearly delineated strip. Its outline is generally barely perceptible. It would certainly not be recognisable at first glance without the movement of those making use of it. And they are often peasants on foot, a cart taking a farmer's wife and her baskets to market, a pedestrian leading an animal by its halter. There is of course the occasional dashing horseman or a carriage drawn by three nimble horses which looks as if it contains a whole middle-class family. But in the next picture the holes in the road are full of water, the horsemen are squelching along, their mounts up to their hocks in water; the carriages move painfully forward, their wheels sunk in the mud. Pedestrians, shepherds and pigs have wisely retired to the safer banks bordering the road. The same scenes, worse perhaps, were enacted in northern China. If the road 'is spoiled' or if it 'makes a considerable bend', 'coolies', carts and horses 'go across tilled land to shorten the route and make themselves a better one, not worrying overmuch whether the grain is risen or already tall'.

Nothing or very little would have changed in these matters between the time of Richelieu or Charles v and China under the Songs or the Roman Empire. Such conditions governed and burdened commercial exchanges and even ordinary human relations. Mail took weeks, months, to reach its destination. The 'defeat of space', as Ernst Wagemann calls it, was only to be achieved after 1857 with the laying of the first intercontinental maritime cable. Railway, steamship, telegraph and telephone inaugurated real mass communication on a world scale very late.

Rigid itineraries

Take any road whatsoever in any period whatsoever. On it there are vehicles, beasts of burden, a few horsemen, inns, a forge, a village, a town. However slightly marked it seems, it was never a flexible line – even in the Argentine pampas or eighteenth-century Siberia. Transporters and travellers remained prisoners of a limited range of choice. Perhaps they could prefer one itinerary to another to avoid a toll or a customs post, but even then they might have to turn back in case of difficulty. They followed one road in winter and another in spring, according to frost or pot-holes. But they could never abandon roads already laid out. Travelling meant drawing on services provided by others.

In 1776 Jacob Fries, a Swiss doctor and a major in the Russian army, made the long journey from Omsk to Tomsk (890 kilometres) in 178 hours, an average speed of five kilometres an hour, changing horses regularly so as not to miss the posting houses. Travellers who missed one in winter ended up buried beneath the snow. In the Argentinian interior, even in the eighteenth century, they had to regulate their progress so as to cross the *despoblados* (the deserts) at the right time and find houses, villages, water points and people selling eggs and fresh meat just at the right moment. And this was the case whether they travelled on board the heavy ox-carts – which arrived in Buenos Aires laden with corn or hides and left empty for Mendoza, Santiago de Chile or Jujuy, in the direction of Peru – or even if they preferred to go on mule- or horse-back. If a traveller got tired of the narrow cabin of his carriole, he could mount a horse, load 'an adequate bed' on to another beast and set off at a gallop in front of the convoy, preferably at between two and ten in the morning to avoid the heat. 'The horses are so well accustomed to making these crossings in a short space of time that they gallop at full tilt without any urging.' The reward? 'The post houses are the best lodgings where the traveller can rest as he pleases.' He arrived there and went to bed. This information makes it easier to understand the comments in *L'Itinéraire de Buenos Aires à Lima* (1776) by Don Alonso Carrio de la Bandera concerning the first part of the road from Buenos Aires to Carcaranal: 'During these three-and-a-half days on the road, with the exception of two crossings, cows, sheep and goats will be found in abundance and at low prices.'

These late pictures of 'new' lands (Siberia, the New World) are fairly accurate descriptions of journeys in the 'old' civilised lands in earlier centuries. Even in the nineteenth century in Argentina the traveller made his will before he set out: this was the custom of European merchants in the middle ages. Whence arise so many repetitions and inevitable regularities over the centuries and at thousands of miles apart.

To reach Istanbul by way of the Balkans, advises Pierre Lescalopier (1574), 'it will be necessary to travel from morning to night, unless some stream or meadow gives you the means of putting foot to ground and taking some cold meat from your saddlebag and a bottle of wine from your saddlebow to feed on lightly around midday, while your horses, unbridled and with hobbles on their feet, graze or eat what they are given'. The next caravanserai where food and drink were to be found had to be reached by evening. These were 'hospitals' (in the sense of hospices – hospitable houses) 'built to mark the limits of each day's journey ... Rich and poor lodge [there] for want of anything better; they are like very large barns; they have loopholes instead of windows'. The people were accommodated on 'projections' (platforms) arranged around this hall, to which the animals were attached. 'Thus everyone sees his horse and puts his food on the projections and to make him eat oats and barley they [the Turks] use leather bags from which the horse eats while the straps of the bag are passed over his ears'. A Neapolitan traveller described these inns more simply in 1693: 'They are nothing but ...

long stables where the horses occupy the central part; the sides are left for the Masters.'

In China a *Public Itinerary* printed in the seventeenth century indicated the roads out of Peking, with their outlines and their stopping places, where mandarins on mission were received at the emperor's expense, entertained, fed and refurnished with mounts, boats or porters. These stopping places, a day's journey away from each other, were large towns or 'second-order' towns, or castles, or *Ye* or *Chin* – places 'of lodging and guarding', 'formerly built in areas where there were no towns'. Towns often grew up there as a result.

Travelling was only pleasant in lands where towns and villages were close together. *L'Ulysse françois* (1643) – a notable guidebook of its day – indicates the good inns (the *Faucon Royal* in Marseilles, the *Cardinal* hostelry in Amiens) and advises (revenge or wisdom?) against lodging at the *Cerf* inn in Péronne! Amenities and speed were the privileges of populated and firmly maintained, 'policed', lands: China, Japan, Europe, Islam. In Persia 'good caravanserai are found every four leagues' and travelling there was 'cheap'. But the same traveller, having left Persia, was complaining about Hindustan in the following year (1695): no inns, no caravanserai, no animals to hire for carriages, no food outside 'the large towns of the Mogul's lands'; 'one sleeps beneath the stars or under a tree'.

More surprising is the fact that sea routes were also invariable. And yet ships were subject to winds, currents and ports of call. Coasting was the rule both in the seas bordering China and the Mediterranean. The coast attracted and guided the procession of coasters. The rules for voyages in the open seas were dictated by experience. The route between Spain and the 'Castilian Indies' had been fixed by Christopher Columbus. Alaminos scarcely improved it in 1519. After that it did not change until the nineteenth century. On the return journey it brushed the thirty-third parallel at a point very far north, bringing the travellers into sudden contact with northern hardships: 'The cold began to make itself severely felt,' noted one of them (1697), 'and certain knights clad in silk and without cloaks found it very hard to bear.' Similarly Urdaneta discovered the route from Acapulco to Manila, from New Spain to the Philippines and back in 1565, and fixed it once and for all. The journey there was easy (three months); the return was difficult and long (six to eight months) and cost the traveller up to 500 pieces of eight (1696).

All being well the ship passed the points and stopped at the places where it was usual to pass and stop. Food and water were taken on at appointed ports of call. It could, if the need arose, careen, repair, replace a mast or remain for a long time in the calm bosom of the ports. Everything was provided for.

If a gust of wind took a ship by surprise before the sail was knotted and broke its mast in the open sea off Guinea, where only low tonnages could reach the shallow coast, it sailed, if possible, to the Portuguese island of the Prince – *a ilha do Principe* – to find a substitute mast, and to take on sugar and slaves. Near the Sunda straits wisdom dictated that ships follow the coast of Sumatra as closely as possible and then reach the Malacca peninsula. The hilly coast of the large island would protect them against squalls and the water was not deep. When hurricanes blew up, as happened during Kämpfer's journey to Siam, in 1690, the ship had to drop anchor and like other vessels in the vicinity cling to the shallow sea floor until the squall had moved a little farther off.

Ups and downs in the history of roads

We should not exaggerate the importance of the ups and downs in the history of roads. They spring to our attention, seem at variance with one another, and often fade into the background. There is no doubt that we cannot explain the decline of the Champagne fairs as the result of the ill-natured interference on the roads leading to the towns of Champagne by the French authorities, particularly Louis x, the Headstrong (1314–16). It cannot even be explained by the establishment of direct and regular maritime connections from the Mediterranean to Bruges, initiated after 1297 by the large boats from Genoa. At this time, in the first decades of the fourteenth century, the structure of large-scale commerce was transformed; the itinerant merchant became scarcer; merchandise travelled alone, its movements between Italy and the Netherlands, the two poles of the European economy, controlled from a distance by written correspondence, without the need thenceforth for meeting or discussion midway. The relay point of Champagne became less useful. The popularity of the Geneva fairs, another rendezvous for settling accounts, became established in the fifteenth century.

Likewise, we should not seek minor explanations for the breakdown of the Mongolian route around 1350. During the thirteenth century the Mongol conquest had established direct overland contact between China, India and the West. They had got round Islam.

And the Polos, Marco's father and uncle, and Marco himself, were not the only ones to reach distant China or the Indies by long but surprisingly safe routes. The breakdown should be attributed to the vast recession in the middle of the fourteenth century. For everything regressed at once, the West just as much as China under the Mongols. Neither did the discovery of the New World immediately transform the major trade routes of the globe. The Mediterranean was still the scene of active international life a century after Columbus and Vasco da Gama. The regression came later.

As for the chronicle of routes over short distances, the ebb and flow of circumstances generally dictated success or lack of it. In 1332 the town of Ghent repaired at its own expense the road leading to the Champagne fairs at the point where it touched Senlis. One can guess with what slight results. It is also open to question whether the 'free trade policy' of the Counts of Brabant between 1350 and 1460, their roads unhampered by heavy tolls, was anything but a search for a way out of a depressing situation. To be sure, Milan was able to get on famously with Rudolph of Hapsburg, who reigned from 1273 to 1291, and organise its traffic across the Alps in agreement with him. Who could have failed to succeed at that time? Likewise, in about 1530 – a propitious moment – the Bishop of Salzburg made the mule path from the Tauern passable for vehicles, without supplanting the St Gothard or the Brenner with Milan and Venice behind them. There was enough work for all roads at that time.

Water transport

A drop of water and everything came to life in the heart of the land. It is easy everywhere to picture life as it was then. We cannot fail to sense the flourishing water transport of former times at Gray, on the wide and empty Saône, transporting wine and 'the merchandise of Lyons' upstream, corn, hay and oats downstream. Without the Seine, Oise, Marne and Yonne, Paris could not easily have eaten, drunk or warmed itself. Without the Rhine, Cologne would not have been the largest town in Germany from before the fifteenth century.

A sixteenth-century geographer talking about Venice would immediately mention the sea and the great waterways converging on its lagoons: the Brenta, the Po, the Adige. Various kinds of boats, some propelled by poles, were constantly arriving at the large town by these routes and by the canals. But the scantiest stretches of water were utilised everywhere. Gunpowder, bullets, grenades and other ammunition manufactured at Navarre were transported on flat boats down the Ebro 'from Tudela to Tortosa and down to the sea' even at the beginning of the eighteenth century and despite many difficulties, notably 'the Flix Fall where the merchandise is unloaded and later taken back on board'.

The great region for water transport in Europe was beyond the Oder in Poland and Lithuania even more than Germany. River transport had developed there from the middle ages, with the aid of immense rafts of tree trunks. Each of them had a cabin for the sailors. This vast traffic led to the building of wharves – Torun (Thorn), Kovno, Brest-Litovsk – and aroused endless disputes.

However, taking the world as a whole, there was nothing to equal southern China, from the Blue River to the borders of Yunnan.

The great internal trade of China, which has no equal in the world, depends on this traffic [noted a witness in about 1733]. One sees a perpetual movement of boats, barks, and rafts everywhere there (some of these rafts are half a league long and fold back ingeniously because of the bends of the rivers) and form so many moving towns at each spot. The drivers of these barks have their permanent home on them, having their wives and children with them there, so one can easily believe the report of most travellers that there are almost as many people on the water in that country as in the towns and countryside.

'No country in the world,' according to Father de Magaillans, 'can equal China in navigation [meaning water transport] ...' In this country 'there are two empires, one on water, the other on land, and as many Venices as there are towns'. The following is the opinion of a witness who went up the Yang-tse-Kiang 'which is called the Son of the sea' as far as Se-tchouan over a period of four months in 1656: 'The Kiang which, like the sea, is limitless, is bottomless as well.' A few years later (1695), a traveller laid it down as a principle that 'the Chinese like to live in the water like ducks ...' One sailed 'amidst timber rafts' for hours, for half a day at a time, he explained. The canals and rivers of a town had to be negotiated desperately slowly 'through great numbers of barks'.

Out-of-date transport

If we collected a series of pictures relating to transport over the whole world between the fifteenth and eighteenth centuries, carefully mixed them up and offered them to the reader without captions, he could accurately identify them. No one would fail to recognise a Chinese sedan chair or a Chinese wheelbarrow equipped with a sail; the pack ox or war elephant from the Indies, the Turkish *araba* from the Balkans (or even Tunisia); or again the caravans of camels from Islam; the files of African bearers; or the two- or four-wheeled carriages of Europe, with their oxen or horses.

But if it came to dating these pictures there would be endless difficulties. The means of transport scarcely developed at all. Father de Las Cortes saw Chinese porters 'lifting travellers' chairs on long bamboos' in the Canton region in 1626. George Staunton described the same thin coolies 'with their rags, straw hats and sandals' in 1793. When his barge had to change canals on the road from Peking it was lifted by arms and winches 'and is thus conveyed into the upper canal with less delay than can be done by locks, but by the exertion of much more human force; a force indeed which, in China, is always ready, of little cost, and constantly preferred to any other'. Likewise one could swap round descriptions of a caravan from Africa or Asia provided by Ibn Batouta (1326), an anonymous sixteenth-century English traveller, René Caillé (1799-1838), or by the German explorer Georg Schweinfurth (1836-1925). The spectacle remained timeless and unchanging. I still saw convoys of narrow four-wheeled peasant wagons on the Cracow roads in November 1957 going to town loaded with people and pine branches, their needles trailing like hair in the dust of the road behind them. This sight, probably now living out its last days, was just as much a feature of the fifteenth-century scene.

The same applies to the sea; Chinese or Japanese junks, Malayan or Polynesian pirogues with outriggers, Arab boats on the Red Sea or Indian Ocean – so many characters that hardly changed. Ernst Sachau, an expert on Babylon, described (1897-8) the Arab boats, as did Belon du Mans (1550) and Gemelli Careri (1695). Their planks were tied with palm fibre without the aid of a single iron nail. Careri noted à propos a boat which he saw being built at Daman (in the Indies): 'The nails were wooden and the caulks cotton.' These sailing ships remained numerous until the introduction of English steamboats. Perhaps they still fulfil the same functions here and there today as they did in Sinbad's time.

Europe

Some chronological discrimination is obviously possible in Europe. We know that vehicles with a movable front carriage, descended from artillery carts, were only really employed from about 1470.

Primitive coaches only appeared with the second half or end of the sixteenth century (they had glass windows only in the seventeenth). Diligences were seventeenth-century institutions. Stagecoaches for travellers and *vetturini* in Italy only appeared in any number in the Romantic period. The first canal locks date from the fourteenth century. But these innovations cannot conceal the innumerable permanencies at the basis of everyday life. The changing realm of ships also had its upper limits – of tonnages and speed – forming a permanency, a 'ceiling'.

As far back as the fifteenth century Genoese carracks had a capacity of 1500 tons; 1000-ton Venetian ships carried bulky bales of cotton from Syria. In the sixteenth century Ragusan cargo ships of 900 to 1000 tons specialised in the salt, wool and corn trades, as well as in carrying cases of sugar and bales of skins. At the same time the giant of the seas, the Portuguese carrack, had a displacement of up to 2000 tons. Counting both sailors and passengers, it carried a complement of over 800 persons. Great disasters ensued if the wood used to build it had not been dry enough and it sprang a leak in its side, if a storm threw it on to the shallows off the Mozambique coast, or if light-weight privateers encircled, seized and set fire to it. The *Madre de Deus* was not able to sail up the Thames when it was seized by the English in 1587 because of its draught.

Broadly speaking the skill of the shipyards had reached its highest point a good century before the Invincible Armada in 1588. Only heavy or long-distance trade, guaranteed by *de facto* or *de jure* monopolies, made the luxury of these large tonnages possible. The majestic Indiamen at the end of the eighteenth century (they specialised in trade with China, despite their name) had a displacement of barely more than 1900 tons. The upper limit was determined by the material used for construction, sails, and the armament on board.

But an upper limit is not an average. Very small ships of thirty, forty and fifty tons were sailing the seas until the last days of the sailing ship. The use of iron made the construction of larger hulls possible only in about 1840. A hull of 200 tons had until then been the general rule, one of 500 an exception, one of 1000 to 2000 an object of curiosity.

Low speeds and capacities

Bad roads, ridiculously low speeds: this is the conclusion modern man jumps to, and his point of view has its validity. He sees the enormous handicap hampering all active life in the past better than a contemporary, for whom it was an everyday fact. Paul Valéry pointed out that 'Napoleon moves at the same slow rate as Julius Caesar'. This is demonstrated by three recently published accounts that make possible an estimate of the speed of news sent to Venice. The period from 1497 to 1537 is covered by the *Diarii* of Marin Sanudo, a patrician of Venice who kept day-to-day notes of the dates when letters received by the Seigniory arrived as well as the dates when they were sent. Then we have hand-written gazettes published in Venice between 1686 and 1701 and between 1733 and 1735. Other calculations would give the same conclusions, namely that with horses, coaches, ships and runners, it was the general rule to cover at the most 100 kilometres in 24 hours. Higher speeds were very infrequent and a great luxury. It was possible, if one was prepared to pay, to have an order taken from Nuremburg to Venice in four days at the beginning of the sixteenth century. If the large towns attracted rapid news in their direction it was because they paid for speed and always had the means to create better communications, one of which was obviously to build stone or paved roads; but such things long remained exceptions.

The road from Paris to Orléans was entirely paved and thus allowed rapid communication with Orléans (despite the brigands who were still feared in the seventeenth century around the area of the Torfou wood). Orléans was the main river station of France, equal or almost so to Paris, the Loire being the most convenient waterway of the realm, with 'the widest bed and the longest course ... on which one can sail for over a hundred and sixty leagues in the Kingdom, which is not found in any other river in France'. This road from Paris to Orléans was the 'King's highway', a great carriageway, *strada di carri* an Italian said as early as 1581. The Stamboulyol, the road from Istanbul to Belgrade via Sofia, also had carriages from the sixteenth century, its luxury *arabas* in the eighteenth.

One aspect of progress in eighteenth-century France was the planned extension of highways. The lease of the French posts rose from 1,220,000 livres in 1676 to 8,800,000 in 1776. The budget of the *Ponts et Chaussées* department was 700,000 under Louis XIV and 7 million as the Revolution drew near. But this budget only took care of construction work – opening new roads. Old roads were maintained by the highway *corvée*, created in about 1730. It was annulled by Turgot in 1776, re-established in the same year and only disappeared in 1787. France then had somewhere around twelve thousand kilometres of completed road and twelve thousand in process of construction.

The time had therefore come for the stagecoach, including the famous 'turgotines'. Contemporaries thought them dangerous, demoniacal. Their 'body is narrow', said one of them, 'and seats get so crowded that everybody asks his neighbour for his leg or his arm back when it comes to getting down. . . . If by ill chance a traveller with a big stomach or wide shoulders appears . . . one has to groan or desert.' They went at an insane speed. Accidents were numerous, and no one compensated the victims. Furthermore only a narrow central carriageway was paved on main routes. Two carriages could not pass at the same time without a wheel plunging into the mud at the side of the road.

Certain unusually stupid comments were already heralding the reactions which later greeted the first railways. There were many protests in 1669 when a stagecoach covered the distance from Manchester to London in a day. It was the end of the noble art of horsemanship; it spelled ruination for saddle and spur manufacturers; it meant the disappearance of the Thames boatmen.

But the trend continued. The first road revolution was sketched out between 1745 and 1760. The price of transport fell, and even more, 'small speculative capitalists' profited by it. They heralded the changing times.

Nevertheless these modest achievements only concerned highways. In France most of the time it was impossible to move heavy loads conveniently outside these 'postal' roads, and even, according to Adam Smith, 'to travel on horseback; mules are the only conveyance which can safely be trusted'. The countryside, generally not well equipped with roads, remained condemned to partial suffocation. We could say that this first rational network of roads represented no more and no less than the canals that spread in England, also in the eighteenth century (the Bridgewater Canal from Manchester to Liverpool in 1755), and grew rapidly in number after 1790.

Carriage and carriers

Carrying was the second occupation of thousands of peasants in the West after the grain or grape harvest or during the winter months, and they were poorly paid for it. The rhythm of their leisure indicates the upper and lower levels of transport activities. Organised or not, these activities were always in the charge of the poor or the very lowly everywhere. In the same way ships' crews were recruited from amongst the wretched classes of Europe and the world. Dutch ships, victorious over all the seas in the seventeenth century, were no exception to the rule. The same was true of the amazing American sailors, 'Englishmen of the second kind' as the Chinese said, who went off to conquer the seas at the end of the eighteenth century in tiny ships, sometimes of 50 to 100 tons, sailing from Philadelphia or New York to China. They were said to be drunk every time they got the chance.

We should add that transport entrepreneurs were not normally high-ranking capitalists: their profits were limited. We will come back to this.

But despite the small scale of costs and returns, carriage was expensive in itself: an average of 10% *ad valorem*, according to a historian of medieval Germany. But the average varied according to country and period. We know the price of cloth bought in the Netherlands and sent to Florence in 1320 and 1321. The cost of carriage (for six known accounts) ranged *ad valorem* between 11·70%, the lowest rate, and 20·34%, the highest. This was for merchandise which was not bulky and carried a very high price. Other types hardly travelled over very long distances. In the seventeenth century it was necessary 'to pay 100 to 200 francs to take a barrel of wine often not worth more than about 40 francs from Beaune to Paris'.

The expenses and problems were generally greater on land than on sea. This led to a certain lack of vitality in inland traffic, except for the waterways, but in that sector nobles and towns imposed numerous tolls that wasted a good deal of time. Merchants often chose overland roads, even in the Po plain or along the Rhine, in preference to waterways broken up by endless series of tolls. There was also the not negligible risk of brigandage which remained common throughout the world, a marginal symptom of permanent economic and social malaise.

The sea route on the other hand signified a sort of explosion of 'free trade'. It represented a bonus to the advantage of the maritime economies. In the thirteenth century the price of English wool increased 1·5% and grain 15% every time these commodities travelled a distance of eighty kilometres overland, while wine from Gascony arriving at Hull or in Ireland via Bordeaux only increased by a total of 10%, despite the long sea journey. 'In 1546 a few leagues overland raised the price of sugar from San Domingo almost more than 8000 kilometres by sea.' In 1828 Jean-Baptiste Say told his audience at the Collège de France that the inhabitants of the Atlantic towns in the United States 'warm themselves with coal from England which is over a thousand leagues away. Carriage over ten leagues overland is more expensive than transport over a thousand leagues by sea.' Steam ships were not yet in use at the time when Jean-Baptiste Say was teaching these elementary ideas (repeating the similar remarks of Adam Smith). Nevertheless maritime transport, with wood, sail and rudder, had long since attained its perfection, its limits of possibility, probably because of its increasing use.

This highlights the delay in road services and makes it all the more surprising. Roads had to wait for the first upsurge of the industrial revolution before men sought to develop their full potential between 1830 and 1840, on the threshold of the growth of the railways. From the 'turgotine' to the time just before the railway took over, a tremendous change on the roads showed what it would have been possible to achieve technically very much earlier. Networks were extended at that time (from one to eight between 1800 and 1850 in the United States, where everything was already assuming enormous proportions; more than doubling in the Austrian Empire between 1830 and 1847). Vehicles and posting houses were improved. Transport became more democratic. These changes were not the result of any precise technical discovery. They were simply the consequence of large investment, of deliberate systematic improvement, because the economic growth of the time made them 'profitable' and necessary.

3 Technology

Is there a history of technology in itself? Yes and no. In our day the answer is yes, to a certain extent: technology is linked with science and is trying to take over the world. But before the seventeenth century, and still in the eighteenth, science was only in its infancy, concerned with itself and its own foundations. It was not concerned with the crafts or with the practical problems of technology. Such exceptions as there were confirm the rule – Huygens' discoveries (the pendulum, 1656-7; the adjusting spiral, 1675) which revolutionised clock-making, or Pierre Bouguer's work, the *Traité du navire, de sa construction et de ses mouvements* (1746). Technology, a collection of recipes drawn from craftsmen's experience, somehow or other evolved unhurriedly. First-rate manuals were slow in coming: *De re metallica* by Georg Bauer (Agricola) in 1556, Agostino Ramelli's book *Le diverse et artificiose machine* in 1588, Vittorio Zonca's *Nuovo teatro di machine ed edifici* in 1621, *The Engineer's Pocket Handbook* by Bernard Forest in 1755. The professional 'engineer' emerged slowly. An 'engineer' in the fifteenth and sixteenth centuries was concerned with military matters, or hired out his services as architect, hydraulics expert, sculptor, or painter. Nor was there any systematic training before the eighteenth century. L'Ecole des Ponts et Chaussées was founded in Paris in 1743; L'Ecole des Mines, opened in 1783, was modelled on the Bergakademie created in 1765 in Freiburg, an old mining centre of Saxony which produced many engineers who later worked in Russia.

Gradual specialisation inevitably took place in the crafts. A Swiss artisan, Jost Amman, listed 90 different crafts in 1568. Diderot's *Encyclopédie* counted 250; the catalogue of the London firm of Pigot listed 826 different activities for the capital in 1826, some of them amusing and clearly marginal. But despite everything such specialisation was extremely slow. Existing solutions constituted a barrier. Strikes of printing workers in France towards the middle of the sixteenth century were 'provoked by changes in the printing press which resulted in a reduction in the number of workers'. No less characteristic was the workers' resistance to the use of the 'beetle', an improvement which made 'spring shears', enormous scissors to cut fabrics, easier to handle. And if the textile industry showed little development from the fifteenth to the midde of the eighteenth century, it was because its economic and social organisation, the elaborate division of operations and the poverty of its workers enabled it to get by somehow without making any change. There were so many obstacles that we can agree with James Watt when he confided to his friend Snell (26 July 1769) 'that in life there is nothing more foolish than inventing'. The reason was that the sanction of society was an invariable prerequisite of success in this sphere.

Nine times out of ten the patents of invention, serious or not, recorded on the pages of registers and dossiers in the Venetian Senate corresponded to the problems of the city: to make the waterways converging on the lagoon navigable; dig canals; raise water; drain swampy land; turn mills without resorting to hydraulic power (inevitable in this land of still water); work saws, millstones, hammers to powder the tannin or raw materials used to produce glass. Social considerations were uppermost.

An inventor who had the good fortune to please the prince could obtain a 'patent of invention or, more accurately, a licence enabling him to exploit an invention as a monopoly'. Louis xiv's government distributed large numbers of them, 'affecting the most varied techniques. For example, the process of economical heating in which Madame de Maintenon invested some capital.' But real discoveries remained all the more a dead letter because people did not need them – or did not think they needed them.

It was in vain that Baltasar de Rios, an ingenious inventor of the first years of Philip ii's reign, proposed to build a large-calibre cannon that could be dismantled and transported in separate pieces on the backs of a few hundred soldiers. The *Histoire naturelle de la fontaine qui brûle près de Grenoble* passed unnoticed in 1618; and yet the author, Jean Tardin, a doctor from Tournon, studied the 'natural gas content of the fountain' and described the distillation of coal in a retort, two centuries before gas lighting. A doctor from Périgord, Jean Rey, explained the expansion of lead and tin after calcination by 'the incorporation of the heavy part of the air' in 1630, over a century before Lavoisier. Schwenteer set out the principles of the electric telegraph as a result of which 'two individuals can communicate by means of the magnetic needle' in his *Délassements physico-mathématiques* in 1635. The magnetic needle had in fact to wait for Oersted's experiments in 1819. And 'to think that Schwenteer is less well known than the Chappe brothers!' An American, Bushbell, discovered the submarine, and a French military engineer, Duperron, the machine-gun, 'the military organ', in 1775.

All this was in vain. It was the same story with Newcomen's steam machine in 1711. Only one was in operation in England thirty years later, in 1742; on the continent two had been assembled. Success came in the following thirty years: sixty machines were built in Cornwall, to drain water from the tin mines. Nevertheless only five were in use for iron-smelting in France at the end of the eighteenth century. The delays in coke-smelting we have already mentioned were no less typical.

Thousands of factors obstructed progress. What could be done with a labour force threatened with unemployment? Montesquieu was already criticising the mills for taking work away from agricultural workers. A letter of 18 September 1754 from the marquis of Bonnac, French ambassador in Holland, asked for 'a good mechanic who can steal the secret of the different mills and machines in

Amsterdam which avoid the expenditure of the labour of many men'. But was it desirable to reduce this expenditure? The mechanic was not sent.

Finally there remains a matter of the greatest interest to the capitalist – the question of costs. Even when the industrial revolution in cotton was already well advanced English entrepreneurs continued to employ hand labour at home for spinning at a time when their mechanical weaving looms were already in full commission. This was because domestic production was sufficient to supply the weaving looms at much lower cost. The tempo of demand had to increase immeasurably before the use of mechanical spinning became general, well after its invention. One might well wonder what would have happened to it if the boom in English cotton had stopped prematurely.

All innovations, therefore, came up ten or a hundred times against the barrier obstructing them. It was a war marked by lost opportunities and in which rudimentary techniques very often outlived their usefulness. 'Hand millstones still turned at the end of the nineteenth century on the borders of regions conquered by the water-mill [in the thirteenth century]' wrote Daniel Faucher, 'and it is probable that this old equipment, which has come down from pre-history, was used again to crush clandestine grain during the Second World War.' Two centuries after Crécy, in July 1545, a small-scale French landing on the English coast in the neighbour-hood of the Isle of Wight was for a time successful – until archers intervened on behalf of the defenders. Just before the Invincible Armada (1588) Spain conceived the war against England on the pattern of Lepanto (1571), the last glorious battle between galleys in history. But Spain was not the only country to have anachronistically fought 'the last war' over again.

7

Money

When we bring money into the discussion we reach a higher level apparently outside the scope of this book. However a view of the whole picture from this vantage point enables us to understand monetary activity as a tool, a 'structure', a deep-seated regular feature of all slightly accelerated commercial life. Above all money is never an isolated reality; wherever it is, it influences all economic and social relationships. This makes it a wonderful indicator: a fairly reliable assessment can be made of all human activities down to the most humble level from the tempo of its circulation, or the way it becomes complicated or scarce. It is an important source of illumination for us.

Although it is an ancient fact of life, an ancient technique, money never ceases to surprise humanity. It seems to them mysterious and disturbing. First and foremost it is complicated in itself, for the monetary economy that goes with money was nowhere fully developed, even in a country like France in the sixteenth and seventeenth centuries, even in the eighteenth. It only made its way into certain regions and certain sectors. It continued to disturb the others. It was a novelty more because of what it brought with it than what it was itself. What did it actually bring? Sharp variations in prices of essential foodstuffs; incomprehensible relationships in which man no longer recognised either himself, his customs or his ancient values. His work became a commodity, himself a 'thing'.

The words Noël du Fail put into the mouths of old Breton peasants (1548) expressed their astonishment and confusion. If there was so much less abundance inside peasant homes, it was because:

both chickens and goslings are hardly allowed to come to perfection before they are taken to sell [to the town market of course] for money to be given either to the lawyer or the doctor (people [formerly] almost unknown), to the one in return for dealing harshly with his neighbour, disinheriting him, having him put in prison; to the other for curing him of a fever, ordering him to be bled (which thank God I have never tried) or for a clyster; all of which the late Tiphaine La Bloye of fond memory [a bone setter] cured, without so much mumbling, messing and antidotes, and almost for a Paternoster.

But now they have 'transferred from the towns to our villages' those spices and sweetmeats ranging from pepper to 'sugar-coated leeks' quite 'unknown' to our predecessors and harmful to man's body, 'without which, however, a banquet this century is tasteless, ill-arranged and graceless'. 'Upon my word,' replies one of the speakers, 'you say true, my friend, and it seems to me I am in a new world.' A fuddled comment, but not without sense. The ramifications it suggests could be applied to the whole of Europe.

Actually every society that is based on an ancient structure and opens its doors to money sooner or later loses its acquired equilibria and liberates forces thenceforth inadequately controlled. The new form of interchange jumbles things up, favours a few rare individuals and rejects the others. Every society has to turn over a new leaf under the impact.

As a result the extension of the monetary economy was a recurring drama quite as much in old countries accustomed to its presence as in countries it reached without their being immediately completely aware of it – Turkey under the Osmanlis at the close of the sixteenth century (when the Spahis' *timars* gave way to pure private property); Japan under the Tokugawas, which was at very nearly the same time in the grip of a typical urban and middle-class crisis. We can get a good picture of these basic processes by examining what is still happening under our own eyes in certain underdeveloped countries today, Black Africa for example, where depending on circumstances in over 60% or 70% of exchanges money is not used. Man can still live there for a time outside the market economy 'like a snail in his shell'. But he is a condemned man on temporary reprieve.

History shows us an endless procession of these condemned men – men destined not to escape their fate. Naïve and astonishingly patient, they suffered the blows of life without really knowing where they were coming from. There were rents for farms and dwellings, tolls, the salt-tax, purchases which had to be made at the town market, and there were taxes. Somehow or other these demands had to be met in cash and, if silver money was lacking, in copper coins. A Breton farmer brought his rent to Madame de Sévigné on 15 June 1680: an enormous weight of copper deniers amounting in all to thirty livres. Tolls were another example of the same process. They had long been levied in kind, but the declaration of 9 March 1547, issued in France at the instigation of the large salt merchants, made collection in money compulsory.

Hard cash thus found its way into everyday life by many different paths. The modern state was the great provider (taxes, mercenaries' pay in money, office-holders' salaries) and recipient of these transfers; but not the only one. Those in favourable positions sat back and received the contributions of others. And who were they? The tax-collector, the salt-tax collector, the pawnbroker, the landowner, the large merchant entrepreneur and the 'financier'. Their net stretched everywhere. And naturally this new wealthy class, like their equivalent today, did not arouse sympathy. The faces of the financiers look down on us from the museums. On more than one occasion the painter has conveyed the ordinary man's hatred and mistrust. But ultimately the course of events was scarcely diverted by such feelings, these keen or muted demands feeding a constant popular mistrust of money itself – a mistrust which the first economists did not easily discard. Over the whole world the great monetary circuits organised their axes and centres and set up profitable deals in 'royal commodities'. Magellan and del Cano sailed round the world in difficult and dramatic conditions. Francesco Carletti and Gemelli Careri, in 1590 and 1693 respectively, travelled round the globe with a bag containing pieces of eight and silver, and bundles of selected merchandise. And they returned.

Money is of course the symptom – as much as the cause – of the changes and revolutions in the monetary economy. It is inseparable from the movements that bring and create it. But former Western explanations too often considered money in isolation and resorted to comparisons, which nine times out of ten amounted to concealing a difficulty instead of tackling it head-on. Money was 'the blood of the social body' (a commonplace image well before Harvey's discovery); it was a 'commodity', a truth repeated over the centuries. 'For Money', according to William Petty (1655), 'is but the fat of the Body-politick, whereof too much doth as often hinder its Agility as too little makes it sick'. In 1820 a French economist explained that money facilitated the circulation of commodities, 'like oil, which makes a machine move more smoothly; when the wheels have been sufficiently greased an excess can only harm their action'. Such images are better than a very questionable proposition by John Locke, a good philosopher but a doubtful economist.

In 1696 he said that 'money was capital': this was more or less to confuse money with wealth, or measurement with the quantity measured.

All these definitions leave out the essential point – the monetary economy itself, the real reason for the existence of money. It is often said that money 'is only a veil'. In fact it only comes into being where men need it and can bear its cost. Its flexibility and complexity are functions of the flexibility and complexity of the economy that brings into being. There will ultimately be as many types of money and monetary systems as there are rhythms, systems and economic situations. Everything holds together in a process which is not mysterious after all, if only we frequently remind ourselves that there was a monetary economy of the *ancien régime*. It was unlike today's, very imperfect, with many levels and not extended to all mankind.

Barter remained the general rule over enormous areas between the fifteenth and the eighteenth centuries. But every time it was needed an early improvement brought the circulation of so-called primitive money, 'imperfect monies', such as cowry shells to its aid. However they are only imperfect in our eyes: the economies that welcomed them would hardly have been able to support any others. And often Europe's metallic money proved very inadequate. Like barter, metal had shortcomings; there was not always enough of it for its task. Then, for better or for worse, paper, or rather credit (*Herr Credit* as they mockingly said in Germany in the seventeenth century), offered its services. Basically this is the same process at a different level. In fact every lively economy breaks away from its monetary language and innovates by very reason of its movement, and all these innovations are then valuable as indications of the state of the economy concerned. Law's system and the contemporary English scandal of the South Sea Bubble were something quite other than post-war financial expedients or unscrupulous speculation, or share-outs between 'pressure groups' (Jakob van Klaveren). In France innovation took the form of the confused and ineffectual but obvious birth of credit, a difficult birth into the bargain. The Princess Palatine exclaimed: 'I have often wished that hell-fire would burn all these notes,' and swore that she understood nothing of the detestable system. This uneasiness was the beginning of the awareness of a new language. For money is a language (we too must be forgiven for using a metaphor); it calls for and makes possible dialogues and conversations; it exists as a function of these conversations.

If China did not possess a complicated monetary system (apart from the strange and long interlude of its paper money) it was because it did not need one in its relations with the neighbouring regions it exploited: Mongolia, Tibet, the Indian Archipelago, and Japan. If medieval Islam towered way above the Old Continent, from the Atlantic to the Pacific for centuries on end, it was because no state (Byzantium apart) could compete with its gold and silver money, *dinars* and *dirhems*. They were the instruments of its power.

If Europe finally perfected its money, it was because it had to overthrow the domination of the Muslim world. Likewise the monetary revolution that gradually invaded the Turkish Empire in the sixteenth century was largely due to its forced entry into the concert of Europe, which did not only consist of high-falutin exchanges of ambassadors. Japan closed its doors to the external world after 1638. But this is only a figure of speech: they stayed open to Chinese junks and Dutch liberty boats. The crack was wide enough for money and merchandise to make their way into the country and to force it to make the requisite response: the exploitation of its silver and copper mines. This effort was, at the same time, linked to its urban progress in the seventeenth century and the growth of a 'real middle-class civilisation' in privileged towns. Everything is connected.

Such evidence reveals a sort of monetary foreign policy in which the foreigner dictated the terms, both by his strength and by his weakness. When you talk to someone you are forced to find a common language, some common ground. The merit of long-distance trade, of large-scale commercial capitalism, was its ability to speak the language of world trade. Even if this trade, as we will see in our second book, was not the most important in volume (trade in spices was much less – even in value – than trade in corn in Europe), it was crucial because of its efficiency and the constructive change it introduced. Long-distance trade was the source of all rapid accumulation of money. It controlled the world of the *ancien régime* and money was at its command, following or preceding it as necessary. Trade steered the economies.

1 Economies and imperfect money

There would be no end to describing the elementary or very elementary forms monetary exchange assumed. It appeared in numerous ways and we must identify them. And the dialogue between perfect (if it exists) and imperfect money sheds light on the very root of our subject. If history is explanation it must come into full play here. But certain errors are to be avoided. It must not be thought that perfection and imperfection do not exist side by side and occasionally mingle; that these two gradations do not form one and the same problem; that all exchange does not necessarily thrive on differences in voltage (it does even today). Money is also a way of exploiting someone else inside and outside his own home, and of accelerating the whole process of exploitation.

A 'synchronic' view of the world in the eighteenth century still proves this to the point of obviousness. Over vast expanses and for millions of people we are still in Homer's period 'when the value of Achilles' shield was calculated in oxen'. Adam Smith pondered over this example. He wrote: 'The armour of Diomede, says Homer, cost only nine oxen; but that of Glaucus cost an hundred oxen.' An economist today would unhesitatingly call these simple types of humanity a Third World: there has always been a Third World. Its regular mistake was to agree to the terms of a dialogue which was always unfavourable to it. But it was often forced to.

Primitive money

A rudimentary form of money appears as soon as commodities are exchanged. A more desired or more plentiful commodity plays or tries to play the part of money, the standard of exchange. For example salt was money in the 'kingdoms' of Upper Senegal and Upper Niger, and in Abyssinia where cubes of salt, according to a French author in 1620, 'cut in the same way as rock crystal, the length of a finger', served indiscriminately as money and food, 'so that they can, with good reason, be said to eat their money in substance'. What a risk, this prudent Frenchman immediately exclaimed, 'of one day finding all their means melted and dissolved into water!' Cotton cloth played the same role on the banks of the Monomotapa and the shores of the Gulf of Guinea where they talked about a 'piece of India' in the Black slave trade to designate the quantity of cotton goods (from the Indies) that was equivalent to the price of a man. Later the term came to designate the man himself. Experts were soon to say that the 'piece of India' meant a slave between fifteen and forty years old.

Copper bracelets, called *manillas*, gold in powder form by weight, and horses were all money on this same African coast. Father Labat (1728) spoke of the magnificent horses the Moors resold to the Blacks.

'They price them,' he wrote, 'at fifteen slaves a piece. This is a quite absurd type of money, but every country has its own ways.' The English merchants established an unbeatable tariff in the first years of the eighteenth century in order to oust their competitors: 'They set the captive "piece of India" at four ounces of gold or thirty piastres [of silver] or three-quarters of a pound of coral, or seven pieces of Scottish cloth.' Meanwhile chickens 'so fat and so tender that they are worth as much as capons and fowl in other countries' were so numerous in some Black villages in the interior that their price was one chicken for a sheet of paper.

Sea-shells were another form of money on the African coasts. They varied in size and colour but the best known are the *zimbos* of the Congo shores, and the cowries. 'The *zimbos*,' wrote a Portuguese in 1619, 'are very small sea snails having no use and no value in themselves. The barbarism of earlier times introduced this money which is still used today.' And what is more it is still used in our day! Cowries too are small sea-shells, blue streaked with red, which were made up into strings. Whole boatloads of them were sent from the lost islands of the Indian Ocean, the Maldives and the Laccadives, to Africa, north-eastern India and Burma. Cowries formerly circulated in China by the routes Buddhism used to win the countries over to its faith. Moreover the cowry was not completely driven out by the Chinese *sapeke*; Yunnan, the wood and copper country, was to retain them for a long time. Recent research there has indicated late contracts relating to hiring and sales fixed in cowries.

No less strange was the money discovered by an astonished journalist who recently accompanied the Queen and Prince Philip to Africa: 'Natives in the interior of Nigeria,' he wrote, 'buy livestock, weapons, agricultural products, cloth, even their wives, not with Her Britannic Majesty's pounds sterling, but with strange coral money minted [or rather manufactured] in Europe. These coins ... come from Italy where they are called *olivette*; they are specially manufactured in Tuscany in a shop working Leghorn coral which has continued in existence to the present day.' *Olivette* are coral cylinders, perforated in the centre and grooved on their outside surface. They are in circulation in Nigeria, Sierra Leone, on the Ivory Coast, in Liberia and even farther afield. In Africa the purchaser carries them at his belt on a string. Everybody can calculate his wealth *de visu*. Behanzin bought a specially manufactured *olivetta*, weighing a kilogram and of a marvellous colour, for a thousand pounds sterling in 1902.

But we could not draw up an exhaustive list of these unexpected forms of money. They are found everywhere. Iceland, according to regulations of 1413 and 1426, had a centuries-old market price list for commodities, payable in dried fish (1 fish for one horseshoe, 3 for a pair of women's shoes, 100 for a barrel of wine, 120 for a cask of butter, etc.). In Alaska, and in Russia under Peter the Great, furs fulfilled the same role, or rather in Russia squares of fur which sometimes cluttered up the military paymasters' desks. In colonial America it was tobacco, sugar, or cocoa, depending on the region concerned. The Indians in North America used little cylinders cut from blue or violet sea shells and threaded on a string. This was *wampum*, which European colonists continued to use legitimately until 1670 and which indeed continued to exist up to at least 1725. Similarly the Congo in the broad sense (including Angola) witnessed the awakening of a series of markets and active trading networks between the sixteenth and eighteenth centuries, both of them probably in the vital service of barter, of trade with the whites and their agents, the *pombeiros*, often settled deep in the interior. Two types of pseudo-money were in circulation: *zimbos* and pieces of material. The sea-shells were standardised: a gauged sieve was used to separate large from small (one large equalled ten small). The cloth money also varied in size; a *lubongo* was as large as a sheet of paper, a *mpusu* the size of a table napkin. This money was usually in sets of tens and therefore formed a scale of values, with multiples and sub-multiples like metallic money. It was thus possible to mobilise large sums. In 1649 the king of the Congo assembled 1500 loads of material, worth approximately 40 million Portuguese *reis*.

The fate of this pseudo-money after the European impact (whether cowries in Bengal, *wampum* after 1670, or the Congo *zimbos*) proves identical in every case where it can be investigated – monstrous and catastrophic inflation, caused by an increase in reserves, an accelerated and even hectic circulation, and a concomitant devaluation in relation to the dominant European money. And 'counterfeit' primitive money was even added to the confusion! The production of counterfeit *wampum* in glass paste in the nineteenth century by European workshops caused the total disappearance of the old money. The Portuguese had shown greater foresight; they had seized 'fishing grounds of money' (that is to say *zimbos*) off the coasts of Loanda island in Angola in about 1650. But *zimbos* had already been devalued by 10% between 1575 and 1650.

It must really be concluded that in every case primitive money was genuine money and had the appearance and properties of money. Its vicissitudes sum up the history of the clash between primitive economies and advanced economies, which is what the eruption of Europeans on the seven seas of the world meant.

Barter: the crux of monetary economies

What is less well known is that almost equally uneven relationships were perpetuated inside the 'civilised' countries themselves. Under the fairly thin skin of the monetary economies, primitive activities continued and blended into the others, in the regular meetings at town markets and the riotous fairs. Rudimentary economies survived in the heart of Europe, encircled by monetary life which did not destroy them but rather kept them as so many internal colonies within easy reach. Adam Smith (1775) spoke of a Scottish village 'where it is not uncommon, I am told, for a workman to carry nails instead of money to the baker's shop or the alehouse'. There are later and even more convincing examples. Corsica, according to the evidence of ethnographers, was not annexed by a really efficient monetary economy until after the First World War. The change had hardly occurred in certain mountainous regions of 'French' Algeria before the Second World War. This was one of the underlying dramas of the Aurès up to the period around the 1930s. We can imagine comparable dramas as the modernity of the monetary order caught up with innumerable small closed worlds in certain rural or mountainous districts in eastern Europe or western America, at different times but by comparable processes despite the chronological difference.

The example of Russia shows the same thing. At Novgorod at the beginning of the fifteenth century 'they still only used ... small Tartar coins, scraps of marten's skin, bits of stamped leather. They only began to mint very coarse silver money in 1425. And Novgorod was still in advance of the Russian economy, within which exchanges were made in kind for a long time.' They only began to mint money regularly with the arrival of German coins and ingots (because the Russian balance of trade was favourable) in the sixteenth century. And then only on a modest scale. And the minting of money still often depended on private initiative. Barter continued in this immense country. It only receded with the reign of Peter the Great. Regions until then isolated were put into contact with each other and a national market took shape. Russia undeniably lagged behind the West: the crucial gold resources of Siberia were only really worked after 1820. But many 'backward' areas were still to be found in the French and English countryside in the eighteenth century and the comments made about Russia by a French economist, Mercier de la Rivière (1775), were certainly exaggerated. 'He thought we walked on all fours,' Catherine II wrote to Voltaire, 'and very civilly took the trouble of coming along to set us on our hind legs.'

Colonial America also presented a highly significant scene. The monetary economy only reached the large towns of the mining countries there – Mexico, Peru – and regions nearer Europe, the West Indies and Brazil (Brazil was soon to be in an advantageous position because of its gold mines). They were not perfect monetary economies; far from it. But prices in them did fluctuate – already a sign of a certain economic maturity – whereas up to the nineteenth century prices did not fluctuate in either Argentina or Chile (which nevertheless produced copper and silver). They were remarkably steady and, one might say, still-born.

Exchanges of commodity for commodity were frequent there. The feudal or semi-feudal grants of the colonial governments were a symptom of the scarcity of hard cash. Imperfect money therefore naturally played its part: bits of copper in Chile, tobacco in Virginia, 'card money' in French Canada, *tlacos* in New Spain. These *tlacos* (from a Mexican word) stood for an eighth of a *réal*. They were small coins, created by retail dealers, proprietors of shops called *mestizas* which sold everything from bread and alcohol to silk fabrics from China. Each of these shop-owners issued small wood, lead or copper coinage with his own mark. The counters were occasionally exchanged against real silver *pesos* and circulated amongst a small public. Some of them got lost. All of them lent themselves to speculation, often sordid. Such a situation arose because silver money only consisted of large coins, which in practice passed over the heads of people of small means. In addition every fleet that reached Spain drained the country of its silver. Finally, the attempt to create copper money in 1542 was a failure. There was really no option but to be content with the defective system of almost primitive money. Was this so different from what happened in France in the fourteenth century? John the Good's ransom was enough to empty the country of its coin, so the king minted leather money which he bought back a few years later!

The same difficulties occurred in the English colonies, both before and after independence. In November 1721 a Philadelphia merchant wrote to one of his correspondents who had settled in Madeira: 'I had intended to send a little corn, but creditors here are reluctant and money so scarce that we begin to be, or rather we have for some time already been, racked by lack of a means of payment, without which trade is quite a puzzling occupation.'

Clavière and Brissot, well-known figures in the French Revolution, described a similar situation in their book on the United States in 1791.

Instead of money incessantly going backwards and forwards into the same hands, there they supply their needs in the countryside by direct reciprocal exchanges. The tailor and bootmaker go and do the work of their calling at the home of the farmer who requires it and who, most frequently, provides the raw material for it and pays for the work in goods. These sorts of exchanges cover many objects; they write down what they give and what they receive on both sides and at the end of the year they settle a large variety of exchanges – which would only be done with a considerable quantity of money in Europe – with a very small quantity of coin. [Thus] a means of wide circulation without coin. . . . [is created].

This eulogy of barter and services paid for in kind as a progressivist innovation of young America is amusing. In the seventeenth century and even in the eighteenth payments in kind were very frequent in Europe; they were the relics of a past in which they had been the general rule. There would be no end to the list (following the example of Alfons Dopsch) – cutlers from Solingen, miners and weavers from Pforzheim, peasant clock-makers from the Black Forest, all were paid in kind, in victuals, salt, cloth, brass wire, measures of grain, all of which were excessively priced. This was the *Trucksystem* (barter) which existed in Holland, England and France just as much as in Germany in the fifteenth century. Even German 'officials' of the Empire, *a fortiori* municipal officials, received part of their salary in kind. And how many schoolmasters were still paid in poultry, butter and corn in the last century! Indian villages at all periods also paid their craftsmen (the craft was handed down from father to son in artisan castes) in foodstuffs, and *baratto* (barter) was whenever possible the prudent rule of all large merchants in the Levantine ports from the fifteenth century. Those experts in credit, the sixteenth-century Genoese, were probably following in the steps of this tradition of barter when they thought of turning the fairs known as Besançon fairs, where bills of exchange from all Europe were settled, into positive clearing-houses. A Venetian in 1602 was astounded by the millions of ducats which changed hands at Plaisance (the site of these fairs), with nothing to show for it in the end except a few handfuls of écus.

2 Outside Europe: early economies and metallic money

Between the primitive economies and Europe, Japan, Islam, India and China represented intermediate stages half-way towards an active and complete monetary life.

Japan and the Turkish Empire

The monetary economy was established in Japan during the seventeenth century. However, the circulation of gold, silver and copper coins barely touched the masses. The old money – rice – continued in use. Loads of herrings were still exchanged for loads of rice. But the changeover gained ground. The peasants soon had enough copper coins to pay their dues in money on new fields not planted with rice (the old system of labour obligations and allowances in kind being in force for the remaining fields). In the western part of Japan, on the *shogun's* domains, a third of peasant dues was paid in money. Certain *daimios* (great nobles) soon owned such large quantities of gold and silver that they even paid their own *samurais* (nobles in their service) with it. This development was slow because of interference by the government, hostile attitudes to the new system and the *samurais'* moral philosophy which forbade 'them to think, let alone speak, of money. The monetary world of Japan, confronted with the peasant and feudal world, was at least threefold: governmental, merchant and urban – which meant revolutionary. The undeniable symptom of a certain degree of maturity was ultimately the fluctuations in prices (with which we are familiar) and especially in the price of rice and the peasants' money dues; or the drastic devaluation of 1695, determined by the *shogun* in the hope of 'increasing money'.

Islam had a monetary organisation at its disposal from the Atlantic to India, but it was old and remained enclosed in its traditions. The only development there benefited Persia, an active junction, the Ottoman Empire, and Istanbul, an exceptional case. In the enormous capital city during the eighteenth century price lists fixed the prices of commodities and *ad valorem* customs duties in national currency.

Exchanges on all the great markets of the West – Amsterdam, Leghorn, London, Marseilles, Venice, Vienna – were clinched there.

The gold currency in circulation were the *sultanins*, called *fonduc* or *fonducchi* (whole coins, half coins, quarter coins); silver money – the Turkish piastres known as *grouck* or *grouch*, the *para* and the *aspre* – had become money of account. A *sultanin* was worth five piastres, a piastre forty *paras*, a *para* three *aspres*; the *mekir* or *gieduki*, worth a quarter of an *aspre*, was the smallest real money (silver and copper) in circulation. This Istanbul currency was sent far afield to Egypt and the Indies via Bassora, Baghdad, Mosul, Aleppo, and Damascus, where colonies of Armenian merchants stimulated trade. A certain monetary deterioration is unmistakable. Foreign coins were at a premium compared with Ottoman money; the venetian *sequin*, a golden coin, was worth 5·5 piastres; the Dutch *thaler* and Ragusan *écu*, silver coins, were quoted at 60 *paras*. The fine Austrian *thaler*, known as *Carl Grouch*, changed hands at 101, even 102 *paras*. A Venetian document of 1688 already indicates that it was possible to make up to 30% on *réals* from Spain (sent to Egypt). Another showed that consignments of *sequins* or *ongari* bought in Venice made from 12% to 17·5% in Istanbul in 1671. The Turkish Empire thus drew money from the West; its own circulation demanded it.

There is another aspect to the matter: in the Levant 'all money [which arrives] is melted down and sent to Persia and the Indies after having been converted into ingots'. They would then be minted in the form of Persian *larins* or Indian rupees. Moreover, other coins from the West arrived intact in either Ispahan or Delhi, and by other routes. This would have proved to Turkey that however badly off you are (and Turkey was) there is always someone worse off. The transformation of coins into ingots shows that confidence did not reign from Syria to Bengal and beyond.

India

An economic system originating in the Mediterranean and spreading as far as Bengal reached the Indian continent very early on. A real monetary 'conquest' was made. Five or six centuries before the Christian era gold and silver coins were minted in Hindustan though immense zones still retained a natural economy, rice being used as a monetary standard for a long time (and not only in religious institutions). Because of its inertia and its size India always withstood a systematic monetary conquest in the same way as it withstood repeated conquests by the barbarians.

There were approximately three attempts at monetary conquest, in the thirteenth, sixteenth and eighteenth centuries. None was complete or had the effect of standardisation. A distinction somehow or other persisted between the north, from the Indus and Ganges valleys, which was the zone of Muslim rule, and the southern peninsula where Hindu kingdoms survived, including the long-prospering kingdom of Vijnayanagar.

Where there was a system operating in the north it was a silver/copper bi-metallism, the lower-ranking copper coins being far and away the most numerous. The silver coins – rupees (or their sub-multiples), sometimes round, sometimes square – appeared in the sixteenth century. They only affected the upper level of economic life: below this level was copper, and also bitter almonds (that curious primitive money which originated in Persia). The south had gold and a few silver and copper coins, and sea-shell money. The gold coins were what were known in the West as *pagodas*, very thick coins but with a narrow diameter, 'which were worth as much as the Venetian *sequin*' (in 1695), their metal being finer 'than that of the Spanish *pistole*'.

Monetary chaos persisted in the eighteenth century. Coins were struck at innumerable mints, the one at Surat, the great port of Gujerat, being the largest. If quality and alloy were equal, local money was at a premium. Since minting was frequent, intervention with an eye to gain on the part of the princes increased the value of recent money even if, as was often the case, it was inferior to the old. Gemelli Careri advised the merchants in 1695 to strike (or rather restrike) their silver coins 'to the coinage of the land . . . and above all the die should be of the same year otherwise a loss of half a per cent will be incurred. This capacity for minting money is found in all the towns on the Great Mogul's frontiers.'

Finally, as India in fact produced no gold, silver, copper or cowries, other countries' money came to it, passed through its ever-open door and provided it with the basis of its monetary raw material. Encouraged by the chaos the Portuguese minted coins to compete with Indian coins. In the same way there were (until 1788) Batavian and Persian rupees.

A systematic drain on precious metals from the whole world continued, primarily to the profit of the Great Mogul and his states.

The reader must take into consideration [explained a traveller (1695)] that all the gold and silver which circulates in the world ultimately goes to the Great Mogul, as if to its centre. It is known that the metals that leave America go partly to Turkey and partly to Persia, via Smyrna, for silk, after having roamed over several European kingdoms. But the Turks cannot do without coffee from Yemen or Arabia Felix. No more can the Arabs, Persians and Turks do without commodities from the Indies. This means that they send large sums of money by the Red Sea to Moka near Bab el Mandeb, to Bassorah at the bottom of the Persian Gulf, to Bandar Abessi and to Gommeron, and from there take it to the Indies on their ships.

The Dutch, English and Portuguese also made all their purchases in the Indies against gold and silver because 'we can only get from the Indians the merchandise we want to transport to Europe with hard cash'.

The picture is hardly exaggerated. But, as nothing is free, India had to pay dearly for its precious metals. This was one of the reasons for its austere life and also for the rise of its compensating industries, notably the textiles of Gujerat, a real driving-force of the Indian economy even before the arrival of Vasco da Gama. A considerable export trade to countries near and far was carried on. Gujerat with its cotton weavers must have been like Netherlands wool centres in the middle ages. From the sixteenth century an enormous burst of industrialisation began there and spread towards the Ganges. In the eighteenth century cotton prints flooded into Europe. They were imported by British merchants in large quantities until the moment came when England preferred to manufacture them itself and competed with them.

Quite naturally the monetary history of India followed the movements of the distant West. It was as though the resumption of the minting of money, at least in Delhi after 1540 or 1542, had to wait for the arrival in Europe and the subsequent departure from Europe of American silver. For the pieces of eight, the famous *reales de a ocho*, soon arrived in India via Persian or Hindu merchants or Portuguese ships on the Cape route. There was thus a recognisable bond unifying the world. Later on India suffered the impact of the great world depression of the seventeenth century. Around 1627, after the reign of Jahangir, minting of copper, hitherto relatively plentiful, slowed down and the part played by cowries increased, although copper *pachas* did not entirely disappear. This obvious crisis, from Surat to Bengal, only receded with the eighteenth century and the European revival.

China

China can only be understood in the context of the primitive neighbouring economies linked to it and on which it depended: Tibet, Japan (almost up to the sixteenth century), the Indian archipelago and Indochina. As exceptions prove the rule we shall exclude certain areas from this general heading of primitive economies: Malacca, a market junction to which money flowed of its own accord; the western point of Sumatra, with its gold towns and spices; and the island of Java, already fairly populated but where copper coins, *caixas*, followed the Chinese pattern. Java was still only at an elementary stage in its monetary life.

China thus lived near to countries that had remained in their infancy. In Japan rice had long served as money; in the Indian archipelago and Indochina it was Chinese *caixas* imported or imitated, copper 'gongs', or gold dust by weight or weights of tin or copper; in Tibet it was coral brought from the distant West, and gold dust.

All this accounts for the backwardness of China itself and at the same time a certain strength of its 'dominant' monetary system. It had been able to enjoy a lazy monetary history with no risks involved simply by preserving its status in relation to its neighbours. But let us not forget that stroke of genius – paper money – which lasted roughly from the ninth century to the fourteenth and was particularly effective in the Mongol period when China was simultaneously opened to the world of the steppes, Islam and the West by routes from central Asia.

Apart from providing the internal facilities for payments between provinces paper money avoided the need to export cash. The emperor collected certain taxes in notes; foreign merchants (Pegolotti recalled) had to change their coin into notes. Paper was the Chinese answer to the situation in the thirteenth and fourteenth centuries – a means of surmounting the difficulties inherent in an outmoded copper or silver circulation.

But the great Mongol route westwards was broken with the depression in the fourteenth century and the victory of the peasant rising that brought to power the national dynasty of the Mings. Issues of notes continued but inflation was making itself felt. In 1378 seventeen paper *caixas* were worth thirteen copper *caixas*. Seventy years later, in 1448, one thousand notes were required for three *caixas* of cash. Inflation got the upper hand all the more easily because paper recalled the hated Mongol regime. The state abandoned it; only private banks still put paper for local needs into circulation.

Thenceforth China had only one type of money, *caixas*, *caches*, or copper *sapekes*, as the Europeans called them. They were an old creation, having appeared 200 years before the Christian era. They had changed slightly over the centuries but had been maintained in the face of strong competition from salt and grain and a more serious challenge from silk in the eighth century.

In the early days of the Ming dynasty these coins were always made of a mixture of copper and lead (four parts lead to six of copper) 'which means that they break very easily in the fingers'. They were circular, stamped on only one side and pierced by a square hole. A small cord was threaded through the hole so that they could be made into strings of a hundred or a thousand. 'It is usual to give,' noted Father de Magaillans (who died in 1677 and whose book appeared in 1688), 'a cord of a thousand deniers for one *écu*, or Chinese *tael*; and this exchange is made in banks and public booths intended for that purpose.' Obviously Chinese 'deniers' were too small to fulfil every function. Silver valued by weight was a sort of superior currency. Coins were not used in the case of gold (which played a very limited role) and silver. Instead, melted-down ingots were employed 'in the shape of a small boat . . . in Macao they are called *paes*, gold or silver "loaves"'. They were of different values, Father de Magaillans continued. 'The gold loaves are worth one, two, ten and up to twenty or a thousand *écus*; the silver ones are half an *écu*, one *écu*, ten, twenty, fifty and sometimes one hundred and three hundred *écus*.' The Portuguese Father persisted in talking in *deniers* and *écus* but his meaning is clear. We will only specify that the *tael* (the *écu*) was most frequently a money of account, an expression we will return to later.

In fact only the silver ingot was important at this upper level. It used to be said of silver and gold in Macao: 'Silver is blood and gold is a commodity.' Europeans made quite large profits by buying gold because for a long time it was worth only four or six times its weight in silver and not twelve times as in the West.

But the silver – 'white as snow' because it was mixed with antimony – was the basic instrument of large-scale exchanges in China, all the more so under the Mings (1368–1644) as a monetary and capitalist economy came to life and tended to enlarge its scope and increase its services. We should remember the rush on the Chinese silver mines (1596) and the enormous scandal that ensued in 1605.

Silver loaves could not always be used whole in everyday life. Buyers 'cut them up with steel scissors they carry for this purpose, and divide them into coins which are large or small according to the price of their purchase'. Each of these fragments had to be weighed. Buyer and seller used small Roman scales.

There is scarcely a Chinaman [one European said (between 1733 and 1735)] however wretched he may be, who does not carry scissors and a precision scale around with him. The first is used to cut gold and silver and is called a *trapelin*; the other, which is used to weigh the materials, is called a *litan*. The Chinese are so adept at this operation that they will often cut two *liards'* [half an old farthing] worth of silver or five sous' worth of gold so accurately that they will not have to do it again.

Our witness admired the system.

Reflecting [he writes] on the multiplicity of our coins in Europe, I deem it an advantage for the Chinese to have neither gold nor silver coins. The reason for this, in my opinion, is that since these metals are considered as commodities in China, the quantity which gets in there cannot effect such a considerable rise in the prices of goods and merchandise as in a country where silver money is very common. . . . Moreover the price of everything is so well controlled in China that one hardly ever buys things at above their usual value in relation to each other. Only Europeans are the dupes of their good faith. Because it is a very common occurrence for the Chinese to sell them what they buy at above the price current in the country.

This is a rather over-simplified explanation: if China experienced a certain relative stability of prices, it was primarily because its metal stocks were low. It attracted many kinds of silver coins in free circulation over the world, but it only possessed a few mines and consequently only melted-down silver brought by 'foreign nations, particularly American silver. This is why the Emperor of China calls the King of Spain the King of Silver' (1695). The coins concerned at this period were piastres or pieces of eight ('the best were those from Mexico . . . in China, they were worth one per cent more than those from Peru'). But they only arrived in limited quantities and were dispersed over its immense market – the first reason why prices did not show a marked rise. China was too vast to have been inundated with silver, as so many historians have maintained. The proof was the enormous purchasing power of a single piece of eight. That it was worth from 700 to 1100 *caixas* according to province (and the many different currencies in circulation) may not tell us a great deal; but in 1695 a single one of these thin silver coins 'could buy the best bread in the world for six months'. The remark obviously refers to one person's consumption, in this case a traveller from the West who took advantage of the extraordinary cheapness of corn flour, not appreciated in China. Yet the same small coin, handed over once a month, also enabled our traveller to hire a Chinese servant 'to do the cooking', and a *taes* (a *tael*, or 1000 *caixas*, still almost equivalent to a piece of eight at that period) bought him the services of a Chinese servant of 'mature' age, who received a further 'four pieces of eight [a lump sum] for the main-tenance of his family' during the servant's absence when he followed Careri to Peking.

The colossal hoarding of wealth in the imperial treasury must also be taken into account (not to mention hoarding by the rich and dishonest). Most of this mass of immobilised money depended on government decisions and measures, and the government used it to influence prices. This is brilliantly explained in a correspondence between Jesuit fathers in 1779. According to them the value of money in relation to things varied under the Tsing dynasty, meaning that prices had on the whole risen. Moreover, whether silver was money in the strict sense or not (of course it was not), China lived under a sort of silver/copper bi-metallism. The internal rate of exchange was between *sapekes* on the one hand and on the other a Chinese 'ounce' of silver, weighed on the so-called kwan-si scales or the emperor's scales, or against some piece of eight sold by a Western merchant. But the silver/copper exchange rate varied from day to day, according to season, year and above all issues of silver and copper ordered by the imperial government. These issues were intended to maintain a normal monetary circulation and to bring the copper/silver relationship back into balance every time it was necessary, by releasing silver when silver was too highly priced, or copper when copper was. 'Our government,' said the Chinese Jesuit, 'makes the respective value of silver and money rise and fall ... it has organised this expedient for the whole Empire.' Control was all the easier in that the state owned all the copper mines in China.

Money cannot therefore be said to have been a neutral tool in China, nor prices always marvellously stable. Intervention was necessary. And furthermore prices of some commodities – notably rice – did move. The Chinese system therefore allowed the possibility of movement. In the eighteenth century prices rose in Canton under the impact of European trade, following a double revolution in money and credit which deeply permeated the old economy of the

Middle Empire. A seaboard economy linked to the piastre over-turned the internal economy linked to the *sapake*. But the *sapake* was not as fundamentally inert and calm as is generally supposed.

In view of this the reader will perhaps accept our way of seeing things: in monetary matters China was more primitive and less sophisticated than India. But its system had much more cohesion and obvious unity. China did not have the rest of the world's cash.

3 Precious metals and metallic economies in Europe

Europe stood alone and was already enormous. It experienced the whole gamut of monetary experience. On the lowest level, and to a greater extent than is usually believed, were barter, self-subsistence and primitive money – old expedients, indirect means of economising on hard cash. At a higher level came relatively plentiful supplies of metallic money – gold, silver and copper. Finally there were many kinds of credit, from the pawnbroking activities of the Lombards and Jewish merchants to the bills of exchange and speculation of the great markets.

But these activities do not give the whole picture. The system was projected over the whole world, a vast net thrown over the wealth of the other continents. It was no minor detail that for Europe's gain the treasures of America were exported as far as the Far East, to be converted into local money or ingots in the sixteenth century. Europe was beginning to devour, to digest the world. We should resist those past and present economists who seem to feel sorry for it, doubting its economic health and maintaining that it suffered a permanent monetary haemorrhage in the direction of the Far East. Europe certainly did not die of it. In any case a man who bombards a town about to be captured loses bullets, powder and effort in the process.

What precious metals?

A metallic 'money' is at first glance a collection of related coins: one is worth a tenth, a sixteenth, a twentieth of another, and so on. In the West, as elsewhere, it is also the simultaneous utilisation of several precious metals. The West retained three metals: gold, silver and copper, with the inconveniences and advantages of such a diversity. The advantages were that it answered the varied requirements of exchange. Each metal with its coins dealt with a series of transactions. In a system exclusively of gold coins it would be difficult to settle small-scale everyday purchases. On the other hand large-scale payments would present difficulties in a system confined to copper. In fact every metal played its part: gold, reserved for princes, large merchants (even the Church); silver for ordinary transactions; copper naturally for the smallest. Copper was the 'black' money of people of small means and the poor. Mixed with a little silver it blackened quickly and deserved its name.

The health of an economy can be guessed almost at first glance from its dominant metal. In Naples in 1751 gold was hoarded and silver left the country. Despite its small volume (1·5 million ducats against 6 million of silver and 10 of gold) copper was used to settle the bulk of transactions because it circulated rapidly and, however inferior it was, 'it stayed where it was'. It was the same story in Spain: in 1724 'the major part of payments is made . . . in alloy [copper with a little silver added]; its transport is very cumbersome and expensive; moreover it is customary to accept it by weight. . . .' This was a deplorable custom, according to a contemporary, at a time when alloy was used only as small change in France and Holland. But the other powers only permitted Spain to remain the apparent mistress of the silver of the New World on condition that it allowed these distant treasures to circulate as a money 'common to all nations', to drain itself for the benefit of others. Spain became 'a mere channel' for silver from its colonies, as Portugal was for gold. Careri called at Cadiz in 1694 with a fleet of galleons; in one day he saw 'over a hundred vessels arrive in the Bay coming to collect silver in return for the goods they had sent to the Indies'. 'The greater part of this metal which goes on the galleons,' he concluded, 'enters the purses of foreign nations.'

On the other hand either silver or gold asserted its role in the thriving countries. In 1699 the London Chamber of Commerce described silver money 'as more useful and with more uses than gold'. But the vast inflation of gold in the eighteenth century was not far distant. In 1774 England recognised gold as legal and common money. Thenceforth silver played only a supplementary role. France, however, continued to back silver, as we shall see.

This is of course a very rough outline of the rules in force. There were obvious exceptions. While the large markets were warding off copper money like the plague in the first part of the seventeenth century, Portugal was deliberately seeking it out – but with the intention of sending it beyond the Cape of Good Hope to the Indies, as was its custom. We should therefore be wary of useful but over-simplified tests. Even gold can mislead us. Thus Turkey under the Osmanli dynasty belonged to a gold zone as far back as the fifteenth century (based on bullion from Africa and Egyptian coins). But gold was relatively plentiful in the Mediterranean and Europe before 1550. It fed a still inactive currency in Turkey and the main thing soon was the transit of silver coins from Europe to the Far East across this separate zone.

In favour of the general application of Gresham's Law

The predominance of one type of money (gold, silver, copper) also came about as a result of constant interaction between the different metals. The structure of the system resulted in their being in competition with each other. Obviously copper normally played the least important role because the value of small change bore no exact relationship to its metal-content. But there was still the possibility of surprises. Precisely because of its reasonable price copper was the convenient medium for powerful and elementary inflations all over Europe in the seventeenth century. This was especially true of Germany and Spain (up to 1680), of economically sick countries that had found no other solution to their difficulties. Even outside Europe, for example in Persia in about 1660, copper small change – 'half scraped away, red as magpie's flesh' – invaded the markets and 'silver is becoming very scarce from day to day in Hispan (Ispahan)'.

Having said this, let us leave copper out of the discussion. There remains the formidable aristocracy of gold and silver. Their production was irregular and never very flexible, so that depending on circumstances, one of the two metals would be relatively more plentiful than the other; then, with varying degrees of slowness, the situation would reverse, and so on. This resulted in turmoils and catastrophes and especially in the slow, powerful oscillations which were a feature of the monetary *ancien régime*. It is a well-known truth that 'silver and gold are hostile brothers'. Karl Marx adopted the formula for his own purposes: 'Wherever silver and gold continue legally side by side as money,' he wrote, 'attempts to treat them as one and the same material have always been in vain.' The dispute has never ended.

Ancient theoreticians would have liked a fixed relationship giving gold twelve times the value of silver for equal weights. This was certainly not the general rule from the fifteenth to the eighteenth century. The ratio at that time varied frequently around and beyond this so-called 'natural' relationship. In the long term, the scales sometimes tipped towards one metal, sometimes towards the other (discounting temporary or local variations that need not detain us at present).

Thus in the long term the value of silver increased from the thirteenth to the sixteenth century, roughly until around 1550. At the risk of straining the meaning of the word, we might say that there was gold inflation at that time lasting for centuries. The gold minted in Europe came from Hungary, the Alps, from the distant gold-washers of the Sudan, then from early colonial America. Gold coins were the easiest of all to gather together, and it was them that the princes used to further their designs, that Charles VIII minted before his expedition to Italy, that Francis I and Charles V spent on their battles.

Who profited from this relative profusion of gold? Inevitably the holders of silver bullion or coins, which means the Augsburg merchants, owners of the silver mines in Bohemia and the Alps. In their midst were those uncrowned kings, the Fuggers. Of the two, silver bullion was the stable value at that time.

On the other hand silver was over-plentiful after 1550 and up to 1680, with the modern technique (amalgam) used in the American silver mines. In its turn silver was the force behind powerful and sustained inflation. Gold became scarce and increased in value. Those who backed gold early, for example the Genoese in Antwerp from 1553, had bet on the winner.

The scales tilted back slightly again after 1680 with the beginning of gold-washing in Brazil. Until the end of the century the situation could best be described as stable; then the slight movement became stronger. The relationship between the two metals in Germany, at the Frankfurt and Leipzig fairs, averaged 1 to 15·27 between 1701 and 1710. It moved to 1 to 14·93 between 1741 and 1750. At least silver no longer fell in value as it had done before the gold from Brazil had come into circulation. This was because world production of gold had at least doubled between 1720 and 1760. A small but significant fact: gold reappeared in Burgundy in peasants' hands around 1756.

In this slow, long-term process, every movement of one of the metals involved governed the movement of the other. This is a simple law. The relative abundance of gold in the last years of the fifteenth century launched the silver mines of Germany. So too the first development of Brazilian gold around 1680 stimulated the silver mines of Potosi (which were in great need of stimulus) and even more the mines of New Spain, with the great wealth of Guanajuato and the Veta Madre vein.

In fact these oscillations simply come under the law known as Gresham's law – although Elizabeth of England's counsellor was in no way its author. Its terms are well known: bad money drives out good. Gold or silver coins took turns, according to the long-term situation, to play the role of the less 'good' money driving the other, the better, into the woollen stockings of speculators or hoarders. Naturally such spontaneous activity could be precipitated by inopportune action on the part of governments who spent their time readjusting money, raising prices of gold or silver coins according to the oscillations of the market, in the hope (rarely realised) of reestablishing equilibrium.

If the rise was economically justified nothing happened, or nothing deteriorated. If the rise was too high, for example when gold currency was concerned, all the gold coins from neighbouring countries flowed to the country where they were at a premium, whether that country were France under Henry III or Titian's Venice. If the situation persisted the inordinately over-valued gold money played the role of bad money. It drove out silver money. This was often the case in Venice and, continuously from 1537, the bizarre situation in Sicily. Since there were advantages to be gained from sending silver from Venice or Sicily to North Africa and even more to the Levant, we can be sure that these apparently absurd movements were never without reason, whatever one might think of them and whatever the theoreticians of the period tell us about them.

In these affairs, circumstances could change overnight. In Paris Edmond Jean François Barbier noted in his journal in July 1723: 'One only sees gold in business; it has reached a point where it costs up to twenty sous ... to change one louis [into silver coins]. ... On the other hand we weigh out the louis ... and it is great nuisance. You need a precision scale in your pocket.'

Flight, saving and hoarding

The monetary system in Europe suffered from two incurable diseases. On the one hand there were external flights of precious metals; on the other, metals were immobilised by being saved and hoarded. As a result the engine incessantly and irreparably lost some of its fuel.

Precious metals had never stopped leaving the Western circuits, primarily for the Indies and China, even in the far-off times of the Roman Empire. Silk, pepper, spices, drugs and pearls from the Far East had to be paid for in either silver or gold to force them westwards. As a result Europe's balance remained in deficit in this respect, especially – until about the 1820s – in relation to China. This perennial flight became part of the economic structure of the world: precious metals flowed to the Far East by the Levant route, the Cape route, even across the Pacific. They went in the form of Spanish pieces-of-eight, *reales de a ocho*, in the sixteenth century; in the form of *pesos duros* (those strong piastres which were moreover identical with the *reales de a ocho* – another sign of permanence; the name alone had changed) in the seventeenth and eighteenth. It matters little whether shipment was arranged from the Bay of Cadiz, on so vast a scale as to favour fraudulent practice, from Bayonne by means of smuggling across the Pyrenees, or from Amsterdam and London, meeting places for world silver. It even happened that silver from America was transported from the coasts of Peru to Asia on French boats.

Other movements acted in favour of eastern Europe. The West, in fact, gradually stimulated the monetary circulations of those backward countries which supplied corn, wood, rye, fish, hides and furs, and which bought on a very small scale in exchange. Such movements were foreshadowed in the sixteenth century by the trade with Narva, Muscovy's window to the Baltic (opened in 1558 then closed in 1581) and the trade at Archangel on the White Sea initiated in 1553 by the English; and they were continued in the eighteenth by the trade with St Petersburg. These infusions of foreign money were necessary so that the anticipated exports of raw materials could be arranged in exchange. The Dutch, who persisted in wanting to pay for them in textile products, fabrics and herrings, quickly lost their ascendancy in this field.

In short, metallic money had to flow and even increase its rate of flow to accomplish its manifold tasks. But it often stagnated, and frequently in Europe itself, as a result of many forms of saving, against which François Quesnay protested (like Lord Keynes very much later!), and also as a result of illogical and widespread hoarding.

Europe in the middle ages had a passion for precious metals and gold ornaments. Later came the new 'capitalist' passion for minted coins in the thirteenth century, or about the middle of the fourteenth at the latest. But the old passion for precious objects persisted.

Spanish princes in Philip II's period bequeathed chests of gold coins and innumerable objects in gold and silver work to their heirs. Even the Duke of Alba, who died in 1582 without a reputation for wealth, left his heirs 600 dozen silver plates and 800 silver platters. Two centuries later Galiani estimated the reserves hoarded in the kingdom of Naples in 1751 at four times the monetary stock in circulation there. 'Luxury,' he explained, 'has made all silver objects – watches, snuff-boxes, sword and cane handles, forks and spoons, cups, plates – so common that it is unbelievable. The Neapolitans, like the Spaniards of yore in almost all their customs, derive very great pleasure from keeping ancient silver objects in their chests known as *scrittori* and *scarabattoli*.' Sébastien Mercier spoke of the 'worthless and idle' wealth in Paris 'of gold and silver furniture, jewellery and plate dishes' (silver dishes).

There are no reliable statistics on the subject of hoarding. An old study by W. Lexis assumes a ratio of three to four between precious metals hoarded and minted metal in circulation at the beginning of the sixteenth century. The ratio must have changed in the eighteenth century, perhaps not in the proportion of four to one suggested by Galiani, anxious as he was to demonstrate that the demand for precious metals did not only depend on their monetary use. It is true that the world's stocks of metals increased enormously from the sixteenth to the eighteenth century – from one to fifteen according to a rough ratio suggested by W. Lexis, and known examples do not contradict it. In 1670 monetary circulation in France was in the order of 120 million francs; a century later it was 2000 million. Monetary stock in Naples in 1570 was 700,000 ducats; it was 18 million in 1751. Naples and Italy in the seventeenth and eighteenth centuries had huge reserves of unemployed currency. Bankers in Genoa in about 1683 were forced to offer their money to foreigners at 2% and 3%. Many religious orders borrowed from this miraculous source to pay off old debts, at 5%, 6% and 7%.

And the governments chipped in: Sixtus V's treasure, piled up in the Castel Sant Angelo, Sully's treasure at the Arsenal; the treasure of the Sergeant-King, Frederick William I, which he did not know how to use any more than his army. All these are known and often cited examples. There were others, like those cautious banks created or recreated at the end of the sixteenth and beginning of the seventeenth century. A keen observer said of the prestigious Bank of Amsterdam in 1761: 'All the silver metal and coin is to be found in the bank . . . this is not the place to examine whether the silver shut up there is not as useless to circulation as when it was buried in the mines. I am convinced that it could be made to circulate to the advantage of trade without altering credit or violating good faith . . .' All the banks deserved this criticism, except the Bank of England, founded in 1694, which was revolutionary in its own way, as will be seen.

America's rôle

European monetary stock as a whole (gold, silver, copper) had to confront a series of tasks. It had to supply the Far East and Eastern Europe, swell the reserves of the money-hoarders, above all provide the raw material necessary for the transactions of the European economy and make good the follies of monetary policy. The same answers came up every time: increase production and speed up circulation. The two accelerations were usually concomitant. When precious metals became plentiful coins passed more quickly from hand to hand. There was thus only a single problem – one historians have solved a little too hastily.

According to them everything from the beginning of the sixteenth century to the end of the eighteenth depended on the quantities of gold and silver delivered by the New World, the New World being the sole motive force. Again, the situation in America is said to have controlled and caused the world situation – that is to say monetary stocks in Europe, their movement and variations in prices and incomes. The Indies began to 'disgorge their wealth' in the sixteenth century. The pace of Europe's economic life immediately accelerated. Inflations followed in quick succession. But a slump in mining production in the seventeenth century as a result of the catastrophic drop in the Indian population was enough to plunge Europe into the series of difficulties of that period. Everything was re-established sooner or later with the reversal of the American situation, if not exactly simultaneously with the beginnings of Brazilian gold in about 1680. One historian unhesitatingly sees the upsurge of the eighteenth century in Europe and even the French Revolution as logical consequences of gold-washing at Minas Gerais and Goyaz. All this reasoning would seem to imply that the new continent had acted of its own accord and given old Europe its fabulous metals as a gift, or as if Europe had won them at a lottery or free of charge through the inhuman exploitation of the Indians and Black slaves.

In fact Europe paid for these metals, no doubt not their full price, but it paid for them. Furthermore the American supply never grew of its own accord. It was operated by remote control according to European demand. The situation was at least produced by both sides of the Atlantic together, there were reciprocal arrangements and a division of responsibilities. We can think of the precious metals as fuel for an engine: in order for them to arrive the engine had to be turning; but the engine only turned when they arrived. Both explanations are valid and the second is not the worse of the two. One historian suggests: 'One could even ask oneself [following the same lines as our reasoning] whether it was not the movement of prices, once it had begun [with the second half of the sixteenth century], that made it necessary to create additional money.'

Money of account

The intermingling of the various types of European money necessitated money of account, known as 'imaginary' money. Inevitably currencies needed a common measurement. Money of account consists of units of measurement, like the hours, minutes and seconds on a clock. France, for example, had the *livre tournois*.

When we say nowadays that the *Napoléon d'or* is worth 44·70 francs on the Paris Bourse we are not making a statement difficult to grasp. But firstly, the average Frenchman is generally not concerned with such a quotation and does not meet with old gold coins everyday of his life; secondly, the franc, the actual money of account, is really in his wallet in the form of notes. Some Parisian bourgeois gentleman in a certain month of the year 1602 might have pointed out that the gold *écu* was worth sixty-six sous, or if you prefer three livres six sous. But such a man met with gold and silver coins in his everyday life much more often than Frenchmen today. They were legal currency for him. On the other hand he never came across the livre, nor the sou which was a twentieth of it, nor the denier, a twelfth of a sou: these were imaginary units used to reckon up and estimate the respective values of the coins, to fix prices and wages, and to keep commercial accounts that could later be translated into any real money, local or foreign, when it came to moving over from book-keeping to actual payment. A debt of 100 livres could be paid in so many gold coins, so many silver, with the addition of copper as required.

No contemporary of Philip the Fair, Louis XIV or Turgot had ever held a *livre tournois* or sou in the palm of his hand (the last *deniers tournois* were minted in 1649). One would have to go back a very long way to find the coins corresponding to the money of account. All money of account was in fact real money at some given moment in the past. This is true of the *livre tournois*, the *livre parisis*, the pound sterling, the livre of the Italian towns (the Venice ducat became money of account in 1517), or the Spanish ducat which ceased to be real money in 1540, contrary to what historians and men of letters have found to say on the subject. The 'gros', the money of account of Flanders, was the old silver *gros* minted by Saint Louis in 1266, which had ceased to be real money. Look at an eighteenth-century trade note relating to India. The country may be different but the problem is the same: 'All India reckons by the standard rupee which is worth thirty sous.' (As this is a Frenchman speaking, he means thirty *sous tournois*.) He adds: 'This is imaginary money like livres in France, the pound sterling in England or the 'gros' livre of Flanders and Holland; such ideal money is used to settle the business one does and one has to state whether one is dealing in the standard rupee or rupees from some other country . . .'

The explanation will be complete if it is added that real coins did not cease to rise in value, governments constantly putting up the price of currency and therefore devaluing money of account. If the reader has followed this reasoning and found it clear, he should approach the following small problem.

A French example demonstrates how the device of money of account could be avoided. In 1577 Henry III, one of the most discredited French kings, decided to revalue the *livre tournois* under pressure from the Lyons merchants. Nothing was simpler than to link the money of account to gold. This was what the weak government succeeded in doing when it decided that accounts henceforth should be kept in *écus* and no longer in livres. The *écu* was a real gold coin, 'hard cash', valued at three livres or sixty sous. The result would be the same if a French government decided tomorrow that the French fifty-franc note would henceforth be equivalent to a *louis d'or* and that all accounts would be kept in *louis d'or*. (But would such a measure be successful?) The 1577 operation succeeded until the dark years which followed the assassination of Henry III (1589). Then everything broke down, as foreign exchange rates showed. The real *écu* broke away from the *écu* of account, which always remained equivalent to 60 sous; the former was quoted at 63, 65, even over 70. The return to accounts in *livres tournois* in 1602 was the recognition of inflation; the money of account was again separated from gold.

And this was so until 1726. Louis xv's government not only put an end to a long series of monetary movements. It tied the *livre tournois* to gold, and except for slight changes, the system no longer stirred. The last change came when the declaration of 30 October 1785 raised the ratio between gold and silver, on the pretext of the flight of gold. Until then it had been established at 1 to 14·5. Then it was fixed a point higher at 1 to 15·5.

Thus France did not completely abandon its preference for silver, since the ratio in both Spain and England was 1 to 16. This is no trifle. As gold was cheaper in France than England it was a lucrative operation to take it across the Channel (from the French market) so that it could be coined in English mints. Silver left England in the opposite direction for the same reasons: between 1710 and 1717, to the value of 18 million pounds sterling. English mints minted sixty times more gold (by value) than silver coins between 1714 and 1773.

Eighteenth-century Europe could at last allow itself the luxury of these stabilisations. Until then all money of account, whether it had a high or low intrinsic value, had been subject to continual devaluation; some, like the *livre tournois* or the Polish *grosz*, more rapidly than others. These devaluations were probably not fortuitous for there was a sort of dumping of exports in countries like Poland and even France, which were primarily exporters of raw materials.

In any case devaluation of money of account regularly stimulated the rise of prices. An economist (Luigi Einaudi) calculated that during the price rise in France between 1471 and 1598 the devaluation of the *livre tournois* was responsible for at least 209·6% of the total rise of 627·6%. Devaluation of money of account did not stop until the eighteenth century. President Pasquier said as early as 1641 that he did not much care for the proverb: 'He is discredited like an old coin, to describe a man who has a bad reputation . . . because as things go in France old money is better than new, which has been getting continually weaker for a hundred or so years . . .'

Metallic reserves and the velocity of monetary circulation

France on the eve of the Revolution possessed a monetary stock of perhaps 2000 million *livres tournois*, or 100 livres per person for some 20 million inhabitants. Taking round figures for Naples – 18 million ducats and 3 million inhabitants in 1751 – each person would have had 6 ducats at his disposal. There had perhaps been 2000 tons of gold and 20,000 tons of silver in Europe in 1500 before the arrival of metals from America (these figures are obtained by a highly questionable calculation). About 40,000 tons of silver for 60 million inhabitants, or a little over 600 grammes per person; a derisory figure. Between 1500 and 1650, according to *official* figures, fleets from the Indies landed 180 tons of gold and 16,000 tons of silver at Seville. This was enormous and, yet again, very modest.

But the magnitude was relative. What was involved was stimulating channels of low demand, despite what contemporaries imagined. And above all, the money passed from hand to hand, 'cascading' as a Portuguese economist said (1761). It was multiplied by its velocity (the velocity of circulation probably first brought to light by William Potter in 1650). Every rebound meant a new account settled, money completing exchanges 'like a pin closing a joint', as a present-day economist has noted. It is never the whole price of sales or the whole price of purchases that is settled, only the difference between them.

In Naples almost 18 million ducats were in circulation in 1751 – 1·5 million ducats in copper money, 6 million in silver coins and 10 million in gold coins (including 3 million in the banks). Total purchases and sales in one year can be estimated at 288 million ducats. The figure can be reduced by 50% if auto-consumption, salaries in kind and sales by exchange are taken into account; if it is remembered, as Galiani explained, 'that the peasants who form three-quarters of our people do not settle a tenth of their consumption in hard cash'. This gives rise to the following problem: how to settle payments of 144 million with a monetary stock of 18 million? The answer: each coin must change hands eight times. The speed of circulation is therefore the quotient of total payments by the total of circulating currency. Must we assume that money would 'cascade' faster if total payments increased?

Irving Fisher's law helps to set out this problem. If the total of goods exchanged is Q, their average price P, total money M, its speed of circulation V, the equation for budding economists briefly reads: $MV = PQ$. If total payments increase and the monetary stock remains stationary, the velocity of circulation must rise, if everything is adjusted in the economy in question (Naples or any other).

Thus it seems to us that during the economic advance accompanied by the 'price revolution' in the fifteenth century the velocity of circulation increased at the same tempo as the other elements in Irving Fisher's equation. If, *lato sensu*, production, monetary mass and prices quintupled, the speed of circulation itself probably also quintupled. We are obviously dealing with averages which ignore short-term variations (such as a serious slump in business in 1580–4) and local variations.

On the other hand, circulation could achieve abnormal and exceptional speeds at certain points. A contemporary of Galiani's said that an *écu* could change hands fifty times in twenty-four hours in Paris: 'The whole world does not contain half the money spent in one year in the town of Paris alone, if one counts every statement of expenses made and paid for in currency from the first day of January to the last day in December, in all the orders of state, from the Royal Household to the beggars consuming a sou's worth of bread a day. . . .'

This circulation of money puzzled classical economists. They saw it as the fountain of all wealth, the explanation of absurd paradoxes. 'As communications were cut during the siege of Tournay in 1745 and for some time before,' one of them explained, 'lack of money made it difficult to pay the garrison. Someone thought of borrowing the sum of seven thousand florins [proof that Tournay was at that time in the hands of the Dutch] from the canteens. It was all there was in them. At the end of the week, the seven thousand florins had returned to the canteens from which the same sum was once more borrowed. This was then repeated for seven weeks until the surrender, so that the same seven thousand florins had the effect of forty-nine thousand. . . .'

Like all examples this one is not decisive. What it indisputably demonstrates is that money returns by preference into certain hands. But if currency circulates fast it necessarily extends its field of action.

Outside the market economy

Let us return to the Kingdom of Naples in 1751. The monetary stock in motion settled half the transactions. This was a great deal, but the residue was enormous. Peasants and wages in kind (bacon, salt, salted meat, wine, oil) made money unnecessary. The wages of workers in textile industries, soap works and alcohol distilleries in Naples and elsewhere only involved money incidentally. The workers in these industries certainly played a part in the distribution of currency but they spent it in the time it took to go from their hands to their mouths, *della mano alla boca*. The German economist Schrötten as early as 1686 mentioned it as one of the advantages of factories 'to make more money pass from hand to hand because in this way they [the factories] provide food for more people'. Transport was also paid in currency, however poorly. All this, in Naples as elsewhere, did not prevent the existence of a barter and subsistence economy of equal importance to the flexible modern economy.

The key word is often *baratto*, or *barattare* or *dare a baratto*. *Baratto* was barter, standard practice at the very heart of Levantine trade. From before the fifteenth century the skill there had lain in trading spices, pepper or gall nuts for fabrics or glass ornaments from Venice, and therefore in not paying cash. Commodities were generally exchanged for one another in Naples in the eighteenth century, everybody falling in with prices which the authorities fixed later (prices called *alla voce*). Then each consignment of merchandise was valued in money, and exchanged according to the ratio of these values. What a mine of problems there was for the schoolboys in the *Arithmetica Pratica* by Father Alessandro delle Purificazione, which appeared in Rome in 1714. *Barattare* meant applying the rule of three – *la regola di tre* – but to one of the following: simple barter, wax against pepper for example; barter half in money and half in kind; and barter with a time limit, 'when a date for settlement is fixed'. The fact that the operation figured in an arithmetic book indicates that merchants also practised barter and this, as we know, 'made it possible to cover up the price of interest', just like the bill of exchange.

All this reveals the inadequacies of monetary life even in the active eighteenth century which we tend to regard as a paradise in comparison with earlier times. But the bonds of money and market did not encompass all human life. The poor evaded them. It was possible to say in about 1713 that 'variations in money hardly interest the greater part of the peasants [Burgundians], who do not possess currency'. This was true almost always for peasants everywhere.

On the other hand other sectors were well advanced and already at grips with all the complications of credit. But these sectors were narrow.

4 Paper money and instruments of credit

Economists distinguish between metallic money (which we have discussed fully), fiduciary money (bank notes) and scriptural money (created by the process of book-keeping, by clearing one bank account against another: a practice known to the Germans as

Buchgeld, book money. Economic historians would say there was an inflation of *Buchgeld* as early as the sixteenth century).

A clear but very theoretical frontier separates money (in all its forms) from credit (taking into consideration all instruments of credit). Credit is the exchange of two deferred promises: I will do something for you, you will pay me later. The lord who advanced seed-corn to a peasant, on condition that he were repaid at harvest, opened a credit. So did the tavern-keeper who did not claim the price of his drinks from his customer immediately but put it down to the drinker's account by means of a chalk-mark on the wall, or the baker who delivered bread and marked up the payment to come by notching a double piece of wood (one part being kept by the giver, the other by the taker). Merchants in Segovia and elsewhere who bought standing corn from peasants or wool from sheepbreeders before the sheep were shorn were doing the same thing. And this is also the principle behind 'bills of exchange': the seller of a bill on any market whatsoever – at a fair at Medina del Campo in the sixteenth century for example – received the money immediately. The taker would be repaid at another market, three months later, according to the rate of exchange at the time. It was up to him to calculate, make sure of his profits and work out his risks.

If most contemporaries found money a 'difficult cabbala to understand', this type of money, money that was not money at all, and this interplay of money and mere writing to a point where the two became confused, seemed not only complicated but diabolical. Such things were a constant source of amazement. The Italian merchant who settled in Lyons in about 1555 with a table and an inkstand and made a fortune represented an absolute scandal, even in the eyes of people who understood the handling of money and the process of exchange fairly well. Even in 1752 a man of the intellectual calibre of David Hume (1711–76), philosopher, historian and moreover an economist, spoke of 'that new invention of paper money' when the Bank of England had been issuing notes since it was founded in 1694. The comment is enough to indicate how greatly the problem disconcerted observers. Obviously the main thing is to set it in its right perspective.

Old practices

These arrangements that by-passed money in the strict sense were very old inventions. They were techniques that really had only to be rediscovered. But they were on the whole more 'natural' than they seemed, if only on account of their very great age.

In fact as soon as men had known how to write and had had coins to handle they had replaced cash with written documents, notes, promises and orders. Notes and cheques between market traders and bankers were known in Babylon twenty centuries before the Christian era. There is no need to exaggerate the modernity of such systems to admire their ingenuity. The same devices were found in Greece and Hellenistic Egypt, where Alexandria became 'the most popular centre of international transit'. Rome was familiar with current accounts and debit and credit in the *argentarii* books. Finally, all the instruments of credit – bills of exchange, promissory notes, letters of credit, bank notes, cheques – were known to the merchants of Islam, whether Muslim or not. This is shown by the *geniza* documents from the tenth century AD, principally found in the Old Cairo synagogue. And China used bank notes from the ninth century AD.

These distant antecedents must guarantee us against a state of rather naïve wonderment. When the West rediscovered the old instruments, it was not a discovery like the discovery of America. In fact every economy that found itself hard up for metallic currency fairly quickly opened up instruments of credit of its own accord, as if it were part of its natural development. They sprang from its commitments.

So in the thirteenth century the West rediscovered bills of exchange, a long-distance method of payment that spread through the whole length of the Mediterranean with the success of the Crusades. The bill of exchange came to be endorsed earlier than is usually thought. The recipient signed it and sold it. Obviously at the time of the first known endorsement in 1410 the circulation of bills of exchange was not what it later became. A further advance came when the bill of exchange was no longer restricted to a simple journey from one market to another, as when it was first used. Businessmen caused it to be moved about from market to market, from fair to fair, known by the French as *le change et le rechange*, by the Italians as *ricorsa*. These advances, which meant prolonging credit, became widespread during the difficulties of the seventeenth century. Fictitious bills were in circulation at that time with the connivance of businessmen. It even became common for a man to draw upon himself. This was the open door to many abuses. In fact these abuses even preceded the seventeenth century. We know of re-exchanges to the profit of the Fuggers in 1590 and on the Lyons market in 1592, and even more so in Genoa, the city of innovations, in the fifteenth century.

Neither can we say that the bank note made its appearance at the counters of the Bank of Stockholm in 1661 – which in any case quickly suspended it in 1668 – or on the counters of the Bank of England in 1694, though this is more realistic. There are notes and notes. In the first place governmental orders, prototypes of bank notes, had multiplied in England from 1667 and the use of goldsmiths' notes, later called bankers' notes, was common earlier, in the middle of the century, for the London goldsmiths received silver on deposit against notes. In 1666 one of these goldsmiths alone had the sum of 1,200,000 pounds sterling circulating in notes. Cromwell himself had recourse to their credit. The bank note was born almost spontaneously from commercial usage. It was a matter of urgent necessity. In 1640, when Charles I had seized the ingots deposited in the Tower of London by the city merchants, the merchants found asylum for their property with the goldsmiths, whose fortune they made until the Bank of England was created.

But England did not have a monopoly in these matters. The *Casa di San Giorgio* had its *biglietti* at least from 1586 and they were payable in gold or silver currency after 1606, according to the nature of the deposit which guaranteed them. In Venice the banks *di scritta* (of writing) had from the fifteenth century had their notes which could be exchanged and redeemed.

But the innovation of the Bank of England was that it added to the functions of deposit and clearing banks those of a deliberately organised issuing bank, capable of offering ample credit in notes (whose total amount in fact far exceeded actual deposits). By doing this, said Law, it did the greatest good to trade and the state, because it 'increased the quantity of money'.

We will return to scriptural money. It appeared with the very beginnings of the banking profession: one account was cleared against another, as the customer desired. There were even what we would call overdrawn accounts, if the banker consented to it. This form of money was, therefore, established from the beginning of the period covered in this book.

Cash and credit

Of course notes and paper did not always reach a wide public. David Hume's comment must not be forgotten. Even after the late foundation of the Bank of France (1801), its notes only interested a few Parisian merchants and bankers, practically no one in the provinces.

However, there were many kinds of paper and credit and by indirect means they incessantly rejoined and mingled in the stream of the monetary circulation. A bill of exchange circulated like real money when it was endorsed, that is when it had been made over by its owner by means of a reference and a signature. Contrary to the custom with present-day French cheques, these endorsements were on the front of the paper on which the bill was drawn up, not on the back. Even government bonds were sold wherever they were to be found – in Venice, Florence, Genoa, Naples. We have an impressive number of proofs. So too in France with the *rente* certificates of the Hôtel de Ville de Paris, which were created in 1522 and suffered numerous vicissitudes. When the *connétable* of Montmorency bought an estate (the manor of Marigny) on 1 November 1555, he paid for it with Hôtel de Ville *rentes* or bonds. Nine times out of ten Philip II and his successors met their liabilities to the businessmen in *juros*, government bonds, reckoned at par. When the businessmen had been repaid in this way, they in their turn settled their debts to a third party in the same sort of 'money', making someone else bear the risks and disappointments of their profession. As far as they were concerned this meant changing short-term debts (loans to the king, *asientos*) into funded perpetual or life debts. But shares in the *asientos* were themselves transferred, inherited and distributed. They were on the market, even if not quite openly. Shares in the Amsterdam Bourse were also on the market in their time and so were the innumerable rents that money from the towns had drawn in from peasant fields, vines and houses in all the lands of the West. An immense panorama reveals itself if we take care to perceive it. Even the *cedole* (the cedula) which Sicilian *caricatori* (grain warehouses) gave landowners who deposited their grain there, were sold. In addition, false *cedole* circulated with the complicity of the warehouse owners and high authority. One last detail: in Naples the viceroy issued *tratte*, authorisations to export cereals and even vegetables. He issued too many and it was regular practice for Venetian merchants to buy them at below the nominal rate and thus pay their customs duties at a discount. Every time there was a breakdown in metallic money anything was pressed into service and paper money flowed in or was invented.

In Paris 'it is worthy of note that there was such a shortage of currency in trade in 1647, 1648 and 1649 that people only gave a quarter in hard cash when they made a payment and three-quarters in notes or bills of exchange, which were signed uncompleted so as to serve as an endorsement and not as an order to pay. Thus merchants, traders and bankers had developed the custom amongst themselves of paying each other in this way.' The text would call for comment (for example on the way they signed the bills uncompleted), but the interest of the document does not lie there. Cash was short and credit was resorted to: it was improvised. And, on the whole, this was William Petty's advice in his strange *Quantulumcumque Concerning Money* (1682), which may be freely translated as 'The least that can be said about Money'. He proceeded by question and answer. Question 26: 'What remedy is there if we have too little money?' Answer: 'We must erect a Bank ...' that is create a machine to produce credit, to increase the effect of the money in existence. As Louis XIV, grappling with continual wars, did not succeed in creating a bank, he had to manage with the help of financiers, 'tax farmers and partisans', who advanced him the enormous expenses of his armies abroad by way of bills of exchange. In fact these lenders advanced their money and the money deposited with them by third parties. It was then up to them to get their money back in royal revenues. As for the king, how could he have acted otherwise when his kingdom was drained of precious metals?

It was always metallic money, slow to fulfil its functions or absent altogether (standing idle), that had to be pushed forward or some-how replaced. A repeated effort was improvised in the gaps and on occasions of breakdowns in currency, bringing with it reflections and hypotheses concerning its very nature. What was actually involved here? In fact it soon involved the artificial manufacture of money, of ersatz money, or if you like a manipulated and 'manipulable' money. All those English bank promoters and finally the Scot John Law gradually realised 'the economic possibilities of this discovery, whereby money – and capital in the monetary sense of the word – were capable of being manufactured or created at will'. It represented a sensational discovery and a huge temptation. And what a revelation to us! It was the slowness of the heavy metallic money that created the necessary profession of the banker from the very dawn of economic life. He was the man who repaired or tried to repair the mechanical breakdown.

Schumpeter: everything is money, everything is credit

We come to the last and the most difficult of our comments. Is there really any absolute difference in nature between metallic money, substitute money and instruments of credit? It is normal to make immediate distinctions between them; but thereafter should they not perhaps be related and intermingled? The problem opens the door to so much debate. It is also the problem of modern capitalism, which deploys itself in this domain and finds its tools here – and even becomes 'aware of its own existence' in the very act of defining them. Of course, we are opening the discussion with no intention of examining it fully. We will return to it later.

Up to at least 1760 all economists gave careful attention to the analysis of the early stages of the monetary process. Later, during the whole of the nineteenth century, and afterwards, until Keynes' reversal, they tended to consider money as a neutral element in economic exchanges, or rather as a veil. To tear away the veil and observe what it concealed was one of the customary standpoints of 'real' economic analysis; no longer to see money with its personal attributes, but the underlying realities: exchange of goods and services, flow of income and expenditure, and so on.

Let us start with something approaching this (nominalist) way of looking at things in the period before 1760 and keep a deliberately mercantilist perspective already several centuries old then. This perspective gave exclusive attention to currency, considered as wealth in its own right, like a river, whose power set in motion and completed exchanges, and whose volume accelerated or slowed them. Money, or rather the monetary stock, was both volume and momentum, both its own and that of the trade it induced, as a car's momentum is that of its engine and its wheels. If the volume increased or if the momentum of the whole thing accelerated, the result was almost the same; everything rose (prices and more slowly wages; also the volume of transactions). If the reverse occurred, everything regressed. In these conditions, at a time when direct exchange of commodities (barter) was in operation, if a substitute money made possible the conclusion of a deal without resort to currency, if credit facilitated a transaction, it must be concluded that there would actually be a rise in the volume in circulation. In short, if all the instruments capitalism uses come into the monetary process in this way, they are pseudo-money or even real money. A general reconciliation ensues, of which Cantillon gave the first lesson.

But if it is possible to say that everything is money, it is just as possible to claim that everything is, on the contrary, credit – promises, deferred reality. Even this *louis d'or* was given me as a promise, as a cheque (real cheques, drawn on specific accounts, only came into current use in England towards the middle of the eighteenth century). It is a cheque on the collection of tangible goods and services within my reach and amongst which, tomorrow or later, I will finally make my choice. It is only then that this coin will have fulfilled its purpose in the framework of my life. As Schumpeter said: 'Currency in its turn is nothing other than an instrument of credit, a title which gives access to the only means of definite payment, namely consumer goods. Today [1954] this theory, which naturally can assume various forms and demands much elaboration is, we can say, in the process of prevailing.' All in all the brief can legitimately be argued either way.

At this point capitalism is neither completely integrated in the normal life of money nor excluded from it, nor explained or explicable in itself. Theoretical discussion forced it to take cognisance of itself, to define the ideas of wealth, of stock, before the idea of capital fully emerged. But the discussion will never produce a simple answer to satisfy our curiosity. Because money and pseudo-money are in fact techniques amenable to the history of technology, in which cause and effect intermingle, and we are not wholly concerned with questions of pure technology. It is obvious that the enormous expansion of the volume of currency. the improvement and expansion of substitute money – in a word the arrival of paper – accompanied the establishment of capitalism and of an increasingly vigorous and complicated economy, a society secretly shaken and distorted down to its foundations. And all of these form so many correlated phenomena which cannot possibly be explained in terms of an unequivocal relationship.

The banks

Banks are theoretically quite simple machines, either private or public. The pendulum swung steadily between the two, sometimes favouring risk and sometimes caution. The bankers' principle almost without exception consisted in collecting other people's money. The Hochstetters of Augsburg, who tried to monopolise mercury in the sixteenth century and foundered completely in the process, had accepted money from depositors who were sometimes very humble, ordinary craftsmen, even servants from their town. The prestigious Genoese bankers employed by Philip II and his successors used the savings of the clergy and nobility of Spain or investors in Italy. And, as we have said, when the Castilian monarchy was bankrupt (in 1557, 1575, 1597, 1607, 1627 and 1647) it repaid its creditors in *juros* (bonds the state had given them to clear its debts), pleading the right to pay in the same money in which they themselves had been paid off. But with the last years of the sixteenth century, and more still the first years of the seventeenth, the public's money was collected in a dictatorial manner. Public banks foisted their services on their clients.

The same was true in Venice, at the Rialto Bank founded in 1584 and replaced in 1617 by the Banco Giro; and in Amsterdam's bank. 'The town of Amsterdam,' Samuel Ricard wrote much later in 1706, 'without embarrassing freedom of trade, has made itself mistress of the money of all its inhabitants, without inconveniencing them, no one thinking himself any the less rich because his possessions are only to be found in the bank.' The 'ideal' bank money, the *florin de banque*, was quoted higher than real money in circulation, because of the inadequacies of circulating currency. It was rather as if we put our money into a bank where it would then be converted into dollars of account, and that there was an 'agio', a difference between our current francs and these dollars in favour of the bank money. The difference varied incessantly: in 1703 the agio was between 1·5% and 2%. It had been as high as 5·6%, and in 1963 even rose 'to 12% and 13% because of bad *shellings* of six sous which were reduced to five and a half sous'. This was a further reason to be a customer of the bank and to participate in the buying and selling of money which took place between merchants or at the Bourse. 'Cashiers with whom one negotiates for the *asio* [*sic*] at the highest selling price and the lowest buying price . . .' are normally to be found 'between ten and eleven in the morning, on the Dam market, in front of the Town Hall and the Bank'. It may be presumed that the Bank profited from the deals, and likewise the *Oost Indische Companie* which was behind it. Founded in 1602, the Company allowed itself considerable overdrafts. The *Monte de Pieta* of Florence (an important bank over and above its role as a pawnbroker), which was under the control of the Medicis, did the same. In Genoa, where capitalism was extremely alert, it supported the *Casa di San Giorgio*, which in its turn supported the weak state of the *Dominante*.

As for the Bank of England, it was like no other, except perhaps in a certain way like the *Casa di San Giorgio*. Its originality lay in the fact that it put into circulation notes of over twenty pounds sterling to begin with, and of five, ten and fifteen pounds later. Eventually the smallest notes were for ten pounds, the largest for a thousand, all bearing the signatures of the directors of the Bank. The Bank was fully involved in discounting bills of exchange and in massive loans to the State and to South Sea and East Indies companies. It collected taxes in the form of bills of exchange and, though exceeding its reserve, was only seriously bothered in 1745 when the Pretender marched victoriously on London and everyone rushed to its counters to obtain payment in cash. The shareholders then took it into their heads to have their shares repaid in notes. They betook themselves to its counters and managed to block them. At the same time ordinary bearers of notes were intentionally paid in small change, which took up time in every case. There was general delay and in the meantime the Pretender was defeated.

The machine for manufacturing credit was eventually completed in the provinces and in Scotland by a proliferation of small local banks, 'country banks' (there were over 500 in 1803–4, 800 in about 1809) and private banks in London itself. These banks, which specialised in discount, also issued notes, taking advantage of the circulation of the notes of the Bank of England, which had accustomed the British public to their use. All in all they formed a pyramid of credit with the Bank of England, a construction at once solid and fragile, at the top. Napoleon and his advisers vainly hoped to destroy it.

This English originality was long recognised as a point of superiority. Sébastien Mercier often repeated: 'So long as we do not have notes in public circulation we will not have the advantages we ought to be enjoying. . . . We should perhaps have begun by . . . modelling ourselves on the Bank of London.' Moreover look at the obsolete spectacle of cash payments in Paris:

From ten o'clock until midday on the tenth, twentieth and thirtieth of the month, you meet bearers with bags full of money, bent beneath their burdens: they are running as if an enemy army were about to take the town by surprise; which proves that the successful political symbol [meaning the note] that would replace those metals, which should be only immobile symbols instead of travelling from cashbox to cashbox, has not been created in our midst. Unhappy the man who has a bill of exchange to pay on that particular day and who has no funds! Happy the man who has paid for it and has an *écu* of six livres left over.

The scene was concentrated entirely on the Rue Vivienne where 'there is more money . . .,' comments the informant, 'than in all the rest of the town; it is the pocket of the capital city. The great banks are situated there and in particular the Discount Bank [the first rough version of what later became the Bank of France]. Bankers, bill-brokers, jobbers, everyone in fact who makes a commodity out of minted money, is to be found there. . . .'

Bills of exchange

The bill of exchange was the most important of all the instruments of credit during the centuries covered by this book. Unfortunately we hardly have the means of assessing its volume in relation to the general movement of transactions and monetary payments. If we work backwards from the eighteenth century, its share decreases progressively, but we do not know in what proportion.

Venice's war loans (during the Turco-Spanish-Venetian war of 1570–3) amounted to some 5 million ducats in about 1575, invested by the taxpayers (because these were forced loans). But only 2% of the total was settled by bills of exchange. This may be thought to be a bad example: the bill of exchange was not the ideal instrument for a payment on the Venice market itself by Venetian merchants. The great period of paper and speculation at the Besançon fairs only came ten or fifteen years later. However, it is a fact that in this respect Venice was behind Genoa, or even Florence. Naples offers us another statistic: 5,600,000 ducats in cash payments against one million payments of bills of exchange in 1570 (if we assume that the velocity of circulation was then already as much as eight).

In any case the popularity of the bill of exchange grew more and more. In the eighteenth century, a little earlier in some places, a little later in others, it had reached the market places of the whole world. Thus bills of exchange were sent from Batavia to Amsterdam and in such quantities that in 1719 it was already a cause of concern to the *Zeventien Herren*, the Seventeen Gentlemen who presided over the destiny of the *Oost Indische Companie*. In fact skilful speculators unlawfully loaded *ducatons*, pieces of silver minted in Holland, on to the Company's boats when they were leaving Europe. When they arrived in Batavia the silver coins found their way into 'government' coffers against remittance of bills of exchange to be drawn in Amsterdam. This took advantage of the difference between the quotations for silver in Amsterdam, where it was cheap, and in Batavia where the price was high and resulted in a 24% to 30% premium, plus the 4% or 5% interest the Company allowed in order to take the duration of the return journey into account. Likewise bills of exchange were drawn from Canton on London from 1760 onwards and on all the markets of Europe: this was a way for companies trading in China to borrow there the profits of Canton's trade with India, by selling, at advantageous prices, bills of exchange to the holders drawn principally on London.

These somewhat aberrant examples magnificently observe the first rule for bills of exchange, that of *distancia loci*, which forced them to move about from one point to another. French law maintained that imperious rule, *sine qua non* of canon law, up to 1894. The Church in fact forbade borrowing at interest (usury) and only permitted the bill of exchange because of the risks to which it was exposed on its travels.

As a rule, a bill of exchange required the intervention of four people – *Primus, Secundus, Tertius, Quartus* – for the conclusion of the 'compact of exchange' of which the bill of exchange was the expression (the purchaser, *remittans*; the drawer, *trahans*; the bearer, *praesentans*; the drawee, *solvans* or, when he has accepted, *acceptans*). This last man, who closed the deal, could refuse to pay the bill; the 'protestation' then gave place to *protests*, often to law suits.

I could in certain circumstances agree for my bill to be protested. I could even be purchaser and drawer at one and the same time and send the bill to one of my correspondents who would send it back to me. The process involving four parties would then be reduced to two. Better still, I could come to an agreement to make some bill of exchange pass from hand to hand, by 'exchange and re-exchange', as the Fuggers did for a period of seventeen years from 1590 to 1607. Having lent money to Philip II, they circulated the total of this debt by bills of exchange from market to market. The royal debt was thus recorded – swollen by those remittances which disguised but did not do away with interest.

Actually bills of exchange had a dual nature: firstly, they were a means of payment at long distance, necessary to large-scale trade; that was their official role. Secondly, they were a concealed instrument of credit at interest, an opportunity for some to lend and make their money earn profits, and for others to obtain the advances indispensable to any trade. Other means, for example sham rents, have sometimes been used for this purpose. But bills of exchange ultimately became the normal method of borrowing. It was obviously a 'usurious' transaction but it was allowed, in view of the risks involved in the journey between the two markets connected by the bills of exchange.

These liaisons between market and market, between fair and market, or between fair and fair, were arranged in a business-like manner. Simon Ruiz, in Medina del Campo in about 1590, was an old man with a long and happy career behind him, quite a large part of which had been spent travelling. He had dealt in merchandise between Nantes and Lisbon and then engaged in finance, playing his part in Philip II's attempt in 1575 (which came to an abrupt end) to free himself from his Genoese lenders. He then negotiated loans, *asientos*, with the Catholic King. In the eighteenth century he would have been described for this short time as a 'financier'. When the crisis was over he once again became a banker, lending his money here and there, receiving correspondence and business notes from his friends, working on commission. But in the 1590s producers in Castile were no longer able to find intermediaries to buy their wool in Spain itself. They therefore had to make their own arrangements to send their bales to Leghorn and Florence, to agents who would only pay them after the actual sale of the merchandise, sometimes after long periods of delay. They therefore needed advances.

Ruiz lent them the money at one of the two fairs at Medina del Campo. He bought *treaties* from them (meaning bills of exchange) to be drawn on their correspondents in Florence, repayable three months later in the Tuscan capital. Of course Ruiz bought the bill at a price below that for which it was underwritten. This was his first profit. Then he sent it to a Spaniard settled in Florence, Baltasar Suarez, whom he had every reason to trust. Suarez collected the sum of the bill (he was the *tertius* in the deal according to our explanatory model). In Florence he received the money from the sale of the wool. To send the money back to Spain, he bought a bill of exchange, this time payable at Medina del Campo – on a Saturday at the Florence market and sent it to Ruiz, who in his turn would be the *tertius* in this new deal, the return deal. He most frequently collected the sum from a merchant in Medina del Campo (the *quartus*).

If the bill had been bought at a favourable rate in Florence, Ruiz could make a profit of 5% on this backward and forward business in six months (that is an annual rate of 10%). There were obviously upsets, failures to make money which the old man regarded as losses. If 'hard cash' was too plentiful in Florence when the time for the return to Medina came round, bills of exchange sold at very high prices and were so scarce that Baltasar could find none to buy and was forced to draw on himself to clinch the return operation. Ruiz eventually abandoned this business and during the last years of his life went back to trade in commodities: pepper, wool and above all cochineal, for which Seville was the great market.

Let us imagine this process repeated innumerable times, and more and more so as the eighteenth century approached, and we will have some idea of what commercial credit, sometimes centred on one market, sometimes on another, could be like at that period. Despite the flexibility of re-exchange and the channels that were organised (also depending on trade balances, as we will see), the bill of exchange remained a not too supple instrument, difficult to handle and with inherent risks – the impossibility of calculating exchange rates in advance. And the loss of time is obvious.

The practice of discount, which grew up in England around the 1680s, marked decisive progress. Protestant England – heir no doubt to the old innovations of Antwerp – achieved what Catholic Europe had not dared, nor legally been able to do, and what Amsterdam, a traditional market, had not initiated. Usury, in short, lowered its mask. I do not believe that morals lost thereby. In any case trade gained greater freedom of movement. The Bank of England specialised in discounting sixty-day bills of exchange very early on. It had innumerable imitators.

Credit: a technique not in general use

The situation in eighteenth-century Europe had improved considerably, taking everything into account, although there was no real technical innovation in means of payment (except for discount). What had happened in these spheres, especially the sphere of money, was that everything had enormously increased in scale, by a multiple of twenty or thirty since the sixteenth century. 'Today people talk about a million,' noted Sébastien Mercier (1788), 'in the same way as they talked about a thousand *louis d'or* a hundred years ago.' The miracle cannot be attributed to money, or to paper, 'flying money', as the Chinese in Canton called it, or even to the increase, however real, in silver or gold (gold from Brazil, silver from New Spain). A general acceleration in exchanges, in the velocity of circulation of money, has to be admitted.

But even in Europe these developments only happened in a few market places, a few nations, a few groups. When Frederick II was looking for emergency resources for a war treasury (his *Kriegskasse*, during the Seven Years War, 1756–63 – his third war with Silesia), he did not dare resort to the amenities of paper money (he was perhaps influenced by Law's notorious failure). He minted money of bad alloy, not in his own states – which he vainly hoped to preserve from the plague – but in the conquered lands, particularly Saxony (occupied from the outset), in Leipzig and Dresden, where he had the supplementary resources of silver ore from Freiburg. The King of Prussia resorted to the powerful Jewish firm of Ephraim and Sons in these transactions. The red of the copper very quickly showed through the dazzling white of the silver coins minted in Saxony (sometimes ante-dated). The public joke ran: 'Frederick on the outside, Ephraim inside' (*Von aussen Friedrich, von innen Ephraim*). These bad coins were even used to pay the Austrian troops. They flooded Poland, curiously defenceless from the monetary point of view. They did not spare the Prussian state. When peace returned Frederick II set to work to limit the damage.

This is the proof that the tempo of life was not the same throughout all Europe from West to East in the eighteenth century, at least in 1763. Berlin had become a city rotten with speculation by the end of Frederick's reign (1787).

But in Russia the clock was still tremendously slow, even in about 1783. While merchants were trying to attract south-going trade with Cherson and the Crimea, a reliable French authority recorded *de visu*: 'Minted silver is entirely absent from Cherson and the Crimea: all that is to be seen there is copper and paper money [notes issued by the Bank of Moscow] with no circulation, because of the lack of means of discount . . .'

Once again we find the picture of coexistent worlds, modern or very modern, backward or very backward, apparently far removed from each other and yet living in an economic symbiosis, sometimes of town and countryside, sometimes of an advanced country and a region still rooted in traditional life (the two cases are in fact analogous).

Here perhaps we might emphasise that the impetus of modern centuries also carried the rudimentary economies themselves along in its momentum. It was sometimes a painful process for the more backward regions who were forced to progress as best they could, but progress at all costs. Alfons Dopsch's central theme should be recalled in this context: namely that the natural economy benefits from a general impetus. It accelerates and develops its primitive or rudimentary money wherever other forms of money are not yet possible. This buoyancy of rudimentary money and the economies up to the eighteenth century also appeared in the relationship between man and man in the rise in statutory labour across the countries eastwards of a line drawn from Venice to the mouth of the Elbe. This 'second serfdom' was in no way the maintenance of a traditional structure. The Eastern countries had already experienced a regime of quasi-liberty for the peasant, with very light statutory labour. The second serfdom was rather the effect of imperative outside demand on an unprepared, old, almost primitive structure, making it work to increase production whatever the cost. But these are problems which will require further discussion.

At the risk of being monotonous we repeat our conclusion once more. What were money and credit if not luxuries in which the majority of men had only a minute share? Evolutions taking place were far from unimportant, but they required time. In the interim the old habits of barter, self-sufficiency, statutory labour, slavery and everyday material life continued. Men were more aware of this division than might be thought. In 1620 Scipion de Gramont wrote: 'Money, said the seven sages of Greece, is the blood and soul of men and whosoever has none wanders dead amongst the living.'

8

Towns

The towns are so many electric transformers. They increase tension, accelerate the rhythm of exchange and ceaselessly stir up men's lives. They developed out of the oldest and most revolutionary division of labour: the fields on the one hand and the activities described as urban on the other. 'The contrast between town and country begins with the transition from barbarism to civilisation, from the tribal régime to the state, from the individual locality to the nation, and recurs in all history of the world until our own days.' Karl Marx wrote these lines in his youth.

Towns are also oppressive, parasitical formations. 'Herodotus was already speaking of the millet-eaters north of the Black Sea who grew corn for the Greek cities.' This town–country confrontation is the first and longest class struggle history has known. We should not pass censure or take sides: these parasitic towns also embodied the intelligence, risk, progress, and modernity towards which the world was slowly moving. They had the finest foods, the luxury industries, brisk currencies and soon calculating, clear-sighted capitalism. To the rather unwieldy body of the state they lent their irreplaceable vitality. They were the accelerators of all historical time. Which does not mean that they did not make men suffer throughout the centuries, including the men who lived in them.

1 The town: a definition

The ideal would be to define the town in itself, outside the economy or civilisation containing it. There are two conditions for this: that all towns have certain common characteristics, and that such characteristics more or less persist from one period to another. But who would seriously deny it? As historians, we have put the original and creative power of Western towns too much in the limelight and unintentionally under-estimated and neglected the others. None the less, a town is a town wherever it is. 'Only primitive or undeveloped societies have not experienced the urban phenomenon,' and this urban phenomenon necessarily presupposes certain recurring features. Even Black Africa had its towns. Even the pre-Columbian civilisations had their successes: Tenochtitlan (Mexico), Cuzco.

We ought therefore to rediscover one basic language for all the cities of the world within their very depths and beyond their varied and original images – the uninterrupted confrontation with the countryside, a prime necessity of daily life; the supply of manpower, as indispensable as water to the mill-wheel; the aloofness of the towns, that is to say their desire to be marked off from others; their situation necessarily at the centre of a network of communications; their relation to suburbs, secondary cities often their servants and even their slaves.

Minimum size

The town, an unusual concentration of men and houses, close together, often joined wall to wall, is a demographic anomaly. Not that it is always 'full of people' or, as Ibn Batouta said, admiring Cairo, a 'restless sea' of men. There are towns that have barely begun being towns and also some extensive villages that exceed them in numbers of inhabitants. Examples of this are the enormous villages in Russia, now and in the past, the country towns of the Italian *Mezzogiorno* or the Andalusian south, or the loosely-woven clusters of hamlets in Java, which has remained an 'island of villages up to the present time'. But these inflated villages, even when they were contiguous, were not necessarily destined to become towns.

Numbers are not the only consideration involved. The town only exists as a town in relation to a form of life lower than its own. There are no exceptions to this rule. No privilege serves as a substitute. There is no town, no townlet without its villages, its scrap of rural life attached; no town that does not supply its hinterland with the amenities of its market, the use of its shops, its weights and measures, its moneylenders, its lawyers, even its distractions. It has to dominate an empire, however tiny, in order to exist.

Varzy, now in the Nièvre, barely numbered two thousand inhabitants at the beginning of the eighteenth century. But it was well and truly a town, with its own bourgeoisie. There were so many lawyers there that one wonders what they could really have done, even in the midst of an illiterate peasant population who obviously had to resort to the pens of others. But these lawyers were also land-owners. Other members of the bourgeoisie were masters of iron-works or tanneries, or wood merchants profiting from the traffic in 'lost logs' along the rivers, sometimes involved in the colossal pro-visioning of Paris, and owning forests as far as the distant Barrois. This is really a typical case of a small Western town. There are thousands of similar examples.

Numbers certainly determine the character of the town. All the same, they have to be specified with a certain accuracy. Present-day statistics use an arbitrary figure – 2000 inhabitants for French censuses – to distinguish between towns and smaller rural communi-ties. If we wanted to follow this procedure for the past – a risky method – the dividing line would need to be lowered considerably. Before 1500, 90% to 95% of the towns known in the West had fewer than 2000 inhabitants. A fairly reliable calculation for the 3000 places in Germany that had been granted the status of cities gives an average population of no more than 400 individuals. There were, therefore, some very small towns there, well below the size of Varzy, caught up in a rural life which submerged them but which they none the less transformed, preparing the way for certain develop-ments for the benefit of more important towns which they supplied with manual labour, apprentices and even skilled workers.

This was the case in the West, where so many urban constellations revolved around one dominant town. But China had similar hierar-chies (*Fou*, town of the first order, *Tcheou* of the second, *Hien* of the third), and in poor provinces there were rudimentary towns, because of the 'need to control half-savage peoples who were impatient of the yoke of authority'. A German doctor who passed through a small town on the road from Yedo (Tokyo) in Japan in 1690 counted 500 houses there, including the suburbs – a detail that alone would prove it really was a town. But, of course, these figures are only valid when seen in relation to the whole population.

In English America, around 1700, Boston numbered 7000 inhabitants, Philadelphia 4000, Newport 2600, Charlestown 1100, New York, 3900. However bricks had replaced wood in house-building after 1642 in New York (at that time Nieuwe Amsterdam), an obvious symptom of urbanisation. Moreover no one would not acknowledge the urban character of these centres – even when they were still small-scale. In 1690 the urban concentra-tion made possible by a total population of some 200,000 people dispersed over a vast expanse represented 9% of the population.

There probably was more or less the same proportion between towns and villages in Germany in 1500 (10%).

Nevertheless the urban population in Flanders and Brabant a century earlier is said to have already been 50% of the total population, the proportion for western and central Europe towards the end of the eighteenth century being 20% to 25%; for France, which had remained rural, only 16%. On the other hand, half the population of England according to certain calculations was grouped in the towns in about 1700. But this remains questionable (it would be more accurate to say 30%).

With a non-rural population in the vicinity of 50% or even 40%, an entire region automatically and under its own impetus moved into the category of a modern economy, freed from the rural hold and relieved of a heavy primary sector. And this shift was a considerable event in itself. The census of 1795 recorded a rural population of only 45·6% of the total in the Netherlands province of Overijssel; it had crossed the line. In the East, in Muscovy where everything was behind, towns represented 2·5% of the total population in 1630, 3% in 1724, 4% in 1796, and 13% in 1897.

Division of labour

The essential problem at the beginning and throughout the life of towns in Europe and elsewhere remains the same: the division of labour between the countryside and the urban centres, a division which has never been perfectly defined and which calls for continual reassessment, because the positions of the partners change incessantly. The formula is always being recast in one or the other direction.

The urban problem consists of separating out certain activities in a partnership which was originally a joint one. Economists would describe it as detaching the specialised 'secondary' sectors from a primary sector incorporating the whole. In theory (and only in theory), the merchants, the functions of political, religious and economic control, and the craft activities, would move over to the town side. However the complete span of professions can only spread out in a town of a certain size, for instance Frankfurt-am-Main or Strasbourg. Numbers alone allow this elementary rationalisation. It cannot occur in the small towns where manpower is too limited and which all continue to ensure the exploitation of their own land.

In fact town and countryside never separate like oil and water because the bond uniting them neither breaks nor pulls one way only. They separate and draw closer together at the same time, split up and then regroup. Even in Islamic lands the town does not ignore or exclude the countryside, despite the steep gulf separating them. It even develops efficient agriculture and market-gardening activities around it. Certain water-channels along urban streets are extended to the gardens of nearby oases. The same symbiosis occurs in China where the countryside is fertilised with refuse and rubbish from the town.

But there is little point in trying to demonstrate what is self-evident. Until very recently every town had to have its foodstuffs within easy reach. An economic historian familiar with the statistics estimates that from the eleventh century a centre holding 3000 inhabitants had to have the lands of some ten villages at its disposal in order to live, or approximately 8·5 square kilometres, 'in view of the low yield of agriculture'. In fact the countryside has to support the town if the town is not to live in a constant state of anxiety with regard to its subsistence. It can be fed by large-scale trade only partially and in rare circumstances. And this applies only to privileged towns such as Florence, Bruges, Venice, Naples, Rome, Peking, Istanbul, Delhi, and Mecca.

Moreover even the large towns continued to engage in rural activities up to the eighteenth century. In the West they therefore housed shepherds, gamekeepers, agricultural workers and vine-growers (even in Paris). Every town generally owned a surrounding area of gardens and orchards inside and outside its walls, and fields farther away, sometimes divided into three breaks, as in Frankfurt-am-Main, Worms, Basle and Munich. In the middle ages the noise of the flail could be heard right up to the *Rathaus* in Ulm, Augsburg or Nuremburg. Pigs were reared in freedom in the streets. And the streets were so dirty and muddy that they had to be crossed on stilts, unless wooden bridges were thrown across from one side to the other. The main streets of Frankfurt were hurriedly covered with straw or wood shavings on the eve of the fairs.

As for the innumerable small towns, they were barely outside the framework of country life. All the same, Weinsburg, Heilbronn, Stuttgart and Esslingen in vine-growing lower Swabia took it upon themselves to send the wine they produced to the Danube, and wine was an industry in itself. Jerez de la Frontera, near Seville, stated in answer to an inquiry in 1582 that 'the town has only its harvests of wine, corn, oil and meat', which were enough for its well-being and to keep its trade and its workers alive. Algerian pirates were able to take Gibraltar by surprise in 1540 because they knew the customs of the place and chose the time of the grape harvest. All the inhabitants were outside the walls, sleeping in their vineyards. True, towns everywhere guarded their vineyards jealously. Hundreds of municipal magistratures every year – in Rothenburg in Bavaria or in Bar-le-Duc, for example – proclaimed the opening of the grape-harvest when the 'vine leaves have taken on that yellow hue that proclaims their ripeness'. Florence itself received thousands of barrels every autumn and was transformed into an enormous market for new wine.

Townsmen in those days were often only semi-townsmen. At harvest-time artisans and others left their houses and trades behind them and went to work in the fields. This was true of busy, over-populated Flanders in the sixteenth century. It was also true of England, even on the eve of its industrial revolution; and of Florence where the very considerable art of wool was primarily a winter activity in the sixteenth century. A diary kept by Jean Pussot, master-carpenter of Rheims, shows greater interest in vintages, harvests, the quality of the wine, and corn and bread prices, than in the events of political or craft life. At the time of the French Religious Wars the people of Rheims and the people of Epernay were not on the same side and both harvested their vines well escorted. But our carpenter notes, 'the thieves of Epernay took the herd of pigs away from the town [of Rheims] ... they took them to the aforesaid Epernay on Tuesday the thirtieth day of March 1593'. It was not only a question of knowing who would win, the Leaguers or Henry IV, but of who would salt and eat the meat. Things had barely changed in 1722 when a treatise on economy deplores the fact that artisans instead of peasants took a hand in agriculture in small and even princely towns in Germany. It would be better if everyone 'kept in his own station'. Towns would be cleaner and healthier if they were cleared of livestock and their 'large stores of manure'. The solution would be 'to ban agriculture to towns and craftsmen and to put it in the hands of those suited to it'. Artisans would have the advantage of selling to the countrymen in proportion to what the countrymen would be assured of selling regularly to the town. Everyone would gain thereby.

If the town did not completely surrender the monopoly of crops or stock-raising to the countryside, conversely the countryside did not give up all its 'industrial' activities in favour of nearby towns. It had its share of them, although they were generally those activities the towns were glad enough to leave to them. For a start the villages had never been without craftsmen. Cartwheels were manufactured and repaired locally in the village itself by the wheelwright and ringed with iron by the blacksmith (the technique spread at the end of the sixteenth century). Every large village had its shoeing smith. Such activities could still be seen in France until the beginning of the twentieth century. Moreover, in Flanders and elsewhere, where the towns had established a sort of industrial monopoly in the eleventh and twelfth centuries, town industries surged back towards the rural outskirts on a vast scale in about the fifteenth and sixteenth centuries in search of cheaper manpower, outside the protection and meticulous supervision of the urban craft guilds. The town lost nothing thereby, controlling as it did the wretched rural workers outside its walls and managing them as it wanted. But the ungenerous division provoked quarrels. In any case in the seventeenth century, and even more in the following century, villages resumed a very large part of craft activities.

The same division was to be found elsewhere, but organised differently – in Russia, India and China for example. In Russia the greater part of the industrial tasks fell upon the villages, which were self-supporting. Urban agglomerations did not dominate or disturb them as in the towns in the West. There was as yet no real competition between townsmen and peasants. This is clearly explained by the slow rate of urban growth. There were probably a few large towns, despite the accidents they suffered (Moscow, burned by the Tartars in 1571 and set alight by the Poles in 1611, would appear to have contained not fewer than 40,000 houses in 1636). But in a poorly urbanised country, villages were necessarily forced to do everything by themselves. Apart from which the owners of large estates organised certain paying industries with their serfs. The long Russian winter therefore did not bear the sole responsibility for the lively activity of these country-dwellers.

The village in India was similarly self-sufficient. A lively community, capable on occasion of moving en bloc to escape some danger or too heavy oppression, it paid taxes to the town but only called on it for rare commodities (iron tools for example). In China the country craftsman supplemented his hard life by work in silk or cotton. His low standard of living made him a formidable competitor with the town craftsman. An English traveller (1793) registered surprise and delight at the unwonted sight of peasant women near Peking breeding silk worms and spinning cotton: 'which is in general use for both sexes of the people, but the women are almost the sole weavers throughout the Empire'.

The town and newcomers (the poor)

A town would probably cease to exist without its supply of new people. It attracts them. But they often come of their own accord towards its lights, its real or apparent freedom, and its higher wages. They come too because first the countryside and also other towns no longer want them and reject them. The standard stable partnership is between a poor region with regular emigration and an active town: Friuli in relation to Venice – the *Furlani* supplied it with its common labourers and servants; the Kabylias in relation to Algiers under the pirates – the mountain-dwellers went down to dig the gardens in the town and surrounding countryside; Marseilles and Corsica; the towns of Provence and the *gavots* of the Alps; London and the Irish. But every big town would have many different places of recruitment.

In Paris in 1788:

> The people known as common labourers are almost all foreigners. The Savoyards are decorators, floor polishers and sawyers: the Auvergnats ... almost all water-carriers; the natives of Limousin are masons; the Lyonnais are generally porters and chair-carriers; the Normans, stone cutters, pavers and pedlars, menders of crockery, rabbit-skin merchants; the Gascons, wigmakers or *carabins* [barbers' assistants]; the Lorrainers, travelling shoemakers or cobblers .... The Savoyards live in the suburbs; they are organised by rooms, each run by a chief or an old Savoyard who is treasurer and tutor to the young children until they reach an age to govern themselves.

A certain Auvergnat who hawked rabbit skins, buying them individually and reselling them in quantity, travelled around 'so overloaded that one looks [in vain] for his head and arms'. And of course, all these poor people bought their clothes at the second-hand shops on the quai de la Ferraille or the Mégisserie where everything was bartered. 'Someone [goes into] the shop as black as a crow and leaves it green as a parrot.'

But the towns did not only welcome poor wretches such as these. They also recruited at the expense of the bourgeois in neighbouring or distant towns: rich merchants, masters and craftsmen (whose services were sometimes fought over), mercenaries, ships' pilots, professors and doctors, engineers, architects, painters. Thus the points from which apprentices and masters of its *Arte Della Lana* came to Florence in the sixteenth century could be marked on the map of northern and central Italy. In the preceding century they had come in a steady stream from the Netherlands. The origins of new citizens in a lively town like Metz or Constance for example (the latter from 1367 to 1517) could equally well be marked on a map. In each case it would disclose a wide area associated with the life of the town concerned. Perhaps this might after all be the same area that would be marked out by the radius of its commercial relations, if we put in the villages, towns and markets that accepted its systems of measures or money, or both, or which, failing that, spoke its dialect.

Such constant recruitment was a matter of necessity. Before the eighteenth century the town had scarcely any excess of births over deaths. It suffered from too high an incidence of mortality. If it was to grow, it could not do so by itself. Socially as well, it left the lowly tasks to new arrivals. Like our over-pressurised economies today, it needed North Africans or Puerto Ricans in its service, a proletariat which it quickly used up and had quickly to renew. The existence of this wretched and lowly proletariat is a feature of any large town.

An average of 20,000 people died in Paris every year, even after the 1780s. Some 4000 ended their days in the poor-house, either at the Hôtel-Dieu or the Bicêtre. The dead were 'sewn up in sacking' and buried unceremoniously in the paupers' grave at Clamart, which was sprinkled with quick lime. A hand-drawn cart carried the dead southwards from the Hôtel-Dieu every night. 'A mud-bespattered priest, a bell, a cross' – such was the true funeral procession of the poor. Everything about the poor-house 'is hard and cruel'; 1200 beds for 5000 to 6000 sick people. 'The newcomer is bedded down beside a dying man and a corpse . . .'

And life was no kinder in its beginnings. Paris had 7000 to 8000 abandoned children out of some 30,000 births around 1780. Depositing these children at the poor-house was an occupation in itself. The man carried them on his back 'in a padded box which can hold three. They stand in their swaddling clothes, breathing through the top . . . When [the carrier] opens his box, he often finds one of them dead; he completes his journey with the other two, impatient to be rid of the load. . . . He immediately sets off once more to start the same task, which is his livelihood, over again.' Many of these abandoned children came from the provinces. Strange immigrants indeed.

The aloofness of towns

Every town is and wants to be a world apart. It is a striking fact that all of them or nearly all between the fifteenth and eighteenth centuries had ramparts. They were held in a restrictive and distinctive geometry, hence cut off even from their own immediate surrounds.

Insecurity and ramparts

The first point is security. Protection was only superfluous in a few countries; in the British Isles, for example, there were practically no urban fortifications. They were thus spared a lot of useless investment, according to economists. The old city walls in London had only an administrative function, although temporary fear on the part of the Parliamentarians in 1643 caused fortifications to be hurriedly built around the town. Nor were there any fortifications in the Japanese archipelago, which was also protected by the sea, nor in Venice, an island in itself. There were no walls in self-confident countries like the vast Osmanli Empire which had ramparted towns only on its threatened frontiers – in Hungary facing Europe, in Armenia facing Persia. Both Erivan (where there was a small force of artillery) and Erzerum (crowded by its suburbs) were surrounded by double walls (though not earthworks) in 1694. Everywhere else the *pax turcica* brought about the ruin of the ancient ramparts. They deteriorated like the walls of abandoned estates, even the wonderful ramparts at Istanbul inherited from Byzantium. Opposite, in Galata, in 1694, 'the walls [are] half-ruined and the Turks do not seem to be thinking of rebuilding them'.

No such confidence was to be found anywhere else. Urban fortification became the general rule across continental Europe (Russian towns were ramparted to a greater or lesser degree and depended on a fortress as Moscow depended on the Kremlin), across colonial America, Persia, India and China. Furetière's *Dictionnaire* (1690) defined a town as the 'home of a large number of people which is normally enclosed by walls'. But the definition was not valid for the West alone.

In China only second-rate or declining towns no longer had or never had had walls. Ramparts were usually impressive, and so high that they concealed 'the tops of the houses' from view. Towns there were all built in the same way and in a square [said a traveller (1639)] with fine brick walls which they cover with the same clay from which they make porcelain; this hardens so much in the course of time that it is impossible to break it with a hammer. ... The walls are very wide and flanked with towers built in the classic style, almost in the same fashion as one sees Roman fortifications depicted. Two large wide roads generally cut the town crosswise and they are so straight that, although they run the whole length of a town, however large it may be, the four gates are always visible from the crossroads.

The wall of Peking, said the same traveller, much more than the walls of European towns, is 'so wide that twelve horses could run abreast on it at full speed without colliding [let us not take his word for it: another traveller (1697) mentions a width of only twenty feet]. It is guarded at night as if it were war-time, but in daytime the gates are not guarded except by Eunuchs who stay there rather to collect entrance fees than for the safety of the town.' On 17 August 1668 a torrential flood submerged the countryside around the capital and 'a quantity of villages and country houses [were carried away] by the momentum of the water'. The new town thereby lost a third of its houses, but the old town escaped. 'Its gates were promptly closed ... and all holes and all cracks were stuffed with lime and bitumen mixed together.' Here is proof of the almost impervious stability of the walls of Chinese towns.

It was a curious thing in these centuries of *pax sinica*, when danger no longer threatened the towns from outside, that the walls had almost become a system for supervising the townspeople themselves. Soldiers and horsemen could be mobilised in an instant up the wide ramps giving access from within to the heights of the ramparts where they could overlook the whole town. There was no doubt that the town was firmly held by the responsible authorities. Moreover every street in both China and Japan had individual gates and internal jurisdiction. Any incident whatsoever, any misdeed, and the gates of the street were closed and the guilty or arrested person immediately, often bloodily, punished. The system was all the more foolproof in China in that everywhere the square of the Tartar town stood next to the Chinese town and watched closely over it.

The wall frequently enclosed a portion of fields and gardens together with the town. This was for obvious reasons of supplies in case of war. Such was the case with the ramparts rapidly constructed in Castile in the eleventh and twelfth centuries around a group of villages at some distance from each other, with enough space left between them to hold the flocks in case of emergency. The rule is valid wherever, in anticipation of a siege, ramparts enclosed meadows and gardens, as in Florence, or arable land, orchards and vineyards, as in Poitiers. In fact Poitiers' walls, even in the seventeenth century, were almost as extensive as those of Paris, but the town took a long time to grow into this outsize garment. Similarly, Prague took a long time to fill up the space left between the houses of the 'small town' and the new ramparts built in the middle of the fourteenth century. The same applied to Toulouse from 1400; and to Barcelona, which took two centuries (until about 1550) to reach the ramparts reconstructed around it in 1359 (on the site of the present-day Ramblas).

The scene was the same in China: one town on the Yang-tse-Kiang 'has a wall ten miles in circumference, which encloses hills, mountains and plains uninhabited because the town has few houses and its inhabitants prefer to live in the very extensive suburbs'. In the same year, 1696, the upper part of the capital of Kiang-Si sheltered 'many fields and gardens, but few inhabitants'.

The West had long ensured security at a low cost by a moat and a perpendicular wall. This did little to interfere with urban expansion – much less than is usually thought. When the town needed more space the walls were moved like theatre sets – in Ghent, Florence, and Strasbourg for example – and as many times as was required. Walls were made-to-measure corsets. Towns grew and made themselves new ones.

But constructed and reconstructed walls did not cease to encircle towns and to define them. They were boundaries, frontiers, as well as protection. The towns pushed the maximum of their craft activity, and particularly their heavy industries, to the periphery, so much so that the wall was an economic and social dividing line as well. As the town grew it generally annexed some of its suburbs and transformed them, pushing activities foreign to strictly urban life a little farther away.

Plans in a chessboard design

Western towns developed gradually and in a haphazard way. That is why their plans are so complicated. Their winding streets and unexpected turnings are quite unlike the pattern of the Roman town, as it still survives, in fact, in a few cities descended from the classical period: Turin, Cologne, Coblenz, Ratisbon. But the Renaissance marked the first development of deliberate town planning, with the flowering of a series of supposedly 'ideal' geometric plans in chessboard pattern or concentric circles. This was the spirit in which the widespread urban development in the West remodelled squares and rebuilt districts acquired from the suburbs.

This new coherence and rationalisation were even better expressed in the new towns where builders had a free hand. Furthermore it is curious that the few examples of chessboard-pattern Western towns before the fifteenth century corresponded to deliberate constructions, built *ex nihilo*. Aigues-mortes, a small port that Saint Louis bought and reconstructed in order to have an outlet on the Mediterranean, was an example. So was the tiny town of Mompazier (in the Dordogne), built by order of the King of England at the end of the thirteenth century. One of the squares of the chessboard design corresponded to the church, another to the market place, surrounded by arcades and equipped with wells. Other examples were to be found in the *terre nuove* of Tuscany in the fourteenth century, Scarperia, San Giovanni Valdarno, Terranuova Bracciolini, and Castelfranco di Sopra. But the town planning honours lists gets rapidly longer from the sixteenth century. One could give a long list of the towns built on a geometric plan, like the new Leghorn after 1575, Nancy, reconstructed from 1588, or Charleville from 1608. The most extraordinary case was still St Petersburg, to which we will return. Founded late, almost all the towns of the New World were similarly constructed on a pre-arranged plan. They formed the largest family of chessboard towns. Those in Spanish America were particularly characteristic, with their streets cutting the *cuadras* at right angles and the two main roads converging on the *Plaza Mayor* where stood the cathedral, the prison, and the town hall – the *Cabildo*.

The chessboard plan poses a curious problem, taking the world as a whole. All the towns in China, Korea, Japan, peninsular India and colonial America (not forgetting those in Rome and certain Greek cities) were planned according to the chessboard pattern. Only two civilisations built confused and irregular towns on a large scale: Islam (including northern India) and the West in the middle ages. One could lose oneself in aesthetic or psychological explanations of these choices by civilisations. There is no doubt that the West was not harking back to the needs of the Roman camp in America in the sixteenth century. What it established in the New World was the reflection of modern Europe's interest in town planning, an urgent taste for order. It would be fascinating to go beyond the numerous manifestations of this taste and investigate its living roots.

Towns, artillery and carriages in the West

Western towns faced severe problems from the fifteenth century onwards. Their populations had increased and artillery made their ancient walls useless. They had to be replaced at all costs, by wide ramparts half sunk in the ground, extended by bastions, terrepleins, 'cavaliers', where loose soil reduced possible damage from bullets. These ramparts were wider horizontally and could no longer be moved without enormous expense. And an empty space in front of these fortified lines was essential to defence operations; buildings, gardens and trees were therefore forbidden there. Occasionally the empty space in the requisite spot had to be recreated by pulling down trees and houses. This was done in Gdansk (Danzig) in 1520, during the Polish-Teutonic war and in 1576 during its conflict with King Stefan Batory.

The town's expansion was thus blocked and it was often, more often than previously, condemned to grow vertically. Houses were very early on being built in Genoa, Paris and Edinburgh with five, six, eight and even ten storeys. Prices of plots rose incessantly and high houses became the general rule everywhere. If London long preferred wood to brick it was also because it made possible lighter, less thick walls at the time when four- to six-storey houses were replacing the old buildings, which generally had two. In Paris 'it was necessary to restrain the excessive height of houses ... because a few individuals had actually built one house on top of another. Height was restricted [just before the Revolution] to seventy feet not including the roof.'

Having the advantage of being without walls, Venice could expand in comfort. A few wooden piles sunk in, stones brought in by boat, and a new district rose up on the lagoon. Heavy industry was very soon pushed back to the periphery, knackers and curriers to the island of Giudecca, the arsenal to the far end of the new district of Castello, glassworks to the island of Murano as early as 1255. It was a kind of modern 'zoning'. Meanwhile Venice spread out its public and private splendour on the Grand Canal, an old and abnormally deep river valley. Only one bridge, the Rialto bridge, made of wood and with a drawbridge (until the construction of the present stone bridge in 1587), linked the Fondaco dei Tedeschi (the present central post office) side of the canal to the Rialto square. This marked out the lively axis of the town – from St Mark's Square to the bridge via the busy street of the Merceria. It was thus a town with plenty of room, a comfortable town. But in the ghetto – a narrow, walled and artificial town – space was cramped and houses shot upwards five or six storeys high.

When the carriage made its massive entry into Europe in the sixteenth century it posed urgent problems and made severe measures necessary. Bramante, who destroyed the old district around St Peter's in Rome (1506–14), was one of Baron Haussmann's first predecessors in history. Towns inevitably regained a little order, more air, better circulation, at least for a time. Pietro di Toledo (1536) chose the same type of reorganisation when he opened a few wide streets across Naples where, as King Ferdinand of Naples had said earlier, 'the narrow streets were a danger to the state'. The completion of the short but sumptuous rectilinear Strada Nuova in Genoa in 1547 represented a similar process, as did the three axes dug across Rome from the Piazza del Popolo at Pope Sixtus v's wishes. It was not by chance that one of them, the Corso, became the commercial street *par excellence* of Rome. Carriages and soon coaches entered the towns at top speed. John Stow, who was present during the first changes in London, prophesied (1528): 'The world runs on wheels.' Thomas Dekker said the same thing in the following century: 'In every street [in London] carts and Coaches make such a thundering as if the world ran upon wheels.'

Urban geography

We have no need to be apprehensive about calling on geography for its contribution. It probably has too much to say, but what it says is clear; it deals in known facts. There is no difficulty in summarising them.

The sites

Every town grows in a given place, is wedded to it and does not leave it, except for very rare exceptions. The site is favourable, to a greater or lesser degree; its original advantages and drawbacks stay with it for ever. A traveller who landed at Bahia (Salvador), then capital of Brazil (1684), mentioned its splendour, the number of slaves 'treated', he added, 'with the utmost barbarity'. He also remarked on the defects of its site: 'The roads slope so steeply that horses harnessed to carriages would not be able to cope with them.' There were therefore no carriages, but beasts of burden and saddle horses. A more serious disadvantage was the sharp drop which cut off the city proper from the lower commercial town by the sea, so that it was necessary to 'use a sort of crane to bring merchandise up and down from the port to the town'. Today lifts accelerate the process, but it still has to be done.

In the same way Constantinople on the Golden Horn, the Sea of Marmara and the Bosporus, divided by large expanses of sea water, had to maintain a tribe of boatmen and ferrymen to make incessant crossings – not always without danger.

But these drawbacks were compensated by important advantages – if not, they would have been neither accepted nor tolerated. The advantages were generally those inherent in the location of the town in relation to neighbouring regions. The Golden Horn was the only sheltered port in an immense stretch of squally sea. The vast All Saints' bay facing Bahia (Salvador) was a miniature Mediterranean, well sheltered behind its islands and one of the easiest points on the Brazilian coast for a sailing ship from Europe to reach. The capital was only moved south to Rio de Janeiro in 1763 because of the development of the Minas Gerais and Goyaz gold mines.

Of course all these advantages could eventually be nullified. Malacca had century after century of monopoly; 'it controlled all the ships which passed its straits'. Then Singapore emerged from nowhere one fine day in 1819. A much better example still is the replacement of Seville (which had monopolised trade with the 'Indies of Castile' since the beginning of the sixteenth century) by Cadiz in 1685. This occurred because ships with too great a draught could no longer pass the bar of San Lucar de Barrameda, at the entrance to Guadalquivir. A technical reason was thus the pretext for a ruthless, though perhaps reasonable change, which none the less gave watchful international smuggling its chance in the vast Bay of Cadiz.

In any case, whether these advantages of location were liable or not to be superseded, they were indispensable to the prosperity of the towns. Cologne was situated at the meeting point of two separate shipping routes on the Rhine – one towards the sea, the other upstream – which met up along its quays. Ratisbon on the Danube was a reloading point for ships with too great a draught coming from Ulm, Augsburg, Austria, Hungary and even Wallachia.

Perhaps no site anywhere in the world was more privileged for short- and long-distance trade than Canton. The town was 'thirty leagues from the sea' but still felt the throb of the tide on its numerous stretches of water. Sea vessels, junks, or three-masters from Europe could therefore link up there with the small craft, the sampans, which reached all (or nearly all) interior China using the canals. 'I have quite often contemplated the beautiful views of the Rhine and the Meuse in Europe,' wrote J-F Michel of Brabant (1753), 'but these two perspectives cannot provide a quarter [of what] that river of Canton alone offers for admiration.' Nevertheless Canton only owed its big chance in the eighteenth century to the Manchu empire's desire to keep European trade as far to the south as possible. Left to themselves, European merchants would have preferred to reach Ning Po and the Yang-tse-Kiang. They had a presentiment of Shanghai and the advantage of reaching the middle of China.

Geography in conjunction with the speed – or rather the slowness – of transport at the time also accounts for the very many small towns. The 3000 towns of all kinds which Germany counted in the fifteenth century were so many relay points – four or five hours' journey away from each other in southern and western regions of the country, seven or eight hours' in northern and eastern. And these breaks were not only situated at ports, between *venuta terrae* and *venuta maris*, as they said in Genoa, but sometimes between carts and river craft, the 'pack saddle used on mountain paths and the cart in the plain'. So true was it that every town welcomed movement, recreated it, scattered people and goods in order to gather new goods and new people, and so on.

It was this movement in and out of its walls that indicated the true town. 'We had a great deal of trouble that day,' complained Careri, arriving at Peking in 1697, 'because of the multitude of carts, camels, and mares which go to Peking and return from it, and which is so large that one has difficulty in moving.'

Town markets

Town markets everywhere made this movement tangible. A traveller could say that Smyrna in 1693 'is only a bazaar and a fair'. But every town, wherever it may be, is first and foremost a market. If there is no market, a town is inconceivable. But a market can be situated near a village, even at a point in the open road or at an ordinary crossroads, without giving rise to a town. Every town, in fact, needs to be rooted in and nourished by the people and land surrounding it.

Daily life within a small radius was provided for by weekly or daily markets in the town; we use the word in the plural, remembering the various markets in Venice, for example, listed in Marin Sanudo's *Cronachetta*. There was the great market in the Rialto square, and near it the specially constructed *loggia* where the merchants assembled every morning. The market sagged under the weight of fruit, meat and game. Fish was sold a little farther on. There was another market in St Mark's Square. But every district had its own, in its main square. Supplies came from peasants from surrounding areas, gardeners from Padua, and boatmen, who even brought ewes' cheese from Lombardy.

A whole book could be written on the Halles in Paris and their offshoot, set aside for game, on the Quai de la Vallée; on the regular dawn invasion of the town by bakers from Gonesse; on the five to six thousand peasants who came in the middle of every night half-asleep on their carts 'bringing vegetables, fruit, flowers', and the hawkers shouting: 'Live mackerel! Fresh herrings! Baked apples! – Oysters! Portugal, Portugal!' (i.e. oranges). The ears of the servants on the upper floors were well attuned to get their bearings in the midst of these noises and not to go down at the wrong moment. During the Fair of the Hams, which took place on the Tuesday of Holy Week, 'a crowd of peasants from the areas around Paris gather in the square and in the Rue Neuve-Notre-Dame early in the morning, equipped with an immense quantity of hams, sausages and black puddings, which they decorate and crown with laurels. What a desecration of Caesar's and Voltaire's crown!' This, of course, is Sébastien Mercier speaking.

But a whole book could equally well be written on London and the many markets which were gradually organised there. A list of these markets fill over four pages of the guide drawn up by Daniel Defoe and his successors (*A Tour through the Island of Great Britain*), reissued for the eighth time in 1775.

The space nearest the town, from where, as in Leipzig, came delicious apples and much-prized asparagus, was only the first of the numerous circles surrounding it. In fact no town was without large gatherings of people and various assets, each involving a particular area around it and often spread out over wide distances. In every instance town life was linked to diverse areas that only partly overlapped. Powerful towns would very quickly, certainly from the fifteenth century, bring innumerable spaces into play. They were the instruments of long-distance relationships forming a kind of overall civic economy which they brought to life and from which they profited.

All these extensions belonged to one family of interrelated issues. Depending on the period, the town affected spaces that varied according to its size. It was by turns inflated and emptied according to the rhythm of its existence. Vietnamese towns were 'little populated on ordinary days' in the seventeenth century. But twice a month on days when the great markets were held they were the scene of very great animation. At Hanoi, then Ke-cho, 'the merchants are grouped in different streets according to their specialities; roads for silk, leather, hats, hemp, iron'. It was impossible to move amidst such a mob. Some of these market streets were shared by people from several villages who 'had sole privilege to set up shop there'. A historian has rightly said that these towns were markets rather than towns. We would prefer to call them fairs rather than towns, but town or market or fair, the result was the same – movements towards concentration, then dispersion, without which a somewhat accelerated economic life could not have been created, either in Vietnam or in the West.

The suburbs

All the towns in the world, beginning with those in the West, had their suburbs. Just as a strong tree is never without shoots at its foot, so towns are never without suburbs. They are the manifestations of its strength, even if they are wretched fringes, shanty towns. Shoddy suburbs are better than none at all.

Suburbs were made up of the poor, the craftsmen, the watermen, the noisy malodorous industries, cheap inns, posting houses, stables for post horses, porters' lodgings. Bremen turned over a new leaf in the seventeenth century: its houses were constructed in brick, roofed with tiles, its streets paved, a few wide avenues built. In the suburbs around it the houses still had straw roofs. To reach the suburbs was always to take a step downwards, in Bremen, London and elsewhere.

Triana, a suburb or rather an extension of Seville often mentioned by Cervantes, became the rendezvous for low-lifers, rogues, prostitutes and dishonest agents of the law. The suburb began on the right bank of the Guadalquivir, level with the bridge of boats which crossed the river towards the upper waters rather as London Bridge – on a different scale – crossed the Thames. Sea shipping arriving on the tide at Seville from San Lucar de Barrameda, Puerto Santa Maria or Cadiz was unable to go beyond this point. Triana would certainly not have had its violent character nor its pleasure gardens beneath their vine arbours if it had not had Seville by its side – Seville with its foreigners, 'Flemish' or otherwise, and its *nouveaux riches*, the *peruleros* who returned there from the New World to enjoy the fortunes they had made. A census in 1561 counted 1664 houses and 2666 families in Triana with four people per family – which meant really overcrowded accommodation and over 10,000 inhabitants, the substance of a town.

As dishonest work did not suffice, to support itself, Triana had its artisans who produced varnished faience tiles – the blue, green and white *azulejos*, with their Islamic geometric patterns (these *azulejos* were exported all over Spain and to the New World). It also had craft industries producing soap – soft soap, hard soap and lye. Careri, who passed through it in 1697, noted that the town of Triana 'has nothing notable except a Carthusian monastery, the Palace and the prisons of the Inquisition'. It is true that by then Seville had been dethroned by Cadiz and was no longer the same.

The relay town

Small towns inevitably grew up at a certain distance from large centres. The speed of transport, which moulded space, laid out a succession of regular stopping points. Stendhal was surprised at the relative tolerance large Italian towns showed towards the average and second-rate towns. They were opposed to these rivals – Florence seized half-dead Pisa in 1406; Genoa filled in the port of Savona in 1525 – but they did not suppress them, and for the excellent reason that they could not; they needed them. A large town necessarily meant a ring of secondary towns, one to weave and dye fabrics, another to organise haulage, a third as a sea port, like Leghorn in relation to Florence for example (Florence preferred Leghorn to Pisa, which was too far inland and hostile); like Alexandria or Suez to Cairo; Tripoli and Alexandretta to Aleppo; Jeddah to Mecca.

In Europe the phenomenon was particularly marked, and small towns were numerous. Richard Häpke was the first to use the expression an 'archipelago of towns' in relation to Flanders, showing its cities linked to each other and more still to Bruges in the fifteenth century, later to Antwerp. 'The Netherlands,' Henri Pirenne repeated, 'are the suburb of Antwerp,' a suburb full of active towns. The same was true, on a small scale, of the markets around Geneva in the fifteenth century; of the local fairs around Milan at the same period; the series of ports linked to Marseilles on the Provence coast in the sixteenth, from Martigues on the pool of Berre up to Fréjus; or the large urban complex that connected San Lucar de Barrameda, Puerto de Santa Maria and Cadiz to Seville; or Venice's urban ring; or Burgos' links with its outer harbours (notably Bilbao) over which it long exercised control, even in its decline; or London and the Thames and Channel ports; or finally the classic example of the Hansa towns. At the lowest limit one could point to Compiègne in 1500 with its single satellite, Pierrefonds; or Senlis, which only had Crépy. This detail in itself passes judgement on the stature of Compiègne and Senlis. A series of these functional connections and dependencies could thus be drawn up: regular circles, lines and intersections of lines, single points.

But these patterns had only a limited duration. If traffic moved faster without changing its favourite routes, relay points were by-passed and went out of use.

Sébastien Mercier could even see this in Paris (1782): 'Second- and third-class towns are imperceptibly becoming depopulated and the immense pit of the capital is not only devouring the gold of the parents but even the honesty and native virtue of their sons who pay dearly for their imprudent curiosity.' But it was a slow process.

François Mauriac tells of an English visitor he welcomed in south-west France:

He slept at the Lion d'Or hotel in Langon and walked about the small sleeping town in the night. He told me that nothing like it exists in England any more. Our provincial life is really a survival, what continues to exist of a world in the process of disappearing and which has already disappeared elsewhere. I took my Englishman to Bazas. What a contrast between this somnolent straggling village and its vast cathedral, evidence of a time when the capital of the Bazadais was a flourishing bishopric. We no longer think about that period when every province formed a world which spoke its own language and built its monuments, a refined and hierarchical society which was not aware of Paris and its fashions. Monstrous Paris which fed on this wonderful material and exhausted it.

In the event Paris was obviously no more to blame than London. The general movement of economic life alone was responsible. It deprived the secondary points of the urban network to the advantage of the main ones. But these major points, in their turn, formed a network amongst themselves on the enlarged scale of the world. And the process began again. Even the capital of Thomas More's island of Utopia, Amaurote, was surrounded by fifty-three cities. What a fine urban network! Each city was less than twenty-four miles from its neighbours, or less than a day's travelling. The whole order would have changed if transport had accelerated, however slightly.

Towns and civilisations: the case of Islam

Another feature common to all the towns, and one which was furthermore at the origin of their profound differences in appearance, was that they were all products of their civilisations. There was a prototype for each of them. Father du Halde writes in 1735: 'I have already said elsewhere that there is almost no difference between the majority of towns in China, so that it is almost enough to have seen one to get an idea of all the others.' We might well apply this rapid but by no means impetuous judgement to the towns of Muscovy, colonial America, Islam (Turkey or Persia), and even – but with much greater hesitation – Europe.

There is no doubt that there was a specific type of Islamic town to be found all over Islam from Gibraltar to the Sunda Isles, and this one case is a sufficient example of the obvious relationships between towns and civilisations.

Islamic towns were generally enormous and far away from each other. Their low houses were clustered together like pomegranate seeds. Islam prohibited high houses, deeming them a mark of odious pride (there were certain exceptions: in Mecca, Jedda, its port, and Cairo). As they could not grow upwards, they invaded public road systems, poorly protected by Muslim law. The streets were lanes which became blocked if two asses with their pack-saddles happened to meet.

[In Istanbul] the streets are narrow, as in our old towns [said a French traveller (1766)]; they are generally dirty and would be very inconvenient in bad weather without the pavements running along either side. When two people meet they have to step off the pavement or get out of the way into a doorway. You are sheltered from the rain there. The majority of houses have only one storey which projects over the ground floor; they are almost all painted in oil. This decoration makes the walls less dark and sombre. . . . All these houses, including even those belonging to the richest nobles and Turks, are built of wood and bricks and whitewashed, which is why fire can do so much damage there in so short a time.

Despite the enormous difference of location the scene was the same in Cairo, described by Volney in 1782, and in the Persian towns which another Frenchman, Raphaël du Mans, uncharitably contemplated a century earlier (1660): 'The streets of the town are . . .

winding,' he wrote, 'uneven, full here and there of the holes those villains dig to piss in, according to the law, so that the urine should not make them unclean by spurting up at them.' Gemelli Careri had the same impression some thirty years later (1694). The streets in Ispahan, as in all Persia, were not paved, resulting in mud in winter and dust in summer. 'This great filthiness is still further increased by the custom of throwing dead animals, together with the blood of those killed by butchers, on to the squares and of publicly relieving oneself wherever one happens to be. . . .' No, this was not Palermo, as has been suggested; Palermo where 'the smallest house . . . is better than the best in Ispahan. . .'.

Every Muslim town was an inextricable network of badly maintained lanes. Slopes were used to the utmost so that rain and streams took charge of the refuse. But this confused topography involved a fairly regular plan. The Great Mosque stood in the centre, with shopping streets (*souqs*) and warehouses (khans or caravanserai) all around; then a series of craftsmen ranged in concentric circles in a traditional order which always reflected notions concerning that which is clean and that which is unclean. For example, perfume and incense merchants, 'clean according to the canonists because devoted to the sacred', were next to the Great Mosque. Near them were silk weavers, goldsmiths and so on. At the outer limits of the town were to be found the curriers, blacksmiths, shoeing smiths, potters, saddlers, dyers and the men who hired out asses. Then at the gates themselves were the country people who came to sell meat, wood, rancid butter, vegetables, 'green herbs', all products of their labour 'or their pilfering'. Another regular feature was the division of races and religions into districts. There was almost always a Christian district and a Jewish district, the latter generally under the protection of the prince's authority and sometimes as a result situated in the very centre of the town, as in Tlemcen.

Of course every town varied slightly from this pattern, if only because of its origins and its importance as a market or craft centre. The main market in Istanbul, the two stone *besistans*, was a town within a town. The Christian districts of Pera and Galata were another town beyond the Golden Horn. The stock exchange stood in the middle of Adrianople. 'Near the stock exchange [1693] is Serachi Street, a mile long and full of good shops selling all sorts of commodities; it is roofed with planks, one on top of the other, with several holes at the sides to let in daylight.' Near the mosque was 'the covered street where the goldsmiths are'.

2 The originality of Western towns

The West was, as it were, the luxury of the world. The towns there had been brought to a standard hardly found anywhere else. They had made Europe's greatness. But although this fact is very well known, the phenomenon is not simple. Specifying that something is superior means referring either to something inferior or to an average in relation to which that thing is superior. It means moving on sooner or later to an uncomfortable and deceptive comparison with the rest of the world. It is impossible, following Max Weber, to discuss costumes, money, towns and capitalism and avoid comparisons, because Europe has never stopped explaining itself 'in relation to other continents'.

What were Europe's differences and original features? Its towns were marked by an unparalleled freedom. They had developed as autonomous worlds and according to their own propensities. They had outwitted the territorial state, which was established slowly and then only grew with their interested co-operation – and was moreover only an enlarged and often insipid copy of their development. They ruled their fields autocratically, regarding them as positive colonial worlds before there were such things and treating them as such (the states did just the same later on). They pursued an economic policy of their own via their satellites and the nervous system of urban relay points; they were capable of breaking down obstacles and creating or recreating protective privileges. Imagine the fine goings-on there would be if modern states were suppressed so that the Chambers of Commerce of the large towns were free to act as they wanted!

These old realities leap to the eye without the help of doubtful comparisons. They lead up to a key problem which can be formulated in two or three different ways: What stopped the rest of the towns in the world enjoying the same relative freedom? Or again – another aspect of the same problem – why was change a striking feature of the destiny of Western towns (even their physical existence was transformed) while the other cities have no history by comparison and seem to have been shut in long periods of immobility? Why were they like steam-engines while the others were like clocks, to parody Lévi-Strauss? In short, comparative history compels us to look for the reason for these differences and to attempt to establish a dynamic 'pattern' of turbulent urban evolution in the West, while the pattern of life in cities in the rest of the world runs in a long, straight and unbroken line across time.

Free worlds

Urban freedom in Europe is a classic and fairly well documented subject; let us start with it.

In a simplified form we can say:

(1) The West well and truly lost its urban framework with the end of the Roman Empire. Moreover the towns in the Empire had been gradually declining from before the arrival of the barbarians. The very relative animation of the Merovingian period was followed, slightly earlier in some places, slightly later in others, by a complete halt.

(2) The urban renaissance from the eleventh century was precipitated by and superimposed on a rise in rural vigour, a growth of fields, vineyards and orchards. Towns grew in harmony with villages and clearly outlined urban law often emerged from the communal privileges of village groups. The town was the country revived and remodelled. The names of a number of streets on the map of Frankfurt (which remained very rural until the sixteenth century) recall the woods, clumps of trees and marshland amidst which the town grew up.

This rural rearrangement naturally brought to the nascent city the representatives of political and social authority: nobles, lay princes and ecclesiastics.

(3) None of this would have been possible without a general return to health and a growing monetary economy. Money was the active and decisive element, come perhaps from afar (from Islam, according to Maurice Lombard). Two centuries before Saint Thomas Aquinas, Alain de Lille said: 'Not Caesar but money is everything now.' Money is the same as saying towns.

Thousands of towns were founded at that time, but few of them went on to brilliant futures. Only certain regions therefore were urbanised in depth, immediately distinguishable from the rest, and played an obvious central role: these were between the Loire and the Rhine, in upper and middle Italy, and at vital points on the Mediterranean coasts. Merchants, craft guilds, industries, long-distance trade and banks were quick to appear there, as well as a bourgeoisie and even some sort of capitalism. The formula so often used to describe this strong and privileged urban body can be repeated without misgivings: 'The town is a world in itself.' But to complete the process it had to break away from other human groups, from rural societies, and from old political connections. It even had to stand apart from its own countryside. The break was achieved either violently or amicably, but it was always a sign of strength, plentiful money and real power. Moreover towns only flowered at vital trade junctions.

Soon there were no more states around these privileged towns. This was the case in Italy and Germany, with the political collapses of the thirteenth century. The hare beat the tortoise for once. Elsewhere – in France, England, Castile, even in Aragon – the earlier rebirth of the territorial state restricted the development of the towns, which in addition were not situated in particularly lively economic areas. They grew less rapidly than elsewhere.

But the main, the unpredictable, thing was that certain towns made themselves into autonomous worlds, city-states, buttressed with privileges (acquired or extorted) like so many juridical ramparts. Perhaps in the past historians have insisted too much on the legal factors involved, for if such considerations were indeed sometimes more important than, or of equal importance to, geographical, sociological and economic factors, this latter category did count to a large extent. What is privilege without material substance?

In fact the miracle in the West was not so much that everything sprang up again from the eleventh century after having first been almost annihilated with the disaster of the fifth. History is full of those slow secular up and down movements, urban expansion, birth and rebirth: Greece from the fifth to the second century BC; Rome too; Islam from the ninth century; China under the Songs. But these revivals always featured two runners, the state and the town. The state usually won and the town then remained subject and under a heavy yoke. The miracle of the first great urban centuries in Europe was that the town won entirely, at least in Italy, Flanders and Germany. It was able to try the experiment of leading a completely separate life for quite a long time. This was a colossal event. Its genesis cannot be pinpointed with certainty, but its enormous consequences are visible.

Modern features of towns

The large cities, and the other towns they touched and to which they served as examples, built an original civilisation on the basis of this freedom and spread techniques which were new, or revived or rediscovered after centuries. They were able to follow fairly rare political, social and economic experiments right through to the end.

In the field of finance the towns organised taxation, finances, public credit and customs and excise. They invented public loans: the first issues of the Monte Vecchio in Venice could be said to go back to 1167, the first formulation of the Casa di San Giorgio to 1407. One after another they re-invented gold money, following Florence which minted the florin in 1252. They organised industry and the crafts; they re-invented long-distance trade, bills of exchange, the first forms of trading companies and accountancy.

They also quickly set in motion their class struggles. Because if the towns were 'communities' as has been said, they were also 'societies' in the modern sense of the word, with their pressures and civil wars: nobles against bourgeois, poor against rich ('thin people', *popolo magro*, against 'fat people', *popolo grasso*). The struggles in Florence were already more deeply akin to those of the French industrial early nineteenth century than conflicts of the Roman type (classical Rome of course). The drama of the *Ciompi* (1378) demonstrates it.

This society divided within itself also faced enemies from without – the worlds of the nobles, princes, peasants, everybody who was not a citizen. These towns were the West's first 'fatherlands'. And certainly their patriotism was for a long time to be more coherent and much more conscious than territorial patriotism, which was slow to appear in the first states. One can ponder this subject looking at an amusing picture representing the battle on 19 June 1502 between the Nuremburg burghers and the Margrave Casimir of Brandenburg-Ansbach who was attacking the town. Most of the townspeople are depicted on foot, in their ordinary clothes and without armour. Their leader, on horseback and dressed in a black suit, is chatting to the humanist Wilibald Pirckheimer, who is wearing one of the enormous hats of the period with ostrich feathers, and who (the fact is also significant) is leading a band of men to assist the rightful cause of the attacked town. The Brandenburg assailants are heavily equipped, armed horsemen, their faces hidden by the visors of their helmets. One group of three men in the picture could be taken as a symbol of the freedom of the towns against the authority of princes and nobles: two burghers with unshielded faces proudly frame an armoured horseman they are taking away – a prisoner and ashamed of the fact.

'Burghers', little 'bourgeois' fatherlands: these are convenient terms but highly imprecise. Werner Sombart has placed a good deal of emphasis on this birth of a society, and more still of a new state of mind. 'It is in Florence towards the end of the fourteenth century, if I am not mistaken,' he wrote, 'that we meet the perfect bourgeois citizen for the first time.' Perhaps. In fact the assumption of power (1293) by the *Arti Maggiori* – those of wool and of the *Arte di Calimala* – was the victory of the *nouveaux riches* and the spirit of enterprise in Florence. Sombart, as usual, preferred to place the problem on the level of states of mind and the development of rational spirit, rather than on the plane of societies, or even of the economy, where he was afraid of following in Marx's footsteps.

A new state of mind was established, broadly that of an early, still faltering, Western capitalism – a collection of rules, possibilities, calculations, the art both of getting rich and of living. And also gambling and risk: the key words of commercial language, *fortuna, ventura, ragione, prudenza, sicurta*, define the risks to be guarded against. It was certainly no longer a question of living from day to day, like the nobles, by somehow or other raising returns to the level of expenditure and letting the future take care of itself. The merchant was economical with his money, calculated his expenditure according to his returns, his investments according to their yield. The hour-glass had turned back the right way. He would also be economical with his time: a merchant could already say that *chi tempo ha e tempo aspetta tempo perde*, which means much the same thing as 'time is money'.

Capitalism and towns were basically the same thing in the West. Lewis Mumford humorously claimed that capitalism was the cuckoo's egg laid in the confined nest of the medieval towns. By this he meant to convey that the bird was destined to grow inordinately and burst its tight framework (which was true), and then link up with the state, the conqueror of towns but heir to their institutions and way of thinking and completely incapable of dispensing with them. The important thing was that even when it had declined as a city the town continued to rule the roost all the time it was passing into the actual or apparent service of the prince. The wealth of the state would still be the wealth of the town: Portugal converged on Lisbon, the Netherlands on Amsterdam, and English primacy was London's primacy (the capital modelled England in its own image after the peaceful revolution of 1688). The latent defect in the Spanish imperial economy was that it was based on Seville – a controlled town rotten with dishonest officials and long dominated by foreign capitalists – and not on a powerful free town capable of producing and carrying through a really individual economic policy. Likewise, if Louis XIV did not succeed in founding a 'royal bank', despite various projects (1703, 1706, 1709), it was because the merchants 'were afraid . . . that the king would lay hands on the deposits in the bank'. Paris did not offer the protection of a town free to do what it wanted and accountable to no one.

Urban patterns

Let us imagine we are looking at a comprehensive history of the towns of Europe covering the complete series of their forms from the Greek town to the eighteenth-century town – everything Europe was able to build at home and overseas, in the Muscovite East and across the Atlantic. The abundant material could be classified in many ways according to political, economic or social characteristics. Politically a differentiation would be made between capitals, fortresses and administrative towns in the full meaning of 'administrative'. Economically, one would distinguish between ports, caravan towns, market towns, industrial towns and money markets. Socially, a list could be drawn up of *rentier* towns, and Church, Court or craftsmen's towns. This is to adopt a series of fairly obvious categories, divisible into sub-categories and capable of absorbing all sorts of local varieties. Such a classification has its advantages, not so much for the overall problem of the town itself as for the study of particular economies limited in time and space.

On the other hand some more general distinctions arising out of the very process of town development offer a more useful classification for our purpose. The West has had three basic types of town in the course of its evolution (we are, of course, over-simplifying) : open towns, that is to say not differentiated from their hinterland, even blending into it (A); towns closed in on themselves in every sense, their walls marking the boundaries of an individual way of life more than a territory (B); finally towns held in the whole known gamut of subjection by prince and state (C).

Roughly, A preceded B, and B preceded C. But there is no suggestion of strict succession about this order. It is rather a question of directions and dimensions shaping the complicated careers of the Western towns. They did not all develop at the same time or in the same way. Later we will see if this 'grid' is valid, as I think it is, for classifying all the towns of the world; if one of our categories (either simple or composite) can be invoked at the right moment to take in no matter what specific case no matter where.

Open towns: Ancient Greece and Rome

The ancient Greek or Roman town was open to its countryside and on terms of equality with it. Athens accepted within its walls as rightful citizens the Eupatride horse-breeders as well as the small vine-growing peasants so dear to Aristophanes. As soon as the smoke rose above the Pnyx, the peasant responded to the signal and attended the Assembly of the People where he sat beside his equals. At the beginning of the Peloponnesian war the whole Attic country-side automatically converged on Athens, where it was swallowed up and settled, while the Spartans ravaged fields, olive groves and houses. When the Spartans fell back at the approach of winter, the small country folk retrod the road to their homes. The Greek city was in fact the sum of the town and its wide countryside. If this were so, it was because the town had only just been born, only recently become a distinct entity in a given rural area (a century or two is very little on this scale). Moreover the division of industrial activities, source of discord in the future, did not enter into the matter. Athens did have the Ceramic suburb where its potters lived, but they had only small shops. It also had a port, Piraeus, swarming with foreigners, freed men and slaves, where craft activity – we cannot call it industry or pre-industry – was becoming firmly established. But this activity came up against the prejudices of an agricultural society that mistrusted it; it was therefore left to foreigners or slaves. Above all Athens' prosperity did not last long enough for social and political conflicts to come to a head there and push 'Florentine-type' conflicts to the fore. We can just discern a few symptoms. Moreover the villages had their craftsmen and forges where it was pleasant to go and get warm when winter came. In short, industry was rudimentary, foreign and unobtrusive. Likewise, roaming the ruins of old Roman towns, you leave the gates and immediately find yourself in open country: there are no suburbs, which is as good as saying no industry or active well-organised crafts in their proper place.

Towns closed in on themselves: the medieval cities

The medieval city was the classic type of the closed town, a self-sufficient unit, an exclusive Lilliputian native land. Crossing its ramparts was like crossing one of the still serious frontiers in the

world today. You were free to thumb your nose at your neighbour
from the other side of the barrier. He could not touch you. The
peasant who uprooted himself from his land and arrived in the town
was immediately another man. He was free – or rather he had
abandoned a known and hated servitude for another, not always
guessing the extent of it beforehand. But this mattered little. If the
town had adopted him, he could snap his fingers when his lord
called for him. And though obsolete elsewhere, such calls were still
frequently to be heard in Silesia in the eighteenth century and in
Muscovy up to the nineteenth.

Though the towns opened their gates easily it was not enough to
walk through them to be immediately and really part of them. Full
citizens were a jealous minority, a small town inside the town itself.
A citadel of the rich was built up in Venice in 1297 thanks to the
serrata, the closing of the Great Council to new members. The *nobili*
of Venice became a closed class for centuries. Very rarely did anyone force its gates. The category of ordinary *cittadini* – at a lower level
– was probably more hospitable. But the Seigniory very soon created
two types of citizen, one *de intus*, the other *de intus et extra*, the latter
full, the former partial. Fifteen years' residence were still required to
be allowed to apply for the first, twenty-five years for the second. A
decree by the Senate in 1386 even forbade new citizens (including
those who were full citizens) from trading directly in Venice with
German merchants at the Fondego dei Todeschi or outside it. The
small folk in the town were no less mistrustful or hostile to newcomers. According to Marin Sanudo, in June 1520 when too many
wretched peasants came looking for jobs or just a little bread, the
street people attacked them. '*Poltroni*,' they shouted, '*ande arar.*'
('Poltroons, go away and till the land.')

Of course Venice was an extreme example. Moreover it owed the
preservation of its own constitution until 1797 to an aristocratic and
extremely reactionary régime, as well as to the conquest of Terra
Firma at the beginning of the fifteenth century, which extended its
authority as far as the Alps and Brescia. It was the last *polis* in the
West. But citizenship was also parsimoniously granted in Marseilles
in the sixteenth century; it was necessary to have 'ten years of domi-
cile, to possess property, to have married a local girl'. Otherwise the
man remained amongst the masses of non-citizens of the town. This
limited conception of citizenship was the general rule everywhere.
The town was none the less a whole, with its own statutes and its
privileges in relation to state and nearby countryside. Even in a still

poorly urbanised country like France these distinctions only disappeared with the abolition of privileges on the memorable night of 4 August 1789.

The main source of contention can be glimpsed throughout this vast process: to whom did industry and craft, their privileges and profits, belong? In fact they belonged to the town, to its authorities and to its merchant entrepreneurs. They decided if it were necessary to deprive, or to try to deprive, the rural area of the city of the right to spin, weave and dye, or if on the contrary it would be advantageous to grant it these rights. Everything was possible in these interchanges, as the history of each individual town shows.

As far as work inside the walls was concerned (we can hardly call it industry without qualification), everything was arranged for the benefit of the craft guilds. They enjoyed exclusive contiguous monopolies, fiercely defended along the imprecise frontiers that so easily led to absurd conflicts. The urban authorities did not always have the situation under control. Sooner or later, with the help of money, they were to allow obvious, acknowledged, honorary superiorities, consecrated by money or power, to become apparent. The 'Six Corps' (drapers, grocers, haberdashers, furriers, hosiers, goldsmiths) were the commercial aristocracy of Paris from 1625. In Florence it was the *Arte de la lana* and the *Arte di Calimala* (engaged in dyeing fabric imported from the north, unbleached). But town museums in Germany supply the best evidence of these old situations. In Ulm, for example, each guild owned a picture hinged in triptych form. The side panels represented characteristic scenes of the craft. The centre, like a treasured family album, showed innumerable small portraits recalling the successive generations of masters of the guild over the centuries.

An even more telling example was the City of London and its annexes (running along its walls) in the eighteenth century, still the domain of fussy, obsolete and powerful guilds. If Westminster and the suburbs were growing continually, noted a well-informed economist (1754), it was for obvious reasons: 'These suburbs are free and present a clear field for every industrious citizen, while in its bosom London feeds ninety-two of all sorts of those exclusive companies [guilds], whose numerous members can be seen adorning the Lord Mayor's Show every year with immoderate pomp.' Let us come to a halt here before this colourful scene. And also for the moment let us pass over the free crafts around London and elsewhere which kept outside the guild-masterships and their frameworks, outside their constraint and protection. We will have occasion to mention them again.

Subject towns in the early modern period

Everywhere in Europe, as soon as the state was firmly established it disciplined the towns with instinctive relentlessness, whether or not it used violence. The Hapsburgs did so just as much as the Popes, the German princes just as much as the Medicis or the kings of France. Except in the Netherlands and England obedience was imposed, sometimes with compensations and profitable agreements, as we have already said.

Take Florence as an example: the Medicis had slowly subjugated it, almost elegantly in Lorenzo's time. But after 1532 and the recapture of the town by Cosimo the process accelerated. Florence in the seventeenth century was no more than the Grand Duke's court. He had seized everything – money, the right to govern and to distribute honours. From the Pitti Palace, on the left bank of the Arno, a gallery – a secret passage in fact – allowed the prince to cross the river and reach the Uffizi. This elegant gallery, still in existence today on the Ponte Vecchio, was the thread from which the spider at the extremity of his web supervised the imprisoned town.

In Spain the *corregidor*, the urban administrator, subjected the 'free towns' to the will of the Crown. Of course the Crown left the small profits and the vanities of local administration to the small local nobility. It summoned the delegates of the town *regidores* (in which office could be bought) to meetings of the Cortes – formal assemblies eager to present their grievances but unanimously voting the king his taxes. In France the 'good towns' were just as much under orders. Though enjoying the privileges of their municipal corporations and their manifold fiscal exemptions, they did not prevent the royal government from doubling the *octrois* by its declaration of 21 December 1647 and allocating a good half of them to itself. Paris, equally under the royal thumb, helped – had to help – the royal treasury. Even Louis XIV did not give up the capital. Versailles was not really separate from nearby Paris, and the monarchy had always been accustomed to centre itself upon the powerful, redoubtable city. The monarch spent some time at Fontainebleau, Saint-Germain and Saint-Cloud. At the Louvre he was on the outskirts of Paris; at the Tuileries, almost outside Paris proper. In fact it was advisable to govern these over-populated towns from a distance, at least from time to time. Philip II spent all his time at the Escorial, and Madrid was only at its beginnings. Later the Dukes of Bavaria were in Nymphenburg; Frederick II in Potsdam; the emperors next to Vienna in Schoenbrunn. Moreover to return to Louis XIV, despite everything he did not forget to assert his authority in Paris itself nor to maintain his prestige there. The two great royal squares, the Place des Victoires and the Place Vendôme, were built during his reign. The 'prodigious construction' of Les Invalides was undertaken at that time. Thanks to him, wide access roads where carriages flowed and military marches were organised opened Paris to its nearby countryside on the pattern of Baroque towns. Most important from our point of view was the creation in 1667 of a Lieutenant of Police with exorbitant powers. The second holder of this high office, the Marquis d'Argenson, nominated thirty years later (1697), 'assembled the machine – not the one that exists today', explained Sébastien Mercier, 'but he was the first to think of its main springs and mechanisms. One can even say that today this machine runs by itself.'

We know that later on the large towns blew up in their masters' hands: Paris in 1789, Vienna, Munich and Prague in 1848. We also know that the means of restoring them to order were quite slowly but effectively perfected: to abandon the town to the riots and then return there in full force. Windischgraetz set the example in Prague and Vienna. Versailles applied the method against the Commune in 1871.

Does the rule work?

The triple rule (A, B, C) was only given as a rough model. It outlines a sort of diagram of the development of the Western towns – from A to B and then to C. But it is, of course, understood that urban evolution did not take place by itself, that it was not an endogenous phenomenon, developing in isolation. It also goes without saying – and we have already made this point – that our classification is very much too simple. How does it work outside Western Europe? This is a good opportunity to test its accuracy.

(1) *Towns in colonial America.* We should say 'in Iberian America', because the English towns remained a separate case. They had to live by themselves and leave their wilderness to find a place in the vast world; they constituted what might be called medieval towns. The towns in Iberian America had a much simpler and more limited career. Built like Roman camps inside four earth walls, they were

garrisons lost in the midst of vast hostile expanses, linked together by communications which were slow because they stretched across enormous empty spaces. Curiously, at a period when the privileged medieval town had spread over practically the whole of Europe, the ancient rule still prevailed in all Hispano-Portuguese America outside the large towns of the viceroys: Mexico, Lima, Santiago de Chile, Salvador – that is to say the official, already parasitical organisms.

There were scarcely any purely commercial towns in this part of America, or if there were they were of minor importance. For example Recife – the merchants' town – stood next to aristocratic Olinda, town of great plantation owners, *senhores de engenhos* and slave owners. It was rather like Piraeus or Phalera in relation to Pericles' Athens. Buenos Aires after its second foundation (the successful one in 1580) was still a small market village – like Megara or Aegina. It had the misfortune to have nothing but Indian *bravos* round about, and its inhabitants complained of being forced to earn 'their bread by the sweat of their brow' in this America where the whites were *rentiers*. But caravans of mules or large wooden carts arrived there from the Andes, from Lima, which was a way of acquiring Potosi silver. Sugar, and soon gold, came by sailing ship from Brazil. And contact with Portugal and Africa was maintained through the smuggling carried on by sailing ships bringing Black slaves. But Buenos Aires remained an exception amidst the 'barbarism' of nascent Argentina.

The American town was generally tiny, without these gifts from abroad. It governed itself. No one was really concerned with its fate. Its masters were the landowners who had their houses in the town with rings for tethering their horses fixed on the front walls overlooking the street. These were the 'men of property', *os homens bons* of the municipalities of Brazil, or the *hacendados* of the Spanish *cabildos*. These towns were so many small Spartas or small Thebes of Epaminondas' day It could safely be said that the history of the Western towns in America began again from zero. Naturally there was no separation between the towns and the hinterland and there was no industry to be shared out. Wherever industry appeared – in Mexico for example – it was dependent on slaves or half-slaves. The medieval town would not have been conceivable with serf craftsmen.

(2) *How should Russian towns be classified?* It is indisputably evident at first glance that the towns that survived or grew up again in Muscovy after the terrible catastrophes of the Mongol invasion no

longer lived according to the Western pattern. They were large towns nevertheless, like Moscow or Novgorod, but kept in hand sometimes in a ferocious manner. In the sixteenth century a proverb still asked: 'Who can set his face against God and the mighty Novgorod?' But the proverb was wrong. The town was harshly restored to order in 1427 and then in 1477 (it had to deliver 300 cartloads of gold). Executions, deportations, confiscations followed in quick succession. Above all, these towns were caught up in the slow circulation of traffic over an immense, already Asiatic, still wild, expanse. In 1650, as in the past, transport on the rivers or overland by sledge or by convoys of carts moved with an enormous loss of time. It was often dangerous even to go near villages, and a halt had to be called every evening in open country – as on the Balkan roads – deploying the carriages in a circle, with everyone on the alert to defend himself.

For all these reasons the Muscovy towns did not obtrude on the vast surrounding countryside; quite the reverse. They were unable to dictate their wishes to a peasant world which was biologically extraordinarily strong, but poverty-stricken, restless and perpetually on the move. The important fact was that 'harvests per hectare in the European countries of the East on an average remained constant from the sixteenth to the nineteenth century' – at a low level. There was no healthy rural surplus and therefore no really prosperous town. Nor did the Russian towns have serving them those secondary towns that were a characteristic of the West and its lively trade. All these weaknesses were, as it were, high-lighted by the demographic rise that afflicted Russia in the eighteenth century.

There were innumerable peasant serfs practically without land, insolvent in the eyes of their lords and even the state. It was of no importance whether they went to towns or to work in the houses of rich peasants. In the town they became beggars, porters, craftsmen, poor tradesmen, or very rarely merchants who got rich quickly. They might also stay put and become craftsmen in their own villages. 'In 1760, 62% of the peasants in the Moscow region combined agriculture with home industry: weaving, pottery, passementerie.' Villagers everywhere tried to find in craft, peddling and transport (that peasant industry) the supplementary income they needed for subsistence. Nothing could stop this irresistible search, neither government ukases (sometimes at the demand of town merchants) nor urban controls, nor threat of punishment, the mildest form of which was a whipping.

These examples and others indicate a fate which resembles what could have occurred at the beginning of Western urbanisation. It was something comparable (though more conspicuous) to the caesura between the eleventh and thirteenth centuries, that interlude when almost everything was born of the villages and peasant vitality. We might call it an intermediate position between A and C, the middle stage not having arisen. The prince was there immediately, like the ogre in the fairy tale.

Western historians are too quick to take the stubborn stand that Russia was not European. It is a poor argument. Certainly Novgorod before the fifteenth century owed its Western appearance to its contact with the Hanseatic League. And it was more than a town; it was an empire thrust deep into the heart of Muscovy. Its merchants led expeditions there, as the Canadian and Siberian trappers did later. Furthermore they exploited primitive tribes of huntsmen. Few monetary achievements could be accomplished in such conditions. It was also true that large landowners from the hinterland had their place and their word to say in the popular assembly, the *Vetchi* (was Novgorod 'a feudal republic'?). But there had been similar régimes in both the classical and the Ibero-American city. It has been claimed that deforestation was carried out rapidly and badly, without the stumps being extracted. But there is nothing to suggest that similar practices did not occur here and there in medieval Europe, and we know what brutal treatment the peasant in America even today metes out to his foe the forest.

In short, these arguments seem to carry little weight. There undoubtedly was a time-lag in the destiny of West and East Europe. The European East was trailing behind the West in the eighteenth century, but was rejoining it, moving towards it, wanting to move towards it.

(3) *Imperial towns in the East and Far East.* The same problems and ambiguities – only deeper – arise when we leave Europe to go eastwards.

Towns similar to those in medieval Europe – masters of their fate for a brief moment – only arose in Islam when the empires collapsed. They marked some fine moments for Islamic civilisation. But they only lasted for a time (to the advantage of the marginal towns). Such was certainly the case in Cordoba, or in those fifteenth-century towns which were real urban republics, like Ceuta before 1415 and Oran before 1509. The general rule was the huge town of the prince, or the Caliph: a Baghdad or a Cairo.

Towns in distant Asia were of the same type, imperial or occasionally royal towns – enormous, parasitic, soft and luxurious, Delhi as much as Vijnayanagar or Peking or Nanking before it (although one imagines Nanking as quite different). We are not surprised at the enormous importance the prince enjoyed. And if one of them were swallowed up by the town or rather by his palace, another rose up and the subjection began again. It no longer seems astonishing that these towns were incapable of taking the whole body of their crafts from the countryside: they were both open towns and subject towns at the same time. The sole original feature, which Max Weber strongly emphasises, is that the social structures in both India and China automatically rejected the town and offered, as it were, refractory, sub-standard material to it. Therefore if the town did not win its independence it was not only because of the mandarins' beatings or the prince's cruelty to merchants and ordinary citizens. It was because society was well and truly frozen in a sort of irreducible system, a previous crystallisation.

In the Indies the caste system automatically divided and broke up every urban community. In China the cult of the *gentes* was opposed to a mixture comparable to that which created the Western town – a veritable machine for breaking up old bonds and placing individuals on the same level, the arrival of immigrants creating an 'American' environment where the people already installed set the tone and taught the way of life.

No independent authority represented a Chinese town taken as a whole in its dealing with the state or the enormously powerful countryside. The countryside was the very centre of living, active, thinking China, 'the vegetable mould which continues to feed Chinese thought'. The town, residence of officials and nobles, was not the property of either craftsmen or merchants. There was no comfortably expanding middle class there. No sooner did this middle class evolve than it thought about desertion, being fascinated by the splendours of the mandarins' life. The towns would have lived their own life, would have filled in the contours of their own destiny if individuals and capitalism had had a clear field there. But the tutelary state would hardly consent to this. It had a few moments of inattention, deliberate or not: at the end of the sixteenth century a middle class and a fever for business came into being (one can guess at the part they played in the large iron-works near Peking, in the private porcelain workshops that developed in King-te-tchen, and more still in the rise of silk in Sou-tcheou, the capital of Kiangtsou). But this was only a flash in the pan. With the Manchu conquest the Chinese crisis was resolved in the seventeenth century in such a way as to be against urban freedom.

Only the West swung completely over in favour of its towns. The towns caused the West to advance. It was, let us repeat, an enormous event, but the deep-seated reasons behind it are still inadequately explained. What would the Chinese towns have become if junks had discovered the Cape of Good Hope at the beginning of the fifteenth century, and had made full use of such a chance of world conquest?

3   Large towns

For a long time the only large towns had been in the East and Far East. Marco Polo's wonderment proclaimed the fact: the East was then the site of empires and enormous cities. With the sixteenth century, and more still during the following two centuries, large towns grew up in the West, assumed positions of prime importance and retained them brilliantly thereafter. Europe had thus made up for lost time and wiped out a deficiency (if deficiency there had been). In any case there it was, tasting the luxuries, the new pleasures and the bitterness of large, already over-large, towns. Was it necessary or advantageous to recreate Romes in the classical style? Or to imitate the very expensive luxury of the East?

The states

This late growth would have been inconceivable without the steady advancement of the states: they had caught up with the forward gallop of the towns. It was their capitals which were privileged, whether they deserved it or not. Thenceforth they vied with each other in modernity: which would have the first pavements, the first street lamps, the first steam pumps, the first effective system for supplying and distributing drinking water, the first numbered houses. All this was taking place in London and Paris during the period roughly preceding the French Revolution.

The town that did not grasp this opportunity was necessarily left behind. The more its old shell remained intact, the greater its chance of becoming empty. In the sixteenth century demographic growth had still favoured all the towns indiscriminately whatever their size – large or small. In the seventeenth political success was concentrated on a few towns to the exclusion of others. Despite the depressing economic situation they grew unceasingly, and continually attracted people and privileges.

London and Paris led the movement, but Naples was also in the running with its long-established privileges and with already as many as 300,000 inhabitants in the last years of the sixteenth century. Paris, which the French quarrels had reduced to perhaps 180,000 inhabitants in 1594, had probably doubled by Richelieu's time. And others fell into step behind these large towns: Madrid, Amsterdam, soon Vienna, Munich, Copenhagen and even more St Petersburg. America alone was slow to follow the movement, but its overall population was still very thin. The anachronistic success of Potosi (100,000 inhabitants around 1600) was the temporary success of a mining camp. However brilliant Mexico, Lima or Rio de Janeiro were, they were slow to collect sizeable populations. Rio had at the most 100,000 inhabitants around 1800. As for the hard-working and independent towns in the United States, they fell well below these princely achievements.

This growth of large agglomerations, coinciding with the first modern states, to some extent explains the older phenomenon of the large Eastern and Far Eastern cities – their size was not a function of the density of population, which would have had to be higher in the East than in Europe (we know this is not true), but due to their role as powerful political concentrations. Istanbul probably had 700,000 inhabitants as early as the sixteenth century, but an enormous empire stood behind the enormous town. Behind Peking, which numbered three million inhabitants in 1793, there stood a single and united China. Behind Delhi there stood an almost united India.

The example of India shows how much these official towns were bound up with the prince – to the point of absurdity. Political difficulties, even the prince's whim, uprooted and transplanted the capitals several times. Apart from exceptions which confirm the rule – Benares, Allahabad, Delhi, Madura, Trichinopoly, Multar, Handnar – 'they have wandered like nomads over quite large distances in the course of the centuries'. Even Delhi was moved small distances on its own site two or three times, but its movements consisted of a kind of whirling dance around itself. The capital of Bengal was Rajinahal in 1592, Dacca in 1608, Murshihad in 1704. In each case and in the same way, as soon as its prince abandoned it the town was jeopardised, deteriorated and occasionally died. A stroke of luck was necessary for it to revive. Lahore in 1664 had houses 'much vaster than those at Delhi and Agra, but in the absence of the Court, which had not made this journey for over twenty years, most of them had fallen into ruin. Only five or six sizeable streets remained, two or three of which were over a league long and contained a number of broken-down houses.'

Moreover Delhi was undoubtedly much more the Great Mogul's town than Paris was Louis XIV's. The bankers and tradesmen in the great Chandni Tchoke street, however rich they sometimes were, did not count in relation to the sovereign, his court and his army. When Aurenge-Zebe embarked on the journey which brought him as far as Kashmir in 1663 the whole town followed him because they could not live without his favours and liberality. An improbable crowd formed, estimated at several hundred thousand people by a French doctor who took part in the expedition. Can we imagine Paris following Louis XV during his journey to Metz in 1744?

The flowering of the Japanese towns in the same period was more similar to European growth. In 1609, when Rodrigo Vivero crossed the archipelago and marvelled at it, the largest town was still Kyoto, the old capital and seat of a somnolent Mikado. In the seventeenth century – a great century for Japan as for Holland – censuses for 1626 place Osaka first (300,000 inhabitants and 18,473 houses); Kyoto next (240,000) and Yedo (present-day Tokyo) third (150,000 in 1637). Nagasaki only numbered 40,000 people. Osaka was a meeting place for Japanese merchants. The seventeenth century was the 'Osaka age', a middle-class age, with what could be called Florentine aspects accompanied by a certain simplification of patrician life and the blossoming of a realistic and in some ways popular literature. This literature was written in the national language and no longer in Chinese (the language of letters) and drew enthusiastically on the news and scandals of the Flowers district (the courtesan area).

But Yedo soon moved to the fore. It was the Shogun's capital and very authoritarian with its administration and its concentration of rich landowners, the *daimyo*, who were forced to live there for half the year, under mild supervision, and who regularly came or returned to the city in long and ostentatious processions. After the Shogun's reorganisation at the beginning of the seventeenth century they built their Yedo homes in a district apart from the rest of the population and reserved for the nobles, 'the only people to have their arms painted and gilded above their doors'. Some of these emblazoned doors cost more than twenty thousand ducats, according to our Spanish informant (1609). From then onwards Tokyo (Yedo) did not stop growing. In the eighteenth century it was perhaps twice as large as Paris, but Japan at that period had a larger population than France and its government was much more dictatorial and centralised than that of Versailles.

The function of capital towns

By the laws of a simple and inevitable political arithmetic, it seems that the vaster and more centralised the state, the greater the chance its capital had of being populous. The rule is valid for imperial China, Hanoverian England and the Paris of Louis xiv and Sébastien Mercier. It is even valid for the reasonably large town of Amsterdam, though abandoned by the Courts of the Stadtholder at the end of the seventeenth century.

These towns, as we will see, represented enormous expenditure. Their economy was only balanced by outside resources; others had to pay for their luxury. What use were they therefore, in the West, where they sprang up and asserted themselves so powerfully? The answer is that they produced the modern states, an enormous task requiring an enormous effort. They produced the national markets, without which the modern state would be a pure fiction. For, in fact, the British market was not born solely of the political union of England with Scotland (1707), or the Act of Union with Ireland (1801), or because of the abolition of so many tolls (advantageous in itself), or because of the speeding-up of transport, or the 'canal craze' or the surrounding sea (a natural encouragement to free trade). It was primarily the result of the ebb and flow of merchandise to and from London, an enormous demanding central nervous system which caused everything to move to its own rhythm, overturned everything and quelled everything. Added to this was the enormous cultural, intellectual and even revolutionary role of these hothouses. But the price demanded was very high.

Unbalanced worlds

The right balance had to be struck. Amsterdam was thus an admirable town. It had expanded fast: 30,000 inhabitants in 1530, 115,000 in 1630, 200,000 at the end of the eighteenth century. It aimed at comfort rather than luxury, intelligently supervising the enlargement of its districts. Its four semi-circular canals, like the concentric rings of a tree, marked out the wide physical growth of the town between 1482 and 1658. Light and airy, with its rows of trees, quays and stretches of water, it kept its original character intact. Only one mistake, but a revealing one, was made: the Jordaan districts in the south-west were handed over to unscrupulous contracting companies. Foundations were badly made, canals were narrow; the whole district was situated below the level of the town. And naturally this was the chosen place for a mixed proletariat of Jewish immigrants, *marranos* from Portugal and Spain, Huguenot refugees fleeing France and the wretched of all nationalities.

There is a risk that the retrospective traveller may be disappointed in London, the largest town in Europe (860,000 inhabitants at the end of the eighteenth century). The life of the port was less active than he would suppose. Moreover the town had not taken full advantage of its misfortune (if one can put it that way) after the fire of 1666 to reconstruct itself in a rational manner, despite the plans put forward, in particular the very beautiful one submitted by Wren. It had grown up again haphazardly and only began to improve at the end of the seventeenth century when the large squares in the west were completed: Golden Square, Grosvenor Square, Berkeley Square, Red Lion Square, Kensington Square.

Trade was obviously one of the driving forces behind the monstrous agglomeration. But Werner Sombart has shown that 100,000 people at the most could have lived on the profits of trade in 1700. Taken all together, profits did not add up to the civil list allocation granted to William III, £700,000. London, in fact, lived primarily from the Crown, from the high, middle-grade and minor officials it maintained (high officials were paid in a lordly fashion, with salaries of £1000, £1500 even £2000). It also lived from nobility and gentry who settled in the town, from representatives to the House of Commons who had been in the habit of staying in London with their wives and children since Queen Anne's reign (1702–14), and from the presence of bearers of government bonds whose numbers grew as the years went by. An idle tertiary sector proliferated, turned its stocks, salaries and surplus to good account and unbalanced the powerful life of England to the advantage of London, making it into a unity and creating artificial needs.

The same thing happened in Paris. The expanding town outgrew its walls, adapted its streets to the traffic of carriages, planned its squares and collected an enormous mass of consumers. After 1760 it was full of building sites, where high lifting wheels, 'which raised enormous stones into the air' near Saint-Geneviève and in 'the parish of the Madeleine', were visible from afar. The elder Mirabeau, the 'Friend of Men', would have liked to drive 200,000 people out of the town, starting with royal officers and large landowners and ending up with litigants, who perhaps would have liked nothing better than to go back home. It was true that these wealthy classes and these unwilling spendthrifts supported 'a multitude of merchants, crafts-men, servants, unskilled labourers' and many ecclesiastics and 'tonsured clerics'! 'In several houses,' Sébastien Mercier reported, 'one finds a priest who is regarded as a friend and who is only an honest valet. . . . Then come family tutors who are also priests.' Not to mention bishops breaking residence requirements. Lavoisier drew up the balance sheet for the capital: under the heading of expenditure, 250 million livres for humans, 10 million for horses; on the credit side, 20 million in commercial profits, 140 in government bonds and salaries, 100 million from ground rents or from business activities outside Paris.

None of these facts escaped the observers and economists of the time. 'The wealth of the towns attracts the gay life,' said Cantillon. 'The great and the wealthy,' noted Dr Quesnay, 'have withdrawn to the capital.' Sébastien Mercier listed the endless 'unproductive elements' in the enormous town.

No, [said an Italian text in 1797] Paris is not a real market place, it is too busy supplying itself; it only counts because of its books, the products of its art or fashion, the enormous quantity of money which circulates there, and the speculation on the exchanges, unequalled except by Amsterdam. All industry there is devoted exclusively to luxury: carpets from the Gobelins or the Savonnerie, rich covers from the rue Saint-Victor, hats exported to Spain and the East and West Indies, silk fabrics, taffetas, galloons and ribbons, ecclesiastical habits, mirrors (the wide silvering of which comes from Saint-Gobain), gold work, printing. . . .

The same thing happened in Madrid, Berlin and Naples. Berlin counted 141,283 inhabitants in 1783, including a garrison of 33,088 people (soldiers and families), 13,000 bureaucrats (officials and families), and 10,074 servants; with the addition of Frederick II's court that made 56,000 state 'employees'. All in all, an unhealthy situation. Naples is worth looking at in greater detail.

Naples, from the Royal Palace to the Mercato

Both sordid and beautiful, abjectly poor and very rich, certainly gay and alive, Naples counted 400,000, probably 500,000 inhabitants on the eve of the French Revolution. It was the fourth town in Europe, coming equal with Madrid after London, Paris and Istanbul. A major breakthrough after 1695 extended it in the direction of Borgo di Chiaja, facing the second bay of Naples (the first being Marinella). Only the rich benefited, as authorisation to build outside the walls, granted in 1717, almost exclusively concerned them.

As for the poor, their district stretched out from the vast Largo del Castello, where the burlesque quarrels over the free distribution of victuals took place, to the Mercato, their fief, facing the Paludi plain that began outside the ramparts. They were so crowded that their life encroached and overflowed on to the streets. As today, washing was strung out to dry between the windows. 'The majority of beggars do not have houses; they find nocturnal asylum in a few caves, stables or ruined houses, or (not very different from the last) in houses run by one of their number, with a lantern and a little straw as their sole equipment, entry being obtained in exchange for a *grano* [a small Neapolitan coin] or slightly more, per night.' 'They are to be seen there,' continued the Prince of Strongoli (1783), 'lying like filthy animals, with no distinction of age or sex; all the ugliness and all the offspring which result from this can be imagined.' These ragged poor numbered at the lowest estimate 100,000 people at the end of the century. 'They proliferate, without families, having no relationship with the state except through the gallows and living in such chaos that only God could get his bearings among them.' During the long famine of 1763–4 people died in the streets.

The fault lay in their excessive numbers. Naples drew them but could not feed them all. They barely survived. Next to them an undeveloped lower bourgeoisie of half-starved craftsmen also just managed to get by. The great Giovanni Battista Vico (1668–1741), one of the last universal minds of the West capable of speaking *de omni re scibili*, was paid forty ducats a year as professor at the University of Naples and only managed to live by private lessons, condemned 'to go up and down other people's staircases'.

Above this totally deprived mass let us imagine a super-society of courtiers, great landed nobility, high-ranking ecclesiastics, dishonest officials, judges, advocates, and litigants.

One of the foulest areas of the town, the Castel Capuaro, was situated in the legal district. It contained the *Vicaria*, a sort of Parliament of Naples where justice was bought and sold and 'where pickpockets lie in wait for pockets and purses'. How, asked a too rational

Frenchman, how was it that the social structure remained intact when it was 'laden with an excessive population, numerous beggars, a prodigious body of servants, considerable secular and regular clergy, a military force of over 20,000 men, a multitude of nobles, and an army of 30,000 lawyers'?

But the system held as it had always held, as it held elsewhere and at small cost. In the first place these privileged people did not always receive rich livings. A man got a little money and moved up into the ranks of the nobles. 'The butcher we used to use has no longer practised except through his assistants since becoming a duke,' meaning since he bought a title to the nobility. But we are not forced to take *le Président de Brosses* literally. Above all, thanks to state, Church, nobility and goods, the town attracted all the surplus from the Kingdom of Naples, where there were many peasants, shepherds, sailors, miners, craftsmen and carriers inured to hardship. The town had always fed on this hardship outside its boundaries since Frederick II, the Angevins and the Spaniards. The Church – which the historian Giannone attacked in his vast pamphlet, *Istoria civile del Regno di Napoli* in 1723 – owned at the lowest estimate two-thirds of the landed property in the kingdom, the nobility two-ninths. This restored the balance of Naples. It is true that only one-ninth was left to the *gente più bassa di campagna.*

When Ferdinand, King of Naples, and his wife Marie-Caroline visited Grand Duke Leopold and 'Enlightened' Tuscany in 1785, the unhappy King of Naples, more lazzarone than enlightened prince, grew irritated by the lessons set before him and the reforms held up for his admiration. 'Really,' he said one day to his brother-in-law, Grand Duke Leopold, 'I cannot understand what use all your science is to you; you read incessantly, your people do as you do, and your towns, your capital, your court, everything here is dismal and gloomy. As for me, I know nothing, and my people are still the gayest people of all.' But the old capital of Naples was the Kingdom of Naples, together with Sicily. In comparison little Tuscany could be held in the palm of a hand.

St Petersburg in 1790

St Petersburg, a new town built at the Czar's wishes, marvellously demonstrates the anomalies, the almost monstrous structural disequilibrium of the large towns of the early modern world. And we have the advantage of possessing a good guide to the town and its neighbourhood in 1790, dedicated by its author, the German Johann Gottlieb Georgi, to the Empress Catherine II.

There were certainly few more unfavourable and unpromising sites than the one where, on 16 May 1703, Peter the Great laid the first stone of what would be the famous Peter and Paul fortress. It required his unwavering will power for the town to rise up in this setting of islands and land at water level on the banks of the Neva and its four branches (large and small Neva, large and small Nevska). The ground only rose slightly in the east towards the arsenal and the monastery of Alexander Nevsky, while it was so low in the west that flooding was inevitable there. When the river reached a dangerous level a series of customary signals was set off: cannon shots, white flags in daytime, lanterns permanently lit on the Admiralty Tower at night, bells ringing incessantly. The alarm was given but the danger was not overcome. In 1715 and again in 1775 the whole town was flooded. The threat was present every year. The town had, as it were, to rise above this mortal peril menacing it at ground level. Naturally the moment you began to dig you hit water at two feet, or at seven feet at the very most, so that it was impossible to have cellars under the houses. Despite their price, stone foundations were generally imperative even for wooden buildings, in view of the speed with which planks rotted in the damp ground. Canals also had to be dug across the whole town and edged with fascines, banks of granite blocks – like the Moika and the Fontanka, used by boats bringing wood and food supplies.

Streets and squares in their turn had to be raised from two to five feet according to their location by enormous digging operations, brick or stone masonry and arches to carry the paved roadway and at the same time allow water to flow off the road into the Neva. This prodigious task was systematically undertaken after 1770, starting with the 'fine districts' of the Admiralty on the banks of the large Neva, by Lieutenant-General von Bauer, at Catherine II's orders, and at the imperial treasury's expense.

Urbanisation was therefore slow and expensive. The outline of streets and squares had to be revised, inopportune proliferation of houses restricted, and public buildings and churches, even the remote monastery of Alexander Nevsky, rebuilt in stone. Several houses were also rebuilt in stone, although wood long remained the most common material. It had valuable advantages: comparative warmth inside, lack of dampness, cheapness and speed of construction. Walls were not made of squared beams as in Stockholm, but of undressed trunks. Only the façade was sometimes covered with planks: it could then be decorated with cornices and touched up in colour. A final advantage of these wooden houses was that they could be altered easily and even transported whole from one point in the town to another. The ground floor in the more expensive stone houses was often covered with granite slabs and used as a cellar, or if necessary as poor accommodation. The upper rooms were preferred, so that these houses had át least one, often two and sometimes (though rarely) three storeys.

St Petersburg was therefore a very lively building site. Boats loaded with limestone, stone, marble (all from Ladoga or the Wiborg coast) and blocks of granite arrived via the Neva. Pine beams were floated there and in the process, it was repeatedly said, lost their intrinsic qualities. The workmen, all peasants from the northern provinces, masons or carpenters, were the most curious sight. The carpenters or *plotnidki* – which literally means wooden raft peasants (German translates the word as *Flossbauer*) – had hardly any tools except an axe. Labourers, carpenters and masons all arrived to look for work at the appropriate season. A few weeks were all that were needed for 'the foundations of a stone house to spring up' on a hitherto empty square, 'with its walls seeming to grow before one's eyes and all covered with workmen, while the mud huts where they lived stood round in the likeness of a veritable village'.

Of course the site of St Petersburg also had advantages, if only the amenities and the unparalleled beauty of its river, wider than the Seine and with livelier water movements than the Thames itself. It offered one of the most beautiful town and river views in 'the world between Peter and Paul, Vassiliostrov (the island of Vassili) and the Admiralty. The Neva had its boats and barges; it met the sea at Kronstadt, and after the island of Vassili, where the merchant district, stock exchange and customs were, became a very active maritime port. St Petersburg therefore really was the window opened on the West, the town Peter the Great wanted to incorporate into the violent life of his nation. In addition the Neva supplied the town with drinking water, said to be impeccable.

In winter it was icebound, transformed into a route for sledges and a meeting place for popular merrymaking. At Carnival – in 'butter' week – artificial mounds of ice were erected on the river with frameworks of planks and boards. Light sledges set off from the tops of these structures down a long clear track which the driver negotiated at a crazy speed, 'enough to knock the breath out of him'. Similar tracks were set up elsewhere, in the parks or courtyards of houses, but those on the Neva, supervised by the police, brought a fabulous gathering of people. The whole town went along to watch.

The river and its various branches were only crossed by bridges of boats. Two of these straddled the large Neva. The largest was connected to the commercial island of Vassili from near the square where the lifelike and grandiose statue of Peter the Great (by, or rather in the style of, Falconnet) still stands next to the Admiralty today. It consisted of twenty-one boats, secured at both ends by loaded and firmly anchored barges. Lift-bridges between the boats let ships go through. This bridge used to be hauled in like all the others at the beginning of every autumn, but after 1779 it was left frozen in the ice. It was broken up when the ice melted and they then waited until the water was entirely clear to reassemble it.

Its founder had envisaged the town's developing simultaneously south and north of the river, starting from Peter and Paul. But development took place asymmetrically: slowly on the right bank and fairly rapidly on the left bank of the Neva. The Admiralty quarters and Peter the Great Square on the privileged bank formed the heart of the town as far as the Moika canal, the last canal in the south to be fitted with stone quays. It was the least spacious district but the richest, the most beautiful, and the only one where stone houses (with the exception of the odd imperial building) were the general rule (thirty public buildings and 221 private houses, many of which were palaces). It contained the famous streets of the Small and the Large Million, the magnificent road along the side of the Neva, the beginning of the Nevsky Prospect, the Admiralty, the Winter Palace and its immense square, the Hermitage Gallery, the Senate, and the marble church of St Isaac which took such a long time to build in the square of the same name (1819–58).

Deliberate and conscious zoning separated rich from poor, pushing industries and activities that might have led to congestion – the carrying trade for example – back towards the periphery. The carriers had a wretched town of their own beyond the Ligovich Canal, cut by empty spaces and with a livestock market. The gun foundry (a wooden building built in 1713, reconstructed in stone in 1733) was east of the Admiralty and in the vicinity of the Arsenal, erected by Prince Orlov between 1770 and 1778. The town also had its mint, its mills along the Neva, up- and downstream from the town, and its craftsmen, who were fed better than in Sweden or Germany, bein entitled to coffee and vodka every day before their meals. It manufactured excellent cloth in the Dutch style, and a factory at Casinka near by on the pattern of the Gobelins turned out very beautiful tapestries. The most controversial innovation was the grouping of retail shops into vast markets as in Moscow. There had been one such market on 'Petersburg-island' since 1713 (near Peter and Paul) and later another near the Admiralty. Following the fire which destroyed it in 1736 the market was moved to both sides of the 'Great Prospect' in 1784. These concentrations forced the people of St Petersburg to travel long distances. But the aim was achieved: the official and residential character of the beautiful districts was preserved.

Obviously, certain unharmonious features could not be avoided. A sordid hut occasionally stood next door to a palace; market gardens (to which peasants from Rostow flocked) next door to parks where military music was played on public holidays. Things could not have been otherwise in a town that was growing rapidly and favoured by high prices, the scope of employment and the desires of the government. St Petersburg had 74,273 inhabitants in 1750; 192,486 in 1784; 217,948 in 1789. Sailors, soldiers and cadets (plus their families) accounted for 55,621 of the town's population in 1789, or over a quarter of the total. This artificial aspect of the agglomeration was strongly marked in the enormous difference between numbers of male and female inhabitants (148,520 males compared with 69,428 females). St Petersburg was a town of garrisons, servants and young men. If the figures for baptisms and deaths are to be believed, the town had an excess of births from time to time, but the figures are incomplete and risk being misleading. In any case the predominance of deaths between the ages of twenty and twenty-five indicate that the capital imported young people on a large scale and that they often paid their tribute to the climate, the fevers and tuberculosis.

The wave of immigrants was manifold: officials and nobles hard pressed for promotion, younger sons of families, officers, sailors, soldiers, technicians, professors, artists, entertainers, cooks, foreign tutors, governesses and, even more, the peasants, who flocked in from the poor countryside surrounding the town. They came as haulers and food retailers (they were even accused – and what an irony – of being responsible for the high market prices). In winter they came as ice-breakers on the Neva: the broken blocks (the work was done by Finns) were used to supply the ice-houses to be found on the ground floor of every large house. Or else they were snow- and ice-shovellers at half a rouble a day: they were never done with clearing the approaches to the houses of the rich. Or they might be sledge drivers; they drove customers anywhere they wanted in the enormous city for one or two kopeks and stood at the crossroads where the drivers of the high carrioles had stood the summer before. The Finnish women were chambermaids or cooks. They adapted themselves to their tasks well and sometimes made a good match.

'These inhabitants ... composed of so many different nations ... preserved their individual ways of life,' and beliefs. Greek churches stood next to Protestant places of worship and the *raskolniki* churches. 'There is no town in the world,' continues our informant (1765), 'where more or less every inhabitant speaks such a large number of languages. Even the lowest servant speaks Russian, German and Finnish, and amongst people who have had some education one often meets some who speak eight or nine languages ... which they sometimes mix up to quite pleasing effect.'

Indeed this mixture was the basis of St Petersburg's originality. In 1790 J. G. Georgi found himself wondering if the inhabitants of St Petersburg had a character of their own. He acknowledged their taste for novelty, change, titles, comfort, luxury and expenditure – the tastes of men living in a capital, modelled on those of the court. The court set the tone by its requirements and its celebrations, which were as much occasions for general merrymaking, with magnificent illuminations burning at the Admiralty building, the official palaces and the houses of the rich.

Such an enormous town in the heart of a poor region posed endless problems of supply. There was certainly nothing simpler than bringing live fish from Lakes Ladoga and Onega in barges full of water. But sheep and oxen came to the slaughterhouses from the Ukraine and Astrakhan, the Don and the Volga – from 2000 versts away, even from Turkey. A chronic deficit had to be made up by the imperial treasury and the enormous incomes of the nobles. All the money of the empire flowed into the princely palaces and wealthy houses, where there were abundant tapestries, valuable furniture, carved and gilded panelling and ceilings painted in the 'classical' style. As in Paris and London, houses were divided into numerous individual rooms, with a steadily increasing domestic staff here too.

The most characteristic sight was perhaps the noisy passage of carriages and horses in the streets of the town and the surrounding countryside. These were indispensable in a town of enormous proportions, with muddy streets and only short periods of daylight once winter had set in. On this count an imperial order had specified the rights of each person: only generals in chief or those of equivalent rank could harness six horses to their carriage plus two leading horsemen apart from the coachman. At the lower end of the scale were lieutenants and the bourgeoisie, who had the right to two horses, and craftsmen or merchants who had to be satisfied with one. A series of prohibitions also regulated servants' liveries according to their masters' status. At imperial receptions carriages made a small extra turn at the arrival point, which enabled everyone to see and be seen. Thus no one dared to have only a hired carriage, horses with inferior trappings or a coachman dressed in his peasant costume. A final detail: when courtiers were invited to the castle of Peterhof, situated like Versailles to the west and outside the city, there was not a single horse left in St Petersburg.

Penultimate journey: Peking

We could multiply our journeys and still change none of our conclusions. The luxury of the capitals had always to be borne on the shoulders of others. Not one of them could have existed from the work of its own hands. Sixtus V (1585–90), a pig-headed peasant, misunderstood contemporary Rome. He wanted to make it 'work' and plant industries there, a project which the facts rejected without the need for human persuasion. Sébastien Mercier and a few others dreamt of transforming Paris into a seaport in order to attract hitherto unknown activities there. Had it been possible to recreate Paris in the image of London, then the greatest port in the world, it would still have remained a parasitical town.

It was the same in all capitals, all the towns where the enlightenment and excesses of civilisation, taste and leisure glittered: Madrid or Lisbon, Rome or Genoa, Venice, bent on surviving in its past greatness, or Vienna, at the peak of European elegance during the seventeenth and eighteenth centuries. And also Mexico and Lima. And Rio de Janeiro, capital of Brazil since 1763, which grew incessantly, becoming a handsome human creation within an already sumptuous natural setting, so that travellers would not recognise it from one year to the next. Or Delhi where the splendour of the Great Mogul survived, and Batavia where precocious Dutch colonialism put forth its most beautiful and already poisonous flowers.

What finer example than Peking, capital of the Manchu emperors at the gates to the north and in appalling Siberian cold – diabolical wind, snow and ice – for six months of the year? An enormous population (certainly two, perhaps three million) somehow or other made the best of the climate which no one could stand up to without the plentiful supplies of stone coal 'which lasts and keeps the fire in five or six times longer than charcoal'. Furs were absolutely essential on winter days. Father de Magaillans, whose book only appeared in 1688, once saw as many as four thousand mandarins gathered in the royal room of the Palace covered 'from head to toe in extraordinarily expensive sables'. The rich covered themselves in furs, lining their boots, saddles, chairs, and tents with them. The less wealthy made do with lambskin, the poor with sheepskin. When winter came, all the women 'wear caps and coifs, whether they go out in a chair or on a horse: and they are quite right to do so', says Gemelli Careri, 'because I found the cold intolerable despite my fur-lined robe'. 'Too violent for me,' he added. 'I resolved to leave that town (November 19, 1697).' 'The winter is so cold,' noted a Jesuit father a century later (1777), 'that one cannot open a window on the north side, and the ice stays a foot-and-a-half thick for over three months.' The imperial canal which ensured supplies to the town was closed by ice from November to March.

In 1752 the emperor K'ien Long organised a triumphal entry into Peking to celebrate his mother's sixtieth birthday. Everything had been arranged for the arrival of sumptuous barges by river and canal, but an early cold spell interfered with the celebrations. Thousands of servants vainly beat the water to prevent it from freezing and took out the pieces of ice that formed. The emperor and his suite had to 'replace the barges by sledges'.

Peking consisted of two towns, the old and the new, and many suburbs (theoretically one in front of each of its gates, the most developed being in the west where most of the imperial roads reached the town). It spread out in the middle of a vast low-lying plain, beaten by winds and, worse still, exposed to the flooding of the countryside rivers, the Pei Ho and its tributaries. When their water was running high they could break their banks, change course, and move kilometres away from their original channels.

The new town in the south was shaped like a slightly imperfect rectangle and joined to the old town on its wide northern side. The old town was a regular square, with smaller sides than the adjacent rectangle. The square was the old town of the Mings with the Imperial Palace in the centre. During the conquest of 1644 the palace suffered considerable damage; it was restored by the conqueror very much later. He had to turn to distant southern markets, particularly to replace certain enormous beams, with the inevitable delays and disappointments.

The old town had already proved inadequate to house the growing population of the capital during the Ming period, so that the rectangular town in the south was built well before the 1644 conquest. 'It had clay walls in 1524, then brick walls and gates after 1564.' But after his conquest the conqueror kept the old town for himself, thenceforth making it the Tartar town, and the Chinese were pushed down to the southern town.

Both old and new towns have a chessboard pattern and are of recent date, as is indicated by the unaccustomed width of the streets, particularly those running from south to north. In general those running east and west are narrower. Every street had a name:

Such as the street of the King's Parents, the street of the White Tower, the Iron Lions, the Dry Fish, Spirits and so on. A book is on sale dealing solely with the names and positions of the streets and this is used by the valets who accompany the mandarins on their visits and to their tribunals and who carry their presents, their letters and their orders to various places in the town. ... The most beautiful of all these streets [although laid out from east to west] is the one called *Cham gan kiai*, that is to say the street of Perpetual Repose ... flanked on the northern side by the walls of the King's Palace and on the southern side by various tribunals and the palaces of great nobles. It is so vast that it is over thirty toises [almost sixty metres] wide and so famous that scholars use it to indicate the whole town in their writings, taking the part for the whole; because saying that someone is in the Street of Perpetual Repose is the same as saying that he is in Peking. ... .

These wide, airy streets were full of people. 'The multitude of people in this town is so great,' explained Father de Magaillans, 'that I cannot even attempt to give any idea of their number. All the streets of the old and new towns are full of them, the small as much as the large, and those in the centre as much as those leading to the fringes; the crowd is so large everywhere that it is only comparable to the Fairs and Processions in our Europe.' In 1735 Father du Halde noted:

[the] innumerable multitude of people who fill these streets and the congestion caused by the surprising quantity of horses, mules, asses, camels, carts, waggons and chairs, not counting various groups, one hundred or two hundred strong, who gather here and there to listen to fortune-tellers,

conjurors, singers and others reading or telling some tale conducive to laughter or pleasure, or even to charlatans who distribute their remedies and demonstrate the wonderful effects thereof. People who are not of the common run would be stopped every moment if they were not preceded by a horseman who pushes back the crowd, warning them to make way.

A Spaniard found no better way of conveying the congestion of the Chinese streets (1577) than to say: 'Throw a grain of corn and it will not fall to the ground.'

'Tradesmen with their tools, searching for employment, pedlars offering their wares for sale were everywhere to be seen,' noted an English traveller (1793). The multitude was obviously explained by the increased population figure in 1793. Peking at that time did not have anything like the area of London, but it was two or three times more populous.

Furthermore the houses, even those of the rich, were low. If – as they often did – they had 'five or six apartments', they were not 'one on top of the other as in Europe, but one after another and on the same level. Each apartment was separated from the others by a large courtyard.' Thus one should not imagine the magnificent *Cham gan kiai* as a series of arrogant façades facing the imperial palace. In the first place it would have been unseemly to display such luxury opposite the emperor's house. And then it was customary for each of these individual palaces to have only one large gate on to the street, flanked by two fairly low buildings occupied by servants, merchants and workmen. The streets were thus lined with booths and shops, with tall poles, often decorated with cloth streamers, holding up their sign-boards. The high houses of the nobles were away from the street, which was solely commercial and for crafts.

This custom served public convenience, because [as Father de Magaillans notes] a good part of the streets in our towns [in Europe] are lined with the houses of wealthy people; and one is thus obliged to go a very long way to the market or the ports to obtain necessary articles, while in .Peking – and it is the same in all the other towns of China – everything one could want to buy for maintenance, subsistence and even for pleasure, is to be found at one's doorstep, because these small houses are shops, taverns or stalls.

The sight was the same in all Chinese towns. The same scenes appear on any eighteenth-century picture showing the line of low shops along a street in Nanking, or the houses opening on to their courtyards in Tien Tsin, or on some precious twelfth-century scroll –

the same taverns with benches, the same shops, the same carriers, the same wheelbarrows with sails and the same drivers, and the same teams of oxen. Above all they show a hectic form of life where man only (and then grudgingly) made way for man, everyone elbowing his way, subsisting by dint of work, skill and sobriety. They lived on nothing, 'have wonderful inventions for subsisting'.

However cheap and useless a thing may seem, it has its use, and advantage is taken of it. For example there are over a thousand families in the town of Peking alone [about 1656] who have no other trade to live by except selling matches and wicks to light fires. There are at least as many who live on nothing else but collecting rags of silk fabric and cotton and hempen cloth, pieces of paper and other similar things, in the streets and amongst the sweepers, which they wash and clean and then sell to others who use them for various purposes and profit from it.

Father de Las Cortes (1626) likewise saw porters in Cantonese China who supplemented their work by cultivating a tiny garden. And sellers of herb soup were typical characters in every Chinese street. The proverb ran: 'Nothing is thrown away in the kingdom of China.' All these examples show the extent of latent omnipresent poverty. The spectacular luxury of the emperor, the great men, and the mandarins does not seem part of this lowly world.

A whole book would be needed to describe the Imperial Palace, a town of its own in the old town. It was built on the site of the Yuan's (the Mongols) Palace and had almost inherited the sumptuousness of the Mings, although the ruins of 1644 had had to be rebuilt. Two surrounding walls, one within the other, both sizeable, very high and 'in the shape of a long square', separated it from the old town. The outside wall was 'coated inside and out with cement or red lime and covered with a small roof made of bricks' glazed a golden yellow colour . . .'. The inside wall was made 'of large bricks all of equal size and decorated with well arranged battlements'; a long deep moat filled with water and 'inhabited by excellent fish' stood in front of it. Between the two walls were palaces for different purposes, a river with bridges and a rather large artificial lake to the west.

The heart of the palace was behind the second wall. This was the forbidden city, the Yellow City where the Emperor lived protected by his guards, by check points at the gates, protocol, ramparts, moats and the vast corner-pavilions with twisted roofs, the *Kiao leou*. Every building, every gate and every bridge had its own name and, as it were, its own customs and practices. The forbidden town measured 1 kilometre by 780 metres. 'It could hold the Louvre comfortably.' But it is easier to describe the empty, dilapidated rooms after 1900, when European curiosity could draw up inventories at its leisure, than the activity they once contained, which one suspects to have been enormous. The whole town converged on this source of power and bounty.

A fair measure of it can be got from the endless detailed accounts of the emperor's income, as much in money as in kind (note the double heading). We can hardly imagine what could have been represented by the 'eighteen million six hundred thousand silver écus' to which the main part of the imperial income in money had risen in about 1669. Additional income (still in money) was provided by confiscations, indirect taxes and the domains of the crown or empress. Most tangible and most curious were the mass of dues in kind which filled the vast palace storehouses to bursting point – for example 43,328,134 'sacks of rice and corn', over a million loaves of salt, considerable quantities of vermilion, varnish, dried fruit, pieces of silk, light silks, raw silk, velvets, satin, damask, cotton or hempen cloth, bags of beans (for the emperor's horses), innumerable straw boots, live animals, game . . .

Father de Magaillans was deeply impressed by this prodigious mass of products and the piles of gold and silver platters filled with food and perched on top of each other at imperial feasts. Such a feast was held on 9 December 1669 in honour of the burial of Father Jean Adam, a Jesuit father who together with Father Verbiest succeeded in raising an enormous bell to the top of one of the towers of the palace 'to the great astonishment of the court' in 1661. The bell in question was larger than the bell of Erfurt which (probably wrongly) had the reputation of being the largest and heaviest bell in Europe, even in the world. Positioning this Chinese bell necessitated the construction of a machine and the labour of thousands of arms. The bell was struck by the sentinels at regular intervals during the night to indicate the passing hours. A sentinel at the top of another tower struck an enormous copper drum in reply. The bell had no tongue and was struck with a hammer to produce 'such a pleasant and harmonious tone that it seemed to come much less from a bell than from some musical instrument'. Time was measured in China in those days by burning small sticks or wicks made of a certain type of compressed sawdust with a constant rate of combustion. The westerner justifiably proud of his clocks was to have only limited admiration (unlike Father de Magaillans) for this 'invention worthy of the marvellous industry of the [Chinese] nation'.

Unfortunately we know more about these great palace scenes than about the fish market, where the fish were brought live in tanks of water, or the game markets where a traveller saw one day a prodigious quantity of roe deer, pheasants and partridges. Here the unusual conceals the everyday.

London from Elizabeth I to George III

We come back from these far-off shores and return to Europe, where the example of London will enable us to conclude the chapter and, with it, the present volume. Everything about this prodigious urban development is known or knowable.

In Elizabeth's reign observers already regarded London as an exceptional world. For Thomas Dekker it was 'the Queene of Cities', made incomparably more beautiful by its winding river than Venice itself judged by the marvellous view of the Grand Canal (a very paltry sight compared with what London could offer). Samuel Johnson (20 September 1777) was even more lyrical: 'when a man is tired of London, he is tired of life; for there is in London all that life can afford.'

Growth vainly opposed

The royal government shared these illusions, but it was none the less in constant fear of the enormous capital. In its eyes London was a monster whose unhealthy growth had to be limited at all costs. What alarmed the influential and propertied classes was the invasion by the poor and the proliferation of hovels and vermin that meant a threat to the whole population, including the rich. 'And so a danger to the Queen's own life and the spreading of mortality of the whole nation,' wrote Stow, who feared for the health of Queen Elizabeth and the whole population of his town. The first prohibition on new building (with exceptions in favour of the rich) appeared in 1580. Others followed in 1593, 1607 and 1625. The result was to encourage the dividing-up of existing houses and secret construction-work in poor brick in the courtyards of old houses, away from the street and even from minor alleys. What in fact ensued was a whole clandestine proliferation of hovels and shanties on lands of doubtful ownership. It was no great loss if one or other of these buildings fell victim to the law. Everybody therefore tried their luck, and the network, the labyrinth of lanes and alleys, and the houses with double, triple, even quadruple entrances and exits, grew up as a result. In 1732 London was said to have 5099 streets, lanes and squares, and 95,968 houses. Consequently the rising tide of the London population was neither stemmed nor stopped. The town had 93,000 inhabitants in 1563; 123,000 in 1580; 152,000 in 1593–5; 317,000 in 1632; 700,000 in 1700; and 860,000 at the end of the eighteenth century (all these figures are more or less reliable). It was then the largest town in Europe. Only Paris could compare.

The Thames and the pool of London

London depended on its river. The town was shaped 'like a half moon' because of it. London Bridge, which joined the city to the suburb of Southwark and was the only bridge over the river (300 metres from the present bridge) was the outstanding feature of the landscape. The tide flowed up to this point. The pool, the basin, the port of London, was therefore situated downstream from the bridge, with its quays, its wharves and the often mentioned forest of masts (not without reason: 13,444 ships in 1798). Depending on the load to be discharged, these sailing ships made their way to St Catherine's quay, frequented by coal lighters from Newcastle, or to Billingsgate quay if they carried fresh fish or were involved in the regular service from Billingsgate to Gravesend. Feluccas, barges, tilt boats, ferry boats and barks supplied transport from one bank of the river to the other and from sea-going boats to the appropriate quays – an essential service when these quays were situated upstream from the port. Vintry wharf, which received casks from the Rhine, France, Spain, Portugal and the Canaries, was one such case. It was not far from the Steelyard (or Stilliard), which was the headquarters of the Hanseatic League until 1597 and 'reserved for tasting Rhine wines since the expulsion of foreign merchants'. A character in one of Thomas Dekker's plays says, 'I come to entreat you to meet him this afternoon at the Rhenish Wine house in the Stilliard. . . .'

The utilisation of the river tended to extend farther and farther downstream towards the sea, particularly as the docks – basins inside the bends of the river – were not yet dug, except one belonging to the East India Company (1656). A first impression of the commercial port can be gained either at Billingsgate or at the Tower of London wharf, or better still at that essential barrier, the Customs House, burnt down in 1666 but at once reconstructed by Charles II in 1668. In fact the scene extends as far as Ratcliff, 'infamous rendezvous of prostitutes and robbers', as far as Limehouse, with its lime kilns and tanneries, up to Blackwall, where the pleasure of looking at the anchored boats was balanced by 'the very strong smell of tar'. East London – naval, artisan and slightly dishonest – was not a pleasant sight, and its stench was only too real.

A poverty-stricken population saw the riches from the moored ships dangled before their eyes. In 1798: 'The immense depredations committed on every species of commercial Property in the River Thames, but particularly on West India produce, had long been felt as a grievance of the greatest magnitude....' The 'river pirates' who operated in organised bands, stealing an anchor or a rope when the opportunity offered, were not yet the most dangerous of these thieves. The role was reserved for the night plunderers, the water-men and lightermen, the 'mudlarks', who excavated the river ostensibly searching for old ropes, old iron, or pieces of lost coal, and finally, at the end of the line, the receivers.

All these moralising indictments taken from a *Police Treatise* (1801) convey very precisely the atmosphere of the dubious world of the pool – a vast kingdom of water, wood, sails, tar and menial labour on the margin of the life of the capital but linked to it by routes. The Londoner generally only saw the point where these routes converged.

The north bank

London was primarily on the north bank of its river. The only bridge over it was a commercial street, lined with shops and difficult to cross, leading into a poor suburb, Southwark, the 'Bridge Without'. It contained a few taverns, five prisons of ominous renown, a few theatres and two or three circuses (the Bear Garden, the Paris Garden).

The real town was on the north bank, slightly higher than the opposite bank, with its two eminences, St Paul's Church and the Tower of London. It extended like a 'bridgehead northwards', for it was in a northerly direction that the succession of roads, lanes and alleys linking London to the counties and to the flourishing English countryside actually ran. The great axes, old Roman roads, were directed towards Manchester, Oxford, Dunstable (Watling Street) and Cambridge.

London was the concentrated area of houses, streets and squares along the river – all of them turning their backs on the town; but above all it was the city (160 hectares) as marked out by the old city walls. They stood on the site of the ancient Roman wall, but they had disappeared around the twelfth century on the river front, where quays, wharves and floating landing-stages had breached the useless protection very early on. On the other hand they survived in a broken line, very roughly forming an arc of a circle from Blackfriars Steps or Bridewell Dock up to the Tower of London. The line was cut by seven gates: Ludgate, Newgate, Aldersgate, Cripplegate, Moorgate, Bishopsgate and Aldgate. Facing each of these gates, far into the suburbs, there was a gate limiting the authority of London. The inner suburbs were 'liberties', districts (sometimes vast areas) outside the walls. Thus the gate in front of Bishopsgate was situated on the edge of Smithfield, west of Holborn. Likewise, going out of Ludgate, one had to walk right down Fleet Street in order to reach Temple Bar, level with the Temple of the ex-Templars at the entrance to the Strand. Temple Bar was an ordinary wooden gate for a long time. This was the way in which London, or rather the City, overflowed its restricted boundaries even before Elizabeth's reign, reaching places in the countryside near by and joining itself to them by a series of roads lined with houses.

In the time of Elizabeth 1 and Shakespeare the heart of the town beat inside the walls. Its centre was on the axis extending London Bridge northwards to Bishopsgate. The east/west axis was marked out by a series of streets from Newgate in the west to Aldgate in the east. Under Elizabeth the crossing point was situated about 300 yards from the Stock Market, at the west end of Lombard Street.

The Royal Exchange was a couple of steps away on Cornhill. It had been founded by Thomas Gresham in 1566 and at first was called the 'Bourse' (*Byrsa Londinensis, vulgo the Royal Exchange* ran the caption on a seventeenth-century engraving) in memory of the Antwerp Bourse. The name Royal Exchange had been granted to it by the authority of Elizabeth in 1570. According to witnesses it was a veritable Tower of Babel, especially around midday when the merchants arrived to settle their business. However the most elegant shops around its courtyards attracted a rich clientele. Both the Guildhall (more or less London's town hall) and the Bank of England's first home (it was housed in the Grocer's Hall, the grocers' warehouse, before occupying its sumptuous building in 1734) were not far from the Royal Exchange.

The intensity of London life also showed in its markets, West Smithfields for example, the vast area near the ramparts where horses and livestock were sold on Mondays and Fridays; or Billingsgate, the fresh fish market on the Thames; or the Leaden Hall towards the heart of the city, with its lead roof, an old corn warehouse where butchers' meat and leather were sold on a large scale.

But it would be impossible to give a full account of those important centres, those taverns, restaurants and theatres which were generally on the periphery and therefore reserved for the populace, or later, in the seventeenth century, those Coffee Houses which were so well patronised that the government was already thinking about prohibiting them.

A second capital: Westminster

But the City was never the only runner in the race on the banks of the Thames. In comparison Paris had a solitary fate. Westminster upstream from London was quite a different matter from Versailles (a late creation *ex nihilo*). It was really an old and living town. The Palace of Westminster, next to the Abbey, abandoned by Henry VIII, had become the seat of Parliament and the principal tribunals. It was the meeting place for lawyers and litigants. The monarchy had taken up its abode slightly farther away, in Whitehall, in the White Palace beside the Thames.

Westminster was therefore both Versailles and St Denis plus the Paris Parlement for good measure. We have used the comparison to indicate the powerful attraction this second pole exercised in London's development. For example Fleet Street, which belonged to the City, was the district of jurists, solicitors and attorneys and law students. It looked obstinately westwards. Furthermore the Strand, which was outside the City and which, some way away from the Thames, led to Westminster, became the district of the nobility. They established their houses there and soon another Exchange – a group of luxury shops – was opened there in 1609. Articles of fashion and wigs were the rage there from the reign of James I.

In the seventeenth and eighteenth centuries a broad movement pushed the town in all directions at once. Appalling districts grew up on the outskirts – shanty towns with filthy huts, unsightly industries (notably innumerable brickworks), pig raising, accumulations of refuse, and sordid streets. One such place was Whitechapel, where the wretched shoemakers worked. Elsewhere there were silk and wool weavers.

Fields disappeared from the immediate approaches to London except in the western districts where greenery crept in via the stretches of Hyde Park and St James's Park and the gardens of wealthy houses. In Shakespeare's and Thomas Dekker's day the town was still surrounded by green, open spaces, fields, trees and real villages where one could hunt duck and drop in at authentic country inns to drink beer and eat spice cakes or the *Islington White Pot*, a sort of custard which earned the village of Islington a reputation.

At that time 'the wind that blew in the outer districts of the capital', wrote Thomas Dekker's most recent historian 'was not always heavy and impure: in the theatres in the south, north and north-west there was all the gaiety of Merry England, and also its subtle and vibrant imagination which penetrated the suburbs ... and the whole town'. Merry England, that is to say the England of the undisguisedly peasant centuries of the middle ages, was a romantic, not a false vision. But this happy relationship did not last.

The ever-expanding entity of London completed its split into two parts. The movement had begun a long time before. It accelerated after the Great Fire in 1666 which practically destroyed the heart, almost the whole of the City. Before this disaster (1662) William Petty had already explained that London, where the prevailing winds blew from the west, was growing westwards to escape 'the fumes, steams, and stinks of the whole Eastery Pyle. ... Now if it follows from hence that the Palaces of the greatest men will remove westward, it will also naturally follow that the dwellings of others who depend on them will creep after them. This we see in London where the Noblemen's ancient houses are now become Halls for Companies, or turned into Tenements. ...' A westwards slide of the London rich thus took place. If the centre of the town was still in the vicinity of Cornhill in the seventeenth century, today it is not very far from Charing Cross, at the west end of the Strand. It has shifted a long way.

The proletariat: Irish and Jews

Meanwhile the east and certain peripheral districts were becoming more and more proletarian. Poverty moved in and dug itself in wherever it found room in the London world. The darkest pages of the story concern two categories of outcasts: the Irish and the Jews from central Europe.

Irish immigration began early from the most famished districts of Ireland. The exiles were peasants condemned to a bare living at home by the land system and more still by the demographic growth that shook the island until the catastrophes of 1846. They were used to living with the animals, sharing their hovels with them, and feeding on potatoes and a little milk. Inured to hardship, not jibbing at any task, they regularly found work every haymaking time as agricultural workers in the countryside around London. From there a few pushed on up to London and hung on there. They crowded into sordid slums in the parish of St Giles, their fief, to the north of the City, lived ten or twelve to one windowless room and accepted wages well below the general rate, as dockers, milk carriers, labourers at the brickworks, even lodging-house keepers. Brawls broke out amongst them on Sundays during drinking sessions. And they engaged in pitched battles with the competing English proletariat.

The same tragedy was enacted with the Jews of central Europe, fleeing from persecution in Bohemia in 1744 and Poland in 1772. There were as many as six thousand of them in England in 1734 and twenty thousand in London alone in 1800. Against them was unleashed the most ugly and widespread hostility. Attempts by the synagogues to stop this dangerous immigration, which came via Holland, proved useless. What could these wretched people do once they arrived? The Jews already settled helped them but could neither drive them away from the island nor support them. London craftsmen rejected them. They were therefore of necessity dealers in old clothes and old iron – shouting through the streets, sometimes driving an old cart – as well as rogues, filchers, counterfeiters and receivers. Their late success as professional boxers, even as the inventors of a form of scientific boxing, did not restore their reputation, although Daniel Mendoza, a famous champion, founded a school.

The London drama – its festering criminality, its underworld, its difficult biological life – can truly be understood from this worm's eye view of the poor. It is to be noted, however, that the material situation on the whole improved, as it did in Paris, with street paving, water supplies, building controls and advances in lighting the town.

From London to Paris and back

What can we conclude? That London, alongside Paris, was a good example of what a capital of the *ancien régime* could be. A luxury that others had to pay for, a gathering of a few chosen souls, numerous servants and poor wretches, all linked however, by some collective destiny of the great agglomeration.

What did this common lot comprise? There was, for example, the dreadful filth and stench of the streets, as familiar to the lord as to the populace. It was probably the mass of the populace which created it, but it rebounded on everybody. Much of the countryside was probably relatively less dirty than the large towns until the middle of the eighteenth century, and the medieval city was a pleasanter and cleaner place to live in, as Lewis Mumford suggests. It did not sink under the weight of numbers, simultaneously bringing glory and poverty; it was wide open to the countryside and found its water locally inside its ramparts. In fact the enormous town could not cope with its ever-growing tasks or begin by assuring its elementary cleanliness. Security, the fight against fire and flood, supplies and public order took priority. And even if it had wanted to, it would have lacked the means. The worst material ignominies remained the general rule.

The streets [a traveller tells us à propos Madrid (1697)] are always very dirty because it is the custom to throw all the rubbish out of the window. One suffers even more in winter because carts carry several barrels of water which are emptied into the streets in order to carry away the rubbish and let the filth run off; it often happens that one encounters torrents of this evil water which blocks one's way and poisons by its stench.

Paris was no better provided for. To walk in the streets was inevitably to get covered with mud because of the stream loaded with refuse running down the middle of the roadway. The 'height of the pavement' – which courtesy required be left for women and gentlefolk – along the houses offered better protection from this pestilential mud. But it was still necessary to hug the walls to avoid what was poured out of the windows. It was impossible to pay even a slightly ceremonial visit without taking shoes to change into – which was done in an antechamber – unless some means of transport was borrowed. At the beginning of the seventeenth century nobles and the fashionable world were still travelling around on horseback. Elegance required that this be done *en housse*, that is 'in silk stockings and [perched] on a velvet horse cloth'. Such was no longer the case by 1640 except for doctors and 'those who are not very well off'.

The vogue of the coach was launched. There were still no more than three or four in Paris in 1580, but now, if someone prided himself on elegance, 'one immediately asks: has he got a coach?'. Sedan chairs were then invented, economical because they were hired, as hackney carriages were hired later, and 'so useful in that having been shut up inside without dirtying oneself in the street, it can be said that one gets out as clean as out of a magician's box'.

All in all coaches and chairs were a guarantee of staying presentable when crossing the town as much as a means of transport. All the same everyone by this time was familiar with the smell of Paris – 'so detestable that it is impossible to remain there', said the Princess Palatine, desperate each time she had to leave Versailles for Paris. And visitors, even to the Louvre or the Palais de Justice, still relieved themselves publicly, in broad daylight, at a bend in the corridor, without anyone bothering about it. The chambermaids at the Louvre, like everybody else, soiled the façades by throwing the contents of the night-commodes out of the windows.

And things only really changed with the nineteenth century. Viollet-le-Duc tells how in Louis XVIII's time – Versailles by then had made few concessions to modernity – an old lady of the Court of Louis XV passed through a still foul corridor in the palace and regretfully exclaimed: 'That smell reminds me of a very beautiful time.'

Everything was due to numbers, excessive numbers of people. But the large town attracted them. Every person in his own way received a few crumbs from its parasitical life. And look at Paris: 'It attracts all the manufactured goods of the kingdom; but it has few factories because of the high cost of manpower . . . money rushes towards it in a great mass and all the more so in that it does not flow back to the provinces.' Paris 'sucks in all the goods and makes use of the whole kingdom. People there do not feel the calamities which sometimes afflict the countryside and the provinces.' But it was the same in Peking and Nanking, which were also snowed under with food and fruit from their countryside. London too continued to receive corn by boat from the Humber and coal by boat from Newcastle during the plague in 1665.

Their thieves themselves proved that there was always something to be gleaned from these privileged towns. Criminals inevitably gathered in the most luxurious of them.

In 1798 Colquhoun was deploring that: 'The situation . . . has changed materially since the dissolution of the ancient government of France. The horde of sharpers and villains, heretofore resorted to Paris from every part of Europe, will now consider London as their general and most productive theatre of action. . . .' Paris was ruined and the rats left the ship. 'The ignorance of the English language (a circumstance which formerly afforded us some protection) will no longer be a bar. . . . At no period was it ever so generally understood by foreigners; is the French language so universally spoken, by at least the younger part of the people of this country?'

Town life and false prospects

There is no question of falling into step with such a sad conservative as Colquhoun. The enormous towns had their faults and their virtues. They created, let us repeat, the modern state, as much as they were created by it. National markets expanded under their impetus as did the nations themselves and modern civilisation which mingled its varied colours more in Europe every day. For the historian they are primarily a prodigious test of the evolution of Europe and the other continents. Interpreted properly, their study leads to a general and unusually comprehensive view of the whole history of material life.

On the whole what is at issue is growth in the economy of the *ancien régime*. The towns there were an example of deep-seated disequilibrium, asymmetrical growth, and irrational and unproductive investment on a nation-wide scale. Was luxury – the appetite of these enormous parasites – responsible for it? This is what Jean-Jacques Rousseau says in *Emile*:

It is the large towns that drain the state and create its weakness. The wealth they produce is an apparent and illusory wealth; it is a lot of money and little effect. It is said that the town of Paris is worth a province to the king of France; I believe that it costs him several of them; that Paris is fed by the provinces in more than one respect and that most of their incomes pour into that town and stay there, without ever returning to the people or the king. It is inconceivable that in this century of forward-looking people, there has been no one able to see that France would be much more powerful if Paris were annihilated.

This is of course an absurd comment, because the capitals of the *ancien régime* were not aberrant phenomena. They sprang naturally from the institutions of their times. We should rather say that the town was just not able to do better at that time, that it came up against obvious incapacities. It was, in Europe and elsewhere, what society, economy and politics allowed it to be. Suppose that a historian at the end of the eighteenth century, better informed than we are about the contemporary scene, had indulged in long-term forecasts. He would have asked himself whether these urban monsters in the West were not proof of a kind of seizing-up process analogous to what happened to the Roman empire with the deadweight of Rome, and China with the enormous inert mass of Peking in the far north; that is to say he would have asked if they were not ends of evolution instead of promises for the future, the forces they unleashed resulting in nothing more than themselves.

Such a judgement is obviously exaggerated. But it obsessed a historian of the calibre of Camille Julian, and 'the prose of the Roman Empire' which Hegel mentioned was after all the prose of its capital, Rome.

In any case it has been proved that these enormous urban formations are more linked to the past, to accomplished evolutions, faults and weaknesses of the societies and economies of the *ancien régime* than to preparations for the future. Werner Sombart saw the luxury of the large towns and states as an accelerator of capitalism. But what capitalism? Capitalism is protean, a hydra with a hundred heads. The obvious fact was that the capital cities would be present at the forthcoming industrial revolution in the role of spectators. Not London, but Manchester, Birmingham, Leeds, Glasgow and innumerable small proletarian towns launched the new era. It was not even the capital accumulated by eighteenth-century patricians that was to be invested in the new venture. London only turned the movement to its own advantage, by way of money, around 1830. Paris was temporarily touched by the new industry and then released as soon as the real foundations were laid, to the benefit of coal from the north, waterfalls on the Alsace waterways and iron from Lorraine. Sébastien Mercier's Paris was also the end of a material world. That which was born of the middle-class nineteenth century was worse perhaps for the working classes but it was no longer to have the same meaning.

Conclusion

Books, even history books, run away with their authors. This one has run on ahead of me. But what can one say about its waywardness, its whims, even its own logic, that would be serious and valid? Our children do as they please. And yet we are responsible for their actions.

Here and there I would have liked more explanation, justification and example. But books cannot be expanded to order, and to encompass all the many and varied constituents of material life would require close, systematic research, not to mention whole collections of analyses. All that is still lacking. What the text says calls for discussion, addition and extension. We have not talked about all the towns, nor all techniques, nor all the elementary facts of housing, clothing and eating.

A very old bell struck the hour in the small Lorraine village where I grew up as a child: the village pond drove an old mill wheel; a stone path, as old as the world, plunged down like a torrent in front of my house; the house itself had been rebuilt in 1806, the year of Jena, and flax used to be retted in the stream at the bottom of the meadows. I only have to think of these things and this book opens out for me afresh. Every reader, prompted by a chance memory or journey or a passage in a book, can do the same. A character in *Siegfried et le Limousin* riding out at dawn in the Germany of the 1920s gives the impression of still being in the Thirty Years War. A bend in a path or a street can take anyone back to the past in this way. Even in highly developed economies, the residual presence of the old material past makes itself felt. It is disappearing before our eyes, but slowly, and never in the same manner.

This book – the first of a two-volume work – does not claim to have depicted all material life throughout the whole complex world from the fifteenth to the eighteenth centuries. What it offers is an attempt to see all these scenes as a whole – from food to furniture, from techniques to towns – and inevitably to define what is and was material life. At times the definition is difficult: we have sometimes consciously had to go beyond the frontiers in order to identify them better, in connection with the crucial facts of money for example. That gives our undertaking its first purpose: if not to see everything, at least to locate everything, and on the requisite world scale.

Second stage: over a succession of landscapes which historians only rarely depict and which have a kind of descriptive incoherence as their most obvious characteristic, to try to classify, put in order and reduce disparate material to the main lines and simplifications of historical explanation. This concern sheds light on the present volume and defines its scope as far as method is concerned, even if the programme has sometimes been outlined rather than filled in, partly because a book intended for the general public is a house from which all scaffolding has to be removed. But also because what is involved, let us reiterate, is unexplored territory where the springs have to be discovered and checked individually, one by one.

Of course, material life appears first and foremost in the anecdotal form of thousands and thousands of diverse facts. Shall we call them events? No, to do so would be to inflate their importance, to grant them a significance they never had. That Maximilian, emperor of the Holy Roman Empire, put his hand into the dishes at a banquet is commonplace fact, certainly not an event. So is the story about Cartouche on the point of execution preferring a glass of wine to the coffee he was offered. This is the dust of history, micro-history, in the same sense that Georges Gurvitch talks about micro-sociology: chains of small facts indefinitely repeated. Each of them testifies to thousands of others enduring through the depths of silent time.

It is these sequences, these series, that have retained our attention: in all these landscapes of material life they supply the vanishing points and the line of the horizon. All of them introduce a methodical arrangement into it, imply equilibria, separate out permanencies and constants, whatever is more or less explicable in this apparent disorder. 'A law', said Georges Lefebvre, 'is a constant.' Obviously we have been concerned with constants over different periods of time, and especially with the long term in connection with food, plants, clothes, houses, and the very old and vital division between town and country. Material life complies with these slow evolutions even more easily than the other sectors of man's history.

Among the constant elements the reader will have noticed that we have put those appertaining to civilisations and cultures in the foreground. Our book is not called *Material Life* for nothing; it indicates a deliberate choice. In fact civilisations create connections, that is to say, an arrangement between thousands of actually disparate cultural possessions, at first glance foreign to one another – from those that emanate from religion and intellect to the objects and tools of daily life.

An Englishman who travelled in China (1793) notes this:

> In China ... [the most common] tools have something peculiar in their construction, some difference, often indeed slight, but always clearly indicating that, whether better or worse fitted for their purpose than those used in other countries, the one did not serve as a model for the other. Thus, for example, the upper surface of the anvil, elsewhere flat and somewhat inclined, is among the Chinese swelled into a convex form.

He makes the same comment on the subject of forge bellows: 'The bellows are made in the form of a box, in which a movable floor is so closely fitted as when drawn back to create a vacuum in the box, into which, in consequence, the air rushes through an opening guarded by a valve and produces a blast through an opposite aperture.' We are a very long way from the large leather bellows in European forges.

It is a fact that each densely populated world has worked out a group of elementary answers and has an unfortunate tendency to stick to them because of an omnipresent *vis inertiae* which is one of the great artisans of history. So what is a civilisation if not the ancient settlement of a certain section of mankind in a certain place? It is a category of history, consequently a necessary classification. Mankind only shows a tendency to become one (and it has not yet succeeded) from the end of the fifteenth century. Until then, and more and more as we go further back in time, it was divided between different planets, each sheltering an individual civilisation or culture, with its original features and ancient choices. However close to each other, their solutions were never able to intermingle.

These favoured categories established permanencies and civilisations (the latter often immobile); they allow, indeed call for, the supplementary classification inherent in societies (also omnipresent) alongside them. Everything is social or of the social order – for historians and sociologists a reflection worthy of La Palisse or Monsieur Jourdain. But these commonplace and obvious truths have their importance. Moreover we have talked for pages on end about rich and poor, luxury and poverty, the two sides of life. These are humdrum facts, in Japan as much as in Newton's England or pre-Columbian America where, before the Spaniards arrived, very strict prohibitions regulated clothing so that it distinguished the people from their masters. When European domination reduced them all to the rank of subject 'natives', regulations and differences disappeared, or very nearly. The fabric of their clothes – coarse wool, cotton or sisal cloth (we would say sackcloth) – barely distinguished them from one another any longer.

We should really talk about socio-economies more than societies – a vague term. Marx is right: who owns the means of production, the land, the ships, the businesses, the raw materials, the finished products and no less the leading positions? However, it is still obvious that these two co-ordinates – society and economy – are not self-contained; the multiform state, both cause and consequence simultaneously, makes its presence felt, disturbs relationships, affects them, whether it wants to or not. It plays its part, often very heavily, in those architectural structures that can be regrouped across a sort of typology of the different world socio-economies – those with slaves, those with serfs and nobles, those with businessmen and pre-capitalists. This is going back to the language of Marx, and staying with him, even if one immediately rejects his exact words or the strict rule which in his eyes seems to make all society swing from one of these structures to the other. The problem really remains one of classification, of a carefully worked out hierarchy of societies in comparison with each other. No one can escape from this necessity, which imposes itself from the most elementary level of material life.

The fact that such problems – the long term, civilisation, society, economy, the state, the hierarchies of 'social' values – obtrude at the level of the humble realities (or realities which were considered humble) of material life in itself proves that history is already making its presence known with its enigmas and difficulties, the same ones encountered by all the human sciences coming to grips with their subject. Man can never be reduced to one personality who can be summed up in an acceptable simplification. This is everyone's pipe dream. Hardly is he summed up in his simplest form than he re-asserts himself in his customary complexity.

Moreover I have certainly not devoted myself to this phase of history for years on end because I regard it as any simpler or clearer. Nor because it seemed to have numerical priority, nor because it is usually neglected by the mainstream of history, nor (though this reason nevertheless carried some weight with me) because it tied me down to realities at a time when philosophy, social science and mathematicisation are dehumanising history. This return to mother earth attracted but did not decide me. But I did think that it was not possible to achieve an understanding of economic life as a whole if the foundations of the house were not explored first. It is these foundations that the present book has tried to lay down and upon which the two storeys of the volume which follows and completes the undertaking will be built: economy and capitalism.

With economic life we will emerge from the routine, from the unconscious daily round. However, in economic life, the regularities are still with us; an old and progressive division of labour causes inevitable partings and meetings, on which active and concious daily life feeds, with its tiny profits, its micro-capitalism, which is not unattractive, barely distinguishable from ordinary work. Higher still on the top floor we will place capitalism and its vast ramifications, with its gambles that already seem evil to the common run of mortals. What, we will be asked, has this sophistication to do with the humble lives at the bottom of the ladder? Everything perhaps, because it involves them in its gamble. I have tried to say this right from the first chapter of this book by emphasising the variations in level in the unequal world of men. It is the inequalities, the injustice, the contradictions, large or small, which make the world go round and ceaselessly transform its upper structures, the only really mobile ones. For capitalism alone has relative freedom of movement. As the moment dictates, it can bring off coups to right or left, turning, alternately or simultaneously, to profits from trade or manufacture, even ground rent, loans to the state or usury.

Faced with inflexible structures ('those of material life and, no less, of ordinary economic life'), it is able to choose the areas where it wants and is able to meddle, and the areas it will leave to their fate, incessantly reconstructing its own structures from these components, and thereby little by little transforming those of others.

That is why all the economic creativeness of the world stems from pre-capitalism, and why it is the source or characteristic of all great material progress and of all the most burdensome exploitation of man by man. Not only because of the appropriation of the surplus value of man's labour. But also because of that disproportion in strength and position, on a nation-wide as well as a world-wide scale, which means that at the whim of circumstance there will always be one position more advantageous to adopt than the rest, one sector more profitable to exploit. The choice may be limited, but what an immense privilege to be able to choose!

Index

Abyssinia, 330
Acapulco 120, 308
account, money of, 352–4
Aertsen, Pieter, 229
Africa: animals, wild, 34; exploration of, 31; population estimates, 11–13, 15; primitive money, 330–1; tobacco, 191. *See also* Black Africa
Agricola, Georg, 262, 283, 322
agriculture: animals in, 77–8, 249–53; cereal crops, 68–120; crop rotation, 74–7; hoe culture, 114–18; human labour, 246–8; manuring, 77; tools, determinism of, 116
Aigues-mortes, 385
Aix-en-Provence, 135
Alain de Lille, 397
Alaminos, Antonio, 312
Alaska, 61, 332
Alba, Duke of, 256, 291, 350
alcohol, 91, 121, 170–8
Aleppo, 238
Alexandria, 286, 359
Algeria, 197, 333
Algiers, 203, 228
Allevard, 280
Alpini, Prospero, 184
Amboise, Jacques d', 200
America: alcohol, 177; animal life, 35–6; animal power, 249–51; cereals, 70, 72; colonisation of, 60–1, 62; diseases from Europe, 6; epidemics, 45, 46, 51; exploration of, 31; hoe culture, 117–18; immigration, 12; life expectation, 53; maize, 108–12, 113; monetary economy, 351–2; money, primitive, 332, 334–5; population estimates, 5–6, 7; population increase, 17; populations, urban, 375; tobacco, 189, 190; towns, 375, 406–7, 412
Amiens, 288

Amman, Jost, 322
Amsterdam, 190, 398; banking, 350, 365, 367; buildings, 195, 201; as capital town, 414–15; corn exports, 85, 86; plague, 50; poor in, 201; spice trade, 154–5; tea trade, 179, 181
Andes, 110, 111, 112
Angkor Vat, 100
animal life, wild, 32–7
animal power, 249–59
Anne of Austria, 139
Antwerp, 86, 154, 392; printing, 299
aqueducts, 159–60, 261
Aquitaine, 73
Arab horses, 256
arak, 175–7
Arbeau, Thoinot, 129
Archangel, 349
Ardant, Edouard, 173
Argentina: animal life, 35; colonisation of, 60–1; mules, 250; wine, 162
Arles, 84
Armagnac, 172
Armagnac, Cardinal d', and plague, 49
armaments, 285–95
armies, size of, 21–2
arms factories, 291–3
arquebuses, 290–1
artillery, 22, 285, 287–95; mobile, 287–8; production and budget, 291–3; on ships, 288–90; on world scale, 293–5
Artois, 76, 80, 93
Asia: famine, 38, 41; population estimates, 11, 13, 14–15; towns, 375, 377, 382–3, 384, 394, 410–11, 412–14
Astrakhan, 58, 62, 68, 294
astrology, 20
Athens, 400
Atlantic Ocean, 305–6
Attila, 55

Fontana History

Fontana History includes the well-known History of Europe, editied by J. H. Plumb and the Fontana Economic History of Europe, edited by Carlo Cipolla. Other books available include:

The Fontana History of Europe

Praised by academics, teachers and general readers alike, this series aims to provide an account, based on the latest research, that combines narrative and explanation. Each volume has been specially commissioned from a leading English, American or European scholar, and is complete in itself. The general editor of the series is J. H. Plumb, lately Professor of Modern History at Cambridge University, and Fellow of Christ's College, Cambridge.